Second Edition

The Handbook of
HUMAN SERVICES
MANAGEMENT

Second Edition

The Handbook of
HUMAN SERVICES
MANAGEMENT

Rino J. Patti

Professor Emeritus
School of Social Work, University of Southern California

editor

Los Angeles • London • New Delhi • Singapore • Washington DC

For information:

SAGE Publications, Inc.
2455 Teller Road
Thousand Oaks, California 91320
E-mail: order@sagepub.com

SAGE Publications India Pvt. Ltd.
B 1/I 1 Mohan Cooperative
    Industrial Area
Mathura Road, New Delhi 110 044
India

SAGE Publications Ltd.
1 Oliver's Yard
55 City Road
London EC1Y 1SP
United Kingdom

SAGE Publications Asia-Pacific Pte. Ltd.
33 Pekin Street #02-01
Far East Square
Singapore 048763

Printed in the United States of America

Library of Congress Cataloging-in-Publication Data

The handbook of human services management / Rino J. Patti, editor.—2nd ed.
        p. cm.
Includes bibliographical references and index.
ISBN 978-1-4129-5290-3 (cloth)
ISBN 978-1-4129-5291-0 (pbk.)
    1. Human services—Management.   I. Patti, Rino J.

HV41.H324 2009
658.3—dc22   2008017855

This book is printed on acid-free paper.

          14   10   9   8   7   6   5

Acquisitions Editor:	Kassie Graves
Editorial Assistant:	Veronica Novak
Production Editor:	Catherine M. Chilton
Copy Editor:	Diana Breti
Typesetter:	C&M Digitals (P) Ltd.
Proofreader:	William H. Stoddard
Indexer:	Diggs Publication Services
Cover Designer:	Candice Harman
Marketing Manager:	Carmel Schrire

Contents

Preface

The first edition of this book was designed primarily as a reference work that would provide a comprehensive treatment of organizational theory and research in the human services and major aspects of management practice. Although many readers used it as a reference for their scholarly work, or to supplement classroom texts sources, a number of instructors adopted it as a primary text for their management-related courses at both the doctoral and master's levels.

When Sage Publications asked whether I might be interested in doing a revised edition of the book, our initial discussion turned to how we might keep the quality of a broad, scholarly reference work while making it more readily usable as a text for management courses in the human services.

To assist us in thinking about how the book might be revised to be more user-friendly as a text for both instructors and students, Sage commissioned reviews from a number of faculty members who had used the book in this way and several who had not. These reviewers provided richly detailed critiques addressing the strengths and weaknesses of individual chapters and also provided a number of useful suggestions about how the book might be reorganized to align better with the structure and content of management courses. In particular, reviewers thought the book needed more content on subjects like managing agency performance, diversity, supervision, boards, and advocacy. More cases, examples, exercises, and Internet resources were requested. They also suggested that cognate organizational theory and practice chapters should be nested together in topical sections.

Armed with this feedback and the benefit of ideas provided by Armand Lauffer, a consulting editor for Sage, and Kassie Graves, Acquisitions Editor, we proceeded to clarify the core purpose of the book, modify its structure, add content not previously covered, and update chapters that were in the first edition.

The core issue addressed in the book, now more clearly defined and woven throughout most of the chapters, is *how to manage human services organizations in ways that lead to the provision of high quality, effective services to consumers.* This is arguably the most pressing issue confronting the human services in an environment of decreasing resources, increased competition, and growing demands for accountability from public and private funding and policy institutions. It is also an ethical imperative for human services agencies and those who deliver its services. Understanding how managers can best achieve this key goal is the central concern of this book.

The provision of high quality, effective services to consumers necessarily requires management practices and organizational conditions that are strategically directed to this end. There is still much be learned about how management directly and indirectly shapes the service delivery capabilities of an agency, but in recent years, practice wisdom, theoretical scholarship, and empirical research have begun to suggest the key elements of an effectiveness-driven model of management. These include, for example, leadership that develops and maintains work cultures that encourage high performance norms; a capacity to measure service processes and outcomes and use these for improving policies and services; a skilled, motivated, and culturally competent staff; competent governance, planning, marketing, and financial management; and the support and cooperation of funders, collaborators, and other key constituencies. The chapters that follow address these and related issues, bringing to bear the latest information on practice innovations, theoretical perspectives, and empirical research.

In addition to clarifying the major theme of the book, we also restructured it so that chapters dealing with theory and practice in several areas of management are grouped together in topical sections. This should make for easier cross-referencing and mitigate the problem of fragmentation that is often characteristic of edited books with multiple authors.

Finally, the content of the book has been substantially changed to reflect new developments in the field and address some of the omissions in the first edition. Ten chapters (of the original 26) were deleted and 8 new ones added. The authors of the 16 revised chapters (including several who replaced original authors who were deceased or unable to take on the revision) were given the feedback provided by the reviewers, as well as my suggestions. All these chapters were significantly revised. Finally, a number of the chapters provide Internet sites for further reference.

The book is organized around six themes. Part 1 consists of five chapters that attempt to lay out the fundamental dimensions of management in the human services and provide a context for the chapters that follow. Here, we address definitions of management; how the unique characteristics of human services organizations shape management practice; how management practice evolved in the ideological and policy contexts of the last century and a half; the theoretical perspectives that inform management practice; the scope, structure, and financing of human services in the United States; and the roles and functions performed by managers.

Part 2 deals directly with the central concern of the book: how to manage agencies in ways that lead to the delivery of high-quality, effective services to consumers. While all the chapters in the book are at least indirectly concerned with this question, these chapters address necessary (though not sufficient) elements of effectiveness-driven management. The first two chapters critically address the characteristics of agency culture, climate, and leadership that are associated with high-performing human services organizations. We then turn to the complex challenges of how to measure service processes and outcomes and develop information technologies that will enable human services agencies to learn from their experience, make informed decisions, and change practices.

Part 3 consists of five chapters concerned primarily with management processes needed to motivate and empower frontline staff in human services organizations. Because agencies rely on a skilled and empowered frontline staff to deliver effective services, this issue is a central concern of management. Accordingly, in this section, chapters are devoted to the personal and organizational factors that influence the motivation of staff to perform their often difficult work with sensitivity, skill, energy, and commitment. The critical roles of personnel administration and supervision in the selection, development, and support of frontline workers and volunteers are addressed in two chapters. Because human services programs are delivered predominantly by women providers and often include persons of color and those with diverse sexual orientations (and other marginalized groups), social agencies must frontally address issues of equality and inclusion, if the talent and experience of these groups is to be fully utilized. These issues are addressed in most of the chapters in this section and are dealt with at length in two chapters devoted specifically to diversity.

Part 4 consists of five chapters devoted to developing and managing the governance, strategic, programmatic, and fiscal infrastructures necessary to support the agency's core service mission. While these management processes sometimes seem far removed from the service delivery process, they are organically related to it. Indeed, to the extent these processes are not orchestrated, the agency's viability can be at risk. Two chapters are devoted to planning processes at the agency or strategic level and the program level. In the planning process, managers and their governing bodies lay the framework for the agency's long-term goals and objectives and, within this context, the programs and services to be provided. One chapter addresses the governance of nonprofit agencies, with special attention to what managers do to develop and sustain the capacity of boards of directors to govern effectively. We then turn to a key responsibility of management, the challenge of acquiring the financial resources needed to fund agency programs and services. Finally, there is a chapter devoted to the management of agency finances, including allocating, monitoring, and accounting for resources.

Part 5 contains three chapters that are generally related to how managers engage with agency environments to obtain legitimacy and support and to advocate for policies and resources that will benefit the agency and its consumers. This aspect of managerial leadership, which has historically received little attention, is now among the most important functions performed by administrators in an environment characterized by turbulence, scarcity, and competition. One chapter is devoted to theories that seek to explain how human services organizations are affected by, and seek to influence, forces in their environment. A second deals with interagency relations, with particular attention to how managers work to build mutually beneficial collaborations. A third chapter focuses on why and how managers engage in advocacy and lobbying to influence and shape policies affecting their agencies and disenfranchised groups.

Part 6 looks at the likely future direction of human services management from two perspectives: managers themselves and academics who prepare students for administrative careers. The opinions provided to managers in Chapter 23 are especially interesting because they resonate so much of what is presented in previous chapters: the changing nature of practice in areas such as motivating workers, fundraising, competition, technology, and so on. The final chapter critically examines the state of management education in schools of social work. A number of the instructional and structural challenges facing schools are addressed, as are several strategies for strengthening the preparation of graduates for the demands of management practice.

The editor of a book like this relies essentially on the talents of others, the authors who generously contribute their time and expertise to an enterprise for which they receive little extrinsic reward. I have enjoyed and benefited enormously from my collaboration with the able scholars who made this book possible, and I feel a special pride in what they have produced. I am also indebted to Armand Lauffer, who provided creative advice about reorganizing the book to make it more coherent and usable; to Kassie Graves, Sage's Acquisitions Editor, who had the idea for doing a second edition and has been wonderfully supportive throughout the process; and to Veronica Novak, Senior Editorial Assistant at Sage, who provided gentle but persistent guidance about preparation of the manuscript and saw that the rough product made its way into print.

Finally, having dedicated past books to my immediate and extended families, I have the opportunity to pay tribute to my colleagues in both the academic and practice communities over the last four decades, who have stimulated, supported, and contributed to my scholarly work. They are too numerous to mention, but this book is for them.

Rino J. Patti

Acknowledgments

Sage Publications would like to thank the following reviewers:

Lawrence L. Martin
University of Central Florida

Kevin L. DeWeaver
University of Georgia

Marcia Edwards
Adelphi University

Richard L. Beaulaurier
Florida International University

Bud Warner
Elon University

Lucinda Lee Roff
University of Alabama

Katharine Cahn
Portland State University

Bruce D. Hartsell
California State University, Bakersfield

Ruth E. Fleury-Steiner
University of Delaware

PART 1

Dimensions of Human Services Management

This introductory section provides the reader with an overview of human services management. It deals with the scope and characteristics of this practice, the ideological and policy contexts in management that have emerged over the last century and a half, the theoretical perspectives that have and continue to influence the goals of practice, the structure and financing of the human services enterprise, and the roles and functions performed by managers. Taken together, these chapters help the reader to understand the particular purposes, constraints, and challenges that make human services management a distinctive variation of general management.

In Chapter 1, Rino Patti examines the fundamental characteristics of human services management. Included here is a discussion of essential contributions managers make to the operation of the human services institution, the nature and scope of human services, the demographics of the management labor force, and how the special characteristics of organizations in this field shape management practice and give it a unique character. Management issues that arise in the pursuit of providing effective human services are discussed.

In Chapter 2, a revision of David Austin's entry in the first edition, Michael Reisch discusses the emergence of human services management over the last two centuries. Professor Reisch shows how conceptions of management were shaped over the years by political and professional ideologies and the changing character of private charitable and public service institutions. He traces the ways in which management theory and practice were influenced by the welfare state and the subsequent conservative reaction. The evolution of management education in social work and other fields is also addressed.

Chapter 3, Zeke Hasenfeld's update of his chapter in the first edition of this book, analyzes a number of extant theories of organization and management to critically assess their utility as tools for understanding the dynamics and performance of human services agencies. While all of theories have some application to the administration of social service agencies, none provides a comprehensive theory of organization and management. Professor Hasenfeld suggests some of the elements of such a management theory for human services organizations, drawing upon the early work by Mary Parker Follet and recent empowerment scholarship.

In Chapter 4, Leon Ginsberg provides a broad review of the structure, governance, and financing of public, nonprofit, and for-profit human services in the United States. In a chapter originally authored by Margaret Gibelman, who passed away, Professor Ginsberg describes the similarities and differences found in the various sectors of human services, the increasing interdependence of public and private sectors, and some of the policy and management issues that arise in this context.

Chapter 5, David Menefee's update of his chapter in the first edition, provides the latest perspectives on the nature of management practice in the human services. Drawing on his own extensive research and that of others, Menefee describes some of the conditions that have altered management practice and made it as much about addressing external forces as internal processes. The array of roles assumed by managers is defined, and case examples are provided to illustrate how these roles are carried out, perfectly and imperfectly, by practicing managers.

CHAPTER 1

Management in the Human Services

Purposes, Practice, and Prospects in the 21st Century

Rino J. Patti

This chapter looks broadly at human services management or administration, one of the methods of practice employed by human services workers to achieve their professional and organizational objectives. The important contributions managers make to the functioning of the human services system are highlighted. We then describe the nature, size, and scope of the human services enterprise in the United States, to underscore the importance of having a skilled management labor force capable of developing, sustaining, and, where necessary, changing this institution. The demographics of those who ply this craft and issues that bear on the recruitment, development, and competence of this workforce are reviewed. Major dimensions of management practice and variations at several levels are discussed. We then look at several issues associated with managing in a human services context that have particular relevance for improving the quality of services to consumers. The chapter concludes with a brief note on challenges facing practitioners in the years ahead.

The Importance of Management

Management, or what managers do to catalyze and support the capacity of organizations to realize their goals, is critical to the development, implementation, and effectiveness of human services. People may argue about the precise nature of the manager's contribution to these objectives, or how managers can best achieve them, but there is little question that managers are central players in the human services enterprise. These contributions are reflected in four areas.

Managers at all levels are instrumental in implementing the intent of human services policies

3

formulated by public (e.g., Congress, state legislatures, federal and state executives) and private (e.g., boards) governing bodies. Such policies typically set forth broad goals, populations to be served, programs to be delivered, and funding and accountability arrangements, but it is the job of the manager and staff to translate these directives into programs and services that are competently and fairly administered to intended consumers.

Managers are not only implementers of policies, they also inform and influence the policy formulation process (Austin, 2002). Policymakers rely on feedback from administrators who are close to the communities and persons served. Managers participate in the policy process by advocating for changes that will correct flaws in authorizing policies, identifying unmet needs and emerging social problems, and representing the interests of groups that are underserved or disenfranchised. Increasingly, managers, especially those at executive levels, participate in the policy process through special interest associations (e.g., welfare directors, community mental health associations).

Even as managers are responsible for implementing and shaping social policy, they also play a vital role in networking with other agencies serving a common clientele. Human services "systems" are complex and decentralized, with multiple funding sources and lines of accountability that pose potential barriers to consumers. Increasingly, managers act as systems "engineers," seeking multi-agency solutions to such problems as service fragmentation, eligibility barriers, and lack of interagency coordination. In virtually all human fields (e.g., child welfare, mental health, health), there is a continuing search for collaborative modes that enable consumers to more easily access services and allow agencies to share and exchange information and resources (Alter, 2000; Bardach, 1998).

For at least the last 40 years, human services agencies have been under increasing pressure to account for how they expend public and private funds and with what effects. These expectations have been articulated in federal, state, and local policies and in the nonprofit sector. Managers and their staffs are the first line of accountability in the human services, and it is through them, largely, that policymakers and the public learn whether social policies are having the desired effects. In addition, managers at all levels of human services agencies are responsible for seeing that their organizations have the necessary political, fiscal, and human resources to achieve agency goals and objectives. Bringing all these elements together to create and sustain high-performing agencies is the consummate challenge of leadership.

The Human Services Institution

The term *human services* often refers to a wide spectrum of organizations in health, mental health, education, and social services. Here, we confine the definition to those organizations that provide or support personal social services to children and their families, older adults, the mentally ill, substance abusers, the physically and developmentally disabled, the homeless, and others who need assistance in changing behaviors, acquiring skills, resolving personal and interpersonal problems, and accessing the resources and care necessary to sustain themselves. The programs provided include, prominently, services such as income assistance, counseling and therapy, maintenance, social care, socialization, and rehabilitation.

Human services organizations, as a class, share certain fundamental similarities, including the following:

- a heavy reliance on third-party financing, whereby all or some of the cost of the service is paid by a third party, such as the government or an insurance company, rather than directly by the consumer;
- the goal of improving consumers' physical and psychological well-being, behavior, skills, and social conditions;

- the use of technologies that do not have highly predictable consumer outcomes;
- the participation of consumers with unique goals, personal characteristics, and life experiences in the co-production of outcomes;
- a reliance on collaborating agencies to provide essential complementary services to clients;
- a reliance on the skill, personal commitment, judgment, and discretion of front-line professional personnel in service delivery. (Austin, 2002; Hasenfeld, 1992)

Human services organizations vary in the extent to which they possess all these characteristics. For example, many agencies derive some of their income directly from client fees rather than third-party payers. In some agencies, such as public assistance, the technologies employed are fairly routine and the outcomes largely predictable. The qualifications of staff in these several fields tend to vary from little or no professional training to extensive professional education. Despite these variations, the issues confronting managers in these fields are sufficiently similar to justify thinking of human services management as a generic practice applicable across this diverse institution.

The performance of human services organizations is a matter of considerable importance to society. Collectively, the organizations in this sector contribute to the social cohesion of society by redistributing income and resources to the less fortunate, caring for persons whose circumstances fall below what the community has defined as minimally desirable, giving voice to the interests and needs of disenfranchised and powerless persons and groups, and rehabilitating disabled or dysfunctional persons so they can realize their potential and contribute to their families and communities.

The human services sector is also important to society because it is responsible for the management of tens of billions of dollars each year that are used to serve many millions of distressed and needy people of all races and ethnicities from across the social spectrum. A more detailed discussion of the structure and financing of human services will be found in Chapter 4, but it may be useful here to briefly touch on the scope of this enterprise to underscore the critical importance of management to the proper design and operation of human services.

The Scope of Human Services

Human services organizations are found in the nonprofit, public, and for-profit sectors of the economy. The nonprofit sector is a major conveyor of personal social services. In 2003, 100,800 nonprofit human services organizations in the United States filed returns with the government (there are more such organizations; nonprofits with less than $25,000 in yearly income are not required to file returns). In addition, there are many religious, health, and educational organizations with human services programs that are not reflected in this figure. The filing organizations had revenues of $152 billion (rounded) derived principally from program service revenues ($81.4 billion) and from contributions, gifts, and grants ($58.8 billion; U.S. Census Bureau, 2008b).

Public human services organizations are located at the federal level, in every state and territory, and in many local and/or regional jurisdictions. The U.S. Department of Health and Human Services in 2006 spent approximately $48 billion for discretionary and mandated human services including substance abuse and mental health services, services to the aged, services to children and families (including foster care and adoption assistance, child care, and public assistance), and the Social Services Block grant (U.S. Department of Health and Human Services, n.d.). There are also numerous public human services agencies at state and local government levels. The amount spent by these governments for public welfare programs, including cash payments, vendor payments, and social services, was approximately $335 billion in 2004 (U.S. Census Bureau, 2008a).

Finally, there is a substantial for-profit sector in the human services. It is difficult to estimate how much is spent by these agencies, but the U.S. Census Bureau's Survey of Businesses for 2002 provides data on revenues and operating expenses of businesses in the "Health Care and Social Assistance Sector" (U.S. Census Bureau, 2005). Revenues/receipts for businesses that correspond most closely to our definition of human services (e.g., mental health, substance abuse, child care, individual and family services, rehabilitation, social assistance), which does not include medical and health care fields, were nearly $250 billion. These data include both for-profit and nonprofit businesses, so it is not possible to estimate expenditures of the for-profit sector only, but we know based on observation that for-profit firms are substantially involved in the mental health, substance abuse, and child care and other human services fields and that their presence in this sector is substantial and growing (Schmid, 2004).

Even though the amount expended for human services in the U.S. is quite large, it represents only a small percentage of total outlays in the nonprofit, government, and for-profit sectors as a whole. Still, expenditures for human services represent a significant transfer of resources to the poor and disabled populations in this county. How well these services are managed to benefit these groups is a matter of critical importance.

Another perspective on the scope and size of the human services sector is provided by employment figures. In fields roughly corresponding to our definition of human services, which the U.S. Department of Labor refers to as "Social Assistance," in 2006 there were 1.52 million employees in the private sector, including managerial, professional (social workers, marriage and family therapists, psychologists, etc), service, and administrative support workers. Thirty-five percent of these workers, or approximately 530,000, were professional and paraprofessional service providers (U.S. Department of Labor Bureau of Labor Statistics, 2007a). In the state and local governments in 2006 there were

approximately 428,000 professionals and para-professionals offering human services (e.g., public assistance, child abuse and foster care services, probation, home health services). These figures do not reflect the human services program employees in schools and medical institutions (e.g., hospitals, health maintenance organizations). Based on these data, it is fair to estimate that there are well over 1 million human services workers in the public and private sectors. Included in this workforce there were approximately 562,000 social workers (including masters- and bachelor-level personnel), 352,000 social and human services assistants (usually persons with no formal professional training), and 93,000 probation officers and correctional treatment specialists (U.S. Department of Labor Bureau of Labor Statistics, 2007a).

No discussion of the human services labor force should exclude volunteers, who numbered nearly 8 million in 2006 (in organizations defined as "social and community service"). Median yearly hours worked for volunteers of all types of organizations was 50 hours a year (yearly hours for human services are not reported separately), and there is no reason to believe this would be less in social and community services (U.S. Census Bureau, 2008b).

Given the thousands of human services organizations, the billions of dollars spent each year to serve the poor and disadvantaged, and the number of employees and volunteers who work in this field, it is understandable that the performance of this industry draws increasing scrutiny by government officials, academics, and private associations. Central to this concern is the quality of managerial leadership.

The Human Services Managers in the Labor Force: Demographics

Managers in the human services come from a wide variety of educational backgrounds and career paths (Hoefer, 2003). There appear to be three main groups, though their relative numbers and distribution across sectors and subfields in the human services is a matter of speculation. Included are those with a variety of undergraduate and community college degrees who began as frontline personnel and worked their way up the hierarchy. These managers probably represent a substantial proportion of supervisory and administrative personnel in the public human services (but probably a smaller percentage of the comparable positions in the nonprofit and for-profit sectors), where over the last several decades, owing to declassification efforts (Pecora & Austin, 1983), public agencies recruited a large number of frontline workers without professional credentials.

Another significant source of management personnel is persons with specialized management degrees, such as public administration, health administration, business administration, and nonprofit management. The number of human services managers with this kind of educational preparation has probably increased in the last two decades as university-based management programs have given more attention to preparing students for nonprofit and human services careers (Hoefer, 2003; Mirabella & Wish, 2000).

The human services also draw heavily upon graduates of the helping professions to fill management positions. Social workers with masters and bachelor degrees are prominent among this group, which also includes psychologists, gerontologists, nurses, and ministers, among others. Most of these persons are trained to be direct service providers and begin their careers in this capacity before being promoted through the ranks to supervisory, managerial, and executive roles. In social work, a substantial number of the 177 accredited masters programs in the Council on Social Work Education's 2006 *Directory of Accredited Programs* (www.cswe.org) offer specialties in management and related practices, such as planning and community organization (sometimes referred to as macro specializations), often combined with one year of generic preparation in social work practice and core subjects such as human behavior, social policy, and

research. Data on the career trajectories of these graduates are fragmentary (Martin, Pines, & Healy, 1999; Patti, Diedrick, Olson, & Crowell, 1979), but it appears that they are more likely to move into management careers than are graduates who are primarily trained for direct services jobs.

There are no definitive data on the number and characteristics of managerial personnel in the human services, owing partly to the varied ways in which human services is defined. However, we can piece together a rough estimate by looking at several sources. In 2006, as we discussed earlier, there were 1.5 million workers in the nongovernmental private social assistance field. Of these, about 132,000 were in management-related jobs, or about 9% of the total workers in this sector (U.S. Department of Labor Bureau of Labor Statistics, 2007a). The number of management personnel in the public sector human services is more difficult to calculate because employment data for managers by area of government are not reported. However, we know that there were approximately 8 million state and local employees in 2006. Management-related jobs accounted for about 11.7% of this total (U.S. Department of Labor Bureau of Labor Statistics, 2007b). If we assume, conservatively, that one quarter (25%), or 2 million (in California in 2007–08, budgets for health and welfare and corrections accounted for approximately 39% of the budget), of all state and local employees are employed in human services agencies, and assume further that a like percentage of this workforce is in management-related jobs (line and staff), then we may estimate that there are approximately 234,000 managers in public human services agencies (11.7% of 2 million). Thus, it can be roughly estimated that there may be as many as 360,000 management and related jobs in the private and public human services. And this, no doubt, underestimates the size of the management labor force because it does not include the health and education fields that have substantial human services program elements or management positions in the for-profit sector.

Unfortunately, we know very little about the education, gender, and ethnicity of managers in this field, their career trajectories, the similarities or differences in the characteristics of managers in different sectors, and whether the composition of the management labor force is changing (e.g., more or fewer women, more or fewer persons of color, more or fewer social workers or public administrators). In a field that plays such an important role in American society, it is unfortunate that more is not known about those who lead and manage this institution.

While there is little information about all managers in the human services, some data are available on social workers in management. A recent study by the National Association of Social Work (NASW) Center for Workforce Studies and the Center for Health Workforce Studies (Whitaker, Weismiller, & Clark, 2006a), which examined the personal attributes and professional activities of a national sample of *licensed* social workers in the U.S., found that 27% of the respondents in the study spent 20 hours or more each week in management-related functions, including supervision. Extrapolated to the entire population of licensed social workers, this would suggest a total of approximately 84,000 licensed social workers engaged wholly or partly in administrative practice.

Because this study did not include unlicensed social workers, we cannot know for certain how many more social workers are in management-related jobs. However, the workforce study estimates that there are nearly 900,000 self-identified social workers in the U.S. Prior studies of NASW members in 1988 and 1991 found that 24.1% and 22.3%, respectively, were primarily in management work (Gibelman & Schervish, 1993). Based on the NASW workforce study estimates and the earlier NASW membership studies, it is reasonable to assume that 25% of all self-identified social workers are in management-related jobs: somewhere in the neighborhood of 225,000. Even this rough approximation suggests that social workers are a significant source of management in the human services.

While the distribution of social work managers across types of agencies and fields of practice is not well documented, we know from the NASW workforce study that 66% of the respondents worked in private agencies, including nonprofit and for profit, while 33% were employed in public agencies at all levels of government (Whitaker, Weismiller, & Clark, 2006b). These findings are close to the results of a 2000 survey of members of the National Network of Social Work Managers (NNSWM), which showed that 74% of its members were employed in nonprofit and for-profit sectors and 26% in public agencies (Bess & Associates, 2000).

Social work managers in NNSWM are employed in a wide variety of program areas, including child welfare (43.8%) and mental health (39.1%) services, adolescents (32%), aging (21.1%), and community development (20.5%; Bess & Associates, 2000). These figures correspond roughly to the distribution of all licensed social workers in various fields of practice (Whitaker et al., 2006b), so there is some reason to believe that social work administrators are also mostly found in these areas.

Although the number of women in social work far exceeds the number of men, they appear to be underrepresented in the ranks of management. The NASW workforce study of licensed social workers found that men were more likely than women to be spending any of their time in administration (76% to 66%) or supervision (66% to 56%; Whitaker et al., 2006b). In the 1991 survey of NASW members referred to earlier, a significantly higher proportion of males (32.7%) than females (18.7%) reported their primary job functions as management and supervision (Gibelman & Schervish, 1993). A more recent survey of NNSWM members indicates that women are substantially less represented in the membership of that organization than their number in the profession would suggest (Bess & Associates, 2000). This said, there is some evidence that the relative proportion of woman in higher level management may be increasing. A recent study of 121 Texas public organizations showed that the percentage of women in "higher administration" and women CEOs increased significantly over two decades. Women CEOs represented 33.9% of all state agency CEOs in 2005 (Williams & Gray, 2007). While this progress is noteworthy, it appears that there is much to do to achieve gender equality in the ranks of management.

There also appears to be a continuing discrepancy between the salaries of men and women across all types of jobs in social work, including management. Data from the study of licensed social workers indicate that men make substantially more than women in all kinds of full-time jobs (Whitaker et al., 2006b). In a study of social workers in Pennsylvania, the authors found that men's salaries were, on average, $3,500 a year higher than women's, with the discrepancy explained largely by years of experience and management positions (Koeske & Krowinski, 2004). The reasons for gender disparities in the representation and income of men and women in management are complex, but they probably involve some combination of early career choices, gender stereotyping, and hiring discrimination (Austin, 1995). These disparities are persistent and troublesome in a field that employs a disproportionate number of women.

The representation of ethnic and racial minorities in human services management is also a continuing concern, given that agencies serve a large and growing number of people of color. Evidence from a multi-site study of public welfare agencies with a sample of over 1,900 respondents revealed that European (white) American men occupied 40% of all administrative jobs and 21% of all supervisory jobs, but comprised only 15.7% of the sample. European American men and women were more likely to hold high-status agency jobs than their minority counterparts (McNeely, Sapp, & Dailey, 1998). Public policies regarding equal opportunity and affirmative action, and a growing awareness that minority leadership should more nearly reflect the communities being served, seem to have intensified efforts to recruit and develop minority

workers for management responsibilities. However, the relatively small percentage of such professionals in human services management is a continuing challenge for the human services. Additionally, as Mor Barak (2000) has pointed out, efforts to increase the representation of minorities in management must be paired with increased attention to how agencies can fully include such workers in the social and cultural fabric of these organizations so their talents can be fully developed and utilized.

Administration Defined: Functions and Roles

The terms *management* and *administration* will be used interchangeably in this chapter and throughout this book. Although there have been many attempts to distinguish these terms (e.g., level of responsibility, external vs. internal orientation, human services vs. business), there is no widely accepted agreement regarding their usage (Austin & Kruzich, 2004). Indeed, judging from titles of recent textbooks and job titles used in agencies, it appears that the word *management* and its variations (manager, managerial, managing) may be the more popular term. While *administration* is more often used in public services, this is not universally the case.

Whether management or administration, the words are applied in several ways. Management/administration is often employed to describe the particular person or persons high in the organization's hierarchy whose policies and decisions constitute a leadership regime, as in the phrase "the management of this agency is fiscally conservative, or dynamic, or visionary."

Management/administration is also used to address the totality of processes and functions that are performed throughout the organization in order to accomplish its goals. In this sense, the administration of the agency is characterized as a "system of coordinated and cooperative effort" that extends beyond the responsibilities of managers to include all those who have a stake in the performance of the agency (Stein, 1970, p. 7; Weinbach, 1998). This concept of management stresses the notion of collective responsibility, "wherein each person (i.e., role), every functional entity, plays a vital part in the administrative process" (Patti, 1983, p. 25).

Finally, management/administration refers to a set of functions and roles that are largely (though not exclusively) the province of persons in middle and upper levels of organizations. In this meaning, the manager or administrator engages in a purposeful method of practice that is aimed at *helping* the organization to

- develop a mission, goals, strategic and operational plans aimed at meeting important community needs;
- develop an administrative structure that assigns responsibility, allows for accountability, enables communication both laterally and vertically, and defines decision-making processes;
- acquire, allocate, and monitor resources necessary for agency operations;
- represent and advocate for the agency in the community and with external constituencies that provide legitimacy and resources;
- collaborate with other agencies serving a common clientele;
- recruit, develop, train, and supervise a skilled workforce that is committed to the achievement of the agency's goals;
- facilitate an agency environment that values staff and empowers them to give their best efforts in the provision of services to clients;
- develop and implement information technologies that permit the agency to assess the productivity and effectiveness of its own programs and services in the interest of continuously improving its services, meeting the needs of consumers, and accounting to community stakeholders.

Note that we use the word *helping* above to convey the idea that managers seldom accomplish these things unilaterally. Their core function is to lead, to catalyze action, to create circumstances that empower other persons to perform these functions effectively and efficiently.

Management Roles

Human services management or administration is a multi-faceted practice and process that is, or should be, ultimately concerned with delivering services to consumers. The services are aimed at a wide variety of goals but include, prominently, changes in the statuses, social conditions, behaviors, and capabilities of individuals, families, and/or community groups. To help the agency achieve these goals, managers perform a broad array of roles that require political, analytic, interpersonal, and leadership skills.

Managerial roles have been variously defined (Austin & Kruzich, 2004; Mintzberg, 1973; Patti, 1977), but the framework suggested by Menefee and his colleagues (Menefee, 2001) is useful because it grew out of an empirical examination of what social work managers actually do in the human services (see Chapter 5 for a fuller discussion of management roles and tasks). According to Menefee, managers perform the following roles:

- *Communicator:* exchanging information with stakeholders within and outside the organization to keep them informed on matters pertinent to common interests and concerns. This role is instrumental in the performance of all those that follow.
- *Boundary spanner:* creating and sustaining relationships with stakeholders in the task environment to build collaborative arrangements and strategically position the agency to be influential in key decision forums.
- *Futurist-innovator:* understanding and adapting to changes in the social, economic, political, demographic, and technological environments that pose threats and opportunities and planning to anticipate and shape responses to new opportunities.

- *Organizer:* devising agency structures and work processes that define the distribution of authority and responsibility, enabling co-ordination of activities and accountability; planning for, resourcing and implementing programs to implement agency mission and goals; and recruiting, training, and evaluating staff to acquire/develop the skills necessary to competently implement services.

- *Resource administrator:* acquiring and managing the human, financial, technological, and physical resources necessary to carry out agency programs effectively and efficiently. This role involves a wide array of tasks including marketing, fundraising, contracting, financial planning, budgeting and reporting, and accounting for agency performance.

- *Evaluator:* assessing community need for agency programs and monitoring program quality and service outcomes with a variety of research and information technologies.

- *Policy practitioner:* interpreting governmental policies and regulations pertaining to agency operations, providing feedback on the efficacy of policy, and influencing policy decision makers.

- *Advocate:* fostering an awareness of emerging problems and unmet needs; working to organize community action systems to present grievances or press for change; and lobbying for new or amended legislation.

- *Supervisor:* directing, advising, and evaluating immediate subordinates to improve their performance; assigning work, devising efficient work processes, and creating a supportive work climate that is conducive to staff learning and job satisfaction.

- *Facilitator:* enhancing commitment to agency mission and values by promoting an agency culture that encourages participation, collaboration, mutual support, individual development, and effective performance.

- *Team builder-leader:* organizing committees, coalitions, and work groups both in and out of the agency and providing leadership to enable effective group processes that will lead to task accomplishment.

While managerial roles (behaviors) can be disaggregated for purposes of discussion, in practice managers are typically performing at least several roles in any particular context, so that the performance of one is complemented by others in a kind of behavioral configuration. For example, the role of *communicator* is essential to the effective performance of most other roles. The *evaluator* and *resource administrator* roles are organically related because the decisions required to plan and allocate resources depend on the information generated through assessment and evaluation. The *team builder* role comes into play whenever actors inside and/or outside the organization with diverse interests must be brought together to pursue a common purpose, so this role is essential to *advocacy, boundary spanning,* and *organizing.* Likewise, it is inconceivable that a manager could effectively perform his or her role as an *advocate* if he or she was not also proficient at *boundary spanning* and *policy practice.*

Variations in Management

Management roles become more or less salient under different circumstances or contingencies. One important contingency is the organizational level at which the manager is practicing (Thompson, 1967). Organizations generally have at least three levels of management authority and responsibility: executive or institutional, middle or program management, and supervisory management. The division of labor between management levels tends to become more sharply defined as an organization becomes larger and more complex. In a very small agency, for example, a director might perform most of the roles described above, while in a large one, managers at each level are likely to have a more distinct and specialized role profile (Menefee, 2001).

At the *executive* or *institutional* level are persons who carry overall responsibility for directing and coordinating the activities of the entire organization or a major portion thereof (e.g., a division, a regional office). Typical titles for managers at this level include chief executive officer (CEO), chief operating officer (COO), director, associate director, and division manager. These managers will usually be primarily responsible for making strategic decisions about agency direction within the policy parameters set forth by their board of directors (in nonprofits), legislative bodies, or their superiors in the executive branch (in public agencies); acquiring or maintaining funds needed for operations; tracking changes in the agency's environment (e.g., emerging legislation, new funding sources, developing social trends and problems); advocating for underserved or disenfranchised groups; and interfacing with other agencies in the community to develop collaborative agreements. Increasingly, executive-level managers are expected to build organizational cultures that feature values such as the primacy of service to consumers, appreciation of diversity, learning, and innovation (Latting et al., 2004; see also Chapter 7). These managers are likely be most heavily involved in roles focusing on *boundary spanning, innovation, policy practice, advocacy, resource administration, facilitation,* and *team building.* They will also perform other roles, but these are likely to be central to their job responsibilities.

The middle management or program level of management includes persons who have responsibility for directing a major subunit of an agency, such as a department, bureau, or program. Persons at this level are often referred to as department manager, program director, bureau chief, or section chief. Middle managers are typically charged with seeing that organizational goals and priorities are translated into program objectives, planning programs, devising budgets for their programs within limits set by their superiors, allocating resources to different programs or service elements, hiring or approving the hiring of staff, and liaising and coordinating with other departments or community agencies that share a clientele or offer a complementary service. They play a pivotal role in building a working climate conducive to workers' satisfaction and commitment. They do this by seeing that their staff are adequately provisioned, trained, and compensated; by

providing opportunities for employees to participate in decisions that affect their work; and by providing an environment that rewards employee learning, initiative, and innovation. Finally, middle managers have primary responsibility for assessing the effectiveness of the program(s) under their direction. Keys to accomplishing this task include, but are not limited to, devising or approving evaluation protocols, seeing that they are properly implemented and utilizing the information to determine whether performance standards are being achieved, and helping workers to learn from their practice.

Highly salient roles at this level of management are *organizing, administering resources,* and *evaluation. Team building* and *facilitating* with supervisory staff under their direction or with peers in other departments or agencies are also likely to be important. Middle managers are often expert in programs/services they administer and are frequently called upon for *advocacy* and *policy changing* activities.

The supervisory or technical level of management is in closest proximity to the front line, service-providing staff. Often referred to as supervisor, coordinator, team leader, or project manager, these managers are usually responsible for seeing that the smallest work units in the organization operate efficiently and effectively. Supervisory managers have immediate responsibility in their units for delegating and assigning work, overseeing workflow, and ensuring staff compliance with agency rules and procedures. They provide advice and direction on case services and dispositions, help to facilitate worker access to agency resources, and lend emotional and social support to workers. It is at this level of management that performance evaluations of employees occur and recommendations are made on such key personnel issues as hiring, raises, promotions, and retention. Supervisors often buffer or mediate adverse or disruptive conditions in the larger agency and may advocate for staff concerns and requests (Hopkins & Austin, 2004).

Key roles at this level include *supervisor, facilitator,* and *team builder* within their respective units. Where they are delegated responsibility for planning and allocating resources, supervisors may also *organize* and *administer resources.* The *evaluator* role will come into play in assessing the performance of direct service staff. Supervisory managers arguably exert the most important influence on how frontline staff performs because they shape the day-to-day working conditions and climate in their work units (Hopkins & Austin, 2004).

Managers at all levels are assisted in their line responsibilities (i.e., those that involve the direction and implementation of the agency's programs) by staff personnel. Depending on their areas of expertise, staff personnel provide information and supportive services to line personnel in the performance of all the roles discussed here in areas like human resources, development (i.e., fundraising), planning, information systems, financial management, research, and evaluation.

Employees without management portfolios (e.g., service providers and technical support staff) also participate in the managerial processes. Their most common contributions are as *facilitators* and *team builders.* In many agencies, they will serve as members or chairs of standing or ad hoc committees addressing issues such as quality assurance, personnel grievances, and budget planning and reorganization. The direct service staff also are instrumental in providing feedback about the impact of agency policies and programs and assessing the effectiveness of their own interventions.

In sum, the process of management involves players at all levels of the organization who contribute in different, but overlapping, ways to the management of an agency. It is the coordinated execution of these functions, rather than the behavior of one person or one level of management, that produces organizational excellence, though responsibility for particular functions may fall more heavily at one or another level. Not all managers perform their responsibilities completely or effectively. Levels of commitment to organizational goals and objectives vary, and

there is often conflict over substantive policy differences, personal issues, competition for resource, and so on. To the extent these problems are persistent, the quality and effectiveness of services can be compromised.

Management Practice in a Human Services Context

In this section, we address how selected characteristics of human services organizations shape the practice of those who manage them. In particular, we are interested in how managers attempt to develop and sustain effective services to consumers in the face of challenges that are inherent in these types of organizations. As indicated earlier, the auspices, political context, task environments, goals, technologies, and labor force characteristics in this field are unique and suggest that human services organizations are a distinctive variety of organization; they require a management praxis that differs in important ways from business organizations and, to some extent, other public and nonprofit organizations (Austin, 1995, 2002; see also Chapter 3).

The Management of Performance

Over the last three decades or so, there has been a slow but steady shift from managing agency processes to managing for agency performance. Managing for performance refers to what managers do to develop and sustain the resources, structures, and social-psychological conditions in agencies that foster high quality services and produce measurable, intended outcomes for consumers (e.g., changes in social status, living conditions, behaviors, skills, social relationships). Where once human services were considered an "intrinsic good" (Carter, 1983) that need only be made available to the right consumers in the right amounts at a reasonable cost, agencies are now held to a standard that involves accountability for consumer outcomes.

This transition, often halting and unevenly implemented across the field, resulted from the convergence of several developments. The first was the adoption of policies by governments and nonprofit institutions that required setting goals and benchmarks and measuring program results against these standards (Martin & Kettner, 1996). Perhaps the most important of these policies was the federal Government Performance and Results Act of 1993 (GPRA), which required that federal agencies (and state and nonprofit agencies that receive federal funding) develop and measure goals and objectives for their major programs. Given little notice when passed in 1993, GPRA is now operative and is reflected in such important human services policies as the Adoption and Safe Families Act (U.S. Public Law 105-89). At the state level, the growth of managed care systems, purchase of service arrangements between public and nonprofit agencies (McBeath & Meezan, 2006), and performance-based contracting, whereby public agencies insist on evidence of goal achievement from agencies that receive contracts, have hastened the move to performance management (Martin, 2005). Similarly, foundations and federated funders in the nonprofit sector increasingly require that agencies specify, measure, and report on outcomes as a condition of continued funding.

Second, a parallel and sometimes intersecting development has been the recognition by practitioners and academics in the human services that in order to improve services, it is essential to know more about what works, with whom, and under what circumstances. Some of the efforts aimed at helping develop better, more effective interventions are documenting and disseminating "best practices," building agency information systems sensitive to consumer outcomes, designing programs and services based on empirical evidence (empirically based practice, or EBP), and learning how to move interventions proven effective in clinical studies to agency implementation (Johnson & Austin, 2006). This movement also produced a major effort to develop evaluative and information technologies that have advanced the measurement and analysis of performance information for clinical and administrative decision making (Bliss, 2007; Dobmeyer, Woodward, & Olson, 2002; Neuman, 2003; also see Chapters 8 and 9 for further discussion).

Concurrently, developments in management theory and practice began to focus on how to manage for results (Gregoire, Rapp, & Poertner, 1995; Martin, 1993; Rapp & Poertner, 1992). A variety of management models adapted to the human services focused on the relationship between processes and results for consumers. Strategies such as management by objectives (MBO), total quality management (TQM), continuous quality improvement systems (CQI), and leadership strategies (e.g., transformational leadership) were aimed at producing high-achieving organizations (Mary, 2005).

While the definition and measurement of organizational performance and the use of management strategies aimed at consumer outcomes are becoming more common, these practices are still a development in progress in the human services. There remain a number of administrative challenges to seeing that performance management becomes standard practice (Johnson & Austin, 2006). These include the following:

- developing an agency culture that values questions and a willingness to try new interventions suggested by research evidence, where managers and supervisors stress the primacy of client service, focus on client outcomes, and reward practices that are based on the best available empirical knowledge (Poertner, 2006);
- modifying workloads to allow workers time for discovery and the design and implementation of new interventions;
- providing staff training, time, and resources necessary for staff to access service-relevant research data bases, library resources, and information from other agencies working with similar clienteles;
- developing internal agency expertise to monitor and support the use of empirically based practices throughout the agency;

- developing collaborative relationships between agencies and university researchers, such as those that have been successful in California, where the University of California, Berkeley and San Diego State University have partnered with public welfare agencies to conduct research and training (Patti, 2003), and in Illinois, where the University of Illinois at Urbana-Champaign Children and Family Research Center has been involved with the Illinois Department of Children and Family Services in assessing the impact of programs for children and youth (www.socialwork.uiuc.edu/people/Testa.html).

In making the shift to performance management, agency administrators confront a number of issues. The most obvious of these is acquiring the resources necessary to underwrite this effort. Small agencies, in particular, often do not have sufficient resources to purchase advanced information technology, fund training, or free up staff to participate in design and experimentation activities. Transferring funds from current program operations, developing collaborative arrangements with other agencies that are also attempting to change direction in order to share cost, joining with university researchers to acquire research grants, and seeking development grants from foundations can be useful strategies, but they also require resources, vision, and willingness to risk.

The move to performance management has other implications. If funding (reimbursement) is tied to the achievement of service outcomes, then the ability to determine the resources and processes that must be applied to achieve these outcomes is essential. The specification of service technologies, the selection and training of personnel who can implement these services (see Chapter 12), and the development of management information systems to track how service efforts are related to outcomes (see Chapters 8 and 9) all become imperative in this service environment. Moreover, to the extent that funding is

tied to outcomes, the ability of managers to cost services elements will be vital to the financial viability of their agencies.

While all of these developments are now well under way in the human services, implementation of performance management is not without problems and dilemmas that will have to be addressed if the promise of this approach is to be realized.

Consumers come to the service experience with their own goals and ways of assessing the quality and effectiveness of service (Anspach, 1991). As outcomes and the means for achieving them are increasingly predetermined (service protocols) rather than mutually defined in service transactions, it may become difficult to elicit the involvement and cooperation of consumers necessary to realize service objectives. Indeed, such a scenario raises the specter of consumer disempowerment, which is antithetical to the coproduction of desired service outcomes (Hasenfeld, 1992).

Alternatively, the practice of "creaming" may become more attractive as agencies look for consumers who fit best with the service technologies that are thought to be the most effective, though Martin (2005) has argued that creaming may not be as much of a problem as critics have claimed. The significant challenge for human services organizations will be to develop service technologies that allow the exercise of consumer choice and influence in the context of more and more specific service protocols and performance expectations.

Consumers as Partners

In recent years, it has come to be recognized that consumers of social services are necessary partners in the creation of change. Changes in behavior, attitudes, skills, and even environmental conditions are ultimately achieved only with their active participation. While this view is now conventional wisdom, there remain significant forces in organizational and professional practice that work to maintain the power of the organization and its service providers and perpetuate the dependence and disempowerment of clients (Hasenfeld, 1992). Active participation requires information, influence, and choice. In order to empower clients in the service experience, managers and direct service providers must provide consumers or their representatives with a role in agency governance, including program planning and evaluation; recognize and encourage their strengths and capacities in determining the kinds of services they need; allow workers the discretion to collaborate with clients in deciding upon goals and interventions; and afford clients an opportunity to evaluate their experience (Hardina, 2005; Rapp & Poertner, 1992; see also Chapter 14). Social service consumers are often without the political, economic, and organizational power necessary to assert their claims. This, and the fact that most organizations draw their legitimacy and funding from persons other than clients, makes it tempting for managers and providers to disregard or neglect the interests and the contribution of consumers to the service process. The manager plays a vital role in seeing that the agency culture stresses the primacy of client service and recognizing that good service outcomes are more likely when clients are related to as partners.

Frontline Workers and Service Effectiveness

Frontline workers in human services agencies are the principal instruments of service delivery. Their attitudes, perspectives, skills, and willingness to give fully of their energy and talent in delivering services are critical components of the service delivery process and service outcomes. It follows that a central concern of human services managers is fostering an agency climate and culture that promotes job satisfaction and worker commitment to agency goals and programs and protects against high levels of stress and strain that often undermine worker motivation.

There is considerable evidence over several decades that links organizational conditions and processes variously with job satisfaction, commitment, turnover, and burnout (see, e.g., Glisson & Durick, 1988; Glisson & Himmelfarn, 1998; Himle, Jayaratne, & Thyness, 1989; McNeely, 1992; Mor Barak, Nissly, & Levin, 2001; Nissly, Mor Barak, & Levin, 2005; Olmstead & Christenson, 1973).

This body of research cannot be easily aggregated because of different methodologies and measurements, but such variables as job characteristics, work load, job stress, supervisory support, and worker participation and discretion have consistently been associated in various studies with worker attitudes (see Chapters 6 and 10 for detailed reviews of this literature). But additional work is needed in several areas to better inform management practice.

There is a need for further research on the relationships between workers' responses to organizational conditions (climate, culture, leadership) and their effectiveness with clients (see, e.g., Latting et al., 2004; Martin & Segal, 1977; Prager, 1984/5).

A study by Glisson and Himmelfarn (1998) on service outcomes in child services programs is perhaps the best evidence we have to date that a work environment characterized by "job satisfaction, fairness, role clarity, cooperation and personalization and lower levels of role overload, conflict and emotional exhaustion are likely to support caseworker's efforts to accomplish service objectives" (p. 416). A more recent analysis by Glisson and James (2002) found that organizations with a "team constructive culture," characterized by norms that promoted achievement, developed the potential of employees, and encouraged mutual support, were predictive of worker attitudes and worker-assessed service quality and turnover in a one-year follow up.

The role of organizational leadership in enabling positive work conditions and enhancing service quality and effectiveness also needs more attention. Most of this work has been done on supervisory leaders, but relatively little has looked at higher level agency managers in the human services (Poertner, 2006). There has been extensive research on the role of transformational leadership (e.g., ethical behavior, concern for subordinates, high expectations, intellectual stimulation) in building positive organizational cultures in business and public organizations (Bass & Avolio, 2006; Yukl, 2006), but this model has not been extensively tested in human services. There is evidence that this kind of leadership may improve performance in human services organizations. An early study by Glisson (1989), while not a test of transformational leadership, found that some of these leadership qualities were positively related to worker commitment. Latting and colleagues (2004) have shown that leaders who use transformational strategies appear to elicit commitment among workers and perceptions of higher quality client service. Packard's (2001) qualitative study showed that an organization with visionary leadership produced very high commitment among its employees in a program for the homeless.

Additional research is also needed to investigate the effects of the policy environment on internal working conditions and worker responses. Among the conditions commonly found in the human services are multiple and conflicting goals, uncertain funding, frequent policy change, ambiguous policy directives, excessive rule compliance and paperwork requirements, and externally imposed personnel policies (Smith & Donovan, 2003; Smith & Lipskey, 1993). How managers mediate these frequently aversive external influences and how they advocate for changes that will allow agencies to maintain productive work environments have not yet received much attention and yet they are major challenges to human services managers and are likely to become more challenging in the future (see Chapter 22).

Moral Issues, Ethical Choices, and Trust

Trust, or the perception of others that one is fair, responsible, even handed, and nondiscriminatory,

is a vital resource for human services managers as they work both in and outside the organization. In the human services, trust is especially important because such organizations are expected to act in the best interests of clients and because they have a fiduciary responsibility to use community resources effectively and appropriately. As we have seen in cases involving the United Way, Red Cross, and many public agencies in recent years, the violation of these expectations can bring severe media criticism, loss of financial support, legislative or judicial scrutiny, and other sanctions. Managers win and maintain this trust for themselves and their agencies, in part, by acting in accordance with sound ethical principles (Brody, 1993).

Managers are sometimes obliged to implement policies that may be morally questionable (Hasenfeld, 1992), but since policy directives delegate authority to the agency level and leave large areas for discretion, many difficult choices remain under their purview. These range from the most macro level (e.g., whether to focus agency resources on the most needy and frail populations or on those with less urgent needs but perhaps greater potential for rehabilitation), to program- and service-level decisions (e.g., whether to work toward the termination of parental rights in serious child abuse cases so children can be moved into other permanent living situations), to the internal management of resources (e.g., whether to reduce caseloads to prevent worker burnout or increase them to serve more clients).

These and similarly difficult decisions are pervasive in the human services and can have profound implications for the welfare of individuals, families and communities, and employees. The human services administrator is directly or indirectly involved in making such choices (Austin, 1995; Hasenfeld, 1992; Patti, 1983) or defending those made by subordinates. For this reason, his or her values and ethics are constantly being brought into play in decision making. The manager needs a set of principles or an ethical framework to assist him or her in working through these dilemmas (Brody, 1993; Lewis, 1987; Reamer, 2000).

These issues are typically complex and ambiguous and often involve conflicting and equally compelling values. The consequences of one or another choice are not always clear in advance (e.g., will a child fare better with his natural family, with kin, or in foster care?). Moreover, these decisions are often made in an atmosphere of competing interests where constituents, all of whom may speak for clients, have opposing views. They frequently pose ethical dilemmas when two or more important and equally compelling values are at issue as, for example, whether to maintain a high level of service to the current clientele or reduce services so that more people can be served. Moreover, resolutions often entail tradeoffs (i.e., sacrificing or sub-optimizing one value to achieve another). For example, returning a child to his or her biological family with a previous history of abuse or neglect has the advantage of keeping the child out of foster homes or institutions but may entail the risk of re-abuse.

In this decision environment, the manager is pressed to make reasoned choices based on explicitly ethical criteria and the best available information. Opportunistic, self-serving, or inconsistent decision patterns create a morally ambiguous climate and unclear guidelines for decision making by subordinates, and may generate cynicism among the staff that is required to carry out directives. In an important sense, managers model probity and ethical reasoning for the entire organization and, in so doing, create a normative climate for decision making at every level. This is critical because human services organizations conduct a wide range of transactions with consumers, collaborators, and supporters whose long-term success depends, in great measure, on a sense of mutual trust and fairness (Brody, 1993).

But managers do not operate in an unfettered environment that allows them to make independent choices based solely on their own ethical judgments. Human services organizations are responsible to many constituencies, some of whom may have values and interests different from each other and those of the administrator. Human services agencies function in an environment where legitimacy and resources may be dependent on how they conform to institutionalized environment norms and beliefs (see Chapter 3). In this context, it would be easy to conclude that human services managers are not moral agents but simply functionaries who are compelled to respond to all the constituent interests that bear on the organization. While there are managers who see themselves as functionaries who are simply responsible for executing directives from above, a posture of expedient compliance puts the manager, and indeed the organization, into a kind of moral drift. The literature on management and leadership would argue that the human services organization is better served by managers who act to realize certain values and ethical principles within the organization and defend against constituent demands that may compromise core organizational values (Reamer, 2000).

One of the core values in the human services, expressed in the ethical codes of human services professions, such as the National Association of Social Workers Code of Ethics (www.naswdc.org/pubs/code/code.asp) and the American Nursing Association Code of Ethics (www.nursingworld.org/ethics), the management literature (Brody, 1993; Lewis, 1987; Rapp & Poertner, 1992) and mission statements of most agencies, is the notion that service to clients or consumers is a primary obligation. This ethical precept is based on the premise that although there are many "consumers" of human services, including those that fund and authorize them and other agencies who provide cooperation and resources (Austin, 2002), the primary constituents of the agency are those who rely on it for services. This is a value-based premise rooted in the view that social agencies are instruments of social justice and should seek to protect and advance the interests of their least-advantaged constituents (Zammuto, 1984). The social justice perspective on performance is contrasted with a relativist posture, which suggests that no constituency is a priori more important than any other and therefore the interests of all must served, or a power paradigm perspective, which argues that effective organizations serve primarily the interests of those who provide needed resources (Martin, 1987). Indeed, human services agencies rely on a wide variety of groups and organizations, without whom they would be unable to function. The expectations of these groups may conflict with each other, as well as with the goals and objectives of the agency. In some cases, the power of these groups may be so compelling that an agency has little recourse but to acquiesce. But the human services manager is, or should be, an agent of social change who is attempting to construct a social reality that comes closest to his or her organization's concept of social good. The social justice perspective best serves the ethical purposes of human services managers by focusing, in the first instance, on whether clients' interests are served by the decision to be made. This value premise doesn't necessarily reduce the complexity and ambiguity of ethically charged issues, but it may provide a compass for negotiating the thicket.

Managing in an Environment With Multiple Constituencies

Human services organizations rely on a variety of groups for the legitimacy and resources needed to develop, maintain, and improve agency programs (Gummer, 1990; Hasenfeld, 2000; Schmid, 2000). In return for these resources, constituencies make claims on the organization. Managers must engage with these groups to negotiate the exchanges. The number of constituencies in the working environment of the agency is potentially quite large and heterogeneous, and constituencies often have different expectations. Thus, the manager is responsible for not only negotiating with individual constituent groups but somehow reconciling the multiple claims that are made. A typical list of agency constituents illustrates the diverse and potentially conflicting demands that the manager must address:

- Consumers of services who come to the agency with unique problems and concerns.
- Employees of the organization whose skill and cooperation are needed to carry out the agency's goals and objectives.
- Governing bodies, such as boards and legislatures, that provide authorization and policy direction that frame the parameters of consumer eligibility, service delivery, and desired outcomes.
- Legislatures, government agencies, federated funding agencies, donors, and foundations that provide funds needed to sustain agency operations.
- Collaborating agencies that provide services to common clients before, during, and after their involvement with the agency.
- Accrediting bodies that review and legitimate the agency against various criteria of quality.
- Professional organizations, unions, and other associations that promote the interests of agency employees and may promulgate ethical standards that members are obliged to follow.
- Professional schools that train and socialize staff agency employees and provide research that may inform agency decision making.
- Organized community groups that advocate for and/or seek to protect the rights and interests of consumers, for example, the National Alliance for the Mentally Ill (NAMI).

These groups vary in the power and influence they exert on the agency. Those that are in a position to deny the organization basic resources for its programs and services (e.g., a legislative body or government agency) will exert continuing influence on administrative decision making, but others may be only intermittently important to the organization's welfare (e.g., accrediting bodies at periodic accreditation reviews, community advocacy groups when the agency is found to have violated the rights of consumers or provided substandard services).

Under the best of circumstances, these groups would have similar expectations for the focal organization, but this is seldom the case (Anspach, 1991; Finch, 1978; Herman & Renz, 2004; Martin, 1987; Whetten, 1978).

One major source of divergent expectations grows out of the fact that those who consume services typically pay little of the cost of providing them. Financing is usually provided by third parties such as government, foundations, endowments, and insurance. David Austin (2002) points out that the types of outcomes sought by consumers and funders are often different. The former will seek services that provide them a personal or "private good," while the latter will typically expect a community benefit or so-called "public good." For example, a government agency funding mental health services may be intent on minimizing hospitalization rates and see this as an indicator of agency performance, while consumers, let us say relatives of the seriously mentally ill, will be more concerned with using whatever type of program is needed, including hospitalization, to manage symptoms and ensure the safety of the consumer. The problem is complicated if, as is often true, the organization utilizes personal service technologies whose success, as we have seen, depends centrally on achieving agreement between service provider and consumer regarding treatment goals and means. Pursuing the objectives sought by external funders (e.g., reducing access to long-term mental health care) may result in the denial of services to certain groups of consumers and require that providers alter the objectives of existing services and programs.

The human services manager is thus confronted with trying to meet the needs of both groups, imposing the public good definition of outcomes on the consumer, or persuading the funder that the public interest is best served by producing personal goods. A failure to achieve some symmetry of expectations is likely to problematic for the organization because diverse and/or incompatible demands can result in the diffusion of resources. Additionally, there is growing evidence to suggest that agencies (especially nonprofits) sometimes participate in contractual arrangements with public agencies that require them to divert or compromise their core goals and services as they try to meet multiple and incompatible objectives (Hasenfeld & Powell, 2004; Kramer, 1994; McBeath & Meezan, 2006; Mulroy & Tamburo, 2004).

Given the natural diversity of constituencies and interests in and around the human services organization, managers find it necessary to actively engage the environment in order to reconcile or influence constituent expectations (Martin, 1987; Menefee, 2001). It falls to the administrator to understand the needs and interests of these groups, respond to them when possible, seek to shape expectations to achieve greater symmetry with agency interests, and work to achieve a degree of congruence among external groups to avoid exposing the agency to conflicting expectations that will fragment and diffuse its resources (Austin, 1995). There is evidence to suggest that managers who pursue an active strategy of engagement with constituencies are more likely to bring resources to, and protect the core purposes and technologies of, their organizations (Jansson & Simmons, 1986; also see Chapters 20, 21, and 22 for further discussion of strategies used by managers to influence external constituencies).

Advocacy for Disvalued and Marginalized Consumer Groups

Though progress has been made in destigmatizing some groups of human services consumers, society continues to be ambivalent or divided about many groups such as the homeless, substance abusers, and welfare recipients (Gummer, 1990). These attitudes are reflected in public policy and funding decisions and often result in ambiguous, punitive, or underfunded mandates. The classic example is the historic tendency of state legislatures to cut meager welfare benefits as a first option to deal with budget shortfalls. The child welfare system has long had to deal with policies that seek to protect children from re-abuse by their parents while pressing for the reunification of children with their parental abusers.

Given the tenuous nature of public support for humane and enlightened services to these groups, human services managers must often work to change public attitudes and priorities regarding the needs of disfavored or marginalized consumer groups (Ezell, 1991; Turner & Shera, 2005). Menefee's (2001) study of managerial work, cited earlier, found that advocacy was one of the key functions performed by human services managers. The number of managers engaged in this kind of practice has been variously estimated in several studies (see Chapter 22), but there is little question that advocacy is an increasingly important strategy for protecting and advancing the interests of agencies and their consumers in an increasingly competitive and resource-challenged human services industry.

Examples of managerial advocacy are readily observable. The child welfare administrator may need to convince state or county legislators that abusive parents are worth rehabilitating; the mental health manager will work with local government officials to make the case that the homeless mentally ill are not content with their way of life and will respond to outreach services; the director of a delinquency prevention program will seek to inform the public that gang members have aspirations other than crime and can be helped to choose a different lifestyle if provided with opportunities, and so on. The common theme in all these situations is that the consumers of these programs are morally stigmatized. As such, they are perceived by some segments of the public to be unworthy of assistance and/or deserving of punishment. In addition to the manager's own ethical commitment to empowering these groups, there are at least three strategic reasons that the human services manager finds it important to advocate for these consumers.

First, the core purpose of the human services agency, as we have argued, is to change people or their social circumstances. The agency cannot acquire the resources and cooperation it needs to succeed in that mission if community leaders do not believe in the potential of morally disfavored people or see the relationship between the fate of these groups and the welfare of the broader community. Second, providers of services to such consumer groups will receive little recognition or respect because no matter how skilled or challenging their work is perceived to be, the objects of their service are not considered deserving. The aura of disfavor tends to undermine staff morale over time, contributing to feelings of disempowerment, turnover, and related problems (Hardina, 2005; Turner & Shera, 2005). The empowerment of staff has been associated with self-perceived efficacy and success in service delivery (Guterman & Bargal, 1996). Finally, an agency's claim to public resources rests, in part, on the perception that what they do contributes in some way to the quality of life in the community. If perceptions of morally disfavored groups cannot be changed so that they are seen as a potential asset to the community, or at least less of a threat, then the agency's success will have little meaning.

The Need for Collaboration

The care and/or change of human beings is typically coproduced by networks of agencies. Thus, human services managers find it necessary to collaborate with other agencies to mobilize and focus resources on their common clientele in order to achieve the benefits of an enlarged pool of expertise and improved cooperation. Frequently, the outcomes achieved with the consumers of any one agency are dependent on the complementary or supportive services provided by other agencies in the service delivery system (Bardach, 1998). For example, supporting the mentally ill so that they can stay in the community involves the coordination of mental health, housing, employment, and financial assistance services and perhaps others. Reunifying neglected children with parents will likely involve the collaboration of public child welfare, intensive family counseling, foster care, and school services. Words to describe systems of care like "wrap around," "continuum," "coordinated," "integrated," which are now ubiquitous in the human services, reflect the increasing importance of these arrangements and the recognition that complex social problems are usually not adequately addressed with single-agency or single-intervention solutions.

While collaboration has long been desirable as a strategy to fill service gaps, improve access, and achieve economies, recent developments seem to have made it ever more important to the quality and effectiveness of services (Alter, 2000). The forces that have moved human services agencies to greater interagency collaboration in the last three decades have been well-documented elsewhere (Alter, 2000; Bardach, 1998), but four can be highlighted:

- A growing awareness concerning the co-occurrence and interaction of problems that bring clients to human services agencies (e.g., mental illness and substance abuse; poverty and poor health; school failure and dysfunctional families; the relationships between poverty, ill health, and substance abuse, etc.)
- The recognition of "new" social problems and the emergence of agencies to address them (e.g., rape crisis centers, programs for the homeless, domestic violence programs)
- Reduced public funding for human services and the devolution of fiscal and programmatic authority to local governments and the nonprofit sector, which has increased competition among agencies for funds and clients
- The privatization and outsourcing of public human services programs, with a concomitant increase in the number of agencies implementing publicly funded social programs

From these and related developments emerged a keen interest among policymakers and agency managers in collaborative solutions that would not only provide economies in operation, but also yield more comprehensive and integrated program strategies. Managers of human services agencies, who once saw the promotion of their agencies as the highest calling, began to see that their agency's interests and those of consumers could be better served through collaborative service arrangements (Jaskyte & Lee, 2006).

Collaboration is now built into the fabric of policymaking. Where once public, private, and proprietary sectors were reasonably distinct, government now relies heavily on for-profit and nonprofit entities to carry out public policy using a complex set of intersector mechanisms (see also Chapter 4 for an analysis of this development). The human services manager, whether in a public, nonprofit, or for-profit organization, must be able to work effectively at these collaborative intersections.

Much has been learned about the processes of building interorganizational collaboration (Bardach, 1998; see also Chapter 21). There is also considerable case evidence that such arrangements can increase access to, and the comprehensiveness of, services available to consumers (Schorr, 1998). Still, we need more empirical studies to determine whether interagency collaborative arrangements actually result in better service outcomes for clients. One recent study of the impact of interorganizational coordination in a children's mental health/juvenile justice collaboration found that more coordination produced *lower* quality service and had no impact on client outcomes (Glisson & Himmelfarn, 1998). However, another study that examined the relationship between service integration and service access and housing outcomes for homeless mentally ill patients found that patients served in integrated systems had better housing outcomes after one year (Rosenheck et al., 1998). Moreover, a recent study of 36 non-profits showed that the exchange of clients and the provision of technical assistance in interorganizational relationships were associated with the development of service innovations (Jaskyte & Lee, 2006). Clearly, more research is needed to determine whether interagency collaboration produces better services for clients and under what circumstances.

Looking to the Future

For the foreseeable future, human services managers will operate in an increasingly competitive, privatized, diverse, technologically rich, outcomes-oriented environment. Public and private agencies will compete with one another for funding, for consumers, and for influence. Agencies that fare well in this environment will require good information about demographic, economic, and political changes so they can anticipate and plan strategically for the future. Marketing, advocacy, entrepreneurial initiative, and the ability to demonstrate effective performance will enable agencies to seize opportunities and acquire the resources they need to prosper (see Chapter 23 for managers' views on these issues). In the struggle to be competitive, managers will be challenged to maintain a strong moral and ethical compass so that doing well also means doing good.

Closely connected to the competition is privatization. Currently, especially at the highest levels of public policy, privatizing human services is advocated as a way to constrain the growth of public bureaucracies and as a springboard to lower costs, increased efficiency, consumer choice, and effectiveness. There are reasons to be concerned with the unfettered development of privatization in the human services (Gibelman, 2000; see discussion in Chapter 4), but conventional policy wisdom is that the public is often better served when private, for-profit, nonprofit, and faith-based agencies are delivering social services. For public agency managers, this will mean an even greater role in developing community agency capabilities, setting realistic goals, and developing performance contracts that hold private agencies fiscally and programmatically accountable. Private agency managers will be pressed to make good on contractual commitments by managing public monies responsibly and maintaining efficient operations. Managing

multiple grants and contracts, as is now the norm for most private agencies, will require administrators to balance competing interests and build internal cohesion in organizations with loosely coupled programs that pursue varied objectives.

Diversity will be a continuing challenge for human services agencies. As the population of the U.S. becomes more pluralistic, agencies will face a continuing need to adopt policies and practices that are sensitive to the needs of diverse groups. This will require that agencies listen to and involve consumers and community representatives in their decision processes and monitor their service technologies to insure that they are suited to clients' cultural values and sensibilities. An important requisite of cultural competence will be the ability of agencies to hire staff at all levels whose training and life experience enable them to relate effectively to clients from different cultures. While many agencies have made strides in recruitment, persons of color continue to be underrepresented, and the agency workforce is less diverse than the populations they serve. For example, the NASW Workforce Study shows that 86% of licensed social workers in the U.S. are white non-Hispanics, while only 7% of licensed social workers are black and 4% are Hispanic (Whitaker et al., 2006a, p. 9). The challenge for both professional schools and human services agencies is to bring more people of color into the field and to develop inclusive agency cultures that support and value diversity.

Information technology is advancing at a rapid rate and has begun to significantly impact human services (Martin, 2000; Schoech, 1999). The Internet provides ready access to information on community needs, new service technologies, and industry-wide performance standards that will be useful in monitoring the task environment and planning for improved services. Enhanced computing capabilities have, and will increasingly, become a valuable resource to service providers, offering case-specific information on clients served by other agencies or programs, suggesting interventions that might be appropriate in particular types of cases, and directing clients to community services and self-help resources (Schoech, Basham, & Fluke, 2006). Managers will have to become more sophisticated about the use of information technology and how it can be seamlessly woven into agency decision-making practices.

For the past several decades, there has been mounting interest in seeing that consumers of human services agencies are served effectively. As previously discussed, federal, state, and local public authorities, as well as foundations and other private funding sources, are increasingly insistent that agencies demonstrate the effectiveness of their programs. This interest is also evident in social work and other human services professions, where it is now widely recognized that in order to meet external expectations and continuously improve service performance, agencies need to systematically evaluate their practice. The empirically based practice movement (EPB; Johnson & Austin, 2006; Schoech et al., 2006), the growing use of performance contracting, and the deployment of information systems that measure outcomes as well as processes are all indicators of this trend. As agencies are better able to track the results of their programs, administrators will be called upon to create the conditions and processes needed to support these practices.

References

Alter, C. F. (2000). Interorganizational collaboration in the task environment. In R. J. Patti (Ed.), *The handbook of social welfare administration* (pp. 283–302). Thousand Oaks, CA: Sage.

Anspach, R. R. (1991). Everyday methods for assessing organizational effectiveness. *Social Problems, 38*(1), 1–19.

Austin, D. (1995). Management: Overview. In R. Edwards (Ed.), *Encyclopedia of social work* (19th ed., Vol. 20, pp. 1642–1658). Washington, DC: NASW.

Austin, D. M. (2002). *Human services management: Organizational leadership in social work practice.* New York: Columbia University Press.

Austin, M. J., & Kruzich, J. M. (2004). Assessing recent textbooks and casebooks in human service administration: Implications and future directions. *Administration in Social Work, 28*(1), 115–129.

Bardach, E. (1998). *Getting agencies to work together.* Washington, DC: The Brookings Institution.

Bass, B., & Avolio, B. (2006). *Transformational leadership* (2nd ed.). Mahwah, NJ: Lawrence Erlbaum.

Bess, G., & Associates. (2000, July). *National Network of Social Work Managers: Membership survey.* Paradise, CA: Author.

Bliss, L. B. (2007). Implementing an outcomes measurement system in substance abuse treatment programs. *Administration in Social Work, 31*(4), 83–101.

Brody, R. (1993). *Effectively managing human service organizations.* Newbury Park, CA: Sage.

Carter, R. (1983). *The accountable agency.* Beverly Hills, CA: Sage.

Dobmeyer, T., Woodward, B., & Olson, L. (2002). Factors supporting the development and utilization of an outcome-based performance measurement system in a chemical health care management program. *Administration in Social Work, 26*(4), 25–44.

Ezell, M. (1991). Administrators as advocates. *Administration in Social Work, 15*(4), 1–18.

Finch, W. A. (1978). Administrative priorities: The impact of employee perceptions on agency functioning and worker satisfaction. *Administration in Social Work, 2*, 391–399.

Gibelman, M. (2000). Structural and fiscal characteristics of social service agencies. In R. Patti (Ed.), *The handbook of social welfare management* (pp. 113–132). Thousand Oaks, CA: Sage.

Gibelman, M., & Schervish, P. H. (1993). *Who are we? The social work labor force as reflected in the NASW membership.* Washington, DC: NASW.

Glisson, C. (1989). The effect of leadership on workers in human service organizations. *Administration in Social Work, 13*(3/4), 21–37.

Glisson, C., & Durick, M. (1988). Predictors of job satisfaction and organizational commitment in human service organizations. *Administrative Science Quarterly, 33*, 61–81.

Glisson, C., & Himmelfarn, A. (1998). The effects of organizational climate and interorganizational coordination on the quality and outcome of children service systems. *Child Abuse and Neglect, 22*(5), 410–421.

Glisson, C., & James, L. R. (2002). The cross level effects of culture and climate in human service teams. *Journal of Organizational Behavior, 23*(6), 767–794.

Gregoire, T., Rapp, C., & Poertner, J. (1995). The new management: Assessing the fit of total quality management and social agencies. In B. Gummer & P. McCallion (Eds.), *Total quality management in the social services* (pp. 3–32). Albany: State University of New York-Albany.

Gummer, B. (1990). *The politics of social administration: Managing organizational politics in social agencies.* Englewood Cliffs, NJ: Prentice Hall.

Guterman, N., & Bargal, D. (1996). Social workers' perceptions of their power and service outcomes. *Administration in Social Work, 20*(3), 1–20.

Hardina, D. (2005). Ten characteristics of empowerment-oriented organizations. *Administration in Social Work, 29*(3), 23–42.

Hasenfeld, Y. (Ed.). (1992). *Human services as complex organizations.* Newbury Park, CA: Sage.

Hasenfeld, Y. (2000). Social welfare administration and organizational theory. In R. J. Patti (Ed.), *The handbook of social welfare management* (pp. 89–112). Thousand Oaks, CA: Sage.

Hasenfeld, Y., & Powell, L. E. (2004). The role of nonprofit agencies in the provision of welfare-to-work services. *Administration in Social Work, 28*(3/4), 91–110.

Herman, R. D., & Renz, D. O. (2004). Doing things right: Effectiveness in local nonprofit agencies, a panel study. *Public Administration Review, 64*(6), 694–705.

Himle, D. P., Jayaratne, S., & Thyness, P. (1989). The effects of emotional support on burnout, work stress and mental health among Norwegian and American social workers. *Journal of Social Service Research, 13*(1), 27–45.

Hoefer, R. (2003). Administrative skills and degrees: The "best place" debate rages on. *Administration in Social Work, 27*(1), 25–46.

Hopkins, K. M., & Austin, M. J. (2004). The changing nature of human services and supervision. In M. J. Austin & K. M. Hopkins (Eds.), *Supervision as collaboration in the human services* (pp. 3–10). Thousand Oaks, CA: Sage.

Jansson, B. S., & Simmons, J. (1986). The survival of social work units within host organizations: Strategy options. *Social Work, 31*(5), 339–344.

Jaskyte, K., & Lee, M. (2006). Interorganizational relationships: A source of innovation for non profit organizations? *Administration in Social Work, 30*(3), 43–54.

Johnson, M., & Austin, M. J. (2006). Evidence based practice in the social services: Implications for

organizational change. *Administration in Social Work, 30*(3), 75–104.

Koeske, G., & Krowinski, W. (2004). Gender-based salary inequity in social work: Mediators of gender's effect on salary. *Social Work, 49*(2), 309–317.

Kramer, R. (1994). Voluntary agencies and the contract culture. *Social Service Review, 68*(1), 33–60.

Latting, J. K., Beck, M. H., Slack, K. J., Tetrick, L. E., Jones, A. P., Etchegaray, J. M., et al. (2004). Promoting service quality and adherence to service plan: The role of management support for innovation and learning. *Administration in Social Work, 28*(2), 29–48.

Lewis, H. (1987). Ethics and the managing of service effectiveness in social welfare. In R. Patti, J. Poertner, & C. A. Rapp (Eds.), *Managing for service effectiveness in social welfare organizations* (pp. 271–284). New York: Haworth.

Martin, L. L. (1993). *Total quality management in human service organization.* Newbury Park, CA: Sage.

Martin, L. L. (2000). The environmental context of social welfare administration. In R. J. Patti (Ed.), *The handbook of social welfare administration* (pp. 55–67). Thousand Oaks, CA: Sage.

Martin, L. L. (2005). Performance based contracting for human services: Does it work? *Administration in Social Work, 29*(1), 63–78.

Martin, L., & Kettner, P. (1996). *Measuring the performance of human service programs.* Newbury Park, CA: Sage.

Martin, M. E., Pines, B. A., & Healy, L. M. (1999). Mining our strengths: Curriculum approaches for social work management. *Journal of Teaching in Social Work, 16*(1/2), 73–97.

Martin, P. Y. (1987). Multiple constituencies and performance in social welfare organizations: Action strategies for directors. In R. J. Patti, J. Poertner, & C. A. Rapp (Eds.), *Managing for service effectiveness in social welfare organizations* (pp. 223–239). New York: Haworth.

Martin, P. Y., & Segal, B. (1977, December). Bureaucracy, size and staff expectations for client independence in halfway houses. *Journal of Health and Social Behavior, 18,* 376–390.

Mary, N. (2005). Transformational leadership in the human services. *Administration in Social Work, 29*(2), 105–118.

McBeath, B., & Meezan, W. (2006). Nonprofit adaptation to performance based managed care contracting in Michigan's foster care system. *Administration in Social Work, 30*(2), 39–70.

McNeely, R. (1992). Job satisfaction in the public social services: Perspectives on structure, situational factors, gender and ethnicity. In Y. Hasenfeld (Ed.), *Human services as complex organizations* (pp. 224–258). Newbury Park, CA: Sage.

McNeely, R. L., Sapp, M., & Dailey, A. (1998). Ethnicity, gender, earnings, occupational rank and job satisfaction in public social services: What do workers say? In A. Daley (Ed.), *Workplace diversity issues and perspectives* (pp. 144–165). Washington, DC: NASW Press

Menefee, D. (2001). What managers do and why they do it. In R. Patti (Ed.), *Handbook of social welfare management* (pp. 247–266). Thousand Oaks, CA: Sage.

Mintzberg, H. (1973). *The nature of managerial work.* New York: Harper and Row.

Mirabella, R., & Wish, N. (2000). The "best place" debate: A comparison of graduate education programs for nonprofit managers. *Public Administration Review, 60*(3), 219–225.

Mor Barak, M. E. (2000). The inclusive workplace: An ecosystems approach to diversity management. *Social Work, 45*(1), 339–353.

Mor Barak, M. E., Nissly, J. A., & Levin, A. (2001). Antecedents to retention and turnover among child welfare, social work, and other human service employees: What can we learn from past research? A review and meta-analysis. *Social Service Review, 75*(4), 625–662.

Mulroy, E. A., & Tamburo, M. B. (2004). Nonprofit organizations and welfare-to-work: Environmental turbulence and organizational change. *Administration in Social Work, 28*(3/4), 111–136.

Neuman, K. M. (2003). Developing a comprehensive outcomes management program: A ten step program. *Administration in Social Work, 27*(10), 15–21.

Nissly, J. A., Mor Barak, M. E., & Levin, A. (2005). Stress, social support and workers' intentions to leave their jobs in public child welfare. *Administration in Social Work, 29*(1), 79–100.

Olmstead, J., & Christenson, H. H. (1973). *The effects of agency work contexts: An intensive field study.* Washington, DC: U.S. Department of Health Education and Welfare.

Packard, T. (2001). Building commitment through mission and values: The case of a homeless shelter. *Administration in Social Work, 25*(3), 35–52.

Patti, R. J. (1977). Patterns of management activity in social welfare agencies. *Administration in Social Work, 1*(1), 5–18.

Patti, R. (1983). *Social welfare administration.* Englewood Cliffs, NJ: Prentice Hall.

Patti, R. J. (2003). Reflections on the state of management in social work. *Administration in Social Work, 27*(2), 1–11.

Patti, R., Diedrick, E., Olson, D., & Crowell, J. (1979). From direct service to administration: A study of social workers' transitions from clinical to management roles. *Administration in Social Work, 3*(2), 131–151.

Pecora, P. J., & Austin, M. J. (1983). Declassification of social work jobs: Issues and strategies. *Social Work, 28*, 421–426.

Poertner, J. (2006). Social administration and outcomes for consumers: What do we know. *Administration in Social Work, 30*(3), 11–24.

Prager, S. (1984/5). Organizational environments and care outcome decisions for elderly clients. *Administration in Social Work, 17*(1), 59–73.

Rapp, C. A., & Poertner, J. (1992). *Social administration: A client-centered approach.* New York: Longman.

Reamer, F. G. (2000). Administrative ethics. In R. J. Patti (Ed.), *The handbook of social welfare management* (pp. 69–88). Thousand Oaks, CA: Sage.

Rosenheck, R., Morrissey, J., Lam, J., Calloway, M., Johnsen, M., Goldman, H., et al. (1998). Service system integration, access to services, and housing outcomes in a program for homeless persons with severe mental illness. *American Journal of Public Health, 88*(11), 1610–1615.

Schmid, H. (2000). Agency-environment relations: Understanding task environments. In R. J. Patti (Ed.), *The handbook of social welfare management* (pp. 133–154). Thousand Oaks, CA: Sage.

Schmid, H. (2004). The role of non profit human service organizations in providing social services: A prefatory essay. *Administration in Social Work, 28*(3/4), 1–21.

Schoech, D. (1999). *Human services technology.* Haworth.

Schoech, D., Basham, R., & Fluke, J. (2006). A technology enhanced EBP model. *Journal of Evidence Based Social Work, 3*(3/4), 55–72.

Schorr, L. B. (1998). *Common purpose: Strengthening families and neighborhoods to rebuild America.* New York: Anchor Books, Doubleday.

Smith, B. D., & Donovan, S. E. (2003). Child welfare practice in organizational and institutional context. *Social Service Review, 77*(4), 541–564.

Smith, S. R., & Lipskey, M. (1993). *Nonprofits for hire.* Cambridge, MA: Harvard University Press.

Stein, H. (1970). Social work administration. In H. Schatz (Ed.), *Social work administration: A resource book.* New York: Council on Social Work Education.

Thompson, J. D. (1967). *Organizations in action.* New York: McGraw-Hill.

Turner, L. M., & Shera, W. (2005). Empowerment of human service workers: Beyond intraorganizational strategies. *Administration in Social Work, 29*(3), 79–94.

U.S. Census Bureau. (2005). *Health care and social assistance: Revenue and operating expenses by type and kind of business 2002.* Retrieved from http://www.census.gov/csd/bes/25/part1.htm.

U.S. Census Bureau. (2008a). *Federal, state and local governments: State government finances.* Retrieved from http://www.census.gov/govs/www/estimate.html.

U.S. Census Bureau. (2008b). *The 2008 statistical abstract.* Retrieved from http://www.census.gov/compendia/statab/

U.S. Department of Health and Human Services. (n.d.). *HHS.gov: Improving the health, safety, and well-being of America.* Retrieved from http://www.hhs.gov/

U.S. Department of Labor Bureau of Labor Statistics. (2007a). *Career guide to industries: Social assistance, except child day care.* Retrieved from http://www.bls.gov/oco/cg/cgs040.htm

U.S. Department of Labor Bureau of Labor Statistics. (2007b). *Career guide to industries: State and local government, except education and hospitals.* Retrieved from http://www.bls.gov/oco/cg/cgs042.htm

Weinbach, R. (1998). *The social worker as manager* (3rd ed.). Needham Heights, MA: Allyn & Bacon.

Whetten, D. A. (1978). Coping with incompatible expectations: An integrated view of role conflict. *Administrative Science Quarterly, 23,* 254–271.

Whitaker, T., Weismiller, T., & Clark, E. (2006a). *Assuring the sufficiency of a front line workforce: Executive summary.* Washington, DC: National Association of Social Workers.

Whitaker, T., Weismiller, T., & Clark, E. (2006b). *Supplement to the National Study of Licensed Social Workers.* Washington DC: NASW.

Williams, M. S., & Gray, W. L. (2007). Status of women in Texas state government, *Administration in Social Work, 31*(1), 5–25.

Yukl, G. (2006). *Leadership in organizations.* Upper Saddle River, NJ: Prentice Hall.

Zammuto, R. (1984). A comparison of multiple constituency models of organizational effectiveness. *Academy of Management Review, 9*(4), 606–616.

CHAPTER 2

General Themes in the Evolution of Human Services Administration

Michael Reisch

S ince the late 19th century, the administration of human services organizations in the United States has evolved in a unique pattern, reflecting several aspects of "American exceptionalism" (Reisch, 2005). Five major forces have shaped its development: the changing political-economic environment, from the nation's emergence as a major industrial power to today's economic globalization; the influence of organizational "technology," such as the advent of the "limited liability stock corporation" as the model for business organizations, the concept of scientific management, and contemporary management information systems; the different forms that private, nonprofit organizations took in different racial, ethnic, and religious communities and different regions of the country; the professionalization of social work and the accompanying creation of professional training programs;

and the changing role of the public sector in social welfare. This chapter will discuss how these developments shaped the nature of human services administration in the United States.

The Roots of Human Services Administration

By the 14th century, formal social welfare systems based on law rather than custom, and with both secular and religious roots, emerged throughout Western Europe. Over the next several centuries, these systems expanded as European society struggled through the transition from feudalism to capitalism. In Great Britain, the government enacted a series of Poor Laws between 1349 and 1664 to establish social order in this chaotic and rapidly changing environment, control or reduce wages in order to assist capitalist development, and reassert political authority in the face of frequent popular protests (Piven & Cloward, 1995). The North American colonies established by Great Britain modeled their social welfare systems after these laws, sometimes word for word. Before the American Revolution, formal social welfare systems had been established in North America in which local religious and secular authorities shared responsibility for assisting dependent individuals. This reflected civil government's communal concerns and the "charity" missions of religious organizations (Axinn & Stern, 2007; Jansson, 2005).

Even before independence, private benevolent societies and self-help organizations emerged to address the consequences of poverty and immigration because decentralized government responses proved insufficient or ineffective (Axinn & Stern, 2007). Upper class leaders of secular groups and Protestant churches sought to assist the poor through cash assistance, moral suasion, and personal example. The constitutional separation of civil government from religious organization enabled churches to develop their own charitable activities, which often included religious proselytizing. One consequence was the organization of these activities under "lay" rather than clerical leadership, particularly in the congregation-governed Protestant denominations (Leiby, 1978). Another result during the 19th century was the establishment of Protestant missions in crowded urban slum neighborhoods, to serve humanitarian ends and strengthen the role of organized religion in society (Boyer, 1978; Day, 2005). Unlike today's churches, 19th-century churches wanted to maintain, not break down, the wall separating church and state.

While the provision of aid to people in their own homes (called "outdoor relief") continued the Poor Law tradition of categorizing and stigmatizing the needy, the number of state-funded institutions to serve the mentally ill, orphans, the aged, and the able-bodied poor increased in the 19th century. Often called "indoor relief," these "asylums" removed certain classes of persons and

their problems from public view, reinforced the impression that society was helping individuals in need, and labeled those being helped as "deviant." They established a moral tone for the treatment of those in need and a moral justification for social policies. By the mid-century, these morally based ideas acquired scientific and pseudoscientific rationales (Rothman, 1971; Trattner, 1999).

Spurred by reform movements, particularly in the fields of mental health and child welfare, states also began to assume responsibility during this period for the limited distribution of outdoor relief formerly left to towns and counties. By the late 1830s, government leaders also recognized that indoor relief was inadequate to meet the problems of the poor, particularly those produced by cyclical economic depressions or periodic epidemics of infectious diseases, such as cholera or tuberculosis. As social conditions worsened and government responses proved insufficient or ineffective, private benevolent societies and self-help organizations, the antecedents of contemporary nonprofit human services agencies, began to play a leading role in social welfare provision (Mandler, 1990).

Secular reformers hoped organizations like the Association for the Improvement of the Condition of the Poor and the Children's Aid Society in New York City would create a "harmonious community" and protect traditional values in an environment of rapid social and economic change. Both sectarians and secularists considered private social welfare to be a potential deterrent to the excessive accumulation of government power, a tool to strengthen American democracy, and a means to resist the influence of unpopular or foreign political ideas (Wenocur & Reisch, 1989). Although large private organizations, such as the U.S. Sanitary Commission and the Red Cross, emerged during the Civil War, it was only after the war that problems associated with poverty were seriously addressed. States created boards of charity in the 1860s to oversee the management of charitable institutions developed to address such problems as mental illness, delinquency, and pauperism (Axinn & Stern, 2007).

The Emergence of Modern Human Services Administration

During the half century after the Civil War, rapid industrialization and massive immigration produced an uneven pattern of economic and social development in the U.S., transforming cities and urban life itself. New social and public health problems appeared and social unrest intensified. Elites feared that revolutionary ideas imported from Europe, particularly Marxism and anarchism, would lead to class conflict and political upheaval (Lens, 1966). The roots of social work in the United States date back to this period and the efforts of elites in church-based and secular charitable organizations to address the so-called "social question."

At the time, it was widely acknowledged that existing social welfare institutions were incapable of responding to this growing social and political crisis, but the solutions were not immediately clear. Many upper-class reformers held anti-urban, anti-European, and racial and religious prejudices, particularly against Catholics, Jews, and African Americans. Initially, they developed programs with educational or religious overtones to "inoculate" U.S. civilization from the contagion of dark-skinned immigrants and Southern blacks (Reisch, 2008).

The severe economic crises of the 1870s and 1890s, however, stimulated a reappraisal of prevailing attitudes. Old-style charity, designed to enforce the work ethic and based upon a personal relationship between benefactor and recipient, appeared to have little impact on the "new poor." One response of urban elites was to create an alternative social welfare system, with roots in the charitable activities of churches. Modeled after the London Charity Organization Society (COS), formed in 1869 by Octavia Hill, so-called "scientific charity" combined beliefs in business-like organization and efficiency with long-standing charitable principles. In 1877, the first American COS was established in Buffalo, New York. Over the next two decades, COS appeared in virtually all large and mid-sized cities (Lubove, 1965).

In part, this private philanthropic initiative reflected the unwillingness of business elites to support a system of public taxes and services they did not control. At the time, these services consisted largely of state-funded custodial institutions for groups of people viewed as needing special attention: individuals who were mentally ill or developmentally disabled, orphans, people who were blind or deaf, criminals, and, increasingly, the elderly poor (Katz, 1996). This concern intensified as new immigrants became voters, and politically corrupt "ward bosses" acquired urban political control (Bruno, 1957; Leiby, 1978).

Earlier sectarian human services organizations were formed largely as "charitable associations," with limited attention to their legal status. This reflected their underlying philosophy that charity should be based on a personal connection between benefactor and recipient (Lowell, 1884). The introduction of "scientific charity" illustrated how the nation's changing political economy influenced its social institutions. Just as the "limited liability stock corporation" replaced traditional partnerships in the marketplace, the nonprofit "corporation" became the preferred organizational form for philanthropic and civic activities. Through this model, trustees could control these organizations without incurring legal liability for their debts or activities and introduce concepts of administrative efficiency from the business world into the administration of charity (Lubove, 1965). During the last half of the 19th century, this model spread throughout the nonprofit sector in higher education, cultural institutions, public health, and youth-serving organizations. It helped create a form of "welfare capitalism," a pragmatic U.S. alternative to laissez-faire capitalism and European socialism (Jansson, 2005).

In these philanthropic corporations, the chairman of the board of directors held the most important position. Almost always male, he was usually a wealthy businessman and one of the largest contributors to the organization. He often maintained this position for many years, virtually functioning as a volunteer chief executive officer (CEO) and playing a major role in organization management, including most personnel decisions (Leiby, 1978; Waite, 1960).

The Emergence of Management in the 20th Century

By the early 20th century, virtually all nonprofit agencies had adopted "techniques of intra-agency [and interagency] coordination and the incorporation of ideas from business management such as standardized forms, regular reports to 'stockholders,' and the use of 'cost/benefit analysis' to determine the allocation of agency resources." This focus on standardization and efficiency was not confined to the nonprofit sector. Public sector social welfare leaders, such as Homer Folks in New York, "repeatedly stressed the importance of sound administration, . . . control, cost efficiency, and [interorganizational] cooperation" (Wenocur & Reisch, 1989, pp. 49, 51).

The fusion of charitable and corporate principles helped the COS win financial and political sponsors within the business community, as did its embrace of "technology" in its methods of intervention, organizational structure, and administrative procedures (Margolin, 1997). With this support, the COS sought to establish some degree of order and coordination in the human services field and made systematic efforts to eliminate public poor-relief programs (Kaplan, 1978). Some critics argued, however, that the primary purpose of "scientific charity" was to exercise control over relief recipients and reinforce prevailing gender norms in its distribution of roles, differential salary scales, and hierarchical organizational forms (Margolin, 1997; Piven & Cloward, 1995). In addition, many COS clients regarded the "new charity" as alien and preferred the systems of self-help and mutual aid their communities established (Chan, 1991; Hine, 1990; Mandler, 1990; Rivera, 1987).

In the 1890s, as the COS model became more widespread, paid staff—usually called "district agents"—replaced volunteers. Although they lacked specific training in these areas, district agents were responsible for organizational management, fundraising, recruitment, and supervision. Within a generation, most COS no longer used volunteers, although the application of business principles was not universally embraced (Reisch & Wenocur, 1982).

The career of Mary Richmond exemplifies these trends. In many ways, Richmond was the first female career social welfare administrator, holding executive positions in the Baltimore, Philadelphia, and New York COS. Although best known for her books on social casework, she was also a nationally recognized writer and speaker about human services administration who was particularly concerned about the respective responsibilities of the organization's executive and board (Pittman-Munke, 1985).

Settlement houses, which also began to appear in U.S. cities in the mid-1880s, constituted a significant exception to the emerging board-dominated pattern of nonprofit organization. Many settlements, like Hull House in Chicago, were initially created and run by a single individual with a social reform mission, and their boards were essentially fundraising bodies (Carson, 1992). When the original founder retired or died, however, the relationship between the board and the new headworker often resembled that of the director and board in other nonprofit agencies.

The Settlement Movement grew considerably during the Progressive Era, when its reform-oriented goals, particularly around such issues as child labor, the unionization of women workers, education, public health, and housing, received widespread support. By 1910, there were more than 400 settlements, including those established by African Americans. The movement had a national impact on conditions affecting children and women by advocating for the establishment of the juvenile court system, state-funded mothers' pensions, anti-child labor laws, and public health reforms (Chambers, 1963; Davis, 1967; Lasch-Quinn, 1993).

Like the COS, settlement houses emulated many of the features of corporate management, particularly the importance of organization and fundraising. In fact, in their early years, their appeal was enhanced by the application of corporate and scientific methods to social reform, particularly among the educated middle and upper classes. Unlike the COS, however, settlements lacked clarity on their basic organizational form and struggled with persistent contradictions between their democratic values and their reliance on elites for funding and political support (Wenocur & Reisch, 1989).

During World War I, most local nonprofits began to be coordinated by business-dominated Community Chests, the antecedents of today's United Way. The presence of business leaders ensured the primacy of corporate methods and values in the private human services field (Brilliant, 1990). As these agencies professionalized during the 1920s, this federated structure became the logical vehicle to rationalize philanthropy and help nonprofit human services organizations survive financially.

At the same time, there was a shift in the oversight of public services, from volunteer organizations administered by boards to executive-based systems of supervision. This reflected an increase in state and local government involvement in and control of societal change. The emergence of the field of public administration led to increased professionalism in government departments of social welfare. These bureaucracies were receptive to the expertise social workers had acquired in universities and private charitable organizations.

The appearance of "welfare capitalism" in the form of company unions and other employee benefit packages during the 1920s, however, undermined advocates of governmental intervention in the social welfare arena by promoting the image of the socially responsible corporation whose profits were linked to American progress and well-being (Berkowitz & McQuaid, 1980). Other developments that shaped human services administration in this era included the expansion of specialized organizations in such fields as recreation, mental health, juvenile and criminal justice, child welfare, and occupational social

work; the formation of a professional infrastructure through such organizations as the American Association for Organizing Family Social Work, the Child Welfare League of America, the National Social Work Council, the Community Chests and Councils of America, and a wide range of professional associations; the nearly 300% increase in the number of schools of social work between World War I and the Great Depression; the growth of professional journals; and the use of the medical model and corporate management by many human services agencies (Wenocur & Reisch, 1989).

Consequently, the pattern of administration in these organizations changed considerably during this era (McLean, 1927). Agency boards recruited more individuals, primarily men, with technical or professional education in social work and experience in nonprofit agencies as administrators. James F. Jackson, general secretary of the Cleveland Associated Charities from 1904 to 1927, was one example (Waite, 1960).

New executives, like Jackson, often brought their own ideas about the most effective way to organize services. To implement these ideas, they needed to clarify the executive-board relationship. Agency executives asserted that the board's function was to establish policy, while that of the executive was to manage the daily operations of the agency, including the hiring of personnel (Kirschner, 1986). In addition to redefining these roles, nonprofits rationalized their procedures through the rotation of board members and the establishment of board nominating committees, limited terms for board members, and annual elections of board officers (Waite, 1960). These developments were less visible in ethnic agencies, which still contained many features of the self-help and mutual aid traditions (Iglehart & Becerra, 1995).

The growth of federated Community Chests further strengthened the role of agency executives. Business leaders supported the concept of an annual fundraising campaign to replace a continuous, year-long process of individual appeals from each community agency (Cutlip, 1965). In most cities, the creation of a "council of social agencies" soon followed. Its structure enabled participating agencies to establish fundraising goals and implement community "surveys," which documented the need for greater financial support. In this system, executives became their agency's primary representatives and spokespersons and often played leading roles in the creation of national associations in child welfare and family services, which provided consultation assistance for communities in the organization of new service agencies.

In addition to their application of modern efficiency and organization, federations legitimated the work of nonprofit human services agencies among the general public by emulating the methods of corporate advertising in their fundraising campaigns (Lubove, 1965). By the late 1920s, opposition to federation among large organizations, such as the YM-YWCAs and the Red Cross, was largely overcome. The result was the imposition of corporate ideas of community building, which resulted in less democratic means of decision making and planning and the exclusion of reformist organizations, especially settlement houses, from financial support. With a few notable exceptions (Hull House, the Henry Street Settlement, Chicago Commons), they lost considerable autonomy. Their political activism subsided considerably, to be replaced by a growing emphasis on cultural programs, informal education, recreation, and neighborhood services (Fisher, 1994; Trolander, 1987).

The Welfare State and Its Impact on Human Services Administration

During the first quarter of the 20th century, the U.S. made modest efforts to establish a governmental system of social insurance, influenced by the development of such systems in Germany and Great Britain (Rubinow, 1913). In 1911, Wisconsin implemented the first worker's compensation law in the United States. During the 1920s, a number of states established pension programs for the elderly and blind (Chambers,

1963). States and counties developed child welfare programs to take care of abused and neglected children, particularly in rural and small-town communities that lacked private human services organizations (Bremner, 1974).

Perhaps more than any social welfare innovation in the early 20th century, state-initiated mothers' pensions programs changed the nature of government/voluntary sector relationships (Skocpol, 1992). By recognizing family welfare needs, they reduced the stigma of receiving public aid and broke down the 19th-century resistance against outdoor relief. Mothers' pensions formed the policy basis for Title IV of the 1935 Social Security Act, which established the nation's Aid to Dependent Children (ADC) program (Gordon, 1994).

Despite the growth of public welfare during the first decades of the 20th century, states, counties, and cities paid little attention to the structure and management of these programs, particularly in periods of economic crisis and high unemployment, such as the late 1920s (Breckinridge, 1927). Corporate and philanthropic leaders continued to regard tax-supported welfare programs with suspicion. As a result, the U.S. social welfare system in 1930 was an uncoordinated mixture of local and state public relief agencies, supplemented by the modest resources of private nonprofit organizations. Most large cities had public welfare departments, although 19th-century-type "poorhouses" still existed in smaller cities and rural areas (Wagner, 2005). State, county, and city agencies, however, did not necessarily provide the same services or relate to one another administratively. Wide variations in policies, administrative structures, standards, and staffing patterns persisted among and even within states. The quality of interorganizational relationships between public agencies and between public and private sector agencies varied widely, as did the competence and integrity of administrators. Meanwhile, private organizations lacked the resources to address the growing magnitude of social problems with which they were confronted, such as unemployment (Axinn & Stern, 2007).

Although during the two decades prior to the Great Depression private charities provided barely 25% of all income assistance in the U.S., they had a disproportionate influence on social policy because they administered most relief funds (Reisch, 2004). Between 1929 and 1931, federal policymakers hoped that the expansion of such efforts by Community Chests and family service agencies would be sufficient to address the nation's growing economic crisis and preclude the development of large, government-funded relief programs (Bruno, 1957; Lens, 1969). In response, private charity increased by nearly 400% (to $170 million) in two years. By late 1931, however, leaders of the charitable sector recognized the inadequacy of private giving in the face of the unprecedented demand for aid, particularly in major cities. The pressure for more far-reaching action also came from reformers and business leaders, who were threatened by social protest and the rapid growth of militant unions (Lens, 1966).

By the time of President Franklin Roosevelt's inauguration in March, 1933, the economic crisis had reached unprecedented levels. Many cities faced fiscal bankruptcy and conflicts emerged between city officials, who were under increasing pressure to take action against unemployment and poverty, and business leaders, who feared such actions would generate unfavorable publicity. One-third of all private agencies in the country were forced to close, and state governments rapidly exhausted their financial resources. Reluctantly, leaders of business and philanthropy and state officials conceded the necessity of federal intervention (Reisch, 2004).

Through temporary programs of emergency assistance, such as the Federal Emergency Relief Agency (FERA), and longer-term solutions to the problems of unemployment and poverty, in particular the 1935 Social Security Act, the Roosevelt Administration established a diverse public social welfare system that included employer/employee contributory social insurance programs and government-financed, means-tested public assistance programs. Public assistance, a federal and state-administered system, was impersonal and rule-regulated and included individualized social service programs (Gordon, 1994). While the new social insurance programs were administered within a centralized bureaucratic framework based in Washington, the establishment of public assistance programs required the creation of a nationwide system of public social welfare administration at the state and county level, with a mixture of bureaucratic and professional social work characteristics. Over time, the new public welfare agencies turned to the field of public administration for guidance in establishing administrative procedures, rather than casework-centered social work (Street, 1940).

By redefining the role of government in addressing the nation's social welfare, the New Deal profoundly shaped the nature of nonprofit human services organizations. New public welfare programs required more professional social workers, including administrators. Although the government turned initially to private organizations to meet its personnel needs, this proved insufficient and it soon recruited thousands of new workers, many from working class and union backgrounds. As head of the Federal Emergency Relief Administration (FERA) and the Works Progress Administration (WPA), Harry Hopkins hired professional social workers for key administrative posts and used government funds for professional training, as did Frances Perkins in the Labor Department. Through administrative regulations, Hopkins ensured that trained social workers filled at least 25% of key slots in county and municipal departments, where they could apply "scientific" principles to the distribution of government funds (Kurzman, 1974). This enhanced the role of social work in public welfare and drew clear distinctions between its function and that of private social welfare (Wenocur & Reisch, 1989). In many states, however, child welfare programs continued to emulate private, nonprofit "child protection" agencies. Among public child welfare workers, a model of professional leadership and mentoring developed in which prior casework experience became a requirement for administrative positions (Bremner, 1974).

Within less than a decade, therefore, two distinct social welfare sectors emerged. One consisted of relatively small nonprofit organizations with professional staffs and executives and public child welfare services organized around a similar model. The other consisted of larger public welfare offices, which often administered multimillion-dollar "entitlement" programs, but with relatively few staff who possessed specialized training in administration. The creation of the American Public Welfare Association symbolized this separation.

As a result, two models of human services administration emerged. New York was the national headquarters of the private nonprofit social welfare sector; Washington was the headquarters of the public social welfare sector. Proponents of the private model assumed that professional education and direct service experience were prerequisites for administrative positions, particularly in small and medium-size organizations where the executives were directly involved with personnel administration and probably personally acquainted with all of the professional staff. A central element of these executives' role was the maintenance of an effective working relationship with the board of directors and, through them, with wealthy donors and business leaders in the community. In turn, board members maintained most of the responsibility for budget oversight and resource development (Lohman & Lohman, 2002).

In the public administration model, individuals with and without direct service experience were appointed to positions of responsibility in large-scale programs with bureaucratic, standardized services, personnel, and fiscal procedures. Military experience was regarded as a valuable credential, and veterans were given preference in civil service selection procedures. The introduction of a merit system in the public welfare sector through the use of the civil service served several purposes. First, it sought to replace the patronage model, which still existed at all levels of government, with a model based on professional competence (Leighninger, 1987). Second, it aimed to ensure that the distribution of financial assistance was accompanied by careful planning, efficient administration, and effective service delivery. Finally, it attempted to create a common set of standards and bridge the prevailing gap between the administration of public and private agencies. The limited role of administration in the "minimum curriculum" that the American Association of Schools of Social Work had established as a requirement for accreditation, however, hampered efforts to elevate administrative practice in public welfare.

After World War II, economic growth, low unemployment, programs such as Social Security, and a moderately progressive income tax improved the economic well-being of many Americans (Patterson, 2000). Dramatic demographic shifts, especially the northern migration of over four million African Americans, accompanied this rapid economic expansion. Yet, the long-term implications were little understood by policymakers at the time (Lemann, 1991). Prosperity, the isolation of suburbs, and media images of a consumer-oriented society masked the persistence of poverty (Danziger & Weinberg, 1994). Under increasing pressure from corporate-dominated boards, conservative politicians, and the media, private and public agencies shifted the focus of their services from low income to middle and upper income groups and reduced the role of community-based volunteers in organizational decision making and service delivery. Social activism declined and openly anti-welfare attitudes reemerged (Jones, 1992; Reisch & Andrews, 2001).

In the early 1960s, however, well-publicized exposés (Caudill, 1963; Harrington, 1981) helped Americans "rediscover" the poverty of over 40 million people, nearly one-third of them children (Patterson, 2000). The U.S. responded to this challenge in two different ways. One response explained poverty as the product of individual or cultural deficiency, rather than institutional deficiency, and, thus, as "normal" for large segments of the population (Lewis, 1966). This justified the focus of many antipoverty policies on changing individual behavior.

At the same time, new "structuralist" perspectives on social problems—which addressed the absence of opportunity rather than pathology—began to emerge. They inspired the development of a new kind of human services organization, such as Mobilization for Youth in New York (Gillette, 1996; Lemann, 1988-1989). Acknowledging the complexity of the problem, President Johnson's "war on poverty" included economic stimuli, full employment and health care programs, urban and rural rehabilitation, expanded educational opportunities for youth and adults, and increased assistance for the elderly and the disabled, primarily via the Economic Opportunity Act (Danziger, 1991; Gillette, 1996). In 1965, Congress enacted Medicare and Medicaid, established the Department of Housing and Urban Development (HUD), funded an array of services for the aged through the Older Americans Act, created the Food Stamp Program under the auspices of the Department of Agriculture, and, through the Elementary and Secondary School Education Act, overturned longstanding precedents and directed federal aid to local schools to equalize educational opportunities for children (Matusow, 1984). These legislative initiatives increased the demand for skilled administrators and greater fiscal accountability (Gillette, 1996).

During the 1960s, there were also dramatic increases in child welfare, income maintenance, and community mental health programs, many of which were implemented by government-funded nonprofit "community action" agencies, which often drew on the cadre of experienced social work administrators for leadership. Perhaps the most important policy shift was the separation of the administration of federally funded social services and cash assistance, which occurred between 1969 and 1972 (Gillette, 1996; Ginzberg & Solow, 1974).

Through the 1970s, policymakers assumed that public social welfare expenditures would continue to increase. The Food Stamps program became a nationwide, universal program of financial assistance. The consolidation of Aid to the Blind, Aged, and Disabled in the federally administered Supplementary Security Income (SSI) program in 1972 removed these programs from state control and converted them into a single, federally administered rule-regulated program with a bureaucratic administrative structure. Social Security benefits were indexed to the cost of living. In 1975, Title XX of the Social Security Act provided funding for a variety of "hard" social services for AFDC parents, including day care and family planning, intended to replace "soft" social work counseling services.

Although he initially maintained many of Johnson's social policies, President Nixon soon attempted to reduce domestic spending, in part by shifting the administration of antipoverty programs to states and localities where their funds were controlled largely by elected officials rather than the directors of community action programs or community residents. The failure to curtail federal expenditures also shaped the administration of Title XX by reinforcing the concept of federal "revenue sharing," which provided states with maximum flexibility in planning services while promoting fiscal accountability (Bixby, 1990; Derthick, 1975).

Through its attempt to alter service provision to low-income persons without creating any new programs, Title XX shaped the direction of both public and private human services. In the late 1970s, it led to a rapid increase in federal expenditures while economic "stagflation" (high unemployment and high inflation) undermined government's ability to sustain such costs. These political and economic constraints froze state Title XX budgets and prevented the development of innovative and comprehensive forms of service. In addition, fiscal inefficiency, program redundancy, uneven regulations and standards, and lack of integration often plagued states' Title XX programs. Ironically, the success of earlier efforts to increase the accessibility of services to those most in need led nonprofit agencies to depend largely on government revenues to maintain fiscal solvency. During the Carter administration, this reliance on public funds began to backfire as economic growth stalled and growing numbers of clients sought help for increasingly complex and chronic problems (Gilbert, 1977).

Economic stagnation and declining political support for social spending also led to a withdrawal of government support for antipoverty programs (Katz, 1989). As urban areas became more dramatically segregated by income and race, nonprofit community-based organizations that served low-income areas had fewer sources of potential revenue (Salamon, 1993). Consequently, in the late 1970s, when policymakers promoted privatization and agency self-sufficiency, nonprofit organizations lacked the resources to respond effectively to the burgeoning social costs being thrust upon them. In the 1980s, this hampered their ability to respond to dramatic increases in homelessness and drug abuse (Blau, 1992).

During this period, a large number of new, nonprofit, community-based or "alternative" service organizations emerged in cities. These organizations responded to newly identified needs: violence against women; the plight of displaced homemakers; homelessness; the lack of services for deinstitutionalized mental health patients, and, later, for persons with HIV/AIDS. They were generally "antiestablishment," antibureaucratic, and hostile to standard forms of hierarchical administrative practice. Often influenced by feminist theory, these organizations blurred traditional distinctions between board, paid staff, and volunteers and substituted collective or consensual decision making for formal lines of authority (Perlmutter, 1988; Powell, 1986).

In sum, policy changes in the 1970s altered the government's role in social service delivery and its relationship to nonprofit human services agencies. Through the creation of block grants, the Carter administration combined formerly categorical programs into broad programmatic areas and established a ceiling on total state expenditures in return for increasing state control of spending patterns. This was particularly significant in the 1980s, when political leaders tried to reverse the policies of the New Deal and the War on Poverty.

The Demise of the Welfare State and Human Services Administration

The "Reagan Revolution" of the 1980s launched an unstinting attack on the role of government in the human services field, which had two basic purposes, one economic, the other political. It shifted the social costs of economic change on to the most vulnerable segments of the population (Abramovitz, 1992). It also compelled communities to rely increasingly, if not exclusively, on private sector solutions for complex, seemingly intractable problems.

The Reagan administration justified the rollback of social welfare policies by asserting that previous government attempts to reduce poverty had failed (Gilder, 1981; Murray, 1984). Proponents of cutbacks ignored, however, the dramatic economic changes that had occurred during the previous two decades. These included the trend toward monopoly control over key industries and the growing power of multinational corporations (the beginnings of today's "globalization"); the rise of the "sunbelt" states, fueled by spending increases in the military or energy industries; the transition from a goods-producing to a service economy; and the growing inequality of income and wealth in the United States. These economic shifts were accompanied by a shift in the center of political influence from "rustbelt" states to regions dominated by conservatives and, within states, from urban areas to the suburbs (Katz, 2001).

The Reagan and Bush administrations also attacked the concept of entitlement that lay at the heart of U.S. social welfare since the New Deal. They sought to reduce the scope of social services and benefit levels and shift as much responsibility for social welfare as possible to the private sector. They eliminated or drastically reduced entire welfare programs, including community action and urban renewal. Federal categorical programs in child welfare, community mental health, and community development were converted into block grants with 25% fewer total dollars, and the movement toward the contracting out or privatization of publicly funded programs accelerated (Kamerman & Kahn, 1989). Expenditures on public housing were reduced over 80%, the minimum wage was frozen, and because of cuts, freezes, or changes in AFDC regulations, the purchasing power of people living on public assistance declined by one-third. Funding crises in Social Security and Medicare were forestalled through modest tax increases and benefit reductions (Center on Budget & Policy Priorities, 1984).

At the same time, ballooning federal deficits—primarily caused by a combination of large tax cuts and increases in military spending—precluded the passage of any major new social welfare initiatives. Consequently, despite the prosperity of the mid- and late 1980s, poverty rates soared, particularly among children, young families, and persons of color (Children's Defense Fund, 1996). By the mid-1990s, the U.S. had the highest level of economic and social inequality of any industrialized nation and the greatest degree of social stratification in half a century (Office of Economic Cooperation & Development, 1996).

As a result of the devolution of responsibility for policymaking and implementation to states and localities and the increasing emphasis on privatization, the role of nonprofit organizations as direct service providers expanded in such areas as community mental health. By the end of the 1980s, government contracts, rather than charitable contributions, had become the major funding source for many established nonprofits and even for some of their newer, community-based alternatives (Salamon, 1989). Although new challenges appeared, such as the crack cocaine epidemic, the spread of HIV/AIDS, and increased homelessness, reductions in overall public funding imposed increased financial pressures and led to the emergence of "cut-back management" strategies (Edwards, Lebold, & Yankey, 1998;

Kettner & Martin, 1996; Perlmutter, 1984). Some nonprofits began to place greater emphasis on earnings from user fees and ancillary, profit-making activities, which produced both practical and ethical dilemmas (Weisbrod, 1998; Reisch & Taylor, 1983). In this context, professional social work qualifications were viewed as less useful for administrative positions than financial management and technical skills in program evaluation and cost-benefit analysis.

During this period, the role of the United Way changed considerably. For decades, it had served as the major funding source for many nonprofit agencies. In the 1980s, however, it developed a more specifically targeted contract model under which the proportion of its funds in most agencies' budgets was substantially reduced (Brilliant, 1990). The introduction of "donor option," which permitted donors to designate to which agency their contributions should go (including agencies that were not United Way members), reduced the importance of the United Way allocation process and weakened its overall influence on the nonprofit human services. A series of national and local scandals at the United Way of America in the 1990s further diminished its impact (Salamon, 2002).

The trend toward privatization required public social welfare administrators, particularly in child welfare and mental health services, to become involved in contract management (Gibelman & Demone, 1998). Responsibilities for the daily operation of such programs shrank as they were declassified, deprofessionalized, and privatized. Conversely, the development of contract proposals for government funders and foundations became a major function of nonprofit administrators (Green, 1998). Although the responsibility for agency funding now rested fully on the shoulders of the agency executive (Grønbjerg, 1993; Kramer, 1985), boards often took on an expanded fundraising role, in part because many grants and contracts did not cover the full costs of service provision or core administrative expenses.

These changes intensified and accelerated in the 1990s in both public and private human services. The commercialization of health care and mental health care services through managed care, which began with private employer health insurance contracts, was soon extended to government-funded services. The appearance of for-profit managed care and behavioral health care organizations created some new management opportunities for social workers with professional experience in these service areas. There were also greater opportunities for social work administrators in for-profit business firms and for-profit service organizations, which provided specialized services through contracts with corporate employee assistance programs (Akabas & Kurzman, 2005).

The process of privatization also expanded in most states to include many publicly funded child welfare services. The additional complexities in funding arrangements, particularly for obtaining government funds, contributed to a process of merger and consolidation among traditional nonprofit social service and health organizations (Singer & Yankey, 1991; Wernet & Jones, 1992; Yankey, Wester, & Campbell, 1998) and an increased emphasis on the financial management responsibilities of nonprofit CEOs (Alperin, 1993; Strachan, 1998). In 1996, the Personal Responsibility and Work Opportunity Reconciliation Act (PRWORA) further devolved the responsibility for welfare program development to the states and increased the role of the private sector in program implementation. The impact of such changes was particularly devastating for small and mid-sized agencies and settlement houses and altered "the traditional character" of nonprofits as a whole (Abramovitz, 2005; Alexander, 2000; Fabricant and Fisher, 2002).

Theories of Human Services Administration

The evolution of administrative theory has been affected by the diverse settings in which human services administration has been practiced and the diverse problems it has confronted during the past century. In the early 20th century,

administration was primarily viewed as a facilitating function that supported the organization's service mission as defined by the board of directors. It was generally assumed that the services developed to implement this mission were beneficial for and appreciated by service users; in other words, that the objectives of all the organization's stakeholders were largely compatible. In this model, the administrator interpreted each group's perceptions to the other to maintain agency harmony.

During the 1920s and early 1930s, Mary Parker Follett, a graduate of Radcliffe College and former settlement house resident in Boston, challenged the popular engineering version of scientific management, which emphasized a rational, machine-like organization of production with a hierarchical, command-and-control model of administration, like that of a military organization (Graham, 1995; Metcalf & Urwick, 1941). Instead, she stressed the importance of the human relationships involved in organizational management, including the role of power, constructive conflict, leadership, and coordination (Follett, 1924). Follett asserted that conflict is an opportunity to understand, rather than defeat, an opponent; that management is not exclusive to business; that management is a functional process, rather than a series of technical competencies; and that businesses and other administrative organizations are primarily social organizations (Kanter, 1995; Metcalf & Urwick, 1941). After a brief period of influence, these concepts were largely ignored from the 1930s until the 1990s, when they were rediscovered by writers on business management and social work, such as Kanter (1997), Drucker (1992), Weiner (1990), and Selber and Austin (1996).

Apart from Follett, administration theorists paid little attention to the motives of board members, professional staff, or service users. Consequently, discriminatory or stigmatizing service patterns were seldom questioned (Morton, 1998). The community-based or alternative human services programs created in the 1960s and 1970s, however, challenged many underlying assumptions of traditional nonprofits on the grounds that their administrative structures and programs reinforced institutional racism and sexism (Hyde, 1992). This led to a more careful examination of the interests represented by stakeholders in such organizations.

The development of public social services in the early 20th century introduced alternative conceptions of the role of social welfare administration. The official theory of public administration, originally set forth in this period by Woodrow Wilson (1887/1987) as an alternative to the spoils system, emphasized the role of administrators as politically neutral implementers of public policies established through democratic processes; personal judgments about the soundness, fairness, or humaneness of those policies were to be ignored. This perspective was compatible with views regarding "good government" held by social workers during the Progressive Era (Carson, 1992; Chambers, 1963; Davis, 1967).

Proponents of public administration asserted that political independence facilitated effective service delivery even during periods of political transition. Tensions emerged after World War II, however, when administrators in the South attempted to rationalize the implementation of their states' racially discriminatory policies. Today, similar tensions exist over policies regarding services to immigrants.

Contemporary theories of administration largely fall into two categories. Some, like organizational ecology and institutional theory, emphasize the role of deterministic social processes within organizations and society at large in shaping the organizational context. To a substantial degree, they have been generated by social scientists who focus on the generalities of social dynamics across a population of organizations (Tucker, Baum, & Singh, 1992; see Chapters 3 and 21 for further discussion of these theories).

By contrast, voluntaristic theories place more emphasis on the role of leaders and other organizational participants in shaping organizational development (see Chapter 7 for further discussion of these theories). They have been developed primarily by researchers in professional schools of business and social work or by organizational consultants. These theories are more likely to be based on qualitative and single-case studies than on quantitative research with larger samples (Drucker, 1992; Graham, 1995; Kanter, 1997; Metcalf & Urwick, 1941; Mintzberg, 1989; Peters & Waterman, 1982; Quinn, 1988; Sayles, 1976). They assume that through entrepreneurial initiatives, individual actors can play a decisive role in improving organizational effectiveness and efficiency. Consequently, they emphasize such behaviors as initiating, controlling, interacting personally, and adapting under conditions of unpredictable change and opportunity (Edwards & Yankey, 1991; Edwards, Yankey, & Altpeter, 1998). In the early 21st century, the growing emphasis on the CEO's role has led to greater concern about executive development in the human services.

While these theoretical perspectives offer different views on the dynamics of agency change, together they underline the importance of understanding the political and economic constraints on agency performance and the key role of administrative advocacy in shaping the policy context of human service programs (see Chapters 21 and 23 for further discussion of these issues).

Education for Human Services Administration

In the early 20th century, efforts to improve the effectiveness of nonprofit human services agencies led to the development of training programs for their agents, now identified as "social workers" instead of "friendly visitors" (Richmond, 1897). During this period, colleges and universities established social science programs, which became a new source of administrators for these organizations (Leighninger, 2000). A number of graduates of Johns Hopkins' Ph.D. program and Harvard's undergraduate program became influential nonprofit executives.

Among them was Amos Warner, who was appointed general secretary of the Baltimore

COS in 1887 while a doctoral student at Johns Hopkins and later became the superintendent of charities for the District of Columbia. In his book, *American Charities* (1894), Warner promoted the dominance of private human services agencies, modeled after the COS. Another influential university-trained executive, Edward T. Devine, a graduate of the University of Pennsylvania's Wharton School, was appointed general secretary of the New York COS at the age of 29. He played a leading role in developing professional education for social workers.

In 1893, Mary Richmond, who had been employed initially as an assistant treasurer at the Baltimore COS, replaced Warner as its general secretary. She quickly became a leader in the development of "scientific philanthropy" and systematic professional training (Richmond, 1899). Through the influence of Richmond and Devine, social work practice in the COS increasingly focused on casework with individuals and families, while settlement houses emphasized group work and community organization. Specialties emerged in medical, psychiatric, and school social work, and formal training programs soon affiliated with existing universities. By 1919, 17 schools of social work formed the Association of Training Schools of Professional Schools of Social Work. After World War I, as casework emerged as the dominant form of professional social work, educators paid scant attention to the administration of the organizations that delivered casework services (Leighninger, 2000).

Some of the earliest training materials dealing specifically with the administration of nonprofit human services organizations, other than the materials produced by the Charity Organization Department of the Russell Sage Foundation (Glenn, Brand, & Andrews, 1947), were developed by the YMCA, through training programs at George Williams College in Chicago and Springfield College in Massachusetts. Financial support for these programs came from business leaders who served on the Y's boards of directors, and the YMCA taught its general secretaries to apply businesslike management methods in their work (Johns, 1954).

However, there was no systematic training in the 1920s for human services administration in either schools of social work or social science departments, despite recommendations that such training be developed (Hagerty, 1931). On-the-job experience in a private social welfare agency, including staff supervision, was regarded as the primary qualification for executives. In 1929, the Milford Conference Report, which attempted to define the nature of social work, included administration as a fundamental technique but did not specify what administrators should know and be able to do (Patti, 1983). As Dunham (1939) stated, "Administration was not ordinarily distinguished from direct practice, nor thought of as a separate function" (p. 16). The major responsibilities of the executive were internal, overseeing staff with varied educational preparation and experience. The board was responsible for policy issues brought to it by the executive, fundraising, and budget oversight.

The expansion of social welfare during the 1930s led to increased recognition of the need for enhanced professional education. In 1932, the Association of Professional Schools of Social Work adopted a minimum curriculum involving one year of full-time study; in 1934, it required that all schools aiming for accreditation be affiliated with a college or university; and in 1939, required a two-year curriculum for accreditation.

During the post-war period, there was a movement toward increased standardization in the social work field, reflected in the development of interdisciplinary doctoral training programs and the creation of core curricula involving behavioral and social science, research, and social policy knowledge (Leighninger, 2000). This led to the development of graduate research training programs at the Ph.D. level but added little required content on administrative practice. The "functional school of social work," developed at the University of Pennsylvania in the 1930s, introduced the importance of the agency in service delivery but never achieved the influence of the "diagnostic school" developed by the New York School of Social Work (Dore, 1990; Meier, 1954).

Shortly after World War II, questions emerged about the role of social work education in the preparation of individuals for administrative positions in the public sector. In response to these concerns, the Hollis and Taylor (1951) study recommended that social work curricula give more attention to "administration, supervision, teaching, and research" (p. 397). The prevailing educational model, however, assumed a focus on the preparation of entry-level caseworkers and that selection for administrative positions should continue to be based on casework experience rather than formal training in administration (Spencer, 1959). In 1952, the newly established Council on Social Work Education (CSWE) issued a "limited and timid" curriculum policy statement that required schools to teach about organizations and administrative procedures but declared that only schools with "adequate resources" could offer a concentration in administration (Dinerman & Geismar, 1984, p. 11).

Over the next decade, these fundamental assumptions remained virtually intact. Although a national curriculum study (Boehm, 1959) recommended that administration be included as one of five professional practice methods, CSWE's 1962 curriculum policy statement referred to administration only as an "enabling method," to be treated as an informational knowledge area for direct service practitioners (1962). A footnote added, "Provision may be made by schools with adequate resources for a concentration in administration . . . for specially selected students" (p. 5).

Nevertheless, a growing number of schools began to offer concentrations in administration. In 1959, the establishment of a Ph.D. program at the Florence Heller School for Advanced Studies in Social Welfare at Brandeis University played an influential role in this regard. The largest of the new social work doctoral programs, its curriculum focused on a social science approach to social welfare, emphasizing political science, policy analysis, and quantitative research. Many of its early graduates became deans and senior faculty members in schools of social work in the 1970s, where they developed macro practice concentrations.

The expansion of categorical federal social welfare programs in the 1960s and 1970s underscored the need to prepare more social welfare managers and promote interorganizational coordination. In the 1970s, the APWA received funds for a national in-service training program for managers in the public social services, and some schools of social work established short-term training programs with Title XX funding. Despite these initiatives, expanded efforts to recruit racial minorities, and an increase in the number of interdisciplinary and joint degree programs with schools of business, urban planning, public health, public policy, public administration, education, and law (at schools like Columbia, Michigan, Washington University, the University of Pennsylvania, and the University of California), there has been little progress in increasing the number of students who study administration or management. A CSWE report in the 1970s found that while a substantial number of schools had macro practice concentrations, including administration, only 10–15% of the students in the schools that had such concentrations opted for macro practice, and only 5% of all graduate social work students in the United States were enrolled in such concentrations (Kazmerski & Macarov, 1976).

During the past quarter century, despite a dramatic increase in graduate programs, the number of schools with macro practice concentrations has leveled off. A 1991 study suggested that several technical areas, such as financial management and personnel management, were either ignored or treated superficially (McNutt, 1995). In 1998, CSWE reported that 14% of the more than 34,000 students enrolled in MSW degree programs selected macro practice concentrations, including administration, planning, and community organization (CSWE, 1998). Although the professional literature has repeatedly pointed out that many entry-level social workers would become supervisors and administrators after a few years of direct practice experience (Patti, 1983), neither schools' curricula nor students' concentration choices have significantly changed during the past decade. Students who select administration are still more likely to have prior professional experience (CSWE, 2007).

Since the 1980s, the growing emphasis on financial management and entrepreneurialism has raised new issues about the conceptual connections between training for agency administration and the focus of professional social work education (Weinbach, 2008). This led to the development of new graduate programs in other fields that specifically focus on nonprofit management. By 2006, there were 50 nonprofit academic centers in the U.S. and Canada, and more than 250 colleges and universities offer undergraduate, graduate, and postgraduate courses in nonprofit management, primarily through schools of public administration, public policy, and business administration (Mirabella, 2007). These programs cover the entire range of nonprofit organizations, and, unlike schools of social work, include extensive curriculum content on economics, fundraising, public finance, fiscal management, law, and information technology (Rimer, 1987; Stein, 2004; Wish & Mirabella, 1998).

In the future, the ability of schools of social work to prepare individuals for administrative positions is likely to be affected by broader curriculum developments such as the growth of generalist and "advanced generalist" concentrations and increased awareness of the importance of diversity and the global context of practice (Mor Barak, 2005). In combination with broader shifts in the nature of U.S. social welfare, these developments may reinforce the long-standing assumption that direct-service experience should be the primary criterion for supervisory or administrative positions. If this occurs, it is likely that many graduates from schools of social work will increasingly pursue careers in private, or contract, advanced professional practice rather than supervision or administration and that only a limited number of schools will retain concentrations in administration. Recent studies of social workers in administrative practice appear to confirm that the percentage of professional social workers in management and supervision has stayed largely constant over the last decade or so (Gibelman & Schvish, 1993; Whittaker, Weismiller, & Clark, 2006).

The Future of Human Services Administration

During the past century, public and private human services organizations have served three major purposes in U.S. society. As "complementary" or "supplementary" forces, and, on occasion, in an adversarial role, they have provided a broad range of services to address the social costs generated by a market economy (Young, 1999). U.S. public policy has supported the growth of private nonprofit human services organizations both directly and indirectly for many years (Grønbjerg, 2001). The tax code gives direct support through incentives for individuals and corporations to make charitable contributions and through provisions that grant nonprofits certain advantages over their for-profit counterparts, such as exemption from paying sales tax. Since the late 1960s, through the "public use of the private sector," federal and state governments have provided them with billions of dollars in direct support (Lynn, 2002). This has produced a dramatic transformation of their administrative practices (Alexander, 2000; Salamon, 2002).

Between the early 1930s and the mid-1970s, government-funded social welfare programs increased dramatically and, in response, the role of private nonprofit human services agencies changed. A dual, parallel, but largely separate private and public structure of welfare capitalism in the U.S. existed from the late 1930s until the 1970s and 1980s, when the creation of quasi-governmental nonprofit service organizations and the use of purchase-of-service contracts between governmental organizations and private nonprofit organizations began to blur the distinctions between these two sectors. This process culminated in the 1990s with the large-scale privatization of governmental health and human services programs.

Initially, these policy shifts increased the accessibility of services to needy populations, although they made the nonprofit sector more dependent on government funding. Since about 1980, however, as a result of the retrenchment of government social welfare spending and the restructuring of fiscal policies—which made charitable giving less attractive to wealthy individuals—the nonprofit sector has become somewhat more dependent on fees-for-service and unrelated business income. At the same time, nonprofits have found themselves serving ever-increasing numbers of low-income individuals and families who can least afford to pay for their services (Abramovitz, 2005). The entry of for-profit companies into service areas previously dominated by nonprofits, such as child care, services to the elderly, hospitals, recreation, and education, has further complicated the picture. Consequently, the funding of many nonprofits is now in jeopardy despite recent increases in philanthropy (Salamon, 2002).

In addition, from 1987 to 1997, fueled in part by the dramatic growth in foundations, the number of nonprofit organizations increased over 5% per year. They now number approximately 1.3 million, nearly three times as many as in 1990, and about 13 times as many as 50 years ago. Small organizations, with annual budgets of $25,000 or less, account for most of this growth. Thousands of mutual aid or self-help organizations have also emerged, many staffed entirely by volunteers. Between 1999 and 2003, over 35,000 groups formed, an increase of 140% (Gose, 2005).

One concern created by this recent growth is that finite resources are being distributed across more organizations. Another is that many small agencies operate less efficiently, are financially fragile, attempt to survive with small staffs, and become excessively dependent on a few funding sources (Gose, 2005). This produces overlapping and wasteful services that may raise questions about the efficacy of the entire nonprofit human services sector.

A third concern is that over time, the community-based leadership of such organizations is replaced by individuals with vastly different orientations toward the human services. For these reasons, some analysts and nonprofit leaders have proposed tougher federal criteria for receiving a 501(c)(3) designation from the Internal Revenue Service, which focus more on results or the distinct contribution an organization adds to an already crowded nonprofit sector (for further discussion of IRS regulations for nonprofits, see Chapters 19 and 20).

There have been several recommendations to strengthen administrative practices in the nonprofit sector through a balance between self-regulation and greater government oversight (Panel on the Nonprofit Sector, 2005, 2006). The former would involve increased education within the sector and reform of some of its practices, such as those regarding boards of directors. The latter would include more vigorous enforcement of existing federal and state tax laws, tighter record-keeping requirements, performance disclosure, and auditing and the revision of the tax code to encourage more charitable giving (Panel on the Nonprofit Sector, 2005). Other recommendations address concerns about the diversion of charitable funds for noncharitable purposes and fraudulent fundraising or embezzlement by sanctioned charities.

Today, one of the more controversial areas of government involvement in the human services has been its support for religious charities, which has grown significantly recently, in part for ideological reasons and, in part, to deliver services to "hard to reach" populations (Chaves & Tsitsos, 2001; Cnaan, Wineburg, & Boddie, 1999). These organizations are exempted from Title VII of the 1964 Civil Rights Act that forbids religious discrimination in employment. The inclusion of "charitable choice" in the 1996 Personal Responsibility and Work Opportunity Reconciliation Act further validated this exemption. Federal and state laws also exempt sectarian organizations from education, training, and licensing requirements.

Given the complexity of today's environment, any effort to anticipate the events of the next century is speculative, at best. Several contemporary issues, however, will probably shape the administration of the human services during the next several decades. Economic globalization will continue to affect government's ability to ameliorate the social costs of rapid economic change. Globalization has already revealed the anachronistic structure of many U.S. political institutions and altered the publicly funded social safety net. At the same time, major social and cultural transformations, such as longer life spans, the influx of millions of immigrants, the impact of new technologies, changing gender roles, and the persistence of economic inequality, have produced new individual and social needs, which require new methods of intervention.

There may be a wide range of societal responses to these challenges. The public sector will attempt to control the growth of social insurance programs, particularly Social Security and Medicare, whose financial viability will be challenged by the aging of the baby boomer generation. Another development will be increased privatization in the fields of health, mental health, child welfare, and family assistance. A third development will be increased reliance on government as a monitor of service quality.

If the human services sector is to survive as a socially beneficial force in the U.S. in the 21st century, agency administrators will have to address multiple challenges. These include increased pressure to transfer the social costs of globalization from corporations and government to the nonprofit sector and to prioritize cost-benefit efficiency over service effectiveness. Another is the tendency to respond to demographic diversity by assuming that patterns of need and helping are identical across cultures. There is also evidence that the emulation of for-profit organizations may jeopardize nonprofits' traditional character, threaten the interorganizational cooperation essential for their effectiveness, and endanger the survival of small agencies that often play a critical role in service provision (Abramovitz, 2005; Alexander, 2000; Fabricant & Fisher, 2002; Reisch & Sommerfeld, 2003). If the administrators of human services organizations can overcome these challenges, they could continue to play a critical role in healing the wounds of an increasingly divided and acrimonious society.

References

Abramovitz, M. (1992). The Reagan legacy: Undoing race, class, and gender accords. In J. Midgley (Ed.), *The Reagan legacy and the American welfare state* [Special issue]. *Journal of Sociology and Social Welfare, 19*(1), 91–110.

Abramovitz, M. (2005). The largely untold story of welfare reform and the human services. *Social Work, 50*(2), 175–186.

Akabas, S. H., & Kurzman, P. A. (2005). *Work and the workplace: A resource for innovative policy and practice.* New York: Columbia University Press.

Alexander, J. (2000). Adaptive strategies of nonprofit human service organizations in an era of devolution and new public management. *Nonprofit Management and Leadership, 10*(3), 287–203.

Alperin, D. E. (1993). Family service agencies: Responding to need in the 1980s. *Social Work, 38*(5), 597–602.

Axinn, J., & Stern, M. (2007). *Social welfare: A history of the American response to need* (7th ed.). Boston: Allyn and Bacon.

Berkowitz, E., & McQuaid, K. (1980). An atmosphere of organization: The rise of welfare capitalism, 1910–1930. In *Creating the welfare state: The political economy of 20th century reform* (pp. 44–58). New York: Praeger.

Bixby, A. K. (1990). Public social welfare expenditures, 1965–1987. *Social Security Bulletin, 53,* 10–26.

Blau, J. (1992). *The visible poor: Homelessness in the United States.* New York: Oxford University Press.

Boehm, W. (1959). *Objectives for the social work curriculum of the future, Vol. 1.* New York: Council on Social Work Education.

Boyer, P. (1978). *Urban masses and moral order in America, 1820–1920.* Cambridge, MA: Harvard University Press.

Breckinridge, S. (1927). *Public welfare administration.* Chicago: University of Chicago Press.

Bremner, R. H. (Ed.). (1974). *Children and youth in America: A documentary history: Vol. III. 1933–1973.* Cambridge, MA: Harvard University Press.

Brilliant, E. L. (1990). *The United Way: Dilemmas of organized charity.* New York: Columbia University Press.

Bruno, F. J. (1957). *Trends in social work 1874–1956: A history based on the proceedings of the National Conference of Social Work* (2nd ed.). New York: Columbia University Press.

Carson, M. J. (1992). *Settlement folks: Social thought in the American settlement movement.* Chicago: University of Chicago Press.

Caudill, H. (1963). *Night comes to the Cumberlands: A biography of a depressed area.* Boston: Little Brown.

Center on Budget and Policy Priorities. (1984). *Dramatic shifts in the budget.* Washington, DC: Author.

Chambers, C. A. (1963). *Seedtime of reform: American social service and social action, 1918–1933.* Minneapolis: University of Minnesota Press.

Chan, S. (1991). The social organization of Asian immigrant communities. In *Asian Americans: An interpretive history* (pp. 63–78). Boston: Twayne.

Chaves, M., & Tsitsos, W. (2001). *Congregations and social services: What they do, how they do it and with whom.* Washington, DC: Aspen Institute.

Children's Defense Fund. (1996). *The state of America's children.* Washington, DC: Author.

Cnaan, R., Wineburg, R., & Boddie, S. (1999). *The newer deal: Social work and religion in partnership.* New York: Columbia University Press.

Council on Social Work Education. (1962). *Official statement of curriculum policy for the master's degree program in graduate professional schools of social work.* New York: Author.

Council on Social Work Education. (1998). *Statistics on social work education in the United States: 1997.* Alexandria, VA: Author.

Council on Social Work Education. (2007). *Statistics on social work education in the United States: 2006.* Alexandria, VA: Author.

Cutlip, S. M. (1965). *Fundraising in the United States: Its role in American philanthropy.* New Brunswick, NJ: Rutgers University Press.

Danziger, S. (1991, September/October). Relearning lessons of the war on poverty. *Challenge,* 53–54.

Danziger, S., & Weinberg, D. (1994). The historical record: Trends in family income, inequality, and poverty. In S. Danziger, G. D. Sandefur, & D. H. Weinberg (Eds.), *Confronting poverty: Prescriptions for change* (pp. 18–50). Cambridge, MA: Harvard University Press.,

Davis, A. (1967). *Spearheads for reform: The social settlements and the progressive movement.* New York: Oxford University Press.

Day, P. (2005). *A new history of social welfare* (5th ed.). Boston: Allyn & Bacon.

Derthick, M. (1975). *Uncontrollable spending for social services grants.* Washington, DC: Brookings Institution.

Dinerman, M., & Geismar, L. L. (Eds.). (1984). *A quarter-century of social work education.* Washington, DC: NASW Press.

Dore, M. (1990). Functional theory: Its history and influence on contemporary social work practice. *Social Service Review, 64*(3), 358–374.

Drucker, B. F. (1992). *Managing the nonprofit organization: Principles and practices.* New York: HarperCollins.

Dunham, A. (1939). The administration of social agencies. In *Social work yearbook* (Vol. 16). New York: Russell Sage Foundation.

Edwards, R. L., Lebold, D. A., & Yankey, J. A. (1998). Managing organizational decline. In R. L. Edwards, J. A. Yankey, & M. A. Altpeter (Eds.), *Skills for effective management of nonprofit organizations* (pp. 279–300). Washington, DC: NASW Press.

Edwards, R. L., & Yankey, J. A. (Eds.). (1991). *Skills for effective human services management.* Washington, DC: NASW Press.

Edwards, R. L., Yankey, J. A., & Altpeter, M. A. (Eds.). (1998). *Skills for effective management of nonprofit organizations.* Washington, DC: NASW Press.

Fabricant, M., & Fisher, R. (2002). *Settlement houses under siege: The struggle to sustain community organizations in New York City.* New York: Columbia University Press.

Fisher, R. (1994). *Let the people decide: A history of community organizing in the United States* (Rev. ed.). Boston: Twayne.

Follett, M. P. (1924). *Creative experience.* New York: Longmans, Green.

Gibelman, M., & Demone, H. W., Jr. (1998). *The privatization of the human services.* New York: Springer.

Gibelman, M., & Schvish, P. H. (1993). *Who are we? The social work labor force as reflected in NASW membership.* Washington, DC: National Association of Social Workers.

Gilbert, N. (1977). The transformation of social services. *Social Service Review, 53*(3), 75–91.

Gilder, G. (1981). *Wealth and poverty.* New York: Basic Books.

Gillette, M. (1996). *Launching the war on poverty: An oral history.* New York: Twayne.

Ginzberg, E., & Solow, R. M. (Eds.). (1974). *The great society: Lessons for the future.* New York: Basic Books.

Glenn, J. M., Brand, L., & Andrews, F. E. (1947). *Russell Sage Foundation 1907–1946.* New York: Russell Sage Foundation.

Gordon, L. (1994). *Pitied but not entitled: Single mothers and the history of welfare.* Cambridge, MA: Harvard University Press.

Gose, B. (2005, January 6). America's charity explosion. *The Chronicle of Philanthropy, 17*(6), 23–28.

Graham, P. (Ed.). (1995). *Mary Parker Follett: Prophet of management: A celebration of writings from the 1920s.* Boston: Harvard Business School Press.

Green, R. K. (1998). Maximizing the use of performance contracts. In R. L. Edwards, J. A. Yankey, & M. A. Altpeter (Eds.), *Skills for effective management of nonprofit organizations* (pp. 78–97). Washington, DC: NASW Press.

Grønbjerg, K. A. (1993). *Understanding nonprofit funding: Managing revenues in social services and community development organizations.* San Francisco: Jossey-Bass.

Grønbjerg, K. (2001). The U.S. nonprofit human service sector: A creeping revolution. *Nonprofit and Voluntary Sector Quarterly, 30*(2), 276–297.

Hagerty, J. E. (1931). *The training of social workers.* New York: McGraw-Hill.

Harrington, M. (1981). *The other America: Poverty in the United States* (Rev. ed.). New York: MacMillan.

Hine, D. C. (1990). "We specialize in the wholly impossible": The philanthropic work of black women. In K. McCarthy (Ed.), *Lady bountiful revisited: Women, philanthropy, and power* (pp. 70–95). New Brunswick, NJ: Rutgers University Press.

Hollis, B. V., & Taylor, A. L. (1951). *Social work education in the U.S.* New York: Columbia University Press.

Hyde, C. (1992). The ideational system of social movement agencies: An examination of feminist health centers. In Y. Hasenfeld (Ed.), *Human services as complex organizations* (pp. 121–144). Newbury Park, CA: Sage.

Iglehart, A., & Becerra, R. (1995). *Social services and the ethnic community.* Needham Heights, MA: Allyn & Bacon.

Jansson, B. (2005). *The reluctant welfare state: American social policies—Past, present, and future* (5th ed.). Belmont, CA: Brooks/Cole.

Johns, R. (1954). *Executive responsibility.* New York: Association Press.

Jones, J. (1992). *The dispossessed: America's underclasses from the civil war to the present.* New York: Basic Books.

Kamerman, S. B., & Kahn, A. J. (1989). *Privatization and the welfare state.* Princeton, NJ: Princeton University Press.

Kanter, R. M. (1995). Preface. In P. Graham (Ed.), *Mary Parker Follett: Prophet of management: A celebration of writings from the 1920s* (pp. 4–8). Boston: Harvard Business School Press.

Kanter, R. M. (1997). *Frontiers of management.* Boston: Harvard Business School Press.

Kaplan, B. J. (1978). Reformers and charity: The abolition of public outdoor relief in New York City, 1870–1898. *Social Service Review, 52*(2), 202–210.

Katz, M. B. (1989). *The undeserving poor: From the war on poverty to the war on welfare.* New York: Pantheon Books.

Katz, M. B. (1996). *In the shadow of the poorhouse: A social history of welfare in America* (Rev. ed.). New York: Basic Books.

Katz, M. B. (2001). *The price of citizenship.* New York: Henry Holt.

Kazmerski, K., & Macarov, D. (1976). *Administration in the social work curriculum.* New York: Council on Social Work Education.

Kettner, P. M., & Martin, L. L. (1996). The impact of declining resources and purchase of service contracting on private, nonprofit agencies. *Administration in Social Work, 20*(3), 21–38.

Kirschner, D. S. (1986). *The paradox of professionalism: Reform and public service in urban America, 1900–1940.* Westport, CT: Greenwood Press.

Kramer, R. M. (1985). The future of the voluntary agency in a mixed economy. *Journal of Applied Behavioral Science, 21*(4), 377–392.

Kurzman, P. (1974). *Harry Hopkins and the New Deal.* Fairlawn, NJ: Burdick.

Lasch-Quinn, E. (1993). *Black neighbors: Race and the limits of reform in the American settlement house movement, 1890–1945.* Chapel Hill: University of North Carolina Press.

Leiby, J. (1978). *A history of social welfare and social work in the United States.* New York: Columbia University Press.

Leighninger, L. (1987). *Social work: Search for identity.* New York: Greenwood.

Leighninger, L. (2000). *Creating a new profession: The beginnings of social work education in the United States.* Alexandria, VA: Council on Social Work Education.

Lemann, N. (1988–1989, December/January). The unfinished war. *Atlantic Monthly, Parts I & II,* 37–56, 53–68.

Lemann, N. (1991). *The promised land: The great black migration and how it changed America.* New York: Alfred Knopf.

Lens, S. (1966). *Radicalism in the United States.* New York: Thomas Y. Crowell.

Lens, S. (1969). *Poverty: America's enduring paradox: A history of the richest nation's unwon war.* New York: Thomas Y. Crowell.

Lewis, O. (1966). *La vida: A Puerto Rican family in the culture of poverty—San Juan and New York.* New York: Random House.

Lohman, R. A., & Lohman, N. (2002). *Social administration.* New York: Columbia University Press.

Lowell, J. S. (1884). *Public relief and private charity.* New York: G. P Putnam's Sons.

Lubove, R. (1965). *The professional altruist: The emergence of social work as a career, 1890–1930.* Cambridge, MA: Harvard University Press.

Lynn, L. E., Jr. (2002). Social services and the state: The public appropriation of private charity. *Social Service Review, 76*(1), 58–82.

Mandler, P. (Ed.). (1990). *The uses of charity: The poor on relief in the 19th century metropolis.* Philadelphia: University of Pennsylvania Press.

Margolin, L. (1997). *Under the cover of kindness: The invention of social work.* Charlottesville: University of Virginia Press.

Matusow, A. J. (1984). *The unraveling of America: A history of liberalism in the 1960s.* New York: Harper and Row.

McLean, F. (1927). *The family society: Joint responsibilities of board, staff and membership.* New York: American Association for Organizing Social Work.

McNutt, J. G. (1995). The macro practice curriculum in graduate social work education: Results of a national study. *Administration in Social Work, 19*(3), 59–74.

Meier, F. (1954). *A history of the New York School of Social Work.* New York: Columbia University Press.

Metcalf, H. C., & Urwick, L. F., (Eds.). (1941). *Dynamic administration: The collected papers of Mary Parker Follett.* Bath: Management Publications Trust.

Mintzberg, H. (1989). *Mintzberg on management: Inside the strange world of organizations.* New York: Free Press.

Mirabella, R. M. (2007). *Current offerings in university-based programs.* South Orange, NJ: Seton Hall University Nonprofit Management Education. Retrieved August 30, 2007, from http://tltc.shu.edu/npo/

Mor Barak, M. E. (2005). *Managing diversity: Toward a globally inclusive workplace.* Thousand Oaks, CA: Sage.

Morton, M. J. (1998). Cleveland's child welfare system and the "American dilemma," 1941–1964. *Social Service Review, 72*(1), 112–136.

Murray, C. (1984). *Losing ground: American social policy, 1950–1980.* New York: Basic Books.

Office of Economic Cooperation and Development. (1996). *Report on income inequality in industrial nations.* Geneva, Switzerland: Author.

Panel on the Nonprofit Sector. (2005, June). *Strengthening transparency, governance, accountability of charitable organizations: Final report.* Washington, DC: Independent Sector.

Panel on the Nonprofit Sector. (2006, April). *Strengthening transparency, governance, accountability of charitable organizations: Supplement to the final report.* Washington, DC: Independent Sector.

Patterson, J. (2000). *America's struggle against poverty in the 20th century.* Cambridge, MA: Harvard University Press.

Patti, R. (1983). *Social welfare administration: Managing social programs in a developmental context.* Englewood Cliffs, NJ: Prentice Hall.

Perlmutter, F. D. (1984). *Human services at risk.* Lexington, MA: Lexington Books.

Perlmutter, F. D. (1988). Administering alternative social programs. In P. R. Keyes & L. H. Ginsberg (Eds.), *New management in human services* (pp. 203–218). Silver Spring, MD: NASW Press.

Peters, T. J., & Waterman, R. H. (1982). *In search of excellence.* New York: Warner.

Pittman-Munke, P. (1985). *Mary Richmond and the wider social movement, Philadelphia 1900–1909.* Unpublished doctoral dissertation, University of Texas at Austin.

Piven, F. F., & Cloward, R. (1995). *Regulating the poor: The functions of public welfare* (Rev. ed.). New York: Vintage Books.

Powell, D. M. (1986). Managing organizational problems in alternative service organizations. *Administration in Social Work, 10*(1), 57–70.

Quinn, R. E. (1988). *Beyond rational management: Mastering the paradoxes and competing demands of high performance.* San Francisco: Jossey-Bass.

Reisch, M. (2004). Charity. In R. McElvaine (Ed.), *The encyclopedia of the great depression* (pp. 159–161). New York: Oxford University Press.

Reisch, M. (2005). American exceptionalism and critical social work: A retrospective and prospective analysis. In I. Ferguson, M. Lavalette, & E. Whitman (Eds.), *Globalisation, global justice and social work* (pp. 157–171). London: Routledge.

Reisch, M. (2008). From melting pot to multiculturalism: The impact of racial and ethnic diversity on social work and social justice in the U.S. *British Journal of Social Work, 38*(4), 788–804.

Reisch, M., & Andrews, J. L. (2001). *The road not taken: A history of radical social work in the United States.* Philadelphia: Brunner-Routledge.

Reisch, M., & Sommerfeld, D. (2003, Fall). Welfare reform and the future of nonprofit organizations. *Nonprofit Management and Leadership, 14*(1), 19–46.

Reisch, M., & Taylor, C. (1983). Ethical guidelines for cutback management: A preliminary approach. *Journal of Social Administration, 7*(3–4), 59–72.

Reisch, M., & Wenocur, S. (1982). Professionalization and voluntarism in social welfare: Changing roles and functions. *Journal of Voluntary Action Research, 11*(2–3), 11–31.

Richmond, M. E. (1897). The need for a training school in applied philanthropy. In *Proceedings of the National Conference of Charities and Correction.* Boston: George H. Ellis.

Richmond, M. E. (1899). *Friendly visiting among the poor: A handbook for charity workers.* New York: Macmillan.

Rimer, E. (1987). Social administration education: Reconceptualizing the conflict with MPA, MBA, and MPH programs. *Administration in Social Work, 11*(2), 45–55.

Rivera, J. A. (1987). Self help as mutual protection: The development of Hispanic fraternal benefit societies. *Journal of Applied Behavioral Science, 23*(3), 387–396.

Rothman, D. J. (1971). *The discovery of the asylum: Social order and disorder in the new republic.* Boston: Little, Brown.

Rubinow, I. M. (1913). *Social insurance.* New York: Henry Holt.

Salamon, L. M. (1989). The changing partnership between the voluntary sector and the welfare state. In V. Hodgkinson & R. K. Lyman (Eds.), *The future of the nonprofit sector: Challenges, changes, and policy considerations* (pp. 41–60). San Francisco: Jossey-Bass.

Salamon, L. M. (1993). The marketization of welfare: Changing nonprofit and for-profit roles in the American welfare state. *Social Service Review, 67*(1), 16–39.

Salamon, L. M. (Ed.). (2002). *The resilient sector: The state of nonprofit America.* Washington, DC: Brookings Institution Press.

Sayles, L. (1976). *Leadership: What effective managers do and how they do it.* New York: McGraw-Hill.

Selber, K., & Austin, D. M. (1996). Mary Parker Follett: Epilogue to or return of a social work management pioneer? *Administration in Social Work, 21*(1), 1–15.

Singer, M., & Yankey, J. (1991). Organizational metamorphosis: A study of eighteen nonprofit mergers, acquisitions, and consolidations. *Nonprofit Management & Leadership, 1*(4), 357–370.

Skocpol, T. (1992). Understanding the origins of modern social provision in the United States. In *Protecting soldiers and mothers: The political origins of social policy in the United States* (pp. 1–62). Cambridge, MA: Harvard University Press.

Spencer, S. (1959). *The administration method in social work education: Vol. 3, A report of the curriculum study.* New York: Council on Social Work Education.

Stein, T. J. (2004). *The role of law in social work practice and administration.* New York: Columbia University Press.

Strachan, J. L. (1998). Understanding nonprofit financial management. In R. L. Edwards, J. A. Yankey, & M. A. Altpeter (Eds.), *Skills for effective management of nonprofit organizations* (pp. 343–370). Washington, DC: NASW Press.

Street, B. (1940). *The public welfare administrator.* New York: McGraw-Hill.

Trattner, W. I. (1999). *From poor law to welfare state* (6th ed.). New York: Free Press.

Trolander, J. (1987). *Professionalism and social change: From the settlement house movement to neighborhood centers, 1886 to the present.* New York: Columbia University Press.

Tucker, D. J., Baum, J. A. C., & Singh, J. V. (1992). The institutional ecology of human service organizations. In Y. Hasenfeld (Ed.), *Human services as complex organizations* (pp. 47–72). Newbury Park, CA: Sage.

Wagner, D. (2005). *The poorhouse: America's forgotten institution.* Lanham, MD: Rowman and Littlefield.

Waite, B. T. (1960). *A warm friend for the spirit.* Cleveland, OH: Family Service Association.

Warner, A. G. (1894). *American charities: A study in philanthropy and economics.* New York: Thomas Y. Crowell.

Weinbach, R. W. (2008). *The social worker as manager: A practical guide to success* (5th ed.). Boston: Allyn & Bacon.

Weiner, M. B. (1990). *Human services management: Analysis and applications* (2nd ed.). Belmont, CA: Wadsworth.

Weisbrod, B. A. (Ed.). (1998). *To profit or not to profit: The commercial transformation of the nonprofit sector.* New York: Cambridge University Press.

Wenocur, S., & Reisch, M. (1989). *From charity to enterprise: The development of American social work in a market economy.* Urbana: University of Illinois Press.

Wernet, S. P, & Jones, S. A. (1992). Merger and acquisition activity between nonprofit, social service organizations: A case study. *Nonprofit and Voluntary Sector Quarterly, 21*(4), 367–380.

Whittaker, T., Weismiller, T., & Clark, E. (2006). *Assuring the sufficiency of a front-line labor force: Executive summary.* Washington, DC: National Association of Social Workers.

Wilson, W. (1987). The study of administration. In J. M. Shafritz & A. C. Hyde (Eds.), *Classics of public administration* (2nd ed., pp. 10–25). Oak Park, IL: Moore. (Original work published 1887)

Wish, N. B., & Mirabella, R. M. (1998). Curricular variations in nonprofit management graduate programs. *Nonprofit Management & Leadership, 6*(1), 99–109.

Yankey, J. A., Wester, B., & Campbell, D. (1998). Managing mergers and consolidations. In R. L. Edwards, J. A. Yankey, & M. A. Altpeter (Eds.), *Skills for effective management of non-profit organizations* (pp. 504–520). Washington, DC: NASW Press.

Young, D. (1999). Complementary, supplementary, or adversarial? A theoretical and historical examination of nonprofit-government relations in the United States. In E. Brosi & E. Steuerle (Eds.), *Nonprofits and government: Collaboration and conflict* (pp. 31–67). Washington, DC: Urban Institute Press.

CHAPTER 3

Human Services Administration and Organizational Theory

Yeheskel Hasenfeld

Human services administration has a distinguished history, dating back to the Charity Organization Societies (COS). One of the early studies of the administrative practices was done by Charles Richmond Henderson (1904), who examined in detail the operations of the COS. In the ensuing years, as social service agencies became more institutionalized, there were calls within social work for increased efficiency and effectiveness in administration and with them a search for appropriate management theories (Lubove, 1965). For example, in 1907, Lewis W. Hine published an article in *The World Today* titled "Charity on a Business Basis: The Modern Methods of Applying Business Principles to Social Services" (cited in Lubove, 1965, p. 161). The push for efficiency was coupled with efforts to professionalize the charity workers, to delimit the role of the board

of directors, to focus on policy issues, and to centralize administrative control in the hands of the executive director (pp. 161–170). Administrators and scholars became, therefore, interested in issues such as leadership, role of the board, and supervision. The formation of councils of social agencies and the subsequent financial federations such as the Community Chests drew attention to issues of interorganizational relations and coordination (Lubove, 1965).

Nonetheless, in contrast to social casework with its focus on person-environment, no distinct theory of human services administration has emerged that the profession could claim as its own. If anything, it missed a unique opportunity to have its own voice, had it followed the pioneering work of Mary Parker Follett, whose theories of administration stem directly from her experiences as a community social worker (Fox, 1968; Selber

& Austin, 1997). It is worth sketching her approach to management because as we shall see, much of what passes as management theory in the human services has shallow roots, either in actual practices or in organizational theories that are distinctive to this field.

Follett's concept of organization is relational rather than structural. It is a system of interdependencies (Ansell, 2007) in which the interactions of individuals with each other are the building blocks of the organization (Selber & Austin, 1997). As a relational system, the constituent parts of the organization reciprocally influence each other to produce a whole that, in turn, influences its parts. A key concept, which should be familiar to social workers and other helping professionals, is "circular response," which means that as individuals interact with each other in an unfolding situation, they react and respond to each other; they alter their own and the other's perceptions of themselves and the situation; and they change the situation, which, in turn, affects their own perceptions and behavior. As cited by Barclay (2005), Follett put it this way: "In human relations. . . . I never react to you but to you-plus-me; or to be more accurate, it is I-plus-you reacting to you-plus-me" (p. 748). Therefore, the organization is not a static or fixed entity because individuals in it (including clients) constantly change it through their experiential relations with each other. Hence, paraphrasing Follett, Barclay writes, "We must understand how the actions of managers or organizations affect employees [and, I would add, clients] and how employees' behavior, in turn, impacts managers" (p. 748).

Key to Follett's theory of management, and particularly to human services administration, is her notion of integrative unity. As Fox (1968) put it,

> integration is a harmonious marriage of differences which, like the nut and the screw, or the parts of a watch come together in a way that produces a new form, a new entity, a new result, made out of the old differences and yet different from any of them. (p. 524)

Integration is an evolving process, and to be successful, it requires management practices that acknowledge that differences exist and are legitimate; that differences are open to change; and that differences should be explored openly and freely with contributions from all sides (Fox, 1968, p. 524). In other words, it arises when the individuals in the organization recognize their interdependencies and joint responsibilities and seek common interests. It further means that conflict can be positive, if it is resolved through integration rather than domination or compromise (Selber & Austin, 1997, p. 6). To achieve integration, Follett conceptualized power not as "power over" but rather as "power-with," which she defined as "a jointly developed power, a co-active, not coercive power" (cited in Selber & Austin, 1997, p. 8). It is closely akin to the concept of empowerment in social work. To achieve power-with, organizational leaders cannot enforce orders from above. According to Follett, "One person should not give orders to another person; but both should agree to take their orders from the situation" (cited in Ansell, 2007, p. 23). Leaders and subordinates need to achieve integration through "circular response." Therefore, a key role for leaders is to develop an organizational culture that promotes integrative unity through the joint activity of managers and workers. This is what Follett means by "the law of the situation," which "emphasizes the integrative nature of decision making, stresses the importance of empowerment of the employees, and implies that fair decisions are those that involve all individuals who have a stake in the decision and its outcomes" (Barclay, 2005, p. 743). In her final lecture, Follett (1940, p. 297) articulated her idea of management as "evoking, interacting, integrating, and emerging" through these four principles:

1. Coordination by direct contact of the responsible people concerned

2. Coordination in the early stages

3. Coordination as the reciprocal relating of all the factors in a situation

4. Coordination as a continuing process

Follett's theory of management failed to gain adherence in an era dominated by Taylorism and scientific management. Preoccupied with issues of control and efficiency, scientific management, with its ideological underpinnings of the moral superiority of scientific reasoning and the view of individuals as rational actors motivated to work for economic gains, was antithetical to Follett's views (Barley & Kunda, 1992).

Thus, since its inception, human services (or what has historically been referred to as social welfare) administration theory and practice has echoed general trends in managerial theories and ideologies embraced by business organizations and public bureaucracies (Austin, 2002). An implicit assumption guiding these theories is that management practices developed for business organizations are equally applicable to human service organizations. Below, I question that assumption. As a result, it is difficult to identify a human services management theory that springs from the distinctiveness of the field.

Moreover, a recent review of major textbooks in human services administration notes that neither organizational theory nor empirical research seems to inform the management practices enunciated in the textbooks (Austin & Kruzich, 2004; see also Au, 1994). Yet, if we are to have a theory-based practice that can be verifiable, it must emanate from an empirically grounded organizational theory. Still, encouragingly, we are witnessing an increasing body of empirical research on organizational factors that influence the administration and outcomes of social services (e.g., Poertner, 2006; see also Chapters 6 and 8). Hopefully, such research will anchor human services administration in stronger empirical foundations. In this chapter, I examine the use of organizational theory and research in developing models of human services administration as expressed in the leading textbooks in the field.

It can be argued that the management of human service organizations is not appreciably different from the management of other organizations (e.g., Drucker, 1990). Indeed, with the increasing commercialization of the human services and the blurring distinctions among public,

private nonprofit, and for-profit organizations (e.g., Salamon, 1995; Weisbrod, 1998), there is greater pressure on human service organizations to adopt management practices and principles that have been developed for business organizations and have stood the test of the competitive marketplace (e.g., Total Quality Management, transformational leadership). Still, management strategies that gain widespread acceptance may not deliver on their promises because they lack a strong grounding in organizational theory and research. The management field, including management in the human services, is very susceptible to fads and fashions, which, under critical theoretical and empirical analysis, are revealed to be of limited merit (Mintzberg, 1996). Most important, a seemingly appropriate management tool for business organizations may not work for human service organizations. To guard against such pitfalls, administration practices must first and foremost recognize the unique attributes of their organizations. Second, they must be anchored in organizational theories that take these attributes into account. Third, they must be empirically verifiable.

What sets human service organizations apart from many other organizations is a combination of attributes emanating from the fundamental fact that they work on people in order to transform them (Hasenfeld, 1992). As a result, human service organizations engage in moral work, upholding and reinforcing moral values about "desirable" human behavior and the "good" society. Therefore, human service organizations are embedded in an institutional environment from which they derive their legitimacy and license to work on people. It is also from the institutional environment that human service organizations must obtain their service technologies, technologies that are inherently indeterminate and fraught with ambiguities. Moreover, the success of these technologies depends greatly on the reactivity of the clients. That is, clients present various contingencies and constraints that affect the trajectory of the service delivery process, making it uncertain. And the clients' degree of compliance is critical to the effectiveness of the technology. Hence, a dominant feature of human service organizations is the centrality of client-staff relations in determining service outcomes. It is through these relations that workers attempt to bring about change in their clients and attain compliance. Therefore, workers invariably engage in emotional labor (Lopez, 2006; Maynard-Moody & Musheno, 2003). Following Hochschild (1983), the organization sets rules and expectations about the appropriate and required expressions of feelings and emotions (e.g., empathy) toward the clients that it deems necessary for its service technology. A related point is that the work in human service organizations is gendered; that is, the majority of the front-line workers are women. In part, this is due to a gendered ideology that women have greater nurturing capabilities that are needed for the effective provision of social care. Finally, the definition and measurement of service effectiveness is equally indeterminate, ambiguous, and multidimensional. While other types of organizations may exhibit one or more of these attributes, it is the combination and interaction of all of them that makes human service organizations distinctive.

One can readily see how, in such an organizational context, human services are exceedingly complex. They have to cope with a turbulent environment, grapple with service design and management issues that are highly value-laden, lack clear and unambiguous end-states, and manage staff and clients who cannot be readily controlled. Moreover, although there is a consensus that the primary aim of management in this field is to promote service effectiveness (e.g., Patti, 1987; Rapp & Poertner, 1992), the definition of service effectiveness typically is a contested terrain that greatly affects administrative strategies and choices. As human service organizations become more dependent on government funding, they face greater pressures to meet definable and typically quantifiable effectiveness measures. These measures, reflecting dominant institutional rules, may not concord with the original raison d'être of the organization, yet they are enforced through the evaluation criteria demanded by the external funders.

To address these challenges, human services administration looks for practice principles. These, in turn, implicitly or explicitly are guided by the choice of an underlying organizational theory that offers a rationale for these principles. As shown in Table 3.1, each theory tends to focus on a major administrative theme, and several theories may address the same theme by offering very different perspectives, conceptualizations, and possible solutions.

Table 3.1   Administrative Themes and Organizational Theories

Administrative Theme	Organizational Theories
Goal attainment	Rational—legal, scientific management
Management of people (staff and clients)	Human relations, feminist perspective
Proficiency and efficiency	Contingency, technology and structure, network
Adaptation and resource mobilization	Political economy
Founding and survival	Population ecology
Institutionalization	New institutionalism
Integration and social cohesion	Culture, sense making
Knowledge, power, and control	Postmodern, structuration
Social change	Critical theory, radical feminism

Goal Attainment

The rational approach views the organization as an efficient machine to attain specific goals (Morgan, 1997). The model assumes that once the goals are specified, an efficient service technology can be chosen to meet them. Such a technology can be implemented through an internal division of labor where roles and authority relations are clearly specified and formalized. The organizational structure is *rational* because it can be shown that the service technology and its attendant division of labor ensure the most efficient way to attain the organizational goals. This engineering approach has its roots in Taylor's scientific management and what has been labeled as "Fordism," after Henry Ford's innovations in mass production (Zuboff, 1998). In addition, the organizational structure is *legal* (Weber, 1924/1968) because the division of labor and exercise of authority are based on legally accepted normative rules (e.g., professional expertise, administrative law).

Kettner, Moroney, and Martin (2007) exemplify this approach in their "effectiveness-based" approach to social welfare administration. As they state,

> Effectiveness-based program planning involves taking a program through a series of steps designed to produce a clear understanding of the problem to be addressed, to measure client problem type and severity at entry, to provide a relevant intervention, to measure client problem type and severity at exit. (p. 15)

Similarly, Lewis, Packard, and Lewis (2007, p. 8) picture human services management as a rational process. It includes (a) developing a vision for the future, creating strategy, setting goals and objectives; (b) structuring and coordinating the work that needs to be done; (c) mobilizing the people needed to make the program work; (d) enhancing the skills and motivation of service providers; (e) planning the use of financial resources to reach the goals; (f) tracking progress on program objectives and activities; and (g) comparing program accomplishments with the standards set at the planning stages. Again, the purpose of management is to produce a highly efficient and effective service delivery system that is governed by norms of rationality.

Despite the predominance of the rational model of organizations in human services administration, it has been shown to be theoretically weak and empirically untenable (for a review, see Scott & Davis, 2007). The organization is conceptualized as a closed system, with little attention to the broader social system in which it is embedded. Decision making is based on an economic model of organizational behavior that lacks empirical validity (Pfeffer, 1997). Structure is devoid of the processes of sensemaking and interpretative interactions by organizational actors (Weick, 1995). One can also readily see how a rational model fails to take into account the unique attributes of human service organizations. For example, the model assumes that goal attainment would be measured through feedback loops from workers and, most important, from the clients or consumers. Yet, this is often not the case because line staff use their discretion to control such feedback, and clients are typically powerless and their voices are seldom heard (Brodkin, 1997). Critics have also argued that the rational model has provided the ideological and intellectual justification for the concentration of power in large organizations and the hierarchical authority of a managerial class (Creed & Miles, 1996). Feminist scholars, for example, argue that the rational approach to organizations implicitly legitimizes gender inequalities and male domination (Acker, 1990). It runs counter to the emphasis in social work on empowerment (discussed below). Hence, questions arise regarding the compatibility of the rational model with social work values and ethics.

Nonetheless, the rational model remains dominant in the management of human services, for several reasons. First, it is a reflection of the prominence of control and efficiency in managerial discourse. This is increasingly the case in an environment of devolution and privatization of social services (Frumkin & Andre-Clark, 2000). Second, it provides legitimacy to administrative practices by appealing to norms of technical rationality. In particular, by casting clients needs, service responses, and desired outcomes in technical terms, the rational approach masks the implicit moral and value choices made by those who wield power in the organization. Third, it does offer pragmatic solutions to the problematic relations between ends and means, albeit with potentially unintended consequences.

Managing People

The rational approach assumes an economic model of human behavior. Such a model cannot adequately explain the complex interdependencies, social ties, and forms of cooperation that exist among members of the organization. The human relations perspective, in contrast, assumes that behavior is embedded in a web of social relations. How members relate to each other within and without the organization will influence their motivation, patterns of work, productivity, and identity. Therefore, to the extent there is consonance between the needs of the individual and the needs of the organization, both will flourish (Argyris, 1964). According to the human relations perspective, such consonance is attained when the workers find meaning and satisfaction in their work, when they actively participate in the management of the organization, and when leadership is person-oriented.

The human relations approach has produced a very rich body of theory, research, and management practices. Contemporary theorizing and research within this perspective have focused on four major interrelated areas: (a) job satisfaction, (b) human resource practices management, (c) trust, and (d) leadership. Job satisfaction has been shown to be correlated with such job attributes as relations with supervisors, work

conditions, pay and promotion opportunities, job security, coworkers' attitudes, and personal growth (for a review, see Jayaratne, 1993; also see Chapter 6). Related studies have explored the idea of person-environment fit, especially between individual predispositions and job requirements (Chatman, 1989). The relationship between human resource practices and performance, including participatory management, has been the focus of many studies (Pfeffer, 1997). Factors such as decentralization, participation, teamwork, job enrichment, autonomy and flexibility, high-level training, and performance-based rewards have been correlated with organizational performance. Similarly, trust is viewed as a key to cooperative relations and teamwork within the organization (Creed & Miles, 1996). Leadership skills are viewed as vital to organizational success. Hart and Quinn (1993) showed that high-performance organizations have executives with high levels of "behavioral complexity" playing four critical roles—vision setter, motivator, analyzer, and task master.

The appeal of the human relations perspective to the human services is obvious considering the centrality of worker-client relations. Trust, values, emotions, and feelings are critical to these relations, and they are assumed to be influenced by how workers feel about their work, how their self-actualization needs are being met, and how the internal environment facilitates their work. Indeed, considerable research from the human relations perspective has been done in the human services. The concept and much of the research on burnout has been done on human services workers (Maslach & Schaufeli, 1993). Role conflict and lack of support from colleagues and supervisors were found to be the main determinants of burnout. Participatory management, often recast in the human services as the empowerment of workers, has been shown to contribute to organizational effectiveness (Whiddon & Martin, 1989). Guterman and Bargal (1996) found that there is a relationship between the sense of empowerment social workers feel and their perceptions of service outcomes. Leadership in the social services is also seen as important in empowering the workers. Keller and Dansereau (1995) proposed that when superiors empower subordinates, they reciprocate by performing in accordance with the preferences of the supervisors. Glisson (1989) showed that the more workers perceive their leaders to have power and maturity, the greater their commitment to the organization.

Despite the extensive research, the application of human relations theory and research to human services administration has been uneven. As we have seen, participatory management and staff empowerment are taken to be important administrative practices. Similarly, the role of leaders in articulating a vision and a nurturing culture for the agency is viewed as a central administrative function (e.g., Pearlmutter, 1998; Weil, 1988). But only Skidmore (1995) articulates a model of administration that fully embraces the human relations perspective. Indeed, he begins his book with the following introduction:

> Administration in social work is changing from a pyramid to a circle. No longer does one person at the top have absolute power to dictate and control agency policies and practices. Such power is being shared more and more with staff and clients. . . . In many agencies, in varying patterns, administrators, staff, and clients are working cooperatively together to make decisions and delivery agency services. (p. 1)

Skidmore (1995) proposes three guiding principles that are very consonant with the human relations perspective—acceptance of leaders and staff, democratic involvement in formulation of agency policies and procedures, and open communication. Accordingly, the human services manager is described as accepting, caring, creating, democratizing, trusting, approving, maintaining personal equilibrium and balance, planning, organizing, setting priorities, delegating, interacting with the community, decision making, facilitating, communicating, timing, building, and motivating. Teamworking and motivating strategies are central to his model.

There is something surreal about such a model, being so removed from the complex and difficult realities of human services work. This is not surprising because the human relations perspective tends to view the organization in isolation from its environment, thus diminishing the importance of external factors in shaping organizational dynamics. It assumes that both the organization and its people are highly malleable and that changes in how people behave will have great impact on organizational performance. Yet the empirical evidence is quite weak. For example, leadership studies have been able to show modest impact, at best, on organizational performance (Pfeffer, 1997). In addition, the human relations perspective presents an image of the effective organization that is presumed to be applicable to most situations. Again, it does so by neutralizing much of the impact of the external environment. It is difficult to see, for example, how in public welfare agencies, characterized as street-level bureaucracies (Handler & Hasenfeld, 2007; Lipsky, 1980), human relations strategies can have but limited effects.

This is not to imply that using strategies to reduce job stress, empowering workers and clients, and having charismatic leaders are not valuable. Indeed, organizations that use such strategies do exist, as exemplified by feminist and collectivist organizations (Bordt, 1998). However, as social movement organizations, they arise in a particular environmental context (Hasenfeld & Gidron, 2005). Therefore, they are far less common than the bureaucratic and professionally dominated human services. Thus, the applicability of human relations must be assessed within the organizational and broader context in which they are to be undertaken. Otherwise, their application might have the opposite effect, resulting in frustration and cynicism. Yet little consideration of these factors is built into proposed human relations practices for management practice in this field.

Proficiency and Efficiency

Contingency theory attempts to overcome some of the limitations of the rational approach by embracing an open systems perspective and discarding the normative structure inherent in the model. Instead, structure is made variable and contingent on the characteristics of the organization's environment, including environmental heterogeneity and stability, technological certainty, organizational size, and power (Mintzberg, 1979). Organizational effectiveness and efficiency is assumed to be a function of the *fit* between the contingency and the internal structure. Therefore, as the environment becomes more heterogeneous and unstable, the internal structure shifts from a centralized bureaucracy to a decentralized and organic structure (e.g., flexible, informal). Similarly, as the task becomes more variable and the knowledge more uncertain, the structure will move from a simple bureaucracy to a professional mode (Perrow, 1967). In the same vein, increase in size leads to greater internal differentiation and specialization by function, a finding that has been widely replicated (Donaldson, 1996). Finally, Mintzberg (1979, p. 288) proposed that as the external control of the organization increases, there is more internal centralization and formalization. A burgeoning field of organizational design has emerged, showing how strategic choices regarding markets, clients, and products influence the internal design of the organization (e.g., Galbraith & Kazanjian, 1986).

Although contingency theory has produced an impressive body of studies, including management practice principles, it has lost much of its luster (Pfeffer, 1997). In part, the empirical research, especially on the relationship between technology and structure, has failed to provide a convincing verification of the theory (Glisson, 1992; Schoonhoven, 1981). In addition, the theory is quite complex, and there is considerable difficulty in clearly defining and operationalizing all its variables. Still, Donaldson (1987) showed that organizations that achieve a fit between a particular contingency and an aspect of their structure (e.g., strategy and structure) outperform organizations that lack such a fit.

More recent developments in contingency theory (for a review, see McGrath, 2006) relevant to the human services stress the multiplicity of contingencies the organization needs to address as it designs its structure. These include the embeddedness of the organization in many networks, the internal interdependencies among units within the organization, and the capacity of the organization to shift its location in the environment (e.g., leaving a resource-poor neighborhood or opening a satellite in an emerging neighborhood). Moreover, there is greater recognition that there is no one best way to accomplish the organization's service mission (the principle of equifinality).

Little attention has been given to contingency theory in human services, despite the importance of designing structures that can optimally achieve service effectiveness. This is even more ironic because some important research testing the contingency model has been done on human services. A series of empirical studies by Glisson and colleagues (1978, 1980) are particularly noteworthy. In a groundbreaking study, Glisson (1978) showed that in the human services, it is structure that determines how the workers will implement the technology. That is, if the structure is centralized and formalized, the workers will treat the clients in a uniform and routine manner (see also Glisson, 1992). In a later study, Glisson and Martin (1980) found that productivity and efficiency were highly correlated with a centralized authority structure. Hence, human services administrators face a dilemma of focusing on productivity and efficiency at the expense of staff and client satisfaction. In a study of addiction treatment programs, Savage (1988) identified four different technologies, which she classified as limited, specialized, individualized, and encompassing. She showed how internal structures varied by technology and that the greater the scope of the technology, the higher the service effectiveness. More recent work by

D'Aunno and colleagues examined the effects of hybrid structures as mental health agencies diversified into drug treatment (D'Aunno, Sutton & Price, 1991).

Yet despite such research, Patti (1983) and Austin (2002) are among the few that refer to contingency theory when discussing the development of an organizational structure to implement a program. Weiss (1989) incorporates findings from contingency theory in explicating management strategies to structure the organizations. Weinbach (1990) offers several alternative structures and a list of factors to consider in selecting an appropriate model. But he makes only an opaque reference to contingency theory and research. In contrast, Austin (2002) makes an explicit and detailed use of Mintzberg's framework as well as empirical research in articulating administrative strategies to synchronize structure with service technology. In particular, he identifies several program strategies that emanate from different theories of intervention. That is, he shows how each intervention theory, such as the medical model or the developmental rationale, calls for a distinct program design, such as a professional or systems strategy.

The emergence of network organizations in the human services presents new challenges to administration. Driven, in part, by devolution, privatization, contracting out, and managed care, human service organizations, public and private, face an environment that encourages and often demands the formation of network exchange relations, collaborations, and alliances (Milward & Provan, 2000). Moreover, innovations in information technology, especially the Internet, have supported the transformation from traditional models of bureaucracy to network organizations (Ho, 2002). With the rise of managed care in the provision of mental health services, participating agencies become members of a formal and vertically organized network under the auspices of an oversight organization. Because the participating agencies must assume some of the financial risks if they experience cost overruns, they have an incentive to strengthen horizontal relations among themselves, and they indeed respond by developing greater collaborations and denser network relations. This enables the providers to cope with the financial pressures of managed care without sacrificing quality of care (Provan, Isett, & Milward, 2004). Interorganizational collaboration in the form of alliances has been shown to increase the quantity and breadth of client and information exchanges, thus fostering a more integrated service network (Foster-Fishman, Salem, Allen, & Fahrbach, 2001). Service coordination, however, can have a dark side to it. A longitudinal study of child welfare service coordination by Glisson and Hemmelgarn (1998) showed that service coordination teams had a negative effect on the quality of services the children received, possibly because caseworkers relinquished many of their responsibilities by assuming that they would be taken over by the coordination teams. It may also be that coordination teams cannot substitute for effective interorganizational exchanges built on trust and reciprocity.

Research suggests that in addition to external networks, internal networks, rather than hierarchical structures, may have greater advantages, especially in reducing costs and improving quality. They may also provide a more hospitable work environment to women (for a review, see Podolny & Page, 1998). More broadly, guided largely by norms of reciprocity and trust, network organizations also promote greater organizational learning and innovation (Goes & Park, 1997; Jaskyte & Lee, 2006).

Despite the critical importance of networks to human services administration, they receive limited attention. Austin (2002), as noted below, presents a systematic treatment of network relations and their importance to the management of human services. Hardina and colleagues also emphasize the importance of building network relations, both with the community and with other organizations, as a way to mobilize power (Hardina, Middleton, Montana, & Simpson, 2006; also see further discussion of interorganizational collaboration in Chapter 21).

Adaptation and Resource Mobilization

A political economy perspective recognizes the importance of environmental contingencies, but it rejects the rational model implicit in contingency theory. Rather, it views the organization as a collectivity that has multiple and complex goals; paramount among them are survival and adaptation to the environment. Moreover, internal processes and structures also reflect diverse and possibly conflicting interests and relations. As a result, the organization in operation is quite different from its official or formal design (Perrow, 1986). As articulated by Wamsley and Zald (1976), the capacity of the organization to survive *and* to provide services depends on its ability to mobilize power, legitimacy, and economic resources (e.g., money, personnel, clients). To obtain these resources, the organization must interact with elements in its task environment that control them. The ensuing processes of negotiations and their outcomes will reflect the degree of organizational dependency on the resources controlled by each element (Pfeffer & Salancik, 1978). The greater the resource dependency of the organization on an element in the environment (e.g., governmental funding agency, regulatory organization, professional association, providers of clients), the greater the ability of the element to influence organizational policies and practices. Therefore, many organizational practices, such as the service delivery system, will reflect the constraints and contingencies imposed by those who control needed resources (Cress & Snow, 1996).

The internal dynamics of the organization will also reflect the power relations of different interest groups and individuals within the organization. Some of these groups (e.g., professional staff, executive cadre) derive their power from relations with important external organizations, others because they possess personal attributes, control internal resources (e.g., information and expertise), or carry out important functions (e.g., manage the budget) that are not easily substituted (Lachman, 1989). The emerging power relations shape the internal structure and the resource allocation rules. These, in turn, reinforce the power relations (e.g., Astley & Sachdeva, 1984; Pfeffer, 1992).

Disturbances in the external and internal political economies will result in changes within the organization. The power of external groups may rise or fall as the environment changes, altering the power relations between the organization and its task environment. These, in turn, will affect the operative goals and the service delivery system. Similarly, the need for different internal resources or functions to meet new environmental challenges or the rise of new alliances will modify internal power relations and, with them, structure and processes (Pfeffer, 1992).

The political economy perspective has served as a platform for extensive research on human service organizations, beginning with Zald's pioneering study of the YMCA (Zald & Denton, 1963). More recent research looked at innovations in community mental health centers (Sheinfeld Gorin & Weirich, 1995), the implementation of welfare-to-work programs (Handler & Hasenfeld, 2007), and the changing environment of human services nonprofit organizations (Grønbjerg, 2001). In addition, the perspective has been applied to analyze organizational issues ranging from understanding the dynamic relations between human service organizations and their task environment (e.g., Benson, 1975; Hasenfeld & Cheung, 1985) to the position of women in social welfare agencies (Arnold, 1995). One can readily see the appeal of the political economy perspective to human services administration. The relatively high dependence of human service organizations on their external environment for legitimacy and resources makes them particularly susceptible to external influences. Hence, concerns with survival and adaptation must be balanced against the goal of service effectiveness (e.g., Brodkin, 1997; Hyde, 1992; Smith & Donovan, 2003). Moreover, having to respond to multiple external and internal constituencies with conflicting interests is also a common experience for most administrators.

Internally, agency administrators typically have to balance among the interests and claims for resources of different program components, each with its own constituent staff and clients. This is particularly the case in multiprofessional organizations.

Gummer (1990) presents the most systematic application of political economy to administration in the human services. It is also a model of how the field can be enriched by a thoughtful articulation between organizational theory and administrative practices. Paying close attention to the distinct issues facing social service agencies—scarcity of resources, multiple goals, uncertain technologies—Gummer proposes that their solutions can best be addressed from a political economy perspective. Effectively handling budgetary constraints through strategic planning requires several power resources, such as centralized authority, continuity of top management, rapid and accurate feedback, budget flexibility, and incentives to conserve resources. Recognizing that program implementation is a political process, Gummer argues that effective implementation requires administrators to assume several broad roles—policy advocate, negotiator of organizational linkages, and manager of worker discretion (p. 107). To mobilize power and use it to influence organizational processes, administrators must employ various political strategies ranging from controlling agendas to building network relations and managing impressions. Because administrators rarely have sufficient power to impose their will on other actors, they must negotiate and bargain, and Gummer enunciates a number of strategies and tactics for successful negotiations (pp. 153–183). Undoubtedly, use of power to achieve administrative objectives raises many ethical issues, but as Gummer points out, it is not the use of power per se that is at stake, but rather the ends for which power is used, that is, the extent to which it benefits the clients.

Austin (2002) also uses political economy to analyze the impact of different stakeholder constituencies on administrative practices and, particularly, to offer a framework to analyze the agency's service delivery network. He provides administrators with analytic tools to map out several internal and external networks based on the exchange relations between their constituent elements. He is explicit on how power dependence relations influence the structure of such networks and the capacity of administrators to manage them.

Founding and Survival

The political economy perspective has its limitations. First, it understates the importance of values and cultural norms in the survival of the organization, an issue addressed by the new institutionalism. This is a particularly critical issue for human service organizations because they engage in moral work. Moreover, by emphasizing survival and adaptation, less attention is given to the desired outcomes the organization is expected to attain. Second, the unit of analysis remains the single organization. Yet administrative practices must pay attention to industry-wide or sectoral patterns and the dynamics that shape their organizational forms (Scott, 1985). Because organizations are embedded in industries or networks and are part of a population of similar organizations, their survival is influenced by the extent to which their organizational features are consonant with those characterizing the industry or population. For example, because community mental health agencies are constituent elements of the mental health sector, they acquire structural and operative features that are systemic to that sector (Scott & Meyer, 1983). As members of a population consisting of community mental health agencies, their survival is affected by the characteristics and dynamics affecting the entire population (Tucker, Baum, & Singh, 1992).

The ecological perspective addresses this central issue. The unit of analysis is a population of organizations, defined as a set of organizations engaged in similar activities and with similar patterns of resource utilization (Baum, 1996, p. 77). The ecological approach wants to explain the conditions that generate (or inhibit) diversity of organizations and change over time. Using the metaphor of evolutionary biology, Hannan and Freeman (1989) state that "current diversity of organizational forms reflects the cumulative effect of a long history of variation and selection, including the consequences of founding processes, mortality processes, and merger processes" (p. 20). Over time, successful variations are retained as surviving organizations come to be characterized by them. Rates of organizational founding and failure are explained by two interrelated ecological processes: *population dynamics* and *density dependence* (Baum, 1996). Population dynamics posits that prior organizational founding signals existence of opportunities in the environment, which stimulates new founding. However, as new organizations enter the field, competition increases, thus discouraging new founding. Similarly, prior failures release resources that also stimulate new founding, but further failures signal a hostile environment, discouraging founding. Density dependence (i.e., the number of organizations in the population) proposes that an initial increase in density signals institutional legitimacy (e.g., favorable governmental policies) for such organizations that enables them to secure resources. However, as density rises, competition over the resources increases, leading to higher rates of failure and discouraging further founding.

The ecological processes are not the only determinants of organizational founding and failure. Technological developments influence the importance of various resources, creating new opportunities while rendering the competencies of existing organizations obsolete (Tushman & Anderson, 1986). Institutional developments, such as changing government policies and funding, will also affect rates of founding and failure (Tucker et al., 1992). Similarly, linkages to community and public institutions provide resources and legitimacy that reduce failure rates (Baum & Oliver, 1991). Finally, demographic characteristics—age and size—also affect rates of failure. Older and larger organizations are less likely to fail.

The ecological perspective has produced a substantial body of research, including important studies on human service organizations. A key concept that is particularly relevant to human service organizations is organizational identity, defined as consisting "of social codes, or sets of rules, specifying the features that an organization is expected to possess" (Hsu & Hannan, 2005, p. 475). An example might be "community mental health center" or "child protective services." Because human service organizations depend on external audiences such as state authorities, donors, and foundations for legitimacy and resources, the expectations of these audiences about what the organization must do and in what manner greatly influence its character or form. Organizational identities become critical to the survival of the organization. A simple identity reduces the problem of mobilizing legitimacy from a specific audience. However, it restricts the opportunities available to the organization. A complex identity makes legitimacy more difficult but gives the organization greater flexibility to exploit its environment (Hsu & Hannan, 2005, p. 480). Organizational identity locates the organization in a specific niche in which it competes with other organizations for legitimacy and resources. For the human services, changes in the niche and the resulting emergence of new organizational identities typically arise from major legislative initiatives, social movements, and the discourse among the organizations themselves (Ruef, 2000).

The ecological perspective has implications for administrative practices (Schmid, 2004; also see Chapter 20). It demonstrates how environmental forces set considerable limits on the success of administrative practices. It proposes that individual managers are constrained by existing organizational forms, scarcity of resources, and forces at the population level that cannot be readily manipulated or fully understood by each manager (Hannan & Freeman, 1989, pp. 42–43). Especially for the administration of human service organizations, there is a dual message. First, while administrators can make a difference in improving the agency's chances to survive and be effective, their capacity to do so is highly constrained. At best, they can try to locate the organization in a more favorable niche or improve their position in a niche through changes in organizational identity. But, this is clearly a risky strategy. Second, macro-level strategies that affect an entire population of agencies are far more important for their overall survival and effectiveness. These strategies include influencing governmental policies, supporting social movements, coalescing and lobbying to alter funding patterns and legislative rules, and developing extensive institutional linkages that increase the legitimacy of the organizations (see Chapter 22 for further discussion of advocacy and lobbying). One can readily understand, for example, that to rescue urban child protection agencies from the almost chronic crisis they encounter depends much less on the behavior of any single administrator than on macro-changes in the social, economic, and political environment in which these agencies are embedded. With the exception of Lohmann and Lohmann (2002), limited attention has been given to this message in the current state of theorizing in human services administration. They, however, point to the imperative role of administrators as institutional leaders to be proactive in formulating policy, to establish strategies to implement it, and to manage the process of institutionalizing the policy (Lohmann & Lohmann, 2002, p. 150).

One of the chief limitations of the ecological perspective, especially concerning human service organizations, is its failure to fully acknowledge and incorporate the importance of these macro-level strategies. In particular, the theory understates the role organizations play, individually and collectively, in constructing the environment in which they operate. While at any given point in time the environment is taken as given, from a historical perspective one can see how organizations, acting as industries, influence the policies, flows of resources, and the very processes of selection and retention of certain organizational forms. This can be gleaned, for example, from the history of the evolution of the medical or mental

health "industry" (e.g., Grob, 1991; Starr, 1982). Related, the theory fails to address the processes by which organizations mobilize legitimacy that is so vital to their survival (Zucker, 1989). The new institutional perspective addresses some of these issues (Scott, 1995).

Institutionalization

The underlying premise of the new institutional perspective is that the survival of organizations depends on the degree to which their structures reflect and reinforce institutional rules. Institutional rules include (a) regulative rules and laws, (b) normative rules (i.e., values and expectations), and (c) cognitive rules (i.e., categories and typifications) shared by the community of organizations (Scott, 1995). In contrast to political economy, with its emphasis on resources, the new institutionalism places primary emphasis on legitimacy and the dominant role of cultural institutions (regulative, normative, and cognitive) in the survival of organizations. It proposes that the more organizations adhere to the rules of these institutions—by embedding the rules in their structures—the greater will be their legitimacy and chances of survival (similar to the idea of organizational identity discussed above).

Meyer and Rowan (1977) also make an important distinction between technical and institutional organizations. Technical organizations have highly specified production systems designed to produce explicitly defined outputs. Institutional organizations have neither explicit output goals nor concrete technologies to attain them. Therefore, human services are institutional organizations par excellence. Their success depends less on the efficacy of their service technologies than on designing structures that conform to dominant institutional rules. Consequently, structure is only loosely coupled with the technology. Schools, for example, must employ only certified teachers, adhere to sanctioned curricula and textbooks, and establish approved graduation requirements. Yet these have little to do with the educational technology teachers are likely to use in the classroom (Meyer & Rowan, 1983). In other words, many of the activities of human service organizations involve the production of myths and ceremonies whose function is to uphold institutional rules. These will take precedence over actual service performance because they are more important to the survival of the organization. For example, in keeping with the new cultural rules of welfare reform, welfare departments ostensibly have transformed themselves into employment agencies by adopting the language of "work first" and "self-sufficiency." But mostly, it has been an exercise in myth and ceremonies without truly shedding their primary function of determining eligibility, limiting entry, and hastening exit from cash aid (Handler & Hasenfeld, 2007). A key difficulty with the new institutionalism is its failure to explain how institutional rules come about (Zucker, 1988). Tolbert and Zucker (1996) proposed that the organizations themselves are not passive in conforming to institutional rules, but are actually active in shaping the institutionalization process itself. Oliver (1991) also points out that organizations can actively respond to institutional processes by negotiating with various stakeholders, disguising their nonconformity, challenging institutional rules, and attempting to influence them.

The new institutionalism is a powerful framework for the analysis of human service organizations precisely because it focuses on the critical relations between these organizations and cultural institutions, the values and norms these organizations are expected to promote (i.e., institutional rules), and how institutional rules affect their internal structures. And yet, theorizing in social welfare administration has, by and large, failed to capitalize on the rich insights and research from this framework. An important exception is a paper by Martin (1980), who uses the new institutional perspective to outline the role of administrators in balancing the need to adhere to dominant cultural values with responding to the needs of other constituents, especially clients. Neugeboren (1991) briefly

mentions the importance of managing the institutional system and the role of boards in linking the agency to legitimizing institutions. Lohmann and Lohmann (2002), as noted above, also emphasize the administrative importance of institutionalization.

Rapp and Poertner (1992) make the moral entrepreneurship of social service agencies the centerpiece of their administrative approach, an approach that is highly compatible with new institutionalism. Yet they fail to use it to anchor and buttress their model. By advocating for a client-centered management, they articulate four guiding principles: (1) venerating the people called clients, (2) creating and maintaining the focus on clients and client outcomes, (3) developing a healthy disrespect for the impossible, and (4) continuing to learn more effective ways to help people. Nonetheless, most of the administrative practices they enunciate have little bearing on these principles, especially in laying out strategies to implement them. Had they based their model on new institutionalism, they could have formulated administrative practices, supported by theory and research, on how to institutionalize these laudatory principles.

Integration and Social Cohesion

The new institutionalism points to the importance of organizational culture and sensemaking as major forces in shaping organizational structure and processes. Organizational leaders, motivated to increase the legitimacy and the resources of the organization, seek to shape the culture of the organization to conform with dominant institutional rules. In addition, organizational culture also provides an internal integrative mechanism by having a common interpretative schema. It enables members of the organization to make sense of their work and to construct a common understanding of their internal and external environment (Weick, 1995). Trice and Beyer (1993) distinguish between substance of culture—shared emotionally charged belief systems (i.e., ideologies)—and cultural forms—observable entities, including actions, through which members of a culture express, affirm, and communicate the substance of the culture to one another. Similarly, Weick's (1995) concept of sensemaking provides members of the organization with a frame that consists of (a) ideologies that combine beliefs about cause-effect relations, preferences for certain outcomes, and expectations of appropriate behavior; (b) vocabulary that provides premise control, especially when the technology is nonroutine; (c) paradigms such as standard operating procedures, shared definitions of the environment, and agreed-upon systems of power and authority; (d) vocabularies of coping, which are theories of action to guide behavior; (e) tradition; and (f) stories that describe how difficult situations were handled, providing sequencing and facilitating diagnosis.

> Sensemaking is an effort to tie beliefs and actions more closely together as when arguments lead to consensus on action, clarified expectations pave the way for confirming actions, committed actions uncover acceptable justifications for their occurrence, or bold actions simplify the world and make it clearer what is going on and what it means. (Weick, 1995, p. 135)

Therefore, sensemaking is retrospective. Organizations also have subcultures. Trice and Beyer (1993) suggest that organizational subcultures consist of distinctive clusters of ideologies, cultural forms, and practices exhibited by identifiable groups. Occupational subcultures are most common, and they have powerful socialization functions.

For human service organizations, the concept of culture extends beyond shared assumptions and beliefs. It also incorporates moral assumptions about the clients as well as practice ideologies of how to work with them that are embedded in the service technology. Both have important consequences on how service delivery systems will be organized (Hasenfeld, 2000). Moreover, the notion of occupational subcultures, each with its own distinct moral conceptions and practice ideologies, is important in understanding how services are organized to accommodate them (Strauss, Fargerhaugh, Suczek, & Wiener, 1985). Hence, viewing the agency as a multicultural system is particularly apt in understanding many of its structural and operational features.

Organizational culture has become a rhetoric and an all-embracing concept in management theory preoccupied with social controls and performance (Czarniawska-Joerges, 1992, pp. 168–170). There is a burgeoning field of management literature on the competitive advantages of fostering a "strong" organizational culture (e.g., Cameron & Quinn, 1996; Peters & Waterman, 1982). Such a culture is said to inculcate a sense of vision and mission that is deeply felt by all members, a commitment to organizational values that guides personal behavior, and self-fulfillment derived from identification and participation in the organization. Management experts have also argued that a strong culture is correlated with high performance (e.g., Wilderom, Glunk, & Maslowski, 2000), although the empirical evidence is inconclusive (Pfeffer, 1997, p. 122). Advocates of "strong" culture postulate that it is a critical tool in the hands of managers to foster organizational integration. Yet the assumption that organizational culture can be a unifying and integrating force has been challenged by numerous ethnographic studies (for a review, see Martin & Frost, 1996). The theme of these studies is cultural inconsistencies—organizations are beset by value conflicts, disjunctures between norms and actual behavior, and frail consensus. This theme is taken up again when I discuss postmodernist approaches to organizations. The idea of cultural ambiguity should not come as a surprise to social work and other helping professions. Meyerson (1992) showed that one cannot appreciate the professional culture of social work without paying close attention to the many value ambiguities, multiple goals, indeterminate technology, and uncertainty of results that characterize the field.

In this context, it is not clear how much organizational culture can be "managed."

In the human services, Glisson and colleagues have done pioneering research on the relationship between organizational culture and climate on service effectiveness (see Hemmelgarn, Glisson, & James, 2006). Culture, according to Glisson (2000),

> comprises the norms and values of that social system that drive the ways things are done in the organizations. These norms include how employees interact, how they approach their work, and what work behaviors are emphasized in the organization through rewards and sanctions. (p. 198)

Glisson and Green (2006) show that a constructive culture (i.e., workers are mutually supportive, develop their individual abilities, maintain positive interpersonal relations, and are motivated to succeed) leads to better service outcomes. Moreover, Glisson and colleagues (Glisson, Dukes, & Green, 2006) also show that an organizational intervention strategy (availability, responsiveness, and continuity) can improve organizational climate (defined as workers' perceptions of their work environment) and reduce staff turnover. Still, it remains to be determined what organizational factors generate a constructive vs. a defensive culture. Although organizational leaders do influence the culture of the organization, it cannot be simply enforced from top down. Rather, it is more likely to be a manifestation of the institutional context and the external and internal political economy of the organization (Glisson, 2002).

Much of the research cited above is yet to be incorporated into human services administration. (For further discussion of organizational culture and leadership, see Chapters 6 and 7.) When culture is addressed, the integrative perspective on organizational culture prevails. (Later, we will see that the feminist perspective also addresses culture, but from a very different angle.) Rapp and Poertner (1992) argue that in a client-centered approach, the organizational culture should promote organizational learning, especially through the use of information on client services and outcomes. They are mindful that staff encounter many contingencies and constraints that must be taken into account in how an information system is designed, what data are collected, and how they are used and interpreted. Brody (2004) recognizes that a strong culture may not always be associated with effectiveness, unless it is harnessed to promote a climate of job ownership among the workers, a sense of higher purpose, emotional bonding, trust, and pride in one's work (not dissimilar to Follett's argument). Few would object to these values and the lofty strategies to attain them, and that is precisely the difficulty with the approach. There is exceedingly limited verifiable knowledge on how to change organizational culture; however, it is acknowledged that the process is complex, difficult, and multifaceted (Trice & Beyer, 1993). Because culture emerges out of dialectic processes in which members attempt to make sense of their external and internal environments, changing it requires addressing these institutional, political, and economic environments (see, e.g., Snyder, 1995).

Knowledge, Power, and Control

The notion that culture is a major source of social control in the organization; that it objectifies the values, norms, and knowledge of those in power; and that it perpetuates patterns of dominance is a central theme in the postmodern conception of organizations. Postmodernism argues that what is assumed to be "rational" is a cultural construction that gives preference to certain culturally defined discourses over others (e.g., masculine or Anglocentric over feminist or Afrocentric). It also contends that what is passed off as empirical knowledge is, in fact, socially constructed because language itself is value-laden, and "meaning is not universal and fixed, but precarious, fragmented, and local" (Alvesson & Deetz, 1996, p. 208). Finally, language acquires meaning through its use in action. "To 'tell the truth,' on this account, is not to furnish an accurate picture of 'what actually happened' but to participate in a set of social conventions"(Gergen & Thatchenkery, 1996, p. 361). Consequently, power is embedded in how knowledge is produced. "Power resides in the discursive formation itself—the combination of a set of linguistic distinctions, ways of reasoning, and material practices that together organize social institutions and produce particular forms of subjects" (Alvesson & Deetz, 1996, p. 209).

Postmodernism has important implications for organizational theory and research. It makes problematic the very concept of organization and its constituent elements such as structure, technology, division of labor, staff, and clients. A postmodernist approach is to examine how such concepts come into being and how they acquire their self-reifying qualities (Chia, 1995). The emphasis is on microprocesses of actions, interactions, and emergence of local patterns of relations. Studying the processes of organizing, the researcher is concerned with how certain interaction patterns become stabilized, dominant, and self-reproduced. The focus is on the heterogeneous material, the multiple identities, and the ongoing struggles and resistance that are inherent in organizing processes. Put differently, what we take for granted as "organization," "staff," and "client" are actually reflective of these dynamic and ever-changing microprocesses. When we objectify the organization, we not only ignore these processes, but we fail to recognize the struggles, meanings, and identities that have been silenced. Moreover, the language we use to describe organizational properties and processes is actually a form of social control because of its self-reifying qualities. Thus, for example, a feminist analysis critiques the concept of gender as political, organizational hierarchy as oppressive, and "bounded rationality" as devaluing emotional experiences (Mumby & Putnam, 1992). Some have argued that even theories and research

about organizations, once deconstructed, can be shown to objectify bureaucratic organizations and justify their power (Cooper, 1989).

The postmodernist perspective can offer important insights on human service organizations. The moral work and the maintenance of cultural symbols—the essence of these organizations—typically become objectified and acquire a taken-for-granted quality in the service technologies and staff-client relations. Only when deconstructed can we study the dynamics of how they have become dominant, how they exclude alternative conceptions, and how they control the very language used by the professionals. Indeed, professional knowledge and language can be seen as powerful tools of social control, or what Foucault sees as a disciplinary mode of domination (Foucault, 1977). Schram (1995), for example, showed how food shelters, unable to meet the flood of people asking for food, embraced prevailing definitions of dependency. As he put it,

> Food shelf personnel must invoke discursive practices that enable them to shift responsibility for hunger back onto the poor themselves. Imputing deficiencies to the poor allows food shelf staff the room to justify the regulations of clients' behavior and the rationing of food and to maintain a sense of control over their own operation. (p. 64)

The result is that the food shelters adopt the dominant moral assumptions of "blaming the victim."

Therefore, the language that is used in the organization becomes a powerful tool of managerial control, both over staff and clients. Following Bourdieu and Wacquant (1992), the organization can be viewed as a contested relational and stratified field in which different actors compete and struggle for access to valued resources by using their economic, social, and cultural capital. Those in the organization that gain greater power also accumulate symbolic capital, which provides legitimacy to their world view and their hierarchical status in the organization (Everett, 2002).

Symbolic power is expressed in the language, cultural codes, and the classification and categorization schemas used in the organization (e.g., how service goals and objectives are expressed, how clients are defined, and how workers rationalize their work). Therefore, powerful actors in the organization acquire a common "habitus," which is a set of internalized mental schemata and structured dispositions, that gives stratification and the practices it reinforces a taken-for-granted character. Subordinates, accepting the legitimacy of symbolic power, misrecognize the arbitrariness of these cultural codes and incorporate them in their own habitus. According to Bourdieu, subordinates experience "symbolic violence" because against their own interests they accept the logic of practice and thus conspire and give tacit acceptance to the unequal distribution of resources and patterns of dominance in the organization (Everett, 2002, pp. 66–67).

The postmodern approach asks us to deconstruct the prevailing models of human services administration and their underlying assumptions. For example, in the name of consumer empowerment and service effectiveness and efficiency, the "New Public Management" (NPM) approach to human services embraces several themes (Hood, 1995): reorganizing public organizations into product and cost centers; shifting toward competition within and between public organizations and the private sector; adopting corporate management strategies; seeking alternative and less costly modes of service delivery; adopting "hands-on management"; using explicit and measurable standards of performance; and using explicit output measures. Its adoption has resulted in the devolution and privatization of social care. Yet Vigoda (2002) argues that the emphasis of NPM on a quasi-market relationship between citizens and public bureaucracies actually reduces the participation of citizens as partners. Citizens are viewed as individual consumers who pursue self-interest in seeking the optimal services for themselves. Service providers, whether public or private, in turn, become entrepreneurs who rely on market strategies to gain desirable

consumers and enhance their competitive position. As a result, other values such as fairness, social justice, participation, collective responsibility, and community are crowded out.

Similarly, the adoption of evidence-based practice assumes that agencies have the obligation and clients have the right to receive services that have been shown, through careful empirical research, to produce the desired outcomes. Yet, left unchallenged are the very criteria of "desired outcomes" and who defines them (Webb, 2001). From a postmodern perspective, the criteria typically reflect, on the one hand, the invisible power of the profession, as manifest in the language and categories it employs and, on the other hand, the powerlessness of the clients who accept them as normal practices. At the same time, postmodernism recognizes that both workers and clients can resist dominant discourse by exercising their agency capacities and, by doing so, modify practices (Ungar, 2004).

The idea that there is a reciprocal relationship between human agency and social structure is developed by Giddens' (1984) structuration theory. It is based on the notion of "the *duality of structure*, which relates to the *fundamentally recursive character of social life, and expresses the mutual dependence of structure and agency*" (Cassell, 1993, p. 122). In other words, social structure both enables and constrains human agents whose actions produce and reproduce the structure. Human agents are viewed as capable of reflexive action, of being knowledgeable about the conditions and consequences of what they do in their daily lives (Giddens, 1984, p. 281). In particular, agents are not only able to observe and understand what they are doing, but they can also adjust their observation rules. For example, workers, knowing that their decisions about their clients are affected by their own moral beliefs, can modify such decisions. When agents do so, they can effect change in the social structure. Structure is conceptualized as recursively organized rules and resources that agents draw on and reconstitute in their daily activities. Therefore, "structure has no existence independent of the knowledge that agents have about what they do in their day-to-day activity" (Giddens, 1984, p. 26). As a result, "the structural properties of social systems are both the medium and outcome of the practices they recursively organize" (Giddens, 1984, p. 25). This implies that structure is not something external of human agents but is both enabled by them and constrains them. An important element of the theory is the idea of modalities—interpretative schemes that include meaning, normative elements, and power—that agents draw upon in the reproduction of social interactions that also reconstitute their structural properties. Again, these schemes sanction certain modes of social practices, but they also enable the change of such practices. Structuration theory has been incorporated into organizational analysis in numerous ways. Orlikowski (1992) showed how technology can be conceptualized both as being socially constructed by members of the organization and, once constructed, as a reified and objectified structure that constrains their behavior. Sarason (1995) showed how it could be used to understand organizational change. More recently, Sandfort (2003) used the theory to explain how welfare workers, constrained by the administrative policies they find difficult to accept, develop their own interpretive schemes, which enable them to continue to work in a difficult environment. These schemes, in turn, affect and alter the structure of their work, in ways that may not have been intended by the policies. As she puts it,

> In organizations charged with developing their own interventions, staff themselves must craft what they perceive to be legitimate means for achieving the organizations' goals. In turn, this technology comes to have structuring properties; it helps direct staff action, minimizes their distractions, and provides them a standard to rely on to interpret daily events and experiences. In this way, the structuration process actually allows street-level workers to carry out their day-to-day tasks in spite of the technological

> uncertainty of how to move welfare recipients into the workforce. (pp. 617–618)

Structuration theory can provide an important analytic approach to understand human services organizations. It draws attention to how workers in their daily activities reproduce and reify organizational assumptions and conceptions about the clients, but also how they change them. It pays close attention to the interpretative schemes that workers use because these determine how clients are morally constructed, how actions are justified, and how they become reproduced in the structural properties of the agency. At the same time, the theory also provides important insights into the processes of organizational change, especially in the capacity of the workers to be knowledgeable and reflexive about the rules they use, and how reflexive action can bring about change in organizational structure. Therefore, it has the potential to both understand and inform management practices in the human services.

Social Change

Critical theorists echo the postmodernist critique of organizations as repressive systems. Accordingly, modernism, embracing science and technical rationality, only produces new forms of domination, inauthentic social relations, and technocratic consciousness. As a result, according to Habermas (1971), moral and reflexive social interactions have been displaced. The domination of technical and instrumental reasoning is reproduced because those subjugated by it actively accept its hegemony (Alvesson & Deetz, 1996). According to Alvesson and Deetz,

> The central goal of critical theory in organizational studies has been to create societies and workplaces which are free from domination, where all members have equal opportunity to contribute to the production of systems which meet human needs and lead to the progressive development of all. (p. 198)

Thus, unlike other theoretical approaches, critical theorists are quite explicit about the purpose of their research: to achieve social change by turning the organizations from instruments of domination to authentic, dialogic communities (Handler, 1990). Such communities are characterized by communicative rationality; that is, viewpoints are freely exchanged and accepted on the basis of the strength of the argument rather than on the basis of power, status, and ideology.

The main strategy of critical theory, not unlike postmodernism, is to critique the underlying ideologies that legitimate our social institutions, showing how they maintain and reinforce patterns of domination, including those based on gender and ethnicity, and foster distorted and inauthentic communication patterns that repress emancipation and justice. Looking at the organization, Alvesson and Deetz (1996, p. 198) suggest that critical analysis focuses on four major themes, showing that (a) organizational forms need not be accepted as the natural order of things, (b) management interests are not universal, (c) the emphasis on technical rationality represses understanding and mutual determination of the desired ends, and (d) the organizational culture fosters the hegemony of dominant groups. In studies of management practices, Alvesson and Willmott (1996) tried to show how strategic management, for example, is actually a form of domination because strategic discourse and the decision-making process are controlled by the managerial elite, thus legitimizing its hegemony. Similarly, a critical analysis of information systems is likely to show how it controls patterns of communication and stifles reflexive thinking.

The usefulness of critical analysis of human services and administrative practices lies in its ideology critique. Ideologies play a dominant role in the moral construction of the clients, in defining the desired ends, in shaping the service technologies, and in the socialization and control of the staff. Administrative practices inherently reinforce these ideologies. As Handler (1990) demonstrated, a legal-bureaucratic ideology fosters hierarchy, domination, and distrust between staff and clients. In contrast, an ideology of dialogism based on autonomy, shared decision making, and equality promotes trust and staff-client relations that empower both. While such ideology is an exception in the organization of human services, it does occur, and it is predicated on three conditions: (a) professional norms that embrace dialogism, (b) a service technology in which success requires shared decision making with clients, and (c) reciprocal financial incentives for both staff and clients to cooperate.

If the aim of human services administration is to improve and protect the well-being of clients, it must critically examine its own ideologies. With the exception of the feminist critique, discussed below, administrative practices have not been subject to such analysis. A critique in the human services might show that the preoccupation of management with technical rationality, such as Total Quality Management, strategic planning, and evidence-based practice, reinforces the domination of powerful interest groups that control the agency's resources. It will show that such practices prevent an open, authentic, and reflexive discourse about the goals of the agency by all its constituents, including workers and clients. Such a critique can also point to administrative practices that can foster a more dialogic and, therefore, client-oriented organization.

The feminist critique, rooted in critical theory, is well-suited to undertake such a discourse, particularly because much of the work in the human services is gendered. Women constitute the majority of human services workers, and yet men are more likely to assume the key administrative positions. There are, of course, several feminist approaches to explain and remedy gender inequality in organizations, and each offers a different perspective on the organization itself (for a review, see Calas & Smircich, 2006). Liberal feminism, for example, with its theme of women in management, does not challenge mainstream conceptions of organizations, but acknowledges that inequality is a result of stereotypes and discriminatory practices that block job and advancement opportunities. The remedies are legal-rational, such as antidiscrimination and sexual harassment policies, equal worth pay, gender-free performance appraisals, and unbiased promotion criteria (e.g., Kanter, 1977; Powell, 1992; Reskin & Hartmann, 1986). As noted by Calas and Smircich (2006), such a perspective "documents the persistence of sex segregation in organizations, looking for explanations as to why it continues within what is assumed to be fundamentally a just system" (p. 291).

In contrast, radical feminism, building on the notion of gender domination and repression, has a distinctive conception of the organization and offers an alternative organizational form. As a result, it has attracted particular attention in social welfare administration. Acker (1990) proposed that organizations are inherently gendered. They reproduce male domination through (a) divisions along gender lines, (b) construction of symbols and images that explain and reinforce these divisions, (c) interaction between men and women including patterns of dominance, (d) production of gendered components of personal identity, and (e) expression in ongoing social structure. In other words, gendered organizations subordinate women via structural arrangements and power relations that give primacy to male dominance while suppressing feminist values. These values are "egalitarianism rather than hierarchy, cooperation rather than competition, nurturance rather than rugged individualism, peace rather than conflict" (Taylor, 1983, p. 445).

Radical feminism is committed to the development of alternative organizations imbued with feminist values that "focus on the primacy of interpersonal relations; empowerment and personal development of members; building of self-esteem; the promotion of enhanced knowledge, skills, and political awareness; personal autonomy; and the politics of gender" (Martin, 1990, p. 192). The most important characteristics of these alternative organizations are (a) participatory decision making, (b) a system of rotating leadership, (c) flexible and interactive job designs, (d) equitable distribution of income, and (e) interpersonal and political accountability

(Koen, 1984, cited in Calas & Smircich, 1996). A number of such alternative organizations have emerged in the human services, ranging from feminist health centers (Hyde, 1992; Schwartz, Gottesman, & Perlmutter, 1988) to rape crisis centers (Martin, DiNitto, Byington, & Maxwell, 1992) and schools (Rothschild & Whitt, 1986). They have demonstrated that human service organizations can be designed to be nonhierarchical and egalitarian, where social controls are noncoercive and rewards are intrinsic, and where relations among workers and between workers and clients are nurturing, caring, and based on mutual responsibility and accountability (Iannello, 1992; Rothschild & Whitt, 1986).

Nonetheless, such organizations remain the exception in the human services because of serious external and internal obstacles (Hyde, 1992). Indeed, there are numerous studies that point to the inherent conflict between feminist ideals of empowerment and the need of the organization to survive, grow, provide services efficiently, and remain competitive (Aschraft, 2001; Bordt, 1998; Zilber, 2002). As a result, such organizations gravitate toward a hybrid form, which is "the merger of hierarchical and egalitarian modes of power"(Aschraft, 2001, p. 1303), but they face a dialectic tension between inequality/equality and centralization/decentralization (Aschraft, 2001, p. 1305). In her case study of a feminist organization to assist survivors of domestic violence, Aschraft (2001) points out that despite an ideology of "ethical communication" that encouraged equal and open communication, members experienced reluctance to challenge the authority and expertise of the supervisors.

The challenges to articulate an empowerment perspective for human services administration, based on a feminist theory of organization, is evident in the empowerment approach to management advocated by Hardina and colleagues (2006). Several underlying premises guide their project, such as creating a structure that ensures participation of clients in organizational decision making; making all program beneficiaries (clients, staff, board members) equal partners;

reducing cultural, ethnic, and gender barriers; ensuring that managers are committed to an empowerment ideology; promoting the use of teams; involving all constituencies in program evaluation and renewal; and mobilizing power to increase the political influence of all beneficiaries (Hardina et al., 2006, pp. 9–16).

Steeped in social work values, Hardina and colleagues (2006) articulate detailed and specific management strategies from an empowerment perspective. They stress the importance of embedding social work values and ethics in management ideologies; suggest ways to create an internal structure that fosters decision-making partnerships with clients, line staff, and boards; offer guidelines to program design that incorporate the clients' perspectives and concerns; point to ways to promote a culturally competent organization; advocate for internal structures that empower the workers; detail an evaluation model that is participatory; and suggest ways the organization can mobilize power through advocacy, collaboration, and community organization. The authors are quite cognizant and explicit about the hurdles that managers committed to an empowering approach may face. They are also aware of the limited research currently available to inform such a project.

Undoubtedly, an empowering approach to management attempts to define a unique vision for human services and give it a distinct voice apart from the general management literature. Still, it is a highly idealized model that has very limited empirical references. While there are, indeed, some examples of human service organizations that practice an empowering management, even they, as noted above, face serious challenges in maintaining it. What is particularly problematic with an empowerment approach to management is that it is not solidly anchored in organizational theories that treat power as a key variable in defining organizational structure, processes, and services. While Hardina and colleagues (2006) give some attention to political economy and power dependence relations, they do not systematically apply them as does

Gummer (1990). Yet what is needed is to secure such a model of management in a theory of power in organizations (see Clegg, Hardy, Lawrence, & Nord, 2006) that defines the many sources and shapes of power, addresses the dynamics of how power is mobilized and exercised in the organization, and identifies the forces and the struggles that enable different constituent elements to acquire and use power. Unless empowering management is informed by such a theory and related research, the underlying assumption that it can distribute power equally in the organization remains unsustainable.

It is quite remarkable that nearly a century after Follett (1940) enunciated her theory of management, many of her ideas are indirectly echoed in the empowering approach espoused by Hardina and colleagues (2006). Yet there is no mention of Follett and her theory of power in organizations and its critical role in management. In particular, no attention is given to her pioneering vision that effective management requires that power not be used "over" but "with," to the managerial responsibilities and strategies to transform power from being coercive to being coactive, and, most important, to her emphasis on integrative unity and the "law of the situation."

Conclusion

While human services administration is maturing as a field of practice, its intellectual foundations still remain poorly defined. On the one hand, models of practice are often rationalized on the basis of organizational theories that have questionable validity, especially when applied to human service organizations. On the other hand, important theoretical developments and empirical research that could inform management in this field remain neglected. With a few important exceptions, when models of practice refer to organizational theories, the use of such theories to inform practice principles is superficial and uncritical. Equally serious is the tendency to emulate popular management models that lack empirical validity or sensitivity to the attributes of human service organizations. For the field to flourish, it must be grounded in theory and research. It need not embrace any particular theoretical orientation. To paraphrase Weick (1995), over time, administrators will act as if they are feminist, rationalist, political economists, or radicalist. Therefore, human services administration should embrace and adapt organizational theories that most effectively address its particular administrative issues within the social welfare context. In doing so, however, it needs to study and assess the implementation and consequences of such practices. Moreover, it needs to find its own voice by staying very close to the actual administrative practices in the field, as Mary Parker Follett did, and to derive its models, such as empowerment management, from a continuing dialogue with the field. That is, it needs a heavy dose of reality testing. With such accumulated knowledge, human services administration will enrich and be enriched by organizational theories and research while finding and maintaining its own distinct voice.

References

Acker, J. (1990). Hierarchies, jobs, bodies: A theory of gendered organizations. *Gender & Society, 4,* 139–158.

Alvesson, M., & Deetz, S. (1996). Critical theory and postmodernism approaches to organizational studies. In S. Clegg, C. Hardy, & W. Nord (Eds.), *Handbook of organization studies* (pp. 191–217). London: Sage.

Alvesson, M., & Willmott, H. (1996). *Making sense of management.* London: Sage.

Ansell, C. (2007). *Mary Parker Follett, pragmatist.* Paper presented at The Sociology Classics and the Future of Organization Studies, Philadelphia.

Argyris, C. (1964). *Integrating the individual and the organization.* New York: Wiley.

Arnold, G. (1995). Dilemmas of feminist coalitions: Collective identity and strategic effectiveness in the battered women's movement. In M. Feree & P. Y. Martin (Eds.), *Feminist organizations.* Philadelphia, PA: Temple University Press.

Aschraft, K. L. (2001). Organized dissonance: Feminist bureaucracy as hybrid form. *Academy of Management Journal, 44,* 1301–1322.

Astley, W. G., & Sachdeva, P. S. (1984). Structural sources of intraorganizational power: A theoretical synthesis. *Academy of Management Review, 9*(1), 104–113.

Au, C. (1994). The status of theory and knowledge development in social welfare administration. *Administration in Social Work, 18,* 27–58.

Austin, D. M. (2002). *Human services management: Organizational leadership in social work practice.* New York: Columbia University Press.

Austin, M. J., & Kruzich, J. M. (2004). Assessing recent textbooks and casebooks in human service administration: Implications and future directions. *Administration in Social Work, 28,* 115–129.

Barclay, L. J. (2005). Following in the footsteps of Mary Parker Follett. *Journal of Management History, 43,* 740–760.

Barley, S. R., & Kunda, G. (1992). Design and devotion: Surges of rational and normative ideologies of control in managerial discourse. *Administrative Science Quarterly, 37,* 363–399.

Baum, J. A. C. (1996). Organizational ecology. In S. R. Clegg, C. Hardy, & W. R. Nord (Eds.), *Handbook of organizational studies* (pp. 77–114). London: Sage.

Baum, J. A., & Oliver, C. (1991). Institutional linkages and organizational mortality. *Administrative Science Quarterly, 36,* 187–218.

Benson, J. K. (1975). The interorganizational network as a political economy. *Administrative Science Quarterly, 20*(2) 229–249.

Bordt, R. L. (1998). *The structure of women's nonprofit organizations.* Bloomington: Indiana University Press.

Bourdieu, P., & Wacquant, L. J. D. (1992). *An invitation to reflexive sociology.* Chicago: University of Chicago Press.

Brodkin, E. Z. (1997). Inside the welfare contract: Discretion and accountability in state welfare administration. *Social Service Review, 71*(1), 33.

Brody, R. (2004). *Effectively managing human service organizations.* Thousand Oaks, CA: Sage.

Calas, M. B., & Smircich, L. (1996). From "the woman's" point of view: Feminist approaches to organizational studies. In S. R. Clegg, C. Hardy, & W. R. Nord (Eds.), *Handbook of organizational studies* (pp. 218–257). London: Sage.

Calas, M. B., & Smircich, L. (2006). From "woman's point of view" ten years later: Toward a feminist organization studies. In S. R. Clegg, C. Hardy, T. B. Lawrence, & W. R. Nord (Eds.), *The Sage handbook of organization studies* (pp. 284–346). Thousand Oaks, CA: Sage.

Cameron, K. S., & Quinn, R. E. (1996). *Diagnosing and changing organizational culture.* San Francisco: Jossey-Bass.

Cassell, P. (Ed.). (1993). *The Giddens reader.* Stanford, CA: Stanford University Press.

Chatman, J. A. (1989). Managing people and organizations: Selection and socialization in public accounting firms. *Administrative Science Quarterly, 36,* 459–484.

Chia, R. (1995). From modern to postmodern organizational analysis. *Organization Studies, 16,* 580–604.

Clegg, S. R., Hardy, C., Lawrence, T. B., & Nord, W. R. (Eds.). (2006). *The Sage handbook of organization studies.* Thousand Oaks, CA: Sage.

Cooper, R. (1989). Modernism, post modernism and organizational analysis 3: The contribution of Jacques Derrida. *Organization Studies, 10,* 479–502.

Creed, W. E., & Miles, R. E. (1996). Trust in organizations. In R. M. Kramer & T. R. Tyler (Eds.), *Trust in organizations* (pp. 16–38). Thousand Oaks, CA: Sage.

Cress, D., & Snow, D. A. (1996). Mobilizing at the margins: Resources, benefactors, and the viability of homeless social movement organizations. *American Sociological Review, 61,* 1089–1109.

Czarniawska-Joerges, B. (1992). *Exploring complex organizations: A cultural perspective.* Newbury Park, CA: Sage.

D'Aunno, T., Sutton, R. I., & Price, R. H. (1991). Isomorphism and external support in conflicting institutional environments: A study of drug abuse treatment units. *Academy of Management Journal, 34,* 636–661.

Donaldson, L. (1987). Strategy and structure adjustment to regain fit and performance: In defence of contingency theory. *Journal of Management Studies, 21,* 1–24.

Donaldson, L. (1996). *For positivist organization theory: Proving the hard core.* London: Sage.

Drucker, P. (1990). *Managing the non-profit organization.* New York: HarperCollins.

Everett, J. (2002). Organizational research and the praxeology of Pierre Bourdieu. *Organizational Research Methods, 5,* 56–80.

Follett, M. P. (1940). *Dynamic administration: The collected papers of Mary Parker Follett* (H. C. Metcalf & L. Urwick, Eds.). New York: Harper.

Foster-Fishman, P. G., Salem, D. A., Allen, N. A., & Fahrbach, K. (2001). Facilitating interorganizational collaboration: The contribution of interorganizational alliances. *American Journal of Community Psychology, 29,* 875–905.

Foucault, M. (1977). *Discipline and punish: The birth of the prison.* New York: Pantheon Books.

Fox, E. M. (1968). Mary Parker Follett: The enduring contribution. *Public Administration Review, 28,* 520–529.

Frumkin, P., & Andre-Clark, A. (2000). When missions, markets, and politics collide: Values and strategy in the nonprofit human services. *Nonprofit and Voluntary Sector Quarterly, 29,* 141–163.

Galbraith, J. R., & Kazanjian, R. K. (1986). *Strategy implementation.* St. Paul, MN: West.

Gergen, K. J., & Thatchenkery, T. J. (1996). Organization science as social construction: Postmodern potentials. *Journal of Applied Behavioral Science, 32,* 356–377.

Giddens, A. (1984). *The constitution of society: Outline of the theory of structuration.* Berkeley: University of California Press.

Glisson, C. A. (1978). Dependence of technological routinization on structural variables in human service organizations. *Administrative Science Quarterly, 23,* 383–395.

Glisson, C. A., & Martin, P. Y. (1980). Productivity and efficiency in human service organizations as related to structure, size and age. *Academy of Management Journal, 23,* 21–37.

Glisson, C. (1989). The effect of leadership on workers in human service organizations. *Administration in Social Work, 13,* 99–116.

Glisson, C. (1992). Structure and technology in human service organizations. In Y. Hasenfeld (Ed.), *Human services as complex organizations* (pp. 184–204). Newbury Park, CA: Sage.

Glisson, C. (2000). Organizational climate and culture. In R. J. Patti (Ed.), *Handbook of social welfare management* (pp. 195–218). Thousand Oaks, CA: Sage.

Glisson, C. (2002). The organizational context of children's mental health services. *Clinical Child and Family Psychology Review, 5,* 233–253.

Glisson, C., Dukes, D., & Green, P. (2006). The effects of the ARC organizational intervention on caseworker turnover, climate, and culture in children's service systems. *Child Abuse & Neglect, 30,* 855–880.

Glisson, C., & Green, P. (2006). The effects of organizational culture and climate on the access to mental health care in child welfare and juvenile justice systems. *Administration and Policy in Mental Health and Mental Health Services Research, 33,* 433–448.

Glisson, C., & Hemmelgarn, A. (1998). The effects of organizational climate and interorganizational coordination on the quality and outcomes of children's service systems. *Child Abuse & Neglect, 22,* 401–421.

Goes, J. B., & Park, S. H. (1997). Interorganizational links and innovation: The case of hospital services. *Academy of Management Journal, 40,* 673–696.

Grob, G. N. (1991). *From asylum to community: Mental health policy in modern America.* Princeton, NJ: Princeton University Press.

Grønbjerg, K. A. (2001). The U.S. nonprofit human service sector: A creeping revolution. *Nonprofit and Voluntary Sector Quarterly, 30,* 276–297.

Gummer, B. (1990). *The politics of social administration: Managing politics in social agencies.* Englewood Cliffs, NJ: Prentice Hall.

Guterman, N. B., & Bargal, D. (1996). Social workers' perceptions of their power and service outcomes. *Administration in Social Work, 20,* 1–20.

Habermas, J. (1971). *Toward a rational society: Student protest, science and politics.* London: Heinemann.

Handler, J. F. (1990). *Law and the search for community.* Philadelphia: University of Pennsylvania Press.

Handler, J. F., & Hasenfeld, Y. (2007). *Blame welfare, ignore poverty and inequality.* New York: Cambridge University Press.

Hannan, M. T., & Freeman, J. (1989). *Organizational ecology.* Cambridge, MA: Harvard University Press.

Hardina, D., Middleton, J., Montana, S., & Simpson, R. A. (2006). *An empowering approach to managing social service organizations.* New York: Springer.

Hart, S. L., & Quinn, R. E. (1993). Roles executives play: CEOs, behavioral complexity, and firm performance. *Human Relations, 46,* 543–574.

Hasenfeld, Y. (1992). The nature of human service organizations. In Y. Hasenfeld (Ed.), *Human services as complex organizations* (pp. 3–23). Newbury Park, CA: Sage.

Hasenfeld, Y. (2000). Organizational forms as moral practices: The case of welfare departments. *The Social Service Review, 74,* 329–351.

Hasenfeld, Y., & Cheung, P. (1985). The juvenile court as a people-processing organization: A political economy perspective. *American Journal of Sociology, 90,* 801–824.

Hasenfeld, Y., & Gidron, B. (2005). Understanding multi-purpose hybrid voluntary organizations: The contributions of theories on civil society, social movements and non-profit organizations. *Journal of Civil Society, 1,* 97–112.

Hemmelgarn, A. L., Glisson, C., & James, L. R. (2006). Organizational culture and climate: Implications for services and interventions research. *Clinical Psychology-Science and Practice, 13,* 73–89.

Henderson, C. R. (1904). *Modern methods of charity: An account of the systems of relief, public and private, in the principal countries having modern methods.* New York: Macmillan.

Ho, A. T.-K. (2002). Reinventing local governments and the e-government initiative. *Public Administration Review, 62,* 434–444.

Hochschild, A. R. (1983). *The managed heart: Commercialization of human feeling.* Berkeley: University of California Press.

Hood, C. (1995). The "new public management" in the 1980s: Variations on a theme. *Accounting, Organizations & Society, 20.*

Hsu, G., & Hannan, M. T. (2005). Identities, genres, and organizational forms. *Organization Science, 16,* 474–490.

Hyde, C. (1992). The ideational system of social movement agencies: An examination of feminist health centers. In Y. Hasenfeld (Ed.), *Human services as formal organizations* (pp. 121–144). Newbury Park, CA: Sage.

Iannello, K. P. (1992). *Decisions without hierarchy.* New York: Routledge.

Jaskyte, K., & Lee, M. (2006). Interorganizational relationships: A source of innovation in nonprofit organizations? *Administration in Social Work, 30,* 43–54.

Jayaratne, S. (1993). The antecedents, consequences, and correlates of job satisfaction. In R. T. Golembiewski (Ed.), *Handbook of organizational behavior* (pp. 111–140). New York: Marcel Dekker.

Kanter, R. M. (1977). *Men and women of the corporation.* New York: Basic Books.

Keller, T., & Dansereau, F. (1995). Leadership and empowerment: A social exchange perspective. *Human Relations, 48,* 127–146.

Kettner, P. M., Moroney, R. M., & Martin, L. (2007). *Designing and managing programs: An effectiveness-based approach* (3rd ed.). Thousand Oaks, CA: Sage.

Lachman, R. (1989). Power from what? Reexamination of its relationships with structural conditions. *Administrative Science Quarterly, 34*(2), 231–251.

Lewis, J. A., Packard, T. R., & Lewis, M. D. (2007). *Management of human service programs.* Belmont, CA: Thomson Brooks/Cole.

Lipsky, M. (1980). *Street level bureaucracy.* New York: Russell Sage Foundation.

Lohmann, R. A., & Lohmann, N. (2002). *Social administration.* New York: Columbia University Press.

Lopez, S. H. (2006). Emotional labor and organized emotional care. *Work & Occupations, 33,* 133–160.

Lubove, R. (1965). *The professional altruist: The emergence of social work as a career, 1880–1930.* Cambridge: Harvard University Press.

Martin, J., & Frost, P. (1996). The organizational culture war games: A struggle for intellectual dominance. In S. R. Clegg, C. Hardy, & W. D. Nord (Eds.), *Handbook of organizational studies* (pp. 599–621). London: Sage.

Martin, P. Y. (1980). Multiple constituencies, dominant societal values, and the human service administrator: Implications for service delivery. *Administration in Social Work, 4,* 15–27.

Martin, P. Y. (1990). Rethinking feminist organizations. *Gender & Society, 4,* 182–206.

Martin, P. Y., DiNitto, D., Byington, D., & Maxwell, S. M. (1992). Organizational and community transformation: The case of a rape crisis center. *Administration in Social Work, 16,* 123–145.

Maslach, C., & Schaufeli, W. B. (1993). Historical and conceptual development of burnout. In C. Maslach, T. Marek, & W. B. Schaufeli (Eds.), *Professional burnout: Recent developments in theory and research* (pp. 1–16). Washington, DC: Taylor & Francis.

Maynard-Moody, S., & Musheno, M. C. (2003). *Cops, teachers, counselors: Stories from the front lines of public service.* Ann Arbor: University of Michigan Press.

McGrath, R. G. (2006). Beyond contingency: From structure to structuring in the design of the contemporary organization. In S. R. Clegg, C. Hardy, T. B. Lawrence, & W. R. Nord (Eds.), *The Sage handbook of organization studies* (pp. 577–597). Thousand Oaks, CA: Sage.

Meyer, J., & Rowan, B. (1977). Institutional organizations: Formal structure as myth and ceremony. *American Journal of Sociology, 83,* 340–363.

Meyer, J. W., & Rowan, B. (1983). The structure of educational organizations. In J. W. Meyer, W. R. Scott, B. Rowan, & T. E. Deal (Eds.), *Organizational environments: Ritual and rationality* (pp. 71–98). Beverly Hills, CA: Sage.

Meyerson, D. (1992). "Normal" ambiguity? A glimpse on an occupational culture. In P. Frost, L. Moore, M. Louis, C. Lundberg, & J. Martin (Eds.), *Reframing organizational culture* (pp. 131–144). Newbury Park, CA: Sage.

Milward, H. B., & Provan, K. G. (2000). Governing the hollow state. *Journal of Policy Administration Research and Theory, 10,* 359–379.

Mintzberg, H. (1979). *The structuring of organizations.* Englewood Cliffs, NJ: Prentice Hall.

Mintzberg, H. (1996). Musings on management. *Harvard Business Review, 74,* 61–67.

Morgan, G. (1997). *Images of organization.* Beverly Hills, CA: Sage.

Mumby, D. K., & Putnam, L. L. (1992). The politics of emotion: A feminist reading of bounded rationality. *Academy of Management Review, 17,* 465–486.

Neugeboren, B. (1991). *Organization, policy, and practice in the human services.* Binghamton, NY: The Haworth Press.

Oliver, C. (1991). Strategic responses to institutional processes. *Academy of Management Review, 16,* 145–179.

Orlikowski, W. J. (1992). The duality of technology: Rethinking the concept of technology in organizations. *Organization Science, 3,* 398–427.

Patti, R. (1983). *Social welfare administration: Managing social programs in a developmental context.* Englewood Cliffs, NJ: Prentice Hall.

Patti, R. J. (1987). Managing for service effectiveness in social welfare organizations. *Social Work, 32,* 377–383.

Pearlmutter, S. (1998). Self-efficacy and organizational change leadership. *Administration in Social Work, 22,* 23–38.

Perrow, C. (1967). A framework for the comparative analysis of organizations. *American Sociological Review. 32*(2), 194–208.

Perrow, C. (1986). *Complex organizations: A critical essay* (3rd ed.). New York: Random House.

Peters, T. J., & Waterman, R. H., Jr. (1982). *In search of excellence.* New York: Harper & Row.

Pfeffer, J. (1992). *Managing with power: Politics and influence in organizations*. Boston: Harvard Business School Press.

Pfeffer, J. (1997). *New directions for organizational theory: Problems and prospects*. New York: Oxford University Press.

Pfeffer, J., & Salancik, G. R. (1978). *The external control of organizations: A resource dependence perspective*. New York: Harper & Row.

Podolny, J. M., & Page, K. L. (1998). Network forms of organization. *Annual Review of Sociology, 24,* 57–76.

Poertner, J. (2006). Social administration and outcomes for consumers: What do we know? *Administration in Social Work, 30,* 11–24.

Powell, G. N. (1992). *Women and men in management*. Newbury Park, CA: Sage.

Provan, K. G., Isett, K. R., & Milward, H. B. (2004). Cooperation and compromise: A network response to conflicting institutional pressures in community mental health. *Nonprofit and Voluntary Sector Quarterly, 33,* 489–514.

Rapp, C. A., & Poertner, J. (1992). *Social administration: A client-centered approach*. White Plains, NY: Longman.

Reskin, B. F., & Hartmann, H. I. (1986). *Women's work, men's work: Sex segregation on the job*. Washington, DC: National Academy Press.

Rothschild, J., & Whitt, A. J. (1986). *The cooperative workplace*. Cambridge: Cambridge University Press.

Ruef, M. (2000). The emergence of organizational forms: A community ecology approach. *American Journal of Sociology, 106,* 658–714.

Salamon, L. M. (1995). *Partners in public service: Government-nonprofit relations in the modern welfare state*. Baltimore, MD: Johns Hopkins University Press.

Sandfort, J. R. (2003). Exploring the structuration of technology within human service organizations. *Administration & Society, 34,* 605–631.

Sarason, Y. (1995). A model of organizational transformation: The incorporation of organizational identity into a structuration theory framework. *Academy of Management Journal, 47*–51.

Savage, A. (1988). Maximizing effectiveness through technological complexity. In R. J. Patti, J. Poertner, & C. A. Rapp (Eds.), *Managing for service effectiveness in social welfare organizations* (pp. 127–143). New York: Haworth Press.

Schmid, H. (2004). Organization-environment relationships: Theory for management practice in human service organizations. *Administration in Social Work, 28,* 97–113.

Schoonhoven, C. B. (1981). Problems with contingency theory: Testing assumptions hidden within the language of contingency "theory." *Administrative Science Quarterly, 26,* 349–377.

Schram, S. (1995). *Words of welfare: The poverty of social science and the social science of poverty*. Minneapolis: University of Minnesota Press.

Schwartz, A. Y., Gottesman, E. W., & Perlmutter, F. D. (1988). Blackwell: A case study in feminist administration. *Administration in Social Work, 12,* 5–15.

Scott, W. R. (1985). Systems within systems: The mental health sector. *American Behavioral Scientist, 28,* 601–618.

Scott, W. R. (1995). *Institutions and organizations*. Thousand Oaks, CA: Sage.

Scott, W. R., & Davis, G. F. (2007). *Organizations and organizing: Rational, natural, and open systems perspectives*. Upper Saddle River, NJ: Pearson Prentice Hall.

Scott, W. R., & Meyer, J. W. (1983). The organization of environments: Network, cultural, and historical elements. In W. R. Scott & J. W. Meyer (Eds.), *Organizational environments: Ritual and rationality* (pp. 129–154). Beverly Hills, CA: Sage.

Selber, K., & Austin, D. M. (1997). Mary Parker Follett: Epilogue to or return to social work management pioneer? *Administration in Social Work, 2,* 1–13.

Sheinfeld Gorin, S. N., & Weirich, T. W. (1995). Innovation use: Performance assessment in a community mental health center. *Human Relations, 48,* 1427–1453.

Skidmore, R. A. (1995). *Social work administration: Dynamic management and human relationships*. Boston: Allyn & Bacon.

Smith, B. D., & Donovan, S. E. F. (2003). Child welfare practice in organizational and institutional context. *Social Service Review, 77,* 541–563.

Snyder, N. M. (1995). Organizational culture and management capacity in a social welfare organization: A case study of Kansas. *Public Administration Quarterly, 19,* 243–264.

Starr, P. (1982). *The social transformation of American medicine*. New York: Basic Books.

Strauss, A., Fargerhaugh, S., Suczek, B., & Wiener, C. (1985). *Social organization of medical work*. Chicago: The University of Chicago Press.

Taylor, V. (1983). The future of feminism in the 1980s: A social movement analysis. In L. Richardson & V. Taylor (Eds.), *Feminist frontiers: Rethinking sex, gender and society.* Reading, MA: Addison-Wesley.

Tolbert, P. S., & Zucker, L. G. (1996). The institutionalization of institutional theory. In S. R. Clegg, C. Hardy, & W. R. Nord (Eds.), *Handbook of organization studies* (pp. 175–190). London: Sage.

Trice, H. M., & Beyer, J. M. (1993). *The cultures of work organizations.* Englewood Cliffs, NJ: Prentice Hall.

Tucker, D., Baum, J., & Singh, J. (1992). The institutional ecology of human service organizations. In Y. Hasenfeld (Ed.), *Human services as complex organizations* (pp. 47–72). Newbury Park, CA: Sage.

Tushman, M. L., & Anderson, P. (1986). Technological discontinuities and organizational environments. *Administrative Science Quarterly, 31,* 436–465.

Ungar, M. (2004). Surviving as a postmodern social worker: Two Ps and three Rs of direct practice. *Social Work, 49,* 488–496.

Vigoda, E. (2002). From responsiveness to collaboration: Governance, citizens, and the next generation of public administration. *Public Administration Review, 62,* 527–540.

Wamsley, G. L., & Zald, M. N. (1976). *The political economy of public organizations.* Bloomington: Indiana University Press.

Webb, S. A. (2001). Some considerations on the validity of evidence-base practice in social work. *British Journal of Social Work, 31,* 57–79.

Weber, M. (1968). *Economy and society: An interpretive sociology.* New York: Bedminister Press. (Original work published 1924)

Weick, K. E. (1995). *Sensemaking in organizations.* Thousand Oaks, CA: Sage.

Weil, M. (1988). Creating an alternative work culture in a public service setting. *Administration in Social Work, 12,* 69–82.

Weinbach, R. W. (1990). *The social worker as manager: Theory and practice.* White Plains, NY: Longman.

Weisbrod, B. A. (Ed.). (1998). *To profit or not to profit: The commercial transformation of the nonprofit sector.* New York: Cambridge University Press.

Weiss, R. M. (1989). Organizational structure in human service agencies. In L. E. Miller (Ed.), *Managing human service organizations* (pp. 21–38). New York: Quorum Books.

Whiddon, B., & Martin, P. Y. (1989). Organizational democracy and work quality in a state welfare agency. *Social Science Quarterly, 70,* 667–686.

Wilderom, C., Glunk, U., & Maslowski, R. (2000). Organizational culture as a predictor of organizational performance. In N. M. Ashkanasy, C. Wilderom, & M. F. Peterson (Eds.), *Handbook of organizational culture & climate* (pp. 193–210). Thousand Oaks, CA: Sage.

Zald, M. N., & Denton, P. (1963). From evangelism to general service: The transformation of the YMCA. *Administrative Science Quarterly, 8,* 214–234.

Zilber, T. (2002). Institutionalization as an interplay between actions, meanings, and actors: The case of a rape crisis center in Israel. *Academy of Management Journal, 45,* 234–254.

Zuboff, S. (1998). *In the age of the smart machine.* New York: Basic Books.

Zucker, L. (1988). Where do institutional patterns come from? Organizations as actors in social systems. In L. Zucker (Ed.), *Institutional patterns and organizations* (pp. 23–52). Cambridge, MA: Ballinger.

Zucker, L. G. (1989). Combining institutional theory and population ecology: No legitimacy, no history. *American Sociological Review, 54,* 542–545.

CHAPTER 4

The Structure and Financing of Human Services Organizations

Leon Ginsberg and Margaret Gibelman

Organizations, especially organizations specialized for the delivery of social services, are fundamental in the human services. Even private practitioners who deliver social services are often employed by organizations or group themselves into organizations. So understanding organizations is fundamental to understanding all human services programs.

This chapter, which is a revision of a 2000 chapter written by the late Margaret Gibelman for the first edition of this book, focuses on the structure and the financing of human services organizations, which is essential information for those who work in, manage, or simply want to understand human services.

It should be clear in this discussion that management roles are varied and operate at diverse levels. Although management is sometimes understood to be the role of only the top management of an organization, in reality it is also the role of those who direct units at every level of the organization. Certainly, the top manager who has a major role in all elements of the organization must have managerial skills. However, that is also true of line supervisors who work directly with only a handful of operational staff on a day-to-day basis.

Organization and Structure

Organizational structure has been defined as "the formal arrangement of people and functions necessary to achieve desired results" (Page, 1988, p. 46). R. H. Hall (1982) sees structure as the "formal

EDITOR'S NOTE: This chapter, originally written by Dr. Margaret Gibelman (who passed away in 2005) of Yeshiva University for the first edition, has been revised by Dr. Leon Ginsberg.

positional distribution and role relations of persons in a human service organization" (p. 53). Skidmore (1990) further defines structure as the "actual arrangements and levels of an organization in regard to power, authority, responsibilities, and mechanisms for carrying out its [organizational] functions and practices" (p. 97).

Human services organizations, the vehicle through which most human services are provided, "are viewed as those organizations that assist in the growth and development of individuals and families" (Wellford & Gallagher, 1988). The services offered by human services organizations are, typically, "uniquely intimate and personal in nature" (p. 49). These organizations may be public (governmental) at the federal, state, or local level; proprietary (for-profit); or nonprofit.

Table 4.1, which is adapted from a table prepared by the Council on Accreditation of Services for Families and Children, Inc., provides a description of the primary typologies of human services organizations and the authority under which they operate. In recent years, the demarcation of these organizations has, to borrow the term used by Dr. Gibelman, blurred. In an earlier time, prior to the Great Depression and the passage in 1935 of the Social Security Act, the three types of organizations were much more distinct. In more recent times, the differences are less striking and, in fact, the three kinds of organizations each may provide services that appear to be in each other's bailiwicks. That is, not-for-profit organizations may carry out functions normally expected of the public sector, and public agencies may engage in the delivery of services traditionally provided by not-for-profits. For example, early childhood programs, which have typically been in the province of the not-for-profit, often sectarian, sector, also are often organized and run by government agencies. Proprietary organizations may partly or primarily engage in services that are often considered the function of public or not-for-profit human services programs.

Table 4.1   Operating Authority of Human Services Organizations

Type of Organization	Operating Authority
Not-for-profit	• Incorporation in the state or locality in which it operates, with a charter, constitution, and bylaws *and* • Has its own governing body *and/or* • Is organized as an identified organization of a religious body with legal status or is an identified organization of another legal entity that is recognized under the laws of the jurisdiction
Public	• Authorized and established by statute *or* • Is a subunit of a public organization with which a clear administrative relationship exists
Proprietary (for-profit)	• Organized as a legal entity as a corporation, partnership, sole proprietorship, or association *and* • Has a charter, partnership agreement, or articles of association and a constitution and bylaws

SOURCE: Adapted from Council on Accreditation of Services for Families and Children, Inc. (1997).

The Complexity of Human Services Provisions in the United States

For a variety of reasons, understanding, delivering, and receiving human services in the United States are complicated. The federal system is complex, and it, in turn, grafts complexity onto states and local governments, such as cities and counties. Most Americans have little understanding of the complete nature of human services and their provision until they need them. Even when they need such services, many people do not grasp their complexity and therefore do not gain access to services to which they may be entitled. Ask most Americans (this writer's sample is graduate social work students answering examination questions) how much money is provided monthly for people with disabilities under the Americans With Disabilities Act and few have the correct answer, which is "none." Few Americans seem to know the distinction between Medicaid and Medicare or the fact that low-income elderly people can receive benefits from both. Many fewer citizens receive food stamp benefits than are eligible for them (Quindlen, 2006), and few nonrecipients realize that in most states, the stamps were replaced by electronic cards long ago. The Temporary Assistance for Needy Families program, which replaced Aid to Dependent Children over a decade ago, is the source of even more misunderstanding than most other programs.

A cynic might assume these programs are deliberately complicated to deny public knowledge of and access to them. However, it is more likely that programs have been changed, and changed again, in response to political pressures. Those pressures include opposition to assistance programs; concerns about spending more money than is appropriate for the federal revenues; demands that government address specific issues, such as the financial needs of older adults or people with health conditions such as kidney failure or AIDS; as well as the classic need for legislators and executive branch officials to demonstrate their achievements to those who elected them.

The result is that the American system of human services, though generous in many ways, is nearly incomprehensible to the nonexpert. Critics of this system call for a comprehensive national policy to support family needs or a policy to guarantee health care to all or a policy to deal with the needs of children. However, there is no formally declared "family policy" or other overarching statement of the nation's intent to meet the social welfare needs of its citizens. At the same time, there are statements and documents in which one may readily discern such a policy as well as programs to implement it. The first is in the preamble to the U.S. Constitution, which includes the phrase, "To promote the general welfare" as a purpose of the creation of the United States. Such strong language in the nation's most basic legal document is evidence of the historically powerful intention to promote the well-being of American citizens. A second source of welfare policy is, especially, in the Social Security Act of 1935, which, with its 70 years of history and amendments, is the basis for most of the nation's social welfare programs for older adults, people with disabilities, children and their families, and health care needs. The statement of purpose of that Act says, using the language of the preamble to the Constitution,

> To provide for the general welfare by establishing a system of Federal old-age benefits, and by enabling the several States to make more adequate provision for aged persons, blind persons, dependent and crippled children, maternal and child welfare, public health, and the administration of their unemployment compensation laws; to establish a Social Security Board; to raise revenues; and for other purposes.

So America's policy of social welfare can be found in the Constitution and the Social Security Act. These provide the basic framework for the development of many human services programs. Over the years, other authorizing statutes have been enacted that provide the bases for social services, such as the Older Americans Act, as well as specific statutes that deal with mental health, public health, addictions, violence, AIDS, and other social problems.

The 21st-Century Mixed Economy

Although it is not often discussed by elected officials or codified in United States statutory law, the United States economy is increasingly mixed. A mixed economy is defined in the *Social Work Dictionary* as "A society or environment in which services and transfers of funds occur through the participation of public, nonprofit, and proprietary organizations" (Barker, 2003, p. 276). The *Shorter Oxford English Dictionary* (2002) says it is "an economic system containing both private and State enterprise" (p. 1801).

The traditional conception of the American economy is an economy that is strictly a free enterprise system. There is an idealized strict separation between government and nongovernment activities. That is, government, especially the federal government, is not conceived to directly deliver services to citizens except in carefully defined areas. Of course, education is a public function provided through state and local governments. And local governments also provide recreation services, as well as many other services to citizens. The ideal model, however, especially when discussing the national or federal government, is one in which government is strictly limited in its functions.

Although it is beyond the scope of this chapter, readers may be interested in finding out more about the economic philosophy that discourages government involvement in human services. One of the primary proponents of that viewpoint was Milton Friedman, who died in 2006 (Van Riper, 2006). Charles Murray (2006) is another proponent of eliminating government from most human services (also see Ginsberg, 1998).

It is perhaps sufficient to say that human services programs are both governmental and nongovernmental and that American government has, to some degree, for much of its history been a financer as well as a provider of human services.

Government's role as taxer, developer, and administrator of programs has a long history.

Federal Human Services Agencies

In keeping with the federal government's tendency to devolve human services to state and local governments (see below), most such programs are delivered by these governments. However, there are a few federal agencies that provide services directly to citizens and residents. The largest and most important is the Social Security Administration, which administers the federal Old Age, Survivors, and Disability Insurance program, commonly called by its initials, OASDI. That agency also administers the Medicare program for persons aged 65 and over and the Supplemental Security Insurance program (SSI) for low-income older adults and people with disabilities.

The federal government also provides services to veterans through the Veterans Administration and services for some Native Americans through the Bureau of Indian Affairs and the Indian Health Service, although many Native American groups are now served through state government agencies, rather than through federal organizations.

Perhaps the most significant role of the federal government is the provision of funds, usually in the form of matching grants or block grants, to states and localities for services to citizens. Normally, those have been limited to the provision of aid to governmental and nonsectarian private organizations, but in recent years, the federal government also established "faith-based" programs to aid religious organizations in their delivery of human services, a subject that is discussed later in this chapter.

State Public Human Services Organizations

Every state has one or more public organizations that organize and deliver services to its citizens pursuant to legislation that is enacted by the state legislature and approved by the governor.

Such departments are typically accountable to the governor, but they also rely on the legislature to appropriate their budgets and oversee their performance.

The most prevalent state-wide organization, historically called the "department of welfare," is more commonly known today as the "department of social [or human] services." These organizations receive federal and state funds for the delivery of services such as Temporary Assistance for Needy Families, Food Stamps, and Medicaid.

Some states administer these programs directly, while others do so through local governments such as counties. The designations are "state-administered" and "locally administered and state supervised." Federal funds, in both cases, must come first to the state government.

As is discussed under the section on the financing of services, almost all of these programs also rely on state funds for a portion of their budgets, with the federal government providing at least half, and often more, of the costs through matching formulas or grants. There are differing formulas for different programs, as is discussed later in this chapter.

The services are divided between economic assistance programs and social services, which are discussed in greater detail below. Many clients use both elements of the agency program to obtain concrete assistance and to help themselves with family or personal problems they encounter. A major portion of the social services are for children—child protection, foster care, and adoption—as is illustrated below. A substantial portion provides various services for older adults and people with disabilities.

Many states have larger, more comprehensive agencies (sometimes referred to as "umbrella organizations") that incorporate the social and economic services into a structure that may include some other state government services, such as public health, mental health, services for adults and children with disabilities, workers' compensation, and work and employment programs.

Mental Health and Disability Services. Beginning in the 19th century, states began providing services for people with mental disabilities, both mental illness and developmental disabilities such as mental retardation. Over the years, beginning in the mid-20th century, those services began to change to include both institutional care and outpatient services to clients and their families, with increasing emphasis on the latter.

Some states have separate departments of mental health and disabilities. Others combine them, and still others make such services part of a larger human services agency structure. The financing of such services is appropriated by state legislatures and is augmented by some federal grants.

Employment and Unemployment Services. Every state has a program of financial assistance for persons who are unemployed because of employer retrenchment or prevailing economic slowdowns. The same agency also administers an employment service to help those who are unemployed find work as well as training programs to help equip unemployed people for the workforce.

Employment programs are generally financed entirely by a federal tax on employers, with some special assistance provided by the federal government for training programs.

Most human services agencies are part of the executive branch of government, although some at state and local levels, such as probation services, may operate under court jurisdiction. In the federal government, the president appoints secretaries of the cabinet-level agencies (e.g., the Department of Health and Human Services) as well as directors and other executives of agencies that are part of departments in the cabinet. Presidential appointments generally must be approved or confirmed by the U.S. Senate before they are finalized. In most states, the governor is the key authority of state agencies. The state chief executive appoints the department heads, who may be called directors or, in some cases, commissioners. Some states have less direct lines between agencies and governors. In those states, the governor appoints a board of directors, which, in turn, appoints the agency chief executive. In many states, the agency chief executive or the board members, whichever holds the top authority for managing the agency, must be approved—a process called confirmation—by the state legislature, most typically the state upper house or senate.

Not-for-Profit Organizations

Nonprofit organizations are usually governed by boards of directors, although some are subsidiary entities of larger organizations that have boards of their own. In most states, nonprofit organizations must be chartered or licensed by the state government, depending on the type of service they provide. Many are also supervised or monitored by state health departments, social services departments, or other agencies of state government. In some states, the charitable contributions received by the organizations are evaluated by state government agencies, usually in terms of the proportions of the contributions spent for fundraising and administration. Board members may be appointed by the chair or president of the board, selected by outgoing board members, or elected by the members in membership organizations. The board of directors has the legal authority to operate the organization and carries out its goals through the appointment of a chief executive, who may be called director, executive director, president, chief executive officer, executive vice-president, or any number of other designations chosen by the organization.

Generally, the chief executive implements the organization's purposes by directing program operations; employing staff members; raising, budgeting, and administering operating funds; and ensuring the organization's mission is carried out.

Nonprofit organizations use a wide array of administrative structures. Some operate with a chief executive officer, who is primarily responsible for external and board relations, and an associate executive director, who manages the day to day operations of the program. Sometimes those roles are delineated as executive director and program director.

Not-for-profit agencies are typically organized in departments corresponding to groups of clients served (e.g., children, youth, couples, older adults), or kinds of service offered (group counseling, recreation, outdoor programs, health services), or times of the services (day care, after-school care, evening programs), or functions (development and fundraising, client activities, information and education, nursing services).

Sometimes called the private sector, nonprofit organizations may be classified in a number of ways, but two of the most significant types are sectarian and nonsectarian. Sectarian organizations, such as Catholic Charities, Lutheran Social Services, Jewish Community Centers and Jewish Family Services, the Salvation Army, and organizations that operate under the Church of Jesus Christ of Latter Day Saints (Mormons), operate, at least partially, with funds from their parent religious organizations. Nonsectarian private organizations operate without regard to religious affiliation or religious norms.

As discussed earlier, some government funds, including federal funds, are provided to nonsectarian nonprofit organizations to carry out various kinds of programs. Such funds are increasingly available to sectarian organizations for human services they provide, such as homeless shelters, recreation programs, and social and financial assistance to families. Generally, sectarian organizations that receive federal funds are required to provide those funded services without regard to the religious affiliation of the recipients.

There is no general Federal law that prohibits faith-based organizations receiving Federal funds from hiring on a religious basis. Nor does the Civil Rights Act of 1964, which applies regardless of whether an organization receives Federal funds, prohibit faith-based organizations from hiring on a religious basis. This Act protects Americans from employment discrimination based on race, color, religion, sex, national origin, age, and disability. But the Civil Rights Act also recognizes the fundamental rights of faith-based organizations to hire employees who share their religious beliefs. The United States Supreme Court unanimously upheld this special protection for faith-based groups in 1987, and it has been the law since then. Thus, a Jewish organization can decide to hire only Jewish employees, a Catholic organization can decide to hire only Catholics, and so on, without running into problems with the Civil Rights Act (The White House, n.d.). Of course, public funds cannot be used for the discharge of purely religious activities, such as conducting worship services.

Not-for-profit organizations generally do not pay taxes, just as government organizations do not. They are exempt under one or more of the federal and state tax exemptions that are provided for nonprofit organizations. Some are classified as charitable nonprofits, which can receive the exemption classification of 501(c)3 under the U.S. Internal Revenue Code. Others, such as membership organizations (the National Association of Social Workers is an example), receive special exemptions as nonprofits, although they are not charities. Of course, the concept behind these tax exemptions is that such organizations do not distribute income from profits to owners or shareholders (which is the usual basis for taxation of businesses). For nonprofits, money earned in excess of expenses may be put back into the organization's operations but cannot be distributed or used as income for employees or board members. The tax exemption of nonprofits is often controversial. Some nonprofits own large quantities of resources, such as real estate. Some universities own extensive tracts of urban property, which they may rent to others for real estate ventures. Their earnings on the real estate are not taxable. Some hospitals may, under the reimbursement regulations of Medicare, Medicaid, and private insurance companies, collect more than they spend on patient care. So long as the earnings are not treated as income and distributed to individual owners or stockholders, nonprofit status continues.

Private foundations (e.g., Ford Foundation, The Bill and Melinda Gates Foundation, and many others of all sizes at regional and national levels), to which many people and corporations contribute parts of their earnings, are also tax exempt, provided they distribute specified portions of their earnings to pursue health and social objectives.

Tax exemptions are often significant subjects for debate by government entities. For example, when a public university or another kind of public or nonprofit organization acquires property, that property is removed from the tax rolls. Local governments often rely heavily on property taxes for their revenue, which they use to pay for education, law enforcement, roads, and other government functions. When property becomes nontaxable, the government loses funds or has to raise the rates on the remaining taxable property and/or on income.

Nonprofit as well as public organization employees are, of course, subject to income tax as well as other taxes paid by individuals. Simply working for a religious organization, government, or social agency does not exempt employees from paying the same taxes as their counterparts in for-profit social services organizations or other businesses.

Although most of the nonprofit organizations operate in particular cities or regions, some, such as the Red Cross and Salvation Army, are national in scope. Nonprofits such as Holt International Children's Services; the Christian Children's Fund; Caritas, a sectarian agency associated with the Roman Catholic Church; and World Vision operate in countries around the world.

Nonprofits are regularly studied and reorganized for the purposes of reforming them and their functioning. Paul C. Light (2000, 2002) has written two books during his time as a vice-president of the Brookings Institution, which discuss the evolution and functions of nonprofits. Other books on the subject include Bray (2005), Grobman (2005), and Harman and Associates (2005). There are also journals dedicated to the study of and management of nonprofits, such as Jossey-Bass's *Nonprofit Management and Leadership* and Haworth's *Journal of Nonprofit and Public Sector Marketing*. Some Internet resources on nonprofits are also available, such as http://www.supportcenteronline and http://www.nonprofitmanagementgroup.

Another organization of nonprofits is called the Independent Sector, a coalition of corporations, foundations, and private voluntary organizations that work to strengthen America's nonprofit organizations, which collectively are often called the third or independent sector. Its Web site provides information on the nonprofit industry.

Proprietary Organizations

Many human services are delivered by proprietary organizations, which are established to earn a profit for their owners in the process of delivering services. The distinctions between proprietary and not-for-profit organizations are sometimes less clear and dramatic than they seem. A nonprofit may actually collect significantly more than it expends in providing services, which is often the case with large health care financing organizations such as Blue Cross and Blue Shield agencies. In such cases, the additional funds may be spent in providing new services, upgrading staff salaries, constructing new buildings, and other activities chosen by the organization. In proprietary organizations that are publicly held as well as those that are privately held, a primary purpose is to earn profits so they may be distributed to owners and shareholders. In publicly held organizations, the owners may be members of a corporate board of directors or simply stockholders. Proprietary organizations also pay taxes on their earnings.

Proprietary human services organizations are quite varied in their structures and in the services they provide. Virtually any social service may be provided by a private organization. Some of the more typical private organizations are long-term care facilities (Barker, 2003), which may serve people with disabilities and chronic health conditions. Hospitals, both medical and psychiatric, and health care financing organizations, such as insurance companies, are other examples of proprietary human services organizations. In recent years, for-profits have become major players in the provision of mental health services, child residential services, and income maintenance programs, usually under contract with public agencies.

Many social workers are also employees or owners of private social work practices, which provide counseling to individuals, couples, and groups. In some cases, the social workers are part of incorporated service organizations with other providers such as nurses, psychologists, and psychiatrists. In other cases, a social worker may set up a "solo" practice on either a full or part-time basis. Another common pattern is for social workers to form private group practices, sometimes sharing the rental costs of offices and administrative services, for example, billing clients or "third party providers" such as insurance companies or government agencies that contract for their services.

Although mental health private practices appear to be the most common, a variety of other private practice arrangements are often developed. Some social workers provide studies of homes of prospective adoptive parents on behalf of adoption agencies. Others may operate residential care facilities for children who cannot live with their own families. Still others operate private foster care organizations, especially foster care programs for children with physical, intellectual, or emotional disabilities.

In recent years, for-profit organizations have increasingly entered into the human services enterprise, particularly in such settings as nursing homes, home health, residential treatment centers, and adult and child day care. These organizations employ social workers and other mental health professionals. For-profits are owned and operated like any other business (Morales & Sheafor, 2002). The entrance of for-profits as providers of human services can largely be explained by changes in federal funding regulations in the late 1960s, which began by allowing for-profit organizations to apply for and receive contract funds (Gibelman, 1995). Furthermore, such changes in federal regulations reflect a growing preference for things private (a phenomenon known as privatization), based on the hope that the free market and heightened competition will increase efficiency and reduce costs. One observer of the growth of for-profit social service programs asserts that "For better or worse, for-profit social-service providers—in mental health, welfare, and medical care—are driving fundamental change in an industry previously driven largely by humanitarian concerns" (Skwiot, 2007, p. 17).

Skwiot (2007) quotes several executives of for-profit human services programs that provide services to recipients of Medicaid, Supplemental Security Income, and State Children's Health Insurance Programs. One source, Peter Frumkin of the LBJ School of Public Affairs at the University of Texas, suggests that nonprofits should consider changing their client bases, the nature of their interventions, and the types of staff they employ if they are to compete with for-profit agencies (p. 21).

Organizations such as Maximus, Magellan, and Centene are among the corporations discussed in Skwiot's (2007) article. The article does not report the extent of for-profit activity in the human services. Such figures are difficult to calculate because of the current decentralization of financing of human services.

Generally, a modern prescription for organizational structure effectiveness is that provided by Peters and Waterman (Ginsberg & Keyes, 1995). They suggest that organizations should be mission-driven and that the structure should be simple rather than complicated. Within those concepts, many different kinds of structures can be effective.

One principle of organization that seems to be well accepted is the existence, especially in large organizations, of external and internal managerial roles. In organizations such as universities and large social agencies, both public and private, a top official, such as a university president, assumes an external role and interacts with the board of directors, the governing persons or institutions, and the larger public, while an internal official such as a university provost or an agency program director manages the day-to-day operations of the institution. In smaller organizations, the chief executive officer is often required to play both roles—managing the internal operations and interfacing with the larger organizational environment.

Financing Patterns for Human Services

Human services programs are financed in various ways. Table 4.2 explains the sources of funds that support public, nonprofit, and for-profit organizations.

Financing Federal Programs

Federal human services are financed through the various ways in which the federal government obtains revenue. For the OASDI program of Social Security, the funds come from a trust fund that is supported by employee and employer contributions. Medicare is similarly financed by taxes contributed by employees and employers. All the rest of the services, such as Supplemental Security Income, block grants for human services, education programs, and law enforcement, are supported through "general revenues," which include personal and corporate income taxes, tariffs, fees, fuel taxes, admissions fees for federal parks, passport fees, and many others, as well as the tax on employer payrolls, which supports the unemployment compensation program, as discussed earlier in this chapter.

Financing State and Local Programs

The financing of state and local governments is derived largely from taxes, although fees for services are perhaps proportionately a larger source of funds than is the case in the federal programs. Most states have state income taxes. As noted earlier, property taxes are likely to be levied by local

Table 4.2   Sources of Funding by Type of Organization

Organizational Type	Primary Source of Funding
Public	• Government (legislative) allocations • Occasional private funds for special purposes (such as Fannie Mae support for computerization)
Nonprofit	• Direct contributions (bequests, donations) • Fees for services • Government grants and contracts • Foundations • Campaigns (e.g., United Way, Combined Federal Campaign) • Medicaid/Medicare
For-profit	• Fees for services • Government grants and contracts • Medicaid/Medicare

governments, although some also have income taxes—including taxes on commuters who work in cities but are not residents of those cities. In terms of fees for services, higher education tuition and fees are a major source of state government financing.

Another major form of support of state and local government is federal grants and matching funds, which are devoted to specific governmental activities, especially public assistance, social services, aging programs, child welfare, and public education.

Another example of a state program that is largely paid for by federal funds is Food Stamps. The federal government provides the Food Stamps (which, as indicated earlier, are increasingly issued to recipients on an electronic card) according to federally defined benefit levels. The states receive a grant from the federal government for administering the program.

See Table 4.3 for the projections for federal expenditures for various human services programs for 2007 and for 2009.

Table 4.3   Projected Federal Expenditures 2007 and 2009

Program	Expenditures (in billions of dollars)
Medicaid	395 (2009 projection)
Supplemental Security Income	36 (2009 projection)
Food Stamps	33 (2007 expenditures)
Family Support (TANF and related programs)	26 (2009 projection)
Foster Care	7 (2007 projection)
OASDI	520 (2009 projection)
Medicare	420 (2009 projection)

SOURCE: U.S. Census Bureau (2008); The White House, Office of Management and Budget (n.d.).

Financing Private, Nonprofit Organizations

Private, nonprofit organizations derive significant portions of their funding from direct contributions; fundraising activities such as bequests, fundraising campaigns, solicitations of supporters through direct requests, and events such as dinners or socials; sales of products; and auctions. Some agencies also receive funds from united campaigns such as United Way drives. A major portion of private financing comes from contracts with government, which is discussed in more detail later in this chapter.

According to Independent Sector (http://www.independentsector.org), there are 1.9 million nonprofit organizations, which include religious institutions and foundations. They employ 9.4 million people, whose earnings represent 6.6% of the wages paid in the U.S. The approximately trillion dollars in annual expenditures by nonprofits are funded as follows: 38% by dues, fees, and charges; 31% by government; and 20% by contributions. However, social service programs receive more than half—52%—of their incomes from government.

Financing For-Profits

For-profit organizations derive much of their income from fees but also from contracts with government agencies as well as from donations and dues. A typical kind of financial support for organizations that provide specialized foster care for children with disabilities is contracts with state or local departments of social services. Similarly, adoption placement studies may also be funded by state or local child welfare agencies. Mental health counseling programs, including those that provide services to people who abuse or are addicted to drugs, may be financed, in part, with funds from Medicaid, a federal-state program for low-income clients who need health care. Some public health-oriented organizations may receive all or part of their financing from Medicaid. Organizations that serve persons with AIDS may also be supported through Medicaid funds.

Federal-State Matching Programs

Many state and local programs are supported by federal and state government matching programs. That is, the federal government provides part of the funds and the state the balance for programs the state determines it wants to operate—as all states do. For example, the Temporary Assistance for Needy Families (TANF) program, which provides financial assistance, at levels determined by the state, to low-income families with children, is financed, in large part, by a block grant to the states. The formula for financing the Medicaid program is set by the federal government, based on the per capita income of the state. In the Food Stamp program, the financial assistance is provided by the federal government and the administrative costs of determining eligibility and managing the program are shared between the state and federal government.

There are federal provisions that permit states to request exceptions to federal regulations so that they can operate programs that deviate, to an extent, from federal guidelines. For example, Medicaid services, which often pay for long-term nursing home care, may be modified to provide for in-home services that would prevent the placement of a person in a nursing home.

Other Federal Funds

There are other federal programs designed to serve children, and some of those are open-ended federal appropriations that only require a state matching percentage. Title IV-E of the Social Security Act finances children's programs that provide foster care assistance payments, placement services, and administrative costs, as well as training for child welfare workers. In fact, many child welfare workers in state departments of social services are trained with those funds, as are many social work students through contracts between state agencies and social work education programs. Table 4.4 shows that the foster care assistance payments are unlimited, although the state must contribute the same percentage as it contributes for Medicaid.

Table 4.4   Major Federal Programs Dedicated to the Support of Child Welfare Activities

Program	Budgetary classification	Federal support of total
Title IV-E Foster Care program		
Foster care assistance payments	Entitlement	Open-ended Federal match at Medicaid rate
Placement services and administrative costs	Entitlement	Open-ended Federal match of 50 percent
Training expenses	Entitlement	Open-ended Federal match of 75 percent
Title TV-E Adoption Assistance Program		
Adoption assistance payments	Entitlement	Open-ended Federal match at Medicaid care
Nonrecurring adoption expenses	Entitlement	Open-ended Federal match of 50 percent (up to $2,000 per adoption)
Placement services and administrative costs	Entitlement	Open-ended Federal match of 50 percent
Training expenses	Entitlement	Open-ended Federal match of 75 percent
Title IV-E Independent Living		
Chafee Foster Care Independence Program	Entitlement	80 percent Federal funding, total capped at State allotment
Educational and Training Vouchers	Discretionary	80 percent Federal funding, total capped at State allotment
Title IV-B child welfare Services Program		
Subpart 1 Child welfare services	Discretionary	Federal match of 75 percent, total capped State at allotment
Subpart 2 Promoting Safe and Stable Families	Entitlement	Federal match of 75 percent, total capped State at allotment
	Discretionary	Federal match of 75 percent, total capped State at allotment
Mentoring Children of Prisoners	Discretionary	Federal match of 75 percent in the first two fiscal years in which the grant is awarded and 50 percent in the third and each succeeding year, total capped at State allotment

SOURCE: Adapted from Committee on Ways and Means, U.S. House of Representatives (2004).

Placement services and the administrative costs are also unlimited but are shared 50-50 between the state and federal governments. Child welfare training expenses can receive 75% from the federal government—without limits. Adoption assistance is paid for similarly.

Much of the money used for contracting comes from the federal Social Services Block Grant, which is provided under Title XX of the Social Security Act. In 2003, the amount of money provided overall from that block grant was $1.7 billion. The history of Title XX funding is complicated and varied. During the 1970s, there was no limit on the amount of Title XX money a state could receive from the federal government, so long as the state was able to provide matching funds of approximately one-third. Because the expenditures were great and because state government social services agencies were able to obtain funds from voluntary agencies to match the federal funds, a cap was eventually imposed.

The ceilings on the Title XX Social Services Block Grant changed periodically. In 1996, the ceiling was $2.8 billion, but Congress only appropriated $2.381 billion. (Committee on Ways and Means, U.S. House of Representatives, 2004) For 1997–2002, the ceiling was $2.38 billion, but Congress actually appropriated $2.5 billion for 1997. In 1998, the appropriation was reduced to $2.299 billion, and in recent years, the ceiling was reduced to $1.7 billion. According to The Workforce Alliance (2006), the appropriation for the Social Services Block Grant has remained at $1.7 billion.

The Social Services Block Grant is allocated to states on the basis of population. Although it represents a large portion of the funds that are used in social services contracting, the Social Services Block Grant is only one source of funds that state governments use in contracting for human services. It is possible for states to transfer funds from other block grants to the Social Services. For example, the TANF program described earlier is a block grant to the states. If they wish to do so, states may transfer up to 30% of the TANF grant to the Social Services Block Grant. There is also a Child Care and Development Block Grant (CCDBG). When states transfer funds to the Social Services, they must also transfer two dollars for every dollar transferred to the Social Services to the CCDBG.

Table 4.5 shows the ways in which states spent their Title XX funds in 1998–2001.

In 2001, about 10% of the funds were used for administration. The bulk of the funds were used for children and youth to provide child protection, day care, residential treatment, and foster care. Case management used 6.5% of the funds and substantial portions of that service are devoted to children. A second portion of the funds was used for adult protection and day care. So, by and large, the Title XX Block Grant program serves children and adults, most of whom are elderly and in need of special services. Services for people with disabilities were also a large portion of the expenditures, 8.5%.

Public-Private Collaboration

The Private Provision of Public Services: Trends and Issues

Perhaps the most significant development in the latter part of the 20th century, which continues in the 21st century, is the contracting for services by government with nonprofit and proprietary organizations. The 1967 amendments to the Social Security Act authorized states, for the first time, to purchase services from nonprofit or proprietary agencies. Initially, government was looking for service providers, and nonprofits were in a positive negotiating position.

Governments often contract with nonprofit or proprietary organizations for service delivery as a means of promoting efficiency. Programs may be begun and ended without the complexities of creating government agencies and civil services positions. Federal and state government procedures for establishing services and employing

Table 4.5   Use of Title XX Funds, by Expenditure Category, Fiscal Years 1998–2001

Services	Percent of Funds			
	1998	*1999*	*2000*	*2001*
Adoption services	0.7	0.9	1.4	1.3
Case management	3.5	4.3	6.4	6.5
Congregate meals	0.1	0.1	0.3	0.3
Counseling services	1.5	1.4	1.6	1.6
Day care—adults	0.5	0.5	0.5	0.9
Day care—children	9.5	13.0	5.9	7.6
Educating/training services	0.3	0.3	0.6	0.3
Employment services	2.3	1.8	2.0	0.8
Family planning services	1.5	1.6	1.5	1.6
Foster care services—adults	0.2	0.3	0.3	0.3
Foster care services—children	8.0	10.6	10.7	10.1
Health-related services	0.4	0.4	0.6	0.9
Home-based services	9.5	6.8	7.2	7.6
Home-delivered meals	0.6	0.6	0.7	0.7
Housing services	0.1	0.6	0.6	0.3
Independent/transitional living services	0.7	0.7	0.6	0.1
Information and referral services	0.6	1.1	1.3	2.6
Legal services	0.3	0.4	0.5	0.6
Pregnancy and parenting	0.4	0.3	0.2	0.2
Prevention/intervention	5.1	9.1	7.4	7.7
Protective services—adults	2.8	3.6	4.9	5.7
Protective services—children	7.1	8.8	10.8	11.8
Recreation services	0.1	0.0	0.1	0.1
Residential treatment	3.8	2.7	2.7	4.0
Special services—youth at risk	1.2	2.6	3.1	2.3
Special services—disabled	8.4	7.7	7.8	8.3
Substance abuse services	0.3	0.5	0.5	0.6
Transportation	0.6	0.8	1.0	0.7
Other services	5.7	5.2	5.6	4.3
Administrative costs	11.6	7.7	8.6	10.1
Uncategorized TANF transfer expenditures	12.5	5.5	4.5	—
Total	100	100	100	100

SOURCE: Table prepared by the Congressional Research Service, based on data submitted by 50 states and the District of Columbia to the U.S. Department of Health and Human Services.

personnel are time-consuming, which may delay the delivery of services. It is also difficult for government to end a program once it is part of the government structure. In addition, personnel procedures, fringe benefits, and other complex governmental processes are avoided when government contracts with an external entity to deliver its services.

In light of the concurrent movements to decentralize decision making and service delivery, to de-bureaucratize and de-federalize and to privatize human services, among other enterprises, purchasing services from the private sector is a favored means of delivering social services. As indicated earlier, over half—52%—of the services offered by nonprofit human services agencies are financed by government through grants and contracts. These funds are a significant portion of the expenditures detailed above for family support and foster care. Adding to this is the billions of dollars annually spent on health and human services through Medicaid and Medicare, in which consumers are given the responsibility of selecting their own provider.

The old adage "he who pays the piper calls the tune" is an apt description of one end result of these contracting arrangements. On the positive side, nonprofits have, as a condition of government funding, had to develop new management competencies, including negotiating skills and financial accountability systems. Nonprofit agencies have been able to introduce new programs and services. In some cases, voluntary agencies have come into being as a direct result of the availability of public funds to finance particular types of services, such as assistance to victims of crime (Smith, 1989). The negative byproducts of these public-private relationships, however, are formidable. Questions about the autonomy of nonprofits have increasingly been raised (Gibelman, 1995), as these contracted agencies modify their service delivery systems to align with public program priorities and as the public sector becomes more vigilant in its accountability requirements. The consequences of contracting have been seen as so pervasive that nonprofits

have been accused of becoming agents of the state (Goldstein, 1993). The key factor in this transformation has been the growing reliance of nonprofits on contract funds, making them resource-dependent on government. (For an extensive discussion of actual and perceived effects of this resource dependence, see Foundation Center, 2008; Kadlec, 2007; Kramer, 1994; Poertner & Rapp, 2007.)

Purchase-of-service arrangements have also led some nonprofits down the road of goal displacement. As nonprofits sought to take advantage of existing or new public funds, they initiated some programs that may not have been on target or consistent with their mission. The end result has been a dilemma: To what extent should the need for organizational maintenance and growth take precedence over organizational mission (Gibelman, 1995)? Such questions are less pertinent to for-profit organizations engaged in contracting because their mission is defined as profitability.

Besides their relationship with government through contracts, nonprofits are also the beneficiary of public policy on their behalf. For example, nonprofits benefit from government largesse in regard to special postage rates that are federally subsidized. (However, a 1993 law changed the way that Congress subsidizes the U.S. Postal Service for delivering nonprofit mail; federal subsidies are gradually being phased out; Hall, 1998.) The Internal Revenue Service sets tax rates (typically below market rates) for computing charitable deductions for trusts, gift annuities, charitable lead trusts, and some other deferred gifts (Billitteri & Stehle, 1998). And, of course, taxpayers benefit from their ability to claim tax deductions for charitable giving in cash and kind. There is increased pressure on Congress to pass new tax incentives to encourage charitable giving, particularly at a time in which nonprofit organizations are seen as key players in solving the country's problems ("Panel on Civic Renewal," 1998). Such positive impacts of public policy further highlight the interdependence between the sectors.

For-profits, too, continue to extend their boundaries, as the human services are now fair game for private enterprise. Despite authorization to contract with for-profits dating back to the 1960s, government's closer relationship with nonprofits favored purchase of service from the nonprofit sector. However, lawmakers continued to look for service delivery options as social problems remained intractable. A viable option was to open the door to businesses to compete for government contracts for a larger array of social service programs, with the hope that newer alternatives might be found and increased competition would lead to better cost-efficiency (Moore, 1998).

In 1996, Connecticut became the first state to retain a private company, Maximus, Inc. of McLean, Virginia, to manage its entire program of child care benefits and services for families on welfare and the working poor (Rabinovitz, 1997). A year later, the company was at risk of losing the $12.8 million contract because the system it was hired to fix had become more, rather than less, problem-plagued. Such an outcome is not a surprise, nor unique to for-profits. A primary rationale for using purchase-of-service arrangements is their ability to implement new programs quickly and effectively (Gibelman, 1995). However, what constitutes rapid response time on the part of the government agency paying the bill may be perceived as unreasonable and unrealistic by the contracted party. Nevertheless, in this instance, Connecticut remained committed to privatization of its welfare system, whether with the current company or another for-profit.

The service arenas once dominated by nonprofit programs are thus dissipating as a direct result of public policy choices. The 1996 welfare reform law furthered the competition among the sectors by allowing for-profits to bid against nonprofits and state and local public agencies for billions of dollars in job training contracts. For-profits were also allowed to compete for about $3 billion a year in contract funds to run foster care programs (Moore, 1998). Even privatization of Head Start is being considered by Congress, with the first step taken by the Senate in July, 1998 to approve legislation that would allow for-profits to apply for funds heretofore restricted to nonprofits and government agencies (Moore, 1998).

As we look toward the future, we are likely to see increased competition between not-for-profit and for-profit organizations, as well as the continued decline in the direct-service role of the public sector, except as it delivers its services through contracts. Indeed, one of the hallmarks of the last decade has been the proliferation of for-profit companies offering services previously provided primarily by nonprofit and government organizations, including, most recently, job training (Moore, 1998). Such competition has already been experienced by nonprofit hospitals, many of which were taken over by for-profit chains or were forced to merge or restructure their operations to continue on a fiscally sound basis (Moore, 1998). Conversion of organizations from one type to another—profit to nonprofit or nonprofit to profit—is also having the effect of dissipating the traditional distinctions among and between the sectors. Such conversions have been notable in the health field, not only in hospitals and nursing homes but also in the health maintenance industry.

An example of public-private partnerships is in the Child Support Enforcement program, in which governments assist parents entitled to child support to collect those funds. According to the U.S. House Committee on Ways and Means (2004) and the General Accounting Office, an arm of the U.S. Congress, 15 states have turned to private organizations to collect child support in some of their offices. The GAO also found 38 private firms that regularly collected child support payments.

Boundary-blurring between the sectors continues to be a pervasive phenomenon, and government has inserted itself even more to ensure that nonprofits maintain their unique charitable focus. A current example of such government oversight can be seen in Section 4958 of the Internal Revenue Code, enacted as an amendment on July 30, 1996. Known as the Taxpayer

Bill of Rights 2, Pub. Law 104-168 (110 Stat. 1452), this amendment seeks to control "excessive" pay of nonprofit executives. Excess benefits are subject to tax and penalties and are defined as "any transaction in which an economic benefit . . . provided by an applicable tax-exempt organization . . . to or for the use of any disqualified person . . . exceeds the value of consideration received for providing such benefit" (UncleFed's Tax Board, 2004). The independence of the independent sector is further diminished to the extent that government can now decide on the limits of nonprofit executive pay.

Analyses of Contracting

In the years since contracting for services began, scholars have studied the processes and the formats used by government in delivering services through private organizations. More than half of nonprofit organization social services are paid for with government funds, whereas none were in 1960. The magnitude of the impact of contracting is dramatic. Kamerman and Kahn (1998), writing for the Finance Project, say that 90% of the workers in New York State social services agencies worked for organizations that were supported to some extent by public funds. Massachusetts had twice as many social services workers in agencies funded in that way than it had publicly employed workers. According to Martin (2005, p. 65), citing his own 2001 estimates and Lauffer (1997), "more publicly funded human services are provided via contractual arrangements than are provided directly by public employees. By some estimates, upwards of 80% of all human services funding may involve contracting by the year 2010."

Lawrence L. Martin (2005) has studied the performance-based contracting approach now gaining widespread popularity in the human services. Performance contracting, developed by the Office of Federal Procurement Policy and state purchasing officers as well as The National Association of State Purchasing Officials, essentially specifies standards of performance, such as quality, timeliness, and quantity, and the expected outcomes of contracts. Based on his analysis of performance-based contracting in several states, he concluded that the process had accomplished its primary objective of requiring contractors to focus on performance results. Martin also found that quality, outcomes, and outputs could be considered and treated together in determining the conformity to performance standards of a contract and that all contractor compensation need not be tied to performance. There was also evidence that performance-based contracting did not necessarily lead to "creaming," where cases more likely to be successful are chosen in order to improve performance outcomes. Martin asks whether performance-based contracting works, and he concludes, based on studies in several states, that it does and that it is accomplishing its objectives.

The American Public Human Services Association (2005), which is largely an association of state public agencies, agrees that the federal expectations for public services and contracts should be focused on outputs of services. One of their recommendations is that "the focus of performance measurement and assessment should be a set of simple requirements and outcome measures that emphasize the positive incentives for high performance" (p. 113). They further suggested the avoidance of narrow process measures and a focus on actual outcomes for clients.

Roland Zullo (2006) studied contracting in the child welfare field. He sought to determine whether the nature of contracts was coercive, competitive, or collaborative. Coercive contracts, he suggested, were those in which the more powerful of the parties attempted to delegate the more difficult cases to the less powerful. Competitive contracting is designed, Zullo suggested, to resolve governmental delivery system shortcomings. In collaborative contracts, both parties work for long-term agreements for the purpose of best using their joint resources.

Zullo (2006) concluded that the relationships were more collaborative than coercive or competitive. He analyzed 500 foster care cases drawn from a population of 750 private agency cases and 4,900 public cases and found that private sector cases were most likely to have been children who needed protection, cases that involved two-parent families, and cases in which there were fewer siblings in the family. He initially hypothesized that private sector cases would be most likely to involve parent-child conflicts, while the public sector would have more cases that involved difficult parental behavior such as a lack of parenting skills, drug and alcohol problems, and situations in which children were involuntarily removed from the home—areas in which states have responsibility. He found that his conclusions about the differences between private and public child protection agencies were essentially correct.

In the initial version of this chapter, when contracting was relatively new, it appeared to the author, Dr. Gibelman, that there were more problems than subsequent experience has actually shown. Martin (2005) and Zullo (2006) both demonstrate that contracting, although not perfect, has not led to many of the problems that were earlier anticipated. Contracting has evolved into a variety of approaches, some more advantageous to some agencies than others, and some that lend themselves to accountability more readily than others. There are capitation contracts, a form of purchase of service, which provide services to specified numbers of eligible clients, paid for by the government entity and delivered by the contract agency. There are performance-based contracts such as those described by Martin (2005).

Although contracting has had positive effects, problems do arise. In some cases, agencies have incentives to use less costly arrangements for services, such as those already being provided in the community. One of the negative elements of such incentives, according to Poertner and Rapp (2007), is to discourage agencies from taking on clients with more severe needs.

Poertner and Rapp (2007) also caution that some contracts do not benefit agencies. For example, when contracted services reimburse only for services provided to clients that were referred to the agency, income depends on the number of referrals actually made. If there are few or no referrals, the income is less than expected. The agency may have tooled up to provide the services by employing more staff, renting additional offices, or otherwise dedicating resources to the activities of the contract. Without activity, the resources may have been dedicated, but there will inadequate funds to pay for these costs.

As is the potential case with any service delivery, contracted or public agency-provided, the most necessary help may not be provided and the services available may be limited to those that are not central to the client's need. For example, the client may need transportation to service providers or medical facilities, but the contract may not provide for such assistance.

The States and Contracting

In its 2005 report, the American Public Human Services Association drew several conclusions about contracting. For example, they call for federal regulations to be prospective rather than retroactive so that states are not penalized for actions or failures to act on requirements about which they had no prior warning. One of their main concerns, one that is often mentioned in public discussions of federal legislation, is that the federal government should refrain from making states responsible for activities for which there is no federal funding. Called "unfunded mandates," such requirements are a major area of contention between the state and federal governments. They also call for the federal government to be reasonable in its demands for data and reports on federally funded human services programs.

Conclusion

Few elements of human services management are quite as important as the organization, financing, and structure of social agencies of all kinds—federal, state, and local; public, nonprofit, and proprietary. These are the issues that preoccupy those who serve in management roles, whatever the kind of organization or unit they manage.

Organizational success is often a function of the structure chosen by the organization. The nature and extent of the organization's financing are also always perennial and critical issues in organizational effectiveness. The relatively new process of governmental support for human services, usually through contracting, is a direction that is making a significant difference in human services funding. It is also demonstrating ways in which government and the nonprofit and for-profit human services sectors may blend their objectives and activities.

The other chapters in this book necessarily allude to the structure and financing of the organization, always critical—perhaps the most critical—issues in the management of organizations.

References

American Public Human Services Association. (2005). *Crossroads II: New directions in social policy.* Washington, DC: Author.

Barker, R. (2003). *Social work dictionary* (3rd ed.). Washington, DC: NASW Press.

Billitteri, T. J., & Stehle, V. (1998, July 16). Charities breathe easier after court decision on gift annuities: Model law delayed. *Chronicle of Philanthropy,* p. 40.

Bray, I. M. (2005). *Effective fundraising for nonprofits: Real world strategies that work.* Berkeley, CA: Nolo.

Committee on Ways and Means, U.S. House of Representatives. (2004, March). *2004 Green book: Background material and data on the programs within the jurisdiction of the Committee on Ways and Means.* Washington, DC: U.S. Government Printing Office.

Council on Accreditation of Services for Families and Children. (1997). *Behavioral health care standards: United States edition.* New York: Author.

Foundation Center. (2008). *Get started.* Retrieved from http://www.foundationcenter.org

Gibelman, M. (1995). Purchasing social services. In R. L. Edwards (Ed.), *Encyclopedia of social work* (19th ed., pp. 1998–2007). Washington, DC: NASW Press.

Ginsberg, L. H. (1998). *Conservative social welfare policy.* Chicago: Nelson-Hall.

Ginsberg, L. H., & Keyes, P. L. (1995). *New management in human services* (2nd ed.). Washington, DC: NASW Press.

Goldstein, H. (1993, July 13). Government contracts are emasculating boards and turning charities into agents of the state. *Chronicle of Philanthropy,* p. 41.

Grobman, G. M. (2005). *The nonprofit handbook* (4th ed.). Harrisburg, PA: White Hat.

Hall, H. (1998, July 16). Non-profit groups gird for double-digit increases in postage rates. *Chronicle of Philanthropy,* p. 39.

Hall, R. H. (1982). *Organizations: Structure and process* (3rd ed.). Englewood Cliffs, NJ: Prentice Hall.

Harman, R. D., & Associates. (2005). *The Jossey-Bass handbook of nonprofit management.* San Francisco: Jossey-Bass.

Kadlec, D. (2007, March 5) Rethinking nonprofits. *Time,* p. 74.

Kamerman, S. B., & Kahn, A. (1998, June). *Privatization, contracting and reform of child and family social services.* Retrieved November 17, 2006, from http://76.12.61.196/publications/private.htm

Kramer, R. M. (1994). Voluntary agencies and the contract culture: "Dream or nightmare?" *Social Service Review, 68*(1), 33–60.

Lauffer, A. (1997). *Grants, etc.* Thousand Oaks, CA: Sage.

Light, P. C. (2000). Making nonprofits work: A report on the tides of nonprofit management reform. Washington, DC: The Aspen Institute, Brookings Institution Press.

Light, P. C. (2002). Pathways to nonprofit excellence. Washington, DC: The Aspen Institute, Brookings Institution Press.

Martin, L. L. (2005). Performance-based contracting for human services: Does it work? *Administration in Social Work, 29*(1), 63–78.

Moore, J. (1998, August 13). A corporate challenge for charities. *Chronicle of Philanthropy,* pp. 1, 34–36.

Morales, A. T., & Sheafor, B. W. (2002). *The many faces of social workers.* Boston: Allyn & Bacon.

Murray, C. (2006). *In our hands: A plan to replace the welfare state.* Washington, DC: AEI Press.

Page, W. J. (1988). Organizational structure and service delivery arrangements in human services. In J. Rabin & M. B. Steinhauer (Eds.), Handbook on human services administration (pp. 45–75). New York: Marcel Dekker.

Panel on civic renewal adds another voice to calls for tax incentives to promote giving. (1998, July 16). *Chronicle of Philanthropy,* p. 51.

Poertner, J., & Rapp, C. A. (2007). *Textbook of social administration: The consumer centered approach.* Binghamton, NY: Haworth.

Quindlen, A. (2006, December 11). Real food for thought. *Newsweek,* p. 110.

Rabinovitz, J. (1997, October 24). Company hits snags running welfare plan. *New York Times,* p. A25.

Shorter Oxford English dictionary. (2002). New York: Oxford University Press.

Skidmore, R. A. (1990). *Social work administration* (2nd ed.). Englewood Cliffs, NJ: Prentice Hall.

Skwiot, R. (2007). For love or money: The rise of for-profit social services. *Social Impact,* pp. 16–23.

Smith, S. R. (1989). Federal funding, nonprofit agencies, and victim services. In H. W. Demone, Jr., & M. Gibelman (Eds.), *Services for sale: Purchasing health and human services* (pp. 215–227). New Brunswick, NJ: Rutgers University Press.

UncleFed's Tax Board. (2004). *1996 Taxpayer Bill of Rights II.* Retrieved May 19, 2008, from http://www.unclefed.com/TxprBoR/1996/index.html

U.S. Census Bureau. (2008). *The 2008 statistical abstract.* Retrieved May 19, 2008, from http://www.census.gov/compendia/statab/

Van Riper, T. (2006, November 16). *Milton Friedman dies.* Retrieved November 20, 2006, from http://www.forbes.com/business/2006/11/16/economist-milton-friedman-dies-biz-cx_tvr_1116friedman.html

Wellford, W. H., & Gallagher, J. G. (1988). *Unfair competition: The challenge to charitable exemption.* Washington, DC: The National Assembly of National Voluntary Health and Social Welfare Organizations.

The White House. (n.d.). *Partnering with the federal government: Some do's and don'ts for faith-based organizations.* Retrieved March 1, 2007, from http://www.whitehouse.gov/government/fbci/guidance/partnering.html#10

The White House, Office of Management and Budget. (n.d.). *Fiscal year 2009 budget of the U.S. government.* Retrieved May 16, 2008, from http://www.whitehouse/gov/omb

The Workforce Alliance. (2006). Retrieved November 21, 2006, from http://www.workforcealliance.org

Zullo, R. (2006). Is social service contracting coercive, competitive, or collaborative? Evidence from the case allocation patterns of child protective services. *Administration in Social Work, 30*(3), 25–42.

CHAPTER 5

What Human Services Managers Do and Why They Do It

David Menefee

Hasenfeld (1983) tells us that human services organizations have unique characteristics that set them apart from organizations in the private, for-profit sector. Human services are in the business of restoring, maintaining, and/or enhancing the welfare of individuals. Changing people is a very value-laden mission subject to a wide variety of interpretations, sometimes leading to a great deal of conflict among opposing interest groups. Human services also tend to have ambiguous and conflicting goals that are especially difficult to quantify and relate to the processes that serve them. It is difficult to know the effects that a particular human services technology has on client outcomes, especially when outcome measures are absent, unreliable, or invalid. It is also difficult to manage the work of human services agencies because the work usually takes place in a private relationship between the client and his or her caseworker. Finally, human services management in these organizations is often not viewed by frontline workers as essential to the welfare of clients. These characteristics make human services organizations among the most difficult to manage (Drucker, 2006).

This chapter defines human services management as a set of informed and competent management responses to environmental (internal and external) demands that continuously improve an agency's capacity to serve its customers. The chapter begins by describing the shape of human services management practice illuminated by the pioneering studies of the late 1970s and early 1980s. Subsequent investigations of management practice based upon this foundation are presented and integrated into a comprehensive three-dimensional core competencies practice model. Each dimension and its associate competencies are described in detail. The reader is then challenged with responding to several case studies that bring alive the way in which the management roles, competencies, and skills are played out in actual situations and get at the question, why managers do what they do. Finally, the last section of the chapter explores the relationship between what managers do and why they do it with a particular emphasis on service effectiveness, the raison d'être of human services.

The Shape of Management Practice in the Human Services

Early Studies

What do human services managers do and why do they do it? To answer this question, Patti (1977) conducted one of the earliest and most definitive empirical studies of what human services managers do. He used interview data provided by 90 managers in human services agencies to identify and prioritize 13 activities according to the amount of time they devoted to each during a typical work week. Supervising, information processing, controlling, direct practice, planning, and coordinating were among the most time-consuming activities, whereas less time was spent in extracurricular activities, representing, evaluating, negotiating, budgeting, staffing, and supplying. Cashman (1978) found that human services managers spent the greater part of their time administering, communicating, planning, and implementing, while less time was spent in such activities as counseling, evaluating, and temporary assignments. In a similar study, Files (1981) identified and prioritized 14 management tasks according to the proportion of time devoted by each of 50 human services managers. She then organized these tasks under the eight management functions of supervising, planning, coordinating, negotiating, evaluating, investigating, staffing, and representing.

These early studies set the stage for many management books and published articles over the last three decades. These publications address a wide variety of management competencies and

skills, ranging from communication to evaluation. However, very few are empirical works; most are normative studies that prescribe what managers should do and why they should do it (Wimpfheimer, 2004). Further, since these studies of management activity use different conceptual and descriptive frameworks, it is difficult to comparatively analyze them. Therefore, in order to organize and better understand these normative and empirical works, we will introduce an integration of two popular human services management practice models (1) the Triangle of Practice Model (TPM; Austin, Kettner, & Kruzich, 2002) and (2) the Core Competencies Model (CCM; Menefee, 2000, 2004; Menefee & Thompson, 1994). The integration of these two models produces a clear conceptual framework for human services management practice, education, and future research. We will refer to this integrated model as the Triangle of Practice Core Competencies Model (TPCCM). Before integrating them, we will introduce each of these models separately.

The Triangle of Practice Model (TPM)

The TPM (Austin et al., 2002) was developed using a qualitative research process by which the authors reviewed and assessed recent textbooks and casebooks in human services administration. This extensive study produced a model of human services management that rests on three fundamental roles: leadership, interactional, and analytic. Effective performance of the leadership role requires the human services manager, working collaboratively with internal and external stakeholders, to (1) define the mission of the agency, (2) create a vision for the future, and (3) construct a bridge or plan for moving the agency from its current mission to its future state. Effective performance of the interactional role requires the human services manager to (1) build productive relationships and communicate effectively with key constituencies; (2) advocate for agency goals, objectives, and action plans; and (3) garner support for achieving predetermined program outcomes. Effective performance of the analytic role requires the human services manager to (1) secure and manage resources needed for realizing the mission and vision through everyday operations; (2) analyze and influence policy that may have direct effect on operations; and (3) evaluate the clinical, managerial, organizational, and environmental impact of services.

The Core Competencies Model (CCM)

The CCM (Menefee, 2000, 2004; Menefee & Thompson, 1994) was developed and validated empirically over the course of 15 years of research in the field. This model identifies 12 core practice competencies and their associated skill sets necessary for effective human services management. The competencies are communicating, boundary spanning, futuring, organizing, leveraging resources, managing resources, evaluating, policy practice, advocating, supervising, facilitating, and team building. Each of these core competencies and their associated skill sets are described below.

Manager as Communicator. The importance of effective communication in organizations cannot be overemphasized. Managers are directly responsible for the effectiveness of communication, both within the organization and between the organization and its external stakeholders. The skills of communication include exchanging written and verbal information between the agency and its external stakeholders; writing reports, memos, newsletters, and instructional materials; making formal presentations to groups outside the agency; and exchanging information with internal staff (Menefee & Thompson, 1994). New modes of communication like fax, electronic mail, voice mail, Internet conferencing, and telecommuting are now common management practices.

Manager as Boundary Spanner. Establishing interorganizational relations, developing partnerships, and integrating service delivery systems

are essential activities for agency survival (Healy, 1991; Moore, 1992; O'Looney, 1994). Managers need to know how to network, collaborate with, and influence political figures, collateral service providers, government officials, funding sources, and other key persons in order to establish and maintain support and funding for their agencies. Managers need to use these same skills with agency staff in order to enlist their support of the agency's ever-changing priorities. Some authors refer to this cluster of activities as boundary spanning (Menefee & Thompson, 1994), which involves managing relationships, networking, and influencing others. Managing relationships is the work a manager does to establish and maintain mutually beneficial and supportive relationships with internal and external stakeholders. When networking, a manager creates and nurtures linkages between his or her agency and major stakeholders in the environment (Kenney, 1990). Finally, influencing is the work a manager does to engender support for a particular perspective or action through the appropriate use of personal or organizational resources.

Manager as Futurist. There is an increased emphasis placed on the human services manager's ability to forecast trends in the external environment and develop alternative and innovative strategies for responding to these forces (Thompson & Kim, 1992). This is a time of great uncertainty and instability in the industry. These conditions require that human services managers identify and interpret emerging national, state, and local trends, that they anticipate the impact of these trends on their agency, and that they continuously realign their agency structures, processes, and conditions. The human services manager needs to define and communicate the agency's vision, mission, and strategic goals (Arndt, 1996; Steiner, Gross, Ruffolo, & Murray, 1994). In addition, managers need to build a structure and process for ensuring that the agency's strategic plans are realized (Menefee, 1997) and not simply retired on a shelf. This will demand that human services managers seek creative ways to structure and manage programs and services and identify ways to influence service quality. They have to translate strategic goals into action plans that spawn new programs and prepare staff for helping the agency accomplish these changes. In sum, the agency director and program manager must focus the agency on futuring (Menefee & Thompson, 1994) while simultaneously maintaining the effectiveness of current programs and services. The process of futuring demands skill in "reading the environment" (Morgan, 1988), strategic planning (Bryson, 2004), and innovating (Keys, 1988). When a manager "reads the environment," he or she identifies emerging national, state, and local trends and anticipates their impact on the agency. Strategic planning is the work a manager does to create a vision and purpose for the agency and to make the vision actionable through the efforts of others. A manager is innovative when he or she introduces or encourages others to introduce creative ideas that solve current problems and prevent future ones.

Manager as Organizer. Turbulent environments require organizations to change their internal structures, processes, and/or conditions in order to adapt. This is referred to as *aligning* (Menefee & Thompson, 1994). Aligning includes organizing, delegating, and staffing. Organizing is the work a manager does to arrange and structure the work of the agency so as to optimize the use of its human and material resources. Organizing involves a full range of skills, including establishing an organizational structure, developing formal work relationships among positions, determining workflow, and designing/redesigning jobs for individuals and groups (Bennett, Evans, Tattersall, 1993; Hartman & Feinauer, 1994). In delegating work, a manager assigns formal responsibility and authority to those whose role it is to perform the work. The manager helps to clarify the role of the job incumbent and reviews his or her performance expectations, holding him or her accountable for predetermined outcomes. The ability to recruit, hire, orient and train, reward, and discipline people effectively is called staffing or human resource management. Staffing is a critical skill for the human services

manager (Levine, 1995; Musser-Granski & Carrillo, 1997; Perlman, 1994). It involves successful creation of a high-performing team of workers that comes to the agency not by accident, but by careful and purposeful matching of the right skills with the job requirements. Good staffing maximizes the contributions of the worker to the team and to the organization (Kraus & Pillsbury, 1994).

Manager as Resource Administrator. (Leveraging and Managing Resources). Managers must also acquire and manage the resources necessary to operate the agency and serve the client. Leveraging resources (Menefee & Thompson, 1994) involves securing appropriate inputs, including human, financial, information, physical, and the like. Once secured, these resources must be managed efficiently and effectively. We saw earlier how staffing and human resource management are critical functions of the human services manager. Managers must also secure and manage revenue (governmental and philanthropic) such that agency funding streams are diversified, thus reducing dependency on any single source (Jaffe & Jaffe, 1990). Cultivating funding sources often involves developing relationships, networking, and influencing potential contributors over extended periods of time, not just during financial crises. Moreover, the manager must be able to track and respond to funding opportunities when they present themselves. This demands a host of skills including research and grant writing, conducting fundraising drives, and successful marketing (Kaye, 1994; Segal, 1991). It also requires that the manager represent his or her agency to the community and the broader environment through effective marketing (Bilbrey, 1991; Segal, 1991), public relations (Loring & Wimberley, 1993), and mass media campaigns. Maintaining a good image is critical to continued funding. More and more, revenue sources are requiring managers to show evidence of results achieved with donor monies as a condition of continued funding (Courtney & Collins, 1994). Valid and reliable performance data is, therefore, a vital resource for fund development and other management functions. Sophisticated management information systems that inform the agency of internal and external conditions have to be developed and maintained if the human services manager is to comply with these requests and take advantage of opportunities in the environment (Berman, 1989).

Physical resources have to be secured and managed in order to provide the materials necessary for accomplishing work. Securing and managing these resources requires an understanding of procurement and purchasing; accounting and bookkeeping; and financial planning, budgeting, and reporting. Even if the manager is not directly involved in these activities, he or she must understand such concepts as breakeven analysis, cost accounting, alternative choice decisions, pricing, operations budgeting, and interpretation of financial reports (Anthony & Young, 2002). In fact, in today's complex accountability environment, the human services manager who is accountable for the performance of a formal responsibility center (cost, revenue, profit, or investment) must know and apply these technologies well beyond the basic level.

Manager as Evaluator. Evaluating is the work a manager performs to ascertain service needs and determine the agency's effectiveness in providing services (Menefee & Thompson, 1994). Needs assessment is used extensively in HSOs to design community drug prevention programs (Colby, 1997), identify family service needs, improve service delivery systems (Cheung, 1993), develop cultural sensitivity training (Chau, 1993), assess maternal and child health (Julia, 1992), and so on. Program evaluation is a management tool used to determine the effectiveness and efficiency of individual program components or entire service systems (Grasso & Epstein, 1992). Although still not a common management practice, this technology is used to investigate program cost-effectiveness, program stabilization, agency functioning, and a variety of other outcomes (Martin & Kettner, 1996). The research skills for planning and conducting good needs assessments and program evaluations are sophisticated and complex. They

include quantitative and qualitative methods such as survey research, experimental and quasi-experimental designs, single-system designs, time-series designs, and field studies (Rossi, Freeman, & Lipsey, 2003). They may require the manager to develop surveys, perform various statistical operations, interpret statistical tests, or write research reports for consumers. At the very least, the manager should know how to screen, hire, and participate with others in the design, implementation, and interpretation of needs assessments and program evaluations. In the future, however, the basics will not be enough. Recently, management and information systems technologies have converged to shift the evaluation paradigm from the now typical annual study to the continuous evaluation of cost and quality at any and all levels of operation (Hicks, 2002; Kinlaw, 1992; for a discussion on performance evaluation techniques, see Chapter 9). Annual assessments are likely to be replaced by monthly performance reviews and ad hoc evaluations, and these will be intimately tied to decisions related to agency legitimization and funding, which come from external sources.

Manager as Policy Practitioner. Policy practice is the work a manager does to develop, interpret, comply with, and influence local, state, and federal policy (Menefee & Thompson, 1994). Managers who engage in policy practice are involved in reading and interpreting federal, state, and local policies and translating these policies into agency structures, conditions, or processes that ensure compliance with federal and state laws. It is often the case that managers must design and implement new programs and services that either blend with current organizational arrangements or necessitate their change. Managers must also act as policy interpreters for agency employees, helping them understand the implications of new and modified policy for organizational arrangements and for service delivery. There is also a need for the human services manager to actively participate in the formulation and administration of policy (Wyers, 1991) at both the state and federal level. Because agencies, their managers, staff, and clients are the recipients of policy legislation, they need to have a hand in crafting policy by influencing policy-making groups with their knowledge and experience in social problems. In addition, human services managers need to be savvy in organizing community and advocacy groups for the purposes of influencing federal and state policy. Finally, the role of the human services manager in policy implementation analysis overlaps his or her role as evaluator (Copeland & Wexler, 1995).

Manager as Advocate. Advocating is an essential activity of human services managers (Menefee & Thompson, 1994). Advocating is the work a manager performs to further the cause of individuals or groups before major stakeholders. Managers may advocate inside the organization or in the environment, and they may do so at the case or class level (Ezell, 2000). Case advocacy pertains to representing or lobbying for individual rights, whereas class advocacy is concerned with representing or lobbying for the rights of groups. Skills include representing significant others; representing the agency; expressing management's viewpoint to staff and vice versa; lobbying at local, state, and national level; testifying; and establishing contact with legislators and government administrators (Ezell, 2000). Using these skills, managers may advocate for community services (Mancoske & Hunzeker, 1994), high-risk clients (Klein & Cnaan, 1995), Medicaid managed care recipients (Perloff, 1996), environmental health (Landrigan & Carlson, 1995), and other important arenas where the disenfranchised my not have the capacity to speak for their own rights. In the future, human services managers as a group must take a more organized and proactive approach to influencing the premises upon which social policy is founded as well as the substance, implementation, and evaluation of that policy (for additional discussion of administrative advocacy, see Chapter 22).

Manager as Supervisor. Supervision is regarded as the cornerstone of clinical practice (Pepper, 1996). The overall objective of supervision is to maximize service effectiveness and efficiency through the day-to-day operations of the unit. Supervising is the work a manager does to direct and guide the delivery of services while simultaneously attending to the socio-emotional needs of the workers. Kadushin and Harkness (2002) present a model of social work supervision that includes three functions: administrative, educational, and supportive. Menefee and Thompson (1994) support this observation with empirical evidence that supervision is composed of coordinating, supporting, and consulting/advising activities. Much of the literature on supervision can be organized using this framework. Effective supervision demands skills in motivating employees (Walsh, 1990), coordinating work and workload (Rauktis & Koeske, 1994), setting goals and limits (Kurland & Salmon, 1992), giving corrective feedback (Latting & Blanchare, 1997), monitoring and improving work processes, educating and consulting with employees (Greene, 1991), controlling outcomes, and supporting the socio-emotional needs of staff. Today's traditional form of supervision will gradually give way to a supervisory partnership between workers who perform tasks and one who coordinates, supports, and advises workers. Some authors have even suggested that, in the near future, the supervisory function will be in jeopardy, with the advent of self-directed work teams (Orsburn, Moran, Musselwhite, & Zenger, 1990; for further discussion of supervision, see Chapter 13).

Manager as Facilitator. Facilitation includes all of the strategies the manager uses to enlist the efforts of workers in accomplishing the vision, mission, and goals of the agency. Facilitating is the work a human services manager performs to orient and enable others to carry out the work required (Menefee & Thompson, 1994) to achieve agency goals. Although this definition sounds much like leadership, we have divorced it from the concept as a precaution to avoid confusion with other multiple and vague definitions of that term (Bass, 1990). Activities associated with facilitating are empowering, developing, and modeling. Human services managers empower their employees by helping them influence agency operations, programs, and services (Staples, 1990). When staff is empowered, they perform better and are more innovative (Guterman & Bargal, 1996; Shera & Page, 1995). Collaborative practice, staff development, and supervisory leadership are all-important elements in building and maintaining an agency that is empowered (Gutierrez, GlenMaye, & Delois, 1995). Furthermore, an agency that is empowered will promote greater job satisfaction and service effectiveness (Shera & Page, 1995). Managers also develop their employees by providing training and education opportunities that improve their expertise (Berman, 1994). Lee (1984) offers managers a process for implementing staff development programs. Using staff participation, training needs are assessed, developmental priorities are identified, training programs are designed, resources are acquired, and training efforts are initiated and subsequently evaluated. Staff training is also used as a strategy for developing the organization as well as its management practices. Finally, human services managers model the practices, beliefs, values, and ethics to which all other employees aspire. Modeling is one of the most important roles of the human services manager because through modeling, workers learn and internalize appropriate behaviors, values, and ethics in the workplace. Collectively, these behaviors, values, and ethics comprise what is known as the organizational culture (Deal & Kennedy, 2000). Active and conscious management of the organizational culture will become increasingly important as the American nonprofit workforce continues to diversify (see Chapter 6 for further discussion of organizational culture).

Manager as Team Builder. Human services managers make extensive use of administrative and clinical groups in agencies and in communities (Gummer, 1995) to accomplish the work of their agency. Coalition and team building is what a manager does to organize and enlist the work of groups to ensure that agency operations are effective and services are available (Menefee & Thompson, 1994). Teams take many forms. They

may be interagency (Iles & Auluck, 1990), multidisciplinary, interdisciplinary (Gibelman, 1993), or intradisciplinary. Managers use teams for a variety of reasons: to identify, analyze, and solve problems related to agency performance (Hodge-Williams, Doub, & Busky, 1995); to promote creativity and innovation (Pavilon, 1993); to improve the quality of services; to orient and train interdisciplinary service delivery teams; and many others. Building high-performing teams is no easy task. The manager must be well versed in group processes and able to help groups master the tasks inherent in every stage of development. This requires skills in managing the socioemotional as well as the task dimensions of group behavior. In addition, managers need to plan and manage meetings of administrative and clinical groups. They must prepare and disseminate agendas, arrange meeting facilities, notify participants, set meeting objectives, ensure full and balanced participation, focus the group on task, accomplish the intended outcomes, and follow up on meeting decisions. These steps are critical if group members are to have confidence in the value of teamwork. Managers use these same skills to organize coalitions. Coalitions are a major vehicle for organizing and accomplishing social change. Coalitions are used to spearhead citizen rights to housing (Ferlauto, 1991), to improve delivery of services to rural areas (Miner & Jacobsen, 1990), to expand social work's role in genetic services (Black & Weiss, 1990), to influence urban policy agendas (Sink & Stowers, 1989), and for many other purposes. Building coalitions and teams is expected to persist as a major social work vehicle for accomplishing change in organizations and communities well into the 21st century.

The Triangle of Practice Core Competencies Model (TPCCM): An Integrated Perspective and Case Study Challenge

Figure 5.1 represents a conceptual integration of the two models discussed above, thus forming

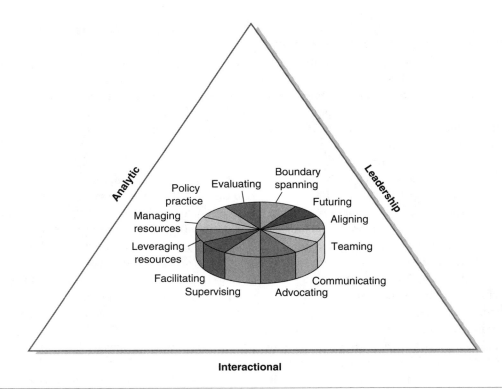

Figure 5.1   The "triangle of practice" model. Twelve competencies model of management based upon original research conducted by Menefee and Thompson (1994) and organized by the Austin, Kettner, & Kruzich (2002) framework.

SOURCE: Austin and Hopkins (2004, p. 139).

the TPCCM. The remainder of this chapter will integrate the two models using three case studies to demonstrate each of the three roles of the TPM along with their respective core competencies. The case studies are real-life management situations in human services organizations experienced by the author as manager, consultant, or researcher. The names of the characters in the case studies have been changed, but the story lines are factual.

A "Case Analysis" follows that is designed to inform the reader of the author's opinion regarding alternative strategies that might be used to remedy the management problems inherent in the case. Let us begin with the case study related to the leadership dimension of the model.

Case Study in the Leadership Role

In early 2006, it was announced by the newly appointed Executive Director of the Office of Behavioral Health and Housing (OBHH) that the Division of Mental Health (DMH) and the Alcohol and Drug Abuse Division (ADAD) of the Department of Human Services were to be merged into a Behavioral Health Services (BHS) Division. The new Director of Behavioral Health Services held a meeting following the announcement and distributed a two-page memorandum explaining the purpose of the merger. The entire staff of both divisions attended the meeting to listen to the rationale and ask questions regarding the new division's mission, vision, and structure. No answers to their questions were forthcoming, at least for several months.

In the interim, a great deal of informal discussion about the merger took place in hallways, break rooms, and behind closed doors. Staff wanted to know why and how the decision was made. Personnel in each division wanted to know what they were doing wrong to warrant such a merger. Scenarios designed to inform all possible futures were rampant, some optimistic, others not. Staff from both divisions became confused, threatened, and withdrawn from each other and members of the other division. Interpersonal conflict emerged on just about every decision item because staff no longer knew their formal roles, role relationships, responsibilities, lines of authority, or decision processes. Within the year, there were multiple resignations on both the management and staff levels. It seemed as though the division was disintegrating before their very eyes.

Case Study Analysis

What went right? The Director of OBHH and the new Director of BHS had a shared vision (futuring). They envisioned a new organization that would address statewide mental health issues, alcohol and drug abuse issues, and co-occurring disorders (futuring). They saw it as a new opportunity to address unmet mental health needs while capitalizing on the human resource expertise that currently existed in both divisions. They saw the potential for improving efficiencies through economies of scale (organizing). They looked forward to improved communication in their new organizational structure (organizing). Staff would be working together more effectively, meeting the needs of a new genre of clients (teaming). They spanned several boundaries to garner support for their vision. They obtained support from the State Director of Human Services, the State Mental Health Planning and Advisory Council, and the Community Behavioral Healthcare Council (boundary spanning). Even the Governor's office was in support of the concept.

What went wrong? The Directors of OBHH and BHS failed to span the boundaries within their own divisions (boundary spanning). They did not involve key staff in the decision to merge the two divisions at the initial phases of conceptualization (teaming). The merger was considered a foregone conclusion by many staff, and they were resentful that they were not included from the start (teaming). This resulted in a tremendous amount of resistance to the merger and a rapid increase in role confusion and conflict (organizing). Without the help of those with the expertise, it was difficult to develop a concrete plan to achieve the merger, and without a concrete plan, the merger was difficult to justify and accomplish (futuring).

What could have been done differently? The merger would have received much greater support from divisional staff had they been involved in the decision and conceptualization of "BHS" from the beginning (teaming). If all key stakeholders recognize and agree on the need for change, the probability of their supporting the change is increased greatly (boundary spanning). Recognizing the need for change is the first essential step in moving an organization from a current to a future state (futuring). The collaborative model of change management involves engaging key stakeholders in envisioning the future and creating a concrete plan to realize that vision. A major byproduct of realizing a vision is a new organizational arrangement (organizing). (For further discussion of leadership in change situations, see Chapter 7.)

What now? It is time for the Directors of OBHH and BHS to openly recognize and communicate the error of their change strategy (teaming) and to reengage the staff in developing a new function and form of organization (futuring and organizing). They might do this by including key internal stakeholders in designing and implementing the change process (teaming) that will result in a merger of the two divisions. In addition, it will be extremely important for the directors to include external stakeholders', especially clients', input into the design of future programs and services (boundary spanning). These steps become the foundation for strategic planning and management to realize the vision of the new BHS (futuring).

Case Study in the Interactional Role

It's 2:30 AM and Paul, the director of a human services consulting firm, is at his computer trying to finish a quarterly site visit report and multimedia PowerPoint presentation for the Council on Accreditation (a nonprofit that accredits human services agencies based on a site audit of performance standards) that is due this morning at 10:00 AM. It is the fourth COA report he and his staff have produced in the last year, and somehow he always ends up having to write it himself. His staff goes home early and he sits up until the wee hours of the morning finishing *their* work! He must be doing something wrong. Let's see. . . .

Several years ago when they first opened their human services consulting firm, Paul sat down with Samantha, the Research Associate, and explained to her what her role was with respect to the COA report. She is responsible for collecting the data on site visits by conducting structured telephone interviews, disseminating and collecting scannable optical mark reader mail surveys from site visit team leaders and members, scanning the surveys as they come in the mail, recording narrative input, and creating an integrated database for data analysis using the Statistical Package for the Social Sciences (SPSS). Once the database is completed, Samantha notifies Roger, the Data Analyst, so that he can begin the analysis. How could that be any clearer?

Paul also met with Roger when the firm first opened to show him exactly what he needed to do with respect to data analysis and report writing. The statistical analysis was basic, though lengthy, frequency tables, descriptive statistics,

charts, and graphs on each agency that had a site visit during the quarter (N = 100). The narrative data had to be analyzed using a special computer application and integrated into the findings of the quantitative analysis. The format of the approximately 130-page report had already been designed, with a section on the overall findings followed by individual agency reports. When Roger finishes the report, he notifies Susan and she uses it to create a presentation. That's pretty straightforward.

Susan, the Research Liaison, is responsible for putting together the PowerPoint presentation summary of all of the findings, printing all documents to be distributed at the meeting, and making the proper arrangements for the meeting (time, place, equipment, invitations, etc). Paul reviewed the specifications of the standard COA PowerPoint presentation with her. It is about 20 minutes long, highlighting the main points found in the first section of the report and integrating and summarizing the findings at the individual agency level. Pretty simple, wouldn't you say?

About two weeks before the quarterly report was due, Samantha went to Paul and complained she had not been able to get all the data in from the agencies and she was behind in creating the database Roger needed to do the analysis and report. Paul told her to keep trying and to do the best she could given the circumstances. Meanwhile, Roger was visibly stressed out because Paul asked him how the report was "coming along." Toward the end of the week, he went to Paul's office and told him that the report was not going to be ready in two weeks and asked whether Paul could call COA to negotiate an extension. Paul told him that Samantha said she would have the database in a couple more days and that Susan had already made arrangements for the meeting and was waiting for the report to complete the PowerPoint presentation. Roger shook his head and walked out of Paul's office, seemingly furious. Susan poked her head in and said, "What's wrong with Roger? He seems upset by something. By the way, could you speak with him about getting me that report; we are running out of time for me to complete the COA PowerPoint Presentation."

The day before yesterday, Samantha, Roger, and Susan scheduled a meeting with Paul in his office. Each had an explanation for why he or she couldn't get the job done. "I can't get all the data in (Samantha); I can't do the report without the data (Roger); I can't do the PowerPoint presentation without the report" (Susan). Paul said, "Here we are again; we've been here before; why can't we get this report completed without going through all this?"

It's now 3:30 AM and Paul is fast asleep on his keyboard, having dreams of statistical problems he cannot solve. Perhaps next time he will be able to accomplish this work without having to stay up all night the night before to get it done!

As the director, what steps will you take now to remedy the situation?

Case Study Analysis

What went right? Not much. Paul, the director, oriented each of his staff to particular jobs and his expectations of performance (facilitating). He listens actively to his staff's communications regarding their concerns about the report (communicating).

What went wrong? The director is not doing a very good job of conveying critical task information to his staff (communicating); he appears to be somewhat preoccupied and lacks concern for task and socio-emotional aspects of the work group (supervision); he is not enabling his workers to successfully complete all of the tasks required of the work (facilitating); and finally, he is not advocating for his work group by engaging in an active pursuit of the task details that led to the current situation (advocating).

From the start: The director could have identified all of the tasks required to produce the report (supervising), determined which of his staff were willing and able to complete the tasks (supervising), provided on-the-job training to those who needed it (facilitating), and developed a team approach to project planning and management (communicating and advocating). These steps would have assisted the director and team to quickly identify and evaluate the particular problems that repeatedly affected the team's ability to produce the report. In this particular case, Samantha, although willing to do all that was required to create a usable database for Roger, did not have the necessary skills to do the job. She needed training (facilitating) in optical mark reader technologies; she was having a great deal of difficulty scanning the hundreds of surveys that were arriving daily.

What now? It would be prudent for the director to become more involved in supervising the work of his staff so that he could understand where the problems were with task completion (supervising). This would enable him to provide more immediate corrective feedback on performance (supervising), improve the workflow from data collection to report generation (supervising), and monitor task completion through to project completion.

Case Study in the Analytic Role

Joint resolution 1084 is sitting on Pam's (the Director of Data and Evaluation) desk. A group of legislators in the house and senate have been lobbied by a local child welfare advocacy group to support a "promising" intervention designed to reduce the recidivism rate of juveniles who are held in detention centers for anything from truancy to grand theft auto (policy practice). In this pilot program, mental health services will be provided to children in two detention centers. These services are designed to improve the mental health status of the juvenile and thereby reduce the chance that he or she will return to detention subsequent to leaving the center (policy practice). The legislative committee is asking for input into the final bill and fiscal note to be review by the house and senate (leveraging resources). They want to know what services (case management, group therapy, individual counseling, etc.) will be provided as part of the intervention; what specific objectives will be accomplished; what action steps (program steps, schedules, accountabilities, budgets) will be taken to implement the intervention; and what outcomes will be achieved as a result of the intervention (managing resources). They also want an estimate of what it might cost to support such a pilot program; where the costs will be allocated by line item; how the central question in the joint resolution will be answered (evaluating); and what implications the findings might have for future state policy concerning juvenile justice (policy practice). Pam has to complete this request by 6:00 PM before today's close of the legislative session.

Case Study Analysis

The service package proposed in this intervention is called *wraparound services*. These include a host of social service technologies depending upon the clinician's assessment of the individual client's needs. Examples of these technologies are functional family therapy, anger management counseling, multisystemic therapy, and dialectic behavioral therapy, as well as others. In fact, the agency expects to rely on many of the multiple service technologies it currently has in its service portfolio to treat the detainee population. It is expected that 150 youth will receive "individualized wraparound services" under this program.

Specific Goals, Objectives, and Outcomes. The goals and objectives of the program are shown in Table 5.1. The outcomes expected from these programs and services are shown in Table 5.2.

The resources required to support 150 clients for a period of one year are 2 Mental Health Counselor FTEs, .25 FTE administrative support staff, and .25 FTE program coordinators. Psychiatric services will be obtained contractually at a cost of approximately $12,000 per year. Operating expenses include administrative overhead, professional liability insurance, medication and testing, telephones, data access, furnishing, postage, and computers and computer software.

Table 5.1   Program Goals and Objectives

Program Goals	Program Objectives
Reduce recidivism among detained program youth	• Identify detained youth in need of mental health treatment. • Test detained youth and provide clinical recommendations on treatment. • Provide recommended treatment to youth and their families. • Prepare youth and families with transitional plan to move youth from detention to community. • Support detained youth and families with educational/vocational opportunities.
Improve mental health among detained program youth	• Develop treatment plans based on client needs and strengths. • Provide evidence-based practice interventions to clients. • Make 24-hour crisis intervention services available.
Reduce substance abuse among detained program youth	• Include substance abuse treatment goals in treatment. • Include substance abuse counseling in treatment. • Educate youth on strategies to avoid substance abuse.

Table 5.2   Expected Outcomes From Programs and Services

Program Goals	Expected Program Outcomes
Reduce recidivism among detained program youth	65% of detained youth who complete the program remain living in their homes and are not readmitted to another detention facility as a result of new charges.
Improve mental health among detained program youth	65% of detained youth completing the program will evidence improved mental health functioning as measured by the Mental Health Functioning Index.
Reduce substance abuse among detained program youth	65% of detained youth who complete the program will show reduced substance use as measured by a self-report substance abuse questionnaire.

The total expenses to serve 150 detained youth, improve their mental health, and keep them from recidivating is $450,000 for the first year of operation (leveraging and managing resources).

The evaluation designed to inform the major question of whether or not the program achieved its outcomes is a simple pre-test post-test pre-experimental design (evaluating). Using a comprehensive mental health evaluation instrument, researchers will assess the mental health status of the detainee on multiple psychosocial dimensions before and after services are delivered (evaluating). Researchers will also calculate the rate of recidivism among detainees who received program services and compare this rate to those who did not receive services while in detention (evaluating). Finally, a post-detention self-report survey will be administered to determine the extent to which adolescents are using illegal substances six months after they complete the program (evaluating).

The actual effects on state juvenile justice policy are not yet determined because the program is currently underway. Legislative interest in the initiative tends to ebb and flow (policy practice). Program reports to inform the legislature are due every year, and special interest groups such as mental health advocates, juvenile justice advocates, government representatives from the Division of Mental Health and the Department of Juvenile Justice, and State financial officers meet regularly to review program services, goals, objectives, outcomes, costs, and effectiveness (policy practice). Of course, at this point, there is much conjecture about the effects of the program; some are rooted in fact, other in fantasy, but in the end, either will certainly impact legislative decision making.

By using three case studies, this chapter has demonstrated how TPCCM can be used to conceptualize, analyze, and resolve a variety of human services management conundrums occurring in actual practice. More important, though, the model can be used as a tool for preventing ineffective management practice by considering the potential impact a manager's or management team's decision and/or action under one role might have on remaining roles and/or competencies. Certainly, how management practices the leadership role affects practice in all the other key roles and competencies. For example, before launching into the role of leadership to create mission and vision, strategic plans, and organizational structure, the manager or management team must consider the importance of involving key constituencies (internal and external) in the planning process and garnering their support for achieving predetermined program outcomes (interactional role), as this will affect management's ability to secure and manage resources needed for realizing the mission and vision and demonstrating the impact of agency performance on service effectiveness (analytic role). Hence, the TPCCM model, understood as a set of complex integrated roles and competencies, is a valuable tool not only for solving management problems but for preventing them as well. Before making your next management decision, revisit this model and consider the potential impact of that decision in relation to your other roles and competencies. Does your decision and its associated actions reflect consistency and continuity of management practice from your perspective and from that of others?

What Managers Do and Agency Outcomes

What managers do inevitably affects agency outcomes in some way at various points in time (for further discussion on this topic, see Chapter 8). These outcomes can be organized into several categories: productivity/efficiency, service quality, client change, employee morale, client satisfaction, and financial viability. Although the primary reason for human services is service effectiveness (service quality + client change + client satisfaction), this cannot be achieved without concern for efficiency, employee morale, and financial viability. The decisions that managers make and the actions they take have a direct and/or indirect impact on all of these important outcome areas. Through performing the leadership, interactional, and analytic roles and competencies (TPCCM), managers secure and manage resources that are consumed by services and activities that generate outputs and achieve outcomes. This is truly a complex and difficult job.

References

Anthony, R. N., & Young, D. W. (2002). Management control in nonprofit organizations (7th ed.). Burr Ridge, IL: Irwin.

Arndt, E. M. (1996). Creating organizational vision in a hospital social work department: The leitmotif for continuous change management. *Administration in Social Work, 20*(4), 79–87.

Austin, M. J., & Hopkins, K. M. (2004). *Supervision as collaboration in the human services: Building a learning culture.* Newbury Park, CA: Sage.

Bass, B. M. (1990). *Bass & Stogdill's handbook of leadership: Theory, research, and managerial applications* (3rd ed.). New York: Macmillan.

Bennett. P., Evans, R., & Tattersall, A. (1993). Stress and coping in social workers: A preliminary investigation. *British Journal of Social Work, 23*(1), 31–44.

Berman, R. I. (1994). Staff development in mental health organizations. *Administration and Policy in Mental Health, 22*(1), 49–55.

Berman, Y. (1989). The structure of information in organizational frameworks—The social service department. *British Journal of Social Work, 19*(6), 479–489.

Bilbrey, P. (1991). Marketing in mental health services [entire issue]. *Administration and Policy in Mental Health, 19*(2).

Black, R. B., & Weiss, J. O. (1990). Genetic support groups and social workers as partners. *Health and Social Work, 15*(2), 91–99.

Bryson, J. M. (2004). *Strategic planning for public and nonprofit organizations: A guide to strengthening and sustaining organizational achievement* (3rd ed.). San Francisco: Jossey-Bass.

Cashman, J. F. (1978). Training social welfare administrators: The activity dilemma. *Administration in Social Work, 2*(3), 347–358.

Chau, K. L. (1993). Needs assessment for group work with people of color: A conceptual formulation. *Social Work with Groups, 15*(2/3), 53–66.

Cheung, K. F. M. (1993). Needs assessment experience among area agencies on aging. *Journal of Gerontological Social Work, 19*(3/4), 77–93.

Colby, I. C. (1997). Transforming human services organizations through empowerment of neighbors. *Journal of Community Practice, 4*(2), 1–12.

Copeland, V. C., & Wexler, S. (1995). Policy implementation in social welfare: A framework for analysis. *Journal of Sociology and Social Welfare, 22*(3), 51–68.

Courtney, M. E., & Collins, R. C. (1994). New challenges and opportunities in child welfare outcomes and information technologies. *Child Welfare, 73*(5), 359–378.

Deal, T. E., & Kennedy, A. A. (2000). *Corporate cultures: The rites and rituals of corporate life.* New York: The Perseus Books Group.

Drucker, P. F. (2006). *Managing the non-profit organization: Principles and practices.* New York: Collins.

Ezell, M. (2000). Administrators as advocates. *Administration in Social Work, 15*(4), 1–18.

Ferlauto, R. C. (1991). A new approach to low-income housing. *Public Welfare, 49*(3), 30–35.

Files, L. A. (1981). The human services management task: A time allocation study. *Public Administration Review,* 686–692.

Gibelman, M. (1993). School social workers, counselors, and psychologists in collaboration: A shared agenda. *Social Work in Education, 15*(1), 45–51.

Grasso, A. J., & Epstein, I. (1992). Toward a developmental approach to program evaluation. *Administration in Social Work, 16*(3/4), 187–203.

Greene, R. R. (1991). Supervision in social work with the aged and their families. *Journal of Gerontological Social Work, 17*(1/2), 139–144.

Gummer, B. (1995). Go team go! The growing importance of teamwork in organizational life. *Administration in Social Work, 19*(4), 85–100.

Guterman, N. B., & Bargal, D. (1996). Social workers' perceptions of their power and service outcomes. *Administration in Social Work, 20*(3), 1–20.

Gutierrez, L., GlenMaye, L., & DeLois, K. (1995). The organizational context of empowerment practice: Implications for social work administration. *Social Work, 40*(2), 49–58.

Hartman, E. A., & Feinauer, D. (1994). Human resources for the next decade. *Administration and Policy in Mental Health, 22*(1), 27–37.

Hasenfeld, Y. (1983). *Human service organizations.* Englewood Cliffs, NJ: Prentice Hall.

Healy, J. (1991). Linking local services: Coordination in community centres. *Australian Social Work, 44*(4), 5–13.

Hicks, D. T. (2002). *Activity-based costing: Making it work for small and mid-sized businesses* (2nd ed.). New York: John Wiley & Sons.

Hodge-Williams, J., Doub, N. H., & Busky, R. (1995). Total quality management (TQM) in the non-profit setting: The Woodbourne experience. *Residential Treatment for Children and Youth, 12*(3), 19–30.

Iles, P., & Auluck, R. (1990). Team building, interagency team development and social work practice. *The British Journal of Social Work, 20*(2), 151–164.

Jaffe, E. D., & Jaffe, R. (1990). Resource development and social work: Funding early intervention through homemaker services for brain-damaged children in Jerusalem. *International Social Work, 33*(2), 145–156.

Julia, M. (1992). Understanding how to assess maternal and child health needs in a developing country. *Social Development Issues, 14*(2/3), 28–40.

Kadushin, A., & Harkness, D. (2002). *Supervision in social work* (4th ed.). New York: Columbia University Press.

Kaye, L. W. (1994). The effectiveness of services marketing: Perceptions of executive directors of gerontological programs. *Administration in Social Work, 18*(2), 69–85.

Kenney, J. J. (1990). Social work management in emerging health care systems. *Health and Social Work, 15*(1), 22–31.

Keys, P. R. (1988). Administrative entrepreneurship in the public sector. *Administration in Social Work, 12*(2), 59–68.

Kinlaw, D. C. (1992). *Continuous improvement and measurement for total quality: A team-based approach.* Homewood, IL: Irwin.

Klein, A. R., & Cnaan, R. A. (1995). Practice with high-risk clients. *Families in Society, 76*(4), 203–211.

Kraus, A., & Pillsbury, J. B. (1994). Streamlining intake and eligibility system. *Public Welfare, 52*(3), 21–29.

Kurland, R., & Salmon, R. (1992). When problems seem overwhelming: Emphases in teaching, supervision, and consultation. *Social Work, 37*(3), 240–244.

Landrigan, P. J., & Carlson, J. E. (1995). Environmental policy and children's health. *The Future of Children, 5*(2), 34–52.

Latting, J. K., & Blanchare, A. (1997). Empowering staff in a poverty agency: An organization development intervention. *Journal of Community Practice, 4*(3), 59–75.

Lee, L. J. (1984). Self-study: Organization resource in staff development preparation. *Social Casework, 65*(2), 67–73.

Levine, C. H. (1995). Managing human resources: A challenge to urban governments. *Urban Affairs Annual Reviews, 13,* 1995.

Loring, M. T., & Wimberley, E. T. (1993). The time-limited hot line. *Social Work, 38*(3), 344–346.

Mancoske, R. J., & Hunzeker, J. M. (1994). Advocating for community services coordination: An empowerment perspective for planning AIDS services. *Journal of Community Practice, 1*(3), 49–58.

Martin, L., & Kettner, P. (1996). *Measuring the performance of human service programs.* Newbury Park, CA: Sage.

Menefee, D. (1997). Strategic administration of nonprofit human service organizations: A model for executive success in turbulent times. *Administration in Social Work, 21*(2), 1–19.

Menefee, D. (2000). ABM: An innovative business technology for human service organizations. *Administration in Social Work, 24*(2), 67–84.

Menefee, D. (2004). The managerial roles of the supervisor. In M. J. Austin & K. M. Hopkins (Eds.), *Supervision as collaboration in the human services.: Building a learning culture.* Newbury Park, CA: Sage.

Menefee, D. T., & Thompson, J. J. (1994). Identifying and comparing competencies for social work management: A practice driven approach. *Administration in Social Work, 18*(3), 1–25.

Miner, E. J., & Jacobsen, M. (1990). Coalition building in human services: Enhancing rural identity in the shadow of the big apple. *Human Services in the Rural Environment, 14*(1), 5–9.

Moore, S. (1992). Case management and the integration of services: How service delivery systems shape case management. *Social Work, 37*(5), 418–423.

Morgan, G. (1988). *Riding the waves of change: Developing managerial competencies for a turbulent world.* San Francisco: Jossey-Bass.

Musser-Granski, J., & Carrillo, D. F. (1997). The use of bilingual, bicultural paraprofessionals in mental health services: Issues for hiring, training, and supervision. *Community Mental Health Journal, 33*(1), 51–60.

O'Looney, J. (1994). Modeling collaboration and social services integration: A single state's experience with developmental and non-developmental models. *Administration in Social Work, 18*(1), 61–86.

Orsburn, J. D., Moran, L., Musselwhite, E., & Zenger, J. H. (1990). *Self-directed work teams: The new American challenge.* Burr Ridge, IL: Irwin.

Patti, R. J. (1977). Patterns of management activity in social welfare agencies. *Administration in Social Work, 1*(1), 5–18.

Pavilon, M. D. (1993). Cultural and organizational considerations of TQM: Notes on American and Japanese companies. *Employee Assistance Quarterly, 8*(4), 151–156.

Pepper, N. G. (1996). Supervision: A positive learning experience or an anxiety provoking exercise? *Australian Social Work, 49*(3), 55–64.

Perlman, B. (1994). Personnel management in mental health services. *Administration and Policy in Mental Health, 22*(1), 3–5.

Perloff, J. D. (1996). Medicaid managed care and urban poor people: Implications for social work. *Health and Social Work, 21*, 189–195.

Rauktis, M. E., & Koeske, G. F. (1994). Maintaining social work morale: When supportive supervision is not enough. *Administration in Social Work, 18*(1), 39–60.

Rossi, P. H., Freeman, H. E., & Lipsey, M. (2003). *Evaluation: A systematic approach* (7th ed.). Newbury Park, CA: Sage.

Segal, U. A. (1991). Marketing and social welfare: Matched goals and dual constituencies. *Administration in Social Work, 15*(4), 19–34.

Shera, W., & Page, J. (1995). Creating more effective human service organizations through strategies of empowerment. *Administration in Social Work, 19*(4), 1–15.

Sink, D. W., & Stowers, G. (1989). Coalitions and their effect on the urban policy agenda. *Administration in Social Work, 13*(2), 83–98.

Staples, L. H. (1990). Powerful ideas about empowerment. *Administration in Social Work, 14*(2), 29–42.

Steiner, J. R., Gross, G. M., Ruffolo, M. C., & Murray, J. J. (1994). Strategic planning in non-profits: Profit from it. *Administration in Social Work, 18*(2), 87–106.

Thompson, J. J., & Kim, Y. W. (1992). Forecasting AFDC caseloads and expenditures. *Social Work Research and Abstracts, 28*(4), 27–31.

Walsh, J. A. (1990). From clinician to supervisor: Essential ingredients for training. *Families in Society: The Journal of Contemporary Human Services, 71*(2), 82–87.

Wimpfheimer, S. (2004). Leadership and management competencies defined by practicing social work managers. *Administration in Social Work, 28*(1), 45–56.

Wyers, N. L. (1991). Policy-practice in social work: Models and issues. *Journal of Social Work Education, 27*(3), 241–250.

PART 2

Managing for Performance

P art 2 addresses the central theme of this book: how to manage human services organizations in ways that lead to the provision of high quality, effective services to consumers. This is arguably the most pressing issue confronting the human services in an environment of decreasing resources, increased competition, and growing demands for accountability from public and private funding and policy institutions. It is also an ethical imperative for human services agencies and those who deliver its services. The chapters here are devoted to the organizational conditions and management practices that are thought essential to the delivery of effective services.

Chapter 6 addresses the central question: how to create organizational conditions that will lead to positive worker perceptions, attitudes, and behaviors and ultimately the delivery of high quality, effective services. In this discussion, Charles Glisson provides a detailed examination of the constructs of organizational climate and culture, showing their similarities and differences, how they emerge and are maintained, and how they link to critical worker attitudes and behaviors, such as job satisfaction and commitment to client service. A review of the empirical literature suggests that climate and culture have a significant impact on worker performance in human services agencies and suggests how they might be managed to improve service performance. This chapter might well be read in conjunction with Chapter 10 on motivation.

In Chapter 7, Tom Packard addresses the same question but from the vantage point of managerial leadership, or what managers can do to enable conditions that lead to organizational excellence. Professor Packard provides a broad review of classic and emerging leadership theories, critically examines their relevance to human services organizations, and examines their impact on workers and their performance. He also addresses the role of leadership in producing innovation and change.

Key to improving the quality and effectiveness of social services is the availability of information about agency performance. In Chapter 8, John Poertner provides a detailed examination of the types of information that agency managers and front-line staff need to learn about the effects of their effort, in order to improve services. The measurement of agency performance—common methods and some available instruments—is discussed at length along with the challenges agencies confront as they undertake this task.

In Chapter 9, we learn of the many recent developments in information technology that have helped, and could in the future help, organizations not only monitor their performance, but also link to the vast resources available in cyberspace. Increasingly, this information-rich environment can be harnessed for the empirical research on intervention efficacy, industry-wide data on program performance, proven service protocols, and so on. One such service protocol is illustrated. Yet, with all these possibilities, Professor Schoech cautions that agencies must take care not to adopt these technologies without the necessary resources, expertise, and structural support.

CHAPTER 6

Organizational Climate and Culture and Performance in the Human Services

Charles Glisson

O rganizational climate and culture are popular constructs that receive a great deal of attention in both the trade and academic press. Researchers and practitioners alike are attracted to the potential that climate and culture offer for understanding and improving the work environments of organizations. Organizational climate has a longer history in the research literature, but organizational culture is more frequently mentioned in trade texts on organizations and currently receives as much, or more, attention in the academic literature. Of particular interest to both researchers and practitioners are the ways that climate and culture contribute to or detract from individual performance and organizational effectiveness.

What Is Organizational Climate and Culture?

The general notion that climate and culture describe critical, palpable dimensions of organizational life that members experience is widely accepted. Moreover, the concepts of climate and culture have generated interest in the power of organizations to influence and affect the behavior, attitudes, and performance of members. Some especially influential books have gained popularity in both the research and practice worlds by developing conceptual links between organizational culture and effectiveness. Of these, Peters and Waterman's (1982) *In Search of Excellence* was one of the first and most successful

AUTHOR'S NOTE: Research for this chapter was supported by NIH R01-MH66905.

and can be credited for spawning much of the current interest in organizational culture. Their emphasis on norms and values in the workplace (i.e., culture) as the key predictors of organizational success attracted the attention of numerous writers and fueled the organizational development efforts of several *Fortune* 500 businesses. *In Search of Excellence* was published at a time when it was generally believed that American businesses were competing unsuccessfully in the increasingly globalized market. By giving case examples of some of America's most successful businesses, Peters and Waterman offered the promise of improving American competitiveness in the global marketplace and inspired a nationwide infatuation with culture as the key to success.

A decade later, Osborne and Gaebler's (1992) *Reinventing Government* extended the work of Peters and Waterman to the public sector by describing the importance of culture to the performance of government agencies. After visiting and assessing a number of government agencies and programs, Osborne and Gaebler identified several culture-based principles that are characteristic of successful public organizations. They emphasized the importance of workplace cultures that focus on results rather than process, emphasize mission over bureaucratic rules, and promote worker autonomy and discretion rather than control. During the Clinton administration, Vice President Al Gore led the implementation of these principles in a number of federal agencies (Gore, 1993).

Schorr's (1997) *Common Purpose* built directly on Osborne and Gaebler's work by explaining the roles that organizational culture can play in revitalizing the nation's public child and family service systems. Her focus on transforming the bureaucracies that manage these services so that social workers and other service providers are freed to focus on results and are less hampered by red tape and other bureaucratic barriers directly links organizational culture to social service outcomes. Her book and the previous two provide many real world examples of how culture and climate (although the latter term is rarely used in these three texts) contribute to organizational performance. Recent research findings support the observations made in the case studies reported in these books and adds to the evidence that culture and climate are critical to organizational performance in a variety of manufacturing and service areas (Broome, Flynn, Knight, & Simpson, 2007; Brown & Leigh, 1996; Chen, Kirkman, Kanfer, Allen, & Rosen, 2007; Denison & Mishra, 1995; Gordon & DiTomaso, 1992; Greener, Joe, Simpson, Rowan-Szal, & Lehman, 2007; Liao & Chang, 2007; Petty, Beadles, Lowery, Chapman, & Connell, 1995; Simpson, Joe, Rowan-Szal, 2007; Zamanou & Glaser, 1994).

The challenge for both researchers and practitioners, however, is to understand the intuitively appealing constructs of culture and climate in a way that clearly defines them, distinguishes them from other organizational characteristics, and establishes convincing links to performance and outcome criteria. The constructs, although extremely popular, continue to be used inconsistently by researchers as well as practitioners. They are applied in ways that confuse them with related organizational characteristics such as structure, technology, and leadership and with individual worker characteristics such as job satisfaction, motivation, and commitment (Verbeke, Volgering, & Hessels, 1998).

Definitions of Climate

Today, organizational climate is widely defined in terms of employees' perceptions of their work environment (Schneider, 1990). The distinction between *psychological* and *organizational* climate developed by Larry James and colleagues drives much of the current theoretical and empirical work concerning climate (James & James, 1989; James, James, & Ashe, 1990; James & Jones, 1974; James & Sells, 1981). Psychological climate is an employee's perception of the psychological impact of the work environment on his or her personal well-being. Brown and Leigh (1996) and Edmondson (1999) operationalize a positive psychological climate in terms of psychological safety and meaningfulness. They emphasize that positive climates are those in which workers perceive that their work environment poses no threat to their self-image or career and provides a return on their investment of personal effort.

All work environments create psychological climates, but organizational climates are created by shared psychological climates. In other words, the psychological climate of a work environment is a worker's perception of how the work environment is negatively or positively affecting him or her. So it is an employee's perception of the work environment, and not the environment itself, that is most important. An organizational climate exists to the extent that employees agree on their perceptions. When employees in a particular work environment agree on their perceptions of their work environment, their shared perceptions can be aggregated to describe the organization's climate (Jones & James, 1979; Joyce & Slocum, 1984). Workers' perceptions of work environment stress, functionality, and engagement are dimensions of climate included in the Organizational Social Context (OSC) measure, which has been tested in mental health and social service organizations (Glisson, Landsverk et al., 2008; Glisson, Schoenwald et al., 2008).

Definitions of Culture

Definitions of organizational culture have depended to a great extent on definitions of societal culture, which emerged from anthropological research. Definitions commonly used in the organizational literature emphasize that culture includes the shared values, beliefs, and behavioral norms in an organization (Ouchi, 1981; Swartz & Jordan, 1980; Van Maanen & Schein, 1979). But there is much more disagreement surrounding definitions of culture than climate, and there is overlap in the definitions of the two constructs that blurs the boundaries that separate them. Climate has been distinguished from culture by emphasizing that culture is a property of the social system (the norms and values that drive behavior in the system), as compared to climate,

which is a property of the individuals (their perceptions) within that system (James et al., 1990; James & McIntyre, 1996).

There are other, related definitions of culture that emphasize different properties and characteristics. Rousseau (1990) describes culture as the social process by which members share their values, beliefs, and norms. Schein (1992) defines culture as the shared assumptions that are taught to new members, but he restricts this socialization process to perceptions, thinking, and feelings, specifically excluding behavior. Jelinek, Smircich, and Hirsch (1983), in their introduction to a special issue of *Administrative Science Quarterly* devoted to culture, describe culture as both product and process, the shaper of human interaction and the outcome of it.

Common to most definitions of culture are the values and norms that drive behavior in an organization. However, there is disagreement about whether culture is a property of the individual or the social system, whether it includes perceptions as well as behavior, and whether it is a social process, social structure, or both. Proficiency, rigidity, and resistance are dimensions of culture that are included in the OSC measure (Glisson, Landsverk et al., 2008; Glisson, Schoenwald et al., 2008). But other elements of culture that are included in some measurement instruments, such as fairness, overlap with many elements that are included in some measures of climate, creating confusion about the differences and similarities between climate and culture.

Similarities and Differences Between Climate and Culture

Although many questions remain unresolved, culture and climate continue to be popular constructs in both the practice and research literatures. Yet the question of what differentiates culture from climate, or what unites them, has not been adequately answered (Denison, 1996). A review of the history of the terms in the research literature, as well as of recent findings about their links with other variables, provides insight into their similarities and differences, but more work remains to be done to fully understand their value to organizational performance (Aarons & Sawitzky, 2006).

This chapter defines organizational climate as a property of the individual (perception) that is shared by other individuals in the same work environment. That is, organizational climate is the shared perceptions that employees have of the psychological impact that their work environment has on those who work there. In contrast, culture is defined as a property of the collective social system. It comprises the norms and expectations of that social system that drive the way things are done in the organization. These norms and expectations include how employees interact, how they approach their work, and what work behaviors are emphasized in the organization through rewards and sanctions. Thus, culture captures patterns of social interaction and behavior, and climate captures the personal meaning that individual workers give to those interactions and behaviors for their own well-being and functioning.

It would be misleading to imply that there is widespread agreement on the distinction made here between climate and culture. Both climate and culture have been described in the literature at one time or another as properties of the organization and as properties of the individual. However, as described in the next section, a review of the history of the development of the two constructs offers support for the distinction made here. The key to understanding the distinction is found in the roles that perception and behavior play in climate and culture, respectively.

The norms and expectations of the organization as a social system reflect its culture, guide the way things are done in the organization, and establish what is most important in the work of the organization. When we ask individuals in an organization to describe their organizational activities and interactions, we are attempting to understand the behavioral norms and expectations established in the organization. If workers in the same organization agree that a particular norm or expectation characterizes their organization,

we conclude that it is a part of that organization's culture. Here, we could use a measure of interrater agreement among respondents to assess whether we are indeed tapping a cultural dimension that members agree is characteristic of their organization. If there is disagreement among the respondents about a certain norm or expectation, then we would conclude that that norm or expectation is not characteristic of the organization's culture—or perhaps that there are multiple subcultures.

In contrast, when we define organizational climate as shared perceptions, we are not using the term *shared* to refer to interrater reliability. The construct we are measuring is an individual property, similar to asking whether respondents experience the temperature of a room as hot, comfortable, or cold. If most respondents feel hot, but others feel comfortable, we don't challenge the accuracy of the perceptions of those who feel comfortable. Those who are comfortable are merely experiencing the temperature of the room differently from those who feel hot. So even if we characterize the temperature of the room as hot for most respondents, we could still conclude that others do truly feel comfortable because the characteristic we are assessing remains a property of the individual. It is in this sense that climate remains a property of the individual, whether there is agreement or disagreement among the respondents' perceptions of the work environment.

The History of Culture and Climate as Organizational Constructs

Organizational Climate: 1950s–1970s

Although climate and culture are now often mentioned in tandem (Ashkanasy, Wilderom, & Peterson, 2000; Barker, 1994; Hoy, 1990; Rentsch, 1990; Schneider, 1990; Schneider, Gunnarson, & Niles-Jolly, 1994; Verbeke et al., 1998), their individual histories within the organizational literature are quite distinct (Denison, 1996; Reichers &

Schneider, 1990). Climate has a significantly longer history. Articles as far back as the 1950s identify organizational climate as a key factor in worker performance (Argyris, 1958; Fleishman, 1953). Early work emphasizing the roles of leadership and group dynamics in the development of workgroup climate coincided with the surge of academic interest in leadership and group behavior that followed World War II. Scholarly work on organizational climate began to mature during the 1960s, when key texts were published that focused specifically on climate (Litwin & Stringer, 1968; Tagiuri & Litwin, 1968). Empirical research on climate flourished during the 1970s, with numerous articles appearing in many different journals (e.g., Hellriegel & Slocum, 1974; James, Hater, Gent, & Bruni, 1978; James & Jones, 1974; Payne & Mansfield, 1973; Schneider, 1972; Schneider & Bartlett, 1970). A number of scales for measuring climate were developed and refined during this time, and linkages with an array of antecedents and consequences of climate were explored (Hellriegel & Slocum, 1974).

The Emergence of Organizational Culture: 1970s–1980s

Although the notion that organizations are social systems with varying norms and expectations is found in such early classics as Gouldner (1954) and Selznick (1949), the concept of *organizational culture* did not appear in the organizational literature until the late 1970s (Handy, 1976; Pettigrew, 1979). Borrowing heavily from anthropology as well as sociology, the early approach to studying organizational culture can be contrasted sharply with the psychological focus of the climate studies. As a result of its academic roots, the study of organizational culture had and continues to have a decidedly qualitative focus.

Although a relatively recent development, the interest in organizational culture expanded quickly. During the 1980s, several texts on culture emerged that emphasized the importance of culture to the performance of business and industrial organizations (Deal & Kennedy, 1982;

Frost, Moore, Louis, Lundberg, & Martin, 1985; Ott, 1989; Sathe, 1985; Schein, 1992). These texts and the large number of articles on culture that appeared in the 1980s in a variety of journals served to place culture in a position of prominence in the organizational literature equal to or surpassing that of climate (Ouchi & Wilkins, 1985).

The Evolution of Culture and Climate in the 1990s

During the 1990s, the constructs of culture and climate began to appear in print together, and their similarities and differences began to be discussed. Schneider (1990) devoted an entire text to this issue, and articles in a variety of disciplines examined both constructs simultaneously (Barker, 1994; Hoy, 1990; Johnson & McIntyre, 1998; Rentsch, 1990; Schneider et al., 1994; Verbeke et al., 1998).

As the two constructs were increasingly discussed and examined together, it became clear that theorists and researchers were not in agreement about several important issues. Perhaps the most important issue is simply whether climate and culture are actually distinct concepts or are merely two views of the same concept (Ouchi & Wilkins, 1985). Although the debate continues among some scholars, if culture and climate are defined as they have been described above, the two are clearly distinct. That is, the norms and expectations that guide work in an organization can be distinguished from the perceptions that individual workers have of the psychological impact of their work environment on their own well-being. This distinction has been supported empirically and conceptually (Glisson, Landsverk et al., 2008).

A second issue—if it is assumed that climate and culture are distinct concepts—concerns the relationship between the two. Does one affect the other, is there a reciprocal effect, or are the two associated by their respective relationships with a common third variable? Although there are undoubtedly common variables that affect norms and affect workers' perceptions, it is likely that the concepts affect each other in a number of ways. Workers' perceptions of the impact of their work environment on their well-being and functioning are most certainly affected by the norms and expectations that drive behavior in that environment (Aarons & Sawitzky, 2006; Schneider et al., 1994). For example, if a hospital emphasizes billable hours and profitable procedures at the expense of individualized care, health care providers may perceive their work environment as depersonalized and as having a negative psychological impact on their well-being.

It is also possible that workers' perceptions of their work environment affect behavioral norms and expectations in the organization. For example, if most child protection workers in a state agency perceive that their work environment is extremely stressful due to intense critiques from government officials, common norms for defensive practice in that agency may develop. Case managers might then emphasize extensive written documentation and routinized, by-the-book protocols in order to defend their actions as based on required procedure if a decision or action is challenged by the court or a client advocate.

A third issue concerns whether culture can be quantitatively assessed in an organization in the way that climate has traditionally been assessed (Ouchi & Wilkins, 1985). This issue is rooted in the respective histories of the two concepts and has originated with some theorists who have criticized quantitative approaches as inappropriate for assessing culture (Deal, 1986; Schein, 1986). The qualitative versus quantitative methods debate is familiar to many social scientists, but in this case, qualitative methodologists argue that each organization has a unique, complex culture that can only be understood by extensive observation and dialogue with its members. Moreover, it is argued that the information gathered in that dialogue cannot be quantified but can only be described in qualitative terms. Others argue that both methods can be used and, in fact, complement each other (Denison & Mishra, 1995; Hofstede, Neuijen, Ohayv, & Sanders, 1990; Rousseau, 1990). For example, in a study of the cultures of hospital emergency rooms, the results of extensive, open-ended interviews were used to compare emergency room cultures qualitatively. The results were then used to develop questionnaires that became the basis of quantitative comparisons of the emergency room cultures, which confirmed the qualitative observations (Hemmelgarn, Glisson, & Dukes, 2001).

Why Are Culture and Climate Important to Social Services?

The success of human services organizations generally depends on the relationships and interactions between service providers and service recipients. Whether the organizations provide social, mental health, medical, educational, or other human services, these relationships and interactions are central to the quality and outcomes of the service. Culture and climate are important to human services because the nature and tone of these relationships and interactions are molded by and reflect the organizational culture and climate in which they occur (Blau, 1960; Broome et al., 2007; Greener et al., 2007; Hoy, 1990; Johnson & McIntyre, 1998; Rentsch, 1990).

The Role of Service System Norms and Expectations in Social Services

The norms and expectations that drive service provider behavior and communicate what is valued in organizations and the shared perceptions of service providers about the impact of their work environment on their well-being and functioning create a social and psychological context that shapes the tone, content, and objectives of the service (O'Reilly & Chatman, 1996; Perkins, Shaw, & Sutton, 1990). Interestingly, one of the early classic studies of work group norms and employee perceptions was conducted in a state social welfare agency (Blau, 1960). This study provided the first evidence of the connections between the norms and expectations of a social service organization, the perceptions of work group members, and the quality and outcomes of service. Although we need to understand more about these connections, recent studies have added to the evidence that they exist (Glisson, 2007; Glisson & Green, 2006; Glisson & Hemmelgarn, 1998; Glisson & James, 2002; Glisson, Schoenwald et al., 2008).

In the study of emergency rooms mentioned previously, the organizational cultures were found to prescribe significant differences in the way emergency rooms provide emotional support to the families of children with serious medical emergencies (Hemmelgarn et al., 2001). In some emergency rooms, parents and children are rarely separated from each other, health care providers are careful to respond fully to the concerns and questions raised by parents, and it is common for physicians and nurses to comfort parents during the most serious pediatric cases. These are important components of family-centered care, which has been linked to effective pediatric health care, but the study shows that the extent to which they are practiced varies as a function of the culture of the emergency room in which the physician, nurse, or social worker is working.

The emergency room research provides evidence that the nature and tone of physicians', nurses', and social workers' interactions with pediatric patients and parents are determined by their organization's culture rather than by their profession, training, or experience. In some emergency rooms, providing support to the families of children who are seriously injured or ill is valued and is the norm. In other emergency rooms, it is neither valued nor the norm, so it does not occur regardless of the training or experience of the individual health care provider.

In addition to molding the nature and tone of interactions between service provider and service recipient, organizational culture can affect technical aspects of service. For example, the service and custodial decisions made by case managers about children placed in state custody have been found to be dictated more by organizational norms than by the actual needs of the children

(Glisson, 1996; Martin, Peters, & Glisson, 1998). In these studies, case managers ignored the results of standardized needs assessments and instead followed the organization's established norms for referring children to placements and mental health services, regardless of actual need. For example, it was the norm for males to be placed in more restrictive placements than females, even when matched on age, reason for custody, and problem behavior.

We have known for decades that workers in many human services organizations operate within "well-worn paths" that routinize service delivery in a way that prevents individualized care (Glisson, 1978). These well-worn paths constitute sets of behavioral norms for an organization. Well-worn paths are created because organizations generally value certainty and predictability, whereas many organizations discourage innovation and unique approaches to work. As will be discussed below, formal and informal, tangible and intangible rewards and sanctions exert pressure on workers to behave in ways that conform to these norms, independently of the actual needs of those who are being served.

The Role of Service Provider Perceptions in Social Services

Brown and Leigh (1996) emphasize that it is employees' perceptions of their work environment, rather than the environment itself, that mediate employee attitudes and behavior (see also Aarons & Sawitzky, 2006). Perceptions are particularly important in social services because of the nature of the helping relationships that are central to the work. Social service relationships consist of human interactions that are focused on enhancing human functioning. As a result, the attitudes and perceptions that service providers carry into these interactions can dramatically influence the nature and tone of the interactions (Broome et al., 2007; Greener et al., 2007; Schneider, White, & Paul, 1998). If a work environment is nonsupportive, impersonal, and stressful, employees' interactions with those who receive their services will reflect the lack of support, impersonality, and stress that the employees perceive in their work environment. Whether the employees are teachers, nurses, social workers, psychologists, or bank tellers, employees' perceptions of the impact of their work environment on their well-being influence how they interact with those they serve in that environment (Schneider et al., 1998).

Much of the work in many social service organizations also requires that social workers interact with others outside their organization. Many times, this includes advocacy on behalf of individual clients, information seeking, or service coordination activities. Particularly in public social services, effectiveness in completing these types of tasks requires a great deal of personal and extended effort on the part of individual workers. In addition to knowledge and skill, tenacity and innovation can be critical to solving unexpected problems or navigating complex barriers to services. It is more likely that social workers will be tenacious and innovative in the face of unexpected problems or barriers if they perceive that their work environment treats them fairly and provides personal support for their effort. In short, if workers perceive that their organization stands behind them and can be counted on when the going gets tough, they are more likely to put the extra effort into the work that is required for success. In short, positive organizational climates complement and encourage the type of service efforts that lead to success (Glisson, 2007; Glisson & Hemmelgarn, 1998).

A very close relationship has been found consistently between organizational climate and worker attitudes toward their job and organization (Glisson & James, 2002; Glisson, Landsverk et al., 2008; James & Tetrick, 1986; Johnson & McIntyre, 1998). Workers who perceive their organizational climate in positive terms report higher job satisfaction and greater commitment to their organization. As found in other types of organizations, research on mental health and social service organizations has shown that social workers' perceptions of their work environment affect both their job satisfaction and organizational commitment (Glisson & Durick, 1988; Glisson, Landsverk et al., 2008).

How Culture and Climate Link Organizations to Service Outcomes

Culture and climate link organizations to outcomes through the behaviors, perceptions, and attitudes that are associated with employee performance (Denison & Mishra, 1995; Glisson, 2007; Glisson & Hemmelgarn, 1998; Hoy, 1990; Joyce & Slocum, 1984; Petty et al., 1995; Schneider et al., 1994; Wilkins & Ouchi, 1983). Two issues are especially important to understanding how culture and climate affect social service outcomes. The first is that social services employ soft technologies, which are particularly vulnerable to the behavioral norms that make up an organization's culture. The second is that social service core technologies depend on human interaction and relationships, which are especially sensitive to the perceptions that service providers have of the psychological impact of their work environment. Both culture and climate influence human interaction, and human interactions compose the core technologies of social service organizations (Denison, 1996).

The core technology of any organization includes the skills, activities, and materials that are required to produce the product or create the service for which the organization is remunerated. Some technologies are "harder" and some are "softer." Harder technologies include more concrete processes and materials that can be clearly specified in advance and have more predictable and determinate outcomes. The harder the technology, the more workers can rely on their knowledge of the raw materials and their skills for using those materials to successfully create the product or service. For example, the quality of stainless steel, the performance of a personal computer, or the beauty and durability of a house painting project is a direct function of the quality of the materials and the skill of those who use the materials to create the steel, build the computer, or paint the house. In contrast, softer technologies include fewer concrete processes, more variable raw material, and have less predictable and determinate outcomes. Even highly knowledgeable and skilled workers are not always successful in the use of soft technologies. Moreover, there is much more variability in the way experienced workers implement soft technologies than hard technologies. For example, skilled mental health professionals in the best-equipped residential facilities treat drug addiction in distinctly varied ways, and all experience many failures. As another example, highly regarded oncologists treat specific malignancies in very different ways and have a high ratio of failures to successes in the treatment of some types of cancer.

Factors that make technologies harder or softer also make them more or less vulnerable to the cultures in which they are implemented. Soft technologies are molded to fit within existing organizational norms with few visible consequences. They can be molded by an organization because the best way to implement the technology is not widely agreed on, outcomes are unpredictable, and it is difficult to determine whether an organization is implementing the technology effectively. Hard technologies, on the other hand, are more resistant to organizational differences. For hard technologies, there are widely known and agreed on practices that consistently result in predictable outcomes, and it is therefore possible to determine whether an organization is implementing a hard technology appropriately according to those practices. But even in companies that rely on hard technologies, the culture and climate of the company has a profound influence on performance and success, as documented in extensive studies of the car manufacturer Toyota (Liker & Morgan, 2006).

We have known for some time that social service systems incorporate soft technologies that are especially vulnerable to the organizational context in which they are implemented (Blau, 1960; Glisson, 1978, 1992; Street, Vinter, & Perrow, 1966). Organizations that have identical missions and that provide similar services to the same target population can have core technologies that are implemented in very different ways. For example, when organizational norms emphasize the importance of extensive paperwork, following bureaucratic rules, and obtaining prior approval for all decisions, social workers place more importance on following bureaucratic procedures and documenting their activities with a paper trail than on meeting the individual needs of their clients. When organizational norms place more emphasis on the importance of social workers' discretion and flexibility in addressing unique problems, social workers focus more on the individual needs of each client. In the former organizations, the core technology is highly routinized, with work proceeding in an assembly line fashion. Social workers in those organizations perceive their clients as having similar problems and believe that they know what each client needs, even before learning about the characteristics of the individual case. In the latter organizations, the core technology is nonroutinized, and social workers describe their clients as having many unique problems that they cannot anticipate and that require individualized plans of care (Glisson, 1978, 1992; Glisson & Green, 2006).

Workers' perceptions of their work environment reflect a general appraisal of whether they view their work environment as beneficial or detrimental (James & James, 1989). This general appraisal determines their attitudes about their work and how they approach it (James & McIntyre, 1996). Workers' perceptions of their work environment, therefore, affect how they perform in that environment (Brown & Leigh, 1996; Chen et al., 2007; James, Demaree, Mulaik, & Ladd, 1992; Liao & Chang, 2007). Because human interaction and human relationships are central to successful social services, social workers' perceptions of their work environment are particularly important to that success.

A study of public children's services systems found that positive, less restrictive climates complement and encourage the type of service provider activities that lead to improved outcomes (Glisson & Hemmelgarn, 1998). The success that social workers had in improving children's psychosocial functioning depended on their consideration of each child's unique needs, their responsiveness to unexpected problems, their tenacity in navigating complex bureaucratic and judicial hurdles, and their personal relationships with each child they served. Among agencies that provided the same service to the same target population, those in which caseworkers reported higher levels of work environment fairness, role clarity, cooperation, and personalization and lower levels of work environment conflict and stress provided higher quality service and achieved better outcomes. A recent nationwide study of child welfare agencies replicated the effect of organizational climate on service outcomes, finding that the well-being of children served by agencies with the least engaged climates deteriorated over time, while the children served by agencies with the most engaged climates improved over time (Glisson, 2008).

Why Organizations Have Different Climates and Cultures

We know that organizations that do the same work can have different cultures and climates (Glisson, Landsverk et al., 2008). It is less clear why organizations develop different cultures and climates, how those cultures and climates are maintained over time, and what differences in culture and climate distinguish different types of organizations. If, in fact, certain cultures and climates lead to success, as explained above, why do organizations not adopt those that are most effective? Herbert Simon's (1957) Nobel prize-winning work several decades ago explained that organizational decision making is not rational and not always in the long-term best interests of the organization. Rather than selecting the best alternative, many organizations tend to "satisfice," or adopt the first acceptable approach or solution that emerges. The first acceptable approach or solution usually addresses one or more relevant issues for the organization, but

frequently, those that are addressed are merely the easiest or most accessible issues, not the most important ones. This is central to understanding why organizations have different cultures and climates.

As explained above, because of the complexity and challenges inherent to the work itself, social service organizations incorporate core technologies that cannot guarantee success in every case. Moreover, even if they are successful, the success of the organizations is difficult to document. Consider the importance of this reality for social service organizations when combined with their constituents' demands for accountability, efficiency, or responsiveness. For these organizations, for example, the demand for accountability may create an organizational emphasis on documenting the process of the work rather than its outcome, the demand for efficiency may create an emphasis on reducing the cost per person served regardless of effectiveness, and the demand for responsiveness may result in an emphasis on increasing the number of people who receive the service rather than the number who are helped by the service (Glisson & Martin, 1980). Although such strategies may well address concerns raised by boards of directors, funders, legislators, or public interest groups, these strategies do not address effectiveness or outcomes. This is to say that the factors contributing to the development of an organization's culture or climate (such as an emphasis on documenting process or decreasing costs) may be unrelated, or at times detrimental, to its effectiveness, while at the same time being central to its survival.

How Climate and Culture Develop in an Organization

There are three groups of factors that contribute to the norms and expectations that define an organization's culture and to the perceptions of its members that define its climate. These three groups of factors are individual differences among workers, the characteristics of the organization's external environment, and the design of the organization as a sociotechnical system.

The contribution of individual differences to climate and culture. Individual workers have personal traits that can influence the norms and values that develop within an organization and the perceptions that they have of their work environment (Bareil, Savoie, & Meunier, 2007; Broome et al., 2007; James & McIntyre, 1996; Wiener, 1988; Wilkins & Ouchi, 1983). For example, if enough new workers are hired whose personality traits include high levels of achievement motivation, an organization's culture could develop new behavioral norms for achievement that did not previously exist. Other worker traits such as reliability, competitiveness, risk taking, or perfectionism could exert similar influences on culture. Such individual traits can redefine organizational norms as more employees are hired who share those traits. Administrators use selective hiring and firing as means of either maintaining existing norms or changing them (Bareil et al., 2007; Wiener, 1988). Of course, to do so suggests that administrators have a sense of the traits they desire in their employees and are then able to identify workers or applicants who have the traits (James & McIntyre, 1996). (See Chapter 12 for further discussion of recruitment.)

Climate can also be influenced by individual differences in workers' perceptions of the impact of their work environment. Research has documented that an individual's perceptions can be consistent across different work environments (Bareil et al., 2007; Staw & Ross, 1985). That is, individuals who view their work environments more positively relative to other employees also tend to view former and future work environments more positively. Also, employees who view their work environments more negatively relative to other employees tend to view former and future work environments more negatively. In other words, if an employee perceives his or her work environment as less supportive and less fair

than do other employees in that organization, then in subsequent jobs, the employee is likely to perceive the new work environments as less supportive and less fair than other employees in those organizations perceive them (Arvey, Bouchard, Segal, & Abraham, 1989). If new employees are selected who share tendencies to perceive their work environments either more positively or more negatively, the organization's climate is affected by the perceptions that are shared by the new employees.

Importing climate and culture from the external environment. Organizations adopt ways of doing things that resemble other organizations in their external environment with which they compete or cooperate (Hannan & Freeman, 1977; Martin & Glisson, 1989; Pennings, 1980; Pennings & Gresov, 1986). The similarities among competing or cooperating organizations have been described as the result of certain practices ensuring survival in given environments, regional differences in management practices, or organizational mimicry (DiMaggio & Powell, 1983; Martin & Glisson, 1989; Weiss & Delbecq, 1987; also see Chapter 20 on organization-environment relations). Organizational mimicry occurs when the norms of one organization that is seen as more successful are adopted by another organization in an effort to emulate that success. For example, a mental health center may receive positive attention and attract new funding as the result of developing innovative ways of reaching previously underserved populations. As a result, the board of directors and chief executive officer of another mental health center may begin to promote similar approaches to service among its own employees.

Another way culture is imported from the external environment is through the norms that workers have internalized as members of the society in which the organization is embedded (Martin & Glisson, 1989; Smircich, 1983). This is demonstrated by differences in interaction patterns, relationships with authority figures, openness in communication, and other characteristics of societal culture that determine how individuals relate to others (Hofstede et al., 1990). This explains why attempts to replicate certain Japanese models of management (such as those that had been so successful in manufacturing Toyota automobiles) encountered barriers in the United States that did not exist in Japan (Liker & Morgan, 2006).

Workers' perceptions of their work environments can also be affected by characteristics of their external environment that either offer additional options, provide new information, or create threats. Because workers' perceptions of their organizations are subjective appraisals, they can be influenced by the social, political, and economic realities in their organizations' external environments. For example, if the number of schools hiring social workers increases dramatically because of a need newly recognized by principals and school boards responding to increased school violence, then the recruitment of social workers with experience in schools becomes more competitive. As a result, social workers already working in schools may begin viewing their own work environments more critically as they begin to examine new job opportunities. Or, employees of a home health care agency may begin to perceive their work environment more positively after their own agency survives decreases in federal and state funding that result in the demise of other agencies with which it has competed.

The impact of organizational design: structure, technology, and leadership. The structure, core technology, and leadership of a human services organization describe the patterns of interactions among practitioners, the nature of the interactions between practitioners and clients, and the administration's style of organizational governance, respectively. These interactions create behavioral norms and expectations that compose its culture and stimulate the shared perceptions that compose its climate (Birleson, 1998; James & Tetrick, 1986; Pennings & Gresov, 1986; Rentsch, 1990; Schein, 1996).

Cultural dimensions affected by an organization's structure include such behavioral norms as flexibility, approval seeking, risk taking, and innovation. Hofstede and colleagues (1990) found that centralization, formalization, and specialization in structure were linked with a variety of cultural dimensions, particularly the extent to which workers were process oriented rather than results oriented. A highly centralized formal structure that restricts participation in decision making and maintains a narrow hierarchy of authority promotes approval seeking and reduces risk taking among employees. Highly formalized structures that narrowly divide labor and rely on strict written procedural specifications will tend to place little value on worker flexibility.

Characteristics of an organization's core technology influence norms and values in the organization when workers generalize behaviors required by the core technology throughout the organization. For example, the careful attention to detail required in certain engineering core technologies has been found to influence the broader organizational culture, encouraging senior managers to give excessive attention to detail and control in nontechnology as well as technology matters (Barker, 1994; Schein, 1996). Changes in core technology, such as those that accompany the introduction of computer systems, can transform the cultures of human services organizations by changing the norms that govern and direct interactions among workers (Gundry, 1985).

The characteristics of the core technology can also affect climate dimensions such as employees' perceptions of personal accomplishment, role conflict, and depersonalization. If the core technology in a public child welfare system is a routinized, assembly line approach to service delivery that does not allow individualized attention to the needs of each child, social workers are likely to experience high levels of role conflict and depersonalization. On the other hand, if the core technology emphasizes individualized attention to the needs and well-being of each child, encouraging social workers to attend to unexpected problems in innovative ways, social workers may experience higher levels of personal accomplishment.

Organizational leaders can manipulate their organizations' cultures by implementing new structural and technological characteristics that determine how work is done in the organization. In fact, the manipulation (or maintenance) of culture is believed to be an essential function of leadership (Bryman, 1996; Peters & Waterman, 1982; Schein, 1992; Trice & Beyer, 1993). However, there is a difference of opinion between those who conclude that leaders manage meaning and values and those who argue that leaders dictate practices, not meaning. Hofstede and colleagues (1990) conclude that organizational founders and key leaders shape organizational cultures by creating shared practices in the organizations. Distinguishing between the values of the organizational leaders and the values of organizational members, they provide evidence that the leaders' values influence the members' practices without necessarily changing the members' values. This separation of members' values and practices underscores the difference between assessing common practices in an organization and assessing personal values (Hofstede, 1998). Rousseau (1990) and others have linked practices and values of organizational members in a direct way with the assumption that practices reflect deeply held values. But Hofstede et al. (1990) conclude that the values reflected in observed practices are more likely those of the leaders than of the members. (See Chapter 7 for further discussion of leadership effects on organizations.)

An organization's leadership has an important impact on workers' perceptions of fairness and psychological safety in their work environment. When leaders are considerate of their employees in their decisions, are open to communication from employees regarding policies and procedures, and recognize their employees' accomplishments, the employees are more likely to perceive their work environment as fair and psychologically safe (Edmondson, 1999). Sheridan (1992) found that employees in firms emphasizing interpersonal relationships were much more committed to remaining with the firm. In social service organizations, good leadership has been identified as one of the few factors that contribute to both employee job satisfaction and commitment, each of which is highly correlated with positive organizational climate (Findler, Wind, & Mor Barak, 2007; Glisson & Durick, 1988; Glisson & Hemmelgarn, 1998).

How Are Climate and Culture Maintained in an Organization?

We know that culture and climate are stable characteristics of an organization that are maintained over time and gain considerable inertia as generations of workers come and go (Wiener, 1988). The mechanisms that explain the stability of the concepts are important to understanding the challenge of improving services by changing the behavior and perceptions of service providers. These mechanisms include the need for certainty, the need for power, and socialization.

The Need for Certainty

James Thompson (1967) has said that "organizations abhor uncertainty" (p. 99). More accurately, perhaps, individuals in organizations abhor feeling uncertain about what they are doing and about how they fit within the organization. Most people want to be clear on what they should be doing in a job, and they want to believe that what they are doing contributes to a meaningful goal. Culture contributes to certainty in an organization through shared norms and expectations (Louis, 1990; Trice & Beyer, 1993). Even when confronted with the uncertainty of a soft technology, a nonspecific mission, and unpredictable outcomes, organizations can create certainty through shared norms and expectations. This creation of certainty may have positive or negative repercussions for outcomes. Bureaucracies can create certainty through rites and ceremonies and by establishing norms that focus on process, routinization, regulations, and procedures that are unrelated to effectiveness (Trice & Beyer, 1984; Wiener, 1988).

This is not to say that norms and expectations only contribute to red tape and routinization. Shared norms and expectations can work in other ways to help create certainty in the face of confusion and challenge (Schein, 1992). Whether it is a combat team in battle, an emergency room team following a natural disaster, or a child protection unit determining whether a child should be immediately removed from a home, individuals' certainty about decisions and actions is enhanced by shared norms and expectations. Even if there is no one right decision or action, the perception of certainty is engendered by individuals in an organization sharing common ideas about the way they get things done.

The emergency room research described above found that among hospitals, norms about providing emotional support to families varied significantly, but in each emergency room, the existing norms and expectations had what Schein (1992) describes as "survival value." That is, the demands on medical personnel in emergency rooms require strategies for adapting to the associated stress. The cultures that evolve in response to these demands serve important functions that are valued by the members and are resistant to change (Hemmelgarn et al., 2001). Those who attempt to change the cultures of work groups find that even those members who are most vocal about the negative aspects of their work environment can be among the most resistant to change when their adaptive patterns of survival behavior are threatened.

The Need for Power

Whereas individuals in an organization may abhor uncertainty, most appear to be attracted to and influenced by power. Political-cultural analyses of organizations describe power as distributed both formally and informally through processes of conflict that lead to a negotiated order (Lucas, 1987). As a result of this negotiated order, individuals holding the same positions will

not necessarily have the same power because of differences in experience, expertise, access to information, relationships in the organization, and membership in interest groups. These factors contribute to power structures that are built and maintained by the norms that drive behavior in the organization (O'Reilly & Chatman, 1996; Trice & Beyer, 1993). Therefore, many members in an organization have an investment in perpetuating existing norms because those are the basis of their power (Barker, 1994). When existing norms change, an opportunity for shifts in power structures occurs, and changes in norms are therefore resisted by those most invested in the existing power structures (Sherwood, 1988).

For this reason, when organizations are formally restructured, the opportunity for cultural change is presented. Many writers believe that efforts to make significant changes in organizational culture are much more likely to be successful when they coincide with major mergers, reorganizations, or new administrations. Receptivity to change is related to the need for certainty described above, as well as to the dissolution of old power structures. Therefore, members of organizations in the midst of major structural changes are thought to be much more receptive to new norms. On the other hand, the role of existing power structures also explains why large state service systems are so resistant to change. Although top officials in these systems may come and go with different governors or political administrations, most state bureaucracies maintain consistent structures over long periods of time in which existing cultures are firmly entrenched and rarely challenged.

Power also plays a role in the development of perceptions of work environments. Social information-processing theory explains that perceptions are influenced by social interactions (Salancik & Pfeffer, 1978). From this point of view, social interaction is used by the members of the work environment to create shared perceptions of that environment. Each member does not arrive at his or her perception of the work environment independently. Rather, the shared perceptions are arrived at through consensus building in the work group. So, if workers share a perception of a work environment as not supportive, social information-processing theory would argue that the shared perception evolved through a process of social interaction (Louis, 1990; Salancik & Pfeffer, 1978). Moreover, the conclusions arrived at by those interactions may be less a result of any objective weighing of evidence and more a function of the composition of the interaction group (Rentsch, 1990). For example, the interactions are likely to be influenced by persuasive individuals with strongly held views. Informal power contributes to persuasiveness in social interactions, and the shared perceptions that develop from those interactions reflect the views of those with more informal power.

Socializing New Employees to Culture and Climate

We have known for almost half a century that employees in social welfare agencies are socialized by the organizations in which they work. A number of decades ago, Blau (1960) documented that the attitudes and behavior of social workers in social welfare systems are affected by the norms, values, and perceptions typical of their work groups. Perhaps even more important was the finding that this occurred even when the group's norms, values, and perceptions were anti-client. Through social information processing as described above, the need for social support, rites and ceremonies, and the rewards and incentives provided by the organization, most new employees are either socialized into the culture and climate of their work group or they resign (Carroll & Harrison, 1998; Chatman, 1991; Hebden, 1986; Louis, 1990; Schneider, 1987; Sheridan, 1992; Trice & Beyer, 1984). The need to reduce uncertainty is a primary motivation in the socialization process (Falcione & Wilson, 1988; Lester, 1986). However, not all new employees experience the same pressure to adopt the shared norms, values, and perceptions of their coworkers. For some, social acceptance is less important than for others, and their feeling of certainty about their new jobs is more a function of their individual competence and experience.

Employee selection, therefore, becomes an important issue in maintaining existing cultures and climates as new employees are hired (Chatman, 1991; Hofstede et al., 1990). Although socialization plays an important role in that process, more experienced, competent, or confident new hires may import as many norms, values, and perceptions as they adopt. As Hofstede et al. (1990) point out, employees can follow the prescribed practices in their organization without internalizing the values implied by the practices. Personal values can be more deeply held and carried from organization to organization. As was discussed earlier, there is a cross-situational consistency in the perceptions that employees have of their work environment that will be imported as well. Finally, the fit between the traits and abilities that new employees bring to the job and the expectations of the job can affect the employees' perceptions of their new work environment and their subsequent performance (Broome et al., 2007; Chatman, 1991; James et al., 1992; O'Reilly, Chatman, & Caldwell, 1991).

Climate and Culture Differences Between Types of Organizations

Very little comparative research on organizational culture and climate has been conducted, but there is evidence that different cultures and climates are found in different types of organizations (DiMaggio & Powell, 1983; Glisson, Landsverk et al., 2008; Gordon, 1991; Lucas, 1987). Some of these differences are related to the factors discussed above, whereas others are independent of them. These differences are a function of the missions of the organizations, the way they are funded, and the external environments in which they must survive (Etzioni, 1960, 1964; Gordon, 1991; Pennings & Gresov, 1986). Therefore, three major dimensions can be used as the basis of categorizing organizations according to type. These are human service versus non-human service, profit versus nonprofit, and public versus private organizations.

Human Service Versus Non-Human Service Organizations

For a number of years, human service organizations have been recognized as having distinct qualities (Hasenfeld & English, 1974). These qualities are primarily related to the mission of improving the functioning or well-being of human beings, as opposed to manufacturing, selling, investing, or the many other things that organizations do. This is important because it emphasizes that the raw material that is the focus of the work of human service organizations is human beings who have minds of their own, are highly complex, relatively unpredictable, and very difficult to mold, process, or change. This contributes to many of the qualities of the core technology discussed above. It also contributes to norms, expectations, and perceptions of workers in the organization that are interwoven with the welfare of human beings (Hasenfeld, 1992). This is the most important distinction between the cultures and climates of human service and non-human service organizations. The impact of workers' successes or failures, the frustrations generated by organizational barriers to success, and the motivation to do the core work of the organization are all linked to the workers' need to help other human beings. As a result, the norms and values that drive behavior in human service organizations evolve, in part, as a function of their impact on the welfare of the human beings served.

There has been very little empirical research that directly compares the cultures and climates of human service organizations to those of other types of organizations. In one of those comparisons, Solomon (1986) found that non-service or production organizations in Israel were much more likely to use performance-based reward systems than were service organizations, whether they were profit or nonprofit organizations. This difference is perhaps due, in part, to the fact that quantifying and assessing production performance is a more straightforward and obvious endeavor than quantifying and assessing service performance. But that does not provide either a complete or satisfactory explanation of the difference between human service and non-service organizations. Service can be quantified, assessed, and used as the basis of employee rewards, as most large law offices demonstrate daily. Therefore, the finding that the use of such systems for performance-based rewards is less common in human service organizations than in other types of organizations is undoubtedly linked to norms that distinguish the cultures of human service organizations from other types of organizations.

Profit Versus Nonprofit Organizations

The majority of social welfare organizations are nonprofit organizations. It is not difficult to understand the impact that this has on an organization's culture and climate. When the bottom-line criterion of success is profit, the values and norms that drive behavior in the organization cannot deviate far from increasing earnings and decreasing costs. However, earnings and costs are also a concern for many nonprofit organizations as they struggle to survive in the face of policy changes that threaten their income.

But in nonprofit organizations, as compared to profit organizations, monetary incentives cannot play the same role in providing rewards and incentives. As one person who worked for one year in a nonprofit organization after making a fortune in the business world phrased it, "It was interesting, but the stakes were so small!" Managers of profit organizations have the power to create behavioral norms and mold employee perceptions with monetary rewards and incentives far beyond the power of nonprofit managers. Nonprofit managers can hope to hire or promote people who have the desired norms, values, and traits they would like to see in their workers, and sometimes, they can fire or demote those who do not. But they have limited power to dramatically alter behavior or perceptions with large monetary bonuses, profit-sharing plans, or stock options that can be provided in profit organizations.

On the other hand, nonprofit organizations are freed from the negative aspects of the pressure for profit. As the competition increases or the stakes get larger, the danger is that the motivation behind profit organizations becomes tied increasingly to the stakes rather than the quality and outcomes of the work. This affects the underlying norms and expectations of the organization as well as employee perceptions of the organization. Peters and Waterman (1982) provide descriptive examples of business and industrial organizations that suffer because of managers who focus more on the bottom line and lose touch with the meaning and quality of the work of their organizations. Although there is almost no research comparing for-profit and nonprofit mental health and social service organizations, there were no differences in new program sustainability and therapist turnover between for-profit and nonprofit mental health clinics in a nationwide sample (Glisson, Schoenwald et al., 2008).

Public Versus Private Organizations

Public organizations can provide classic examples of bureaucratic red tape, unresponsive bureaucrats, and large expenditures of taxpayers' money on ineffective services. The comparison of public and private service organizations projects images of inefficiency versus efficiency, incompetence versus competence, and unresponsiveness versus responsiveness (Vestal, Fralicx, & Spreier, 1997). But Osborne and Gaebler (1992) point out that these stereotypes have developed largely as the result of the constraints placed on public organizations by the public, not by the employees. They explain that the public has been so concerned about making sure that everyone is served in exactly the same way and that each employee follows precise procedures that all discretion and entrepreneurial qualities are drained from public work. This is echoed by

Schorr (1997), who describes the nation's social service bureaucracies: "We are so eager, as a body politic, to eliminate the possibility that public servants will do anything wrong that we make it virtually impossible for them to do anything right" (p. 65).

There is also evidence that the quality of social welfare services provided by private agencies is no better than, and in some instances worse than, the quality provided by public agencies that serve the same population in the same geographical region (Petr & Johnson, 1999). The differences, then, in the cultures of public versus private organizations may be rooted less in whether employees are public employees than in the origin and focus of the control of public organizations. Or more precisely, they may be rooted in the fact that managers of public organizations are penalized by the public more for mistakes than they are rewarded by the public for successes. These types of differences between public and private sector organizations are represented in Solomon's (1986) findings that there is a greater emphasis on performance-based rewards and efficiency in the private sector than in the public sector. In addition, she found much higher job satisfaction in the private sector and concluded there is a need for restructuring the reward systems of public sector organizations to improve public sector job performance and job satisfaction. However, a recent nationwide study found no differences in new program sustainability and therapist turnover between public and private mental health clinics (Glisson, Schoenwald et al., 2008). Nevertheless, many public service organizations, such as the social welfare systems described by Schorr (1997), appear to have cultures that focus more on process than results, are rule driven rather than mission driven, and lose sight of the well-being of those they serve in their emphasis on bureaucratic procedures and red tape.

Summary

Organizational climate and culture are important to human service administration because they provide the critical links between organizational characteristics and service outcomes. Their attractiveness as organizational constructs is tied to the way they explain how work environments determine the effectiveness of service providers (Glisson, 2008). No other organizational constructs capture in such a successful way the importance of an organization as a psychosocial system that determines how its members approach and carry out their work.

The behavioral norms and expectations that make up culture and the subjective perceptions that make up climate explain the social and psychological impact of the structural and technological features of organizations. Since the turn of the last century, it has been known that organizational design characteristics associated with its structure and technology can affect an organization's productivity, measured in terms of the number of units produced or the number of customers served. By the latter part of the 20th century, however, it was clear that these characteristics were not as tightly coupled to the quality of the product or to the effectiveness of the service provided by an organization. Climate and culture provide the direct link to product quality and service effectiveness that broadens our understanding of how work environments affect worker performance.

Climate and culture are critical to service effectiveness because work in human services in general, and in social welfare in particular, can be stressful, complex, unpredictable, and indeterminate. So, to be effective, in addition to having the requisite skills and knowledge for the work, social workers and other human service providers must be tenacious, innovative, responsive, cooperative, flexible, committed, and supportive. These qualities are required when social workers face bureaucratic hurdles, difficult clients, conflicting job demands, frequent failures, a critical public, and other barriers to their work. Although individual workers differ in their potential to exhibit these qualities, ensuring that workers exhibit as many of these qualities as possible requires a work environment that promotes and sustains tenacity,

innovativeness, responsiveness, cooperation, flexibility, commitment, and support among its workers. These are promoted and sustained by the social and psychological impact of the work environment's climate and culture.

Although the association between climate and culture on the one hand and organizational effectiveness on the other is intuitively and conceptually appealing, much more empirical work is needed to identify the specific linking mechanisms that join climate and culture to service outcomes in human services organizations. There is a need for research that contributes to defining and differentiating climate and culture as distinct constructs, to understanding the way each affects the behavior and attitudes that lead to successful service outcomes, and perhaps most important, to demonstrate how effective climates and cultures can be created in actual service systems.

Adequately addressing these knowledge gaps is difficult, time consuming, and costly. It requires the use of true experimental designs to test strategies for improving climate and culture in actual service systems. This type of research is rare, but one of our recently completed projects, funded by the National Institute of Mental Health (NIMH), was the first to use a true experimental design to examine the effect of an organizational intervention strategy—labeled ARC for Availability, Responsiveness, and Continuity—for improving organization climate and culture in a child welfare system. The ARC organizational intervention strategy reduced caseworker turnover by two-thirds and improved organizational climate by reducing role conflict, role overload, emotional exhaustion, and depersonalization (Glisson, Dukes, & Green, 2006). This is important because these climate characteristics have been linked to outcomes in child welfare systems (Glisson, 2008; Glisson & Hemmelgarn, 1998). In a current project funded by NIMH (NIH R01 MH66905), the organizational intervention strategy tested in the previous study of child welfare offices was extended to mental health services to support the implementation of an evidence-based practice (EBP) for delinquent youth (Glisson & Schoenwald,

2005). The goal is to assess the contribution of organizational culture and climate to the EBP implementation process.

The excitement and interest generated by popular texts on organizational climate and culture continue to fuel efforts to create positive work environments. Many of these efforts have been doomed by misunderstandings of the constructs, poor interventions, and a lack of investment in the change effort. As explained in this chapter, individual dispositions and traits among workers, pressures from the organization's external environment, the need for certainty among members of a work environment, and existing informal and formal power structures all play roles in maintaining existing climates and cultures. Nevertheless, over time, we witness evolutions in the climates and cultures of organizations in various private and public service sectors. Unfortunately, most of these changes occur without empirical documentation, and we are left with the type of anecdotal evidence that is characteristic of many popular management texts. The challenge now is to submit these ideas to rigorous empirical examination, to more fully explicate the ways in which climate and culture affect the quality and outcomes of social services.

References

Aarons, G. A., & Sawitzky, A. C. (2006). Organizational climate partially mediates the effect of culture on work attitudes and staff turnover in mental health services. *Administration and Policy in Mental Health and Mental Health Services Research, 33*(3), 289–301.

Argyris, C. (1958). Some problems in conceptualizing organizational climate: A case study of a bank. *Administrative Science Quarterly, 2,* 501–520.

Arvey, R. D., Bouchard, T. J., Segal, N. L., & Abraham, L. M. (1989). Job satisfaction: Environmental and genetic components. *Journal of Applied Psychology, 74*(2), 187–192.

Ashkanasy, N. M., Wilderom, C. P. M., & Peterson, M. F. (2000). *Handbook of organizational culture and climate.* Thousand Oaks, CA: Sage.

Bareil, C., Savoie, A., & Meunier, S. (2007). Patterns of discomfort with organizational change. *Journal of Change Management, 7*(1), 13–24.

Barker, R. A. (1994). Relative utility of culture and climate analysis to an organizational change agent: An analysis of General Dynamics, Electronics Division. *The International Journal of Organizational Analysis, 2*(1), 68–87.

Birleson, P. (1998). Learning organisations: A suitable model for improving mental health services? *Australian and New Zealand Journal of Psychiatry, 32,* 214–222.

Blau, P. M. (1960). Structural effects. *American Sociological Review, 25,* 178–193.

Broome, K. M., Flynn, P. M., Knight, D. K., & Simpson, D. D. (2007). Program structure, staff perceptions, and client engagement in treatment. *Journal of Substance Abuse Treatment, 33,* 149–158.

Brown, S. P., & Leigh, T. (1996). A new look at psychological climate and its relationship to job involvement, effort, and performance. *Journal of Applied Psychology, 81*(4), 358–368.

Bryman, A. (1996). Leadership in organizations. In S. R. Glegg, C. Hardy, & W. R. Nord (Eds.), *Handbook of organization studies* (pp. 276–292). Thousand Oaks, CA: Sage.

Carroll, G. R., & Harrison, J. R. (1998). Organizational demography and culture: Insights from a formal model and simulation. *Administrative Science Quarterly, 43,* 637–667.

Chatman, J. A. (1991). Matching people and organizations: Selection and socialization in public accounting firms. *Administrative Science Quarterly, 36,* 459–484.

Chen, G., Kirkman, B. L., Kanfer, R., Allen, D., & Rosen, B. (2007). A multilevel study of leadership, empowerment, and performance in teams. *Journal of Applied Psychology, 92*(2), 331–346.

Deal, T. E. (1986). Deeper culture: Mucking, muddling, and metaphors. *Training and Development Journal, 40*(1), 32.

Deal, T. E., & Kennedy, A. A. (1982). *Corporate cultures: The rites and rituals of corporate life.* Reading, MA: Addison-Wesley.

Denison, D. R. (1996). What is the difference between organizational culture and organizational climate? A native's point of view on a decade of paradigm wars. *Academy of Management Review, 21*(3), 619–654.

Denison, D. R., & Mishra, A. K. (1995). Toward a theory of organizational culture and effectiveness. *Organizational Science, 6*(2), 204–223.

DiMaggio, P. J., & Powell, W. W. (1983). The iron cage revisited: Institutional isomorphism and collective rationality in organizational fields. *American Sociological Review, 48,* 147–160.

Edmondson, A. (1999). Psychological safety and learning behavior in work teams. *Administrative Science Quarterly, 44,* 350–383.

Etzioni, A. (1960). Two approaches to organizational analysis: A critique and a suggestion. *Administrative Science Quarterly, 5*(2), 257–278.

Etzioni, A. (1964). *Modern organizations.* Englewood Cliffs, NJ: Prentice Hall.

Falcione, R. L., & Wilson, C. E. (1988). Socialization processes in organizations. In G. M. Goldhaber & G. A. Barnett (Eds.), *Handbook of organizational communication* (pp. 151–169). Norwood, NJ: Ablex.

Findler, L., Wind, L. H., & Mor Barak, M. E. (2007). The challenge of workforce management in a global society: Modeling the relationship between diversity, inclusion, organizational culture, and employee well-being, job satisfaction and organizational commitment. *Administration in Social Work, 31*(3), 63–94.

Fleishman, E. A. (1953). Leadership climate, human relations training, and supervisory behavior. *Personnel Psychology, 6,* 205–222.

Frost, P. J., Moore, L. E., Louis, M. R., Lundberg, C. C., & Martin, J. E. (1985). *Organizational culture.* Beverly Hills, CA: Sage.

Glisson, C. (1978). Dependence of technological routinization on structural variables in human service organizations. *Administrative Science Quarterly, 23*(3), 383–395.

Glisson, C. (1992). Technology and structure in human service organizations. In Y. Hasenfeld (Ed.), *Human services as complex organizations* (pp. 184–202). Beverly Hills, CA: Sage.

Glisson, C. (1996). Judicial and service decisions for children entering state custody: The limited role of mental health. *Social Service Review, 70*(2), 257–281.

Glisson, C. (2008). *Organizational climate and service outcomes in child welfare agencies.* Manuscript submitted for publication.

Glisson, C., Dukes, D., & Green, P. (2006). The effects of the ARC organizational intervention on caseworker turnover, climate, and culture in children's service systems. *Child Abuse and Neglect, 30,* 855–880.

Glisson, C., & Durick, M. (1988). Predictors of job satisfaction and organizational commitment in human service organizations. *Administrative Science Quarterly, 33*(1), 61–81.

Glisson, C., & Green, P. (2006). The effects of organizational culture and climate on the access to mental health care in child welfare and juvenile justice systems. *Administration and Policy in Mental Health and Mental Health Services Research, 33*(4), 433–448.

Glisson, C., & Hemmelgarn, A. (1998). The effects of organizational climate and interorganizational coordination on the quality and outcomes of children's service systems. *Child Abuse and Neglect, 22*(5), 401–421.

Glisson, C., & James, L. R. (2002). The cross-level effects of culture and climate in human service teams. *Journal of Organizational Behavior, 23,* 767–794.

Glisson, C., Landsverk, J., Schoenwald, S. K., Kelleher, K., Hoagwood, K. E., Mayberg, S., et al. (2008). Assessing the Organizational Social Context (OSC) of mental health services: Implications for implementation research and practice. *Administration and Policy in Mental Health and Mental Health Services Research, 35*(1), 98–113.

Glisson, C., & Martin, P. Y. (1980). Productivity and efficiency in human service organizations as related to structure, size, and age. *Academy of Management Journal, 23*(1), 21–37.

Glisson, C., & Schoenwald, S. K. (2005). The ARC organizational and community intervention strategy for implementing evidence-based children's mental health treatments. *Mental Health Services Research, 7*(4), 243–259.

Glisson, C., Schoenwald, S. K., Kelleher, K., Landsverk, J., Hoagwood, K. E., Mayberg, S., et al. (2008). Therapist turnover and new program sustainability in mental health clinics as a function of organizational culture, climate, and service structure. *Administration and Policy in Mental Health and Mental Health Services Research, 35*(1), 124–133.

Gordon, G. G. (1991). Industry determinants of organizational culture. *Academy of Management Review, 16*(2), 396–415.

Gordon, G., & DiTomaso, N. (1992). Predicting corporate performance from organizational culture. *Journal of Management Studies, 29*(6), 783–798.

Gore, A. (1993). *The Gore report on reinventing government.* New York: Times Books.

Gouldner, A. (1954). *Patterns of industrial bureaucracy.* New York: Free Press.

Greener, J. M., Joe, G. W., Simpson, D. D., Rowan-Szal, G. A., & Lehman, W. E. K. (2007). Influence of organizational functioning on client engagement in treatment. *Journal of Substance Abuse Treatment, 33*, 139–147.

Gundry, L. (1985). Computer technology and organizational culture. *Computers and the Social Sciences, 1*, 163–166.

Handy, C. B. (1976). *Understanding organizations.* New York: Penguin.

Hannan, M. T., & Freeman, J. H. (1977). The population ecology of organizations. *American Journal of Sociology, 32*, 929–964.

Hasenfeld, Y. (1992). *Human services as complex organizations.* Newbury Park, CA: Sage.

Hasenfeld, Y., & English, R. A. (1974). *Human service organizations.* Ann Arbor: University of Michigan Press.

Hebden, J. E. (1986). Adopting an organization's culture: The socialization of graduate trainees. *Organizational Dynamics, 15*(1), 54–72.

Hellriegel, D., & Slocum, J. W. (1974). Organizational climate: Measures, research, and contingencies. *Academy of Management Journal, 17*(2), 255–280.

Hemmelgarn, A. L., Glisson, C., & Dukes, D. (2001). Emergency room culture and the emotional support component of Family-Centered Care. *Children's Health Care, 30*(2), 93–110.

Hofstede, G. (1998). Attitudes, values, and organizational culture: Disentangling the concepts. *Organization Studies, 19*(3), 477–492.

Hofstede, G., Neuijen, B., Ohayv, D. D., & Sanders, G. (1990). Measuring organizational cultures: A qualitative and quantitative study across twenty states. *Administrative Science Quarterly, 35*, 286–316.

Hoy, W. K. (1990). Organizational climate and culture: A conceptual analysis of the school workplace. *Journal of Educational and Psychological Consultation, 1*(2), 149–168.

James, L. A., & James, L. R. (1989). Integrating work environment perceptions: Explorations into the measurement of meaning. *Journal of Applied Psychology, 74*, 739–751.

James, L. R., Demaree, R. G., Mulaik, S. A., & Ladd, R. T. (1992). Validity generalization in the context of situational models. *Journal of Applied Psychology, 77*, 1–44.

James, L. R., Hater, J. J., Gent, M. J., & Bruni, J. R. (1978). Psychological climate: Implications from cognitive social learning theory and interactional psychology. *Personnel Psychology, 31*(4), 783–813.

James, L. R., James, L. A., & Ashe, D. K. (1990). The meaning of organizations: The role of cognition and values. In B. Schneider (Ed.), *Organizational climate and culture* (pp. 40–84). San Francisco: Jossey-Bass.

James, L. R., & Jones, A. P. (1974). Organizational climate: A review of theory and research. *Psychological Bulletin, 18*, 1096–1112.

James, L. R., & McIntyre, M. D. (1996). Perceptions of organizational climate. In K. R. Murphy (Ed.), *Individual differences and behavior in organizations* (pp. 416–450). San Francisco: Jossey-Bass.

James, L. R., & Sells, S. B. (1981). Psychological climate. In D. Magnusson (Ed.), *The situation: An interactional perspective* (pp. 275–450). Hillsdale, NJ: Lawrence Erlbaum.

James, L. R., & Tetrick, L. E. (1986). Confirmatory analytic tests of three casual models relating job perceptions to job satisfaction. *Journal of Applied Psychology, 71*(1), 77–82.

Jelinek, M., Smircich, L., & Hirsch, P. (1983). Introduction: A code of many colors. *Administrative Science Quarterly, 28*, 331–338.

Johnson, J. J., & McIntyre, C. L. (1998). Organizational culture and climate correlates of job satisfaction. *Psychological Reports, 82*, 843–850.

Jones, A. P., & James, L. R. (1979). Psychological climate: Dimensions and relationships of individual and aggregated work environment perceptions. *Organizational Behavior and Human Performance, 23*, 201–250.

Joyce, W. F., & Slocum, J. W. (1984). Collective climate: Agreement as a basis for defining aggregate climates in organizations. *Academy of Management Journal, 24*(4), 721–742.

Lester, R. E. (1986). Organizational culture, uncertainty reduction, and the socialization of new organizational members. In S. Thomas (Ed.), *Communication and information science: Vol. 3. Studies in communication* (pp. 105–113). Norwood, NJ: Ablex.

Liao, H., & Chang, A. (2007). Transforming service employees and climate: A multilevel, multisource examination of transformational leadership in building long-term service relationships. *Journal of Applied Psychology, 92*(4), 1006–1019.

Liker, J. K., & Morgan, J. M. (2006). The Toyota way in services: The case of lean product development. *Academy of Management Perspectives, 20*(2), 5–20.

Litwin, G. H., & Stringer, R. A. (1968). *Motivation and organizational climate.* Cambridge, MA: Harvard Business School.

Louis, M. R. (1990). Acculturation in the workplace: Newcomers as lay ethnographers. In B. Schneider (Ed.), *Organizational climate and culture* (pp. 85–130). San Francisco: Jossey-Bass.

Lucas, R. (1987). Political-cultural analysis of organizations. *Academy of Management Review, 12*(1), 144–156.

Martin, L. M., Peters, C. L., & Glisson, C. (1998). Factors affecting case management recommendations for children entering state custody. *Social Service Review, 72,* 521–544.

Martin, P., & Glisson, C. (1989). Social welfare organizations in three locales: Societal culture and context as predictors of perceived structure. *Organization Studies, 10*(3), 353–380.

O'Reilly, C. A., & Chatman, J. A. (1996). Culture as social control: Corporations, cults, and commitment. *Research in Organizational Behavior, 18,* 157–200.

O'Reilly, C. A., Chatman, J., & Caldwell, D. (1991). People and organizational culture: A profile comparison approach to assessing person-organization fit. *Academy of Management Journal, 34*(3), 487–516.

Osborne, D., & Gaebler, T. A. (1992). *Reinventing government.* Reading, MA: Addison-Wesley.

Ott, J. S. (1989). *The organizational culture perspective.* Belmont, CA: Dorsey Press.

Ouchi, W. G. (1981). *Theory Z.* Reading, MA: Addison-Wesley.

Ouchi, W. G., & Wilkins, A. L. (1985). Organizational culture. *Annual Review of Sociology, 11,* 457–483.

Payne, R. L., & Mansfield, R. (1973). Relationship of perceptions of organizational climate to organizational structure, context, and hierarchical position. *Administrative Science Quarterly, 18,* 515–526.

Pennings, J. M. (1980). Environmental influences on the creation process. In J. M. Kimberly & R. H. Miles (Eds.), *The organizational life cycle* (pp. 135–160). San Francisco: Jossey-Bass.

Pennings, J. M., & Gresov, C. G. (1986). Techno-economic and structural correlates of organizational culture: An integrative framework. *Organization Studies, 7*(4), 317–334.

Perkins, A. L., Shaw, R. B., & Sutton, R. I. (1990). Summary: Human service teams. In J. R. Hackman (Ed.), *Groups that work (and those that don't)* (pp. 349–357). San Francisco: Jossey-Bass.

Peters, T., & Waterman, R. (1982). *In search of excellence: Lessons from America's best run corporations.* New York: Warner.

Petr, C. G., & Johnson, I. C. (1999). Privatization of foster care in Kansas: A cautionary tale. *Social Work, 44*(3), 263–267.

Pettigrew, A. (1979). On studying organizational cultures. *Administrative Science Quarterly, 24,* 570–581.

Petty, M. M., Beadles, N. A., Lowery, C. M., Chapman, D. F., & Connell, D. W. (1995). Relationships between organizational culture and organizational performance. *Psychological Reports, 76,* 483–492.

Reichers, A. E., & Schneider, B. (1990). Climate and culture: An evolution of constructs. In B. Schneider (Ed.), *Organizational climate and culture* (pp. 5–39). San Francisco: Jossey-Bass.

Rentsch, J. R. (1990). Climate and culture: Interaction and qualitative differences in organizational meanings. *Journal of Applied Psychology, 75*(6), 661–668.

Rousseau, D. M. (1990). Assessing organizational culture: The case for multiple methods. In B. Schneider (Ed.), *Organizational climate and culture* (pp. 153–192). San Francisco: Jossey-Bass.

Salancik, G. R., & Pfeffer, J. (1978). A social information processing approach to job attitudes and task design. *Administrative Science Quarterly, 23,* 224–254.

Sathe, V. (1985). *Culture and related corporate realities.* Homewood, IL: Irwin.

Schein, E. H. (1986). What you need to know about organizational culture. *Training and Development Journal, 40,* 30–33.

Schein, E. H. (1992). *Organizational culture and leadership.* San Francisco: Jossey-Bass.

Schein, E. H. (1996). Culture: The missing concept in organization studies. *Administrative Science Quarterly, 41,* 229–240.

Schneider, B. (1972). Organization climate: Individual preferences and organizational realities. *Journal of Applied Psychology, 56,* 211–217.

Schneider, B. (1987). The people make the place. *Personnel Psychology, 40,* 437–453.

Schneider, B. (1990). *Organizational climate and culture.* San Francisco: Jossey-Bass.

Schneider, B., & Bartlett, J. (1970). Individual differences and organizational climate II: Measurement of organizational climate by the multitract-multi-rater matrix. *Personnel Psychology, 23,* 491–512.

Schneider, B., Gunnarson, S. K., & Niles-Jolly, K. (1994). Creating the climate and culture of success. *Organizational Dynamics, 23*(1), 17–29.

Schneider, B., White, S. S., & Paul, M. C. (1998). Linking service climate and customer perceptions of service quality: Test of a causal model. *Journal of Applied Psychology, 83*(2), 150–163.

Schorr, L. B. (1997). *Common purpose.* New York: Doubleday.

Selznick, P. (1949). *TVA and the grass roots.* Los Angeles: University of California Press.

Sheridan, J. E. (1992). Organizational culture and employee retention. *Academy of Management Journal, 35*(5), 1036–1056.

Sherwood, J. J. (1988). Creating work cultures with competitive advantage. *Organizational Dynamics, 16*(3), 5–27.

Simon, H. A. (1957). *Models of man, social and rational.* New York: John Wiley.

Simpson, D. D., Joe, G. W., & Rowan-Szal, G. A. (2007). Linking the elements of change: Program and client responses to innovation. *Journal of Substance Abuse Treatment, 33,* 201–209.

Smircich, L. (1983). Concepts of culture and organizational analysis. *Administrative Science Quarterly, 28,* 339–358.

Solomon, E. E. (1986). Private and public sector managers: An empirical investigation of job characteristics and organizational climate. *Journal of Applied Psychology, 71*(2), 247–259.

Staw, B. M., & Ross, J. (1985). Stability in the midst of change: A dispositional approach to job attitudes. *Journal of Applied Psychology, 70*(3), 469–480.

Street, D., Vinter, R., Perrow, C. (1966). *Organizations for treatment: A comparative study of institutions for delinquents.* New York: The Free Press.

Swartz, M., & Jordan, D. (1980). *Culture: An anthropological perspective.* New York: John Wiley.

Tagiuri, R., & Litwin, G. H. (1968). *Organizational climate: Explanation of a concept.* Boston: Division of Research, Harvard Graduate School of Business.

Thompson, J. D. (1967). *Organizations in action.* New York: McGraw-Hill.

Trice, H. M., & Beyer, J. M. (1984). Studying organizational cultures through rites and ceremonials. *Academy of Management Review, 9*(4), 653–669.

Trice, H., & Beyer, J. (1993). *The cultures of work organizations.* Englewood Cliffs, NJ: Prentice Hall.

Van Maanen, J., & Schein, E. H. (1979). Toward a theory of organizational socialization. In B. M. Staw & L. L. Cummings (Eds.), *Research in organizational behavior* (Vol. 1, pp. 209–264). Greenwich, CT: JAI Press.

Verbeke, W., Volgering, M., & Hessels, M. (1998). Exploring the conceptual expansion within the field of organizational behaviour: Organizational climate and organizational culture. *Journal of Management Studies, 35*(3), 303–329.

Vestal, K. W., Fralicx, R. D., & Spreier, S. W. (1997). Organizational culture: The critical link between strategy and results. *Hospital and Health Services Administration, 42*(3), 339–365.

Weiss, J., & Delbecq, A. (1987). High-technology cultures and management. *Group and Organization Studies, 12*(1), 39–54.

Wiener, Y. (1988). Forms of value systems: A focus on organizational effectiveness and cultural change and maintenance. *Academy of Management Review, 13*(4), 534–545.

Wilkins, H. L., & Ouchi, W. G. (1983). Efficient cultures: Exploring the relationship between culture and organizational performance. *Administrative Science Quarterly, 28,* 468–481.

Zamanou, S., & Glaser, S. R. (1994). Moving toward participation and involvement: Managing and measuring organizational culture. *Group & Organization Management, 19*(4), 475–502.

CHAPTER 7

Leadership and Performance in Human Services Organizations

Thomas Packard

L eadership is commonly seen as an important variable affecting organizational performance. While the concept has been
extensively studied, there is still much to be discovered regarding how leadership affects variables such as organizational culture, climate, and
performance. Most of the research on leadership
has been in for-profit organizations. While
research on leadership in human services organizations is increasing, there is still a limited
amount of research knowledge to guide practice
in our field. One seminal article in social work
described the importance of administrative
"behaviors, attitudes, practices, and strategies" in
ensuring effective service outcomes (Patti, 1987,
p. 377), and subsequent research, some of which
is included below, supports this perspective.

The purpose of this chapter is to provide guidance to human services managers, consultants,
and researchers regarding the ways in which
leadership can improve the performance of
human services organizations. The chapter will
begin with definitions, a conceptual overview,
and a brief discussion of evidence-based practice
applications in management, which will under-
gird the rest of the chapter. Then we will review
the best-known and most studied theories and
models of leadership, with specific attention to
how leadership impacts organizational culture,
climate, and performance. Organizational change
leadership and, specifically, organizational cultural change will receive special attention
because of their key roles in impacting and
improving organizational performance. Related
issues, including diversity and ethics, will be
briefly reviewed. The chapter will conclude with
discussions of implications for practice, education, and future research.

Leadership Defined

In a recent survey of theory and practice in leadership, Northouse (2004) concluded that "there are almost as many different definitions of *leadership* as there are people who have tried to define it" (p. 2). Northouse's definition will be used here: Leadership is defined as "a process by which an individual influences a group of individuals to achieve common goals" (p. 4). The term *followers* will be used to describe those whom the leader is attempting to influence. The term *subordinates* is often used in organizational settings, but the term *followers* suggests that leaders can be in any role or position, and a bureaucratic hierarchy is not necessarily implied. Additionally, the concept of shared leadership contradicts the notion of "solo" or unilateral leadership. According to Gill (2006), shared leadership is characterized by the quality of interactions rather than hierarchical level; team problem solving; "conversation rather than instructions, shared values, and beliefs"; and "honesty and a desire for the common good" (p. 30).

Another useful way to frame leadership is to contrast it with management. According to Kotter (1990), management produces predictability, order, and consistency regarding key results and includes planning, budgeting, organizing, staffing, controlling, and problem solving. Leadership produces change and includes establishing direction through visioning, aligning people with the vision and strategies, and motivating and inspiring staff. One conceptualization for human services organizations defines administration as a combination of leadership and management (Roberts-DeGennaro & Packard, 2002). Leadership includes visioning, change management, strategy development, organization design, culture management, and community collaboration. Management includes program design, financial management, information systems, human resource management, program evaluation, and project management. Effective execution of management functions often requires leadership.

The Context: Leadership, Organizational Dynamics, and Performance

Leadership is often seen as a key factor in coordinating and aligning organizational processes (Lewis, Packard, & Lewis, 2007). As with any aspect of organizational functioning, it should focus on organizational performance, and most important, effectiveness in achieving desired outcomes (see Chapter 8). The conceptual model in Figure 7.1 illustrates the place of leadership in organizational performance. At the far left of the figure, leadership traits, styles, and approaches are a starting point. Leadership can, to a large extent, affect management capacity through the design of organizational systems. A leader must assess contingency factors in the environment and in staff and the situation, considering staff characteristics and using leader-member processes to shape organizational climate and culture. Other factors, including program capacity (e.g., the service delivery model) and client characteristics, will affect ultimate outcomes. Leaders can impact program capacity through the use of evidence-based practice in program design. In this model, job satisfaction is seen as an intermediate outcome that can also affect an organization's effectiveness.

Leadership can be observed at several levels: groups, teams, programs, agencies, communities, societies/countries, and even worldwide (e.g., international affairs). The focus here will be on program/agency leadership: organizational leadership for organizational performance.

Another important aspect of the leadership context in the human services is the growing emphasis on evidence-based practice (McNeece & Thyer, 2004). This plays out in two ways in a discussion of leadership. First, in its traditional usage, evidence-based methods should be used by leaders in the design and implementation of the programs of their agencies. Second, evidence-based practice principles can be used in assessing the theories, models, and practice guidelines for leadership. The newly emerging field of

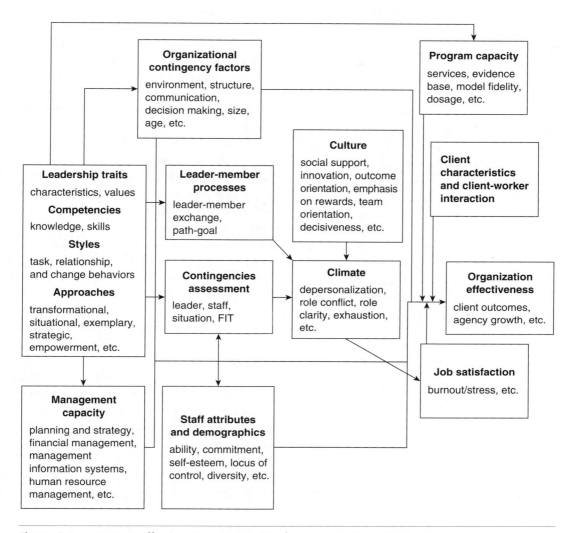

Figure 7.1   Factors Affecting Organizational Performance: A Heuristic Model

evidence-based management is an example of this application (Pfeffer & Sutton, 2006; Rousseau, 2006). When leadership models and principles are discussed below, the relevant empirical literature will be cited wherever possible.

Finally, it should be noted that, while much of the discussion here may imply that leadership is a rational activity, there are powerful contextual factors—including the agency's policy and political arena and economic, social, and technological forces (Lewis et al., 2007, Ch. 2) and internal dynamics such as organizational power and politics (Gummer & Edwards, 1995)—that impact the behavior and effectiveness of leaders. Some of the leadership approaches discussed below, including strategic leadership and contingency theory, provide tactics to deal with these organizational complexities. Other tactics, such as influence skills, are also relevant but beyond the scope of this chapter.

Leadership Theories and Models

This section will summarize the most influential theories and models of leadership, following the historical development of this field. The earliest research on leadership focused on traits, which were originally seen as innate characteristics of leaders. This area of study has broadened to include skills and competencies as well as more innate traits. Next, research in group dynamics examined interpersonal and task behaviors as they impacted group effectiveness. The notion of leadership style evolved from this work, often using a continuum from autocratic or directive styles to participative approaches. Eventually, researchers explored the notion that there is no one "best way" of leading and identified contingencies that would suggest the best approach. Current theories commonly include elements of several of these earlier models.

The Trait Approach

Discussions of leadership in the 20th century essentially began with the trait approach. While this perspective is now seen as incomplete, there has been recent renewed interest in characteristics of effective leaders. In spite of the questionable premise of trait theory as originally conceived, recent research has identified some traits associated with effective leaders: intelligence, self-confidence, determination, integrity, and sociability (Northouse, 2004, p. 19).

In an extensive review of the trait research, Yukl (2006) found several traits that were related to leadership effectiveness: a high energy level and tolerance for stress, self-confidence (including self-esteem and self-efficacy), an internal locus of control orientation, emotional stability and maturity, and personal integrity. Other factors identified by Yukl included emotional intelligence, including self-awareness, empathy, and self-regulation (the ability to effectively channel emotions and behavior), and social intelligence, including the ability to understand needs and processes in a situation and behavioral flexibility in adapting to these situational requirements. Systems thinking and the ability to learn are also seen as important (p. 189).

In evaluating the trait research, Yukl (2006) noted both "considerable progress" and "methodological and conceptual limitations" (p. 207). Little is known about how a combination of traits may impact effectiveness. Researchers do agree that it is important to note that traits are important only to the extent that they are relevant to a particular leadership situation. In fact, one of the weaknesses of the trait approach is that it does not provide detailed descriptions of how traits affect organizational outcomes (Northouse, 2004, p. 24). Regardless of these limitations, Yukl (2006) has offered some general suggestions for applications, including maintaining self-awareness, developing relevant skills through continuous learning and leadership development, remembering that a strength can become a weakness in a different situation, and compensating for weaknesses by using delegation or staff with complementary skills (pp. 208–209).

Leadership Skills and Competencies

The skills approach suggests that leadership abilities can be developed, whereas traits are more inherent in an individual. This approach is most prominent in leadership development programs that focus on identifying specific competencies that are important in a leadership setting. Leadership competencies have been defined as "the combination of knowledge, skills, traits, and attributes that collectively enable someone to perform a given job" (Zenger & Folkman, 2002, p. 83). The use of competencies in leadership development has become somewhat controversial (Hollenbeck, McCall, & Silzer, 2006). For example, the "competency movement," as Zenger and Folkman (2002, p. 85) refer to it, has weaknesses, including, for example, the failure to relate "lists" of competencies to leadership effectiveness in a specific situation and the mistaken assumption that all competencies are equal. Nevertheless, the competencies perspective is generally seen as one valid piece of leadership development.

In their research, Zenger and Folkman (2002, pp. 103–108) found that 16 groups of competencies were seen as associated with organizational effectiveness. These included character (displaying integrity and honesty), technical and professional expertise, problem-solving and analytical ability, innovation, self-development, a focus on results, setting "stretch" goals, taking personal responsibility for outcomes, effective communication, inspiring and motivating others, trust and interpersonal effectiveness, concern for others' development, collaboration and organizational change skills, ability to champion change, and ability to relate well to outside stakeholders.

They also found that leaders with strengths in multiple competencies were most effective, and, significantly, that particular *combinations* of competencies seemed to be more powerful predictors of effectiveness. For example, being able to give feedback did not always correlate with effectiveness, whereas giving feedback while building trust did (Zenger & Folkman, 2002, p. 151). They also found that listening skills alone were not particularly valuable, but listening skills plus other interpersonal skills (e.g., being considerate and caring) did make a difference.

Current thinking uses a "strengths perspective," in which administrators work to build upon their strengths and find situations that optimize them (Buckingham & Clifton, 2001). Zenger and Folkman (2002) agree that magnifying strengths is the best overall approach, but add that "fatal flaws" must be fixed. For example, they found that an inability to learn from mistakes and a lack of core interpersonal skills were fatal flaws (pp. 157–162).

Yukl (2006) has noted that different skill mixes are needed at different managerial levels, with conceptual skills more important at higher levels and technical skills more important at lower levels. Some of each skill will be needed at every level, and interpersonal skills are equally important at every level of management (p. 204).

In social work, a set of generic management competencies, ranging from advocacy to interpersonal skills, has been developed by the National Network for Social Work Managers (http://www.socialworkmanager.org/); they include many of the competencies mentioned in the research and others that are tailored to human services settings.

Leadership Styles

Competencies are also reflected in the style theories of leadership: the notion that certain behaviors make leaders more effective and that these behaviors or styles (e.g., participative or autocratic leadership) can, by and large, be learned and improved. The earliest work in this area, at Ohio State University and the University of Michigan, contrasted task behaviors, such as directing and providing structure for the group and focusing on production, with relationship behaviors, which emphasized building trust, respect, good relations within the team, and an employee orientation. Examples of these behaviors and a newly developing category of change-oriented behaviors are provided in Table 7.1.

Yukl (2006) has concluded that "there are serious weaknesses in much of the behavioral research conducted during the past two decades," noting "a tendency to look for simple answers to complex questions" (p. 75). Researchers "were looking for a universal theory of leadership that would explain leadership effectiveness in every situation" (Northouse, 2004, p. 68), but research in this area turned out to be inconclusive, although "the overall pattern of results suggests that effective leaders use a pattern of behavior that is appropriate for the situation and reflects a high concern for task objectives and a high concern for relationships" (Yukl, 2006, p. 76). Leadership research now more typically recognizes

Table 7.1   Examples of Task-, Relations-, and Change-Oriented Behaviors

---

Task-Oriented Behaviors

- Organize work activities to improve efficiency.
- Plan short-term operations.
- Assign work to groups or individuals.
- Clarify what results are expected for a task.
- Set specific goals and standards for task performance.
- Explain rules, policies, and standard operating procedures.
- Direct and coordinate work activities.
- Monitor operations and performance.
- Resolve immediate problems that would disrupt the work.

Relations-Oriented Behaviors

- Provide support and encouragement to someone with a difficult task.
- Express confidence that a person or group can perform a difficult task.
- Socialize with people to build relationships.
- Recognize contributions and accomplishments.
- Provide coaching and mentoring when appropriate.
- Consult with people on decisions affecting them.
- Allow people to determine the best way to do a task.
- Keep people informed about actions affecting them.
- Help resolve conflicts in a constructive way.
- Use symbols, ceremonies, rituals, and stories to build team identity.
- Recruit competent new members for the team or organization.

Change-Oriented Behaviors

- Monitor the external environment to detect threats and opportunities.
- Interpret events to explain the urgent need for change.
- Study competitors and outsiders to get ideas for improvements.
- Envision exciting new possibilities for the organization.
- Encourage people to view problems or opportunities in a different way.
- Develop innovative new strategies linked to core competencies.
- Encourage and facilitate innovation and entrepreneurship in the organization.
- Encourage and facilitate collective learning in the team or organization.
- Experiment with new approaches for achieving objectives.
- Make symbolic changes that are consistent with a new vision or strategy.
- Encourage and facilitate efforts to implement major change.
- Announce and celebrate progress in implementing change.
- Influence outsiders to support change and negotiate agreements with them.

SOURCE: Yukl (2006), Table 3-1, p. 66.

complexities, which cannot offer simple answers. These insights are reflected in more current style models, including the Leadership Grid and various contingency theories.

The Leadership Grid. Blake and McCanse's (1991) Leadership Grid is considered to be a style approach to leadership, proposing a two-axis model to make a distinction between a concern for people and a concern for production or results. On the Grid, Point 9 indicates a leader's maximum concern, whereas Point 1 denotes minimum concern. The Leadership Grid shows graphically the management styles of leaders, who are identified not by their behaviors but by their attitudes. However, this model assumes that managers' behaviors will reflect their concerns (i.e., a relative emphasis on the task or the people). Managers who are concerned primarily with output, or task, and are less concerned with people are considered 9,1-oriented managers who emphasize task behaviors. Those more concerned with people and who have little concern for production are considered 1,9-oriented managers who emphasize relationship behaviors. It is also possible to be a 1,1-oriented manager or a 9,9-oriented manager. The two axes are independent, so more concern for one factor does not necessitate less concern for the other.

According to the Leadership Grid, the 9,9 management style is seen as the ideal and one toward which managers can and should strive. Survey research has not adequately supported this theory (Yukl, 2006, p. 60). However, the model is compatible with other leadership principles and offers useful intuitive guidance, suggesting that any leader or supervisor should be concerned about both people and results. According to contingency theory, however, leaders can use different combinations of task and relationship behaviors, depending on the situation.

Contingency Theory

Contingency theory suggests that there is no one best way to lead and that different behaviors are appropriate in different situations.

The Decision Approach. One classic, but complex, contingency model is Vroom and Yetton's (1973) Decision Model. In this model, the leader considers several variables in a decision tree format, which eventually suggests a style to use. Factors to consider include the importance of the decision, the amount of relevant information that the subordinates and leader have, the need for decision

quality, subordinate concern for task goals, the extent of structure in the problem, and the importance that subordinates accept the decision. Based on an assessment of these conditions, the leader uses a style ranging from autocratic to consultative to group decision making. While the model is conceptually incomplete, there is some research support for it (Yukl, 2006, pp. 94–95).

Path-Goal Theory. Another contingency theory, the path-goal model (House & Mitchell, 1974), suggests that the leader assess task and follower characteristics and then demonstrate to followers how working toward organizational goals will meet their needs. Leadership style choices are supportive and directive leadership, discussed above; participative leadership, which involves consultation with subordinates; and achievement-oriented leadership, which involves "setting challenging goals, seeking performance improvements, emphasizing excellence in performance, and showing confidence that subordinates will attain high standards" (Yukl, 2006, p. 219). For example, to lead followers with high expectations and a need to excel in ambiguous, challenging, and complex situations (common in human services professions), the achievement-oriented approach is suggested (Northouse, 2004, p. 130).

As is the case with several leadership theories, the path-goal model's complexity makes it difficult to precisely implement and test (Northouse, 2004, pp. 132–133), and research to test it has led to mixed results (Yukl, 2006, p. 221). However, also consistent with other models, it does offer practice principles that may be useful in particular situations.

Leader-Member Exchange Theory. While not explicitly a contingency theory, leader-member exchange (Graen & Uhl-Bien, 1995) is covered here because, like path-goal theory, it places particular emphasis on the relationship between the leader and the follower. In this approach, the leader and individual follower work out an effective relationship of roles and interactions. A favorable relationship is more likely when there is personal compatibility between the leader and follower and the follower is competent and dependable. In such a situation, the leader is supportive, provides mentoring, and uses consultative and delegating styles (Yukl, 2006, pp. 117, 120).

In spite of a good deal of research on this theory, there are still conceptual ambiguities that require further research (Yukl, 2006, p. 121; Northouse, 2004, p. 156). It nevertheless offers a useful perspective for a leader to assess and attend to the relationships formed with individual followers so that subordinate needs and organizational goals can be addressed.

Hersey and Blanchard's Situational Leadership Model. A popular contingency theory is situational leadership (Hersey, Blanchard, & Johnson, 2001). This model suggests that the effectiveness of leadership styles depends, to a great extent, on the situation. The model is unique in its attention to the variable of follower readiness (a combination of ability and willingness to perform a job) level, which is seen as the most important situational factor. Ability is associated with relevant knowledge and skill, and willingness with confidence and commitment. Readiness is measured in terms of the specific task to be performed (e.g., a given follower might be ready regarding one job duty and not ready in another).

Hersey et al.'s (2001) situational model distinguishes between task behavior and relationship behavior on the part of the leader. They contend that varying amounts of relationship and task behaviors (see Table 7.1) can be appropriate, in varying combinations, depending on the readiness level of the follower. According to the situational leadership model, the leader should adapt his or her style to the followers' readiness. A leader dealing with individuals who are at low readiness in terms of the task in question should use a high degree of structure or task behaviors (such as defining tasks and responsibilities) and a low degree of relationship behavior (a guiding, telling, or directing approach). As the follower's maturity level increases, it is appropriate to continue task behaviors and add relationship behaviors, such as two-way communication, facilitation, and emotional support. For followers with

moderate readiness, a selling or persuading style is appropriate. As maturity increases further, to a level at which high relationship and low task behaviors are appropriate, an encouraging or participating style is used. When followers have reached a high degree of maturity, the leader can decrease both supportiveness and structure, using a delegating style.

Consistent with other theories, there is little empirical support for the theory, partly because of conceptual weaknesses such as imprecise definitions of its elements and relationships among them (Northouse, 2004, pp. 93–94; Yukl, 2006, p. 224). Regardless of these limitations, this model can be helpful to leaders in human services agencies, where followers may vary greatly in terms of their readiness levels. Although a person new to an agency might require a high degree of structure, at least temporarily, a seasoned professional might be most effective when led with a delegating style. It is important that the leader assess followers as individuals in terms of their readiness for particular tasks, and then use the appropriate style for each person and situation.

In spite of the limitations in the various contingency theories, Yukl (2006, pp. 240–243) has offered some useful practice guidelines. First, of course, maintaining a situational awareness will help a leader choose an approach appropriate to the follower and situation. More planning will be needed for complex tasks, and more direction will be needed when teams have members with interdependent roles. More direction may also be needed in a crisis situation. This approach suggests a more consultative approach with people who have relevant knowledge and more coaching of an inexperienced follower. Critical tasks or unreliable followers may require closer monitoring, and those working on a stressful task should receive support.

Current Theories

Charismatic Leadership

Charismatic leadership (Conger & Kanungo, 1998) will be briefly discussed here as a prelude to a full discussion of current well-developed models of leadership, some of which include elements of charismatic leadership. A charismatic leader is a strong role model who demonstrates competence and confidence, articulates goals, and communicates high expectations (Northouse, 2004, p. 172). Charismatic leaders foster the development of trust and can inspire followers to a new vision through self-sacrifice, risk taking, and a concern for followers. It should also be noted that charismatic leadership is risky: Power can be misused, and followers can become inappropriately dependent upon a charismatic leader (Yukl, 2006, pp. 250, 262).

Also, as noted by Collins (2001), effective leaders do not need to be strongly charismatic in the traditional sense of "larger than life heroes" such as Lee Iacocca at Chrysler (pp. 28–30). In fact, his research found that leadership attributes included a "paradoxical blend" of humility and a fearless determination to succeed, concluding that "Charisma can be as much a liability as an asset, as the strength of your leadership personality can deter people from bringing you the brutal facts" (p. 89). The challenge here seems to be to demonstrate the characteristics noted without displaying an oversized personal presence, which puts more emphasis on the person than the organization.

Transactional and Transformational Leadership

Currently, one of the most popular and studied models of leadership contrasts two related approaches: transformational leadership and transactional leadership.[1] Much of the current work on this model has been reported by Bass and associates (Bass & Avolio, 2006). In transactional leadership, the more common approach, an exchange process involves the leader and followers agreeing to do or provide things to accommodate each others' needs. In transformational leadership, the leader "transforms and motivates followers by (1) making them more aware of the importance of task outcomes, (2) inducing them to transcend their own self-interest for the sake of

the organization or team, and (3) activating their higher-order needs" (Yukl, 2006, p. 262).

Transactional leadership has two components. First, *contingent rewards* are valued rewards received for performing desired behaviors. A transactional leader identifies factors that motivate a worker and provides the support needed for effective performance. Second, *management by exception* assumes that under normal circumstances, little intervention by a supervisor will be necessary. When exceptions (variations from routine activities) occur, management by exception is used. A leader can use active or passive management by exception. In active management by exception, the leader "arranges to actively monitor deviances from standards, mistakes, and errors that occur and to take corrective action as necessary" (Bass, 1998, p. 7). In passive management by exception, the supervisor does not actively monitor but waits for deviances or mistakes to occur and then acts.

To effectively lead professional staff, transactional leadership will probably not be enough to achieve outstanding performance. Transactional leadership should be augmented by the use of transformational leadership, which includes idealized influence, inspirational motivation, intellectual stimulation, and individualized consideration.

Idealized Influence. Idealized influence "refers to the ability of leaders to display conviction, emphasize trust, take stands on controversial issues, present their most important values, and emphasize the importance of purpose, commitment, and ethical consequences of decisions" (Bargal, 2000, p. 308). According to Bass (1998), a transformational leader serves as a role model who is admired, respected, and trusted. Followers of such charismatic leaders "identify with the leaders and want to emulate them"; perceive them to have "extraordinary capabilities, persistence, and determination"; and see them as risk takers who are "consistent rather than arbitrary" (p. 6). The application of idealized influence essentially amounts to being a role model and exhibiting behaviors that subordinates admire and appreciate.

Inspirational Motivation. A key component of inspirational motivation is vision. The overuse of this concept in the popular press and misapplications in organizations has led to cynicism on the part of some employees. Nevertheless, when properly executed, visionary leadership can be a powerful tool for focusing and energizing staff. Visionary leadership is briefly discussed below as a specific model of leadership. Another important aspect of this element is setting high expectations for the work unit or program. Enthusiasm and encouragement are then used by the leader to pull the team toward the vision and achievement of expected results.

Intellectual Stimulation. Intellectual stimulation involves encouraging innovation and creativity. To enhance this, Bargal (2000) suggests that the leader develop the ability to "question old assumptions, traditions, and beliefs; to stimulate new perspectives and ways of doing things in others; and to encourage expression of new ideas and reasoning" (p. 308). This includes the current management axiom of "thinking outside the box." This principle is particularly important in the early stages of assessing the need for change.

Individualized Consideration. Individualized consideration involves coaching and mentoring workers as individuals and having ongoing personalized interactions with staff. Individual consideration involves finding ways for followers to identify growth goals and providing opportunities for them to achieve them. This can take the form of an explicit discussion with a follower, simply asking what is important to them and how these things can be achieved in a work setting.

According to Avolio and Bass (2002, p. 5), the best leaders use more transformational leadership than transactional leadership, but both used together are optimally effective. Finally, it is also important to note that transformational leadership can be confused with "pseudotransformational leadership," which focuses on personal power, manipulation, threat, and punishment (p. 8).

Yukl (2006, pp. 274–277) has offered several guidelines for the use of transformational leadership. First, articulate a clear and appealing vision, and explain how it can be attained. Act confident and optimistic, and express confidence in followers. Support the vision through resource allocations and emphasizing key values, and lead by example.

Summarizing research over the past 20 years, Bass and Avolio (2006, p. 48) concluded that transformational leadership was positively related to performance in the business, military, educational, government, and not-for-profit sectors. One meta-analysis of Full-Range Leadership, which includes the use of both transactional and transformational leadership (Judge & Piccolo, 2004), found that both transformational leadership and contingent rewards had significant relationships with outcomes, including follower satisfaction and group or organizational performance. In a review of the literature, Tucker and Russell (2004) concluded that transformational leaders can have a major influence on organizational culture and change. Yukl (2006) concluded that, in spite of conceptual weaknesses in the theory, "the available evidence supports many of the key propositions of the major theories of charismatic and transformational leadership" (p. 272).

There have been applications of transformational leadership concepts to human services organizations (Barker, Sullivan, & Emery, 2006; Packard, 2004; Yoo & Brooks, 2005). In one national study, transformational leadership was correlated with perceived leader effectiveness (Mary, 2005). In a hospital study, transformational leadership was significantly correlated with leader outcomes of effectiveness, satisfaction, and extra effort (Gellis, 2001). Another study found significant positive relationships between transformational leadership and job satisfaction, commitment, leader effectiveness, and satisfaction with the leader (Kays, 1993, cited in Mary, 2005, p. 209). Transformational leadership is compatible with human services values and principles regarding valuing and empowering individuals.

Exemplary Leadership

Kouzes and Posner's (2002) popular books on leadership, unlike some of the popular literature, present a model with an empirical base. While they have not formally named their model, we will use here the title of their most comprehensive book on the subject: exemplary leadership. Their model is structured around five "practices" and ten "commitments" of leadership. *Model the way* involves clarifying one's personal values and setting an example by aligning actions with values. *Inspire a shared vision* includes envisioning the future and enlisting others in a common vision. Exemplary leaders *challenge the process* by finding opportunities to innovate, change, and grow and by experimenting and taking risks. These leaders *enable others to act* by fostering collaboration through trust and cooperative goals and sharing power and discretion. Finally, such leaders *encourage the heart* by showing appreciation for individual excellence and celebrating values and victories through a spirit of community. In their research, they found several characteristics that people look for and admire in a leader:

- *Honest*: truthful, ethical, principled, worthy of trust
- *Forward-looking*: articulating a vision and sense of direction for the organization; using strategic planning and forecasting
- *Competent*: having a track record and the ability to get things done, understanding the fundamentals, having relevant experience
- *Inspiring*: enthusiastic, energetic, positive about the future

Kouzes and Posner (2002) conclude that these four make up *source credibility*—people believe in and trust them; they do what they say they will do, represented by the acronym DWYSYWD. "Do what you say you will do" requires that a leader practice what he or she preaches, "walk the talk," and follow through.

Visionary Leadership

Vision has been mentioned in several contexts above, including transformational leadership and exemplary leadership, and because it is mentioned so often in the leadership literature, it will be given special attention here. According to Nanus and Dobbs (1999), a vision is "a realistic, credible, attractive, and inspiring future for the organization" (p. 78). The vision should be challenging, but staff also need to see that, with time and enough of the right kind of work, it is attainable. While a mission statement describes why an organization exists (its purpose) and what it does (its unique niche of programs or activities), a vision statement represents where the organization wants to be, its ideal future.

Articulating a clear and compelling vision is an important aspect of leadership and, as will be discussed below, of change leadership as well. This is important to provide meaning, focus, and clarity of purpose for staff on an ongoing basis, and it may be even more important when organizational change is needed. The organization as a whole typically has a vision statement, and individual programs may have their own vision statements as well. Individual employees come to an organization with their own visions for what they want to accomplish in their careers. It is important for a leader to learn about his or her followers' aspirations, build these into the organization vision as possible, and help followers see how their individual visions can be realized through a common vision (Kouzes & Posner, 2002). Ultimately, all of these visions should be in alignment (Senge, 1990). While an initial statement of vision typically comes from the organization's leader, alignment can be facilitated by having employees involved in creating a final vision statement and then promulgating it throughout the organization. This can occur through a visioning process or, if necessary, through a larger process of culture change or organizational change, as described below.

Servant-Leadership

Servant-leadership, developed by retired AT&T executive Robert Greenleaf (2002), has received increasing attention in the popular literature in recent years. It is a nontraditional model for leadership in several respects. It was developed by a successful career executive; it is explicitly based in philosophical, ethical, and moral principles; and it presents the unorthodox idea that the leader should first serve followers.

Servant-leadership focuses on the leader-follower relationship and can be considered to be in the *style* category of leadership models because it focuses on leader behaviors. Spears (2005, pp. 33–36) has identified 10 characteristics of the servant-leader, many of which are clearly associated with social work and other human services professions: listening, empathy, healing "broken spirits" and "emotional hurts," general and self-awareness, using persuasion rather than positional authority, broad conceptual thinking and visioning, learning from the past and foreseeing future outcomes, stewardship ("holding their institutions in trust for the greater good of society"), commitment to the growth of people, and building community.

Until recent years, much of the writing on servant-leadership emphasized the description of desired behaviors and principles, but research on this model is expanding. A professional journal devoted to it, *The International Journal of Servant-Leadership,* was launched in 2005. Further systematic empirical work on this model should more fully illustrate its potential.

Strategic Leadership

One conceptualization of strategic leadership (Boal & Hooijberg, 2001) contrasts what they call "supervisory theories" of leadership, including contingency, path-goal, and leader-member exchange approaches, with strategic leadership approaches including charismatic, transformational, and visionary models.

> Activities often associated with strategic leadership include making strategic decisions; creating and communicating a vision of the future; developing key competencies and capabilities; developing organizational structures, processes, and controls; managing multiple constituencies; selecting and developing the next generation of leaders; sustaining an effective organizational culture;

> and infusing entical value systems into an organization's culture. (Boal & Hooijberg, 2001, p. 516)

Boal and Hooijberg (2001) further suggest that the "essence" of strategic leadership involves the ability to learn, the ability to change, and managerial wisdom, which includes social intelligence and the ability to take the right action at the right time (pp. 517–518).

As bluntly stated by Gill (2006), "Without strategies, vision is a dream" (p. 174). Leadership and vision are focused on end results, and organizational strategies can provide a road map for reaching them. Students and practitioners of management are aware of the importance of strategic planning (see Chapter 16 on strategic planning). It is addressed here as an aspect of leadership, suggesting that effective leadership can increase the prospects of strategy implementation. Strategic leadership, in this sense, is largely the use of a comprehensive strategic planning process. There can be a leadership dimension to this as well, using participative approaches to leadership by involving staff in the strategic planning process.

Thus far, the discussion of leadership has generally focused on a leader's role in ongoing operations of an agency. An increasingly important role for a leader in an organization is that of a *change leader* (Kotter, 1996). We will now discuss specifics of change leadership, with particular emphasis on organizational change and on creating a high-performance organizational culture.

Leadership and Organizational Culture Change

Organizational culture and climate were addressed in Chapter 6. Here, the discussion will focus on how leaders can create or transform cultures (Hatch, 2000) to deliver high-quality, effective services and on the kinds of leadership associated with a culture that is supportive of effective services. This is a key dynamic because culture is a medium through which leadership travels and impacts organizational performance.

Leaders play an important role in "embedding" and transmitting (Schein, 2004) the culture that they believe will most enhance organizational functioning. Schein (2004, p. 246) has identified six "primary embedding mechanisms":

- What leaders pay attention to, measure, and control on a regular basis
- How leaders react to critical incidents and organizational crises
- How leaders allocate resources
- Deliberate role modeling, teaching, and coaching
- How leaders allocate and reward status
- How leaders recruit, select, promote, and excommunicate

Schein (2004) has also identified six "secondary articulation and reinforcement mechanisms," which a leader can use to shape culture:

- Organizational design and structure
- Organizational systems and procedures
- Rites and rituals of the organization
- Design of physical space, facades, and buildings, including symbols
- Stories about important events and people
- Formal statements of organizational philosophy, creeds, and charters

Administrative mechanisms such as these can help shape a culture as humanistic or bureaucratic, performance or process focused, and team or individual oriented. Specifically, in the human resources area, supervisors as leaders can function as agents of socialization by the ways they assess, develop, coach, counsel, and give feedback to staff (Major, 2000).

Leaders give staff important clues based on the aspects of the organization they pay attention to. For example, if leaders focus on agency outcome data and the functioning of teams, they are likely to get different results than if they focus on following procedures and power struggles for resources. If leaders allocate resources for diversity initiatives and allocate rewards based on improved client outcomes through evidence-based practices and collaboration, employees will get clues regarding what is important. Employees know to look beyond merely what a leader says in meetings or newsletters to see what behaviors the leader models on a daily basis.

Organizational culture change will be addressed more fully in the later section on organizational change. Here, just a few comments will be made regarding the uniquenesses of culture change. Culture change will be presented below as a large-scale transformational change in the way the organization operates. Such a change requires totally new thinking and perspectives on the part of employees, and thus is extremely challenging and complicated and typically can only occur over a period of years.

From an individual employee's perspective, Schein (2004) has used Lewin's classic concepts of unfreezing, changing, and refreezing to illustrate how employees experience the culture change. Unfreezing creates disequilibrium in employees' cognitive structure by presenting disconfirming data, which leads an employee to believe that current conditions are no longer comfortable. This, of course, creates psychological anxiety, which must be addressed by the leader creating psychological safety, so that staff will feel safe in trying out new ways of operating. These new behaviors and attitudes are reinforced and rewarded by leadership, thus refreezing a new or modified organizational culture.

Schein (2004, pp. 332–333) has suggested several tactics to create psychological safety for staff. First, as mentioned above, a compelling vision for a new future can show how the organization can be improved. Formal and informal training, with active involvement of staff in the learning process, can be supported by "practice fields" where it is safe to try new behaviors, supported by coaches and useful feedback. Leaders act as role models for the new ways of thinking, and support groups can aid staff in the learning process. Finally, management systems, including structures and rewards, need to be set up in alignment with the new thinking.

Schein (2004) makes an additional point about how to view "culture change." While leaders often state culture change as the change goal, Schein asserts that a change goal should be stated in terms of desired organizational outcomes, not a process of culture change (p. 334). In other words, culture change is not an end in itself, but a process in service of the larger goal of improving operations and outcomes of the organization.

In summary, Schein (2004) suggests that creating a new culture requires that leaders have vision, persistence, patience, and both flexibility and readiness regarding change (p. 407). They also need the ability to perceive the problem, insight and self-awareness regarding their strengths and limitations, strong motivation for change, emotional strength to handle the inevitable anxiety and criticism, the ability to bring to the surface and change existing culture assumptions, and the ability to involve others in the change process (pp. 414–417).

While the most important goal of culture change is to improve organizational performance, the creation of a culture that is committed to ongoing learning is also a very important intermediate goal because organizational learning is a key aspect of organizational change. Austin and Hopkins (2004) and their colleagues have presented a variety of strategies for creating a learning organization and a culture of learning, including the design of "learning settings" (Garvin, 2000, cited in Austin & Hopkins, 2004). Regular organizational activities, such as staff meetings and outcomes assessments, can be augmented to become arenas for learning by a leader demonstrating a personal investment in learning, asking questions, empowering staff through shared decision making, using data in problem analysis and problem solving, and making time for reflection and the application of new knowledge, fostering dissent and risk taking, regular questioning and listening, and celebrating and rewarding individual learning. The leader should also demonstrate a personal commitment to learning through openness, an awareness of personal biases, a full use of data, and personal humility.

Change Leadership

We will now review a model of organizational change that can be used for any change goal, with our particular interest in improving organizational performance and creating a culture that supports it. A leader may initiate an organizational change process to meet a particular need or goal, such as moving the agency from a process-oriented to an outcomes-oriented culture or implementing evidence-based practice. In addition to such a large-scale initiative, organizational change in a typical human services agency can be a regular activity. Organizations and staffs change in small ways, such as developing new procedures, perhaps without even considering that change is occurring. For larger-scale changes, in which radical changes in the agency's culture or systems are required, the use of change leadership skills should enhance the prospects of the agency reaching its desired new state.

Types of Organizational Change

Costello (1994, cited by Proehl, 2001) identified three levels of organizational change. *Developmental change* involves adjustments to existing operations or improving a skill, method, or process that does not currently meet the agency's standard. This level of change is the least threatening to employees and the easiest to manage. Examples include problem solving, training, and improving communications. *Transitional change* involves implementing something new and abandoning old ways of functioning. This move through a transitional period to a new future state requires patience and time. Examples include reorganizations, new technology systems, and implementing a new program. The most extreme form of change is *transformational change*, which requires major shifts in vision, strategy, structure, or systems.

This might evolve out of necessity, for example, as a result of major policy changes like welfare reform and managed care. The new state involves a new culture, new beliefs, and awareness of new possibilities. Examples include privatization and managed competition.

A Model of Organizational Change

Proehl (2001) has described a change formula, which suggests that change can occur when (a) there is dissatisfaction with the current state, (b) staff have a clear vision of an ideal future state of the organization, (c) there is a clear and feasible process for reaching the desired state, and (d) these factors considered together outweigh the perceived costs of changing. From an employee's point of view, costs of change can include changes in employees' sense of competence, power or status, workplace relationships, rewards, and identity or roles. Therefore, the change leader can create conditions for change by creating dissatisfaction with the status quo, providing a clear and compelling vision for the new state, and establishing and using an effective and efficient process that minimizes the "costs" to participants. This formula is embedded in the following organizational change model.

The organizational change model described here is based largely on Proehl (2001), who created a model adapted from others, including Kotter (1996). Also included here are practice principles from Lewis et al. (2007) and Yukl (2006, p. 303). This model and the related practice principles are primarily informed by case research by author/consultants and a small number of research studies on specific elements of the model.

Imagine an agency executive of a not-for-profit agency who recognizes an important trend in the environment that is now facing the agency: the move in government agencies toward performance-based contracting (see Chapter 8). Most agencies are more accustomed to cost reimbursement contracts, in which the program often has to provide only data on client demographics and services delivered. A move to a performance-based organizational culture is a significant one for most human services organizations. This executive, as a change leader, may increase the prospects of a successful change by using a structured organizational change process, beginning with creating a sense of urgency and ending with institutionalizing and celebrating the change. In a related example, Fisher (2005) has suggested the use of transformational leadership in implementing an outcomes measurement system.

While these steps are presented in a logical linear fashion, they may at some times overlap or be addressed in a different sequence, based on specific agency conditions. Throughout the process, change leaders should be alert to human factors, including staff resistance and need to be informed of activities. Consistent with principles of participative management, involving staff in the process should have a significant effect on creating staff commitment, as well as leading to better ideas and outcomes.

1. *Create a sense of urgency.* The first step for a change leader is to create a sense of urgency among staff regarding the need for change. Staff may be both comfortable and happy with the status quo and feel that they are overworked enough as it is; they may be disinclined to take on a significant change in the way they and their programs operate. The administrator can begin by sharing with staff the important environmental forces impacting the agency. If local government agencies are going to begin requiring performance data in new contracts, the executive can explain the implications for programs and staff; for example, the agency will need to be able to respond to these demands from key funding organizations in order to survive. Cost pressures, while not a popular topic with staff, can be shared, again related to agency growth and survival needs.

As much as possible, existing data should be used to demonstrate the urgency for change. The agency may have staff morale data such as attitude surveys, or at least sick leave and turnover data, which may indicate problems needing attention. More important, if the agency's data systems do not allow the documentation of client outcomes, or if cost effectiveness and efficiency results are below industry standards, staff should see that changes will be needed. This potentially disturbing information may be framed by the executive within a more optimistic and hopeful context by referring to agency and staff visions and ideals for the highest quality of services to the agency's clients, to motivate staff in a more positive way. This step and others below found support in a study of large-scale service integration change efforts in several counties (Patti, Packard, Daly, Tucker-Tatlow, & Prosek, 2003).

2. *Develop an action system.* Large-scale change cannot be accomplished by only the executive or top management team. Building a broad-based action system with designated responsibility for implementing and overseeing the change initiative serves several functions. If many staff are involved, multiple talents can be brought to bear to address the challenges and tasks ahead. Spreading the workload can help ensure that the additional demands of change do not significantly disrupt ongoing work. And, getting staff involved can increase their sense of ownership of the results.

A large-scale change initiative can be guided and overseen by a "change coalition" (Kotter, 1996) such as an organizational change steering committee that has representatives from all key stakeholder groups in the agency, including different levels of the hierarchy (from executives to line staff), different program and administrative areas, and labor organization representation, if appropriate. Specific roles should be delineated (Proehl, 2001). The CEO or other executive serves as a sponsor, who demonstrates organizational commitment to the process and ensures that necessary resources (especially including staff time) are allocated. The key staff person responsible for day-to-day operation of the initiative can serve as a champion who not only oversees implementation but provides ongoing energy and focus for staff. There will probably be multiple change agents who are responsible for implementation at the unit or team level. They may be task force or problem-solving group

chairs, facilitators, or external consultants. Many other staff should be involved as task force or committee members or involved in data collection and analysis and the design and implementation of new systems or processes.

Finally, organizational systems need to be set up to ensure effective functioning of the process. This includes structural arrangements, such as the reporting relationships of the various committees and task forces, and communication processes to ensure that all staff are aware of what is happening. Newsletters, e-mail bulletins, all-staff meetings, and reports at regular unit meetings should all be used, on an ongoing basis.

3. *Clarify the change imperative.* Early in the process, the visions and desired outcomes should be refined and widely communicated throughout the organization. Staffing and resources available for the initiative should be clearly defined. As soon as possible, plans for activities (formation of task forces, data collection and analysis, completion of action plans) should be formalized and put into timelines with deadline dates.

4. *Assess the present.* Next, a more detailed look at the current state of the organization can identify specific areas needing attention. Organizational readiness for change can be assessed by examining existing management and staff competencies, the organization's culture, and the state of existing processes and systems such as, in this example, the agency information system (IS). For example, it may become clear that the existing IS does not measure key factors that will be needed in an outcomes-based system. The existing organizational culture may focus on bureaucratic rules and processes or on interpersonal relationships, rather than on actual results for clients.

This assessment should also consider forces in the agency that will tend to support or resist this change. A key concern will be staff resistance. Proehl (2001, p. 161) has described a "resistance pyramid" to locate areas of resistance. Staff who do not know about the change should be informed and involved in the process. Staff who are not able to change should receive training in new skills, such as the use of outcomes measurement. Finally, change agents can work directly with staff who are not willing to change, by using goal setting, coaching, and feedback while working to show how they can actually benefit from the change. There may be a small group of individuals who may never become committed and who may be ignored or addressed through directive supervision focusing on necessary performance expectations.

A force field analysis (Proehl, 2001; an example of a force field analysis regarding implementation of a program evaluation system is in Lewis et al., 2007, p. 268) can be used to more fully detail the driving forces that will aid the change or make it more likely to occur and the restraining forces, such as specific people, groups, or things getting in the way of change. Using a force field analysis involves identifying key stakeholders, such as managers and staff who may be affected by this change, and planning tactics that will leverage the driving forces and lower the restraining forces (e.g., resisters, as described above).

5. *Develop and implement the plan for change.* After the situation is analyzed, people are involved, and change management processes are in place, strategies and processes can be initiated to implement the change. Teams or task forces can be designated to engage in detailed problem solving and design new processes. In the example here, an information systems task force could identify new data needs from funders and ensure that, based on their program model, all relevant data are collected. Proposed changes may require redesign or replacement of current agency software and changes to recordkeeping systems. When a new system is designed, procedures will need to be written and a staff training program developed. Proposals for change are commonly submitted to the change coalition or steering committee and then forwarded to executive management for final approval.

During implementation of the change plan elements, Proehl (2001, p. 169) recommends "acting quickly and revising frequently," identifying opportunities for short-term successes so that staff can see tangible results from their efforts. And, consistent with principles for organizational learning, the new system should be assessed to ensure that it has the desired results, or is modified as needed.

6. *Evaluate, institutionalize, and celebrate.* Any changes made should be assessed to ensure success and also need to be institutionalized. A new outcomes-based information system can be institutionalized by changing software and record-keeping procedures and reflecting the changes in the procedures manual. Staff will need to be retrained, and training for new staff should reflect the new system. Culture change is harder to institutionalize, but change leaders can, using principles discussed in an earlier section, continually reinforce the new ways of operating. This should include formal and informal reward systems. Job descriptions and performance appraisal systems may need to be modified to include behaviors such as proper use of the new IS and delivering services that obtain desired client outcomes.

Implementation of new systems should be monitored and evaluated, with further adjustments as needed. Finally, changes and successes should be celebrated in ways consistent with the organization's culture. Special events can be held when major milestones are met, and smaller successes can be rewarded and celebrated in staff meetings and other arenas.

Diversity and Ethics Issues in Leadership

Two additional issues related to organizational dynamics warrant more focused attention here: diversity and ethics as they apply to leadership.

Diversity Aspects of Leadership Effectiveness

While diversity issues in organizations have received increasing attention over the past three decades, specifics regarding leadership aspects of diversity have not yet been as fully addressed. In one study, Romero (2005) found that Hispanic leaders were perceived as equivalent to Euro-American leaders in effectiveness, that a leader-subordinate style match was important, and that participative approaches led to higher satisfaction. One expert in the field of workplace diversity, Thomas (2006), has suggested that current notions of diversity need to be broadened to go beyond mere representation to a focus on diversity management: "making quality decisions in the midst of difference, similarities, and related tensions" (p. 50). He adds that leaders will need to acknowledge the challenges in making decisions in diverse organizations and "become more comfortable with tension and complexity" and be more strategic in their thinking, considering diversity issues in the context of mission, vision, and strategy (p. 51).

Mills and Mills (2000) examined the role of gender in organizational culture, highlighting the importance of senior management in shaping culture; they noted that "the commitment of top managers to a program of employment equity, for example, has been shown to have strong influence on outcomes" (p. 64). In a summary of relevant research, Northouse (2004) concluded that "although quite similar to men in behavior and effectiveness, women leaders tend to be more participative and less autocratic, a pattern that is well suited to 21st-century global organizations" (p. 273). Gill (2006) has reported that "several studies have suggested that male and female leaders tend to behave differently but are equally effective" (p. 310). Recognizing the controversies in this field, Eagly and Carli (2003) reviewed meta-analyses of the research on leadership and gender, often examining the use of transformational and transactional leadership, and concluded that "on the average, contemporary female managers manifest a small advantage in leadership style but can face disadvantage from prejudicial evaluation of their competence as leaders, especially in male-dominated leadership roles" (pp. 851–852).

In social work, Austin (1995) has summarized challenges in advancing women and people from diverse backgrounds into management positions. He concluded that both personal strategies, including peer support and career planning, and institutional strategies, including mentoring, management training programs, and explicit organizational policies and initiatives addressing discrimination, will be necessary (pp. 1654–1656). Based on leadership research to date, Yukl (2006) has offered these guidelines: Set an example in appreciating diversity; encourage respect for individual differences; promote an understanding of different values, beliefs, and traditions; explain the benefits of diversity for the organization; encourage and support those who promote tolerance of diversity; address stereotypes and biased beliefs or role expectations for women and "minorities"; and take disciplinary action as needed to stop discrimination or harassment (p. 436).

Ethics Issues in Leadership

The importance of personal values as a component of leadership is part of several of the models of leadership discussed here. While values represent concepts or principles that are considered to be valuable or important, ethics include behavioral guidelines for operationalizing values. The leader's role in developing and encouraging the use of shared values in the organization is worth special emphasis. According to Gill (2006), "creating a sense of shared core values that support the organization's vision, mission and strategies requires their integration into every policy, procedure and process concerning employees: recruitment and selection, performance and management appraisal, training and development, promotion and rewards" (p. 152). A homeless shelter used a process to develop shared organizational values (Packard, 2001), which were built into organizational processes, as Gill suggested. Organizational culture, discussed above, is a useful medium through which to share and disseminate organizational values.

However, actually changing and institutionalizing organizational values, a deep aspect of culture, requires ongoing, concerted leadership over a period of years.

Manning (2003) has asserted that culture is the "context for ethics" in an organization (p. 197), and that leaders must develop an "ethical framework," which includes the agency's mission, values statement, and ethical code, to guide staff (p. 221). She sees leaders as "architects" of organizational structures and processes that "enhance and promote a moral vision and ethical action," concluding that "the essence of ethical leadership is enacting professional values through every decision and action—values that contribute to the common good" (p. 264). The articulation and promotion of organizational values and ethical standards is thus a core aspect of leadership. Leaders can use models of transformational, exemplary, and servant-leadership in their daily behavior and in the ongoing maintenance of an ethical organizational culture.

Summary and Conclusions

Anyone reviewing the overwhelming amount of theory, research, and practice wisdom in this field may end up being confused about ultimate practice implications. At the risk of oversimplification, the following summary of principles for leadership to enhance organizational performance in the human services will be offered.

First, commit yourself to a career-long process of self-awareness, discovery, and learning. Work to "discover your strengths" (Buckingham & Clifton, 2001) and build upon them, discover and fix any fatal flaws in your skills and style, and look for the best fit between yourself and work situations. Use an individual development plan and engage in continuous learning. This should include taking advantage of leadership training and development opportunities (Day, 2001; Hernez-Broome & Hughes, 2004; McCauley & Van Velsor, 2004) and remaining current with relevant research.

Regarding leader traits, higher levels of intellectual, emotional, and social intelligence will enhance prospects for success as a leader, as will high energy, tolerance for stress, self-confidence, an internal locus of control, self regulation, systems thinking, and emotional stability and maturity. Include these factors in your own leadership development as possible and appropriate. Ground your leader behavior in your values, principles, and ethical standards, and demonstrate and articulate these in your work. Integrity, trust, and honesty are especially important.

While individual leaders may have a natural set of strengths or preferences in terms of skills such as task, relationship, and change behaviors, it will help to broaden your style range and develop assessment skills that will enable you to use the appropriate mix of behaviors for particular followers and situations. Remember that a concern for both people and results is important.

Assess individual followers in terms of their strengths, needs, and visions, and work to enable them to see how their goals can be accomplished by working toward organizational goals. Put them in situations that facilitate this. Set challenging goals and high standards, and demonstrate confidence that these can be attained, providing support and development as needed.

As appropriate, use current theories and models including transformational, transactional, exemplary, visionary, and servant-leadership. These include the "four I's" of transformational leadership (idealized influence, inspirational motivation, intellectual stimulation, and individualized consideration) and factors identified by Kouzes and Posner (2002), including honesty and competence, summarized as "Do what you say you will do." Use personal and organizational visions to provide focus and energy in the pursuit of organizational goals. Address the larger context through strategic leadership, including not only strategic planning, thinking, and managing, but also the design of effective organizational cultures, structures, and processes.

Leadership opportunities in an organization are nearly constant, ranging from individual supervision and staff meetings to the oversight and improvement of management and program processes and organizational culture. Additionally, organizational change and organizational learning will be necessary to regularly improve client services and organizational effectiveness. Leaders also need to ensure alignment among organizational processes, including strategy, culture, management systems, programs, and required resources.

Effective leadership is likely to be even more essential in the future to facilitate the growth and adaptation of human services organizations in the constant challenge to improve performance. This will require not only individual leadership development, but also greater attention to teaching leadership in schools of social work and to others preparing human services managers. Finally, as was noted above, there is not extensive coverage of leadership in the human services literature. This warrants more study in its own right, and perhaps more important, as a variable in broader research focusing on factors that affect organizational performance.

Note

1. Some of this section has been adapted from Packard (2004, pp. 152–155).

Internet Sites

The Leader to Leader Institute: http://leadertoleader.org/

The Center for Creative Leadership: http://www.ccl.org/leadership/index.aspx

The Greenleaf Center for Servant-Leadership: http://www.greenleaf.org/

Being First, Inc.: http://www.beingfirst.com/

References

Austin, D. (1995). Management overview. In R. Edwards (Ed.), *Encyclopedia of social work* (19th ed., pp. 1642–1658). Washington, DC: NASW Press.

Austin, M., & Hopkins, K. (Eds.). (2004). *Supervision as collaboration in the human services: Building a learning culture.* Thousand Oaks, CA: Sage.

Avolio, B., & Bass, B. (2002). *Developing potential across a full range of leadership: Cases on transactional and transformational leadership.* Mahwah, NJ: Lawrence Erlbaum Associates.

Bargal, D. (2000). The manager as leader. In R. Patti (Ed.), *The handbook of social welfare management* (pp. 303–319). Thousand Oaks, CA: Sage.

Barker, A., Sullivan, D., & Emery, M. (2006). *Leadership competencies for clinical managers: The renaissance of transformational leadership.* Sudbury, MA: Jones and Bartlett.

Bass, B. (1998). *Transformational leadership: Industrial, military, and educational impact.* Mahwah, NJ: Lawrence Erlbaum Associates.

Bass, B., & Avolio, B. (2006). *Transformational leadership* (2nd ed.). Mahwah, NJ: Lawrence Erlbaum Associates.

Blake, R., & McCanse, A. (1991). *Leadership dilemmas—grid solutions.* Houston, TX: Gulf.

Boal, K., & Hooijberg, R. (2001). Strategic leadership research: Moving on. *Leadership Quarterly, 11*(4), 515–549.

Buckingham, M., & Clifton, D. (2001). *Now, discover your strengths.* New York: The Free Press.

Collins, J. (2001). *Good to great: Why some companies make the leap . . . and others don't.* New York: HarperBusiness.

Conger, J., & Kanungo, R. (1998). *Charismatic leadership in organizations.* Thousand Oaks, CA: Sage.

Costello, S. (1994). *Managing change in the workplace.* New York: Irwin.

Day, D. (2001). Leadership development: A review in context. *Leadership Quarterly, 11*(4), 581–613.

Eagly, A., & Carli, L. (2003). Finding gender advantage and disadvantage: Systematic research integration is the solution. *Leadership Quarterly, 14,* 851–859.

Fisher, E. (2005). Facing the challenges of outcomes measurement: The role of transformational leadership. *Administration in Social Work, 29*(4), 35–49.

Garvin, D. (2000). *Learning in action: A guide to putting the learning organization to work.* Boston: Harvard Business School Press.

Gellis, Z. (2001). Social work perceptions of transformational and transactional leadership in health care. *Social Work Research, 25*(1), 17–25.

Gill, R. (2006). *Theory and practice of leadership.* Thousand Oaks, CA: Sage.

Graen, G., & Uhl-Bien, M. (1995). Relationship-based approach to leadership: Development of leader-member exchange (LMX) theory of leadership over 25 years: Applying a multi-level multi-domain perspective. *Leadership Quarterly, 9*(2), 219–247.

Greenleaf, R. (2002). *Servant-leadership: A journey into the nature of legitimate power and greatness.* Mahwah, NJ: Paulist Press.

Gummer, B., & Edwards, R. (1995). The politics of human services administration. In L. Ginsberg & P. Keys (Eds.), *New management in human services* (2nd ed. pp. 57–71). Washington, DC: NASW Press.

Hatch, M. (2000). The cultural dynamics of organizing and change. In N. Ashkanasy, C. Wilderom, & M. Peterson (Eds.), *Handbook of organizational culture & change* (pp. 245–260). Thousand Oaks, CA: Sage.

Hernez-Broome, G., & Hughes, R. (2004). Leadership development: Past, present, and future. *Human Resource Planning, 27*(1), 24–32.

Hersey, P., Blanchard, K., & Johnson, D. (2001). *Management of organizational behavior: Leading human resources* (8th ed.). Upper Saddle River, NJ: Prentice Hall.

Hollenbeck, G., McCall, M., & Silzer, R. (2006). Leadership competency models. *Leadership Quarterly, 17*, 398–413.

House, R. J., & Mitchell, T. R. (1974). Path-goal theory of leadership. *Journal of Contemporary Business, 3*, 81–97.

Judge, T., & Piccolo, R. (2004). Transformational and transactional leadership: A meta-analytic test of their relative validity. *Journal of Applied Psychology, 89*(5), 755–768.

Kotter, J. (1990). *A force for change: How leadership differs from management.* New York: The Free Press.

Kotter, J. (1996). *Leading change.* Boston: Harvard Business School Press.

Kouzes, J., & Posner, B. (2002). *The leadership challenge* (3rd ed.). San Francisco: Jossey-Bass.

Lewis, J., Packard, T., & Lewis, M. (2007). *Management of human service programs* (4th ed.). Belmont, CA: Thompson/Brooks Cole.

Major, D. (2000). Effective newcomer socialization. In N. Ashkanasy, C. Wilderom, & M. Peterson (Eds.), *Handbook of organizational culture & change* (pp. 355–368). Thousand Oaks, CA: Sage.

Manning, S. (2003). *Ethical leadership in human services: A multi-dimensional approach.* Boston: Allyn & Bacon.

Mary, N. (2005). Transformational leadership in human service organizations. *Administration in Social Work, 29*(2), 105–118.

McCauley, C., & Van Velsor, E. (Eds.). (2004). *The center for creative leadership handbook of leadership development* (2nd ed.). San Francisco: Jossey-Bass.

McNeece, C., & Thyer, B. (2004). Evidence-based practice and social work. *Journal of Evidence-Based Practice, 1*(1), 7–25.

Mills, J., & Mills, A. (2000). Rules, sensemaking, formative contexts, and discourse in the gendering of organizational culture. In N. Ashkanasy, C. Wilderom, & M. Peterson (Eds.), *Handbook of organizational culture and climate* (pp. 55–70). Thousand Oaks, CA: Sage.

Nanus, B., & Dobbs, S. (1999). *Leaders who make a difference: Essential strategies for meeting the nonprofit challenge.* San Francisco: Jossey-Bass.

Northouse, P. (2004). *Leadership: Theory and practice* (3rd ed.). Thousand Oaks, CA: Sage.

Packard, T. (2001). Building commitment through mission and values: The case of a homeless shelter. *Administration in Social Work, 25*(3), 35–52.

Packard, T. (2004). The supervisor as transformational leader. In M. Austin & K. Hopkins (Eds.), *Supervision as collaboration in the human services: Building a learning culture* (pp. 151–163). Thousand Oaks, CA: Sage.

Patti, R. (1987). Managing for service effectiveness in social welfare organizations. *Social Work, 32*(5), 377–381.

Patti, R., Packard, T., Daly, D., Tucker-Tatlow, J., & Prosek, K. (2003). *Seeking better performance through interagency collaboration: Prospects and challenges.* A report commissioned by The Southern Area Consortium of Human Services, San Diego State University: Network for Excellence in the Human Services.

Pfeffer, J., & Sutton, R. (2006). *Hard facts, dangerous half-truths and total nonsense: Profiting from evidence-based management.* Boston: Harvard Business School.

Proehl, R. (2001). *Organizational change in the human services.* Thousand Oaks, CA: Sage.

Roberts-DeGennaro, M., & Packard, T. (2002). Framework for developing a social administration concentration. *Journal of Teaching in Social Work, 22*(1/2), 61–77.

Romero, E. (2005). The effect of Hispanic ethnicity on the leadership process. *International Journal of Leadership Studies, 1*, 86–101.

Rousseau, D. (2006). Is there such a thing as "evidence-based management"? *Academy of Management Review, 31*(2), 256–269.

Schein, E. (2004). *Organizational culture and leadership* (3rd ed.). San Francisco: John Wiley & Sons.

Senge, P. (1990). *The fifth discipline.* New York: Doubleday Currency.

Spears, L. (2005). The understanding and practice of servant-leadership. *International Journal of Servant-Leadership, 1*(1), 29–45.

Thomas, R. (2006). Diversity management: An essential craft for future leaders. In F. Hesselbein & M. Goldsmith (Eds.), *The leader of the future 2* (pp. 47–54). San Francisco: Jossey-Bass.

Tucker, B., & Russell, R. (2004). Influence of the transformational leader. *Journal of Leadership & Organizational Studies, 10*(4), 103–111.

Vroom, V., & Yetton, P. (1973). *Leadership and decision making.* Pittsburgh: University of Pittsburgh Press.

Yoo, J., & Brooks, D. (2005). The role of organizational variables in predicting service effectiveness: An analysis of a multilevel model. *Research on Social Work Practice, 15*(4), 267–277.

Yukl, G. (2006). *Leadership in organizations* (6th ed.). Upper Saddle River, NJ: Prentice Hall.

Zenger, J., & Folkman, J. (2002). *The extraordinary leader.* New York: McGraw-Hill.

CHAPTER 8

Managing for Service Outcomes

The Critical Role of Information

John Poertner

Consumers of social services achieve results through a series of transactions with social workers and other helping professionals. Managers generally do not observe these transactions, yet they are responsible for helping create the conditions that will make this a success for consumers and workers. Information is essential for the manager to know how well the service transaction is working. This chapter discusses the types of information managers need to support the provision of effective services, ways in which this information can be obtained, and how it can be used to create a culture of learning and innovation and expectation for positive consumer outcomes.

Kaplan and Norton (1992) created the "balanced scorecard" as a management tool and use the mixed metaphor of the pilot of a commercial airliner:

Think of the balanced scorecard as the dials and indicators in an airplane cockpit. For the complex task of navigating and flying an airplane, pilots need detailed information about many aspects of the flight. They need information on fuel, air speed, altitude, bearing, destination, and other indicators that summarize the current and predicted environment. Reliance on one instrument can be fatal. (p. 72)

The human services manager is in a similar position. She or he is charged with making a difference in the lives of consumers. The task of managing or piloting a social program is even more complex than that of piloting an airplane. Flying blind or relying on one piece of information can be devastating to consumers.

Human services administrators need to know what information is important and how to use it.

The airplane pilot's tasks are largely mechanical. Pilots respond to the information they receive from their instruments or ground controllers by manipulating systems that change altitude, direction, or speed. Social administrators must respond to the information they receive largely by working with people.

While Kaplan and Norton (1992) concern themselves with identifying the information managers need to produce performance, social administrators need this type of information to use in complex organizational and community environments to benefit consumers. The information that a pilot needs and how it is to be used to successfully transport a group of people from one point to another are well established. This is much less true for human services.

Focusing on the "Right" Information

Determining the information a manager needs to pilot a social program is far from easy. The airline schedule clearly shows where and when the plane is to begin and end a flight. Consumers know where they will end up and about what time. Determining the end or result of a social program for consumers is more difficult.

In an ideal world, public policy identifies society's desired outcome goals. Presumably, these are the goals of consumers and reflect the latest knowledge about the problem. Funding mechanisms now align fiscal incentives with desired results. The world of the human services administrator is not that well ordered. Social policy necessarily lags behind scientific knowledge of social problems and effective interventions. Interest groups are diverse and may have different goals than consumers. We are just beginning to obtain sufficient experience with performance-based contracting to learn how to align fiscal incentives with results.

For example, knowledge of child abuse, mental illness, or addictions is dynamic, with research frequently yielding new insights. Consequently, child welfare, mental health, and addiction

services change as understanding of the problem and testing of interventions demonstrates what works and what does not. The evidence-based intervention movement that seeks to employ interventions with the best evidence of effectiveness has only recently come to social work (Gambrill, 1999). The recency of this concept is demonstrated by a search of Social Work Abstracts. Using the keyword *evidence-based* to search the period 1977 through 2006 returns 155 references; over 90% were published after 2000.

Public policy regarding any social problem is also a moving target. Tracing changes in child welfare or mental health policy over the last 100 to 150 years shows dramatic twists and turns. Juvenile courts of today are far different from the Jane Addams–inspired Cook County Juvenile Court of 1899. Our current public policy goals of safety and permanency for children (Adoption and Safe Families Act [ASFA], 1997) did not exist in 1900. Conditions in mental hospitals of the 19th century would not be tolerated today.

Public policy that expresses society's concern for a social problem is established through the collective actions of interest groups. These groups are constituents of social programs whose concerns cannot be ignored by the human services administrator. Managers of social programs work with many different groups of constituents, from consumers to policy makers (Austin, 2002). Ideas that constituents have about social program goals may coincide with those of managers or they may be different. For example, there may be tension between consumers advocating for particular services and the agency's funding source that does not reimburse for those services.

The National Alliance on Mental Illness (NAMI) is an example of a constituent group. The mission of NAMI is "the eradication of mental illnesses and . . . the improvement of the quality of life for persons of all ages who are affected by mental illnesses" (NAMI, 2008). This organization was founded in 1979 and includes organizations in every state and in over 1100 local communities. NAMI is an important constituent for any manager of mental health services, and their interests need to be considered along with existing mental health policy and funding mechanisms.

Funding mechanisms such as performance-based contracts impact managers and consumers. These contracts are intended to be structured so that the funding agency reimburses the agency when it achieves certain agreed-upon program objectives. However, this may not always work well. There is considerable variation in these contract provisions, and they change over time (Martin, 2005).

The metaphor of a pilot's dashboard is useful for thinking about the information that a social administrator needs to produce results. With the multiple demands on a manager's time and attention, it is a challenge to maintain a focus on program results and key indicators needed to monitor results and prompt action. Envision a manager entering her or his office in the morning where Kaplan and Norton's (1992) balanced scorecard is displayed on the computer. What would be the components of the scorecard?

Critical Information for Managers

Poertner and Rapp (2007) suggest categories of information needs for social programs. These are outcomes for consumers or clients, the service events that are necessary to produce these outcomes, resources needed to produce results, and measures of efficiency and staff morale.

Outcomes for Consumers

It is now widely accepted that social services are expected to produce results for consumers or clients. These results are the principal concern of the human services manager. However, deciding what to measure is not always straightforward because there is often a lack of agreement or clarity on intended results. The degree to which specific outcomes are agreed upon by constituents varies. Where there is agreement, managers have an easier time determining what to measure.

However, how to measure in a way that truly captures the nature and extent of consumer outcomes remains a challenge.

In some cases, public policy explicitly states the intended outcome. The Adoption and Safe Families Act of 1997 (P. L. 105-89) is unambiguous in identifying the intended outcomes of safety and permanency for vulnerable children. Welfare reform was principally concerned with reducing dependence on public assistance and placing recipients in gainful employment. The intended results of public health or mental health policy are less clear.

Service Events

Positive outcomes for consumers generally occur through a series of interactions with a social worker. These are the service events.

Yeaman, Craine, Gorsek, and Corrigan (2000) describe a program improvement project in a psychiatric rehabilitation program that is an example of linking service events to outcomes. Based upon the mental health research literature, the program was designed to include training in medication, symptom, and leisure time management. Training in these skills has been found to produce benefits to consumers, including reductions in incidents of disruptive behavior. Reduction in disruptive behavior was the desired outcome, and skills training in three key areas were the service events. When this program was implemented, both behavior and the number of hours of skills training per month were monitored. The result was a 50% reduction in reported incidents of disruptive behavior.

If service events produce consumer benefits, knowing which events have beneficial results is critical. This is a large and difficult task for managers. Evidence-based practices are a significant development in this regard (Gambrill, 2006; Jenson, 2005; Zlotnik & Solt, 2006). Evidence-based practices emphasize using interventions that have the best available research evidence for their effectiveness. Fortunately, there are an increasing number of research reviews that summarize the available evidence for specific interventions. The research base for an intervention normally identifies the service events, including their frequency, scope, and duration.

Staff Morale

With results for consumers coming largely from their interactions with social workers over time, a concern for the morale of these workers is only natural. Consumers of social services present large and complex problems that have profound effects on their lives. Not surprisingly, the service transaction is frequently emotional. A worker repeatedly engaging in these emotional events needs support and encouragement, not workplace stress.

While it makes sense that there is a connection between job satisfaction and outcomes for consumers, this is not well established in the research literature. Glisson and Hemmelgarn (1998; also see Chapter 6) conducted research that linked organizational climate to positive outcomes for children. Their definition of organizational climate included fairness, role clarity, role overload, role conflict, cooperation, growth and advancement, job satisfaction, emotional exhaustion, personal accomplishment, and depersonalization. This single study linking job satisfaction and outcomes does not warrant strong claims of a positive relationship. Additional research on this important connection needs to be done. However, even without strong empirical evidence linking the two, social administrators seek high staff morale because direct service workers are among the most important resources in the social agency. Creating a positive work environment should be an important value for social administrators.

Resources

The human services manager who disregards resources will quickly go out of business. Social programs require resources to maintain the agency and produce the service events that lead to positive outcomes for consumers. Anything needed to operate a social program is a resource.

Money is the first resource to come to mind. Identification of all of the resources required for consumers to succeed results in a long list. However, only some of them need to be monitored. Some resources need more attention than others. As a general rule, a manager only needs to monitor those resources whose shortage would threaten program success.

For example, the environment where the consumers and workers engage is very important to the success of the service transaction. If the program is designed for workers to engage consumers in their homes, it is probably sufficient to monitor whether there are sufficient funds in the program budget to pay workers' transportation expenses. On the other hand, an employment program for people with severe mental illness will not be successful without jobs and willing employers. Given the ever-changing business environment in most communities, it is likely that the program manager will need to have a gauge counting the number of jobs and/or willing employers.

Efficiency

Human services agencies frequently have more potential consumers than available resources can accommodate. This is the rationale for including efficiency. Efficiency measures are simply ratios of inputs and outputs. Inputs are all of those resources that are required to maintain the program. Outputs include consumer benefits, service events, and staff morale.

The program manager does not need a report for every possible measure of efficiency. Those efficiency measures that can easily deviate from the desired level are the ones needing attention. For example, it is likely in most environments that the number of consumers per worker requires monitoring. Given the large number of people requiring attention from social programs, a worker's caseload can easily become overwhelming. The importance of this efficiency measure is indicated by the many national groups that maintain standards for programs that include caseload size (e.g., see the Child Welfare League of America, http://www.cwla.org).

Another example is the cost per consumer outcome or the cost of a service event. These are also two important ways of budgeting for social programs (Martin, 2001; see Chapter 16). These costs are not likely to change as quickly as the number of consumers per worker; therefore, they may only need to be monitored on an annual or semiannual basis.

Selecting Measures

For the human services administrator to produce benefits to consumers, the information system needs to accurately report on the "right" information. Poertner and Rapp (2007) suggest that in addition to the usual characteristics of validity and reliability, measures need to be understandable, susceptible to change, and efficient. Selecting measures that meet these criteria is not always easy.

Understandable

For staff and consumers to work effectively together, they must communicate effectively. If they do not share common meanings of key terms, they are unlikely to work to achieve common goals. If staff of a child welfare agency do not agree on what is meant by placement stability, they will not all be working to achieve the same result.

While this seems obvious, people in organizations get caught up in professional jargon and communications shortcuts. On a day-to-day basis, it seems to be more efficient to speak in what we consider to be consensually understood shorthand. One difficulty is that we often do not share the same meaning for key words. A work unit might agree that workers should make weekly contact with children in their foster care caseload. However, everyone might not agree on how *contact* is defined. Contact could be face to face, phone, e-mail, or text message. Each may have advantages, but which one is the most important for producing results for children?

Outcome measures should also pass the common sense test for stakeholders. Social services exist because the public invests valuable resources in social problems. A public that does not understand what we are talking about is unlikely to support our efforts.

Susceptible to Change

If a measure does not change, it is not providing information that a manager can act upon. If the weather forecast is "sunny and 75 degrees" every day, people will not pay attention. However, if there are wild variations in weather, people check the forecast first thing every day and act accordingly.

For human services programs, lack of variation in performance measures can be due to the choice of the measure. For example, a measure of some psychological construct is not likely to change. Another reason for lack of variation might be the frequency of the measurement. For example, if the cost of achieving an outcome is reported monthly, it is unlikely to show much change. However, this is likely an important measure on an annual or semiannual basis.

Efficient

Efficiency deserves special attention because measurement is expensive. While it may not be obvious, most people in organizations are aware of the cost of data collection, storage, and retrieval. Much of the data collection cost is staff time, and this is primarily spent filling out forms. The cost of maintaining a staff that stores and retrieves this data is also nontrivial and often hidden (Lohmann & Lohmann, 2002).

For example, SACWIS is a government-supported program to help states improve their child welfare information systems. A General

Accounting Office (GAO) report estimated that states invested more than $2.4 billion in the design and implementation of these information systems (United States General Accounting Office, 2003). This is an enormous amount of money that did not go to services for children and families. These opportunity costs deserve attention when selecting measures. The GAO report did not include the costs of workers filling out forms, which may have an even more important impact on children and families.

Balancing costs and accuracy is a complex task. Measurement costs may lead managers to accept measures based on existing, but inferior, data. Osborne and Plastrik (2000) warn managers against taking these "measurement shortcuts." While most organizations collect a lot of data, Osborne and Plastrik suggest that much of this information is not relevant. They further suggest that managers should devote precious organizational resources to collecting data that is useful. Useful data is that which informs decisions that impact the actions taken to improve the several types of performance mentioned earlier.

Types of Measures

When selecting measures, it is helpful to be familiar with the types of measures that are most frequently used. Each performance area is typically associated with certain types of measures. The most complex of these is consumer outcome, but service events, resources, staff morale, and efficiency also present challenges.

Consumer Outcomes

Identifying measures for consumer outcomes is arguably the most important information for managing a social service program. It is also the most difficult to obtain. Agencies seldom collect these measures as a normal part of doing business, and designing an instrument is a complex and expensive process. When managing an evidence-based

practice, there are manuals and research results that identify appropriate measurement instruments for many types of performance.

There are also books that identify well-designed instruments. Nugent, Sieppert, and Hudson (2001) include descriptions of several measures that are applicable to social programs. Other collections of measures can be found in Corcoran and Fisher's (2000a, 2000b) *Measures for Clinical Practice*. Some instruments are copyrighted and require permission to use. Sometimes this involves a small fee. It is well worth a small cost per consumer to use a well-tested instrument that matches a program's outcome goals.

Social programs are generally designed to produce one or more of a limited number of types of changes. Poertner and Rapp (2007) provide a useful typology of these outcomes:

- changes in psychological states,
- knowledge acquisition,
- behavior change (skills),
- status change,
- environmental changes.

Changes in Psychological States

Helping consumers feel or think differently about something is frequently a desired outcome. Some programs attempt to help people improve their sense of hopefulness or empowerment. Others seek to help people decrease feelings of fear or anxiety. Still others seek to help change discriminatory beliefs such as racism or homophobia.

Typically, measures of this type use a set of questions derived from the definition of the concept. The response dimension is a scale, such as agree to disagree or frequently to never. The number of points on the response dimension varies and can typically range from 5 to 11. The consumer indicates his or her response and these are aggregated.

The Hope Scales of Snyder (2000) are an example. He first derived a definition of hope with three central concepts: Hopeful people tend to have goals, plans to achieve them, and some level of goal-directed energy. Consequently, the overall Hope Scale includes assessment of each of these dimensions. As an example, one item to assess goal-directed plans is "I can think of many ways to get out of a jam." Energy is assessed by items such as "I energetically pursue my goals." The response dimension included eight choices ranging from *definitely false* to *definitely true*.

Program managers identifying a measure of change for a psychological state need to be clear and have the consensus of staff and consumers on the following:

1. the desired state,

2. its definition,

3. the fit between the language of the items and the culture and educational background of consumers, and

4. the evidence of reliability and validity of the scale.

Without consensus on the outcome and its definition, people may be working at cross purposes. If the language of the scale is not understandable and relevant to consumers, results will not be useful. Making certain that instruments are relevant to consumers may be accomplished by testing them with a small group of consumers or a consumer advisory group.

Knowledge Acquisition

Knowledge acquisition is a commonly desired consumer outcome. Examples include parent education and understanding major mental illness or the effects of medications. Given the number of years of education that most managers have obtained, the techniques of assessing knowledge acquisition are well known.

If a manager is overseeing an evidence-based practice, there are probably manuals that specify the knowledge to be gained and how it can be measured. For example, Yeaman et al. (2000) report that research evidence indicates that an effective program for people with severe mental illness includes learning about medication and symptom management. This research base specifies the knowledge that is important for people with serious mental illness. The research that tested this includes measures of the relevant knowledge that managers can retrieve and use in these types of programs.

When a manager does not have the luxury of implementing an evidence-based practice, designing a program-specific assessment approach may be required. Once again, measurement begins with a consensus on what consumers are to learn, identifying an assessment instrument that reflects the language and culture of the consumer, and obtaining evidence of its reliability and validity.

One way to assess knowledge acquisition is the pre-test/post-test technique. While it is not a research method that can establish a causal relationship, it is a useful technique. Pre- and post-tests can be developed using true/false, multiple choice, or open-ended questions. The type of questions used is determined by several factors, such as the verbal skills of the consumer and the level of learning to be assessed.

True or false questions are designed to measure simple recognition or recall. If the questions are written carefully, this format generally does not require a high level of verbal skills. Consequently, this format may work well with children or adults with a lower-than-average reading level.

Multiple-choice questions can evaluate other levels of learning, such as application (problem solving or applying ideas in new situations) or comprehension (restating or reorganizing material to show understanding). Multiple-choice items are useful when the person responding has adequate reading skills. Typically, multiple-choice questions present the problem in one of two formats: the complete question (e.g., What would you do first?) or the incomplete statement (e.g., The first thing you should do is. . .). With these two formats, the respondent selects either the correct answer or the best answer from the list of options provided. In the correct answer form, one answer is correct beyond question or doubt while the others are definitely incorrect. In the best answer version, more than one option may be appropriate in varying degrees; however, it is essential that the best response be the one that competent experts agree upon (Clegg & Cashin, 1986).

While the multiple-choice format is simple, it is difficult and time consuming to construct. Developing a multiple choice test requires writing many questions, using them with the intended audience, and carefully evaluating each item through multiple trials. Fortunately, multiple-choice tests are a popular method of conducting educational evaluation, so a social administrator should be able to obtain expert consultation from educational assessment experts at a nearby college or university.

Open-ended questions are written in a similar manner to multiple-choice questions. Instead of consumers selecting the correct answer, they must supply it. This requires consumers knowing enough to solve a problem or recall the material. Program personnel often like to use open-ended questions. However, this type of question needs to be written and used with great care. When consumers are not highly articulate, it is unfair to expect them to successfully respond to open-ended questions. Social administrators may recall their student days when they wrote volumes on open-ended questions in the hope that the correct response was included. This is a high expectation for consumers. The best open-ended question is the one for which the correct answer can be identified succinctly, clearly, and unambiguously (e.g., Identify the three most common side effects of medication X).

Behavior Change

Many programs work with consumers to help them change a behavior or acquire a new one. Some programs are designed so that the behavior is a result of changes in attitudes and/or knowledge. Measurement of behavior change is typically done with behavior checklists and observation.

It is important to remember that people who can demonstrate a behavior vary in their ability to engage in it according to the environment. What someone can do in an agency setting or in her home, she may not be able to perform in other environments. Consequently, it is important to observe the behavior in a variety of places, especially in the environment where it is most important.

Ollendick, Alvarez, and Greene (2004) identify behavioral interviews, rating and checklists, self-reports, self-monitoring, and behavioral observation as methods for measuring behavior. For a behavior rating instrument to be useful, it must concretely identify the behavior. While this seems obvious, it is not easy and sometimes not possible or practical.

For example, a highly regarded and widely used behavioral measure for children is Achenbach's (2001) Child Behavior Checklist (CBCL). The core of this instrument is a list of over 100 behaviors that the observer rates as 0 = not true, 1 = somewhat or sometimes true, or 2 = very true or often true. The list includes unambiguous items such as "bites fingernails." However, it also includes items such as "easily jealous," "feels he/she has to be perfect," and "not liked by other kids." It is very difficult to make terms such as *jealous* more behavioral. As a result, what is rated as "feelings of a need to be perfect" may depend on the observer. Mothers, teachers, and foster parents may all rate this item differently, and it is nearly impossible to determine whether these differences are observer variance or environmentally specific. Consequently, many programs use multiple observers to rate behavior.

Status Changes

Many social systems involve people changing statuses. The goal of the social program may be the movement of consumers to a desired status. In some cases, it is to maintain the person in a "desirable" status.

Permanency for children in public child welfare programs is a good example. The desired outcome is for the child to move from foster care to a safe, permanent home by returning to his or her legal parents, being adopted, or having someone assume legal guardianship. However, some times a child is so disturbed that he or she needs the added services or structure of a group home or institution. In child welfare, a status change measure might include the following:

Child living at own home or adoptive/guardianship home

Child living in family foster care

Child living in a group home

Child living in an institution

Criteria for status change measures include the following:

1. The identified statuses must be exhaustive (include all possible statuses).

2. A consumer is not able to be in two statuses at the same time (mutually exclusive).

3. There should be a consensus on the hierarchical ordering of the statuses, for example, from the most desirable to the least desirable status.

4. The measures need to be sensitive to change.

Status change measures are useful for several reasons. First, they can unify the expectations of the agency's multiple constituencies. Frequently, status maintenance or change is the avowed goal of public policy (e.g., maintaining children in a safe and permanent home, least restrictive environment). Second, existing agency information systems frequently include the information needed to report on changes in status. This may make them more reliable and valid measures. Third, status change measures can enhance organizational control because personnel at different organizational levels are examining the same information.

One shortcoming is the possibility that status change may be subject to administrative manipulation. For example, it is possible that children could be "dumped" out of foster care due to budget constraints, not because their family situations have improved. These types of actions tend to be rare, and when they occur they are usually accompanied by a public outcry. When status changes are the result of organizational, programmatic, and managerial efforts, then such measures are realistic and helpful.

Environmental Changes

Social workers recognize the importance of the environment in influencing the lives of consumers. Yet, there are few environmental measurement instruments. Assessing an environment is a complex task involving identification and assessment of the features that are important to consumers.

The Multiphasic Environmental Assessment Procedure (MEAP) developed by Moos and Lemke (1994, 1996) is an example. It includes four conceptual categories for evaluating the physical and social environment of residential settings for older adults: objective characteristics of the program (including staff characteristics, physical features, and policy factors), personal factors (including sociodemographic characteristics, health status, and functioning factors), social climate, and residents' coping responses. The fifth category measures the outcome of resident adaptation (adjustment, activity level, and use of services). The authors' extensive research determined that the four environmental scales included conditions that positively predicted resident adaptation. Clearly the concept of environment goes beyond physical features and includes such things as social climate and agency policies.

Each of the categories is operationalized through subscales. For example, the conceptual category of objective characteristics of the program includes the physical and architectural features checklist. This includes the dimensions of community accessibility, physical amenities, social-recreational aids, prosthetic aids, orientational aids, safety features, staff facilities, and space availability. Each of these subscales is a checklist. For example, community accessibility is assessed through a list of 12 items located within a quarter mile of the facility including grocery store, movie theatre, and doctor's office. Each item is simply checked *yes* or *no*.

The MEAP is very long. This is necessary to obtain an accurate assessment of the environment, which is multifaceted and complex. This demonstrates the difficulty of developing and using environmental change measures. Using such a long and complex measure requires extensive resources, including staff time for training in use of the instrument and time for administration and scoring. This can be a major barrier to its use. However, if environmental change is the goal, it is worth the expense.

Developing such a measure is even more resource intense. First, extensive research is needed to identify environmental features that are important to the outcome. Second, these dimensions must be operationalized. Then, the scale must be tested for the usual measurement characteristics of reliability and validity.

Validity testing involves gathering evidence that the scale predicts the desired outcome. Moos and Lemke (1994) and others conducted extensive research linking various MEAP scales to outcomes for residents. For example, Smothers (1987) used the policies and services subscales to examine the relationship between program policies and behavior among long-term psychiatric patients. One result was that patients showed more responsible behavior when they were in programs that were high on expectations for functioning, did not tolerate problem behavior, and were low on policy choice. In addition, low staff acceptance of problem behavior was associated with more socially adaptive behavior.

Service Events

Service events are much easier to measure than outcomes and are frequently captured by agency information systems. Service events are the interactions between workers and consumers that produce the benefit. The key elements are duration or the time workers spend with consumers and the frequency of these interactions.

For example, a child welfare program that seeks to ensure that children reunified with their parents remain in a safe home is likely to monitor the time workers spend in the home and the number of visits during a designated time period. The expectation may be that these home visits are an hour in duration. In addition, experience may have shown that the first three months is the most critical period of adjustment for the child and family, and therefore the number of visits per week during this time period is reported by the information system.

Staff Morale

There are not many social service organizations that measure staff morale on a regular basis, even though worker-client interactions are the source of many types of consumer benefits. This makes workers perhaps the most important resource in the agency and suggests the need for formal attention to their morale.

There are several scales that assess job satisfaction. One that is specific to social work was developed by Koeske, Kirk, Koeske, and Rauktis (1994). The Job Satisfaction Scale consists of 14 items and assesses three dimensions. The first is intrinsic qualities of the work role, such as working with clients and opportunities for really helping people. The second dimension covers satisfaction with supervision, and the third includes salary and promotion. This instrument is short and easy to administer and score.

An interesting scale that is not specific to social work is that of Buckingham and Coffman (1999), who have researched job satisfaction for many years. This has resulted in identifying a "measuring stick" that assesses staff morale. The 12 questions are answered with a *yes* or *no*. This provides a quick and easy way for people to respond. Administrators can easily tabulate the results, construct a report, and discuss the results in a unit meeting.

In smaller units, a somewhat less formal method of assessing staff morale is the use of note cards. Each staff member is given six note cards and instructed to use three of them to write what is going well on the job and the other three to identify things that he or she would like to see done differently. With a small number of staff, it is easy to simply list all of the items from the cards, identify what is going well, and produce another list of things needing change. These lists can then be used to reward staff for what is going well and start collective problem solving to address those items identified as needing to be changed.

Resources

Measures of the resources needed to operate a social service program are likely to be readily available to administrators. The usual categories are funds, personnel, consumers, public support, and knowledge. The categories of funds, personnel, and consumers are easy to measure. Measuring public support and knowledge is more difficult.

Kaplan and Norton (1992) regard knowledge as so critical to organizations staying competitive that one of the four categories of their balanced scorecard is innovation and learning. Social administrators may be somewhat less concerned with global competition than these authors. However, better consumer outcomes come from knowledge of more effective policies and programs. The volume of social work research is increasing, and keeping up to date is challenging.

Traditionally, knowledge acquisition has been monitored by counting the number of training events or hours of continuing education attended. It is difficult for an administrator to know whether these events are based upon the latest research or whether they are effective in providing staff with new skills. The field of health care has been struggling with this same transfer of knowledge from research to practice. Gray (2001) suggests that health care organizations ought to have

an evidence center whose responsibility is to collect and disseminate the latest evidence-based practices. A social work evidence center is an interesting idea that could help identify better measures of agency knowledge acquisition.

The health care field has also conducted extensive research on transferring knowledge to practice. This research suggests that measures of types of transfer events that have been demonstrated to be more effective may be better at assessing knowledge gained (Gira, Kessler, & Poertner, 2004). For example, this body of research showed that outreach visits to physician offices for educational purposes combined with audit and feedback (patient chart reviews with feedback to the physician) were more effective in the transfer of knowledge than just the visits. If these findings were replicated with social service staff, they would suggest the desirability of measuring knowledge gained by counting training visits to local offices, accompanied by a count of events that includes case record reviews with individualized feedback.

Managers engaged with the multiple constituents that are an essential ingredient of every social program gauge public support through a number of informal measures. Interactions with those funding programs, judges, or police are some examples. Indirect measures of community support might be the size of contributions or number of grants and contracts coming to the agency. Number of consumers referred to the agency is another potential measure. The logic is that if constituents stop referring consumers to the program, this may be due to lack of confidence in the agency.

The number and variety of resources required to produce consumer benefits is very large. A manager who systematically lists all of these resources would likely produce a list of more than 20. The manager's information system design challenge is selecting from this list only those requiring constant attention. The resources requiring monitoring through an information system depend, in part, on program design, public policy, and community context. For example, a program funded through a yearly contract is not likely to need to monitor the acquisition of funds on a monthly basis. However, if the program depends on individual donations, ongoing monitoring of funds becomes an important element of the information system.

Efficiency

Efficiency measures are ratios of inputs and outputs. With the large number of inputs needed to operate a social program, the number of potential efficiency measures can be overwhelming. Most of these efficiency measures are not useful to monitor on a regular basis. The challenge is to decide which ones are important. Careful selection of efficiency measures can produce an information system with a few well-targeted indicators.

Those aspects of the social program that are likely to be problematic are the areas to monitor. Carefully selected efficiency measures can serve multiple purposes and help simplify the information system. For example, if a program is easily overwhelmed by consumer demand, some measure of this is needed. This may also have the benefit of monitoring something that contributes to job satisfaction because large caseloads may negatively affect this important dimension of workers' lives. Consumer demand might be monitored by counting the number of consumers per worker, the number of consumers served per month, or the number of hours that workers are in direct contact with consumers. Carefully selecting one measure helps produce an efficient information system.

The Dashboard: A Set of Program Measures

Just as it takes more than one gauge in a cockpit for a pilot to guide a plane to its destination, social administrators require a dashboard with a set of gauges to depict a program. These gauges need to cover all of the performance areas previously discussed. But a cockpit with too many

gauges may be problematic. The following criteria have been proposed for managers to use to judge sets of measures:

1. Use as few measures as possible.

2. All outcomes that occur as consumers move through the system should be captured.

3. Avoid perverse incentives.

4. Capture real changes and avoid manipulation.

5. Counterbalancing measures may be required (Poertner, Moore, McDonald, in press).

Few Measures

A program information system can easily become voluminous. This frequently happens as information systems evolve over time. People see a need for better or different information without eliminating what is not used. Controlling the amount of data collected and reported is difficult.

In an ideal world, a manager would go to the library or the local university expert and locate valid and reliable measures. This is almost never the case. Most available measures have obvious shortcomings. There is a tendency to respond to the deficiencies of one measure by adding additional measures of the same concept. This adds cost, complexity, and confusion to the information system. A system of a large number of measures is not only inefficient; it also produces information overload. Responses to this include ignoring data reports because they are too complex or focusing on a small set of data that makes the agency's performance appear to be positive.

A good example of an evolving information system that is not necessarily efficient or effective is the set of child outcome measures developed by the United States Department of Health and Human Services (DHHS) to assess state performance under ASFA (DHHS, 2001). The original set of 12 outcome measures was heavily criticized (Courtney, Needell, & Wulczyn, 2003; Zeller &

Gamble, n.d.). Some child welfare managers faced with financial penalties for not meeting the DHHS standards developed information systems that reported the federal measures and a set of local measures that they thought were more useful for managing the system. Faced with two sets of outcome measures, it is very difficult to decide which ones to base decisions upon.

In 2006, DHHS issued regulations revising these measures. This resulted in a new system of two measures of child safety and four data composites for permanency (The Data Measures, Data Composites, and National Standards to Be Used in the Child and Family Services Reviews, 2006). At first glance, it appears that the number of measures was cut in half. However, each of the four permanency composites consists of from three to five underlying indicators. The result is a total of 17 measures. From a management point of view, it is difficult, if not impossible, on a monthly basis to respond to a composite without knowing the relative contribution of the underlying measures. Consequently, managers must attend to all 17 measures. If managers find these inadequate or inaccurate, it is likely that they will feel it is necessary to add measures, further increasing the complexity of the information system.

Capture All Outcomes

All consumers and their outcomes need to be represented in the information system. This seems obvious, but there may be pressures that lead to deemphasizing certain outcomes or groups of consumers. For example, child welfare has been plagued with balancing child safety and permanency. When family preservation was emphasized under the Adoption Assistance and Child Welfare Act of 1980, there was concern that child safety was being compromised. ASFA was seen as a response to this perceived imbalance, and child safety was specifically identified as a preeminent outcome. The Act further placed an emphasis on achieving permanency for children spending 15 of 22 months in care. This naturally draws managers' attention to this group of children, with the possibility of less attention to permanency for children who have been in care more than 22 months. However, social administrators need data that tracks all outcomes as long as a child is engaged with the agency.

Avoid Perverse Incentives

Public policy sometimes unintentionally creates incentives for programs to avoid a positive outcome. For example, the ASFA emphasis on the first 15 of 22 months in care may create a perverse incentive to ignore or place less emphasis on permanency for children in care for more than 2 years. Policy analysis includes examining policy effects for unintended consequences. Once managers recognize these unintended consequences and perverse incentives, measures can be included to lessen their effect.

Capture Real Changes and Avoid Manipulation

Management actions can also unintentionally create incentives to manipulate the system to "look good." For example, the longstanding emphasis on "normalization" for people with disabilities may be translated in an employment program as placing people in jobs in "normal" environments. This might be defined as jobs that are not part of a sheltered workshop and that pay at least minimum wage. While this seems reasonable, it may have an undesirable effect. With the difficulty of finding jobs for consumers, staff may find that it is easier to place consumers in janitorial-type jobs within the agency. The agency and its staff are likely to be more understanding and flexible. While not exactly a sheltered workshop, these jobs are very similar and limited. It is unlikely that staff were intentionally manipulating the outcome to disadvantage consumers. However, that could be the result. Changing the definition of "suitable jobs" would emphasize placing consumers in a broader range of competitive settings and jobs. It is also unlikely that a manager would recognize this effect unless she monitored all aspects of the desired outcome.

Counterbalancing Measures

There is a necessary tension between having an information system with as few measures as possible and adding counterbalancing measures. It requires immense discipline and creativity to think about expanding an information system while limiting it. Each measure needs to be carefully examined with respect to its necessity.

The area of child welfare outcomes provides an obvious example. Permanency for children needs to be counterbalanced by measures of safety. Measures of children returning to their legal parents as quickly as possible need to be balanced with the possibility of the child reentering foster care. Overconcern with moving children home quickly may result in a larger number of children reentering care. Overconcern with limiting reentry may result in keeping children in foster care for extended periods.

Sometimes newer reporting techniques can provide more information with fewer indicators. One suggestion is the use of event history graphs. These graphs track events for all consumers who enter a program during a specified time period. These graphs can show the safety outcomes by time in the program (English, Brandford, & Coghlan, 2000).

For example, these graphs can show the permanency outcomes for all children who enter care during a specified time period. It is easy to draw extra lines on these graphs to indicate standards or particularly important time frames. For example, a line drawn at 15 or 22 months can emphasize that policy requirement while at the same time reminding everyone of those children who have been in care longer. It is also easy to show all of the different types of permanency outcomes so that staff receive credit for children returning home and achieving guardianship as well as adoption.

Using Results to Empower Staff

The metaphor of the airplane cockpit dashboard is useful to envision the social program manager's information system. It ceases to be useful when it comes to responding to what the gauges show. A pilot responds to the gauges in a limited number of ways, primarily changing speed, altitude, and direction. Social program managers have many more possible responses and must rely on many others to make decisions. With consumer benefits coming from interactions with workers and the involvement of others in the community, the job of piloting the social program is much more complex.

An administrator's job becomes less complex when policies and practices are in place that workers understand or accept as ways that help consumers achieve results. The concepts of organizational learning and climate are useful in establishing a unit that becomes somewhat self-regulating (see Chapter 6). An important part of the administrator's job is to create the desired conditions.

The value of organizational learning comes from recognition that workers will never be 100% successful with all consumers. The difficulties that consumers bring to their interactions with workers are too complex and varied. However, every interaction between workers and consumers is an opportunity for learning what is succeeding and for brainstorming new and innovative approaches. Friedman, Lipshitz, and Overmeer (2001) observe that organizational learning takes place in a climate that fosters inquiry, openness, and trust. This requires a context that includes a tolerance for admitting errors, judgments based upon substance, egalitarianism, and a commitment to learning.

Latting et al. (2004) conducted a study of managers' support for organizational learning in human services agencies. Consistent with the ideas of Friedman et al. (2001), they found that leaders who created a work environment supportive of learning and innovation tended to influence supervisors to support staff empowerment. This was related to workers' increased trust in management and their commitment to the organization. Finally, worker trust in management was positively related to perceived service quality and ultimately to client adherence to the service plan.

The study by Glisson and Hemmelgarn (1998) also supports the ideas of Friedman et al. (2001). This study demonstrated a link between a positive organizational climate and better service quality and outcomes. Organizational climate refers to employees' perception of their work environment (see Chapter 6). When workers perceive that management supports a positive climate, the social program is more effective in helping consumers achieve positive results.

The organization's information system is one of the manager's tools for creating and maintaining a positive organizational climate. An example of the power of this approach is the study by Yeaman et al. (2000). They used performance enhancement teams that included delegating responsibility for change to the direct service team level and found significant improvement in results for consumers. These teams identified measures of change, collected the data, conducted the data analysis, and responded by modifying the program. All of this was done in the context of the latest information about what intervention strategies were effective for consumers.

A key element of the program improvement approach tested by Yeaman et al. (2000) was the use of feedback on program performance. When used properly, feedback in organizations can have an important effect on performance. Alvero, Bucklin, and Austin (2001) reviewed organizational feedback research covering over 20 years and found that in 58% of the 64 recent studies they reviewed, feedback had consistent positive effects, while 41% of the studies showed mixed effects and only 1% showed no effect. They identified the following six conditions for feedback to be effective in organizations:

- Combined with antecedents such as training, task analysis, or supervisory prompts

- Provided through graphs combined with written and verbal feedback
- Delivered daily, monthly, and the combination of daily and weekly
- Provided to the work group
- Provided both privately and publicly
- Compared group performance with a standard or previous group performance, or individual performance with a standard of individual or previous performance

These conditions are not difficult to achieve in most organizations. The antecedents are simply job descriptions communicating expectations, training that assures that staff have the necessary skills, and supervisory prompts that remind workers of key tasks that may get overlooked in the day-to-day business of the unit.

Another lesson is that the way feedback is provided makes a difference in how people respond. Aggregating data at the team level and providing it in graphic form that compares current performance to a standard is easy to do with today's information technology. When it is necessary to provide negative feedback to an individual, doing this privately can help the worker respond in a positive manner. Positive feedback on a team member's accomplishment may be cause for a more public display.

The findings regarding timing of feedback are a bit confusing. The major lesson is that timing does make a difference and probably depends on the nature of the data. For example, a child welfare unit concerned with child safety probably would like to have daily feedback on any child subject to subsequent abuse or neglect. Feedback on moving children to a safe and permanent home would likely be more effective on a monthly basis.

Summary

Information is essential to the social administrator's job of piloting a social program to achieve benefits with consumers. Yet it is a complex and difficult task to create the necessary information system. Identifying the "right" information to monitor on a continuous basis requires careful consideration of multiple areas of organizational performance. The categories of consumer outcomes, service events, resources, staff morale, and efficiency are suggested as critical to program performance. Each of the five areas includes several subcategories with multiple indicators. Yet too much information obscures rather than illuminates. This requires careful management judgment of what to include.

The lessons of the organizational research literature indicate that determining what information to collect and report is just the beginning. Feedback is effective when it fits into the context of workers' job expectations and skills. Timing and presentation of feedback also influences staff responses. All of this works best in the context of an organizational climate that values learning and growth.

References

Achenenbach, T. (2001). *Child behavior checklist for ages 6-18*. Retrieved from http://www.aseba.org

Adoption and Safe Families Act of 1997, Pub. L. No. 105-89, 42 USC 1305, 111 Stat 2115 (1997).

Alvero, A. M., Bucklin, B. R., & Austin, J. (2001). An objective review of the effectiveness and essential characteristics of performance feedback in organizational settings (1985–1998). *Journal of Organizational Behavior Management, 21*(1), 3–29.

Austin, D. M. (2002). *Human service management: Organizational leadership in social work practice*. New York: Columbia University Press.

Buckingham, M., & Coffman, C. (1999). *First, break all the rules: What the world's greatest managers do differently*. New York: Simon & Schuster.

Clegg, V. L., & Cashin, W. E. (1986). *Improving multiple-choice tests: Idea paper No. 16*. Manhattan: Kansas State University, Center for Faculty Evaluation and Development.

Corcoran, K., & Fisher, J. (2000a). *Measures for clinical practice: A sourcebook vol. 1: Couples, families and children* (3rd ed.). New York: The Free Press.

Corcoran, K., & Fisher, J. (2000b). *Measures for clinical practice: A sourcebook vol. 2: Adults.* (3rd ed.). New York: The Free Press.

Courtney, M., Needell, B., & Wulczyn, F. (2003). *National standards in the child and family series reviews: Time to improve on a good idea*. Paper prepared for the Joint Center for Poverty Research Child Welfare Services Research and its Policy Implications.

The Data Measures, Data Composites, and National Standards to Be Used in the Child and Family Services Reviews, 71 Fed. Reg. 32,969 (June 7, 2006).

English, D. J., Brandford, C. C., & Coghlan, L. (2000). Data-based organizational change: The use of administrative data to improve child welfare programs and policy. *Child Welfare, 79*(5), 499–515.

Friedman, V. J., Lipshitz, R., & Overmeer, W. (2001). Creating conditions for organizational learning. In M. Dierkes, A. G. Antal, J. Child, & I. Nonaka (Eds.), *Handbook of organizational learning and knowledge* (pp. 757–774). Oxford: Oxford University Press.

Gambrill, E. (1999). Evidence-based practice: An alternative to authority-based practice. *Families in Society: The Journal of Contemporary Human Services, 89*(4), 341–350.

Gambrill, E. (2006). Evidence-based practice and policy: Choices ahead. *Research on Social Work Practice, 16*(3), 338–357.

Gira, E. C., Kessler, M. L., & Poertner, J. (2004). Influencing social workers to use research evidence in practice: Lessons from medicine and the allied health professions. *Research in Social Work Practice, 14*(2), 68–79.

Glisson, C., & Hemmelgarn, A. (1998). The effects of organizational climate and interorganizational coordination on the quality and outcomes of children's service systems. *Child Abuse & Neglect, 22*(5), 401–421.

Gray, J. A. M. (2001) *Evidence-based healthcare* (2nd ed.). London: Churchill Livingston.

Jenson, J. M. (2005). Connecting science to intervention: Advances, challenges, and the promise of evidence-based practice. *Social Work Research, 29*(3), 131–136.

Kaplan, R. S., & Norton, D. P. (1992). The balanced scorecard—measures that drive performance. *Harvard Business Review,* 71–79.

Koeske, G. F., Kirk, S. A., Koeske, R. D., & Rauktis, M. B. (1994). Measuring the Monday blues:

Validation of a job satisfaction scale for the human services. *Social Work Research, 18*(1), 27–35.

Latting, J. K., Beck, M. H., Slack, K. J., Tetrick, L. E., Jones, A. P., Etchegaray, J. M., et al. (2004). Promoting service quality and client adherence to the service plan: The role of top management's support for innovation and learning. *Administration in Social Work, 28*(2), 29–48.

Lohmann, R. A., & Lohmann, N. (2002). *Social administration*. New York: Columbia University Press.

Martin, L. L. (2001). *Financial management for human services administrators*. Needham Heights, MA: Allyn & Bacon.

Martin, L. L. (2005). Performance-based contracting for human services: Does it work? *Administration in Social Work, 29*(1), 63–77.

Moos, R. H., & Lemke, S. (1994). *Group residences for older adults: Physical features, policies and social climate*. New York: Oxford University Press.

Moos, R. H., & Lemke, S. (1996). *Evaluating residential facilities: The multiphasic environmental assessment procedure*. Thousand Oaks, CA: Sage.

National Alliance on Mental Illness. (2008). *About NAMI*. Retrieved from http://www.nami.org/template.cfm?section=About_NAMI

Nugent, W. R., Sieppert, J. D., & Hudson, W. (2001). Practice evaluation for the 21st century. Belmont, CA: Brooks/Cole-Thomson Learning.

Ollendick, T. H., Alvarez, H. K., & Greene, R. W. (2004). Behavioral assessment: History of underlying concepts and methods. In S. N. Haynes, E. M. Heiby, & M. Hersen (Eds.), *Comprehensive handbook of psychological assessment. Volume 3: Behavioral assessment* (pp. 19–32). Hoboken, NJ: John Wiley & Sons.

Osborne, E., & Plastrik, P. (2000). *The reinventor's fieldbook: Tools for transforming your government*. San Francisco: Jossey-Bass.

Poertner, J., Moore, T., & McDonald, T. P. (in press). Managing for outcomes: The selection of sets of outcome measures. *Administration in Social Work*.

Poertner, J., & Rapp, C. A. (2007). *Textbook of social administration: The consumer-centered approach*. Binghamton, NY: The Haworth Press.

Smothers, B. (1987). The relationships among patient functional behaviors, patient characteristics, staff practices and social climate in a psychiatric hospital.(Doctoral dissertation, University of Maryland, College Park, 1986). *Dissertation Abstracts International, 48*, 1307–1314.

Snyder, C. R. (2000). Hypotheses: There is hope. In C. R. Snyder (Ed.), *Handbook of hope: Theory, measures, and application* (pp. 3–18). San Diego, CA: Academic Press.

United States Department of Health and Human Services. (2001). *Safety, permanency, well-being*. Retrieved from http://www.acf.hhs.gov/programs/cb/pubs/cwo01/cwo01.pdf

United States General Accounting Office. (2003). *Child welfare: Most states are developing statewide information systems, but the reliability of child welfare data could be improved* (G.A.O.-03-809). Retrieved from http://www.gao.gov/new.items/d03809.pdf

Yeaman, C., Craine, W. H., Gorsek, J., & Corrigan, P. W. (2000). Performance improvement teams for better psychiatric rehabilitation. *Administration and Policy in Mental Health, 27*(3), 113–127.

Zeller, D. E., & Gamble, T. J. (n.d.). *Improving child welfare performance: Retrospective and prospective approaches*. Troy, NY: Hornby Zeller Associates.

Zlotnik, J. L., & Solt, B. E. (2006). The Institute for the Advancement of Social Work Research: Working to increase our practice and policy evidence base. *Research on Social Work Practice, 16*(5), 534–539.

CHAPTER 9

Developing Information Technology Applications for Performance-Oriented Management in a Global Environment

Dick Schoech

This chapter will address the current state of information technology (IT) management and IT application development by first defining applications and how they are changing. Next, it will discuss the application development process and illustrate this process with a statewide child welfare application. Finally, issues and considerations in developing and managing IT applications will be presented.

The Current State of IT in the Human Services

Information technologies collect, process, manipulate, and disseminate information. A book is a paper-based information technology while a computer is an electronics-based information techno logy. The Internet involves many communications-based information technologies. Because information is a basic resource used in delivering human services, managing information is as important to agency success as managing money, personnel, and property. Failure to successfully manage information results in an opportunity loss and can result in poor decision making and reduced goal achievement. The management of information implies that appropriate functions, people, and IT are in place to collect, store, manipulate, and distribute information. It also implies that changes involving IT are managed just as other changes, for example, adding a new service.

Information management is carried out by IT applications. IT applications are systems of people, procedures, computers, and telecommunications that address an agency problem related to management or client services. Typical management applications are e-mail and systems that collect, process, and report information about staff, services, and clients. Typical client applications include educational Web pages and cognitive behavioral protocols that help overcome depression and anxiety (Proudfoot et al., 2004).

Application development in the human services has become much more complex since the previous edition of this book in 2000. Not only do more types of applications exist due to IT developments, but most human services organizations have also changed due to privatization, continued budget cuts, and reorganization and integration of services. Accountability has increased as agencies compete for reduced funds, especially funds at the federal level. IT systems that document accountability are one way agencies compete for scarce funds.

A number of factors have made IT application management more challenging today. For agencies that have applications built years ago, application maintenance adds complexity. Some agencies operate a patchwork of loosely connected old and new applications rather than an integrated system. This patchwork of applications can become so fragile that changing one can cause errors throughout the whole system. Tracking down and fixing errors in old applications can be a time-consuming process. Additional complexity is due to the tendency to use Internet technology in applications. While Internet-delivered applications solve many networking problems for agencies, especially those with staff at multiple locations, Web-enabling applications is difficult, time consuming, and costly. Some traditional application development tools, such as easy-to-use form and report writers, are not yet available for Web-enabling applications. A final reason applications are more complex stems from the increased threats to agencies that are connected to the Internet, namely, computer security, viruses, and firewalls.

Complicating IT application development is the scarcity and high salaries of high tech personnel. In addition, expectations for sophisticated applications have increased because most staff and clients are familiar with very sophisticated and expensive Internet applications (e.g., multi-user games, personal Web sites, interactive maps, online shopping, and shared documents). Another complication is that problems with IT applications are common. IT application failures in an agency can be catastrophic in terms of staff morale, costs, client privacy, and practitioner down time. Add in the trend toward multi-agency information systems from funding sources and globalization of human services, and you can see why most human services executives wish the IT function would go away rather than assume more prominence in human services agencies.

While more funding for IT is not the complete solution to the challenges listed above, it is increasingly evident that agency IT applications have not kept pace with business IT developments. For example, consider the technology available to a travel agent helping a family find a vacation setting. The travel agent puts possible destinations, time restrictions, preferences, costs, and so on into a Web application and quickly presents the user with choices of destination, times, costs, accommodations, and so on. Many organizations worldwide are linked into the travel agent's application, for example, airlines, hotel chains, rental car dealers. Some of these organizations use the information input by the travel agent to further their own goals. For example, booking an airline reservation may trigger an application that continuously optimizes airline profits by ensuring that each plane is full of the highest paying passengers.

Now consider the technology typically used when the same family wants to find counseling services. They can call 211, if implemented in their area, to obtain a list of possible agencies to contact. The family's call to each agency on the 211 list is handled by a receptionist with little or no computer support. Each agency screens clients in or out of its particular agency rather than into a service delivery system that may meet their needs. No IT applications analyze the client's problem and preferences before presenting service options. No applications exist to optimize agency goals, such as the number of services offered, the quality of services, or client outcomes. This comparison shows that human services agencies, which make life-changing or even life and death decisions about people in need, are far behind business use of IT, even businesses providing routine recreational services.

Applications and Application Development

This section discusses IT management and application development from an organizational and a technology perspective. Each perspective helps the reader understand the historical context of agency IT. As with the human services, the field of IT contains many concepts, abbreviations, and definitions. These often overlap, and generalizations result because the IT field is dynamic and influenced by specialists who coin terms and concepts independent of each other. Because not all definitions have agreement, the terms and concepts used in this chapter are included as Appendix 9.A at the end of this chapter.

Historical Perspective on IT Application Development

IT application development in the human services can be divided into five phases. Each phase will be defined and then the underlying hardware, software, and communication technologies identified. The phases are presented from an historical perspective. A new agency may have had a different order of IT development. For example, today a new agency's first applications for staff may be e-mail and a Web site.

Human services IT applications typically begin with an agency acquiring a nonprofit accounting and billing application, often referred to as an automated data processing (DP) system.

Additional administrative data collection and reporting modules are then added, resulting in a management information system (MIS). Since an MIS collects agency-wide data, the IT function is moved out of the accounting department and under a separate IT committee or department. Having an IT department and information system that supports management information needs could be considered the first IT development phase for an agency. The key hardware in Phase 1 is the computer, while the key software is a database management system (DBMS).

The second phase begins when agencies became more comfortable with the MIS and see the need for IT to support staff throughout the organization. In Phase 2, MISs are gradually expanded to serve not only management but all other staff as well. With this broader usage, the MIS is more properly referred to as an agency information system (AIS). Many of the applications developed during Phase 2 focus on supporting staff decisions (i.e., decision support systems [DSS]) or enhancing staff performance (i.e., performance support systems [PSS]). These applications often have their own separate databases, which are linked to produce agency-wide reports. Large agency IT departments develop a data warehouse function that collects, updates, cleans, manages, integrates, analyzes, and reports data from all applications. The data warehouse concept requires agencies to see data as a key resource requiring agency-wide management. In Phase 2, data security, integrity, and integration become key issues that must be continually addressed. Information management becomes a high-level function similar to personnel management, financial management, and facilities management. Top-level managers in each of these areas continually assess how each resource can be better managed to help all staff achieve the agency's mission. Key technologies of Phase 2 include computers, databases, local and wide area networks (LANs and WANs), and tools that make data easy for everyone in the agency to understand, manipulate, and use.

With the pervasiveness of the Internet and the need for staff to enter data and access AIS features from many locations, agencies often enter a third IT development phase that involves integrating AIS applications with the Internet. This phase may begin with the development of one or more interactive input forms for a new program or service. Eventually in Phase 3, all applications are Web enabled, which allows staff to input data and receive information using a Web browser. Some agencies move into Phase 3 by purchasing an Internet-based application. Consequently, they do not have to go through Phases 1 and 2 as did agencies that developed their IT applications before the Internet became a popular platform. This phenomenon illustrates a constant difficulty with IT development, namely, that no matter when systems are developed, major technological changes occur within 5 to 10 years that make the application outdated. These major technological revolutions (e.g., moving from DOS to Windows or moving from a local area network to the Internet) are difficult to anticipate or to plan for during initial IT planning and development. Rapid obsolescence is the rule with IT rather than the exception. The technologies involved in Phase 3 concern Internet technologies such as browsers, HTML Web pages, TCPIP and XML data networking protocols, and WWW3 Consortium standards (O'Looney, 2005). When applications are built on these Internet tools, the agency is said to have an intranet rather than a dedicated LAN or WAN.

Using the Internet or an intranet allows the agency to enter a fourth phase in which applications expand to include other stakeholders and organizations. A typical example of linking a stakeholder to an intranet-based AIS is when a child protective services information system expands with an application that allows judges to interact with agency data to monitor children under their jurisdiction. While Phase 3 might involve a Web site to educate clients, Phase 4 might involve interactive online applications that allow clients to complete agency forms, schedule appointments, or track their services. More sophisticated Phase 4 applications involve Internet-delivered therapeutic interventions, which are often referred to as etherapy.

Technologies involved in this phase include Web-based programming environments such as Java, PHP.net, Ruby on Rails, RSS feeds, and interactive multimedia.

The fifth phase of human services IT development begins when applications in an agency link up and share information seamlessly with similar applications on a state, national, or global level (e.g., cross-agency case management). The hallmark of Phase 5 is a national or global service delivery infrastructure. Because Phase 5 requires agencies to share information, we can expect Phase 5 activities to occur in human services that have strong communication ties, for example, services to victims of human trafficking. Agencies that address problems such as child abuse according to state and local regulations might take a long time to enter Phase 5. While the first three phases involve applications that address social problems from an agency perspective, the last two phases involve applications that address social problems from a societal or community perspective (e.g., multiple agencies working together simultaneously to address a problem). In Phases 4 and 5, agencies retain organizational identify while adding the power of social networks and collaboratives. Clients, client advocacy groups, policy makers, and funding sources become much more integrated into the design and functionality of applications. Key technologies involved in Phase 5 include technologies such as automatic electronic data interchange (EDI), user authentication, data security, encryption, file sharing, wireless communications, data mining, Wikis, drupals, VOIP, and smartphones. Sometimes these are called Web 2.0 technologies, to indicate that they not only use the Internet, but are designed to take advantage of the unique features of the Internet and high-speed access.

In summary, agencies have progressed historically from one or more separate internal applications to many connected internal and external applications supporting multiple stakeholders. The focus of these applications has moved from an agency perspective to a client, societal, and global perspective. The tasks that these applications address have evolved from data processing to decision and performance support. As an agency moves through these phases, applications increasingly use Internet, multimedia, and wireless technology.

Stages of the Application Development Process

IT change is similar to other organizational changes, which are covered in other chapters of this book (see, especially, Chapter 7). The major difference is that changes involving IT are heavily influenced and limited by the capacities and costs of hardware, software, and telecommunications. Another difference is that once automated, applications are less susceptible to change in the future because application development requires agency operations to be specified and systematized before being programmed into software code. While standard programming practices exist, it is often difficult and time consuming for a programmer to understand and fix another programmer's code. Trying to understand a programmer's code is similar to trying to understand the route of a taxicab that drove across a city center in rush hour years earlier (why main roads were avoided, what short cuts were taken, etc.). A final difference is that human services professionals often become fascinated with technology and forget to use the organizational change skills they use when implementing other agency or client changes.

Organizational change is well-documented and researched. Simply stated, the stages of any planned change effort involve feasibility determination, assessment, implementation, and evaluation. When developing IT applications, agencies progress through major stages, activities, and decisions that are summarized in Figure 9.1.

Each stage in Figure 9.1 begins with the setting of goals, objectives, tasks, schedules, checkpoints, responsibilities, and completion criteria for that stage. Each stage ends with the documentation of all activities in a report. This report then becomes the basis for deciding whether to proceed to the next stage. The application development process in Figure 9.1 is both sequential and repetitive. As decisions are made throughout the process, some stages are repeated as other new stages are entered. Each stage builds on and amplifies the activities of the previous stage and addresses some of the tasks in future stages. For example, the first stage, preparedness and feasibility, must be given repeated consideration throughout the process. In addition, success criteria developed in the feasibility stage are used during the evaluation stage.

The time and effort devoted to each activity in Figure 9.1 varies by application type. For example, if an agency purchases an information system from a vendor, it may skip some design phase activities because the vendor has already completed them. However, the agency should compile documentation on all stages no matter when, where, or who completed them (see document preparation under each stage of Figure 9.1). Completing all stages for a relatively small application may take several months. For large applications, such as the development of a comprehensive information system, the process may take several years. In some cases, the time required to develop a complex application is so long that the application is never completed before a redesign is considered.

Guidelines for IT Application Development

While the stages of Figure 9.1 may appear scientific and precise, successful progression through the stages is more an art than a science. Implementing change often becomes a process of "muddling through." In muddling through, the overall plan is kept in mind as one struggles to find the most appropriate solutions to day-to-day problems. While going through the stages is a complex process, many guidelines, laws, and much conventional wisdom exists along with substantial research on what makes an application successful. Success can be defined in many ways, such as whether the application is developed

Stage 1: Exploration of Feasibility and Preparedness

- Communicate about the IT effort to all staff
- Establish an agency IT committee and an application-specific steering committee
- Define the application's purpose, develop timetables, and assign responsibilities
- Review similar efforts in other agencies and request help from national or state associations
- Estimate resources for change (i.e., money, time, expertise, and commitment of key individuals)
- Estimate improved application impacts (positive and negative)
- Assess the expectations and reactions of those who will be affected by the application
- Determine whether the agency can take the risk associated with developing the application
- Draft continuous improvement mechanisms and success measures
- Prepare and circulate a preparedness and feasibility report
- Decide to proceed or terminate effort

Stage 2: Assessment (Systems Analysis)

- Identify the major needs and decisions the application will address
- Define the characteristics of the information needed, its source, and collection methods
- Analyze current and future data input, processing, and output operations and requirements (e.g., forms, data manipulations, files, reports, and flow of information from collection to dissemination)
- Evaluate problems with how things are currently done
- Identify resources on which to build the new application
- Collect baseline data on success measures
- Prepare and circulate assessment
- Decide to proceed or terminate effort

Stage 3: Conceptual Design

- Finalize application scope, goals, objectives, continuous improvement measures, and success measures
- Develop alternative conceptual designs (i.e., fields, records, files, data manipulation, forms, reports, and graphics)
- Apply design specifications such as flexibility, reliability, processing and statistical requirements, growth potential, and life expectancy
- Apply restrictions to designs (i.e., required and desired data frequency, volume, security, confidentiality, turnaround time; money, time, expertise) and tie in with other applications
- Design mechanisms to collect and report continuous improvement information
- Translate designs into software, hardware, telecommunications, and networking configurations
- Detail the advantages, disadvantages, and assumptions of alternative designs
- Prepare and circulate selected conceptual design and decide to proceed or terminate effort

Stage 4: Detailed Design and Development

- Set up controls and technical performance specifications for the chosen design
- Select the software for the chosen design
- Select the hardware to match the software
- Select the necessary networking and telecommunications

- Design and develop data collection forms, data manipulation operations, file specifications, database structures, encryption, error checks, storage mechanisms, backup procedures, and output reports
- Prepare documentation and instruction manuals

Stage 5: Testing and Preparation

- Prepare system operators, users, and others to receive the application
- Develop agency policy and procedural changes necessary for using the new application
- Develop performance specifications and testing plan
- Test programming, forms, operational procedures, instructions, reports, and the use of application outputs
- Educate and train system operators, data users, and others affected on how to perform their role with the application

Stage 6: Implementation

- Develop and approve implementation plan if new system, or plan for conversion from old system (e.g., stop old system when new system starts or run old and new systems simultaneously for comparison)
- Incorporate application into agency standard operating procedures (e.g., performance appraisals, new employee orientation and training)
- Reorganize staff and space if necessary
- Convert from old to new equipment, new processing methods, and new procedures
- Ensure all systems and controls are working

Stage 7: Monitoring and Evaluation

- Compare application performance with initial application objectives and success measures (e.g., outputs used in decision making, users satisfied, client services improved)
- Relate benefits and costs to initial estimates
- Ensure continuous improvement mechanisms are working and remedial action taken if necessary

Stage 8: Operation, Maintenance, and Modification

- Prepare backup and emergency plans and procedures
- Complete documentation (e.g., instructions for adding to, deleting from, or modifying application)
- Assign persons responsible for system maintenance, backup, data integrity, new software appropriateness, virus protection, etc.
- Provide continuous training of users
- Continue to add desired enhancements and to maintain and debug the application
- Begin Stage 1 if additional applications are to be developed

Figure 9.1   Stages in the Process of Developing an IT Application

SOURCE: "Strategies for Information System Development," by D. Schoech, L. L. Schkade, & R. S. Mayers (1982) *Administration in Social Work, 5*(3/4), 25–26. Copyright 1981 by Haworth Press. Adapted with permission.

within budget, completed on time, reliable with minimum downtime or errors, performing according to expectations, integrated with existing applications, easy to maintain and upgrade, and improving agency performance. Successful implementation of the model outlined in Figure 9.1 requires attention to several processes such as the involvement of stakeholders, planning, and a careful consideration of time and resource allocation.

Involving Stakeholders

The clear, consistent, and visible involvement of stakeholders is a powerful determinant of the success or failure of most change, especially change involving IT. These stakeholders include agency top management, the IT department of the agency, IT developers, middle management, frontline service staff, those targeted to use the application, and those impacted by the application. If one of these stakeholders is not involved, the potential for successful IT development decreases. The responsibilities and tasks of each group will be discussed further.

The involvement of top management signals to employees that they should support an application because leaders take it seriously. Top management demonstrates leadership if they

- make certain the organization is reasonably stable so it can take the stress and disruption caused by developing an IT application;
- educate themselves so as not to be dazzled by technology and technicians' promises;
- separate IT changes from other changes; that is, do not blame IT for organizational changes that management has been reluctant to make;
- openly demonstrate commitment and involvement throughout the process by attending important meetings, communicating expectations, assigning quality personnel to the development effort, and making timely and firm decisions such as

approving contracts with vendors and consultants;
- expend the extra time and energy required to maintain involvement and control throughout the application development and implementation process;
- maintain open lines of communication;
- ensure that accountability for results is clearly assigned, openly understood, and that those accountable have the necessary authority to take initiatives and make decisions that impact results;
- quickly resolve conflicts that arise during implementation and the struggles for IT resources;
- demonstrate that the information, data, and the power inherent in any application will not be used for personal gain or to reprimand employees;
- ensure that those participating in the application receive the necessary release time from normal duties, rather than have IT development assigned as extra duties;
- insure all users are provided with training to use IT applications effectively.

An example will illustrate the importance of top management to the IT development process. The clinical training committee of a mental health provider sought the assistance of a consultant to help them integrate clinical IT applications into the organization. They brought in the consultant because they feared the accounting department was controlling and restricting the scope of clinical IT. The executive did not understand the subtleties of technology and the control issues IT raised and took a hands-off approach, saying he did not want to interfere in the details of IT development. However, major IT change could not move forward until the dispute between the training committee and accounting department was resolved. One obvious solution was for the executive to move IT to a separate, top-level department that represented and served all users throughout the agency.

The next stakeholder is the IT department, which is responsible for information management, just as the accounting department is responsible for financial management. The IT department is responsible for managing and coordinating information on a day-to-day basis, developing and maintaining applications, and providing user training and support. The head of the IT department is sometimes called a data administrator, information manager, management information system (MIS) or IT director, or chief information officer (CIO). The CIO needs to understand the workings of all agency departments as well as the technology and the application development process. Therefore, the CIO needs managerial, technical, and communication skills.

For communication, design, and coordination purposes, each major application should have its own steering committee to guide the application development process. The application steering committee represents all affected parties in the development process, sets overall policy, monitors development, fosters communication and feedback, reduces resistance, and improves the chances that the application will meet the needs of all involved. The CIO should be a member of any application steering committee but probably not the chair. All staff should feel they have easy access to information via their representative on the application steering committee. A cardinal rule in organizational change is "no surprises." A Web site or listserv is an excellent way to disseminate application development information.

Users are another stakeholder group to be involved in IT development. Many techniques to involve users exist, for example, involving users on the IT committee, the application steering committee, or teaming key users with consultants to exchange expertise during development. While involving users is essential, others impacted by the application can provide valuable input. If possible, clients or client representatives should be members of the IT committee or application steering committee if many applications involve client services. Client representatives provide a perspective that cannot be obtained inside the agency. For accountability purposes, board members and funding sources may play a role in agency information management and application development. For example, agency board members may have computer, networking, or information management expertise. Or, a funding source may require an agency to use its service definitions or upload service data into a multi-agency information system. Bringing these outside perspectives to the application development process helps insure success.

The term often used to describe end user application development is *distributed IT* because it distributes applications to end users. A significant management challenges is to foster user involvement and creativity while controlling the tendency of users to develop applications that are not well integrated into the total agency information system. It may seem paradoxical at first, but the best route to a properly functioning distributed IT environment is through centralized planning, control, standardization, and training. To avoid the protectionist attitude and independent development of many distributed IT groups, top management, via the IT committee, must decide the desirable balance of distribution and central control. The intent is not to create an adversarial relationship between distributed IT units and the central unit. Rather, the intent is to administer the entire distributed network as one integrated system that takes into account the needs of all users and stakeholders. While centralized control removes some of the advantages of distribution, the gains in coordination far outweigh the losses. Without central control, applications may compete for scarce IT resources, prevent information sharing, and cause agency-wide reports to have inconsistencies due to different definitions and taxonomies. For example, consider a mental health agency that has several state and federally funded services with their own information systems. Each system may need upgrading and enhancements, so each would compete for the agency's IT budget. The agency may discover several different totals for the number of clients the agency serves because each program defines *client* and *service* differently. Without agency-wide shared definitions, agency reports can be inconsistent and confusing to the public.

IT developers are the technical stakeholders who supply the hardware, software, programming, and telecommunications expertise during application development. The technical specialists may be in-house personnel, outside consultants, or a combination. If in-house, most will work in the IT department. Relying on internal expertise may produce an application that is useful but nonstandard and difficult to support. Use of only outside consultants may produce an application that uses industry standards but does not appropriately address user needs. One way to handle the standardization versus usefulness issue is by placing outside consultants under the control of internal staff. This arrangement is especially good at controlling the scope of an IT application, which often tends to expand uncontrollably based on user demands. Outside contractors are good at curbing users' and managers' appetite for expanding the application (Moyer, 1997).

IT developers have many employment opportunities and frequently change jobs. Because agencies can rarely compete with the private sector for permanent IT expertise, it is often feasible to develop IT generalists from existing staff and then contract for the specialized expertise that varies with each application. Another strategy is for a coalition of agencies to share expensive technical expertise.

Vendors are IT technical stakeholders who sell applications to agencies or develop applications for agencies. Many tools and techniques are available for involving vendors in application development. The request for proposal (RFP) provides a format for communicating application requirements and evaluating several vendor proposals. The response to the RFP can become part of the contract with the chosen vendor. A formal signed vendor contract helps remove optimistic promises and prevents user pressure to increase the project scope. A contract specifies responsibilities, jobs, prices, and recourses should things not go as planned. This ensures that both parties understand the nature of the arrangement and eliminates the reliance on general-purpose contracts. If the application is large and complex, a bidders'

conference can allow vendors to tour agency operations and ask questions about the potential application. Buying an application can be compared to buying a car because the agency and vendor are entering a long-term arrangement. Also, buying a standard car/application makes maintenance and changes easier, while buying a highly customized car/application increases maintenance problems and incompatibilities.

Many other external stakeholders may influence application development, but rarely should an application be designed based solely on the information needs of other organizations. Designing applications to support basic agency functions offers flexibility because that information can usually be translated into the format needed and uploaded into the applications of outside organizations. For example, a funding source's application may require entering the number of clients served by age categories. Rather than entering data directly into the funding source's application, the agency's client information system should collect client date of birth and then have its computer convert date of birth into one of the requested age categories and upload the requested data. Funding source information systems are designed around one service and the information needs of the funder, rather than around the agency's information needs for all services. Having agencies use their basic applications to furnish data for outside organizations offers flexibility and reduces dependency on outside applications that the agency cannot control and that might quickly change. However, some funding source applications may be interactive, making this advice hard to follow; for example, a client eligibility module may need to be completed before funding for services can be authorized.

In summary, involving stakeholders can be difficult because involvement is time consuming and "messy," and the payoffs are long term and hard to measure. Involvement is particularly important when agencies quickly purchase and implement prepackaged applications. Purchasing applications bypasses much of the learning that occurs when an agency develops its own application. If the agency purchases sophisticated applications, it must substitute other learning experiences for those that occur with custom application development; for example, staff could familiarize themselves with similar applications by visiting other agencies.

Planning

As with most change, planning is consistently mentioned as a key factor in successful application development and implementation. A three- to five-year agency IT plan should address how applications will be tied together to form an overall system that achieves agency-wide goals. Planning allows modular implementation. The staged introduction of system components lessens risks, increases flexibility, spreads out costs, and provides time to react and adjust. Agencies that are strongly influenced by their environment should plan how to integrate their applications with outside applications they may be required to use (e.g., the homeless management information system [HMIS] sponsored by the U.S. Department of Housing and Urban Development).

Planning helps to decide which of the three design and development approaches to take: top-down, bottom-up, or prototyping. In a top-down approach, an agency first designs the total system and then develops individual applications. In a bottom-up approach, an agency develops small, well-focused applications based on immediate needs. After several bottom-up approaches are taken, coordination and compatibility problems force the agency to take a more top-down approach. In prototyping, an initial "quick and dirty" application is partially developed and given to key personnel for evaluation. Overall specifications are not developed through a formal needs assessment and conceptual design (Stages 2 and 3 of Figure 9.1), but through repeated prototyping cycles of quick analysis, development, trial use, evaluation, and refinement. In prototyping, conventional wisdom and standard practices are often ignored in favor of "what works."

Each approach has advantages and disadvantages. Traditional top-down development is more appropriate for applications that address the routine and well-structured problems of middle management. A bottom-up development approach is useful when an agency has the opportunity to implement several needed applications but does not have the time or expertise to develop an overall IT strategy. Prototyping may be combined with top-down development to allow experimental IT support for nonroutine and ill-structured problems at the top management or direct service levels (e.g., etherapy). For complex applications, combining all three approaches may be desirable. For example, a drug treatment agency may use a top-down approach to develop a strategic plan for technology. The agency may run a state-funded halfway house that includes funds to develop an application that tracks client progress. This application may be developed from the bottom up with little consideration given to the client tracking needs of other agency services. The agency may realize that the halfway house client tracking application may need to be changed when an agency-wide client tracking application is developed later. The steering committee for the client progress tracking application may be unsure of the design of the application. They may propose a prototyping approach where IT technicians teamed with expert case managers use trial and error to produce an application that works.

Allocating Time and Resource

Time and resources devoted to each stage in Figure 9.1 can vary substantially, depending on the size and complexity of the application. Development guidelines for the use of time and resources are often stated as rules or laws.

The *80/20 rule* suggests that agencies can complete 80% of an application using only 20% of total resources. However, to complete the remaining 20% of the application requires 80% of total resources. This final 20% can cause frustration, especially for users who see little progress as they eagerly wait for the completed application. The 80/20 rule applies to IT primarily because the user interface and other visible features are much easier to develop than the detailed programming required to make these features work error free. Vendors are often said to use this 80/20 rule to decide whether to develop a new product. They complete the 20% needed to have a good "demo" system to illustrate the product's features at their conference exhibit. Then, if sufficient sales materialize, they invest the remaining 80% of time and resources to develop the complete application.

Another guideline is contained in the *10/40/50 rule*. According to the National Science Foundation, hardware typically absorbs 10% of the overall IT application costs, while software and software development absorb 40%, and implementation and training absorb 50% (Neilson, 1985). This rule suggests that getting people to use an application is as difficult as designing the application. Given tight budgets, agencies often expect to spend resources in the reverse proportion. That is, they budget 50% for hardware, 40% for software and software development, and 10% for implementation and training. Consequently, much of the training and implementation is added on to existing workloads, thus causing frustration and resentment against the IT application.

Another useful rule stems from analyses of failed IT systems. Approximately 30% of applications are cancelled before completion and roughly half of all applications cost about 200% more than estimated (Rensin, 2005). The universal law of technology project failure states that Big Dollars + Long Time Horizons = Certain Failure (Rensin, 2005). This law suggests that to be successful, an agency should rapidly implement a well-resourced application or gradually implement independent modules of an application. An application development effort may fall into the first category if purchased from a vendor. Many internal applications developed on a restricted budget fall into the second category.

This law warns against the large, long-term projects that are typical of some government funding. In these projects, the time required to go from conceptual design to legislation, to funding, and finally to development and testing is often so long that technology and agencies have changed substantially during the process. An example can be seen when agencies team up with a small business and apply for SBIR (Small Business Innovative Research) funding. SBIR projects often take many months between conceptualization and funding, which comes in phases. After Phase 1 demonstrates success, the team must apply for Phase 2 funding. Thus, many months can pass between the end of Phase 1 and the beginning of Phase 2. During this time, staff may quit the organization or be assigned to other projects. Enthusiasm, expertise, and momentum may falter and the chances of failure increase.

Safeguarding Security and Confidentiality

IT applications have a tendency to make private information public by mistake. For example, a private e-mail may be accidentally distributed to the whole agency, or staff may obtain agency gossip by snooping into computer files. IT applications can be secure and protect client confidentiality as well as any paper and pencil system only if security, confidentiality, and user authentication are part of the initial design and if agencies establish and follow appropriate policies and procedures.

The training of users is as important as passwords, encryption, audit trails, and asking users to verify the last recorded use under their names. Training can address problems such as taping passwords to computer monitors and using spouses' names as passwords. Often agency security is lax until after a violation has occurred. Establishing security and privacy safeguards after an application is developed can be expensive and time consuming.

An Illustration From a Performance Management and Evidence Perspective

While performance management and evidence-based/informed practice (EBP) are important concepts throughout this book, they have special relevance for IT. This section illustrates IT management and application development from a performance management and EBP perspective.

IT, Performance Management, and Evidence-Based/Informed Practice

IT allows for an enhanced EBP model built on a performance management approach (for further discussion of EBP, see Chapter 8). Enhancing EBP using IT involves changing the focus of EBP from an individual practitioner searching for relevant research on each case to a service delivery system supported by IT applications that allow practitioners

to monitor their performance on well-researched, outcome-based practice standards. The traditional EBP model and an IT-enhanced EBP model are summarized in Table 9.1 and discussed below.

In the traditional EBP model, the practitioner's role is to accumulate the evidence for each new case and then formulate best practices based on the evidence. Much of the EBP literature focuses on changing the work patterns of busy practitioners so they review research literature available in journals or databases, such as the Cochrane Library (Gibbs, 2003). However, because work structures and patterns are heavily influenced by agency practices, changes at the organizational level can enhance a practitioner's

Table 9.1   Current and Enhanced EBP Model

Feature	Current EBP Model	IT-Enhanced EBP Model
Focus	Practitioner/client intervention process and outcomes	Organizational intervention process and outcomes for all clients
Location of evidence	Journals, e.g., Cochrane Library	Agency information systems that are continuously updated
Structure of evidence	Research on interventions	Research on performance standards
Questions asked	Best practices to improve outcomes in each case	Agency-wide indicators, benchmarks, and best practices to advance agency's mission
Responsible entity	Individual practitioner	Policy makers, experts, quality assurance staff, and managers
Practitioner's roles	Formulate best practices for each case based on research evidence	Examine evidence from agency information system using agency developed tools to ensure their practice in each case achieves agency goals and outcomes
Manager roles	Similar to traditional roles, e.g., supervision and administration	Formulate agency-wide standards and indicators and monitor to assure practitioner adherence to standards result in best practice
How EBP is disseminated	Diffusion of innovation via training and education	Performance or decision support applications that give practitioners easy access to agency data within a performance context

SOURCE: "A Technology Enhanced EBP Model" by D. Schoech, R. Basham, and J. Fluke (2006) *Journal of Evidence Based Practice, 3*(3/4), p. 61. Copyright 2006 by Haworth Press. Adapted with permission.

use of EBP (Schoech, Basham, & Fluke, 2006; Stetler, 2003). Focusing EBP at the management level allows the agency to implement the IT-enhanced EBP model in Table 9.1.

A difficult, yet critical first step when applying EBP is to ask the right questions (Hinds et al., 2003). In the traditional EBP model, the practitioner has little guidance on the questions to ask. In an IT-enhanced model, policy makers, researchers, clinical experts, quality assurance staff, and managers determine the key questions to be asked, the available evidence, and practice standards based on the evidence. In the traditional EBP model, the key question for the practitioner might be "What does the literature say is the most effective intervention for this case?" In the enhanced model, the key question for the organization might be "On what research-based indicators and standards can the agency provide information to staff to allow them to optimize agency goals and client outcomes when working each case?" When agencies ground performance indicators and standards in evidence and best practices, it is possible to focus EBP on interventions that achieve the agency mission.

DEMOS, an Illustration

A state Child Protective Services performance support system called DEMOS illustrates the IT-enhanced EBP model in Table 9.1. DEMOS is short for Data Enhanced Management Online Support (Schoech, Fluke, Basham, Baumann, & Cochran, 2004). Table 9.2 presents the federal indicators and standards based on two federally mandated information systems, the Adoption and Foster Care Analysis and Reporting System (AFCARS) and the National Child Abuse and Neglect Data System (NCANDS) (U.S. Department of Health and Human Services, 2001).

DEMOS uses OLAP (OnLine Analytic Processing) software to present data in the form of 6,000+ clickable graphs accessed via a Web browser (The OLAP Council, 1997). DEMOS allows all agency staff to obtain information on how well they are performing on the six indicators in Table 9.2. Staff can "drill down" into DEMOS data by organizational level (e.g., statewide, region, program director, unit, and case; Figure 9.2). Staff can also "slice and dice" the data using several explanatory variables such as child's

Table 9.2 Federal Indicators and Standards From the Adoption and Safe Families Act (ASFA) of 1997

Indicator	Standard
Length of time to achieve reunification	At least 76.2% are reunified in less than 12 months from the time of the latest removal from home
Stability of foster care placement	At least 86.7% had no more than two placement settings
Foster care re-entries	Less than 8.6% re-entered foster care within 12 months of a prior foster care episode
Length of time to achieve adoption	At least 32% exited care in less than 24 months from the time of the latest removal from home
Recurrence of maltreatment	Less than 6.1% had another substantiated or indicated report within six months
Incidence of child abuse and/or neglect in foster care	Less than 0.57% were the subject of substantiated or indicated maltreatment by a foster parent or facility staff

age, gender, ethnicity, and month of disposition. That is, by clicking on any of the explanatory variable graphs, staff can view all graphs on a screen recalculated for only that variable. For example, clicking on *females* in Figure 9.3 refreshes all graphs for females only, thus providing context information for any of the indicators.

Discussion of the Illustration

DEMOS illustrates the enhanced EBP model in Table 9.1 by using systemwide performance indicators developed from research along with the experience of experts and policy makers. DEMOS broadened the concept of evidence from published research studies to organized data from the agency's information systems. Practitioners drill down and slice and dice through the DEMOS graphs to discover additional evidence, for example, why some units exceeded while others performed below standards, or what impact gender played on the department's performance on an indicator.

The development of DEMOS followed the eight-stage process in Figure 9.1. Feasibility was discussed by the major stakeholders, which were the state department of child protective services, a private company consultant with expertise in NCANDS and AFCARS data and performance standards, a software vendor, and a university team with expertise in CPS staff training and human services technology. Due to the risk in developing this application, the state agency did not want to take the lead on the project. State staff were interested in seeing whether an OLAP application would appeal to workers, but DEMOS was considered too burdensome and risky for the department to undertake, given all their other critical projects.

A three-year demonstration project was funded through a federal grant for development, testing, user training, and evaluation. The commitment and support of top management was clearly stated in the grant. DEMOS was assigned to the research and quality assurance departments within the state agency, which had strong links with the IT department. The OLAP vendor

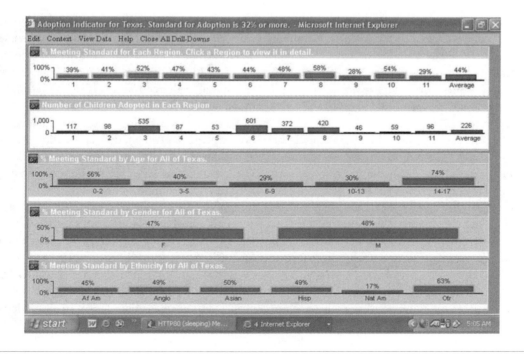

Figure 9.2   DEMOS Screen Showing the Performance of 11 Regions on the Adoption Indicator

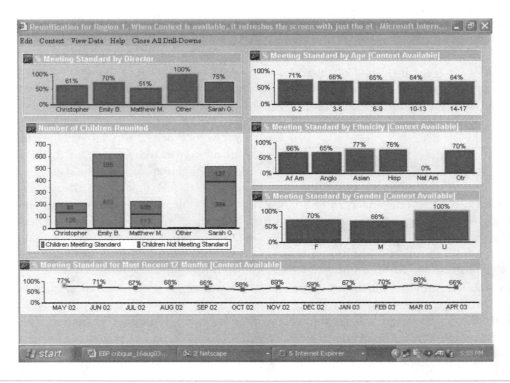

Figure 9.3   DEMOS Screen Showing the Performance of Region 1 Directors on the Reunification Standard

trained the steering committee on the OLAP software and provided technical consultation on the design. While application design used a top-down approach, screen design (Figures 9.2 and 9.3) used a prototyping approach with several screen redesigns based on user testing and technical considerations.

DEMOS development closely mirrored the 10/40/50 rule referred to earlier in terms of resource allocation. The computer server and OLAP software were a small part of the overall budget. Software development concerned getting the appropriate monthly data from the agency's data warehouse, verifying its correctness, and loading it into the OLAP software in a format that addressed the performance standards in Table 9.2. The application steering committee spent considerable time discussing what each of the standards meant and from which agency information system the data needed to be drawn. The user interface was programmed using the

OLAP software by a half-time research assistant who had programming and CPS expertise. Statewide user training took a substantial amount of time, although the project ended after testing and initial evaluation and was not fully implemented statewide.

Since the DEMOS steering committee could not mandate implementation, application success was defined more by user acceptance than use. Users at all levels were excited about having easy access to detailed information about their performance, so DEMOS was considered successful. When asked what new information they wanted from DEMOS, users' answers were summarized by one manager who said they wanted graphs on every decision for which they were responsible. Unfortunately, legislative reorganization of the agency during application development hindered statewide use. The reorganization merged the agency's IT department with many similar state departments and collapsed the 13 regions depicted in Figure 9.2 into 4 regions. Considerable redesign and programming would have been required for DEMOS to reflect these legislature-mandated agency changes. Thus, changes mandated from the agency's environment made DEMOS obsolete before it was implemented. DEMOS did demonstrate the power and acceptance of OLAP, and the DEMOS OLAP programmer was hired by the new department to work on OLAP-type projects in the larger agency.

Management Issues and Considerations

This section discusses some major issues and considerations concerning information management and application development.

Maintenance and Enhancements

While IT support for an agency process can increase efficiency and effectiveness, these benefits come at a cost of increased standardization and processes that are more difficult to change. DEMOS illustrates that keeping IT applications up to date with agency changes can be difficult and costly. Agencies undergoing rapid change are not good candidates for IT applications that go beyond basic information systems for personnel, financial, and service data. An agency must generally require far more standardization when IT applications are involved. Standardization takes many forms, such as the definition of terms, common operational procedures regarding information, and centralized control and access to information. Agencies not willing to undertake this standardization may not be willing to take the risks and pay the costs associated with application development.

Assessing and Controlling Risk

IT failure has been a theme throughout this chapter, for example, in discussing the universal law of technology project failure. Application failure is especially problematic in the human services because clients are involved and securing stable funding is a constant challenge. In the past, some funders preferred to fund client services rather than the agency infrastructure required to deliver these services. Some agency fundraising campaigns suggest that 90-95% of donor contributions will be used for direct client services. Consequently, developing IT systems to support service delivery has been seen as a luxury, and some agencies have not kept up to date with IT (Hudson, 2005). Thus, a key issue that agencies must address is the risk they are willing to take in developing any IT application.

Most human services organizations should avoid implementing the latest IT. The history of IT is littered with pioneering applications that were rarely used. Success is most often reaped by settlers who follow closely behind pioneers and make substantial improvements while avoiding the mistakes of their predecessors. While being on the forefront of IT can be exciting, it is usually frustrating and costly in terms of agency time, effort, and morale. In addition, problems often plague newly developed applications. Cautiously implementing proven applications is safer for agencies not capable of withstanding the "bleeding" that occurs on the "cutting edge." Pioneering in IT is best left to those who can take risks, for example, university researchers and vendors.

To lessen risk, an agency should be prepared psychologically and financially for designing and implementing an IT application. The agency that is most successful in application development will already be functioning well, so it can take the time and risks associated with the changes required. An agency should have formalized and stable goals, procedures, and operations because IT applications become information models of the operations they automate. An agency with frequently changing goals, structures, and procedures will find its IT applications quickly outdated. An organization in crisis or one barely surviving may not have the necessary time, energy, or morale, even if it is highly motivated to change.

Reliance on a few key people for IT applications presents serious risks for an agency.

A consultant may change firms and leave an agency stranded. An in-house designer may quit and set back the IT effort. Given frequent IT personnel changes, it is difficult to assure continuity of technical expertise for the two or three years that are required to develop a major application. A strong application steering committee and teaming outside consultants with in-house staff lessen agency dependency. In choosing the staff to team with outside specialists, it is preferable to select an employee who is expected to be with the agency for a long time. Training the brightest, most interested, or most IT-literate members of the staff may seem logical; however, they are more likely to leave the agency with their newly developed expertise. For example, a vendor developing one statewide MIS hired many key agency staff on the steering committee to work in other states where they functioned as "go-betweens/translators" between agency staff and vendor technicians.

Another way to lessen risk of losing expertise is to have good documentation. Managers often neglect documentation because its value is not immediately apparent. IT technicians neglect it because documentation is a boring and time-consuming task. However, documentation is the basis for evaluating and controlling the IT effort as well as for linking future applications. Documentation is also the key to continuity, especially when technology is changing rapidly and knowledgeable IT personnel change jobs frequently.

In-House Development Versus Outside Vendors

Most human services agencies see themselves as having unique operations. Consequently, the tendency exists to custom design an IT solution rather than purchase a generic packaged solution. Even if internal application developments seem less costly, an outside package should be seriously considered because the purchase/build decision and its consequences are difficult and expensive to reverse. This decision is similar to the automobile purchase decision. A customized one-of-a-kind car may fit the driver's transportation needs best. However, a very common mass-produced car might satisfactorily meet one's transportation needs and be easier and less expensive to repair and maintain. Even if an application is custom designed, generic tools such as those associated with database management systems and intranets should be encouraged. The money invested in these tools often results in less overall programming time and less dependence. However, like most builders, application developers often use the tools they know rather than the most appropriate tools. In addition, application developers have incentives to custom develop every part of an application because custom-developed applications ensure job security.

Working with vendors, from which the agency has purchased an application, is not always easy. Vendors often hype their products and advertise functionality that is not well developed to entice buyers away from competing products. It is common to wait for an essential software module or fix that was promised months earlier. A general rule in working with a vendor is that an application does not exist until it is successfully running on your computers. When considering software from vendors, ask for a complete list of organizations currently using the software and randomly contact several similar to your agency. Be sure that the vendor does not limit the potential list by recommending only a few well-screened possibilities. Also, ensure that if the vendor goes out of business, merges, or is unable to support the product, the agency will have access to the application source code. The above comments are not intended to reflect negatively on vendors. However, human services professionals should not confuse the helping relationship between practitioners and their clients with the business relationship between vendors and their clients.

A popular type of vendor that delivers applications over the Internet is called an application service provider (ASP). ASP applications can be accessed anywhere using standard Internet technology so the agency does not need to develop a database, firewall, LAN, or other IT infrastructure typically needed for in-house applications. However, the dependency that an ASP fosters needs to be countered, if at all possible. Data ownership, access to agency data, use of agency data in other applications, and security and backup need to be negotiated with an ASP. In these days of buyouts and mergers, having an agency dependent on a vendor, with no other options, can lead to problems.

Connectivity and Globalization

Globalization refers to the decline of local forces and the increase of global forces in today's society. Globalization is increasing due to the ease with which information can be automatically and instantly pushed and pulled between networked computers. History tells us that connectivity provides a giant leap forward. For example, the linking of local roads via the high speed interstate highway system is comparable to the linking of computers via the Internet. Besides the Internet, Wi-Fi and WiMAX wireless connectivity allow rural areas and developing countries to connect globally without installing expensive copper or fiber lines.

Internet high speed linking of computers is relevant for human services applications because service delivery involves face-to-face interactions that can be enhanced with two-way audio and video. Equally as important, but not as visible as client oriented video and audio applications, is electronic data interchange (EDI). EDI is the automatic, seamless, and instantaneous exchanging of information between separate organizations based on predetermined data definitions, standards, and protocols. XML (extensible markup language) and World Wide Web consortium (W3C) standards are integral to EDI. When countries develop 100% wireless coverage, information can flow as quickly and easily to a device anywhere in the globe as it does to a device in the same office.

Changes in banking over the past 20 years illustrate how EDI will change human services in the next 20–30 years. Twenty years ago, local banks manually mailed checks and currencies around the world. Today, a global EDI-based banking infrastructure exists with strong authentication, privacy, and confidentiality safeguards. People can pay bills using the Internet or obtain local currency using an ATM machine almost anywhere. Sophisticated computer programs, called agents or bots, analyze financial information for "unusual activity" and trigger the sending of alerts. For example, some banks have bots that analyze transactions and alert customers of large purchases from areas far away from their home. This quiet revolution in banking infrastructure was spurred on by customers who gravitated to banks that offered convenient, reliable, and quick services. Local banks, which chose not to connect to this global infrastructure, have gone out of business.

EDI will allow human services to be linked by an information sharing infrastructure over the next 20–30 years (O'Looney, 2005; Schoech, Fitch, MacFadden, & Schkade, 2002). Using this infrastructure, applications can perform many routine drudgery tasks, for example, scheduling intra-agency meetings, sifting through volumes of information for knowledge, collecting evidence on client progress, keeping everyone informed, updating all appropriate records, conducting six-month client follow-up, and documenting everything. With many routine tasks automated, human services workers can concentrate on high level tasks like those involving observation, sensing, working through "what if" scenarios, and making complex judgments and cognitive leaps. Local social workers can also contribute to the global knowledge base by online involvement with global expert teams to research complex problems.

A global human services infrastructure allows outsourcing, or the transfer of functions from people inside to those outside an organization or to those in different geographic locations. Health and human services functions are just beginning to experience the outsourcing that has changed many other areas of society. While globalization and outsourcing often increase service efficiency and effectiveness, they can increase social problems because communities devastated by the outsourcing of labor have fewer capacities to prevent social problems.

Human services managers and IT application developers need to be aware of the future tendency to link applications globally. Just as local banks that did not become part of the global banking infrastructure eventually went out of business, so too will agencies that ignore the global connectivity of human services information. Linking information does not require agencies to be consolidated; for example, we still have local banks that seem similar to banks before the international financial system was developed.

Conclusion

Managing IT and developing IT applications are key human services management tasks that are becoming more complex and important as we enter an IT-connected global society. Performance management and EBP are useful conceptual frameworks to help with IT management and application development. Standard processes and guidelines also exist to help develop and manage IT, but the advice is not always easy to follow given the limited resources available to most agencies. Some decisions, such as in-house development vs. vendor purchase, will continue to be difficult and tricky because their long- and short-term positive and negative consequences must be explored and balanced. Other difficult tradeoffs exist; for example, agencies are under pressure to support staff with IT, yet IT applications make processes more difficult to change and applications maintenance can consume scarce agency resources that could go into client services. While difficult, management of IT is critical because poorly managed IT can consume far more resources and morale than well-managed IT.

References

Gibbs, L. E. (2003). *Evidence-based practice for the helping professions: A practical guide with integrated multimedia.* Pacific Grove, CA: Brooks/Cole-Thompson Learning.

Hinds, P., Gattuso, J., Barnwell, E., Cofer, M., Kellum, L., Mattox, S., et al. (2003). Translating psychosocial research findings into practice guidelines. *Journal of Nursing Administration, 33*(7), 397–404.

Hudson, M. (2005). *Managing at the leading edge: New challenges in managing nonprofit organizations.* San Francisco: Jossey-Bass.

Moyer, D. (1997). Journey to the brave new world of data automation technology—are we ready? *Computers in Human Services, 14*(2), 17–34.

Neilson, R. (1985). The role of the federal government in social service systems development. *Computers in Human Services, 1*(2), 53–63.

The OLAP Council. (1997). OLAP Council white paper. Retrieved August 20, 2007, from http://www.olapcouncil.org/research/resrchly.htm

O'Looney, J. (2005). Social work and the new semantic information revolution. *Administration in Social Work, 29*(4), 5–34.

Proudfoot, J., Ryden, C., Everitt, B., Shapiro, D., Goldberg, D., Mann, A., et al. (2004). Clinical efficacy of computerised cognitivebehavioural therapy for anxiety and depression in primary care; randomised controlled trial. *British Journal of Psychiatry, 185,* 46–54.

Rensin, D. (2005). The universal law of technology project failure. *Computerworld.* Retrieved July 7, 2007, from http://www.computerworld.com/managementtopics/management/project/story/0,10801,102331,00.html?SKC=project-102331

Schoech, D. (1999). *Human services technology: Understanding, designing, and implementing computer and internet applications in the social services.* New York: Haworth Press.

Schoech, D., Basham, R., & Fluke, J. (2006). A technology enhanced EBP model. *Journal of Evidence Based Practice, 3*(3/4), 55–72.

Schoech, D., Fitch, D., MacFadden, R., & Schkade L. L. (2002). From data to intelligence: Introducing the intelligent organization. *Administration in Social Work, 26*(1), 1–21.

Schoech, D., Fluke, J., Basham, R., Baumann, D., & Cochran, G. (2004). Visualizing multilevel agency data using OLAP technology: An illustration & lessons learned. *Journal of Technology in Human Services, 22*(4), 93–111.

Schoech, D., Schkade, L. L., & Mayers, R. S. (1982). Strategies for information system development. *Administration in Social Work, 5*(3/4), 25–26.

Stetler, C. (2003). Role of the organization in translating research into evidence-based practice. *Outcomes Management, 7*(3), 97–84.

U.S. Department of Health and Human Services, Administration for Children, Youth and Families. (2001). *Background paper: Child and family services reviews national standards.* Retrieved August 20, 2007, from http://www.acf.hhs.gov/programs/cb/cwmonitoring/legislation/background.htm

Appendix 9.A   Basic Information Technology Terms

Term	Definition
Application	A system composed of people and procedures that solve a problem. Automobiles and trains are transportation applications just as word processors and information systems are information technology applications.
Computer	An electromechanical device that accepts data and instructions, manipulates the data according to the instructions, and outputs the results.
Computer network	Linked software and hardware systems that share resources. Computers on a network are called nodes. See Internet, Intranet, LAN, and WAN.
Computing	The total process of collecting, storing, manipulating, communicating, and disseminating information in electronic form.
Confidentiality	The level of secrecy assumed or formally agreed on by two or more parties with the expectation that shared information will be used consistent with this agreement. Confidentiality is a matter of proper levels of authorization, access codes, encryption, and other measures.
Connectivity	The extent of the linkages and the sharing of IT resources between two or more systems.
Data	Numbers that have no inherent meaning. For example, the numbers 76019 are data because they have no meaning other than their arithmetic value or the value assigned by a user.
DBMS—Database management system	A set of software programs for managing data, e.g., a database for storage, a form developer for data input, a query language, and a report writer.
Documentation	Descriptive information, in written or electronic form, which explains the development, use, operation, and maintenance of a computer or application.
DP/ADP—Data processing	The capturing, storing, manipulating, and communication of data. DP is sometimes referred to as automated data processing, ADP.
Drupal	A Web-based content management framework that is often used to build online communities.
DSS—Decision support system	An interactive IT application designed to assist users in making complex decisions. A DSS usually answers "what if" type of questions.
EDI—Electronic data interchange	The automatic, seamless, and instantaneous exchanging of information between separate organizations based on predetermined data definitions, standards, and protocols.
Extranets	Intra-agency networks that use Internet tools.
Firewall	Hardware or software that allows data access while preventing unwanted intrusion based on pre-configured level of trust.

(Continued)

Appendix 9.A (Continued)

Term	Definition
Hardware	The physical, tangible components of a computer, for example, a monitor. One can touch and see hardware.
HTML—HyperText Markup Language	A basic Web programming language.
Information	Data organized to communicate a meaning. If 76019 is a zip code, then this arrangement of numbers is information because it denotes the University of Texas at Arlington.
Information system	A system of people, procedures, and equipment for collecting, manipulating, retrieving, and reporting information.
IT—Information Technology	Technologies that collect, process, manipulate, and disseminate information. For example, a book is a paper-based IT, while a computer is an electronics-based IT. The Internet involves many communications-based information technologies.
Internet	A network of networks that is independent of any application or organization.
Internet2	A nonprofit consortium which provides high-speed computer networking for advanced uses of the Internet, e.g., video conferencing.
Intranets	Inter-agency networks that use Internet tools.
Knowledge	Information in the form of descriptions and relationships. For example, the fact that the University of Texas at Arlington is part of the state university system is a piece of knowledge.
LAN—Local area network	The linking of many computers in the same geographic area. See also WAN.
Organizational intelligence	The capacity of an organization to automate learning about processes while the processes are occurring. If an IT application gets smarter or becomes a better predictor with use, the agency has organizational learning. For example, the Netflix Web site learns your movie preferences as you check out and rate movies and then recommends movies you may like.
Privacy	The rights of individuals to keep their possessions, including information about themselves, away from others.
PSS—Performance support system	An application designed to improve staff performance by providing content specific advice when it is needed and in the format it is needed.
RSS—Really Simple Syndication	A format for automatically disseminating Web content to many users.
Security	The protection of hardware, software, and data by passwords, backup procedures, restricted physical admittance, firewalls, duplicate storage, and protection from fire and electrical interruption.

Term	Definition
Smartphone	A multimedia, full-featured phone that functions as an Internet-connected computer.
Software	Instructions that guide computer operations and their accompanying documentation.
Technology	The combination of tools and actions that are grounded in scientific knowledge, practice, or ideology and that direct or supports one's activities and decisions, for example, interviewing protocols or computer systems. Technology can be hard, involving tangible things, such as camcorders, computers, and other devices. Technology can also be soft, involving non-tangible processes, such as risk assessment systems and nonprofit accounting systems (see Information technology).
WAN—Wide area Network	A network that connects computers to share IT resources in many geographically separate locations.
Wi-Fi	A standard for short-distance wireless mobile computing, e.g., connecting a notebook computer to the Internet in an airport.
Wiki	A Web-based application that stores content and provides tools so that users can access, add, and edit information, e.g., Wikipedia.
WiMAX—Worldwide Interoperability for Microwave Access	A standard for long-distance wireless mobile computing, for example, connectivity hotspots in a city.
XML—Extensible Markup Language	A language designed to allow data sharing across different Internet applications.

SOURCE: *Human Services Technology: Understanding, Designing, and Implementing Computer and Internet Applications in the Social Services* (pp. 409–426), by D. Schoech, 1999. New York: Haworth. Copyright 1999 by Haworth Press. Adapted with permission.

PART 3

Developing and Empowering Staff and Volunteers

In the human services, perhaps more than in any other industry, the provision of high quality, effective services to consumers depends largely on the motivation, attitudes, and commitments of frontline staff. In most human services, the persons who deliver the service and the service itself are inseparable. In this section, we have five chapters that deal with various aspects of how to motivate, develop, and empower frontline workers.

In Chapter 10, Professor Diane Vinokur-Kaplan presents an updated version of her chapter in the first edition to address the central and enduring question of how to motivate workers to perform their best. Taking a multifactorial approach to the question, Vinokur-Kaplan looks at motivational forces that work at the individual, interactional, and organizational levels. Both classic and contemporary theories are examined for their applicability to human services workers. The integration of these theories with a model that incorporates all these elements is suggested. This chapter, as suggested, is a good supplement to Chapter 6.

The increasing diversity of clientele in human services agencies and the staff who provide services raises important questions about how an agency can fully integrate all persons into the mainstream of agency life. In Chapter 11, Michàlle Mor Barak clarifies the various kinds of diversity found in agencies and the social and psychological processes that lead to discrimination and exclusion. The detrimental effects of these processes on both workers and agency capability are examined, and steps that can be taken to create an inclusive agency culture are detailed. This chapter should be read in conjunction with Chapter 14, which also deals with diversity.

Chapter 12 addresses the critical tasks associated with managing personnel in social agencies. In a detailed and practical discussion, Professor Peter Pecora examines management processes of personnel recruitment, selection, and training, as well as how to handle employees with performance problems, and provides examples that can be readily applied. Pecora places all of this in the context of federal policies that are intended to ensure equal treatment for persons of color, women, differently abled persons, and other protected workers and offers suggestions about how to apply these policies in agency personnel practices. This chapter will complement Chapters 11and 14 and broaden the consideration of diversity management.

Perhaps no working relationship is more important to effective job performance than that of the supervisor and supervisee. In Chapter 13, Karen Hopkins provides a broad treatment of the role of first line supervisors in the development and empowerment of frontline staff and volunteers, who are an important part of the human services workforce. The focus of this chapter is how supervisors can develop and support competent workers and volunteers. It addresses effective skills for supervising, training, and staff development in a learning and performing culture. Finally, the chapter explores how personal characteristics shape supervisors' perceptions and developmental and supportive behaviors. This chapter expands on some of the training content in Chapter 12 and also shows the application of leadership skills, addressed in Chapter 7, to supervisory performance.

Chapter 14 provides another perspective: managing for diversity. Professor Alfreda Iglehart examines strategies managers can use to build culturally competent and diverse staffs and develop the agency's ability to deal sensitively with minority groups and communities. Illustrated with case examples, this chapter provides an action framework that can be useful to managers who seek to empower their own staffs and provide a voice in political and organizational decision making for minority clients, who are often disenfranchised. This chapter extends and complements the material in Chapter 11.

CHAPTER 10

Motivating Work Performance in Human Services Organizations

Diane Vinokur-Kaplan

Introduction

Personnel are the most valuable resource in human services organizations, for without them, the organization's mission cannot be meaningfully implemented, nor can its vision of the future be fully realized (see Gummer, 1995). In these types of organizations, social and personal change is achieved, and social value is distinctively added, through the direct interactions between employees and clients.

Human services managers are directly or indirectly responsible for selecting, developing, and retaining a workforce that will carry out the organization's mission and goals efficiently and effectively. If properly carried out, these functions do much to determine the continuity and quality of the organization's services; moreover, they underwrite its reputation in the community as an effective organization that is attractive to future recruits and worthy of moral and financial support. Therefore, a central concern of managers is how best to motivate workers so that agency services are performed well and valuable staff is retained.

AUTHOR'S NOTE: In the first edition of this volume, published in 2000, this chapter was co-authored with Daniel A. Bogin, whom I thank for all his efforts and contributions therein. I totally rewrote the chapter for this edition. I also thank Professors Robert L. Kahn (The University of Michigan) and Robert A. Roe (Tilberg University, The Netherlands) for their comments or help on the 2000 chapter. I also thank Professor Stevan A. Hobfoll (Kent State University) for his comments, suggestions, and encouragement. Finally, I am most grateful to Professor Rino Patti, Editor, both for his thoughtful and helpful comments and for his patient support throughout this chapter's development in both editions of this volume.

Agencies that do not attend to staff motivation often pay dearly for staff turnover, as noted by Mor Barak, Nissly, and Levin (2001, p. 627):

> The direct costs of employee turnover are typically grouped into three main categories: separation costs (exit interviews, administration functions related to terminations, separation pay, and unemployment tax), replacement costs (communicating job vacancies, pre-employment administrative functions, interviews, and exams), and training costs (formal classroom training and on-the-job instruction).

There are also indirect effects that, while difficult to measure, may add to these costs; they include "the loss of efficiency of employees before they actually leave the organization, the impact on their coworkers' productivity [including those to whom the caseload is transferred], and the loss of productivity while a new employee achieves full mastery of the job" (Mor Barak et al., 2001, p. 627). Moreover, an organization can pay dearly and painfully in other, less tangible ways, including possible decrease in staff morale from work overload; a damaged public reputation, leading to fewer interested new job candidates and less access to resources of many kinds; and fewer opportunities to pursue the agency's mission to serve its clients (Robert L. Kahn, Professor Emeritus of Psychology and Public Health, The University of Michigan, personal communication, May 12, 1999; Mor Barak et al., 2001; Mor Barak, Levin, Nissly, & Lane, 2006).

Given the crucial role of employees in determining an organization's success and the high costs of turnover, the following practical question arises: How can human services managers ensure that their employees will continue to bring expertise and vitality to the performance of their jobs and maintain their commitment to the organization? (See Meyer & Allen, 1991; Meyer, Bobocel, & Allen, 1991.)

This chapter seeks to provide some conceptual guidance to managers and students of human services organizations who address this key question. It draws upon a voluminous literature on motivation and work performance in the workplace. Psychologists, sociologists, and other scholars of organizations have addressed this topic from a wide range of perspectives; they range from a micro-level focus on individual personality traits, which predispose individuals' work motivation and their fit with a particular work position (e.g., introversion vs. extroversion), to a macro-level view analyzing the culture and symbols on which an organization relies to promote its employees' motivation and performance (Schein, 2005). Included are classic theories and research, as well as more recent approaches to work motivation that can be applied to human services settings.

This chapter first gives a brief overview of some social trends influencing the current and upcoming human services labor force from which new employees will be drawn, and it cautions that the personal motives and goals of earlier generations might not apply to the new generations of job seekers. This chapter then defines work motivation and performance, emphasizing how past approaches to work motivation sought to link the goals of the organizations with those of individual employees. Illustrations of how such linkages appear in human services are provided. Thereafter, an overview of approaches to work motivation is given, based on three levels of analysis: individual, social interactional, and organizational. The chapter concludes with some general recommendations for enhancing work motivation in the social service workplace.

Current Trends Regarding the Human Services Workplace and Its Employees

Changing Human Services Organizations and Human Resource Relationships

Today's employees in human services (in the United States and other, similar countries) often find themselves serving growing populations facing well-known social problems requiring social care (such as poverty, lack of shelter, unemployment, and poor health). But they are also called upon to serve growing populations with more recently acknowledged or emerging social problems occurring in a more interconnected global context. These challenges include the spread of new infectious diseases (HIV/AIDS and SARS); violations of new standards of human rights; social exclusion of immigrants and displacement of refugees; sexual exploitation of children via the Internet; international terrorism; unforeseen natural, technological, and ecological disasters; and emerging needs related to the growing populations of elders.

At the same time, the organization of human services in the U.S. and some other countries has undergone many changes, including devolution of services to a more local level; contracting out of human services previously delivered by government to various nonprofit and for-profit organizations; public demands for greater accountability; cost reimbursement of services based on predefined performance criteria; greater competition for funding; [1] funders' frequent calls for greater interorganizational collaboration; and social policy changes regarding service delivery, funding, and program procedures, to name but a few (Ascoli & Ranci, 2002; Kearns, 1996; Kramer, 1994; Light, 2000; Panel on the Nonprofit Sector, 2005; Ryan, 1999; Salamon, 1993, 2002).

Furthermore, some human services are following employment trends found in other industries. These developments include eliminating and deprofessionalizing positions (Fabricant & Burghardt, 1992), decreasing job and retirement security, and hiring workers in nonstandard employment relations such as part-time work, employment via a temporary help agency or contract company, short-term and contingent ("only if needed") jobs, and independent contracting (Kalleberg, 2000). These relationships "depart from standard work arrangements in which it was generally expected that work was done full time, would continue indefinitely, and was

performed at the employer's place of business under the employer's direction" (p. 341).

Known examples of such nonstandard employees in human services include those providing direct service or treatment to clients and patients, such as social workers, psychotherapists, nurses, and physicians, as well as administrative staff such as grant writers and project managers. Little research has been done on the motivation and performance of this latter component of the human services workforce, such as whether what they value in their work differs from what salaried employees value (see Ashford, George, & Blatt, 2007).

Changing Personal Values and Opportunity Structures

The realities of the late 20th- and 21st-century workplace, in which employers cannot provide the job security and career paths they used to offer, influence the occupational priorities and expectations of new job candidates. Unlike their parents' generation, today's workers must be more mobile, and they are unlikely to expect to have careers with only one employer. At the same time, they expect adherence to the federal and state legislation passed in the later part of the 20th century that has provided (some) employees with more security than before regarding family leave, physical accessibility, civil rights, and prohibitions against sexual harassment:

Moreover, women, who historically and currently represent the great majority of frontline professionals in human services, now have expanding employment and financial opportunities (Preston, 1990). Thus, human services also will be competing harder for talented personnel, given more and better-paying work opportunities for women and other previously excluded groups (see Mor Barak et al., 2006). Therefore, to successfully recruit, develop, and retain today's and tomorrow's human services workforce, it is important for managers to address the following question: How can a manager continuously enhance each employee's motivation and performance throughout his or her career?

Professional Ethics

Before any further discussion ensues, however, it must be noted that human services managers' efforts to enhance the motivation and performance of their staff must be consistent with relevant professional ethics. Frederic Reamer (2000), the leading scholar of social work ethics, cautions that to function competently, social welfare and, I would add, any other human services administrators

> must have a solid command of three key knowledge areas: (a) ethical issues and dilemmas in administration; (b) ethical analysis, moral reasoning, and decision-making strategies; and (c) ethical risk management—strategies to prevent ethics complaints and lawsuits from being filed against agency staff and organizations themselves. (p. 70)

Specific topics of administrative ethical competence particularly pertinent to work motivation and performance in human services include informed consent and confidentiality, cultural competence and social diversity, conflicts of interest, sexual harassment, labor-management disputes, interdisciplinary collaboration, staff supervision and consultation, and performance evaluation (Reamer, 2000, p. 82; also see National Association of Social Workers, 1996). Thus, human services managers must conduct an ongoing analysis and assessment of current agency employment policies and practices that have an impact on employees and advocate especially for those that improve their knowledge, skills, health, and development.

Defining and Measuring Work Performance and Its Enhancement

While I urge human service administrators to continually develop their knowledge and skills to further enhance their employees' work motivation and performance, I also recognize that just defining and conceptualizing the concepts of work performance is a major challenge in itself.

One definition of work performance, offered by Roe (1999), focuses on "the performance of people carrying out tasks with the purpose of some kind of economic exchange, [who are] typically employees of firms or public organizations" (p. 232). Roe further distinguishes between two interlinked components of work performance: (1) *Process*—"Performance is the process by which people (individually or collectively) try to achieve a given work goal" and (2) *Outcome*—"Performance is the congruence between the work goal and the outcome of the process by which people (individually or collectively) try to achieve that work goal" (p. 234). This conceptualization thus poses two aspects of work performance that managers evaluate in order to improve their employees' performance: to what degree the work goal was achieved, and how effectively, efficiently, and ethically it was done.

To illustrate, let us assume that two social workers are hired for a particular program provided by an agency. That agency's work environment reflects many interacting factors, such as social, legal, political, cultural, and geographic influences and constraints. Let us say that these newly hired social workers are supposed to help implement a program goal (e.g., protect children from further family violence, finalize adoptions, or assess a community's most pressing needs and strengths, each of which is also consonant with the organization's overall mission). They may conduct an intervention (e.g., intensive case management, professional family counseling, asset-based community development mapping; Kretzmann & McKnight, 1993) that promotes and hopefully results in a particular desired outcome (see Roe, 1999, p. 234; also see Hasenfeld, 1983); for example, desired performance outcomes may be that families' children are healthy, not harmed, and developing in an age-appropriate way; abandoned children are successfully adopted; a new community agenda is set to reduce domestic violence and abuse. The performance process would incorporate the workers' direct efforts (such as relationship building and application of relevant knowledge and skills), assistance required from coworkers, relevant legal and ethical consultation, and so forth. If the new workers manage to attain the goal but do not perform tasks appropriately in the process of doing so (or vice versa), their overall performance will be viewed as less than satisfactory. Thus, both of these interlocking aspects of performance—outcome and process—are of concern, especially in human services where high degrees of public trust and confidentiality are required for continued public support of the agency.

Other scholars have highlighted additional key dimensions to consider when evaluating and enhancing work performance. Arvey and Murphy's (1998) review of the work performance evaluation literature from the mid-1990s presented three trends regarding how work performance should be considered when designing appropriate interventions to enhance human services workers' motivation and performance.

First, work performance should be viewed as *multifactorial* in nature and more than just the execution of simple, specific tasks (Arvey & Murphy, 1998). Namely, work performance must capture the complexity and variety of the tasks that workers are expected to perform. In the above example of the newly hired social workers, these tasks could include the complex evaluations required to assess sexual abuse of a child, or the appropriateness of allowing a particular individual or family to adopt a specific child, or the many discrete tasks needed to successfully negotiate with conflicting political factions in a particular community. The evaluation must also assess whether the organization's actions regarding planning and organizing services and selecting, training, and coaching new staff to conduct all official transactions is done in a technically proficient and ethical manner (see Arvey & Murphy, 1998, pp. 145–146; Borman & Brush, 1993).

Second, definitions of job performance are becoming less precise. Both managers and employees must scrutinize both job titles and the attached expectations for successful work performance, for many work positions' requirements

are being changed and broadened. For example, an earlier job title of "Pediatric Social Worker" in a hospital now may be simplified to "Social Worker," so that the employee can be expected to work effectively with patients of all ages. Similarly, the title of "Program Developer," which once focused more on executing technical aspects of program planning inside the agency, has also expanded; the employee with this title may now be expected to also "work extensively with the local community and its political leaders on client advocacy issues in a culturally competent manner," "collaborate actively with numerous local agencies on current and future projects," and "carry a limited caseload of agency clients, as needed." With such changes, managers can more easily rotate—and "stretch"—employees to meet the agency's changing needs. Yet, employees may need new or additional skill sets to accomplish each of these expanded duties successfully.

Moreover, in the past, organizations first recruited and then later evaluated workers' performance on specific duties and observable tasks (see Arvey & Murphy, 1998, p. 148). In human services, these criteria could include questions such as Was the home visit completed? Was the discharge plan written and submitted on time? Was the case file closed? Today, job performance is more than just the execution of specific tasks; it also involves a wider array of important organizational activities (see Arvey & Murphy, p. 141). For example, workers also may need to justify annually how their work relates to the overall mission, goals, and objectives of the agency.

Furthermore, many performance reviews now *also* evaluate workers' "organizational citizenship," the less obvious tasks "that contribute more to the organizational, social, and psychological environment to help accomplish organizational goals" and develop capacity (Arvey & Murphy, 1998, pp. 146–147; also see Organ, 1997). Thus, employees may be evaluated on whether they persist with enthusiasm and extra effort or volunteer to carry out duties not formally part of their job. In social work, these contextual actions may include such tasks as being a positive representative of one's agency to the public, building trust and social capital with potential collaborators, or indirectly promoting the reputation of one's agency through voluntarily serving on a community-wide task force.

Third, much has been learned about the measurement of job performance in terms of the validity of this construct, rating accuracy and rating error, individual versus group evaluation, and issues of rating fairness and bias (see Arvey & Murphy, 1998, pp. 148–159). Today, there is also substantial interest in so-called "360-degree" or "full circle" performance evaluations, which incorporate ratings from the circle of parties with whom the employee interacts, such as supervisors, peers, subordinates, and even customers or clients of an employee (see Morgeson, Mumford, & Campion, 2005). Reviewing all of the multiple perspectives may increase the validity of the evaluation of the employee, and these multiple evaluations can help offset the biases of one person. These various assessments are then used for feedback and/or personnel decisions (Arvey & Murphy, 1998, p. 154). Also, these measures of worker performance vis-à-vis different parties may be integrated within the overall strategy of "balancing the scorecard" of the organization; workers' roles and performance may be analyzed vis-à-vis the financial, customer, business process, and learning and growth perspectives of the organization (see Kaplan, 2001; Kaplan & Norton, 2005; but see Moore, 2003 for a critique when applied to nonprofits).

Another aspect of work performance now being assessed is the various types of personal resources that individuals use in their activities to attain their goals and how they regulate these cognitive, physical, and energetic resources when doing so (Roe, 1999, p. 236). Their expending of these resources "has an impact on people's knowledge, skills, motivation and self-image. . . . it also evokes emotions and produces fatigue—in extreme cases also stress or burnout" (p. 236). Such self-regulation of energies can occur in the various phases of the goal attainment process, which includes

> *goal establishment* (i.e., processes involved in adopting, adapting, or rejecting a goal),

planning (i.e., processes involved in preparing to pursue a goal), *striving* (i.e., processes involved in moving toward or maintaining a goal), and *revision* (processes involved in the possible change or disengagement from a goal). (Italics added; Vancouver & Day, 2005, p. 158)

During this goal attainment process, there are five self-regulating processes that both the anticipated and the actual work performance evoke in individuals and which individuals assess and modulate. Managers must consider this array of workers' self-regulation mechanisms if high work performance is to be initiated and maintained. To help distinguish these different types of self-regulation, I have added illustrations of the internal processes or "self-talk" in which individuals might engage:

1. *Action regulation*: The person decides whether or not to initiate action on a task in accordance with a self-generated cognitive representation of the goal. (Should I or shouldn't I pursue this particular assignment to help attain my goal?)

2. *Energetic regulation*: The person self-regulates the amount of psychic and related energy (perception, thinking, and motor control) to allocate to the action, including how much effort to put forth. (How much personal energy should I use to pursue this task?)

3. *Emotional regulation*: The person's emotions and their regulation will affect his or her performance. (How am I feeling about doing this task?)

4. *Vitality regulation*: The person's long-term mental and physical health affects—and is affected by—performance. (Am I really fit enough to do this task? How is my mental and physical health actually being affected by this task? Would doing this task again really "kill" me?)

5. *Self-image regulation*: The person's performance is a side product of the regulation

of his or her self-image. (Am I doing this task so poorly because it's so contrary to who I think I really am? Am I truly showing those folks "what I'm really made of" by outperforming everyone else doing this task?)

In sum, the conception, definition, and measurement of work motivation and performance has gone much beyond the limited, task-specific, assembly line approach parodied by Charlie Chaplin in the film *Modern Times*. Currently, a much broader perspective is used by many organizational scholars. They "have gradually expanded their focus from 'the worker' to the 'purposeful, goal-striving human' and to the processes by which those purposes are acquired and realized" (Vancouver & Day, 2005, p. 156). They include various types of work performance (observable both directly and indirectly) and workers' cognitive and self-regulative processes, as well as consideration of the impact of workers' attitudes and performance on the organization's internal and external environments.

Still, three major issues remain when interpreting and applying research that seeks correlates or predictors of work performance in human services. First, in reviewing research on this general topic, readers must see whether *work motivation* or *actual work performance* is being measured, or whether some other related but distinct concept is being substituted. For example, because reliable and valid data on work performance outcomes are often difficult or expensive to obtain, some researchers substitute "job satisfaction" as a proxy for actual performance. While job satisfaction and actual work performance are often correlated, they are actually different concepts.

Second, managers must be alert to the particular theoretical perspectives, the points of departure, and the image of the worker and the performance involved. As discussed below, many current approaches are quite cognitive and focus on what is going on "inside the head" of individuals as they decide whether they should initiate, continue, terminate, or otherwise modulate certain activities that may be instrumental to attaining their goals.

For example, such is the case with cognitive perspectives associated with industrial psychology and some scholars of organizational psychology (see Vancouver & Day, 2005). Other approaches give more attention to the emotions of the individuals and the culture and community in which they are nested (Hobfoll, 1998), broadly using more of a community psychology approach. Each approach sheds a particular light on the issues, often reflecting particular types of questions that specific disciplines are particularly interested in investigating. From this author's readings, the time is ripe for greater interdisciplinary integration and mutually enriching discourse. As a very small step in this direction, Figure 10.1 below summarizes key concepts related to work motivation and employee performance currently being investigated; it also illustrates how some of these approaches and concepts could start to be integrated with a recent theory discussed below.

Third, applications of such social science research must consider the complexity of the missions and goals found in human services. In order to enhance the performance of human services workers successfully, organizational theorists have generally recommended blending the organization's performance goals with the worker's personal and career goals (see Weiner, 1990). The human services organization's performance goals may include continuous actualizing of its mission by providing effective, efficient services; enhancing productivity; obtaining needed resources; and maintaining good staff morale. In comparison, the human services worker's personal and career goals may include extrinsic rewards, such as fair pay, and intrinsic rewards, such as feeling successful vis-à-vis his or her work with clients; enjoying challenging, growth-enhancing work; and obtaining a degree of autonomy and self-determination in his or her professional role (see Weiner, 1990, p. 328). This meshing is often referred to as the "motivational fit" of an individual and a job, and it "reflects the continuous and reciprocal influence of personal characteristics and situational factors" (Kanfer & Heggestad, 1997, p. 1), both of which are very dynamic in the field of human services.

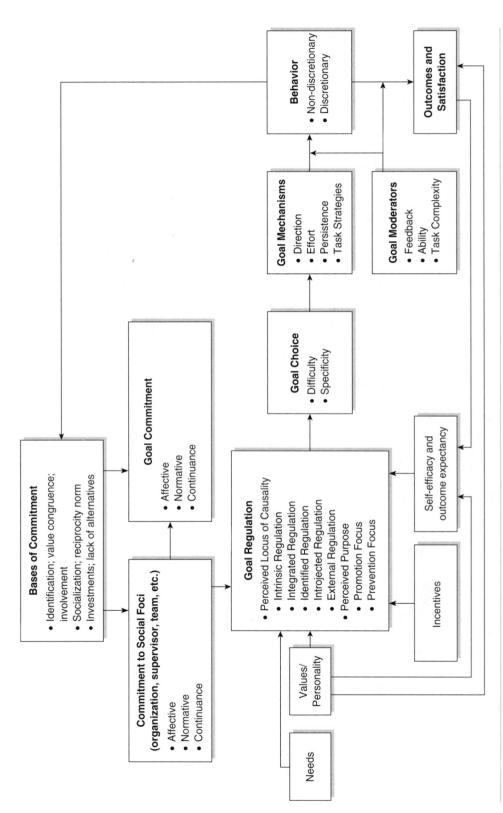

Figure 10.1 An Integrated Model of Employee Commitment and Motivation

SOURCE: This figure is derived and adapted by the author from Meyer, Becker, and Vandenberghe (2004, p. 998), Figure 2: An Integrated Model of Employee Commitment and Motivation, which supplemented E. A. Locke's *The Motivation Process* (1997) in Meyer et al. (2004, p. 993). It also incorporates approaches from Hobfoll (1989, 1998, 2001) and Roe (1999).

Overview of Theoretical Approaches to Motivating Work Performance

Reviews of theoretical approaches to work performance motivation typically present a chronological overview, first noting Taylor's scientific management, followed by behaviorist, human relations, and expectancy theory later in the 20th century. Such an approach has limited success because the diverse approaches to motivation were often overlapping in time, rather than sequential (Robert L. Kahn, Professor Emeritus of Psychology and Public Health, The University of Michigan, personal communication, May 12, 1999). Thus, for the purposes of this chapter, I first provide a schema that categorizes these approaches according to the level of analysis and intervention that they emphasize: individual, interpersonal, or organizational.

Imagine yourself as a manager at a human services organization with which you are familiar. You are concerned about the poor work performance of several employees whom you supervise. How would you go about understanding where the problem may lie? There are three broad lenses, or levels of analysis, that can assist you in analyzing the problem and then planning an intervention to improve their performance:

1. *Individual level:* Managers using this lens focus on the array of relevant personal traits and needs that might be impeding the workers' motivation or performance. For example, these employees may have (or lack) general mental abilities; strong achievement motivation; particular personality components, such as low self-esteem; or an unusual or misunderstood personal need, such as accommodation of an invisible disability. Such an approach requires managers to do much personal observation and tactful probing of their employees.

2. *Interpersonal or social interactional level:* Managers using this lens focus on the social interaction between the focal worker and other individuals in his or her environment and how these experiences may influence a worker's motivation. For example, some scholars have suggested that workers' performance and job retention is aided by social support—and diminished by social undermining—from their coworkers and supervisors. Others have concentrated on social comparison, wherein workers compare themselves or resources to relevant others. For example, how does their salary compare to that of their peers at work? Or to their counterparts at other agencies? How effective are their work efforts compared to those of similar workers in the organization?

3. *Organizational context or work environment level:* Managers using this lens focus on the structure, culture, and policies of the organization and of the particular workplace at hand, and their effects on employees' motivation and work performance. For example, these employees may have low motivation due to their perception that they have little chance for promotion because members of the group to which they belong (e.g., people of color, older workers, women, differently abled individuals) have typically not been promoted. Or, the organization is seen to be systematically unfair when settling workplace disputes. A manager using this level of analysis may benefit from imagining herself or himself to be an anthropologist, studying her or his organization's values, norms, and artifacts. Does the agency present itself one way to the public but act very differently on the inside? Are there informal norms that contradict professional ethics? What kind of structure is in place, highly hierarchical or more egalitarian?

Obviously, there is interaction and overlap between these three levels. For example, the organization's culture can influence the social interactions of employees. Nevertheless, this particular approach to worker motivation and performance is presented specifically for two reasons: (1) These multiple lenses can help managers to explore *various* types of motivational interventions when recruiting, selecting, hiring, training, and evaluating new and current employees. Table 10.1 illustrates how some classic theories in this literature

Table 10.1   Selected Individually, Interpersonally, and Organizationally Focused Approaches to Work Motivation

Theory Type and Major Contributors	Theory's Main Perspective	Mechanism/Aspect of Motivating Work Performance That It Emphasizes	Associated Work Design Principles
A. Individually focused approaches to work motivation			
Reinforcement Theory • Hull (1943) • Skinner (1938)	Interested in stimulus-response associations. Examines how a history of past benefits or punishments modifies job performance.	Work performance improves when contingent upon a certain reward or punishment.	Managers should make workers' valued personal outcomes (i.e., a salary increase or promotion) contingent on their work performance (i.e., improved productivity or effectiveness).
Hierarchy of Needs • Maslow (1954)	Maslow argues that human needs can be understood in terms of a hierarchy of five types of needs. A need that is lower on the hierarchy is stronger and generally must be satisfied prior to the person ascending to a higher level.	Three needs, known as deficiency needs, must be met if an individual is to remain a healthy person. The gratification of the next two needs, known as growth needs, is responsible for helping individuals grow to their fullest potential.	Managers are better informed about the forces driving workers' performance motivation through awareness of their hierarchy of needs. They can then redesign workers' tasks so that they are more harmonious with their current needs.
Job Satisfaction/ Dissatisfaction Two-Factor Theory • Herzberg, Mausner, Snyderman, & Bloch (1959)	Presumes that work satisfaction is related to retention of workers. Proposes that job satisfaction and job dissatisfaction depend on two different and separate sets of factors. The things that cause satisfaction are distinct from those that cause dissatisfaction.	Positive aspects of a job (such as recognition and responsibility) are termed satisfiers, and these are found to be motivating. Negative aspects of a job (such as poor working conditions) are termed dissatisfiers, and their removal is said to be *non*-motivating.	People will only work harder for motivating, nonhygienic measures. Therefore, a manager needs to distinguish between motivating and hygienic measures in the design of job tasks.
Expectancy Theory and Goal Setting • Vroom (1964) • Locke (1984) Later Variant: Locus of Control Theory • Rotter (1966)	Links worker motivation and satisfaction to whether work provides people with what they want, desire, or value. Locke states that the more important a job-related goal is to workers, the greater its potential effect on their motivation.	The process of goal achievement brings fulfillment and such positive externalities as self-esteem and a feeling of self-efficacy.	Managers should set specific, challenging goals by which to target job performance and productivity.

Theory Type and Major Contributors	Theory's Main Perspective	Mechanism/Aspect of Motivating Work Performance That It Emphasizes	Associated Work Design Principles
Social Learning • Bandura (1976)	Emphasizes the impact of others on individuals learning to successfully perform work.	Workers are motivated to aspire to the level of other significant individuals whom they view as models. Observational learning allows individuals to attain and improve their work performance.	Managers should be cognizant of the various significant models influencing workers' learning and performance.
Self-Efficacy • Bandura (1997)	Self-efficacy, or beliefs about one's capabilities to produce designated levels of performance, influences one's self-regulation of personal motivation.	Employees are more motivated to perform when they believe they are capable of doing so.	Managers should understand employees' self-efficacy beliefs and provide interventions to appropriately change their beliefs to match their capabilities.
B. Interactionally focused approaches to work motivation			
Attribution Theory • Heider (1958) • Jones & Davis (1965) • Kelley (1967, 1971, 1972, 1973)	Examines how people perceive and interpret situations, i.e., explain the behavior of others or themselves due to causes (internal or external, stable or unstable, and controllable or uncontrollable), thus influencing their own and others' behavior.	Explanations made by managers, coworkers, and self vis-à-vis causes of workers' performance motivation can strongly influence their subsequent behavior and their evaluation in the organization.	Managers should critically analyze their attributions, consider alternative explanations, and not make attributions too quickly about the causes of others' behaviors, as well as their own.
Organizational Justice Theory • Greenberg & Colquit (2005) • Cohen-Charash & Spector (2001)	Workers' motivation and performance may be affected by their perceptions of fairness in organizations (e.g., allocation of resources, hiring decisions) and the conception of justice applied (distributive, procedural, or interactional).	When workers perceive their position relative to others as being unfair, they will be motivated to correct the inequity.	Managers must be cognizant of the conceptions of justice utilized in their organization, analyze them critically, be consistent in their application, and be clear in communicating decisions and their bases.

(Continued)

Table 10.1 (Continued)

Theory Type and Major Contributors	Theory's Main Perspective	Mechanism/Aspect of Motivating Work Performance That It Emphasizes	Associated Work Design Principles
C. Organizationally focused approaches to work motivation			
Quality of Working Life/Job Design • Deci (1975) • Hackman & Oldham (1980)	Argues that workers can be intrinsically motivated. Suggests that jobs can be made more satisfying through system emphasizing more worker participation.	Proposes that motivation, satisfaction, and quality of performance increase when the following job dimensions are present: skill variety, task identity, task significance, and feedback.	QOL proposes that workers be given more autonomy in doing their jobs. While performance targets are set by management, how these targets are achieved is left to workers.
Total (Continuous) Quality Management Approach • Deming— See Walton (1986), Martin (1993)	Approaches the total system of production of goods or services and seeks to insure and inspire quality throughout the organization.	Invokes participation of all employees in a common purpose of delivering quality; seeks documented root causes of most important, solvable problems in the organization rather than immediate "blaming" of workers.	Management strategies include teams, training, "driving out fear," breaking down barriers between departments, elimination of quotas, and programs of education and self-improvement.
D. Cross-cutting-level approach to work motivation			
Conservation of Resources Theory • Hobfoll (1989, 1998, 2001)	People strive and work to obtain, retain, protect, and foster that which they value; people must invest resources in order to protect against resource loss, to recover from loss, and to gain resources. The threat of loss is a primary motivator.	• Resource loss is disproportionately more salient than is resource gain. • Those with greater resources are less vulnerable to resource loss and more capable of orchestrating resource gain. For them, initial resource gain begets further gain. • Those who lack resources are not only more vulnerable to resource loss, but for them, initial loss begets future loss. They are likely to adopt a defensive posture to guard their resources.	Motivation reflects the individual's energy resources to perform work. Thus, managers must consider employees' actual and perceived types and levels of resources (and especially threatened losses) when developing and assigning tasks and roles, as well as when evaluating employees' work performance. COR Theory is also useful at the interpersonal and organizational levels (e.g., team performance, conflict resolution, and organizational culture change).

can be so categorized and gives suggestions on how they can be used differentially in designing programs, training, and structures in human services workplaces. (2) These different levels of analysis may prevent managers from looking only at individual personality traits—an approach that historically dominated personnel management—which can lead to "blaming the victim." A multilevel analysis also considers interactional and organizational effects.

In addition, this multilevel approach reflects recent management approaches to managerial problem solving and decision making, such as continuous quality improvement (see Arches, 1991; Gummer & McCallion, 1995; Vinokur-Kaplan, 1995b) and high-performance organizations (Ashton & Sung, 2002).[2] It also reflects the concern of human services with enhancing person-in-environment fit. Several theories relevant to each level of analysis are summarized, discussed, and applied below to the human services workplace. (Also see the summary presented in Table 10.1.) Thereafter, a new approach, Conservation of Resources Theory, is presented, which more fully accommodates all three of these lenses.

Individual-Focused Approaches to Worker Motivation

The theories below illustrate how psychologists and others scholars have concentrated on how employees' personal characteristics and their quest to fulfill their basic human needs influence their motivation and work performance. The focus is on individuals and the fundamental processes occurring within them.

Personality Theories

Most researchers would agree that "there are individual differences in motivation, and these differences can be traced to dispositional tendencies" (Judge & Ilies, 2002, p. 797). Some have studied the relationship of general mental abilities

(e.g., intelligence) to work performance (see Luthans & Youseff, 2007, p. 324).[3] Others have explored the so-called "Big Five" personality factors, which some claim as "the most widely accepted structure of personality in our time" (Judge & Illies, 2002, p. 798), even if it does not cover all the domains of personality. Each factor is arrayed on a continuum from a negative to positive: conscientiousness (e.g., undependable vs. dependable); neuroticism (showing poor emotional adjustment, e.g., stress, anxiety, depression, vs. showing emotional stability), extroversion (e.g., sociable, dominant, and positive vs. introverted, nondominant, and negative), agreeableness (e.g., tendencies to be unkind, rough, untrustworthy, cold vs. kind, gentle, trustworthy, and warm), and openness to experience (e.g., rigid vs. flexible; see Judge & Illies, 2002, p. 798; also see McCrae, 1996; Watson & Clark, 1997).

> These traits have previously been found to be related to positive work performance, as well as interpersonal-level outcomes such as quality of relationships with peers, family, and romantic others . . . . and negatively associated with undesirable outcomes such as burnout. (Luthans & Youssef, 2007, p. 325)

Moreover, "the [five-factor] structure has generalized across cultures, sources of ratings, and measures" (Judge & Ilies, 2002, p. 798).

T. A. Judge and his colleagues have also probed employees' self-evaluation regarding their self-esteem, generalized self-efficacy, locus of control, and emotional stability. These investigators have found that "these traits, both independently and when combined into one higher order construct, have been shown to be significant positive predictors of goal setting, motivation, performance, job and life satisfaction, and other desirable outcomes" (Luthans & Youssef, 2007, p. 325).

In actual practice, managers are not likely to significantly change these enduring traits in their workers, although they might take such factors into account when choosing among job candidates. These dispositions can also be considered when managers assess whether current workers have the appropriate qualities to take on new assignments or implement organizational changes resulting, for instance, from welfare reform, performance contracting, managed care, or organizational restructuring.

Needs Theories

Various theorists have tried to specify the types of human needs that must be satisfied to motivate workers. The psychologist Abraham Maslow (1954) put forth perhaps the most famous taxonomy of human needs. Therein, he proposed that human needs could be best understood in terms of a hierarchy of five types of needs and that higher-level needs would come to the fore only after lower-level needs had been met. The hierarchy of needs is, from lowest to highest, (1) physiological needs, at the level of basic survival (e.g., food); (2) safety needs (e.g., a secure job); (3) social needs (e.g., friends); (4) ego needs (e.g., recognition); and (5) self-actualization needs (e.g., becoming the person you know you are capable of becoming; Dessler, 1991, pp. 323–324). The first three needs, which Maslow named "Deficiency Needs," must be met if an individual is to remain healthy. The two higher needs, known as "Growth Needs," are responsible for helping individuals grow to their fullest potential. Once the lower needs have been met, according to Maslow, the human being is increasingly motivated to satisfy higher needs.

Previous approaches to motivating workers were oriented toward the use of economic rewards and the giving or withholding of job security, thereby recognizing only the lower-order needs (see Lewis, Lewis, & Souflée, 1991, p. 201). Thus, a major contribution of the Hierarchy of Needs Theory was that it conceptually broadened the spectrum of human motivation to include more social and existential concerns about which managers would need to be concerned in enhancing their workers' motivation and performance.

Another needs-based approach was put forth in Herzberg, Mausner, and Bloch Snyderman's (1959) Motivator-Hygiene Theory and echoed later in the goal-setting approach of Locke (1984). Herzberg proposed that workers have a lower-level and a higher-level set of needs and that the best way to motivate them is to offer to satisfy their higher-level needs. The lower-level needs, when unrequited, lead to job *dis*satisfaction. Staff are satisfied by "hygiene" factors, which include better working conditions, salary, and supervision. Herzberg contended that these lower-level needs are easily satisfied, but satisfying them does not lead to greater job satisfaction (nor, presumably, to better performance). Rather, it is the higher-level needs, such as achievement, self-esteem, and recognition, which are never entirely satisfied and which lead to job satisfaction. These needs, according to Herzberg, are addressed through "motivator factors" or "job content."

Thus, according to Herzberg, the best way to motivate employees is to provide jobs that offer intrinsic rewards. These motivators are designed into the job by making it more interesting and challenging, thereby increasing the opportunities for experiencing a feeling of responsibility, achievement, growth, and recognition by doing the job well (see Dessler, 1991, p. 326). Characteristics of enriched jobs include new learning, more personalized scheduling, unique experiences, and control over resources (pp. 327–328).

Such job enrichment is costly to agencies, in terms of training resources, personnel, and time, and it also may not be engaging for all workers. However, it seems particularly relevant to human services professionals, who have already made formal investments and commitments to particularly demanding occupations.

Reinforcement Theory

This approach reflects a behaviorist orientation to motivation and examines how different types and patterns of reinforcements (rewards and punishments) modify workers' job performances. Extensive research has been done using this approach, especially with regard to the schedule and contingencies of rewards. In its simplest version, the linkage between the organization's performance goals and the worker's personal and career goals would focus on making receipt of personally valued outcomes, such as a salary increase, directly contingent on work performance, such as improved productivity. Namely, workers are encouraged to work to a defined standard in order to receive a positive benefit (or avoid a punishment). This reward (or avoidance of punishment), in turn, reinforces their motivation to work hard at their jobs, in anticipation of another reward.

Such an approach may be especially appropriate for performance based on piecework efforts—for instance, the more files a social worker closes in a prescribed period of time, thereby meeting the organization's goal of efficiency, the greater her or his bonus pay might be. The limitation of such an approach is that workers adopt behaviors that generate immediate rewards for them, while ignoring other, more long-term goals of the agency, such as service effectiveness or continuity of care. Moreover, because much of the work done by human services professional employees is not piecework but often assessments and interventions in complex social situations, more comprehensive theories seem more applicable to enhancing such workers' performance.

Expectancy Theory

This perspective, also referred to as Expectancy-Value Theory, is more elaborate than Reinforcement Theory, and it casts a more cognitive light on worker motivation. While its roots are found in Kurt Lewin's (1938) Field Theory of Behavior, and it was initially presented in the work of Tolman (1959), its further development is most often associated with Vroom (1964). In its simplest version, two components underlie an individual's motivation: values and expectancies. Generally speaking, values have to do with the person's incentives or reasons for doing a task or

activity, and expectancies refer to beliefs about how one will do on different tasks or activities (see Eccles & Wigfield, 2002, p. 110). Motivation is the product of one component (value) multiplied by the other (expectancy).

For example, a coworker might recommend that some new social workers read a recent book she or he has just finished and found very helpful in understanding substance abuse patterns among local teenagers. If the new social workers are also eager to understand this particular topic better, and feel 100% certain that they can read and understand the book's content, then, according to this model, they will have high levels of motivation to read the book. If, however, they feel either that this book is not very relevant to learning more about the topic of their interest (say, they are most interested in gerontology), or if they expect they won't be able to understand the book (say, it is written in a language they don't understand), or both, then their level of motivation to read the book will be low.

Similarly, if workers perceive strong work performance or high productivity as a highly likely path leading to a distinct goal that they highly value (such as obtaining higher salaries, prestige, or social approval), then they will have a high level of motivation to work hard in order to attain those goals.[4] If, however, they do not value such a goal, or if they believe that no matter how hard they work, it will not lead to the desired result, then they will have a low level of motivation to work hard. Obviously, motivation toward a particular task or activity can include multiple indicators of values and expectancies, and these items could be added up and averaged to find an overall motivation score.

Locus of Control Theories

Another expression of Expectancy Theory emphasizes whether an individual feels in control of his or her life and its successes and failures or, alternatively, feels his or her life is controlled by external conditions. For instance, Rotter's (1966) theory of locus of control has successfully predicted that if an individual has a strong, internal locus of control (e.g., "I am the master of my fate"), then she or he should expect to succeed. This concept of locus of control, or mastery, describes a more general attitude toward one's life, whereas Bandura's approach to self-efficacy, discussed below, pertains to confidence in one's ability regarding more specific behaviors, courses of action, or tasks.

Social Learning and Self-Efficacy Theories

These two social-cognitive theories, both developed by psychologist Albert Bandura, provide a bridge to the next section, Social Interaction-Focused Approaches to Work Motivation. Social Learning Theory emphasizes the impact of others on individuals' learning to successfully perform work. Self-efficacy, or belief about one's capabilities to produce designated levels of performance, influences one's self-regulation of personal motivation, one's activation to take action.

Social Learning Theory emphasized the importance of an individual observing another's behaviors and then modeling them in the performance of tasks, as put forth in the classic works of Miller and Dollard (1941) and Bandura (1971). Such observational learning allows individuals to develop new patterns of behavior, including work performance, without having to resort to trial and error. Also, workers are self-motivated to aspire to the level of other significant individuals, whom they view as models. Thus, by observing coworkers in the workplace, individuals develop attitudes toward the organization, the job as a whole, and specific job aspects. The broad implications of this perspective for human services managers is that they look not only at one individual's behavior, but also at how coworkers, mentors, and influential others affect a particular worker's self-perception and work performance.

Bandura later proposed "a social cognitive model of motivation focused on the role of perceptions of efficacy and human agency" (Eccles & Wigfield, 2002, p. 110; see Bandura, 1997); it emphasizes the importance of self-efficacy as a central cognitive factor motivating behavior, including work performance. This concept focuses on whether a worker believes she or he can succeed in particular tasks, and it emphasizes the role of one's *perceptions* of one's ability to perform. Bandura defined self-efficacy as

> individuals' confidence in their ability to organize and execute a given course of action to solve a problem or accomplish a task.... [It is] a multidimensional construct that varies in strength, generality, and level (or difficulty). Thus, some people have a strong sense of self-efficacy and others do not. Some have efficacy beliefs that encompass many situations, whereas others have narrow efficacy beliefs; and some believe that they are efficacious even on the most difficult tasks, whereas others belief [*sic*] they are efficacious only on easier tasks. (Eccles & Wigfield, 2002, p. 110)

This sense of self-efficacy toward particular actions has broad implications for work life in human services organizations:

> Beliefs in personal efficacy affect life choices, level of motivation, quality of functioning, resilience to adversity and vulnerability to stress and depression. People's beliefs in their efficacy are developed by four main sources of influence. They include mastery experiences, seeing people similar to oneself manage task demands successfully, social persuasion that one has the capabilities to succeed in given activities, and inferences from somatic and emotional states indicative of personal strengths and vulnerabilities. Ordinary realities are strewn with impediments, adversities, setbacks, frustrations and inequities. People must, therefore, have a robust sense of efficacy to sustain the perseverant effort needed to succeed. Succeeding periods of life present new

types of competency demands requiring further development of personal efficacy for successful functioning. (Bandura, 1994)

Thus, we see that managers and supervisors play a critical role in strengthening self-efficacy in their staff, using the techniques Bandura mentions above, so that they feel able to perform various challenging tasks and to continue such work performance over time and across changing circumstances. To encourage such self-efficacy, supervisors and peers can (1) provide coaching and "trial runs" of needed new behaviors so staff can master them; (2) provide examples of how similar others (such as similar staff in another organization) have succeeded in accomplishing such tasks; (3) provide encouragement that affirms that staff members indeed have capabilities they can apply to succeed in new tasks ("Remember how you used your own experience of raising your children to deal with difficult clients? Perhaps you could use the same experience here."); and (4) provide social support and show sensitivity to workers' sicknesses and emotions that may actually indicate frustration ("Yes, indeed, I see how that new computer system could give you a really bad headache!")

Social Interaction-Focused Approaches to Worker Motivation

Several sociopsychological approaches to worker motivation and performance tend to investigate how workers' perceptions and social interactions with relevant others in the workplace, or their comparisons of themselves to such individuals, then influence their own levels of work motivation. While these approaches can overlap with the individual and organizational lenses, they also highlight the importance of social perceptions and evaluations that arise through social interaction in the workplace between two or more people. These approaches also suggest various social interventions to enhance various workers' motivations and performance in the

workplace, such as those facilitating the constructive airing and determination of the perceived causes of staff's behavior, the communication and enforcement of clear norms of fairness, and the conveyance of managers' respect for workers and their needs.

Attribution Theories

Attribution theories also merge the individual and interactional lenses on motivation; they incorporate the general influence of others' behavior on one's motivation, but also note the importance of individuals' cognitions and interpretations of perceived situations. These theories, as developed by such social psychologists as Heider (1958), Jones and Davis (1965), and Kelley (1967, 1971, 1972, 1973), propose that when individuals observe their own or another's behavior, they try to explain what caused it: Was it due to the person's own disposition, an internal force they could somehow control? Or, was it due to an external situation, an external force, beyond or remote from the person's control? For example, managers may attribute their workers' low levels of motivation and performance to such internal causes as workers' dispositions (e.g., undependable), which workers could control, or managers could attribute their workers' low levels of motivation and performance to the hot, muggy weather that day. Managers can similarly make attributions about their *own* behavior: Did I fire that worker because I'm neurotic and did not like him or because he couldn't do the work under the extreme pressure caused by the recent budget cuts? Managers should not make attributions too quickly about the causes of others' behaviors, as well as their own, because (1) upon further consideration, they may find that they erred; and (2) workers' motivation and behavior may well be complex and include a mixture of internal dispositions and external conditions that need to be considered in enhancing their performance. In sum, Attribution Theory can broaden managers' evaluations when explaining workers' performance, as well as their own behavior and that of clients and coworkers; however, it also cautions managers to not oversimplify or overgeneralize their causal explanations.

Organizational Justice Theories

Research in this area has focused on how worker motivation and performance may be affected by perceptions of *fairness* in organizations regarding such concerns as division of monetary resources, hiring decisions, as well as policy and other organizational changes, such as plant closings (see Greenberg & Colquitt, 2005). Steiner and Bertolino (2006) recently summarized three different conceptions of justice that have been included therein: distributive, procedural, and interactional.

Distributive justice focuses on the fairness of distributions or allocations of rewards and the particular decision rule(s) that individuals believe should be used. Generally, research has shown that "both decision makers and the persons affected by these decisions" prefer that the principle of equity be used; namely, "rewards should be proportional to contributions or effort (i.e., merit)" (see Steiner & Bertolino, 2006, 1.1, paragraph 3). However, in some situations, other distributive rules may be seen as more appropriate, such as when group harmony is important. Then, a fair distribution of rewards might give each individual an equal portion, regardless of his or her individual contribution or effort (see Steiner, Trahan, Haptonstahl, & Fointiat, 2006), and in other situations, consideration of special needs may prevail. Thus, whenever possible, managers need to be clear in articulating and applying the rule to be used in decisions such as salary raises and division of other organizational resources, lest workers suspect favoritism or other biases and, as a result, decrease their motivation and performance.

Procedural justice concerns the perceived fairness of the procedures used to make decisions in organizations and began with the work of Thibaut and Walker (1975); they were concerned with "voice," or allowing people to participate in decisions that concern them, thus giving them a sense of control about decisions. "Studies in various domains have shown that people do find procedures more fair when they have had voice. In addition, these studies showed that they found the decisions themselves more fair, irrespective of their valence, when they had voice" (Steiner & Bertolino, 2006, 1.2)

In addition, Leventhal (1976) proposed six rules to strengthen procedural justice: consistency of application of procedures, bias suppression in procedures, accuracy of information used, correctability in case of an error, representativeness of the decision criteria used, and ethicality of procedures. The use of these rules "[has] been studied to various degrees and consistently indicate that procedures which respect these rules are perceived to be fair" (Steiner & Bertolino, 2006, 1.2). Thus, managers do well to scrutinize the procedures they use in making decisions so that a sense of fairness will prevail.

Interactional justice focuses on the role of the interpersonal interactions taking place in exchanges between decision makers and recipients of these decisions, especially emphasizing social sensitivity (treating people with dignity and respect) and informational justice (providing explanations for decisions; see Steiner & Bertolino, 2006, 1.3). These aspects should also be addressed by managers.

These authors conclude:

> A great deal of research has now been conducted taking into consideration these different aspects of organizational justice, and the conclusions are clear: decisions made with respect for organizational justice are unequivocally associated with positive outcomes both for the individuals who are affected by the decisions and for the authorities and the organizations responsible for the decisions. (Cohen-Charash & Spector, 2001; Colquitt, Conlon, Wesson, Porter, & Ng, 2001)

Organizational or Work Environment-Focused Approaches to Work Motivation

This final group of approaches to motivating work performance emphasizes the impact of the overall quality of life in the workplace environment, and it suggests some ways in which organizations can change both jobs and their agency structure, as well as the perceived ambience and image of the workplace. Thus, this organizational lens gives more emphasis to the influence of the external work environment and less emphasis to employees' personal traits or to the influence of social interaction.

Quality of Working Life and Job Redesign

Since the second half of the 20th century, work motivation theorists urged that more attention should be given to creating supportive work conditions and environments that allow the worker's untapped productive tendencies to emerge. For example, the Quality of Work Life approaches (e.g., Deci, 1975; Hackman & Oldham, 1980) argue that workers can be intrinsically motivated when their jobs are made more satisfying through a more participatory system. In particular, it proposed that motivation, satisfaction, and quality of performance all increase when the following job dimensions are present: skill variety, task identity, task significance, and feedback. They also suggest that while management sets performance targets, workers should have more autonomy in choosing the means to achieve them.

Recent work on these various job dimensions has illustrated that they, in themselves, are complex concepts needing greater specification. For example, fairly recent meta-analytic research on "feedback interventions" to improve performance has shown that feedback, a familiar mantra of effective supervision, is actually a "double-edged

sword," and in some cases, it actually diminishes performance (Kluger & DeNisi, 1996, 1998). One of the practical implications these authors recommend is to use feedback intervention only in combination with a goal-setting intervention, which has been found to augment the feedback intervention's effects on performance. Otherwise, overuse of feedback could become distracting or annoying. They note further that "employees who wish to have more feedback than they are receiving often suffer from the absence of clear goals" (1998, p. 71). This latter remark signals the importance of making sure that workers understand the goal (i.e., what they are trying to accomplish through their efforts) and that feedback is given appropriately. Similarly, further research has also been done on "feedback seeking" behavior in organizations (Ashford, Blatt, & Vande Valle, 2003). Its three motives are presented as "the instrumental motive to achieve a goal, the ego-based motive to protect one's ego, and the image-based motive to enhance and protect one's image in an organization" (p. 773). Various aspects of the feedback-seeking process have been conceptualized, and special attention is paid to the context, especially noting influences of culture on whether and how feedback is sought. Thus, such research alerts human services managers to key factors that can influence their feedback encounters with their employees, and how they can best use feedback to motivate employees' work performance.

Total (Continuous) Quality Management

Another approach to systemically altering relationships and processes in the workplace to enhance overall performance is found in the various schools of Total Quality Management (TQM), as proposed by Deming, Juran, Crosby, Feigenbaum and others (Walton, 1986; Martin, 1993, Ch. 2). Therein, such core work practices as customer focus, an organization-wide commitment to continuous improvement, and teamwork are purported to lead to both quality performance (less re-work, more satisfaction of customers' or clients' legitimate requirements) and to greater worker satisfaction, communication, and positive perception of the work environment (Morrow, 1997; also see Dean & Bowen, 1994). In particular, Deming decried punitive, inspection-ridden, worker-blaming American management practices; he urged instead that management "drive out fear" and "remove barriers to pride of work-manship" (see Walton, 1986, Chapters 12 and 16). He emphasized the crucial role management plays in workers' performance: "workers are responsible for only 15% of the problems, the system for the other 85%. The system is the responsibility of management" (p. 94). While originally applied to mostly industrial settings, TQM and its analytic tools have recently been successfully applied in human services as well. (For various human services examples, see Gummer & McCallion, 1995.)

Conservation of Resources Theory as an Integrative Approach

Unfortunately, one recent theory applicable to enhancing motivation and performance, the Conservation of Resources Theory developed and tested by psychologist Steven Hobfoll (see Hobfoll, 1989, 1998, 2001) and others, has not been emphasized previously in the human services literature. To address this oversight, it is included here as a cogent and comprehensive way to address the individual, social interactional, and organizational levels of managerial concerns to enhance workers' motivation and performance in human services workplaces.

Conservation of Resources (COR) Theory originated from the stream of psychological research on stress, coping, and social support; thus, it automatically resonates with concerns of the human services workplace, given the intense human relationships found there. It has been applied successfully to understand the process of stress and burnout in various organizational settings (Freedy & Hobfoll, 1994; Halbesleben &

Buckley, 2004), including social welfare offices (Wright & Cropanzano, 1998). It has become a leading theory of burnout (Halbesleben, 2006; Lee & Ashforth, 1996; Westman, Hobfoll, Chen, Davidson, & Laski, 2005) "and the one that meta-analysis of extant studies suggests best fits the data" (Gorgievski-Duijvesteijn & Hobfoll, in press, p. 1). COR Theory has been further applied by Hobfoll and his colleagues to develop preventive interventions, for example, to prevent burnout among nurses (Freedy & Hobfoll, 1994) and to prevent HIV/AIDS among single, inner-city women (Hobfoll, Jackson, Lavin, Johnson, & Schröder, 2002). Moreover, Gorgievski-Duijvesteijn and Hobfoll's (in press) chapter titled "Work Can Burn Us Out or Fire Us Up" successfully refocused COR Theory to emphasize a more strengths-based perspective regarding organizations and their employees, one already familiar to contemporary human services professions such as social work (e.g., Saleebey, 2005).

Furthermore, this recast perspective, emphasizing employees' vigor and engagement in their work, also dovetails with a current and notable trend in organizational research, referred to as "positive organizational scholarship." Such research is concerned with "the study of especially positive outcomes, processes, and attributes of organizations and their members" (Cameron, Dutton, & Quinn, 2003, p. 4). More specifically, the essence of such positive organizational scholarship is to focus "on the dynamics in organizations that lead to developing human strength, producing resilience and restoration, fostering vitality, and cultivating extraordinary individuals" (Center for Positive Organizational Scholarship, n.d.).[5]

Thus, COR Theory harmonizes with these concerns vis-à-vis preventing stress and endorsing coping and positive social support in human services workplaces. Therefore, it seems especially appropriate to the study of motivation in the human services workplace. Its key concepts are outlined and applied below, and a diagram applying them to an employee in the workplace is presented in Figure 10.2. Further elaboration of COR theory is included in the texts of cited references.

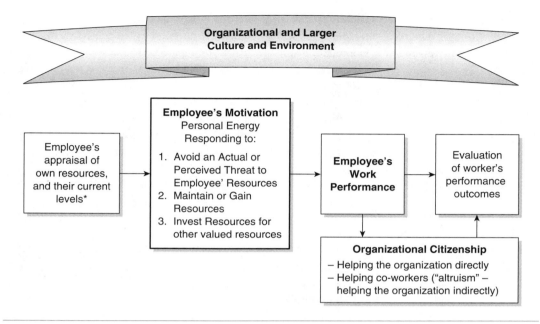

Figure 10.2 Author's Interpretation of An Employee's Process of Motivation, Performance and Self-Evaluation Using Conservation of Resources Theory

SOURCE: Based on Hobfoll, 1998, 2001 and Halbesleben and Bowler (2007).

* For example, sense of achievement buoyed by recent job promotion, mental health depleted through professional burnout, sense of compassion heightened due to engagement in human services with socially excluded target populations.

Basic Tenet

The basic tenet of COR theory is that people have an innate drive, as well as a learned drive, to create, foster, conserve, and protect the quality and quantity of their own resources (Hobfoll, 1998, 2001). While many different things could be thought of as resources, "COR Theory relates to those resources that are key to survival and well-being (e.g., shelter, attachment to significant others, self-esteem) or that are linked to the process of creating and maintaining key resources (e.g., money, credit)" (Gorgievski-Duijvesteijn & Hobfoll, in press, p. 1). The theory then outlines three conditions under which stress occurs. Since work is a major locus of resources and identity for many adult individuals (e.g., salary, benefits, self-esteem), workplace examples are described below. Stress occurs when the following events occur:

1. *Resources are lost:* For example, a close relationship ends through death, departure, or illness; a "sure bet" for investing an agency's endowment goes sour and the funds cannot be recovered; or a sense of personal safety is lost by the staff after a violent client has assaulted a coworker.

2. Individuals' *key resources are threatened with loss:* For example, a forceful natural disaster is forecasted; a dangerous, highly contagious disease is spreading through the local population; human services employees who are also parents are anxious while they work because their own children are not adequately supervised in their absence and have not returned home from school on time; or workers cars are at risk of being stolen the agency's unguarded parking lot.

3. Individuals *fail to gain resources following significant resource investment* (see Gorgievski-Duijvesteijn & Hobfoll, in press, pp. 1–2): For example, a professional degree is not granted after trying hard to complete one's studies; a depressed client commits suicide or a former drug user recidivates, despite a social worker's providing years of supportive counseling and aid; or due to one organization's merger with another, a long-sought promotion does not materialize.

If such stress persists, one outcome is burnout, which typically follows from a process of slow erosion of resources without counterbalancing gain or replenishment of resources (see Gorgievski-Duijvesteijn & Hobfoll, in press, pp. 1–2). Thus, a highly stressed employee can change dramatically, from being a dedicated organizational participant and leader—one who puts forth her or his best efforts, enhances her or his effectiveness, and promotes her or his organization's goals overall—to one who is disengaged, unproductive, or abruptly terminates her or his employment

These authors conclude,

There is something quite central and primitive biologically in the acquisition and maintenance of resources. Clearly, resources of health, family, and those resources related to survival are most central, with psychological resources such as self-esteem, self-efficacy, and optimism being key to overall resource management and maintenance. (Gorgievski-Duijvesteijn & Hobfoll, in press, p. 6)

Three Principles and Their Management Implications

COR Theory also emphasizes three corresponding principles.

The First Principle: Primacy of Resource Loss

This principle vividly explains the tendency of a stressed individual to disengage, turn inward, and become defensive:

Resource loss is disproportionately more salient than resource gain, which means that real or anticipated resource loss has stronger motivational power than expected resource gain. . . . [Moreover,] resource loss is typically accompanied by negative emotions, impaired psychological well-being, and ultimately impaired mental and physical health. Especially when primary resources get threatened, individuals may be inclined to focus on their losses and weaknesses rather than their strengths. In addition, loss experiences are likely to evoke avoidance and loss prevention strategies, rather than an active search for new opportunities for resource gain. (Gorgievski-Duijvesteijn & Hobfoll, in press, p. 7)

The implication of this principle for managers is they should strive to prevent significant resource losses among their employees (Gorgievski-Duijvesteijn & Hobfoll, in press, p. 8). In addition, when employees are faced with significant threats or losses, management may need to actively emphasize the strengths of those employees and encourage them to strive for new resources, or facilitate new ways for their employees to gain them (p. 8).

The Second Principle: Resource Investment

This principle states that "people must invest resources in order to protect against resource loss, to recover from losses, and to gain resources" (Gorgievski-Duijvesteijn & Hobfoll, in press, p. 8). If, however, people employ unsuccessful strategies to offset resource loss, then they may suffer additional, secondary losses. If the situation then becomes chronic, the resources that people have been using may be depleted. In such a case, they may well need to replace the strategies they have been using with other ones that are usually less favorable and require even higher resource costs. For example, they will need to invest resources that are harder to replenish and that embody less chance of success (p. 8). In the worst case, they become much like those people who lose their job and are in a financial crisis. To continue paying their mortgage and avoid losing their home, they may take any money they have and try high-stakes gambling. If that strategy fails, they may have no other means to avoid losing their home. In desperation, they may seek out "loan sharks" who not only charge them exorbitant interest, but also threaten physical harm if they are not quickly repaid.

The implication of this principle for managers is that employees must have the personal capacity and—equally as important—the environmental capacity to invest their own resources so they are not depleted and can enter a process of gaining resources. In other words, exhausted human services workers must feel comfortable that they can ask their supervisors for time off to restore their physical and psychological resources. Equally important, supervisors of employees in high-stress jobs must have the authority, policy support, and organizational resources to help employees restore themselves and, for instance, to grant them some time off.

A related corollary of Principle 2 is "those with greater resources are less vulnerable to resource loss and more capable of orchestrating resource gain. Conversely, those with fewer resources are more vulnerable to resource loss and less capable of resource gain" (Gorgievski-Duijvesteijn & Hobfoll, in press, p. 8). Therefore, supervisors and managers in human services must be mindful of the many demands for personal resources that they place on their employees such as overtime, overload, unnecessary interruptions, and inefficient systems for handling their paperwork. They must advocate for—and adhere to—organizational policies and procedures that keep their workers' interests in mind.

The Third Principle: Acceleration of Loss and Gain Cycles

COR theory envisions the process of motivation and stress as films, not snapshots. This results in an emphasis on loss and gain cycles. Hence, because people have fewer resources as they lose resources, they are decreasingly capable of withstanding further threats to resource loss. These loss cycles are more momentous and move more quickly than gain cycles. (Gorgievski-Duijvesteijn & Hobfoll, in press, p. 9)

Frontline staff members who endure these conditions over time tend to experience downward spirals of lost equilibrium. Thus, managers must also publicly protest such unendurable burdens as unduly high caseloads, archaic office systems, unsafe practices, and grueling schedules. By the same token, when employees gain resources (better schedules, equipment, and systems; more training and continuing education; better financial rewards), such gain cycles "also build on themselves and as people make some resource gains they experience more positive health and well-being and are more capable of further investing resources to sustain, enhance, and increase the speed of the engagement process" (Gorgievski-Duijvesteijn & Hobfoll, in press, p. 9). In this upward spiral, their resource reservoirs will grow, and they will be more capable of devoting themselves effectively to their work.

In conclusion, Conservation of Resource Theory provides an elegant conceptualization of workers' motivation and performance that promotes management responsibilities and actions at all three levels of observation and intervention previously mentioned. On the individual level, it encourages managers to help strengthen workers' capacities (knowledge, skills, assertiveness, self-esteem) so they have a richer set of personal resources to direct toward job challenges. It similarly makes managers more curious and sensitive to their workers' perception of real or threatened losses.

On the interpersonal level, it gives a usable framework to quickly assess the particular gains and losses from which interpersonal conflict may arise. It further cautions about the heavier and accelerating impact of resource loss in terms of ruining health and well-being, when compared to the enhancement rendered by resource gains. On the organizational level, "it calls for the need to nurture and create ecologies that foster resource development, resource growth, and resource protection of individuals and teams," especially if they are to be creative (see Gorgievski-Duijvesteijn & Hobfoll, in press, p. 16).

In particular, Gorgievski-Duijvesteijn and Hobfoll (in press) emphasize the following organizational resources, norms, and policies that can enhance individual and team performance: *flexibility*, expressed both cognitively and emotionally; *balance*, through avoidance of overload on both the individual and environmental level; *time* to think, plan, and strategize without interruption; *hiring people with diverse knowledge and skills* and provision of *opportunities* for continued growth of skills; and *promotion of interdependence and loyalty*, and *tolerance for risk and even failure* (see pp. 17–18, passim).[6]

Summary and Conclusions

This chapter has sought to provide a review of selected contemporary social science theories concerned with motivating work performance and to illustrate how human services managers can apply them. It has addressed these concepts with a requisite multifaceted approach. The three lenses used—individual, interpersonal, and organizational—illuminate multiple points of departure that managers need to consider when addressing the topic of motivating work performance.

If recipients of human services are to receive high-quality attention and care from human services employees, then human services managers may benefit from considering and adopting some of the conceptual, theoretical, and empirical materials reviewed herein. First, for example, Roe's (1999) emphasis that performance contains both process and outcome elements helps to conceptualize work performance in a more sophisticated way. Second, the ongoing research on employees' self-regulation of their personal resources when seeking their goals provides a cognitive model clearly conceptualizing how employees continuously evaluate and seek to control what they are doing and why.

Third, Hobfoll's (1998, 2001; Gorgievski-Duijvesteijn & Hobfoll, in press) Conservation of Resources Theory illuminates new ways of understanding and enhancing employees' motivation and decreasing their stress and burnout, improving their interactions, and considering the community and cultural contexts in which they live and work. Indeed, managers should not presume they already understand what fosters or threatens those resources that employees inherently seek to conserve. Rather, this approach, along with other positive organizational scholarship, encourages managers to consult with their employees about what matters most to them, so that they can perform their work with excellence and dedication. This approach also resonates with Glisson and Hemmelgarn's (1998) work on the impact of more positive organizational climates on clients' outcomes, Total (Continuous) Quality Management approaches, and various authors' growing emphases on establishing "learning organizations" (see Austin & Hopkins, 2004; Latting, Beck, Slack, Tetrick, Jones, & Da Silva, 2004; Senge, 2006). These various conceptualizations and approaches provide means for managers to reexamine the institution in which their employees function and to consider various means to improve it.

Fourth, Hobfoll and other authors draw attention to the corrosive effect of "negatives" on employees' well-being, namely, the overriding power of threats to resources held dear (e.g., possible layoffs, disrespect, or upheavals in valued relationships). Together with other various authors' attention to the deleterious effects of negative social support on employees' stress and mental health, these concerns are a clarion call to action for human services managers (and, indeed, for their funders).

Fifth, rather than providing one sure-fire prescription for motivating work performance in human services, this chapter underlines the variety of possible levels and points of intervention to improve performance.

Finally, I wish to take a step back and ask, "Why motivate human services work performance?

For what?" It is essential that human services managers focus on their organizations' missions and the humane purposes that their employees are expected to achieve. There is growing evidence that outcomes for both clients and employees in human services are better when the staff can conduct their work in a positive organizational climate, with autonomy, respect, and collegiality. Trying to establish and maintain such a work environment in an era of deprofessionalization, contractualization, industrialization, and marketization of human services can be challenging, if not daunting (Bernstein, 1991; Fabricant & Burghardt, 1992; Salamon, 1993). Hopefully, greater public recognition of humanity's shared fate—and the crucial roles that human services employees play in providing compassionate care and treatment and in promoting social development—will provide the support and resources needed for excellent work to be performed in these organizations.

Notes

1. Such competition includes competition among nonprofit agencies, competition between nonprofit and commercial agencies in areas such as child care, health, and nursing homes, and competition among different professions in providing human needs (e.g., social work, nursing, education, public health, and business).

2. There is also a rich literature on group performance and group motivation, which is especially important in light of new management theories that emphasize teams and empowered groups. Due to limitations of space, I pose this discussion in terms of motivating the performance of an individual, but many of the points may also be relevant to groups and teams.

3. Although the positive relationship between general mental ability and human performance has been demonstrated and emphasized in selecting capable employees in the first place (Schmidt & Hunter, 2000), "intelligence" is not discussed further in this chapter, since limitations of space preclude discussing recent attention to the many different types or aspects of intelligence (e.g., emotional intelligence).

4. I am limiting the discussion to work motivation, whereas Expectancy theory has also been applied extensively to study other types of motivation, such as achievement motivation in developmental and educational psychology (see Eccles & Wigfield, 2002, p. 110).

5. "Positive Organizational Scholarship is an exciting new movement in organizational studies that draws on path-breaking work in the organizational and social sciences . . . [It] is based on the premise that understanding how to enable human excellence in organizations will unlock potential, reveal possibilities, and facilitate a more positive course of human and organizational welfare. POS does not adopt one particular theory or framework, but it draws from the full spectrum of organizational theories to understand, explain, and predict the occurrence, causes, and consequences of positivism. Research findings to date indicate that enabling positive qualities in individuals leads to exceptional organizational performance" (Center for Positive Organizational Scholarship, n.d.).

6. Obviously, I am in no way encouraging innovative practices that would fail to protect the health and well-being of human services clients. Rather, there are myriad systems, procedures, paperwork forms, and other activities that bear review and new ways of doing things that could be tried in order to enhance overall efficiency and effectiveness and respect the overall conservation of employees' resources. For example, let's say that social welfare agencies used to employ five-year cycles for planning. They have since found that strategic planning for a year or two at a time yields greater, more specific results; this new procedure also costs less in terms of time spent, and thus promotes better morale and "buy-in" by staff. Even if the first time seems like a failure, the lessons learned may be of greater value for the future than continuing with the past practice of overly long planning cycles.

References

Adams, J. (1965). Inequity in social exchange. In L. Berkowitz (Ed.), *Advances in experimental social psychology* (2nd ed., pp. 267–299). New York: Academic Press.

Arches, J. (1991). Social structure, burnout, and job satisfaction. *Social Work, 36*(3), 202–206.

Arvey, R. D., & Murphy, K. R. (1998). Performance evaluation in work settings. *Annual Review of Psychology, 49*, 141–168.

Ascoli, U., & Ranci, C. (Eds.). (2002). *Dilemmas of the welfare mix: The new structure of welfare in an era of privatization.* New York: Plenum.

Ashford, S. J., Blatt, R., & Vande Walle, D. (2003). Reflections on the looking glass: A review of research on feedback-seeking behavior in organizations. *Journal of Management, 29*(6), 773–799.

Ashford, S. J., George, E., & Blatt, R. (2007). Old assumptions, new work: The opportunities and challenges of research on nonstandard employment. In J. P. Walsh & A. P. Brief (Eds.), *Academy of management annals* (Vol. 1, pp. 79–143). Mahwah, NJ: Lawrence Erlbaum.

Ashton, D. N., & Sung, G. (2002). *Supporting workplace learning for high performance working.* Geneva, Switzerland: International Labour Organization.

Austin, M. J., & Hopkins, K. (Eds.). (2004). *Supervision as collaboration in the human services: Building a learning culture.* Thousand Oaks, CA: Sage.

Bandura, A. (1971). *Social learning theory.* New York: General Learning Press.

Bandura, A. (1976). *Social learning theory.* Englewood Cliffs, NJ: Prentice Hall.

Bandura, A. (1994). Self-efficacy. In V. S. Ramachaudran (Ed.), *Encyclopedia of human behavior* (Vol. 4, pp. 71–81). New York: Academic Press. (Reprinted in H. Friedman (Ed.). (1998). *Encyclopedia of mental health.* San Diego: Academic Press). Retrieved October 18, 2007, from http://www.des.emory.edu/mfp/banency.html.

Bandura, A. (1997). *Self-efficacy: The exercise of control.* New York: W. H. Freeman and Co.

Bernstein, S. R. (1991). *Managing contracted services in the nonprofit agency: Administrative, ethical and political issues.* Philadelphia, PA: Temple University Press.

Borman, W. C., & Brush, D. H. (1993). More progress toward a taxonomy of managerial performance requirements. *Human Performance, 6*(1), 1–21.

Cameron, K. S., Dutton, J. E., and Quinn, R. E. (2003). Foundations of positive organizational scholarship. In K. S. Cameron, J. E. Dutton, & R. E. Quinn (Eds.), *Positive organizational scholarship: Foundations of a new discipline* (pp. 3–13). San Francisco: Berrett-Koehler.

Center for Positive Organizational Scholarship. (n.d.). *The essence of positive organizational scholarship: Unlocking the generative capabilities in human communities.* Ross School of Business, The University of Michigan, Ann Arbor, MI. Retrieved November 21, 2007, from http://www.bus.umich.edu/Positive/PDF/POS%20Essence.pdf.

Cohen-Charash, Y., & Spector, P. E. (2001). The role of justice in organizations: A meta-analysis. *Organizational Behavior and Human Decision Processes, 86*, 278–321.

Colquitt, J. A., Conlon, D. E., Wesson, M. J., Porter, C. O., & Ng, K, Y. (2001). Justice at the millennium: A meta-analytic review of 25 years of organizational justice research. *Journal of Applied Psychology, 86*(3), 425–445.

Dean, J. W., & Bowen, D. E. (1994). Management theory and total quality: Improving research and practice through theory development. *Academy of Management Review, 19*, 392–418.

Deci, E. L. (1975). *Intrinsic motivation.* New York: Plenum Press.

Dessler, G. (1991). *Personnel/human resource management* (5th ed.). Englewood Cliffs, NJ: Prentice Hall.

Eccles, J. S., & Wigfield, A. (2002). Motivational beliefs, values and goals. *Annual Review of Psychology, 53*, 109–132.

Fabricant, M., & Burghardt, S. (1992). *The welfare state crisis and the transformation of social service work.* Armonk, NY: M. E. Sharpe.

Freedy, J. R., & Hobfoll, S. E. (1994). Stress inoculation for reduction of burnout: A conservation of resources approach. *Anxiety, Stress & Coping: An International Journal, 6*(4), 311–325.

Glisson, C., & Hemmelgarn, A. (1998). The effects of organizational climate and interorganizational coordination on the quality and outcomes of children's service systems. *Child Abuse & Neglect, 22*(5), 401–421.

Gorgievski-Duijvesteijn, M. J., & Hobfoll, S. E. (in press). Work can burn us out or fire us up: Conservation of resources in burnout and engagement. In J. R. B. Halbesleben (Ed.), *Handbook of stress and burnout in health care.* Hauppauge, NY: Nova Science.

Greenberg, J., & Colquitt, J. A. (Eds.). (2005). *Handbook of organizational justice.* Mahwah, NJ: Erlbaum.

Gummer, B. (1995). American managers discover secret weapon—their employees! Developing human capacities in organizations; using the Japanese management approach. *Administration in Social Work, 19*, 93–110.

Gummer, B., & McCallion, P. (Eds.), (1995). *Total quality management in the social services: Theory and practice* (Resource guide and publication series on management and supervision). Albany,

NY: Professional Development Program of Rockefeller College.

Hackman, J. R., & Oldham, G. R. (1980). *Work redesign*. Reading, MA: Addison-Wesley.

Halbesleben, J. R. B. (2006). Sources of social support and burnout: A meta-analytic test of the conservation of resources model. *Journal of Applied Psychology, 91*, 1134–1145.

Halbesleben, J. R. B., & Bowler, W. M. (2007). Emotional exhaustion and job performance: The mediating role of motivation. *Journal of Applied Psychology, 92*(1), 93–106.

Halbesleben, J. R. B., & Buckley, M. R. (2004). Burnout in organizational life. *Journal of Management, 30*(6), 859–879.

Hasenfeld, Y. (1983). *Human service organizations*. Englewood Cliffs, NJ: Prentice Hall.

Heider, F. (1958). *The psychology of interpersonal relations*. New York: Wiley.

Herzberg, F., Mausner, B., & Bloch Snyderman, B. (1959). *The motivation to work* (2nd ed.). New York: Wiley.

Hobfoll, S. E. (1989). Conservation of resources: A new attempt at conceptualizing stress. *American Psychologist, 44*(3), 513–524.

Hobfoll, S. E. (1998). *Stress, culture and community. The psychology and philosophy of stress*. New York: Plenum Press.

Hobfoll, S. E. (2001). The influence of culture, community and the nested-self in the stress process: Advancing conservation of resources theory. *Applied Psychology: An International Review 50*(3), 337–396.

Hobfoll, S. E., Jackson, A. P., Lavin, J., Johnson, R., & Schröder, K. E. E. (2002). Effects and generalizability of communally oriented HIV/AIDS prevention versus general health promotion group for single, inner-city women in urban clinics. *Journal of Consulting and Clinical Psychology, 70*, 950–960.

Hull, C. L. (1943). *Principles of behavior: An introduction to behavior theory*. New York: D. Appleton-Century.

Jones, E. E., & Davis, K. E. (1965). From acts to dispositions: The attribution process in person perception. In L. Berkowitz (Ed.), *Advances in experimental social psychology* (Vol. 2, pp. 219–266). New York: Academic Press.

Judge, T. A., & Ilies, R. (2002). Relationship of personality to performance motivation: A meta-analytic review. *Journal of Applied Psychology, 87*(4), 797–807.

Kalleberg, A. L. (2000). Nonstandard employment relations: Part-time, temporary, and contract work. *Annual Review of Sociology, 26*, 341–365.

Kanfer, R., & Heggestad, E. C. (1997). Motivational traits and skills: A person-centered approach to work motivation. *Research in Organizational Behavior, 19*, 1–56.

Kaplan, R. S. (2001). Strategic performance measurement and management in nonprofit organizations. *Nonprofit Management and Leadership, 11*(3), 353–370.

Kaplan, R. S., & Norton, D. P. (2005, July). The balanced scorecard: measures that drive performance. *Harvard Business Review*, 71–80.

Kearns, K. P. (1996). *Managing for accountability: Preserving the public trust in public and nonprofit organizations*. San Francisco: Jossey-Bass.

Kelley, H. H. (1967). Attribution theory in social psychology. In D. Levine (Ed.), *Nebraska symposium on motivation* (15th ed.). Lincoln: Dept. of Psychology, University of Nebraska.

Kelley, H. H. (1971). *Attribution in social interaction*. New York: General Learning Press.

Kelley, H. H. (1972). Attribution in social interaction. In E. E. Jones, D. E. Kanouse, H. H. Kelley, R. E. Nisbett, S. Valins, & B. Weiner (Eds.), *Attribution: Perceiving the causes of behavior* (pp. 1–26). New York: General Learning Press.

Kelley, H. H. (1973). The processes of causal attribution. *American Psychologist, 28*, 107–128.

Kluger, A. N., & De Nisi, A. (1996). The effects of feedback interventions on performance: Historical review, a meta-analysis and a preliminary feedback intervention theory. *Psychological Bulletin, 119*, 276–299.

Kluger, A. N., & De Nisi, A. (1998). Feedback interventions: Toward the understanding of a double-edged sword. *Current Directions in Psychological Science, 7*(3), 67–72.

Kramer, R. M. (1994). Voluntary agencies and the contract culture: "Dream or nightmare?" *Social Service Review, 68*(1), 33–60.

Kretzmann, J., & McKnight, J. (1993). *Building communities from the inside out: A path toward finding and mobilizing a community's assets*. Chicago: ACTA.

Latting, J. K., Beck, M. H., Slack, K. J., Tetrick, L. E., Jones, J. M., & Da Silva, N. (2004). Promoting service quality and client adherence to the service plan: The role of top management's support for innovation and learning. *Administration in Social Work, 28*(2), 29–48.

Lee, R. T., & Ashforth, B. E. (1996). A meta-analytic examination of the correlates of the three dimensions of job burnout. *Journal of Applied Psychology, 81*(2), 123–133.

Leventhal, G. S. (1976). The distribution of rewards and resources in groups and organizations. In L. Berkowitz & W. Walster (Eds.), *Advances in experimental social psychology* (Vol. 9, pp. 91–131). New York: Academic Press.

Lewin, K. (1938). *The conceptual representation and the measurement of psychological forces* (Contributions to psychological theory No. 4). Durham, NC: Duke University Press.

Lewis, J. A., Lewis, M. D., & Souflée, F., Jr. (1991). *Management of human service programs* (2nd ed.). Pacific Grove, CA: Brooks/Cole.

Light, P. (2000). *Making nonprofits work: A report on the tides of nonprofit management reform.* Washington, DC: Brookings Institution/Aspen Institute.

Locke, E. (1984). Job satisfaction. In M. Gruneberg & T. Wall (Eds.), *Social psychology and organizational behavior* (pp. 93–117). Chichester: John Wiley.

Luthans, F., & Youssef, C. M. (2007) Emerging positive organizational behavior. *Journal of management, 33*(3), 321–349.

Martin, L. L. (1993). *Total quality management in human service organizations* (Sage human services guides, No. 67). Newbury Park, CA: Sage.

Maslow, A. (1954). *Motivation and personality.* New York: Harper & Row.

McCrae, R. R. (1996). Social consequences of experiential openness. *Psychological Bulletin, 120,* 323–337.

Meyer, J. P., & Allen, N. J. (1991). A three-component conceptualization of organizational commitment. *Human Resource Management Review, 1,* 61–89.

Meyer, J. P., Becker, T. E., & Vandenberghe, C. (2004). Employee commitment and motivation: A conceptual analysis and integrative model. *Journal of Applied Psychology, 89*(6), 991–1007.

Meyer, J. P., Bobocel, D. R., & Allen, N. J. (1991). Development of organizational commitment during the first year of employment: A longitudinal study of pre- and post-entry influences. *Journal of Management, 17,* 717–733.

Miller, N. E., & Dollard, J. (1941). *Social learning and imitation.* New Haven, CT: Yale University Press.

Moore, M. H. (2003, May). *The public value scorecard: A rejoinder and an alternative to "Strategic performance measurement and management in nonprofit organizations by Robert Kaplan."* Hauser Center for Nonprofit Organizations Working Paper No. 18. Retrieved May 30, 2008, from http://ssrn.com/abstract=402880.

Mor Barak, M. E., Levin, A., Nissly, J. A., & Lane, C. J. (2006). Why do they leave? Modeling child welfare workers' turnover intentions. *Children & Youth Services Review, 28*(5), 548–577.

Mor Barak, M. E., Nissly, J. A., & Levin, J. A. (2001). Antecedents to retention and turnover among child welfare, social work, and other human service employees: What can we learn from past research? A review and meta-analysis. *Social Service Review, 75*(4), 625–661.

Morgeson, F. P., Mumford, T. V., & Campion, M. A. (2005). Coming full circle: Using research and practice to address 27 questions about 360-degree feedback programs. *Consulting Psychology Journal: Practice and Research, 57*(3), 196–209.

Morrow, P. C. (1997). The measurement of total quality management principles and work-related outcomes. *Journal of Organizational Behavior, 18,* 363–376.

National Association of Social Workers. (1996). *NASW code of ethics.* Washington, DC: Author.

Organ, D. W. (1997). Organizational citizenship behavior: It's construct clean-up time. *Human Performance, 10,* 85–97.

Panel on the Nonprofit Sector. (2005). *Strengthening transparency, governance and accountability of charitable organizations.* Washington, DC: Independent Sector. Retrieved July 27, 2008, from http://www.nonprofitpanel.org/Report/final/Panel_Final_Report.pdf

Preston, A. E. (1990). Changing labor market patterns in the nonprofit and for-profit sectors: Implications for nonprofit management. *Nonprofit Management and Leadership, 1*(1), 15–28.

Reamer, F. (2000). Administrative ethics. In R. Patti (Ed.), *The handbook of social welfare management* (pp. 69–86). Thousand Oaks, CA: Sage.

Roe, R. A. (1999). Work performance: A multiple regulation perspective. *International Review of Industrial and Organizational Psychology, 14,* 231–335.

Rotter, J. B. (1966). Generalized expectancies for internal versus external control of reinforcement. *Psychological Monographs, 80,* 1–28.

Ryan, W. P. (1999). The new landscape for nonprofits. *Harvard Business Review,* 127–136.

Salamon, L. M. (1993). The marketization of welfare: Changing nonprofit and for-profit roles in the American welfare state. *Social Service Review, 67*(1), 17–39.

Salamon, L. M. (Ed.). (2002). *The state of nonprofit America.* Washington, DC: Brookings Institute.

Saleebey, D. (Ed.). (2005). *The strengths perspective in social work practice* (4th ed.). New York: Allen & Bacon.

Schein, E. H. (2005). *Organizational culture and leadership* (3rd ed.). San Francisco: Jossey-Bass.

Schmidt, F. L., & Hunter, J. E. (2000). Select on intelligence. In E. Locke (Ed.), *The Blackwell handbook of principles of organizational behavior* (pp. 3–14). Oxford, UK: Blackwell.

Senge, P. (2006). *The fifth discipline: The art & practice of the learning organization.* New York: Doubleday.

Skinner, B. F. (1938). *The behavior of organisms: an experimental analysis.* New York, London: D. Appleton-Century.

Steiner, D. D., & Bertolino, M. (2006). The contributions of organizational justice theory to combating discrimination. *Cahiers de l'Urmis.* Retrieved November 18, 2007, from http://urmis.revues.org/document223.html.

Steiner, D. D., & Rolland, F. (2006). Comment réussir l'introduction de changements: Les apports de la justice organisationnelle. In C. Levy-Leboyer, C. Louche, & J. P. Rolland (Eds.), *RH: Les apports de la psychologie du travail. 2. Management des organisations* (pp. 53–69). Paris: Editions d'organisation.

Steiner, D. D., Trahan, W. A., Haptonstahl, D. E., & Fointiat, V. (2006). The justice of equity, equality, and need in reward distributions: A comparison of French and American respondents. *Revue Internationale de Psychologie Sociale/International Review of Social Psychology, 19,* 49–74.

Thibaut, J., & Walker, L. (1975). *Procedural justice: A psychological analysis.* Hillsdale, NJ: Erlbaum.

Tolman, E. C. (1959). Principles of purposive behavior. In S. Koch (Ed.), *Psychology: A study of a science* (Vol. 2, pp. 92–157). New York: McGraw-Hill.

Vancouver, J. B., & Day, D. V. (2005). Industrial and organization research on self-regulation: From constructs to applications. *Journal of Applied Psychology: An International Review, 54,* 155–185.

Vinokur-Kaplan, D. (1995a). Enhancing the effectiveness of interdisciplinary mental health treatment teams. *Administration and Policy in Mental Health, 21*(6), 525–530.

Vinokur-Kaplan, D. (1995b). Social workers' adoption of quality management in a multi-disciplinary host setting. In B. Gummer & P. McCallion (Eds.), *Total quality management in the social services: Theory and practice* (pp. 231–256). Albany, NY: Professional Development Program of Rockefeller College.

Vroom, V. H. (1964). *Work and motivation.* New York: Wiley.

Walton, M. (1986). *The Deming management method.* New York: Perigee.

Watson, D., & Clark, L. A. (1997). Extraversion and its positive core. In R. Hogan, J. A. Johnson, & S. R. Briggs (Eds.), *Handbook of personality psychology* (pp. 767–793). San Diego, CA: Academic Press.

Weiner, M. E. (1990). *Human services management: Analysis and applications* (2nd ed.). Belmont, CA: Wadsworth.

Westman, M., Hobfoll, S. E., Chen, S., Davidson, O. B., & Laski, S. (2005). Organizational stress through the lens of conservation of resources theory. In P. L. Perrewe & D. Ganster (Eds.), *Research in organizational stress and well-being* (Vol. 4, pp. 167–220). Greenwich, CT: JAI Press.

Wright, T. A., & Cropanzano, R. (1998). Emotional exhaustion as a predictor of job performance and voluntary turnover. *Journal of Applied Psychology, 83*(3), 486–493.

CHAPTER 11

Social Psychological Perspectives of Workforce Diversity and Inclusion in National and Global Contexts

Michàlle Mor Barak

The recent focus on diversity in the management literature takes on special urgency in the context of human services organizations. Human services organizations have traditionally served a wide array of communities with a high representation of diverse, disadvantaged, and oppressed groups. This diversity has not typically been mirrored in the workforce of those organizations. A recent study of a nationally representative sample of 10,000 social workers demonstrates that the profession is not keeping pace with the population it serves in terms of its ability to attract social workers of color (National Association of Social Workers, 2005). The study's findings indicate that 86% of licensed social workers are predominantly non-Hispanic whites. Both African Americans and Latinos are underrepresented relative to their presence in the U.S. population, with 7% African American social workers, compared to 12% in the population, and 4% Latinos, compared to 14% in the population. This workforce data stands in contrast to the social workers' reports about the diversity of their client population: 83% report having black/African American clients in their caseloads and 75% report having Hispanic/Latino clients. In the field of child protective services, agencies have been recruiting professionals outside of social work in order to increase the presence of underrepresented groups in their workforce (Clark & Jacquet, 2003).

Despite advancement in the representation of women and members of minority groups in the human services workforce, there is still a lot to be done to make the workplace more inclusive. The extent to which workers from diverse backgrounds feel included in the organization may have a direct bearing on their job satisfaction and commitment to the organization (Mor Barak, 2000a). As a result, this sense of inclusion or exclusion as well as the overall organizational culture and climate may influence the quality of services that workers provide to their clients (Glisson & Himmelfarn, 1998; Glisson & James, 2002) as well as the workers' health, mental health, and social functioning (McNeely, 1992).

Managers of human services organizations often assume that because their workers' education includes sensitivity to and efficacy in dealing with diverse clients, they should also be skilled in dealing with diversity among their peers, subordinates, and supervisors. This, however, may not necessarily be the case. In an interview I conducted in preparation for a large organizational diversity study, a manager recounted how disappointed she was when she had to reprimand one of her workers for making an offensive remark to a colleague from a different ethnic background. The manager noted that the worker "should have known better; after all, he is an experienced social worker!"

How can we explain both overt and covert incidents of prejudice and discrimination in the workplace, particularly among trained human services professionals? What dynamics dictate intergroup relations? How can we explain conflicts and hostilities among identity groups? The goal of this chapter is to address these questions by exploring social psychological theories of diversity and exclusion. The notion of exclusion can assist in generating a conceptual framework to clarify our understanding of the personal and organizational consequences of workforce diversity in human services organizations.

This chapter is organized into five major sections: (1) background and a definition for diversity in work organizations; (2) exploring some theoretical building blocks—prejudice, discrimination, and exclusion; (3) analyzing theories of diversity and intergroup relations relevant to human services organizations; (4) presenting research evidence on diversity and exclusion; and (5) examining the implications for human services management.

Background and Diversity Definition

In recent decades, many countries around the world, including the U.S., have made significant progress, through legislation and public policies, toward creating a more equitable work environment (Mor Barak, 2005). The combination of antidiscrimination laws and affirmative action programs have helped more women, members of ethnic and racial minorities, gays and lesbians, older workers, the differently abled, and members of other marginalized groups become part of the labor force. Despite progress in increasing the *representation* of diverse groups in work organization, it is the *exclusion* of these groups from circles of influence in the organization that keeps them from fully contributing to, and benefiting from, their involvement in the workplace.

The definition of diversity commonly used in the organizational literature refers to specific categories of human differences such as race, ethnicity, gender, sexual orientation, and disability (see, e.g., Bloom, 2002; Muller & Parham, 1998). However, with increased immigration and worker migration fueled by the global economy, the number and types of groups who are marginalized and discriminated against in the workplace continue to increase. Generating a definition of workforce diversity that will be relevant and applicable in various cultural and national contexts proves to be a challenge. It is important to remember that workforce diversity *is not* about the anthropological differences between people that "make them special"; diversity *is* about belonging to groups that are different from whatever is considered "mainstream" in society. In short, it is about being susceptible to employment consequences as a result of one's association within or outside certain social groups.

Some scholars advocate focusing only on the categories that have been most persistently associated with negative employment consequences across cultural and national contexts (Essed, 1996; Linnehan & Konrad, 1999; Nkomo, 2001). They specifically identify race, gender, and social class as the fundamental diversity categories. For example, Nkomo (2001) asserts that the most fundamental divisions in organizations are along the lines of race, gender, and class and that diversity work must be about ending the domination of these systems of oppression. As another example, Linnehan and Konrad (1999) declare that including many distinct groups in the definition of diversity ends up diminishing the emphasis on intergroup inequality and undermining historical and institutional problems related to stereotyping, prejudice, discrimination, and disadvantage.

There are some general distinction categories that do seem to cut across many (though not all) national and local cultures. These include gender, race, ethnicity, age, sexual orientation, and disability. However, there are two problems in utilizing some of these categories to define diversity: First, some of the categories may have either positive or negative impact on employment and job prospects in different countries. For example, in Western cultures, younger employees are considered more desirable because they are perceived to have new ideas, better technological skills, and a more dynamic and flexible attitude. In Eastern and more traditional societies, such as in China and Korea, the old are revered and believed to possess desirable qualities of wisdom and experience. Therefore, although age discrimination may be relevant in both types of societies, its impact might be very different. And, second, diversity distinction categories are not exhaustive of the domain. Some cultures utilize diversity categories that are not included on this list. For example, religious affiliation in Ireland, regional location (rural vs. urban) in China, and caste in India are powerful diversity categories that are not included in the list.

Perhaps the logical solution to the difficulty of finding a universal definition for diversity that can be relevant in different cultural contexts is to define diversity not by naming specific categories or finding a general rule but by identifying the process and the consequences of diversity.[1] Therefore, the definition of workforce diversity utilized in this chapter is as follows:

Workforce diversity refers to the division of the workforce into distinction categories that (a) have a perceived commonality within a given cultural or national context, and that (b) impact potentially harmful or beneficial employment outcomes such as job opportunities, treatment in the workplace, and promotion prospects—irrespective of job-related skills and qualifications. (Mor Barak, 2005, p. 132)

This definition provides a broad umbrella that includes any categories that may be relevant to specific cultural or national environments without pre-specifying the categories. This approach does not list the distinction categories and therefore does not limit them to specific categories (e.g., to only gender, race, and ethnicity), thus allowing the inclusion of categories that may be relevant in some cultural contexts and not in others (e.g., castes or regional differences). Additionally, this definition emphasizes the importance of the workplace-related *consequences* of diversity. What are the main adverse consequences of the diversity distinction categories? Prejudice, discrimination, and exclusion are all constructs that describe attitudes and behaviors that affect the distribution of resources and privileges in society. They are based on group membership rather than on employment-related characteristics (e.g., level of education, commitment, and job-related skills) and are used as building blocks in the construction of theories relevant to diversity and intergroup relations, as discussed below.

Theoretical Building Blocks: Prejudice, Discrimination, and Exclusion

This section examines several constructs that are often used to express psychological processes and actual behaviors involved in intergroup relations. These constructs are defined as "mechanisms by which advantaged and disadvantaged group members perceive and interpret interactions that appear to be based on their category membership rather than on their individual characteristics" (Taylor & Moghaddam, 1994, p. 159). At the basis of both intergroup attitudes and behaviors are the diversity (or group affiliation) categories used to make the distinction between the advantaged and the disadvantaged in each society. These constructs are helpful in clarifying central aspects of diversity in organizations that could lead to the dominance or advantage of one group over another and, therefore, are central to the construction of theories.

Stereotyping and Prejudice

Often confused, stereotyping and prejudice refer to very distinct psychological processes. All of us hold stereotypical views of groups other than our own and often about our own group as well. For example, "Latino families maintain close relationships"; "Asian-American students excel in math and sciences"; "Women are more attentive to human emotions." These stereotypes serve a very practical function. Rather than starting with no information when we encounter a person from another group, we begin with a framework that gives us a sense of confidence that we know something about the other. Stereotypes are, therefore, a *mental impression* that we form about members of other groups. Although the concept originated to denote negative images of other groups, recent research demonstrates that they could be both positive and negative (McGregor & Gray, 2002; Slabbert, 2001). For example, having closely knit families is typically perceived as a positive attribute, but when it is perceived as a common characteristic of *all* Latino families, it constitutes a stereotype.

The concept of prejudice, on the other hand, refers to people's *attitudes* toward members of other groups—expecting certain behaviors from them that are mostly pejorative. The word *prejudice,* derived from the Latin noun *praejudicium,* means to prejudge. Although it is possible to have positive prejudice as well—that is, to think well about others without sufficient justification (e.g., reverence for the wisdom of the elderly)—the word *prejudice* has acquired a negative connotation. Prejudice is typically described as a schema

of negative evaluations and characteristics that are attributed to groups perceived as racially and culturally different (Essed, 1995, p. 45). For example, in a study of interethnic perceptions, Gilbert, Carr-Ruffino, Ivancevich, and Lownes-Jackson (2003) found that African American males were more likely to be viewed as incompetent and not as courteous as African American women and Asian American women and men. This was despite having similar job-related qualifications and history.

The following definitions summarize the distinctions between a stereotype and a prejudice:

> A *stereotype* is a standardized, oversimplified, and typically negative mental picture held by a person or persons about members of another group and sometimes about their own group as well.

> A *prejudice* is a preconceived judgment or opinion held by members of a group; most commonly it is an irrational attitude of hostility directed against an individual, a group, a race, or their supposed characteristics. (Based on Taylor & Moghaddam, 1994, pp. 159–166)

Discrimination in the Workplace

Negative stereotypes and prejudices make it easier to relate to the other person as different and unworthy of equal rights and treatment. The most extreme psychological mechanism in perceiving members of other groups as inferior is dehumanization, and its behavioral manifestation is oppression. Oppression is the unjust or cruel exercise of authority or power, most often used by one group to dominate another. The psychological process involved in the justification of such practices includes relating to out-group members as inferior or fundamentally different in ways that make them undeserving of equal treatment.

The word *discrimination* is generally neutral in its meaning (e.g., referring to someone as "having a discriminating taste"), but it has a clear negative connotation when applied to the context of employment and is defined as follows:

> *Discrimination in employment and consumer relations* occurs when (a) individuals, institutions, or governments treat people differently because of personal characteristics such as race, gender, or sexual orientation rather than their ability to perform their jobs; and (b) these actions have a negative impact on access to jobs, promotions, or compensation.[2] (Mor Barak, 2005, p. 141)

Around the world, gender has been one of the most commonly used criteria for discrimination in the workplace. The logic used to justify discrimination against women has relied on perceptions of a difference in their "destiny" in life and has often cited religious justification. Consider the following statement made by Justice Joseph P. Bradley when the U.S. Supreme Court threw out a case by a woman who could not become a lawyer simply because of her gender: "The paramount mission and destiny of women are to fulfill the noble and benign offices of wife and mother. This is the law of the creator" (Joseph P. Bradley, U.S. Supreme Court Justice, 1873).[3] One hundred years later, Japan's Prime Minister, Yasuhiro Nakasone, made a similar statement: "First of all, I want women, as mothers, to become 100 percent wonderful mothers. Then I want them to become good wives. And I want them to become ladies capable of making contributions for society also" (Japan Times, 1984).[4]

Members of ethnic and national minorities have been frequent victims of discrimination. A multinational study conducted by the United Nations International Labor Organization (ILO) found that discrimination against migrant and ethnic minority job applicants was widespread (Zegers de Beijl, 1999). The average discrimination rates (i.e., discrimination incidents per application relative to the number of job applications) in the countries studied were around 35%. The study documented that discrimination occurred in each stage of the job application process: during the inquiry stage (minority applicants were told that the job has been filled, when in reality it was not), the job interview (minority applicants were asked for more qualifications than other applicants), and during the job offer (minority applicants were offered inferior salary and benefits). A particularly interesting facet of this study was that it was able to pinpoint the stage during which discrimination had occurred. Most of the direct discriminatory rejections occurred at the first stage of the application process, resulting in these applicants being denied the opportunity to present their credentials. In other words, the discrimination occurred as soon as the applicants introduced themselves using foreign names that were not typical of their country of residence.

The Inclusion-Exclusion Continuum

One of the most significant problems facing today's diverse workforce is exclusion, both the reality experienced by many and the perception of even greater numbers of employees that they are *not* viewed by management as an integral part of the organization (Ibarra, 1993; Kanter, 1992; Mor Barak, 2000b). The inclusion-exclusion continuum is central to the discussion here and is defined below:[5]

> The concept of *inclusion-exclusion* in the workplace refers to the individual's sense of being a part of the organizational system in both the formal processes, such as access to information and decision-making channels, and the informal processes, such as social gatherings and lunch meetings, where information exchange and decisions informally take place. (Mor Barak, 2005, p. 149)

The concept of inclusion-exclusion is an indicator of the way employees experience and perceive their position in the organization relative to its "mainstream." Sometimes the experience of exclusion is blatant. For example, an interviewee in one of my studies, the only woman in a team of engineers, shared with me her experience of not being invited to several team meetings and, when she complained, being told that these were "just informal gatherings, you didn't really need to be there." At other times the experience is more subtle. Another interviewee, an African American social worker in a large human services organization, indicated that she was always "the last to know" about things that were happening in the organization.

Though diversity distinction categories vary from one culture or country to the next, the common factor that seems to transcend cultural and national boundaries is the experience of exclusion, particularly in the workplace. Individuals and groups are implicitly or explicitly excluded from job opportunities, information networks, team membership, human resource investments, and the decision-making process because of their actual or perceived membership in a minority or disfavored identity group.

Yet, inclusion in organizational information networks and in decision-making processes has been linked to better job opportunities and career advancement in work organizations (Morrison & Von Glinow, 1990; O'Leary & Ickovics, 1992), as well as to job satisfaction and well-being (Mor Barak & Levin, 2002). Some scholarly work, though clearly not enough, has examined the interaction between diversity distinction categories, such as race/ethnicity and gender, pointing to the compounding complexity of understanding racial prejudice when entangled with sexism (Bell, 1990, 1992). Research indicates that racial and ethnic minority women commonly believe they are excluded from the organizational power structure and have the least access to organizational resources from among disfavored groups (Kossek & Zonia, 1993; Mor Barak, Cherin, & Berkman, 1998). Similarly, a study of six county welfare departments found that African American women were paid less and had lower occupational rank compared to other workers, controlling for other job-related characteristics (McNeely, Sapp, & Daly, 1998). Employees'

experience and sense of exclusion, therefore, may play a critical role in explaining both their lack of job opportunities and dissatisfaction with their jobs, respectively.

Theories of Diversity and Intergroup Relations

The global trends of immigration and worker migration, coupled with diversity legislation and affirmative action social policies advancements, underscore the need to examine theories that were conceived in different parts of the world and to generate an integrated approach to understanding workforce diversity and intergroup relations. There are several major theories of intergroup relations that are relevant to human services organizations (Taylor & Moghaddam, 1994), including *realistic conflict theory* (RCT), an economic theory that assumes that people act in self-interest and, therefore, intergroup conflicts are caused by people's drive to maximize their own or their group's rewards to the detriment of other groups' interests (Sherif, 1966; Sherif & Sherif, 1953); *equity theory*, which emphasizes that people strive for justice and view perceptions of injustice as the cause of personal distress and intergroup conflict (Walster, Walster, & Berscheid, 1978; Adams, 1965); and *relative deprivation theory*, a theory that focuses on perceptions of inequality between people's access to resources and that of others in the society, resulting in intergroup conflicts and oppression (Crosby, 1976; Stouffer, Suchman, DeVinney, Star, & Williams, 1949). A fourth theory that explains intergroup relations, *social identity theory*, stands out as a mega-theory that can explain the universal effects of social categorization and group membership regardless of the specific type of group. It is this all-embracing orientation of social identity theory that makes it relevant for the study of diversity in human services organizations. The next section describes social identify theory and its usefulness as a tool for explaining exclusion and discrimination in the context of human services organizations.

> ## SOCIAL IDENTITY THEORY: CENTRAL PROPOSITIONS RELEVANT TO WORKPLACE DIVERSITY
>
> - People desire to belong to groups that enjoy *distinct* and *positive* identities.
> - Social identification with certain groups leads to activities that are congruent with the group's collective identity and that foster stereotypical perceptions of self and others.
> - Through *social comparisons* between the in-group and out-group, in-group members will make an effort to maintain or achieve superiority over an out-group in some dimensions.
> - The mere categorization of individuals, either voluntary or assigned, is all that is necessary to create in-group favoritism and out-group discrimination.
> - Those who belong to groups with higher perceived social status will accept and *include* people they consider to be like them, while *excluding* and *discriminating against* those they perceive to be different from them.
>
> SOURCE: Based on Tajfel (1978); Tajfel and Turner (1986); Turner (1987).

Social Identity Theory—Explaining Workplace Exclusion and Discrimination

Social identity theory is a cognitive social psychological theory that originated in Europe and gained popularity in North America and in other regions of the world. It provides the connection between social structures and individual identity through the meanings people attach to their membership in identity groups, such as those formed by race, ethnicity, or gender (Tajfel, 1982). The theory postulates that people tend to classify themselves into social categories that have meaning for them, and this shapes the way individuals interact with others from their own identity group and from other groups (Tajfel, 1978, 1982; Tajfel & Turner, 1986; Turner, 1987).

The central propositions of the theory are noted in the box above.

Social identity is defined as the individual's knowledge that he or she belongs to certain social groups together with some emotional and value significance to him or her of the group membership (Tajfel, 1978, p. 63). Social identity stems from the categorization of individuals, the distinctiveness and prestige of the group, the salience of out-groups, and the factors that traditionally are associated with group formation. Most important, and most relevant to the present discussion, social identification leads to activities that are congruent with the group's collective identity, that support institutions that embody their identity, and that foster stereotypical perceptions of self and others (Ashforth & Mael, 1989).

A person's identity has two components: a personal component that is derived from idiosyncratic characteristics—such as personality, physical, and intellectual traits—and a social component derived from salient commonalities derived from group memberships, such as race, sex, class, and nationality (Ashforth & Mael, 1989; Tajfel, 1982). Social identity is a perception of oneness with a group of persons (Ashforth & Mael, 1989). Sometimes, however, this perception of oneness is the result of being categorized by the larger society as members of a particular group. For example, despite their distinct cultural heritage and complex historical relationships, individuals who emigrate from countries such as Korea, China, and Japan are "lumped" into one group known as "Asian" when they live in the U.S. The differences between these individuals who come from very different countries, backgrounds, and histories are overlooked, with any uniqueness misunderstood at best (Fowler, 1996). However, over the years, individuals from these countries, and particularly the children of these immigrants, have developed a sense of identity that is tied to being Asian Americans.

Social comparison is the process that people use to evaluate themselves by comparing their group's membership with other groups. The basic hypothesis is that pressures to positively evaluate one's own group through in-group/out-group comparisons lead social groups to attempt to differentiate themselves from each other (Tajfel, 1978; Tajfel & Turner, 1986). The aim of differentiation is to maintain or achieve superiority over an out-group on some relevant dimension.

An important aspect of social identity theory that is most relevant to this discussion is the focus on *social categorization* and its connection to *intergroup discrimination*. Social categorization is a cognitive tool that is used to "segment, classify, and order the social environment, and thus enable the individual to undertake many forms of social actions" (Tajfel & Turner, 1986, pp. 15–16). Social categories include groups such as women, Catholics, social workers, gays, and managers. Although categorization may serve to simplify the world, people are complex because of differences in values and norms, as well as one's own group identification, and these differences may influence social categorization. As a result, social categories most often do not fit individuals' sense of who they are. For example, with the increased interracial and interethnic marriages in recent decades, there is a growing awareness that racial and ethnic identification often do not conform to the categories used by social institutions in the past. A person born to an African American mother and a Caucasian father may identify herself as belonging to both groups but, depending on her dominant features, others are more likely to categorize her as belonging to one race or to the other. The mere categorization of individuals and the creation of in-group and out-group is sufficient, according to social identity theory, for discrimination to

occur (for a schematic diagram of social identity theory's basic principles, please see Figure 11.1). Research that examined this proposition showed that even in a minimal group situation experiment (individuals were randomly assigned to experimental conditions, membership was anonymous, and criteria for social categorization were not linked to rewards to be allocated among the groups), people tended to discriminate against members of out-groups simply because they belonged to a different social category (Taylor & Moghaddam, 1994).

An important limitation of social identity theory that is particularly relevant to the discussion here is the theory's very broad and rather generic view of social categories. Because the theory treats all types of categories as equal, it cannot account for the heightened significance of diversity categories such as race, gender, and class in many cultures and nations due to their deep historical roots in both the Western world and in previously colonized countries. Social identity theory conceptualizes identity primarily as self-defined. It, therefore, downplays the consequences of other groups defining individuals and affecting their sense of inclusion or exclusion.

Research on Diversity and Exclusion

The universal human need to be included in social systems has its roots in the way people have traditionally satisfied their basic needs. Because human beings have always depended on cooperation and collaboration with one another for their basic needs (food, shelter, clothing), they are motivated to maintain connections with significant people and social systems in their lives. On the other hand, competition for scarce resources forced people to identify themselves and others into in-groups and out-groups. Being included in a group was central to survival, and sense of inclusion in a group became central to individuals' self-esteem. As a result, self-esteem functions as a psychological gauge, or "sociometer," a

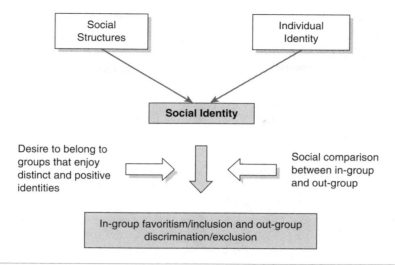

Figure 11.1   A Schematic Diagram of Social Identity Theory's Basic Principles

personal indicator that allows people to monitor inclusion or exclusion reactions toward them from their environment (Baumeister & Leary, 1995; Leary, Schreindorfer, & Haupt, 1995). Triggered by an environment that is exclusionary, threats to one's self-esteem produce behavioral outcomes that are aimed at rectifying the situation by, for example, compensatory efforts to assimilate or disengaging from the exclusionary system and linking with a more inclusive environment.

Research indicates that individuals from diverse groups commonly find themselves excluded from networks of information and opportunity (Cox, 1994; Ibarra, 1993). The reasons are varied. First, overt or covert racism, sexism, ageism, or other forms of discrimination may be the motivation for exclusionary practices. Second, economic self-interest can be the motivation for preventing certain individuals or groups from gaining access to power and economic resources (Larkey, 1996; Morrison, 1992). And, third, prevalent stereotypical perceptions and a general sense of discomfort with those who are perceived as different can be the reason for excluding persons from important

organizational processes and resources (Vonk & Van Knippenberg, 1995). These processes increase the likelihood of exclusion of those who are different (i.e., women, ethnic and racial minorities, and members of groups that may be stereotypically defined or labeled as different).

Research on organizational demography indicates that being in the minority has significant effects on individuals' affective experiences in the workplace, including feelings of isolation and lack of identification in one-on-one relationships (Ely, 1994; Ibarra, 1995; Mor Barak et al., 1998). Milliken and Martins (1996) indicate a strong and consistent relationship between diversity in gender, ethnicity, and age and exclusion from important workplace interactions. One of the most frequently reported problems faced by women and minorities in organizational settings is their limited access to, or exclusion from, informal and yet vital interaction networks (Miller, 1986; Morrison & Von Glinow, 1990; O'Leary & Ickovics, 1992). For example, Bell and Nkomo (2001) note that an important barrier experienced by black women is limited access to informal and social networks in their organizations. The African American women they interviewed felt they had less access to these networks in their organizations than did white men and white women. As a result, they felt cut off from important organizational information and less accepted as full members of the organization. Many of the women spoke of the critical importance of informal networks, including mentorship, sponsorship, and assistance from co-workers, in career advancement. Similarly, the white women managers also believed that exclusion from the "old boy network" was one of the barriers to women's advancement (pp. 152–153). Similar results were found in human services organizations as well, where women and minorities, particularly African American women, are more likely than other employees to occupy the lowest-ranking positions (Dressel, 1987; Gibelman & Schervish, 1993; Martin & Chernesky, 1989; McNeely, 1992).

These networks allocate a variety of instrumental resources that are critical for job effectiveness and career advancement, as well as expressive benefits such as social support and friendship (Ibarra, 1993). Although women and members of minority groups have made some inroads into traditional non-minority male job domains, organizational jobs remain largely structured along race, gender, and class lines, with the more meaningful and prestigious jobs being held by men of the dominant group and of higher social echelons (Beggs, 1995; Tomaskovic-Devey, 1993; McNeely, Blakemore, & Washington, 1993). Research has demonstrated that the extreme overrepresentation of white men in organizational positions of authority may have a negative impact on women and nonwhite subordinates. For example, women in male-dominated organizations may attempt to assimilate—that is, to alter their thoughts, feelings, behaviors, and expectations at work to mirror those typically associated with men (Ely, 1995). The disproportionate representation of men over women in senior organizational positions may highlight for women their limited mobility and reinforce their perceptions of themselves as in a lower status than men.

There is ample evidence of the differential treatment experienced by racial/ethnic minorities and women in the workplace. For example, men believe that gender is a cue to competence and that, in the absence of any definite information to the contrary, the performer's gender becomes relevant in making job-related decisions (Forschi, Lad, & Sigerson, 1994). Women, on the other hand, either do not hold that belief, or do so to a lesser degree. Forschi et al. (1994) concluded that this double standard is a subtle mechanism through which the status quo of gender inequality in the workplace is maintained. For a summary chart of the research outcomes related to diversity and inclusion, see Figure 11.2.

Being in the minority has significant effects on individuals' affective experiences in the workplace, including isolation in work groups and lack of identification in one-on-one relationships (Ibarra, 1995). Similarly, women tend to have less access to a variety of measures of status in the organization, such as income, position, and information, than do men (Alderfer, 1986). Because leadership and management qualities are defined mostly in masculine terms, these barriers persist for women (Nkomo & Cox, 1996). In the context of human services organizations, real participation in the decision-making process has been linked to job satisfaction, which in turn can potentially affect worker retention and effectiveness on the job (McNeely et al., 1998; Whiddon & Martin, 1989).

Implications for Human Services Organizations

Human services organizations are unique in the context of diversity and inclusion because they emphasize sensitivity to diversity in dealing with their clients but often neglect to be sensitive to the diversity of their own workforce (Beckett & Dungee-Anderson, 1998; McNeely, 1992). The theoretical formulations discussed in this chapter demonstrate that people are motivated to seek social inclusion and avoid exclusion. Further, individuals seek to belong to groups that are associated with higher status and prestige in society.

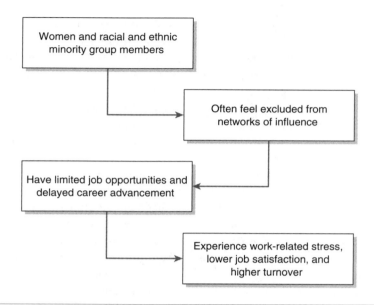

Figure 11.2   Summary Chart of the Diversity and Inclusion Research Outcomes

Belonging to such groups is central to individuals' identity and to their sense of worth. Other people's reactions, particularly the degree to which they accept and include individuals or reject and exclude them, are vital to a person's physical and psychological well-being (Leary & Downs, 1995).

Demographic characteristics of organizations, such as race and gender composition, help to shape the meanings people attach to their identity group memberships at work (Ely, 1994). As social identity theory has demonstrated, the way we perceive our social reality is significantly determined by our group memberships. It, therefore, follows that individual experiences vis-à-vis work organizations and their perceptions of organizational actions and policies will be affected by their identity group memberships. This social psychological perspective is useful to the current discussion because it indicates how identity groups shape worker experiences, perceptions, and behaviors. It is particularly relevant when membership in an identity group is associated with exclusion from employment opportunity and job mobility.

When a social group's status position is perceived to be low, it affects the social identity of group members. There are four paths to addressing the consequences of social exclusion (see Figure 11.3 for a summary):

1. *Individual change:* Individual members of the group may attempt to pass from a lower-status to a higher-status group through disassociating themselves psychologically and behaviorally from their low-status group. When successful, such a strategy will lead to a personal solution, but it will not make a difference in the excluded group's status. For example, an African American woman can rise to the top of an organization through exceptional talent, hard work, and luck, but, without an organizational change, other women, as well as members of minority groups, may not enjoy similar mobility.

2. *Group change:* Members may seek positive status for the group as a whole by redefining or altering the elements of the comparative situations. This could take place by, for example, changing the values assigned to the attributes

of the group so that comparisons that were previously negative are now perceived as positive (such as the slogan used by African Americans, "Black is Beautiful"). Similarly, with the entry of more women into management positions and into management scholarship, there is an effort to reexamine the qualities that are essential for effective management. Rather than expecting effective managers to be "assertive" and "aggressive," qualities that have traditionally been perceived as male characteristics, there is a focus on "people skills" and "emotional intelligence," qualities that have traditionally been perceived as female characteristics. This shift in emphasis opens the door for women as a group to be perceived as qualified for management without having to adopt what are considered more traditionally male characteristics.

3. *Organizational change:* Organizations can implement policies that remove barriers to advancement and promotion of members of disadvantaged groups and thus open up ways for members of these groups, as well as the groups as a whole, to improve their social identity. For example, providing networking opportunities and mentorship programs for members of diverse groups can open up advancement and promotion opportunities. Thus, these opportunities can enhance their access to power in the organizations as well as improve their benefit and salary package. Combined, these elements contribute to improved group status as well as social identity of group members.

4. *Societal change:* Society as a whole can create social mobility of disadvantaged groups through legislation and public policies. Equal opportunity legislation forbids discrimination and is, therefore, negative in that it indicates what individuals and organizations are *not* allowed to do. Public policies such as the Affirmative Action Program in the U.S. or Positive Action initiatives in Europe and in many other regions of the world are positive, in that they indicate what steps organizations *should* actively take in order to become more diverse organizations. Although banning discrimination through legislation is essential for

social mobility, it is not enough to combat persistent, institutionalized, and long-term discrimination against whole groups. Affirmative action policies are aimed at (a) righting past wrongs—compensating groups that have been disadvantaged in the past with better opportunities at present, and (b) achieving social goals of increasing the representation of traditionally disadvantaged groups in more lucrative jobs as well as management and leadership positions (Mor Barak, 2005). Therefore, the combination of antidiscrimination legislation and affirmative action programs can open up social mobility opportunities not only to individuals but to whole groups of society and can potentially create a society-wide change in group and individual social identity.

To provide high quality services to their clients, human services organizations must develop a well-trained, dedicated, responsive, and flexible workforce (Mor Barak & Travis, 2007). Research demonstrates that a combination of compliance with equal employment legislation, active participation in Affirmative Action Programs, and proactive organizational diversity management can have a positive impact on a variety of organizational outcomes (Mor Barak, 2005). Such inclusive practices have been shown to affect employee attitudes and emotions toward the organization, including organizational commitment (Mor Barak, Findler, & Wind, 2001), job satisfaction (Greenhaus, Parasuraman, & Wormley, 1990; Mor Barak & Levin, 2002; Vinokur-Kaplan, Jayarante, & Chess, 1994), and general well-being (Ibarra, 1995; Mor Barak, Findler, & Wind, 2003). They can also impact a variety of financial outcomes, including business growth and productivity (Richard, 2000), cost saving due to lower turnover, less absenteeism and improved productivity (Kirkpatrick, Phillips, & Phillips, 2003), and company image and stock prices (Robinson & Dechant, 1997; Wright, Ferris, Hiller, & Kroll, 1995). In short, inclusive practices not only are the right and ethical thing to do, they are beneficial to the effective management of the organization.

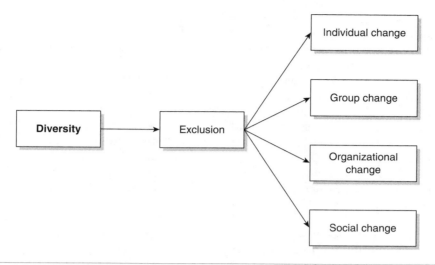

Figure 11.3   Paths to Address the Negative Consequences of Exclusion

Conclusion

Within the context of human services organizations, the need to understand exclusionary practices is particularly important in light of the disproportional representation of women and minorities among their employees (McNeely et al., 1993). A systematic approach to needs assessment and the fit between the community's needs and its goals is the key to a successful and mutually beneficial collaboration. A similar examination of the relationship between a human services agency and the community it serves is also helpful, as often tensions develop between a diverse community and a less diverse social work agency that serves it (McNeely, Sapp, & Meyer, 1998).

The work environment is an important arena in which the mechanisms of intergroup relations are being played out because of individual and group efforts to gain advantage in the competition for (real or perceived) limited resources or out of misguided, ill-informed, or blatantly malicious attitudes toward other groups. Most people derive their livelihood from their jobs, as well as their personal identity, social relationships, and sense of self-fulfillment. The consequences of mechanisms such as discrimination and exclusion can be detrimental to those affected, their families, the organizations that employ them, and their communities.

The inclusion-exclusion continuum, a central concept in this chapter, is linked to important psychological processes such as self-esteem, depression, anxiety, and a general perception that one's life has meaning. This is particularly relevant for members of disadvantaged groups who may suffer the psychological consequences of being excluded. Therefore, this need to be included in social groups is a strong motivator in human behavior. Though one needs to be aware of the inherent competitive nature of identity groups—what one gains in status the other may lose—taken together, these theories tell us that work organizations may gain a more loyal, satisfied, and committed workforce by becoming more inclusive.

Notes

1. For a more detailed discussion of this global definition of diversity, please see Mor Barak, 2005, pp. 119–146.

2. The UN International Labour Organization (ILO) Discrimination Convention of 1958 (No. 111) defines discrimination as "Any distinction, exclusion

or preference . . . which has the effect of nullifying or impairing equality of opportunity or treatment in employment or occupation as may be determined. In this convention the grounds for non-discrimination include race, colour, sex, religion, political opinion, national extraction or social origin" (Zegers de Beijl, 1999, p. 10).

3. A *Time* magazine article from June 4, 1984, "Getting a Piece of the Power: Women Barred From Partnerships Can Now Go to Court," described the 1984 Supreme Court unanimous ruling that in deciding on partnership, it was illegal for law firms to discriminate against women simply because of their gender (p. 63).

4. *Japan Times,* May 15, 1984, p. 2.

5. For research scales that assess this construct in the context of diversity, see Mor Barak, 2005, pp. 293–299.

References

Adams, J. S. (1965). Inequity in social exchange. In L. Berkowitz (Ed.), *Advances in experimental social psychology* (Vol. 2, pp. 267–299). New York: Academic.

Alderfer, C. P. (1986). An intergroup perspective on group dynamics. In J. W. Lorsch (Ed.), *Handbook of organizational behavior* (pp. 190–222). Englewood Cliffs, NJ: Prentice Hall.

Ashforth, B. E., & Mael, F. S. (1989). Social identity theory and the organization. *Academy of Management, 14,* 20–39.

Baumeister, R. F., & Leary, M. R. (1995). The need to belong: Desire for interpersonal attachments as a fundamental human motivation. *Psychological Bulletin, 117,* 497–529.

Beckett, J. O., & Dungee-Anderson, D. (1998). Multicultural communication in human service organizations. In A. Daly (Ed.), *Workplace diversity.* Washington, DC: NASW.

Beggs, J. J. (1995). The institutional environment: Implications for race and gender inequality in the U.S. labor market. *American Sociological Review, 60,* 612–633.

Bell, E. (1990). The bicultural life experience of career-oriented black women. *Journal of Organizational Behavior, 11,* 459–478.

Bell, E. L. (1992). Myths, stereotypes, and realities of black women: A personal reflection. *Journal of Applied Behavioral Sciences, 28*(3), 363–376.

Bell, E., & Nkomo, S. M. (2001). *Our separate ways: Black and white women and the struggle for professional identity.* Boston: Harvard Business School Press.

Bloom, H. (2002, March/April). Can the United States export diversity.? *Across the Board,* 47–51.

Clark, S., & Jacquet, S. (2003). *Demographic profile of the CalSWEC Title IV-E MSW graduates 1993–2002.* Berkeley: University of California, California Social Work Education Center.

Cox, T. (1994). *Cultural diversity in organizations: Theory, research and practice.* San Francisco: Berrett-Koehler.

Crosby, F. (1976). A model of egoistical relative deprivation. *Psychological Review, 83,* 85–113.

Dressel, P. L. (1987). Patriarchy and social welfare work. *Social Problems, 34,* 294–309.

Ely, R. (1994). The effects of organizational demographics and social identity on relationships among professional women. *Administrative Science Quarterly, 39,* 203–238.

Ely, R. (1995). The power in demography: Women's social constructions of gender identity at work. *Academy of Management Journal, 38,* 589–634.

Essed, P. (1995). *Understanding everyday racism.* London: Sage.

Essed, P. (1996). *Diversity: Gender, color, and culture.* Amherst: University of Massachusetts Press.

Forschi, M., Lad, L., & Sigerson, K. (1994). Gender and double standards in the assessment of job applicants. *Social Psychology Quarterly, 57*(4), 326–339.

Fowler, E. (1996). *San'ya blues: Laboring life in contemporary Tokyo.* Ithaca, NY: Cornell University Press.

Gibelman, M., & Schervish, P. H. (1993). *Who we are: The social work labor force as reflected in the NASW membership.* Washington, DC: NASW Press.

Gilbert, J., Carr-Ruffino, N., Ivancevich, J. M., & Lownes-Jackson, M. (2003). An empirical examination of inter-ethnic stereotypes: Comparing Asian American and African American employees. *Public Personnel Management, 32*(2), 251–266.

Glisson, C., & Himmelfarn, A. (1998). The effects of organizational climate and interorganizational coordination on the quality and outcomes of children's service systems. *Child Abuse and Neglect, 22*(5), 401–421.

Glisson, C., & James, L. R. (2002). The cross level effects of culture and climate in human service teams. *Journal of Organizational Behavior, 23*(6), 767–794.

Greenhaus, J. H., Parasuraman, S., & Wormley, W. M. (1990). Effects of race on organizational experiences, job performance evaluations, and career outcomes. *Academy of Management Journal, 33,* 64–86.

Ibarra, H. (1993). Personal networks of women and minorities in management: A conceptual framework. *Academy of Management Review, 18,* 56–87.

Ibarra, H. (1995). Race, opportunity, and diversity of social circles in managerial networks. *Academy of Management Journal, 38,* 673–703.

Kanter, R. M. (1992). Power failure in management circuits. In J. M. Shafritz & J. S. Ott (Eds.), *Classics of organization theory* (3rd ed., pp. ix, 534). Pacific Grove, CA: Brooks/Cole.

Kirkpatrick, D., Phillips, J. J., & Phillips, P. P. (2003, October). Getting results from diversity training—In dollars and cents. *HR Focus, 80*(10), 3–4.

Kossek, E. E., & Zonia, S. C. (1993). Assessing diversity climate: A field study of reactions to employer efforts to promote diversity. *Journal of Organizational Behavior, 14,* 61–81.

Larkey, L. K. (1996). Toward a theory of communicative interactions in culturally diverse workgroups. *Academy of Management Review, 21*(2), 463–491.

Leary, M. R., & Downs, D. L. (1995). Interpersonal functions of the self-esteem motive: The self-esteem system as a sociometer. In M. H. Kernis (Ed.), *Efficacy, agency, and self-esteem.* New York: Plenum.

Leary, M. R., Schreindorfer, L. S., & Haupt, A. L. (1995). The role of low self-esteem in emotional and behavioral problems: Why is low self-esteem dysfunctional? *Journal of Social and Clinical Psychology, 14*(3), 297–314.

Linnehan, F., & Konrad, A. M. (1999). Diluting diversity: Implications for intergroup inequality in organizations. *Journal of Management Inquiry, 8*(4), 399–414.

Martin, P. Y., & Chernesky, R. H. (1989). Women's prospects for leadership in social welfare: A political economy perspective. *Administration in Social Work, 13*(3/4), 117–143.

McGregor, J., & Gray, L. (2002). Stereotypes and older workers: The New Zealand experience. *Social Policy Journal of New Zealand, 18,* 163–177.

McNeely, R. L. (1992). Job satisfaction in the public social services: Perspectives on structure, situational factors, gender, and ethnicity. In Y. Hasenfeld (Ed.), *Human services as complex organizations* (pp. 224–256). Newbury Park, CA: Sage.

McNeely, R. L., Blakemore, J. L., & Washington, R. O. (1993). Race, gender, occupational status and income in county human service employment. *Journal of Sociology and Social Welfare, 20*(1), 47–70.

McNeely, R. L. Sapp, M., & Daly, A. (1998). Ethnicity, gender, earnings, occupational rank and job satisfaction in the public social services: What do workers say? In A. Daly (Ed.), *Work place diversity* (pp. 144–165). Washington, DC: NASW.

McNeely, R. L., Sapp, M., & Meyer, H. (1998). Conflict, cooperation and institutional goal attainment in diversity: How to improve relations between formal organizations and neighborhood residents in changing urban communities. In A. Daly (Ed.), *Work place diversity.* Washington, DC: NASW.

Miller, J. (1986). *Pathways in the workplace.* Cambridge, MA: Cambridge University Press.

Milliken, F. J., & Martins L. L. (1996). Searching for common threads: Understanding the multiple effects of diversity in organizational groups. *Academy of Management Review, 21*(2), 402–433.

Mor Barak, M. E. (2000a). Beyond affirmative action: Toward a model of organizational inclusion. In M. E. Mor Barak & D. Bargal (Eds.), *Social services in the workplace.* New York: Haworth.

Mor Barak, M. E. (2000b). The inclusive workplace: An eco-systems approach to diversity management. *Social Work, 45*(4), 339–354.

Mor Barak, M. E. (2005). *Managing diversity: Toward a globally inclusive workplace.* Thousand Oaks, CA: Sage.

Mor Barak, M. E., Cherin, D. A., & Berkman, S. (1998). Ethnic and gender differences in employee diversity perceptions: Organizational and personal dimensions. *Journal of Applied Behavioral Sciences, 34*(1), 82–104.

Mor Barak, M. E., Findler, L., & Wind, L. H. (2001). Diversity, inclusion, and commitment in organizations: International explorations. *Journal of Behavioral and Applied Management, 2*(2), 72–91.

Mor Barak, M. E., Findler, L., & Wind, L. H. (2003). Cross-cultural aspects of diversity and well-being in the workplace: An international perspective. *Journal of Social Work Research & Evaluation, 4*(2), 145–169.

Mor Barak, M. E., & Levin, A. (2002). Outside of the corporate mainstream and excluded from the work community: A study of diversity, job satisfaction and well-being. *Community, Work & Family, 5*(2), 133–157.

Mor Barak, M. E., & Travis, D. J. (2007). Management: Human resources. In T. Mizrahi & L. E. Davis (Eds.), *Encyclopedia of social work* (20th ed.). Oxford, UK: Oxford University Press.

Morrison, A. H. (1992). *The new leaders: Guidelines on leadership diversity in America.* San Francisco: Jossey-Bass.

Morrison, A. M., & Von Glinow, M. A. (1990). Women and minorities in management. *American Psychologist, 45*, 200–208.

Muller, H. J., & Parham, P. A. (1998). Integrating workforce diversity into the business school curriculum: An experiment. *Journal of Management Education, 22*(2), 44–55.

National Association of Social Workers. (2005, March). *Assuring the sufficiency of a frontline workforce: A national study of licensed social worker.* Washington, DC: NASW Center for Workforce Studies.

Nkomo, S. (2001, July). *Much to do about diversity: The muting of race, gender and class in managing diversity practice.* Paper presented at the International Cross-Cultural Perspectives on Workforce Diversity: The Inclusive Workplace, Bellagio, Italy.

Nkomo, S., & Cox, T., Jr. (1996). Diverse identities in organizations. In S. R. Clegg, C. Hardy, & W. R. Nord (Eds.), *Handbook of organizations studies* (pp. 338–356). London: Sage.

O'Leary, V. E., & Ickovics, J. R. (1992). Cracking the glass ceiling: Overcoming isolation and discrimination. In U. Sekeran & F. Leong (Eds.), *Womanpower: Managing in times of demographic turbulence* (pp. 7–30). Beverly Hills, CA: Sage.

Richard, O. C. (2000). Racial diversity, business strategy, and firm performance: A recourse-based view. *Academy of Management Journal, 43*(2), 164–177.

Robinson, G., & Dechant, K. (1997). Building a business case for diversity. *Academy of Management Executive, 11*(3), 21–31.

Sherif, M. (1966). *Group conflict and co-operation: Their social psychology.* London: Routledge & Kegan Paul.

Sherif, M., & Sherif, C. W. (1953). *Groups in harmony and tension.* New York: Harper.

Slabbert, A. (2001). Cross-cultural racism in South Africa—Dead or alive? *Social Behavior and Personality, 29*(2), 125–132.

Stouffer, S. A., Suchman, E. A., DeVinney, L. C., Star, S. A., & Williams, R. M. (1949). *The American soldier: Adjustment during army life* (Vol. 1). Princeton, NJ: Princeton University Press.

Tajfel, H. (1978). *Differentiation between social groups.* New York: Academic.

Tajfel, H. (1982). *Social identity and intergroup relations.* Cambridge, UK: Cambridge University Press.

Tajfel, H., & Turner, J. C. (1986). The social identity theory of intergroup behavior. In S. Worchel & W. G. Austin (Eds.), *Psychology of intergroup relations* (pp. 7–24). Chicago: Nelson-Hall.

Taylor, D. M., & Moghaddam, F. M. (1994). *Theories of intergroup relations.* Westport, CT: Praeger.

Tomaskovic-Devey, D. (1993). *Gender and racial inequality at work: The sources and consequences of job segregation.* Ithaca, NY: ILR Press.

Turner, J. C. (1987). *Rediscovering the social group: A self-categorization theory.* Oxford, UK: Basil Blackwell.

Vinokur-Kaplan, D., Jayarante, S., & Chess, W. A. (1994). Job satisfaction and retention of social workers in public agencies, non-profit agencies, and private practice: The impact of workplace conditions and motivators. *Administration in Social Work, 18*(3), 93–121.

Vonk, R., & Van Knippenberg, A. (1995). Processing attitude statements from in-group and out-group members: Effects of within-group and within-person inconsistencies on reading times. *Journal of Personality and Social Psychology, 68*(2), 215–227.

Walster, E., Walster, G. W., & Berscheid, E. (1978). *Equity: Theory and research.* Boston: Allyn & Bacon.

Whiddon, B., & Martin, P. Y. (1989). Organizational democracy and work quality in a state welfare agency. *Social Science Quarterly, 70*(3), 667–686.

Wright, P., Ferris, S. P., Hiller, J. S., & Kroll, M. (1995). Competitiveness through management of diversity: Effects on stock price evaluation. *Academy of Management Journal, 38*(1), 272–287.

Zegers de Beijl, R. (1999). *Documenting discrimination against migrant workers in the labour market.* Geneva: International Labour Office.

CHAPTER 12

Managing Human Resources

Administrative Issues

Peter J. Pecora

Introduction

In the human services field, line staff and supervisors constitute the most important resources for maximizing agency productivity and effectiveness. Managing human resources (i.e., personnel management) in human services agencies involves key functions that must be performed to develop and maintain a group of skilled, productive, and satisfied employees:

- Recruitment, screening, and selection of social work and other personnel
- Specification and allocation of job tasks in order to design position descriptions and staffing patterns and requirements
- Designing and conducting performance appraisals

- Orienting, training, and developing staff
- Supervising and coaching ongoing task performance
- Handling employee performance problems
- Enforcing employee sanctions and, when necessary, dismissing workers

In this chapter, a definition of each of these aspects of personnel management will be presented, along with a brief discussion of their importance for supporting effective human services. As part of certain functions, special issues will be briefly addressed, such as affirmative action, equal employment opportunity, protecting Americans with disabilities, and sexual harassment. Because of the importance of recruitment to the success of the work unit and larger organization, we will focus disproportionately

AUTHOR'S NOTE: The author thanks Stacy Radley and Gloria Rendon at the University of Utah, Michael J. Austin of the University of California at Berkeley, Emily Bruce of San Jose State University, David Cherin of California State University of Fullerton, Trinidad Arguello of the University of Utah, Nigel Bristow of Targeted Learning Inc., and administrators at Casey Family Programs for sharing their innovative personnel management ideas.

on it and treat other areas more briefly. Because affirmative action, equal employment opportunity, and Americans With Disabilities Act guidelines have become so fundamental to management practice, they will be addressed as well.

There are a host of issues and tasks associated with these key personnel management functions, such as job classification and wage setting, supporting work teams, promoting worker job motivation and productivity, employee health and safety, labor-management relations, personnel administration law, and merit system reform. Personnel management overlaps greatly with supervision of staff in that many supervisory responsibilities include functions such as promoting teamwork, setting unit goals, promoting and supporting ethnic and cultural diversity, negotiating organizational demands, and managing conflict (see, e.g., Brody, 1993; Patti, 1983; Shulman & Safyer, 2007; Tambor, 1985; Thomas & Ely, 2002; Tsui, 2004; Weinbach, 1998; also see Chapter 13 for further discussion of supervision).

Personnel management should be viewed as part of the organization's approach to human resources. All of the "people systems," such as rewards, work design, succession and promotion, staffing and selection, career development, and training and development, need to be aligned with the overall organizational mission, vision, and strategy in order to insure both programmatic and fiscal success (Bristow, 1999b, p. 16).

There are important efforts under way in the business and technology fields with respect to competency-based and employee-focused human resource systems that we believe have value for the human services with respect to organizational design and personnel management (see, e.g., Bristow, 1999a, 1999b; Collins, 2005; Kettner, 2002; Mathis & Jackson, 2006). To help obtain a sense of the scope of personnel management, an example of the table of contents of a personnel manual is included as Figure 12.1. What this table of contents cannot convey is the dynamic and creative work under way in this area, some of which we will describe in this chapter.

Recruiting and Selecting Effective Employees

Recruiting and screening staff members are two of the most important components of personnel management. The employee selection process requires both analytical and interpersonal skills, as well as knowledge of affirmative action (AA) and Equal Employment Opportunity Commission (EEOC) rules (see "Affirmative Action and Equal Employment Opportunity," below). For example, analytical skills are needed to define the position for which the agency is recruiting in task-specific ways. Task-based job descriptions must be developed, and essential worker "competencies" (knowledge, skills, abilities, and attitudes) must be identified. Well-developed interpersonal skills are required for interviewing job candidates in a courteous and professional manner.

Recruitment involves generating an applicant pool that provides the employer an opportunity to make a selection that satisfies the needs of the organization. *Selection* is concerned with reviewing qualifications of job applicants in order to decide who should be offered the position. *Placement* involves assigning the new employee to the appropriate position and orienting him or her properly so that he or she can begin working (Mathis & Jackson, 2006; Shafritz, Hyde, & Rosenbloom, 1986). The major steps involved in recruitment and selection are presented as a checklist in Figure 12.2.

The interpersonal skills required include being able to work collaboratively with agency staff to develop common expectations for the position and to develop a common set of interview questions. Equally important is the ability to reach an agreement on what constitutes acceptable responses to various interview questions. Supervisory and other administrative personnel must also be able to interview job applicants in a professional and courteous manner. (For additional information on various aspects of employee selection, see Arthur, 2004; Fine & Cronshaw, 1999; Harvard Business School, 2006; O'Leary, 2002; Weinbach, 1998.)

Introduction

Organization philosophy and mission

Major organizational goals and objectives

Organizational programs or types of service

1. **Employment**

   Hiring authority

   Nondiscrimination and affirmative action policies and safeguards (includes safeguards as mandated by EEOC, AA, and ADA)

   Types of employment (full time, part time, temporary, volunteer)

   Probationary period procedures

   Maintenance and access to personnel records

2. **Working Hours and Conditions**

   Work schedule and office hours

   Flexible time

   Overtime or compensatory time

   Types of absence and reports

3. **Salaries and Wages**

   Wages and salary structure and rationale

   Paydays

   Deductions

   Raises (merit and cost of living) guidelines and rationale

   Compensation for work-related expenses

   Employee access to current salary schedule

4. **Employee Benefits**

   Leaves and absences

   Vacations

   Holidays

   Sick days

   Personal days

   Maternity leave

   Paternity leave

   Leave of absence

   Other excused absences

   Insurance

   Social Security

   Medical insurance

   Life insurance

   Disability insurance

Unemployment insurance

Workers' Compensation

Pension or retirement plans

5. **Employee Rights and Responsibilities**

   Employee responsibilities

   Employee rights

   Grievance procedures

6. **Performance and Salary Review**

   Procedures

   Timing

   Use of probation periods or suspension

   Promotion policies and procedures

7. **Staff Development**

   Orientation of new employees

   Planning process for in-service training and related activities

   Educational programs and conferences

8. **General Policies and Procedures**

   Outside employment

   Office opening and closing

   Telephone

   Travel

   Personal property

9. **General Office Practices and Procedures**

   Office coverage

   Smoking

   Use and care of equipment

10. **Termination**

    Grounds of dismissal

    Resignation

    Retirement

    Release

    Reduction in force

Appendixes

   Organizational chart

   Salary ranges by position

   Equal Employment Opportunity Commission guidelines on sexual harassment

   Conflict of interest policies

   Personnel evaluation procedures and forms

Figure 12.1   Typical Table of Contents for a Social Service Agency Personnel Manual

SOURCE: Cox, F. M. (1984). Guidelines for preparing personnel policies. In F. M. Cox et al. (Eds.), *Tactics and techniques of community practice* (2nd ed., p. 275). Itasca, IL: F.E. Peacock; Wolfe, T. (1984). *The nonprofit organization: An operating manual* (pp. 63–64). Englewood Cliffs, NJ: Prentice Hall.

Step 1: Developing a Job Description and Minimum Qualifications

A. Does the job description contain clear and specific task statements that describe the essential duties of this position?

B. Are the knowledge, skills, abilities, educational degrees (if any), and years of related job experience specified anywhere?

C. Do the required minimum qualifications for the job match the work to be performed; that is, can you substantiate the connections between the education and experience required and the tasks of the job?

Step 2: Employee Recruitment

A. Do the job announcements include the necessary details of the position?

B. Are the announcements clearly worded?

C. Is the application deadline realistic, given the usual delays in dissemination and publication; that is, does the deadline allow the applicant sufficient time to respond to the announcement?

D. Have you distributed the announcement to enough community, professional, or other groups? Have you used both formal and informal networks in publicizing the position?

E. Is a record being kept of how and where the position was advertised or posted, including personal recruitment efforts?

Step 3: Screening Job Applicants Using Application Forms and Tests (if Appropriate)

A. Does the application form provide information that helps you determine whether the applicant has related education, training, and experience?

B. Does the application form contain questions that are illegal according to EEO laws?

C. Can you structure the application form and process so applicants are asked to submit a cover letter or other summary statements to highlight how their training and experience qualify them for the position?

Step 4: Conducting the Screening Interview

A. Have you trained the interviewers in the basic phases and principles of the selection process?

B. Have you developed a list of standard questions to be asked of each applicant by the same interviewer?

C. Has a quiet place been set aside for the interview and phone or other interruptions prevented?

D. Have you chosen a person to lead the interview through the opening, information gathering, and closing phases?

E. Have you established a time line for the selection process and informed each applicant of how and when he or she will be notified?

Step 5: Selecting the Person and Notifying the Other Applicants

A. Have you contacted a sufficient number of applicants' references?

B. Has the committee weighed carefully all the information gathered to determine the most qualified and committed applicant?

C. Do you have a firm commitment from the primary candidate before notifying the other applicants?

D. Is your letter notifying the other applicants worded sensitively to ease their disappointment and thank them for their interest in the position?

Figure 12.2   Summary Checklist for Recruiting, Screening, and Selecting Employees

SOURCE: Pecora, P. J. (1998). Recruiting and selecting effective employees. In R. L. Edwards & J. A. Yankey (Eds.), *Skills for effective management of non-profit organizations.* Washington, DC: National Association of Social Workers.

The employment selection process should be considered an important investment of administrative time. If this process is not carried out properly, supervisory staff and managers will spend valuable time and energy later unnecessarily overcoming marginal work performance, increased organizational conflict, and the stress involved in transferring or terminating the staff person. While many local, state, and federal laws and accreditation standards affect minimum qualification requirements and other aspects of employee recruitment, three sets of law and policy, described in a later section of this chapter, will fundamentally help shape what is effective and legal practice in this area: (1) affirmative action, (2) equal employment opportunity, and (3) the Americans With Disabilities Act.

Position Descriptions and Use of Competencies

Specifying Job Tasks and Position Descriptions

A key ingredient of excellence in human services agencies includes attention to the details of human services work. For example,

- the greater the job clarity, the greater the potential for staff members to understand their work and what is expected;
- as worker understanding is increased, there is greater opportunity to connect observations and feedback about job performance with the job description;
- as clarity and feedback are increased, it seems reasonable that worker autonomy can also be increased; and
- as clarity, feedback, and autonomy are increased, there appears to be more opportunity for job enhancement and job enlargement.

Job enhancement adds or changes components of the job to further worker growth and development. Job enlargement involves expanding both authority and responsibility to carry out increasingly more complex and/or sophisticated job functions. Both have been linked with employee motivation and productivity (Baard, Deci, & Ryan, 2004; Howell & Dipboye, 1982), along with other job characteristics and factors associated with employee satisfaction and burnout (see, e.g., Himle, Jaraytne, & Thyness, 1989; Kadushin & Harkness, 2002; Zunz, 1998). One of the basic tools necessary for increasing job clarity or modifying job responsibilities is an accurate job description.

Over the past 50 years, job descriptions have been viewed by workers and administrators as "administrative irritants" in the life of human services organizations. Job descriptions appear to take on importance only when a job vacancy is being advertised and a new worker is hired. Even at these critical points in the recruitment, selection, and orientation process, most human services practitioners pay very little attention to the job description. One approach to assessing task-based job descriptions is to focus on the roles of supervisor and worker. This can be a fairly informal process of sitting down with incumbents and identifying their key job responsibilities (what some personnel experts call "key job parts"), or it can involve a more formal job analysis process that uses a set of steps to analyze the tasks of the job and what is required to perform them (Austin, 1981; Fine & Cronshaw, 1999; McCormick, 1979). Experienced supervisors who use the job analysis have identified several benefits of this approach: (1) it serves as a basis for clarifying job expectations with workers because the job descriptions are often vague and incomplete; (2) it facilitates worker performance reviews because there is specific information about job tasks and competencies necessary for assessing outcome; (3) the analysis is job related and not necessarily worker specific, so it provides continuity during staff turnover; (4) it serves as an information base for assessing staffing needs and for requesting additional staff support based on tasks performed in the unit; (5) it serves as a tool for monitoring the relationship between the work performed by staff and the goals and objectives of the agency; (6) the profiles are useful in identifying training needs of workers; (7) it provides consistency of approach across a range of workers in a unit and can serve as a tool for ensuring equitability of work performed and salary levels; and (8) this approach can be implemented in developmental stages (e.g., one worker at a time) and can save time in the long run by reducing the number of supervisor-supervisee meetings needed to clarify the job expectations for new workers.

Not only do position descriptions provide the foundation for job announcements, the task statements also provide a forum for the supervisor to identify performance standards (see Figure 12.3). A major challenge in human services agencies is the development of performance standards that are meaningful to workers. Performance standards linked to a task or cluster of tasks provide a basis for ongoing worker self-assessment and for supervisory "troubleshooting" when workers do not meet a minimum standard of performance (see Austin, 1981; Del Po, 2007; McCormick, 1979).

Use of Competencies in Personnel Management

A competency can be defined as any knowledge, skill, or attribute observable in the consistent patterns of an individual's behavior, interactions, and work-related activities over time that contributes to the fulfillment of the mission and accomplishment of the strategic objectives of the organization. Through the understanding and incorporation of both core (organization-wide) and domain (job-related) competencies, staff can develop and apply the means to more effectively

- identify concrete valued behaviors within the organization;
- recruit and select new employees;
- assess and enhance their own contribution to the organization, as well as assess and

enhance the contribution of those whom they supervise or team with; and

- focus and manage their own professional development and growth, including setting reasonable goals (Locke & Latham, 1984; Mathis & Jackson, 2006).

To effectively use a competency platform in your personnel program and practices, you must effectively embed competencies in every major system. For example, Casey Family Programs, a child welfare operating foundation headquartered in Seattle, Washington, has followed the example of some major corporations and other types of organizations (Bristow, Dalton, & Thompson, 1996) by adopting nine core competencies for recruiting, supervising, training, and recognizing staff members:

- *Organization and Priority Setting.* Prioritizes, organizes, and monitors work to ensure that goals, objectives, and commitments are met.
- *Flexibility.* Adapts well to changes in direction, priorities, schedule, and responsibilities.
- *Two-Way Communication.* Clearly expresses (verbally and in writing) thoughts, feelings, concepts, and directions; listens effectively to understand communications from others.
- *Teamwork.* Works collaboratively and cooperatively in groups for the purpose of achieving shared objectives, consistent with the organization's mission and strategy and individual work goals.
- *Relationship Building.* Builds and maintains productive associations with others who share a mutual interest in and commitment to achieving Casey's strategic objectives.
- *Valuing Diversity.* In the course of accomplishing the job requirements and strategic objectives of Casey, is sensitive to and competent in working with people who are different from one's self.
- *Developing Self and Others.* Recognizes and acts on the need for life-long learning; takes personal responsibility for building

---

POSITION ANNOUNCEMENT

Family Preservation Service Specialist

Children's Services Society
Seattle, Washington

Function and Location: Provides intensive in-home services to families considering out-of-home placement for one or more members. Is on call 24 hours per day to provide crisis intervention and other family services and problem resolution. Will work out of the Wallingford social services office.

Duties and Responsibilities (Partial List):

1. To prevent unnecessary child placement, provides in-home crisis-oriented treatment and support to families in which one or more family members are at risk of being placed outside the home in foster, group, or institutional care.**

2. Works a 40-hour nonstructured work week (including evenings and weekends) to be responsive to the needs of families.**

3. Provides family education and skills training as part of a goal-oriented treatment plan to prevent the recurrence of or to reduce the harmful effects of the maltreatment of children.**

4. Advocates for family members with schools, courts, and other social service agencies to help family members obtain financial assistance, housing, medical care, and other services.**

**Key duties

Qualifications: Master's degree in social work, psychology, educational psychology, or psychosocial nursing is required. Graduate degree in social work preferred. Experience in counseling families and children is required. Knowledge of crisis intervention, social casework, communication skills, and family therapy techniques is required. Knowledge of cognitive-behavioral interventions, group work, and functional family therapy is desirable. Must have reliable transportation. Required to live in county served. Salary range: $39,000–$45,000.

Application Procedures and Deadline: An agency application form, resume, and cover letter describing related education and experience must be submitted. Position closes April 25, 2009. Starting date is tentatively scheduled for May 25, 2009. Please send application materials to

Annette Jandre
Program Supervisor
Children's Services Society
4601 15th Avenue, NW
Seattle, WA 98103
(206) 263-5857

AN EQUAL OPPORTUNITY EMPLOYER—ALL QUALIFIED INDIVIDUALS ARE ENCOURAGED TO APPLY

Figure 12.3   Sample Position Announcement

professional and organization capability in self and others, consistent with the needs of Casey.

- *Critical Thinking and Judgment.* Gathers, organizes, interprets, and processes information for the purpose of making informed decisions in the course of accomplishing work objectives.

- *Technical Expertise.* Demonstrates both technical and Casey-specific knowledge required to be proficient in one's profession or job classification. (Casey Family Programs, 1998)

A competencies approach can then be linked with a framework for viewing levels of contribution that staff members can make. In fields where employee learning and constant innovation are essential, these contribution levels are being referred to as "levels of knowledge work":

- *Level One: Acquiring Knowledge.* The knowledge acquired is in the form of ideas, theories, methods, principles, skills, and information about the organization, the work of the organization, and its customers. The Level One contributor seeks and acquires knowledge from two primary sources:
  - ○ From supervisors and coworkers (by seeking information, advice, guidance, and feedback)
  - ○ From the codified sources of knowledge in the organization (i.e., systems, guidelines, work manuals, operating procedures, policies, etc.)
- *Level Two: Applying Knowledge.* Level Two contributors use acquired knowledge to independently plan and complete value-added work for the organization. They exercise judgment to make their own decisions, rather than defer those decisions to others. Unless new knowledge is used, it adds little or no value for the organization. By exercising confidence and initiative, Level Two contributors turn previously acquired knowledge into a value-added resource for the organization. (We tend to think of Level Two knowledge workers as the "solid performers" in most organizations. Based on our research, "star" status is usually only conferred on those knowledge workers who contribute at Levels Three, Four, and Five.)
- *Level Three: Creating Knowledge.* The Level Three contributor creates new knowledge by pushing the boundaries of existing knowledge:
  - ○ Asks "What if" questions
  - ○ Takes the risk of doing things that have never been done before

- ○ Solves critical problems that have no predetermined solutions
- ○ Invents new products, processes, technologies, or work methods
- *Level Four: Developing Knowledge in Others.* The Level Four contributor grows intellectual capital in several different ways:
  - ○ Shares knowledge directly with others
  - ○ Helps others apply new or existing knowledge to their work
  - ○ Provides feedback
  - ○ Motivates others to create and apply new knowledge
  - ○ Communicates a sense of direction and purpose
  - ○ Facilitates the face-to-face transfer of knowledge between others
- *Level Five: Leveraging Knowledge.* Level Five contributors help define what the organization does and/or how it does it. They often do this by transforming the knowledge in people's heads into systems that are "owned" by the organization and accelerate the transfer and application of knowledge across the organization. We refer to these systems as *structural capital*. While Level Five contributors may not create this structural capital, they are the ones who get a critical mass of the organization to accept and use the new structural capital. This structural capital could include any of the following:
  - ○ New business or technology strategies and directions
  - ○ New work methods and expert systems
  - ○ New people systems or organization structures
  - ○ New training, communication, or information systems (Bristow, 1999a, pp. 5–6)

These kinds of knowledge are what Bristow (1999a, p. 9) and others refer to as "human capital"—part of the assets that an organization can use to generate future returns. In the human services, human capital is the means for providing high-quality services and achieving desired outcomes with our consumers. Defining a position and developing the staff requires attention to key competencies and to how the employee can grow and contribute to the organization in different ways over time.

Affirmative Action and Equal Employment Opportunity

A number of federal laws provide a legal framework for certain supervisory actions. Among the most significant are those governing affirmative action (AA), the Equal Employment Opportunity Act of 1972 (enforced by the Equal Employment Opportunity Commission [EEOC]), Americans With Disabilities Act (ADA), and those specific civil rights laws that are intended to guard against sexual harassment. Regulations from the Occupational Safety and Health Administration (OSHA) also may apply to many work settings. Knowledge of EEOC, AA, ADA, job descriptions, and key staff competencies are all essential for developing position announcements, screening candidates, and selecting the right candidate. This section will briefly review the key aspects of these policies and statutes.

Affirmative Action

Legislation for affirmative action and equal employment opportunity continues to affect the recruitment, screening, and selection of employees in both for-profit and nonprofit organizations.[1] The distinctive components of equal employment opportunity laws are based on Title VII of the 1964 Civil Rights Act and other laws, including the Age Discrimination in Employment Act of 1967; Sections 503 and 504 of the Rehabilitation Act of 1973, as amended; the Vietnam Era Veterans' Readjustment Assistance Act of 1974 (amended in

2000; P.L. 106-419); and the Equal Pay Act of 1963. As Klingner and Nalbandian (1985) noted,

> With few exceptions, Title VII (EEO) prohibits employers, labor organizations, and employment agencies from making employee or applicant personnel decisions based on race, color, religion, sex, or national origin. Although it originally applied only to private employers, the concern of EEO was extended to local and state governments by 1972 amendments to the 1964 Civil Rights Act. (p. 64)

Equal employment opportunity laws work to reduce discrimination against employees by ensuring that equal opportunity is implemented in all employment actions. These laws require nondiscrimination, which involves the elimination of all existing discriminatory conditions, whether purposeful or inadvertent. Because of their tax-exempt status and because they often depend on government contracts, social service organizations must carefully and systematically examine all their employment policies. They cannot operate to the detriment of any people on the grounds of race, color, religion, national origin, sex, age, or status as a person with a disability, disabled veteran, or veteran of the Vietnam era. These organizations should also prevent and eliminate biases related to gay, lesbian, bisexual, or transgendered employees. Federal and state laws and regulations often specify that managers of those who are responsible for matters of employment, including supervisors, must ensure that practices are nondiscriminatory (Gutiérrez & Nagda, 1996; Swanson & Brown, 1981).

In contrast to equal employment opportunity laws, affirmative action requires that many organizations take steps to ensure proportional recruitment, selection, and promotion of qualified members of groups such as ethnic and racial minority groups and women, who historically have been excluded. Most employers, unions, and employment agencies are required to plan and document, through written affirmative action programs (AAPs), the steps they are taking to reduce the underrepresentation of women and ethnic and racial minority groups. Most public and private organizations that provide goods and services to the federal government and their subcontractors must comply with the affirmative action provisions described in Executive Order No. 11246. Guidelines for working with AAPs are found in Title 41, Part 60-2 (known as "Revised Order No. 4") of the Office of Federal Contract Compliance (U.S. Department of Labor, 2006).

There are four major EEOC concepts to keep in mind:

1. *Equal Employment:* Employment that is not affected by illegal discrimination

2. *Blind to Differences:* Differences among people that have no relationship to job performance should be ignored, and everyone should be treated equally

3. *Affirmative Action:* Employers are urged to hire groups of people based on their race, age, gender, or national origin, to make up for historical discrimination

4. *Protected Class:* Individuals within a group identified for protection under equal employment laws and regulations (Mathis & Jackson, 2006, pp. 98–99)

Knowledge of equal employment opportunity and affirmative action guidelines is essential for designing employment application forms and interviewing protocols that avoid the use of illegal questions.[2] However, court cases such as *Hopwood v. Texas* (1966) and the legislation passed in some states, such as Proposition 209 in California and Proposition 200 in Washington, may alter what is permissible under equal employment opportunity and affirmative action guidelines (Holland, 1999; California State Office of the Secretary of State, 1996; Washington State Office of the Secretary of State, 1998). In fact, some of these kinds of state laws have limited the use of affirmative action

efforts in college admissions and other areas (Alger, 2003). Government updates and legal consultation are important resources for assessing the adequacy of procedures.

Equal Employment Opportunity, Civil Rights Act of 1991, and the Classification of Jobs

In addition to banning certain types of questions for candidates on applications or in interviews, equal employment opportunity guidelines forbid any selection process that has an adverse impact on any social, ethnic, or gender group, unless the procedure is validated through the analysis of jobs or research on the selection of employees. Descriptions and notices of positions that delineate knowledge, skill, ability, education, or other prerequisites require a determination of whether the prerequisites are genuinely appropriate for the job. Some requirements, such as years of experience, certificates, diplomas, and educational degrees, may be considered unlawful for a particular position on the basis of previous court decisions. Specifically, proscriptions against discrimination in employment demand that any requirement, such as education or experience, that is used as a standard for decisions about employment must be directly relevant to the job in question (Uniform Guidelines on Employee Selection Procedures, 1978).[3]

Standards that disqualify women, certain racial or ethnic groups, or other groups at a substantially higher rate than other applicants would be unlawful unless they could be shown to be significantly related to the successful performance of a job and otherwise necessary for the safe and efficient operation of the job for which they are used (e.g., height and strength criteria that are demonstrably related to an individual's capacity to perform the job tasks). The federal government defines educational requirements as a "test," so they must be validated in accordance with EEOC's testing guidelines. In addition, if an organization validates its selection criteria, equal employment opportunity guidelines require it to demonstrate that no suitable alternative with a lesser adverse impact is available:

> The Civil Rights Act of 1991 requires employers to show that an employment practice is *job related for the position* and is consistent with *business necessity*. The act clarifies that the plaintiffs bringing the discrimination charges must identify the particular employer practice being challenged and must show only that protected-class status played *some role*. For employers, this requirement means that an individual's race, color, religion, sex, or national origin *must play no role* in their employment practices. (Mathis & Jackson, 2006, p. 103)

When an adverse impact can be demonstrated with regard to a screening instrument or process (e.g., a test or structured interview), employers should use alternative measures that are equally valid but produce a less adverse impact. Other than background screening to confirm educational qualifications, medical screening, and a criminal background check ("What is employment screening?" 2005), a modest amount of progress has been made in identifying and using screening procedures for skills and attitudes, as alternatives to screening for educational and experience qualifications (Mufson, 1986; "Inside employee screening," 2001). Nonprofit organizations should carefully analyze their jobs and clearly define their tasks in terms of requisite knowledge, skills, and abilities. Certainly, information establishing an individual's minimum qualifications for various positions is essential to certify that the person can be recruited and/or selected. Based on equal employment opportunity and affirmative action regulations, listed below are examples of questions and statements that are acceptable to use in application forms and as interview questions (Jensen, 1981a; Mathis & Jackson, 2006; Pecora, Bruce, Cherin, & Arguello, in press):

Gender, Marital Status, or Family Composition

- Name and address of parent or guardian, if applicant is a minor
- Statement of company policy regarding work assignment of employees who are related

Physical Limitations, Condition, or Handicap

- Statement by employer that offer may be made contingent on applicant's passing a job-related physical examination
- "Do you have any physical condition or handicap that may limit your ability to perform the job applied for? If yes, what can be done to accommodate your limitation?"

Unacceptable inquires are listed below.

- "Do you have any physical disabilities or handicaps?"
- Questions regarding applicant's general medical condition, state of health, or illness
- Questions regarding receipt of workers' compensation, such as, "Have you ever filed for workers' compensation?"
- Questions regarding recent operations, treatments, or surgeries and dates

Arrest or Criminal Record

- "Have you ever been *convicted* of a felony or (within a specified time period) a misdemeanor that resulted in imprisonment?" (Such a question must be accompanied by a statement that a conviction will not necessarily disqualify the applicant for the job.)

Unacceptable inquires are listed below.

- Questions regarding arrest record, such as "Have you ever been arrested?"
- Questions regarding convictions that would *not* be job related

*Gender, Marital Status,
or Family Composition*

- "Are you married?" (marital status)
- Questions that refer to the applicant's sex
- Questions regarding number or ages of children or dependents or provisions for child care
- Questions regarding pregnancy, child bearing, or birth control
- Questions regarding name or address of relative, spouse, or children of adult applicant
- "With whom do you reside?" or "Do you live with your parents?"

Note that the guidelines for screening people who have physical disabilities are being revised, and questions must be carefully considered in light of the Americans with Disabilities Act, described in the next section.

Americans with Disabilities Act

The Americans with Disabilities Act (ADA), enacted July 26, 1990, provides broad civil rights protection to an estimated 43 million Americans with disabilities.[4] The ADA is neither preemptive nor exclusive; stricter requirements of state or federal law will continue to apply.

The purpose of the act is as follows:

- to provide a clear and comprehensive national mandate for the elimination of discrimination against individuals with disabilities (including those coping with obesity);
- to provide clear, strong, consistent, enforceable standards addressing discrimination against individuals with disabilities;
- to ensure that the federal government plays a central role in enforcing the standards established in this Act on behalf of individuals with disabilities; and

- to invoke the sweep of congressional authority, including the power to enforce the 14th Amendment and to regulate commerce, in order to address the major areas of discrimination faced every day by people with disabilities.

The ADA is not an affirmative action law. It is an equal employment opportunity law because it addresses discrimination in hiring, accommodation of a disabled person on the job, and access of people with disabilities to public and private facilities. Even if a person has a disability, he or she still must be qualified under the Act. A qualified individual with a disability is one who, with or without reasonable accommodation, can perform the essential functions of the job. Some examples of these conditions are listed below:

- Cancer
- Deafness
- Diabetes
- Epilepsy
- Back injury or vulnerability to injury
- Wheelchair use

Becoming qualified under the provisions of the ADA is a two-step process that (1) identifies the essential functions of the job and (2) determines whether the individual seeking the position can perform the functions with or without a reasonable accommodation. First and foremost, job requirements should always be expressed in terms of actual job duties and skill requirements and should never be expressed in terms of an applicant's or employee's limitations. An employer should not focus on whether a candidate or employee has a disability or is protected under the Act. Rather, an employer should focus on the essential functions of the position and whether a candidate or employee, with reasonable accommodation, can perform them. An applicant should *not* be asked about the existence, nature, or severity of a disability, but he or she may be asked whether he or she is able to perform each essential job function.

Employers are still free to hire the most qualified candidate for any particular job. Qualifications of all applicants should be reviewed without regard to the disability of one of the applicants. If the applicant with a disability is the most qualified, then an employer should evaluate whether the disability limits or precludes the performance of an essential function of the job and, if so, whether reasonable accommodation will permit the person to perform the essential functions of the job.

Duty of Reasonable Accommodation. The concept of reasonable accommodation is the new, unique distinguishing characteristic of employment practices under the ADA. However, the concept is not well defined in the Act. In simple terms, a reasonable accommodation is an action taken by an employer that assists a person with a disability to perform the essential job functions. In determining whether a person is qualified for a position, employers must evaluate any individual with a disability by assuming all reasonable accommodations will be provided (i.e., the agency would not incur undue hardship). If the individual is then not qualified for the position, he or she may be rejected.

Accommodations Provided by Private Entities. Title III of the ADA prohibits discrimination against individuals with disabilities "in the full and equal enjoyment of goods, services, and facilities, of any place of public accommodation by any person who owns, leases (or leases to) or operates a place of public accommodation." A public accommodation is broadly defined and includes some places of lodging; restaurants and bars; theaters and stadiums; auditoriums, convention centers, or other places of public gathering; sales or retail establishments; service establishments such as banks, insurance offices,

hospitals, and medical offices; public transportation stations; places of recreation; private educational facilities; social services establishments such as day care centers, homeless shelters, food banks, adoption agencies, and senior citizens' centers; and places of exercise or recreation such as gymnasiums, spas, and golf courses.

The alterations and new construction provisions of the ADA also apply to commercial facilities intended for nonresidential use whose operations affect commerce. These facilities include office buildings, to the extent they are not covered by the public accommodations provisions of the Act, factories, and warehouses.

Discrimination. The ADA requires that services be provided to individuals with disabilities in the most integrated setting, appropriate to the needs of the individual. It is discriminatory to deny a person with a disability the opportunity to participate in or benefit from the goods, services, facilities, privileges, advantages, or accommodations offered by an entity or to provide such opportunity in a manner that is not equal to that afforded to other individuals. An entity may provide a service that is different or separate from that provided to other individuals only if such action is necessary to provide a service that is as effective as that provided to others.

Orienting and Developing Staff Members

Orienting, Training, and Developing Staff

The induction process is of critical importance to the new worker and deserves considerable attention by the organization. The impressions generated upon entry into the agency are lasting ones, and it is to the agency's advantage to implement orientation programs that are positive experiences. This section will consider, from the perspective of the organization and the specific job, the major ingredients that should be included in a sound orientation program. Such an orientation would include an introduction to the agency structure and goals, the personnel policies, the director, the job, and the coworkers.

The basic purpose of orientation is to introduce the new worker to the organization, its policies and procedures, his or her colleagues, his or her role and responsibilities, and to the authority structure. The basic components of such an orientation are usually completed in several working days, followed by additional on-the-job orientation that may include reading about policy, agency history, social case history procedures, and sample case studies.

The new worker often enters the agency with only vague notions about its actual programs and procedural operations. Many new workers are not aware of the entry-level skills and knowledge required by human services agencies. Some are hired in public agencies strictly on the basis of good scores on state merit exams. As a result, many human services workers learn about delivering services while on the job. This fact simply underscores the importance of a comprehensive orientation program.

The induction of a new worker to the agency should include a complete description of the agency's structure, with lines of authority/communication, personnel procedures, and career opportunities. The orientation may be conducted, in part, by the supervisor and, in part, by the trainer or staff development specialist. New workers need a full explanation of the purpose, goals, and objectives of the agency. Since most human services agencies are part of a larger network of services, a brief description of the role of the agency in this network is important, including an identification of relevant policies and regulations pertaining to state and federal statutes or agency bylaws. Copies of the organizational chart should be made available to clarify the lines of authority and communication and should be accompanied by the organization's mission statement, strategic plan, and a personnel manual or guidelines, to provide an overall context.

Another component of a comprehensive orientation program is the process of familiarizing the new worker with the personnel policies of the agency. These policies explain what the new worker can expect from the agency and what the agency can expect of the new worker. This part of the orientation should be covered by a personnel specialist or another appropriate person who has knowledge of the personnel system. The worker needs to be informed of the general rules and regulations concerning annual leave, pay, benefits and services, disciplinary procedures, working hours, grievance procedures, and promotional opportunities. Most agencies provide employees with personnel handbooks containing this information, which should be regularly updated.

Orientation programs should also include an introduction to the agency director. An orientation program also involves the supervisor in orienting the new worker to the job. The supervisor should be able to relate the mission, goals, and objectives of the agency and provide information about the unit's role and scope. This information provides the worker with a broad perspective on the organization and lays a foundation for the supervisor's explanation of how the different positions held by coworkers in the unit help both the unit and the agency to meet their goals and objectives. There will probably be few better opportunities for a supervisor to capitalize on the new worker's openness and receptivity and shape a positive attitude toward his or her job. The worker who is already oriented to the organization will be better able to grasp his or her role in carrying out organizational goals and objectives. The orientation process also involves inducting the new employee into the culture of the place, norms, folklore, operating assumptions, and other aspects of the organization and work unit. This is done via both informal and formal work systems.

Supervising and Performance Appraisal

Supervising Ongoing Task Performance

Supervision encompasses a broad range of tasks that involve helping staff set work priorities, establishing work unit goals, working with diverse staff members, monitoring employee performance, providing supportive and education-oriented supervision (Austin & Hopkins, 2004; Brody, 1993; Hays & Kearney, 1983; Kadushin & Harkness, 2002; Levy, 1985; Middleman & Rhodes, 1985; Munson, 2001; Thomas & Ely, 2002; Tsui, 2004), supporting self-directed work groups (Dinkmeyer & Eckstein, 1996; Kruzich & Timms, in press), and other responsibilities. Here, we focus on performance appraisal because so many personnel management functions affect and are affected by this process (see Chapter 13 for further discussion of supervisory functions).

Designing and Conducting Performance Appraisals

Performance evaluations are designed to measure the extent to which the worker is achieving the requirements of his or her position and his or her fit within the team. Evaluations should be based on clearly specified, realistic, and achievable criteria reflecting agency standards (Arvey & Murphy, 1998; Del Po, 2007; Kadushin & Harkness, 2002). Superior performance appraisal methods encourage supervisors and workers to set realistic and measurable goals for job performance. Measurable evaluation criteria also help to motivate, direct, and integrate worker learning while providing staff with examples of how they can evaluate their own performance.

The inability of staff members to meet certain performance standards may be due to dysfunctional or unclear agency policies, a shortage of critical resources, inadequate supervisory feedback,

or other administrative-related shortcomings. Sound performance evaluations help supervisors and manager to distinguish agency-related problems that should be corrected with some form of organizational change from worker-related performance difficulties that may be corrected by in-service training or other strategies (Mager & Pipe, 1970; Waldman, 1994). A systematic approach helps lessen the discomfort of both supervisors and staff (Weinbach, 1998). Evaluating staff at least annually is important for determining pay raises, promotability, future assignments, and the need for discipline.

Sound performance appraisal systems assist agencies in meeting the requirements of equal employment opportunity laws in the areas of promotion or discipline (Brody, 1993; Del Po, 2007; Jensen, 1980; Odiorne, 1984). Finally, given the amount of autonomy and discretion of most social service agency staff, consumers have a right to expect a minimum amount of staff supervision and monitoring as part of agency quality control. As a result of performance evaluations, consumers are more likely to be assured of effective service and protected from continuation of inadequate service (Kadushin & Harkness, 2002).

Despite the multiple advantages of performance evaluation, human services and other organizations continue to struggle with two primary challenges. First is the challenge of specifying the basis on which a worker's job performance is judged (i.e., What performance standards or criteria should be used?) Second, once the criteria have been identified, how and to what extent should they be measured (Howell & Dipboye, 1982)?

A wide variety of process or outcome criteria are being used by human services agencies to evaluate worker performance. Most performance criteria fall into the following general categories: output quality, output quantity, work habits and attitudes, accident rates, learning ability, and judgment or problem-solving ability (Howell & Dipboye, 1982; Mathis & Jackson, 2006). However, many performance evaluations tend to concentrate too much on subjective personality traits or on the peripheral aspects of the worker's performance (e.g., attitude, punctuality, orientation to managers), and not enough time is spent examining the degree of attainment of specific outcome criteria for the job.

Performance appraisal methods can be categorized into two groups: objective or "absolute standards" and subjective or "comparative standards" (Cummings & Schwab, 1973). Objective methods usually focus on some form of quantitative analysis or examination of concrete outputs (e.g., payment error rates, foster homes recruited, children reunified with parents). Subjective performance evaluation methods use one of the three following approaches to measurement: (1) comparisons in which individual performance is judged in relationship to other individuals by using group norms; (2) assessing individual performance based on relatively fixed, independently determined standards; and (3) judging individual performance through careful observation of what people do (Howell & Dipboye, 1982).

Types of Approaches. Although there are many appraisal methods, there appears to be a relatively small number of major approaches (see Figure 12.4).

These approaches can be categorized into five major groups, with some overlap between the first two groups:

1. *Personality-based systems:* Lists of personality traits that are assumed to be significant to the job are rated (essay/narrative, graphic rating scales, ranking, forced choice).

2. *Generalized descriptive systems:* While similar to the personality-based systems, in generalized descriptive systems terms descriptive of good worker performance are used, such as *organizes, communicates, assesses, motivates,* but often without sufficient definition (essay/narrative, graphic rating).

3. *Results-centered systems:* These systems are especially job related as supervisors and subordinates mutually define work objectives and measures (management by objectives and results [MBO/MOR], work standards). (See Pecora et al., in press, for an example.)

4. *Behavioral descriptive systems:* Using detailed job analysis or job descriptions, work behaviors required for success are identified (behaviorally anchored rating scales (BARS), weighted checklist, critical incidents models, assessment centers).

5. *Miscellaneous:* Systems less frequently used that are relatively unique or combine various components of the other methods (forced distribution, field review). (adapted from Odiorne, 1984, pp. 258–259)

The personality-based and generalized description systems, while widely used in human services agencies, have serious limitations. In the past, many performance appraisals concentrated too much on subjective personality traits or on the peripheral aspects of the worker's performance (e.g., general attitude, punctuality) and not enough on the degree of attainment of specific job-related outcomes.

Another criticism of some performance appraisal methods stems from those who focus on applying total quality management (TQM) using Deming's principles. In fact, Deming ranks the traditional evaluation of performance, merit rating, or annual review third in his list of the Seven Deadly Diseases of the western style of management.[5] Deming advocates argue that many of the faulty management practices in performance appraisal originate from a failure to understand variation among workers and a failure to distinguish between the "common causes" and the "special causes" of variation. Deming (1986, 1993) emphasized quality control charts as a proper tool for monitoring the stability of a system, for distinguishing the special causes from the common causes, and for detecting who among the workers is performing within the system, out of the system on the good side, or out of the system on the poor side (Bakir, 2005).

1. *Ability Requirements Scales (ARS):* The Ability Requirements Scales method developed by Fleishman is useful for identifying ability requirements for different occupational specialties.

2. *Assessment Center:* Employees engage in actual or simulated job tasks where their work behaviors can be measured in order to assess current job performance, or more typically, predict their potential for managerial positions.

3. *Behaviorally Anchored Rating Scales (BARS):* Behaviors necessary to achieve program objectives are identified and then used as scale anchors to rate employee performance.

4. *Critical Incident:* Positive and negative work behaviors or incidents are recorded in relation to mutually agreed-upon performance objectives or job tasks.

5. *Essay/Narrative Summary Description Method:* Supervisors develop narrative evaluations of the employee's work behavior or job-related personality traits. In this approach, individual tasks or behaviors are not rated.

6. *Field Review:* Worker appraisal ratings or rankings are reviewed by a small group of supervisors to reassess the appraisal and to develop uniform standards for performance appraisal.

7. *Forced Distribution:* Raters are forced to place staff on a bell curve where only a certain percentage of staff can receive superior, average, and poor ratings.

8. *Forced-Choice Rating:* Key traits or behaviors identified through a form of job analysis are inserted into multiple-choice questions that require supervisors to choose the trait or behavior that best fits the worker.

9. *Graphic (Trait) Rating Scales:* Workers are rated on a 5–7 point scale in relation to a series of personality traits, abilities, and other performance factors.

10. *Management by Objectives Results (MBO/MOR):* Workers and their supervisors establish individual performance objectives to be accomplished in a specific time period along with action plans for attainment and methods for monitoring progress.

11. *Management Position Description Questionnaire (MPDQ):* The MPDQ is a standardized instrument, with about 250 questions, that describes managerial activities to help develop job descriptions, performance appraisal, and job evaluation criteria. Because it is standardized, results can be compared across incumbents and managerial jobs. The MPDQ appears to have several applications, including job analysis and classification as well as providing a sound basis for staff recruitment and selection.

12. *Multisource 360-Degree Systems:* The most comprehensive and costly type of appraisal. It includes self ratings, peer review, and upward assessments by subordinates of the person being rated. Sometimes customer reviews are also included.

13. *Position Analysis Questionnaire (PAQ):* The PAQ is a structured job analysis questionnaire that measures job characteristics and relates them to human characteristics. The information can then be used to identify performance criteria.

14. *Ranking Techniques:* Workers are rank ordered in relation to certain traits and each other using straight, alternative, or paired comparison methods of ranking.

15. *Weighted Checklist:* Work behaviors are assigned weights according to their importance, and supervisors indicate which behaviors are demonstrated by the worker using a checklist where the weights are omitted.

16. *Work Standards:* Uniform, measurable performance standards are developed to evaluate worker behaviors.

Figure 12.4   Major Approaches to Performance Appraisal

SOURCE: Arvey & Murphy (1998), Brannick et al. (2007), Cummings & Schwab (1973), Driskill et al. (1989), Fleishman & Mumford (1991), Haynes (1978), Klingner & Nalbandian (1985), Organizational and Staff Development Unit (2007), PAQ Services (2007), and Rynes et al. (2005).

Thus, various TQM tools, service fidelity assessments, and outcome data are beginning to be used as ways to provide more objective data for worker performance appraisals. For example, a number of mental health and family social services agencies are beginning to implement Evidence-Based Practice (EBP) models of intervention (for more on Evidence-Based Practice, see Chapters 8 and 9). Virtually all of the better EBPs require that a certain amount of fidelity assessment be conducted to help ensure that the EBP is being implemented as it has been designed (Bruns, Rast, Peterson, Walker, & Bosworth, 2006; Jensen, Weersing, Hoagwood, & Goldman, 2005). Consumers receiving the service are often asked about what was provided to them and how the service was provided, so the organization can monitor service fidelity and quality.

In contrast to the more trait- or personality-focused worker performance rating systems, research indicates that the results-centered (e.g., MBO) and behavioral description systems (e.g., BARS) provide more job-related and valid measures of performance and withstand litigation well (Cascio & Bernardin, 1981; Holley & Feild, 1982). Each method, however, has various strengths and limitations. For example, the MBO system appears to work best for jobs in which workers have a large amount of autonomy and use various technical strategies to achieve performance goals. In contrast, the BARS method appears to be very sound for jobs in which the work requirements are known, specific, and repetitive (Odiorne, 1984, p. 259).

Choosing a Performance Appraisal Method for Your Agency. With the exception of certain graphic rating scales, there are no universal appraisal forms in existence today. Most agencies customize a method or form to meet their individual needs, and many commonly use an approach that includes ratings of performance by key task area and a section that rates the achievement of a worker's career development plan (Pecora et al., in press). The critical questions we reviewed at the beginning of this chapter should

guide you in choosing the best method for your agency. In choosing a method and in customizing your form, remember to include space on the form to address modifications based on worker or supervisor feedback, as well as to record accomplishments, worker strengths, areas for improvement, and an overall rating of performance. Now that we have reviewed various performance appraisal methods, this last section will discuss some general strategies and principles for conducting performance appraisal interviews.

Planning and Conducting Performance Appraisal Conferences. There are a few general principles for conducting performance appraisals that, if followed, result in a much more effective *and* comfortable process for the worker and supervisor (see Del Po, 2007; Falcone & Sachs, 2007; Jensen, 1980). For example, staff should be involved in choosing an appraisal system and establishing or modifying evaluation criteria to ensure that more relevant criteria are used, to increase commitment to the evaluation process, and to clarify expectations regarding evaluation. The primary, if not the exclusive, focus of the evaluation should be on the work performance of the supervisee, rather than any evaluation of the worker as a person. In addition, the appraisal method and criteria should be formulated with some consistency, both across workers and supervisors as well as from one evaluation period to the next.

Evaluation should be a continuous process rather than a one-time or occasional event. Time should be allowed to prepare the assessment prior to the formal evaluation. The evaluation needs to occur within the context of a positive working relationship, and the supervisor should discuss the evaluation procedure with the supervisee in advance. Evaluations should be conducted with some recognition and consideration of the total range of factors (worker controlled or not) that may be determining the worker's performance. Both worker strengths and areas for improvement should be reviewed in a way that is fair and balanced.

The appraisal conference must be carefully planned; it requires adequate time and an environment free from unnecessary distractions. This implies that the supervisor will move out from behind the desk, postpone visitors and phone calls, and generally show the worker that the appraisal is a high priority. The evaluation procedure should be a mutual, shared process with worker participation encouraged, but with both taking some responsibility for reviewing the evaluation form and preparing a preliminary assessment. In preparing draft revisions of the performance appraisal, the supervisor and worker should provide some documentation of their views. To facilitate this process, there should be assurances regarding the confidentiality of what is being said and written.

In conducting performance evaluations, supervisors should not merely list excellent and poor work behaviors but should analyze why certain behaviors are desirable or not desirable as well as set goals for future performance. Evaluations should be viewed as part of a continuous assessment process whereby worker job performance is continuously changing and open to improvement.

Finally, performance evaluation often involves providing both negative and positive feedback, as well as negotiation. In providing staff with feedback, it is important to follow some of the principles described by Lehner (n.d., as cited in Austin, 1981). These include focusing feedback on behavior rather than on the person and using observational data rather than inferences. It is helpful to give feedback on behavior as part of a range of possible behaviors (e.g., more or less) rather than simply making qualitative distinctions (e.g., good or bad). In addition, behavior related to a specific situation should be highlighted (e.g., preferably the "here and now" rather than the "there and then").

Feedback is most effective when it is based on sharing ideas and information rather than on giving advice. The focus should be on the exploration of alternatives rather than on producing answers or solutions. Feedback should be based on the value it may have to the recipient, not on the value or release that it provides to the person giving the feedback. Concentrate on the amount of information the worker can process rather than on the amount the supervisor might like to give. In addition, effective interviewers choose a time and place that is unhurried and comfortable so that personal data can be shared at appropriate times. Finally, during those difficult interviewing moments, supervisors focus feedback on what is said rather than why it is said.

Handling Employee Performance Problems

Developing accurate job descriptions, hiring the most qualified personnel, using measurable job-related performance criteria, and conducting effective performance appraisal interviews provide a solid foundation for analyzing and dealing with a variety of employee performance problems. Employee performance problems can be minimized and more easily handled if the personnel functions described in the preceding sections have been adequately addressed. This section will focus on some general principles for handling performance problems, sexual harassment, and employee termination.

Distinguishing Between Worker and Agency Performance Problems

Employee "performance problems" are often viewed as evidence of a lack of worker knowledge or skill (training need), poor attitudes (a lack of commitment to the job), need for more supervision, or poor use of time. However, employee performance difficulties may be also due to a host of agency-related factors such as unclear agency policies, resource limitations, vague work priorities or performance standards, poor supervision, caseload demands, and assignment of inappropriate cases.

Supervisors and managers need to take a close look at both worker and agency factors before deciding on a course of action. More specifically, in analyzing the "performance problem," it is important to determine whether the performance difficulty relates to one or more of the following factors:

- Unclear task assignments
- Unclear performance standards
- Lack of worker ability
- Lack of worker knowledge
- Lack of worker skill (or practice)
- Lack of worker motivation (or conversely, lack of agency rewards for performance)
- Mismatch between worker and agency ideology or approach to practice
- Unclear policies
- Lack of resources
- Poor supervision (e.g., little worker feedback, inconsistent monitoring, little technical assistance provided, poor worker-supervisor relationship)
- Unusually large caseloads
- Assignment of inappropriate cases
- Environmental factors such as excessive noise, poor lighting, lack of privacy, depressing decor
- Demeaning or demoralized organizational climate

All of the above factors are common causes of worker performance problems. Once the real causes have been identified, it is much easier to develop a strategy for addressing them.

The Importance of Personnel Policies

Handling worker performance problems requires specifying certain employee regulations and grievance handling procedures in the agency's personnel policies. Organizations may use a matrix of discipline procedures for various employee performance problems. Explicit policies provide guidelines for expected employee behavior and consequences for noncompliance. As such, they form a foundation for addressing

performance problems within a "developmental discipline" system. In this system, disciplinary standards and procedures are mutually accepted, are designed to shape behavior and not punish, are performance focused, and are periodically reviewed (see Del Po & Guerin, 2005; Odiorne, 1984, pp. 205–217).

When workers are clear about their job assignments and performance standards, it is much less likely that such policies will need to be enforced. As the supervisor and worker examine job performance difficulties and possible causes, it is essential as well that the time, place, and nature of the problems have been carefully documented. Effective handling and prevention of performance problems is a characteristic of high quality supervision. As such, the first line for prevention and remediation is the line supervisor.

Using personnel policies, standard operating procedures, supervision principles, and the job analysis process described earlier, the supervisor can assess the match between worker competencies and the job requisites, seek continuously to clarify performance standards, and remove obstacles to employee success. Supervisors also provide access to training, monitor, and provide feedback and distribute favorable consequences for effective work behaviors (Brody, 1993; Kadushin & Harkness, 2002; Odiorne, 1984; Tsui, 2004). In addition, managers should be sensitive to the possibility that personal factors may be contributing to poor performance. These factors might be a worker's health problems, stress or other emotional difficulties, non-job-related problems (e.g., marital relations, family pressures), or poor work habits (such as unauthorized use of company equipment, carelessness, poor time management).

Human services organizations have a responsibility to assist workers in addressing these problems through referral to medical and mental health programs or, in the case of poor work habits, provision of special on-the-job supervision and coaching. Finally, supervisors should consider whether the employee situation is truly unworkable (worker is rated as having low performance with no potential for further growth) or just "problematic" (performance is at a low level but the potential for improvement is considered good or high; Odiorne, 1984). Depending on your management philosophy, you may fire the "deadwood" employee immediately (see below for processes needed to ensure proper termination) but institute a variety of measures to assist the "problem employee." Thus, in handling performance problems, most agencies rely on progressive discipline consisting of four major phases: (1) counseling and/or training, (2) written reprimands, (3) final warning and a probationary period, and (4) dismissal.

Employee Termination

Discharging staff can be one of the most difficult and unpleasant tasks in managing personnel. Superiors and personnel managers are often given this responsibility with insufficient information and training in planning and carrying out employee terminations. A variety of references provide excellent information and guidelines for handling employee terminations (see, e.g., California Chamber of Commerce, 2006; Coulson, 1981; Jensen, 1981b; Lawrence Berkeley National Laboratory, 2005; Morin & Yorks, 1982; Roseman, 1982; Weinbach, 1998, pp. 171–179). The major challenges for handling the termination process include developing explicit policies, establishing "just cause," conducting termination interviews, and learning from exit interviews.

Clear job specifications and performance standards are essential to evaluating employee performance. Because employee termination can occur for reasons other than poor performance or misconduct, explicit policies must be developed that describe the conditions under which an employee can be terminated. Written policies provide the operational guidelines for termination, protect staff from arbitrary actions, and help ensure that termination decisions are legal and fair. A host of legal issues surround termination, and nearly all groups of employees have

some type of protection under the law that is being enforced by local courts, state human rights agencies, the EEOC, and, in the case of unions, the National Labor Relations Board (Del Po & Guerin, 2005; Ewing, 1983). For example, the "employment at will" doctrine allowing termination without notice and cause in nonunion private jobs is increasingly being narrowed by recent court decisions (Del Po & Guerin, 2005; Heshizer, 1985). Recent changes in case law provide a powerful incentive for careful development and execution of termination policies in human services organizations.

Termination rationales are typically defined in policy statements as resignation, mutual agreement, reduction in force (job elimination), unsatisfactory performance (including the inability to establish effective working relationships with coworkers), misconduct on the job, and retirement (Jensen, 1981b, p. 38). Supervisors need to be aware of the specific items that should be addressed by the organization's termination policies. For example, policies should contain provisions for severance pay and termination notice and should note whether or not an exit interview is required. In terminating long-time employees, it is appropriate to consider more generous termination pay or notice, awarded based on the number of months or years of service to the organization.

Sexual Harassment as Both an Employee Performance Problem and a Grievance

Sexual harassment is discussed here because it has become recognized in recent years as a type of performance problem with significant potential for employee distress and worker grievance.[6] As in the case of racial harassment, sexual harassment is recognized as one of the most sensitive employee situations. Agency supervisors and managers, as well as the organization, are legally liable for damages and penalties when found by local and federal courts to have failed to address problems of sexual harassment (Fisher, Willson, & Young, 2003; O'Connor & Vallabhajosula, 2004; U.S. Equal Employment Opportunity Commission, 1980, 2007).

Sexual harassment involves unwelcome sexual advances, requests for sexual favors, and other verbal or physical conduct of a sexual nature. Harassment can take many forms, including verbal, visual, and physical harassment. For example, visual harassment involves constant leering, suggestive ogling, offensive signs and gestures, or open display of pornographic and/or other offensive materials. Verbal harassment takes the form of dirty jokes, sexual suggestions, highly personal innuendos, and/or explicit propositions. Examples of physical harassment are "accidentally" brushing up against the body, patting, squeezing, pinching, kissing, fondling, forced sexual assault, and/or rape (Code of Federal Regulations, 2001).

In a survey conducted by the Federal Merit System, participants reported whether they had received "any forms of uninvited and unwanted sexual attention" from a person or persons with whom they worked during the 24-month period of the study (U.S. Merit Systems Protection Board [USMSPB], 1981, pp. 26–37). The following forms of behavior were identified:

- Actual or attempted rape or sexual assault
- Pressure for sexual favors
- Deliberate touching, leaning over, cornering, or pinching
- Sexually suggestive looks or gestures
- Letters, phone calls, or materials of a sexual nature
- Pressure for dates
- Sexual teasing, jokes, remarks, or questions

Approximately 42% of the women and 15% of the men reported being sexually harassed during this period. Only 1% reported the severest form (i.e., actual or attempted rape or sexual assault). But that 1% means that nearly 12,000 employees in the federal workforce were victimized in a severe manner during that period

(USMSPB, 1981). In a subsequent study of data from the U.S. Merit Systems Protection Board, Antecol and Cobb-Clark (2004) report that while the pattern of harassment has not changed significantly, employees' attitudes have changed. Federal employees seem to be more willing to recognize a broad range of behaviors as sexual harassment. Letters, e-mails, phone calls, pressure, and touching were identified as less severe sexual harassment. But sexual teasing, jokes, and suggestive gestures were also included as sexual harassment. Sexual harassment appears to occur more than once for each victim.

More recent statistics are available from EEOC based on the total number of charges filed and resolved under Title VII that alleged sexual harassment discrimination as an issue. In fiscal year 2006, EEOC received 12,025 charges of sexual harassment. Slightly more than fifteen percent (15.4%) of those charges were filed by males. EEOC resolved 11,936 sexual harassment charges in fiscal year 2006 and recovered $48.8 million in monetary benefits for charging parties and other aggrieved individuals, not including monetary benefits obtained through litigation (U.S. Equal Employment Opportunity Commission, 2007).

The overall findings from these surveys are that sexual harassment is widespread and occurs regardless of a person's age, marital status, appearance, sex, ethnicity, occupation, or salary level. Based on the above studies, it is apparent that many people are treated unequally, are discriminated against, or are abused severely.

Workers should be informed that in addition to receiving a prompt and assertive response by the supervisor, there are a number of strategies that they can individually employ to discourage or respond to sexual harassment and other forms of discrimination. These include indicating to the person that the behavior is inappropriate and will not be tolerated. Harassing behavior is often repeated even when the victim clearly communicates that the behavior is unacceptable. In addition, staff should begin to keep a private record documenting their interactions with the perpetrator in order to prepare a formal grievance (i.e., documenting who, what, where, when, how, and witnesses to the offenses).

Staff members who perceive discrimination may want to talk with fellow staff members to determine whether others have been victimized and how they have handled the situation. Finally, staff should be encouraged to complain officially. Sexual harassment and other forms of discrimination are a serious personnel problem that often goes unrecognized, or at least, not addressed formally until serious disciplinary measures become necessary. Following some of the preventive measures outlined above can reduce the likelihood of discrimination and allow supervisors to address the problem without resorting to employee dismissal.

Current Issues

Personnel management functions will need to be refined as part of an approach to management and service provision that emphasizes organizational effectiveness and customer-focused refinement of services (Burgess, 2006; Collins, 2005; Rapp & Poertner, 1987). Human services administrators must begin addressing key personnel management functions in new ways. For example, performance standards need to be clarified and strengthened, from a focus on process to more of a balanced focus on the use of more standardized Evidence-Based Practice (EBP) approaches to practice, service quality, and outcomes.

In some cases, practice protocols will need to be used more extensively to help increase consistency in core interventions while allowing maximum worker flexibility in other areas. Recent class action suits in some areas of social services (e.g., child welfare, mental health) have sometimes resulted in increased paperwork demands but little improvement in service quality or outcomes. This has made it difficult for these agencies to implement more streamlined paperwork and other process monitoring systems and increasing their focus on key results. Unions are a powerful constituent group in some agencies, and

depending upon the nature of their leadership and orientation, unions can be a positive force for organizational improvement or pose barriers that must be worked through (Chaison, 2006).

How various personnel management practices support or hinder organizational performance is an area that needs more attention. For example, there is growing evidence that unit managers and supervisors are key to setting a positive organizational culture, interpreting policy, and managing change (Glisson & Hemmelgarn, 1998; Resnick & Patti, 1980; Teather, Gerbino, & Pecora, 1996). But more specific knowledge is needed regarding what specific supervisory behaviors most affect worker and program-wide performance, as well as other aspects of continuous quality improvement (Bruce & Austin, 2000; Sluyter, 1998; Tsui, 2004). (See Chapter 13 for further discussion of this issue.)

On a still more micro level, the field needs to be guided by further research on how to minimize biases of various kinds during the employee selection process and how to refine interviewing approaches. Finally, many supervisors and mid-level human services administrators will continue to need skills-based supervisory training to supplement the clinical skills and experience that they bring to these positions.

Notes

1. Affirmative action is based on Executive Order No. 11246, as amended. Guidelines for handling affirmative action programs (AAPs) are found in the Office of Federal Contract Compliance Programs' Title 41, Part 60-2 (also known as "Revised Order No.4"). Also see the Equal Employment Opportunity Act of 1972, P. L. 93-380, 88 Stat. 514, 2-0 USC 1228 (1976). Executive Order No. 11246, in general, applies to an organization if it has a government contract or subcontract exceeding $10,000. A written AAP is required by this Executive Order (see also 503/38 USC 2012) if the organization has 50 or more employees and a contract in excess of $50,000.

2. See, for example, various articles in the *Labor Law Journal.* Additional resources include the manuals

published by the following organizations, which are regularly updated:

- ○ Commerce Clearing House, Inc.: *Employment Practices, Equal Employment Opportunity Commission Compliance Manual,* and *Office of Federal Contract Compliance Program Manual.*
- ○ Bureau of National Affairs: *Affirmative Action Compliance Manual for Federal Contractors.*
- ○ Prentice Hall, Inc.: *Equal Employment Opportunity Compliance Manual.*
- ○ Federal Programs Advisory Service: *Handicapped Requirements Handbook.*

3. See EEOC's Uniform Guidelines on Employee Selection Procedures (designated as UGESP (1978) §§ 1-18). These guidelines are incorporated into the official regulations of the EEOC, 29 CFR 1607; Office of Federal Contract Compliance Program, 41 CFR 60-3; Department of Justice, 28 CFR 50.14; and the former Civil Service Commission, 5 CFR 300.103(c).

4. This section is adapted from Bruyére (2000); Davis Wright Tremaine LLP (1992); "U.S. says Disabilities Act" (1993); Pardeck (1998); and Perry (1993).

5. See The W. Edwards Deming Institute (TM), http://www.deming.org, or the Kaizen Institute, http://www.kaizen-institute.com/.

6. Special thanks to Dr. Trinidad Arguello for suggesting key articles and strategies.

References

Age Discrimination in Employment Act of 1967, Pub. L. No. 90-202, 81 Stat. 602 (1967).

Alger, J. (2003). What's ahead for affirmative action? *Change, 35*(3), 34–35.

Americans With Disabilities Act of 1990, Pub. L. No. 101-336, 104 Stat. 327 (1990).

Antecol, H., & Cobb-Clark, D. (2004). The changing nature of employment-related sexual harassment: Evidence from the U.S. government, 1978–1994. *Industrial and Labor Relations Review, 57*(3), 443–461.

Arthur, D. (2004). *The employee recruitment and retention handbook.* New York: Amacom Books.

Arvey, R. D., & Murphy, K. R. (1998). Performance evaluation in work settings. *Annual Review of Psychology, 49,* 141–168.

Austin, M. J. (1981). *Supervisory management for the human services.* Englewood Cliffs, NJ: Prentice Hall.

Austin, M. J., & Hopkins, K. M. (Eds.). (2004). *Supervision as collaboration in the human services: Building a learning culture.* Thousand Oaks, CA: Sage.

Baard, P. P., Deci, E. L., & Ryan, R. M. (2004). Intrinsic need satisfaction: A motivational basis of performance and well-being in two work settings. *Journal of Applied Social Psychology, 34*(10), 2045–2068.

Bakir, S. T. (2005). A quality control chart for work performance appraisal. *Quality Engineering, 17*(3), 429.

Brannick, M. T., Levine, E. L., & Morgeson, F. P. (2007). *Job and work analysis: Methods, research, and applications for human resource management* (2nd ed.). Thousand Oaks, CA: Sage.

Bristow, N. (1999a). *The new leadership imperative.* Orem, UT: Targeted Learning.

Bristow, N. (1999b). *Using your HR systems to build organizational success.* Orem, UT: Targeted Learning.

Bristow, N., Dalton, G., & Thompson, P. (1996). *The four stages of contribution* [Mimeograph]. Orem, UT: Novations. (Also reprinted in The Casey Family Program, 1996)

Brody, R. (1993). *Effectively managing human service organizations.* Newbury Park, CA: Sage.

Bruce, E. J., & Austin, M. J. (2000). Social work supervision: Assessing the past and mapping the future. *The clinical supervisor, 19*(2), 85–107.

Bruns, E. J., Rast, J. Peterson, C., Walker, J., & Bosworth, J. (2006). Spreadsheets, service providers, and the statehouse: Using data and the wraparound process to reform systems for children and families. *American Journal of Community Psychology, 38,* 201–212.

Bruyère, S. M. (2000). Civil rights and employment issues of disability policy. *Journal of Disability Policy Studies, 11*(1), 18–28.

Burgess, G. J. (2006). *Legacy living.* Provo, UT: Executive Excellence.

California Chamber of Commerce. (2006). *Recruiting, performance & termination.* Retrieved June 17, 2006, from http://www.calchamber.com/Store/Products/RTT

California State Office of the Secretary of State. (1996). *Proposition 209: Text and analysis.* Retrieved April 7, 2006, from http://vote96.ss.ca.gov/bp/209analysis.htm

Cascio, W. F., & Bernardin, H. J. (1981). Implications of performance appraisal litigation for personnel decisions. *Personnel Psychology, 34*(2), 211–226.

Casey Family Programs. (1998, September). *Competencies recruitment and selection training manual.* Seattle, WA: Author.

Chaison, G. (2006). *Unions in America.* Thousand Oaks, CA: Sage.

Civil Rights Act of 1964, Pub. L. No. 88-352, 78 Stat. 24 (1964).

Code of Federal Regulations, Title 29, Volume 4 [Revised as of July 1, 2001]. U.S. Government Printing Office via GPO Access. CITE: 29CFR1604.11, pp. 186–192. Retrieved May 25, 2005, from http://frwebgate.access.gpo.gov/cgi-bin/get-cfr.cgi?TITLE=29&PART=1604&SECTION=11&YEAR=2001&TYPE=TEXT

Collins, J. (2005, July/August). Level 5 leadership: The triumph of humility and fierce resolve. *The Best of Harvard Business Review,* 136–146. Reprint R0507M; HBR OnPoint 5831.

Coulson, R. (1981). *The termination handbook.* New York: Free Press.

Cox, F. M. (1984). Guidelines for preparing personnel policies. In F. M. Cox et al. (Eds.), *Tactics and techniques of community practice* (2nd ed., p. 275). Itasca, IL: F. E. Peacock.

Cummings, L. L., & Schwab, D. P. (1973). *Performance in organizations: Determinants and appraisal.* Glenview, IL: Scott, Foresman.

Davis Wright Tremaine LLP. (1992). *Special summary of the Americans with Disabilities Act prepared for The Casey Family Program* [Mimeograph]. Seattle, WA: Author.

Del Po, A. (2007). *The performance appraisal handbook.* Berkeley, CA: Nolo Press.

Del Po, A., & Guerin, L. (2005). *Dealing with problem employees: A legal guide.* Berkeley, CA: Nolo Press.

Deming, W. E. (1986). Out of the crisis. Cambridge, MA: MIT Center for Applied Engineering Study.

Deming, W. E. (1993). *The new economics for industry, government, education.* Cambridge: MIT Center for Applied Engineering Study.

Dinkmeyer, D., & Eckstein, D. (1996). *Leadership by encouragement.* Delray Beach, FL: St. Lucie Press.

Driskill, W. E., Weismuller, J. J., Hageman, D. C., & Barrett, L. E. (1989). Identification and evaluation of methods to determine ability requirements for Air Force occupational specialties. San Antonio: Metrica Inc. Retrieved June 3, 2007 from the Defense Technical Information Center: http://stinet.dtic.mil/oai/oai?&verb=getRecord&metadataPrefix=html&identifier=ADA212772

Equal Pay Act of 1963, Pub. L. No. 88-38, 77 Stat. 56 (1963).

Ewing, D. W. (1983). Your right to fire. *Harvard Business Review, 61*(2), 32–34, 38, 40–42.

Falcone, P., & Sachs, R. (2007). *Productive performance appraisals* (2nd ed.). New York: American Management Association.

Fine, S. A., & Cronshaw, S. F. (1999). *Functional job analysis.* Mahwah, NJ: Lawrence Erlbaum Associates.

Fisher, C., Willson, A. J., & Young, R. (2003, August). Is there a "standard of care" to define a reasonable harassment investigation? Society for Human Resource Management White Paper. Retrieved June 24, 2007, from http://www.shrm.org/hrresources/whitepapers_published/Employee%20Relations%20TOC.asp#P234_8677

Fleishman, E. A., & Mumford, M. D. (1991). Evaluating classifications of job behavior: a construct validation of the ability requirement scales. *Personnel Psychology, 44*(3), 523–575.

Glisson, C., & Hemmelgarn, A. (1998). The effects of organizational climate and interorganizational coordination on the quality and outcomes of children's service systems. *Child Abuse & Neglect, 22*(5), 401–421.

Gutiérrez, L. M., & Nagda, B. A. (1996). The multicultural imperative in human services organizations: Issues for the 21st century. In C. A. McNeece & P. Raffoul (Eds.), *Future issues for social work practice* (pp. 203–213). Needham Heights, MA: Allyn & Bacon.

Harvard Business School. (2006). *Workforce wisdom: Insights on recruiting, hiring, and retaining your best people.* Cambridge, MA: Harvard Business School Press.

Hays, S. W., & Kearney, R. C. (1983). *Public personnel administration: Problems and prospects.* Englewood Cliffs, NJ: Prentice Hall.

Haynes, M. G. (1978). Developing an appraisal program. *Personal Journal, 57*(1), 14–19.

Heshizer, B. (1985). The new common law of employment: Changes in the concept of employment at will. *Labor Law Journal, 36*(1), 95–107.

Himle, D., Jaraytne, S., & Thyness, P. (1989). The buffering effects of four types of supervisory support on work stress. *Administration in Social Work, 13*(1), 19–34.

Holland, R. (1999). *Implementing Initiative 200—Keeping faith with the voters*. Seattle, WA: Washington Policy Center. Retrieved April 7, 2006, from http://www.washingtonpolicy.org/ECP/PNKeepingFaithWithVoters99-06.html

Holley, W. H., & Feild, H. J. (1982). Will your performance appraisal system hold up in court? *Personnel, 59*(1), 59–64.

Hopwood v. Texas, 78 F.3d 932 (5th Cir. 1996).

Howell, W. C., & Dipboye, R. L. (1982). *Essentials of industrial and organizational psychology*. Homewood, IL: Dorsey Press.

Inside employee screening. (2001, February). *APESMA Professional Women's Network*. Retrieved April 12, 2006, from http://www.apesma.asn.au/women/articles/inside_employee_screening_feb_01.asp

Jensen, J. (1980). Employee evaluation: It's a dirty job but somebody's got to do it. *Grantsmanship Center News, 8*(4), 36–45.

Jensen, J. (1981a). How to hire the right person for the job. *The Grantsmanship Center News, 9*(3), 21–31.

Jensen, J. (1981b). Letting go: The difficult art of firing. *The Grantsmanship Center News, 9*(5), 37–43.

Jensen, P. S., Weersing, R., Hoagwood, K. E., & Goldman, E. (2005). What is the evidence for evidence-based treatments? A hard look at our soft underbelly. *Mental Health Services Research, 7*(1), 53–74.

Kadushin, A., & Harkness, D. (2002). *Supervision in social work* (4th ed.). New York: Columbia University Press.

Kettner, P. M. (2002). *Achieving excellence in the management of human services organizations*. Boston: Allyn & Bacon.

Klingner, D. E., & Nalbandian, J. (1985). *Public personnel management: Contexts and strategies*. Englewood Cliffs, NJ: Prentice Hall.

Kruzich, J., & Timms, N. (in press). Facilitating learning teams. In P. J. Pecora, E. Bruce, D. Cherin, & T. Arguello, T. (Eds.), *Administrative supervision: A brief guide for managing social service and other non-profit organizations*. Newbury Park, CA: Sage.

Lawrence Berkeley National Laboratory. (2005). *Employee termination process guide*. Retrieved June 17, 2006, from http://www.lbl.gov/LBL-Work/HR/forms/EE_Termination_Process.pdf

Levy, C. S. (1985). The ethics of management. In S. Slavin (Ed.), *Managing, finances, personnel, and information in human services*. New York: Haworth Press.

Locke, E. A., & Latham, G. P. (1984). *Goal setting: A motivational technique that works*. Englewood Cliffs, NJ: Prentice Hall.

Mager, R. F., & Pipe, P. (1970). *Analyzing performance problems*. Belmont, CA: Fearson Pitman.

Mathis, R. L., & Jackson, J. H. (2006). *Human resource management* (11th ed.). Mason, OH: Thomson South-Western.

McCormick, E. J. (1979). *Job analysis: Methods and applications*. New York: Amacom.

Middleman, R., & Rhodes, G. (1985). *Competent supervision: Making imaginative judgments*. Englewood Cliffs, NJ: Prentice Hall.

Morin, W. J., & Yorks, L. (1982). *Outplacement techniques: A positive approach to terminating employees*. New York: AMACOM.

Mufson, D. W. (1986). Selecting child care workers using the California Psychological Inventory. *Child Welfare, 65*, 83–88.

Munson, C. E. (2001). *Handbook of clinical social work supervision* (3rd ed.). New York: Haworth Press.

O'Connor, M., & Vallabhajosula, B. (2004). Sexual harassment in the workplace: A legal and psychological framework. In B. J. Cling (Ed.), *Sexualized violence against women and children: A psychology and law perspective* (pp. 115–147). New York: Guilford Press.

Odiorne, G. S. (1984). *Strategic management of human resources*. San Francisco: Jossey-Bass.

O'Leary, T. (2002). *Using your team for recruiting—A retention strategy for the human resources professional*. Retrieved from http://humanresources.about.com/library/weekly/aa022402a.htm

Organizational and Staff Development Unit. (2007). Guidelines for using 360-degree feedback in the appraisal process London, England: City University of London. Retrieved June 3, 2007 from http://www.city.ac.uk/sd/guidelinesforusing360-degreefeedbackintheappraisalprocess.html

PAQ Services (2007). The PAQ Program. Bellingham, WA: Author. Retrieved May 3, 2007 from http://www.paq.com/?FuseAction=Main.PAQProgram

Pardeck, J. T. (1998). *Social work after the Americans with Disabilities Act*. Westport, CT: Auburn House.

Patti, R. J. (1983). *Social welfare administration: Managing social programs in a developmental context*. Englewood Cliffs, NJ: Prentice Hall.

Pecora, P. J. (1998). Recruiting and selecting effective employees. In R. L. Edwards & J. A. Yankey (Eds.), *Skills for effective management of non-profit organizations* (pp. 115–184). Washington, DC: National Association of Social Workers.

Pecora, P. J., Bruce, E., Cherin, D., & Arguello, T. (in press). *Administrative supervision: A brief guide for managing social service and other non-profit organizations.* Newbury Park, CA: Sage.

Perry, P. M. (1993, Jan/Feb). Avoiding charges of discrimination against the handicapped. *Law Practice Management, 34,* 35–38.

Rapp, C., & Poertner, J. (1987). Moving clients center stage through the use of client outcomes. *Administration in Social Work, 11*(3/4), 23–40.

Rehabilitation Act of 1973, Pub. L. No. 93-112, 87 Stat. 355 (1973).

Resnick, H., & Patti, R. J. (1980). *Change from within: Humanizing social welfare organizations.* Philadelphia: Temple University Press.

Roseman, E. (1982). *Managing the problem employee.* New York: AMACOM.

Rynes, S. L., Gerhart, B., & Parks, L. (2005). Personnel psychology: Performance evaluation and pay for performance. *Annual Review of Psychology, 56,* 571–600.

Shafritz, J. M., Hyde, A. C., & Rosenbloom, D. H. (1986). *Personnel management in government: Politics and process* (3rd ed.). New York: Marcel Dekker.

Shulman, L., & Safyer, A. (2007). *Supervision in counseling: Interdisciplinary issues and research.* San Francisco: Haworth Press.

Sluyter, G. (1998). *Improving organizational performance: A practical guidebook for the human services.* Newbury Park, CA: Sage.

Swanson, A., & Brown, J. A. (1981). Racism, supervision, and organizational environment. *Administration in Social Work, 5*(2) 60–68.

Tambor, M. (1985). The social worker as worker: A union perspective. In S. Slavin (Ed.), *Managing, finances, personnel, and information in human services* (pp. 44–52). New York: Haworth Press.

Teather, E. C., Gerbino, K., & Pecora, P. J. (1996). Making it happen: Strategies for organizational change. In P. J. Pecora, W. Selig, F. Zirps, & S. Davis (Eds.), *Quality improvement and program evaluation in child welfare agencies: Managing into the next century* (pp. 265–288). Washington, DC: Child Welfare League of America.

Thomas, D. A., & Ely, R. J. (2002). Making differences matter: A new paradigm for managing diversity. In R. R. Thomas, D. A. Thomas, R. J. Ely, & D. Meyerson (Eds.), *Harvard Business Review on Managing Diversity* (pp. 33–66). Boston: Harvard Business School Press.

Tsui, M. S. (2004). *Social work supervision: Contexts and concepts.* Thousand Oaks, CA: Sage.

Uniform Guidelines on Employee Selection Procedures (1978), § 60-3, U.G.E.S.P. (1978); 43 FR 38295 (August 25, 1978). Retrieved April 7, 2006, from http://www.uniformguidelines.com/uniformguidelines.html

U.S. Department of Labor. (2006). *Code of federal regulations pertaining to U.S. Department of Labor.* Retrieved April 12, 2006, from http://www.dol.gov/dol/allcfr/Title_41/Chapter_60.htm

U. S. Equal Employment Opportunity Commission. (1980). Title 29: Labor part 1604—Guidelines on discrimination because of sex. *Electronic Code of Federal Regulations.* Retrieved May 30, 2008, from http://ecfr.gpoaccess.gov/

U.S. Equal Employment Opportunity Commission. (2007). *Sexual harassment.* Retrieved June 10, 2007, from http://www.eeoc.gov/types/sexual_harassment.html

U.S. Merit Systems Protection Board. (1981). *Sexual harassment in the federal workplace: Is it a problem?* Washington, DC: Government Printing Office.

U.S. says Disabilities Act may cover obesity. (1993, November 14). *New York Times,* p. Y17.

Vietnam Era Veterans' Readjustment Assistance Act of 1974, Pub. L. No. 93-508, 88 Stat. 1578 (1974).

Waldman, D. A. (1994). Designing performance management systems for total quality management. *Journal of Organizational Change, 7*(2), 31–44.

Washington State Office of the Secretary of State. (1998). *Washington State Initiative 200.* Retrieved April 7, 2006, from http://www.secstate.wa.gov/elections/1998/i200_text.aspx

Weinbach, R. (1998). *The social worker as manager* (3rd ed.). Needham Heights, MA: Allyn & Bacon.

Weiner, M. E. (1982). *Human services management: Analysis and applications.* Homewood, IL: The Dorsey Press.

What is employment screening? (2005). *Beginner's Guide.* Retrieved April 12, 2006, from http://beginnersguide.com/human-resources/employment-screening/what-is-employment-screening.php

Wolfe, T. (1984). *The nonprofit organization: An operating manual* (pp. 63–64). Englewood Cliffs, NJ: Prentice Hall.

Zunz, S. J. (1998). Resiliency and burnout: Protective factors for human service managers. *Administration in Social Work, 22*(3), 39–54.

CHAPTER 13

Supervision, Development, and Training for Staff and Volunteers

Karen M. Hopkins

Supervisors have a direct impact on the success of an organization through their management of employee and volunteer performance and the relationship that employees (and volunteers) have with the organization. Supervisors can be envisioned as conduits through which organizations demonstrate their commitment (or lack of commitment) to employees. If supervisors are competent, supportive, and demonstrate effective coaching and mentoring practices, then employees are likely to perceive the organization as concerned about employee development and a satisfactory place to work. Supervisors play a critical role in humanizing organizations by creating supportive organizational cultures and learning environments that enhance employee development and organizational effectiveness.

The focus of this chapter is how supervisors can develop and support competent workers and volunteers. This chapter begins with an overview of effective supervision, training, and staff development and then describes the ways that supervisors can train, develop, and support staff and volunteers within a learning and performing culture. Finally, the chapter explores how personal characteristics shape supervisors' perceptions and developmental and supportive behaviors.

Effective Supervision

Effective supervision of employees and volunteers has a direct impact on work performance. Effective supervision is best demonstrated by providing workers and volunteers clear performance expectations, fair and consistent feedback, and career development within the context of a learning and performance culture that values communication, innovation, and risk-taking and support

(Corporate Leadership Council, 2005; Hopkins & Austin, 2004b). The actions of supervisors often "determine whether an organization's investment in an employee is salvaged or lost" (Bulin, 1995, p. 301). Likewise, the actions of supervisors toward volunteers are critical to the successful deployment and retention of volunteers. Approximately 80% of nonprofits use volunteers to help extend and enhance paid staff's delivery of services (Hager & Brudney, 2004). Volunteers are increasingly taking on roles that parallel staff functions, and as with human services staff, volunteer turnover is an ongoing problem (Cohen-Callow, 2007). In the general volunteer force, two-fifths of volunteers reported that they stopped volunteering because of poor management practices within organizations (United States Postal Service Foundation, 1998 in Cohen-Callow, 2007).

The work performance of employees and volunteers is primarily determined by whether or not they have the knowledge, skills, and ability to meet the demands of their work or task assignments. Supervisors are responsible for providing the necessary work-related information, instruction, and resources. Other aspects of performance are determined by the attitudes and level of commitment that workers and volunteers have for the job and organization. Therefore, supervisors are also responsible for fostering a culture or environment that positively shapes and supports workers' and volunteers' perceptions of the job and the organization. As their perceptions of the job and organization become more positive, they are more engaged and committed and, thus, more likely to stay with the organization (Corporate Leadership Council, 2005; Hopkins, Cohen-Callow, Salliey, Barnes, Golden, & Morton, 2007).

Satisfaction with volunteering has been found to be positively related to one's experiences and involvement with the organization over time and how much one's motives for volunteering are being fulfilled (Davis, Hall, & Meyer, 2003). Volunteers tend to seek fulfillment of two kinds of motives. These can be categorized as motives focused on helping others (altruistic) and those focused on self-interest (egoistic). Fulfillment of these motives should increase future participation in an organization (Dickinson, 2005). Therefore, supervisors need to learn about the motives of their volunteers and create situations that are likely to lead to their fulfillment.

Volunteer commitment and volunteer task performance have been predicted by attitudes (job satisfaction and perceived organizational support), personality (service orientation and empathy), and customer/consumer knowledge (understanding traits of customers and strategies for interacting with them; Bettencourt, Gwinner, & Meuter, 2001). Research suggests that organizational commitment might be a better predictor of volunteer behavior, over time, than volunteer satisfaction. Organizational factors appear to be an important part of volunteers' organizational commitment. Volunteers have been found to be more committed when they had greater autonomy, were clear about the expected role behaviors, had an opportunity to apply new learned skills, and were highly involved and/or had been at the agency for a greater length of time (Cohen-Callow, 2007).

Whether supervising workers or volunteers (or both), supervisors have to be explicit about what is expected for effective performance. Establishing clear performance guidelines and desired outcomes and helping employees understand the standards that will be used to evaluate them contributes more to improved performance than any other supervisory actions (Corporate Leadership Council, 2005). As with establishing job descriptions for employees, as outlined in Chapter 12, preparing volunteer assignment descriptions (see Table 13.1) lends clarity about volunteers' responsibilities and tasks. This becomes a "tool" that (1) staff can use to work with/alongside volunteers; (2) volunteers use to guide their work; and (3) provides standards for evaluation of volunteers. Supervisors should encourage staff to be involved in designing volunteer assignment descriptions based on their knowledge and understanding of the work and what level and type of assistance they require to get the work done (Cohen-Callow, 1998).

Table 13.1 Components of a Volunteer Assignment Description

- Assignment title
- Supervisor
- Days and hours needed
- Purpose
- Tasks
- Transferable skills
- Type of training provided
- Criteria for success

Supervisors must be able to give both positive and corrective feedback in a manner that is perceived as fair by workers and volunteers. Feedback that is considered fair is accurate, is based on a true understanding of the employee's performance, and contains concrete, specific suggestions for how to do the job better. This feedback should also be delivered consistently, not just during an annual performance review. Supervisors should also provide targeted and detailed feedback for enhancing future performance so that workers are clear about what knowledge and skills they may need to develop to continue to be successful in the organization (Corporate Leadership Council, 2005).

It appears that many supervisors find it difficult to be critical of volunteers, in particular, for a variety of reasons (e.g., fear of losing them). However, it is important that supervisors give ongoing informal feedback and formally evaluate volunteer performance on a periodic basis to give volunteers the opportunity to discuss and process their volunteer experiences. Doing so may also help supervisors improve conditions for better volunteer service (Dickinson, 2005). Supervisors also need to be competent "coaches" with both employees and volunteers to help them solve work-related challenges and problems that may arise between them. Coaching occurs when the supervisor and worker/volunteer (or work group, team) collaboratively explore what behaviors or skills need to change or be enhanced, develop relevant goals, and decide how to evaluate

and maintain the change or improvement (Hopkins & Austin, 2004b).

Progressive management models call for supervisors (and all levels of employees) to "create relationships and conditions that allow both themselves and others to function competently" (Culbert, 1996, p. 82). The best way of doing this involves building a learning- and performance-oriented culture inside human services organizations. A learning culture is an environment that promotes and fosters individual, team, and organizational learning (Garvin, 1998). Supervisors, as unit managers or team leaders, play a critical role in creating a learning culture when they develop mechanisms within their units and teams for facilitating learning and capturing and disseminating knowledge to and from others in the organization. When employees start sharing information, ideas, and knowledge gained, they create a learning culture (Austin & Hopkins, 2004). Supervisors can encourage these employee behaviors by communicating that learning is a continuous cycle; facilitating access to information; encouraging informal learning interactions (e.g., sharing lessons learned or new ideas in team or staff meetings); using a collaborative approach to problem solving; and making individual workers responsible for securing and sharing knowledge/relevant information with colleagues and making it available across service lines, functions, or programs. Supervisors instill a performance culture when they create an environment of open communication, risk-taking, and innovation (based on the shared learning) that enables employee performance and engagement (Corporate Leadership Council, 2005). Through these processes, a learning and performance culture develops over time (see Table 13.2). Organizations tend to seek out employees and volunteers who are self-motivated and responsible, creative problem solvers (Olson, 2000). When members of a work group or team can translate learning into programmatic or service improvements, both consumers and the organization benefit, and the supervisor's sense of personal accomplishment is bolstered.

Table 13.2 Staff and Volunteer Development Activities

Activity	Description
Training	Focused on knowledge, skills, behavior, and attitudes needed for the job, function, or task assignment
Development	Broader in scope than training, and increases potential for advancement or expanded responsibilities through personal and professional growth
Coaching	Focused on formal individual problem solving related to difficulties or opportunities encountered in performing work
Mentoring	Provides informal useful advice and/or application of knowledge

Training and Development

Training and development, as noted in Chapter 12, are key activities in public and nonprofit organizations whose work environments reflect constantly challenging and changing demands. The purpose of training and development is to change or enhance the skills, knowledge, or attitudes of employees and volunteers (Pynes, 2004). Responsibility for training and development may lie with human resource staff, an organizational development department, or a staff development person. However, supervisors are usually held accountable for ensuring that training and development occur because of their responsibility to oversee the performance of staff and volunteers.

Training and development are major indicators of an organization's commitment to staff and volunteers. Both public and nonprofit social service employees want to be acknowledged as professionals within their agencies and supported in their continuing development as professionals. Probably a greater threat to retention than the absence of salary increases or promotion is workers' belief that nothing is changing and they are stagnating (Hopkins, Mudrick, & Rudolph, 1999). To retain volunteers, an organization must provide them with the opportunity to develop personally and to understand more about people around them and the dynamics of the community (Dickinson, 2005).

Although training and staff development are terms that are often used interchangeably, the functions are somewhat different (see Table 13.2). A "trainer" is not necessarily a "developer." While training provides employees with knowledge and skills to use in their current job, development contributes to the overall growth of employees by preparing them for future opportunities, preferably within the organization (Pynes, 2004). Staff development can be conceptualized as broader in scope than training, which is a major activity that falls under this broader function.

Coaching and mentoring are also activities that are encompassed by staff development and are sometimes perceived as being intertwined; however, these are distinct functions as well. Coaching involves "serious and planned discussions" between a supervisor and an employee or volunteer about the need to correct a problem, improve performance, or prepare for a new challenge (Grote, 1995). Through coaching, supervisors clarify performance expectations and help staff and volunteers improve or develop skills and habits in their job or assignment. Mentoring entails sharing one's expertise and experiences and offering guidance to help shape an individual's career. Typically, the supervisor is not an employee's official or formal mentor. A "formal" mentor is more likely to be someone the employee has chosen to facilitate his or her career because of the respect and trust the employee has for the mentor, and who is not in an evaluative position over the employee's work. Sometimes supervisors may provide informal mentoring to talented employees or volunteers who have experience and longevity in the organization and who do not necessarily require coaching. Overall, supervisors play a variety of interrelated roles in training and developing staff and volunteers, including teacher, coach, mentor, evaluator, leader, and learner (see Table 13.3).

Strategies for Training and Developing Staff and Volunteers

Training. There are several logical steps for effectively training staff and volunteers (see Table 13.4). A first step for supervisors (often with the assistance of a human resource or staff development professional) is to identify competency needs in light of agency goals, current policies, and service delivery approaches and match those

with current employee and volunteer competencies. Attention must be paid to needs, wants, and backgrounds of staff (and volunteers) at all levels. A training need "can be defined simply as the difference between what is currently being done and what needs to be done" (Pynes, 2004, p. 285). For example, a worker needs training in client/consumer database management if she is struggling to accurately input and track client data despite an agency mandate for all workers to utilize the management information system. It is the supervisor's responsibility to spot who needs training and assess workload demands and ability to meaningfully engage in training, as well as readiness for using training opportunities. For example, training may not be as helpful if a worker is overloaded with client cases, views training as an added burden, and cannot imagine how he or she is going to incorporate the training into his or her daily work. Supervisors are not facilitating needed or useful "learning" among their workers or volunteers by just sending them

Table 13.3   Supervisor Roles in Training and Developing Staff and Volunteers

Role	Description
Teacher	Help employees/volunteers learn new information, concepts, and skills that will enable them to do the work
Coach	Specifically identify work or task performance problems or opportunities and help employees/volunteers improve their performance to a level that meets the organization's expectations
Mentor	Give personal advice and career guidance
Evaluator	Determine competence and effectiveness of performance and learning of employees/volunteers
Leader	Serve as catalyst for transforming the organization into a learning community through encouraging staff and volunteer participation in problem solving, decision making, taking risks, experimenting, and being learners and performers
Learner	Demonstrate an openness to continued growth and receptivity to challenging environments, and facilitate a culture of learning and information gathering, sharing, soliciting feedback, and being open to succeeding and failing

SOURCE: Adapted from Austin and Hopkins (2004).

to training. Organizational leaders who do not allow supervisors to make judgments about who needs training and what kind of training they need run the risk of wasting resources and/or alienating both supervisors and workers. That's why the next step in the training process is critical.

Table 13.4   Goal Setting Intervention to Facilitate Transfer of Learning

---

1. Worker/volunteer develops one to three goals related to using knowledge and skills learned or enhanced in training

2. The goals are specific, pertinent, attainable, measurable, and observable (SPAMO)

3. Supervisor and employee/volunteer develop (a) transfer objectives with (b) concrete action steps and (c) follow-up review 1–2 months later

---

SOURCE: Foxon (1987) and Tracey and Pecora (1988) in Love (2007).

The second step for supervisors and workers/volunteers is to collaboratively develop meaningful learning objectives prior to attending training. Learning objectives are statements that "provide the standard for measuring what has been accomplished and for determining the level of accomplishment" (Pynes, 2004, p. 286). Essentially, the supervisor and worker/volunteer want to determine what the "trainee" will be able to do differently as a result of the training. For example, a learning objective may be that the aforementioned worker will successfully track the activities and progress of her clients using the agency-supported management information system (MIS). It may be useful for supervisors to keep a log on each employee that notes career goals, learning objectives, examples of successes, and documentation of poor work performance. Together, a supervisor and worker can periodically review the information in the log and plan for future training and development opportunities.

The third step in the training process is for supervisors to select (and/or provide) the appropriate type of training and identify ways in which new learning will be implemented and utilized. For example, after completing training, the aforementioned worker will accurately input client data into the MIS client database and track the activities of her clients over the past three months. Supervisors should encourage and help develop peer support and assistance within work groups to reinforce the learning that occurred through training, especially when the work group members have all received similar training. In the situation just described, the supervisor and worker together could review the client database information and the worker's assessment of her clients' progress after she has finished working on a few cases. The supervisor could also encourage the other team members to help the worker (and each other) when she encounters difficulty with the database.

Finally, supervisors need to evaluate whether the training resulted in changes in workers' knowledge, skill level, attitudes and behavior, and performance effectiveness over time. Incorporating learning activities into daily routines takes practice and is likely to bring success and failure, the two key elements of effective learning experiences (Austin & Hopkins, 2004; Pynes, 2004). Ultimately, training is worthwhile only if successful transfer occurs to the workplace.

Transfer of Training. The research on transfer of training shows that more than 100 billion dollars and 15 billion work hours are spent annually on training programs in all sectors of the economy, but as little as 10% of the expenditures result in long-term behavior change. Only 40% of any training content transfers immediately; after one year, application of new skills drops by another 25% (Curry, 1997; Gregoire, Propp, & Poertner, 1998; Noe & Schmitt, 1986). However, many of the barriers to transfer of training to the work setting are those that the supervisor actually has some degree of control over. For example, workers may lack confidence in using new skills, or the skills learned seem too complex to implement into concrete job tasks, or the practices taught in training do not fit with what really happens in the organization. The key to workers overcoming these barriers is appropriate supervision that includes a goal-setting strategy that can increase transfer initiation and maintenance (Love, 2007; Tracey & Pecora, 1988; see Table 13.4).

Workers are more likely to apply what they have learned in training when supervisors demonstrate support and reinforcement for applying the newly acquired information or skills (Clarke, 2002; Goldstein & Ford, 2002; Love, 2007). Supervisors can and should facilitate the transfer of training by

1. helping workers break down complex skills into smaller components that can be made more relevant to the job and that can be practiced over time;

2. using a goal-setting intervention in which workers identify what and how they will apply and maintain new knowledge and skills gained in training;

3. asking workers to share what they learned in staff meetings;

4. incorporating application of the new learning into job performance evaluations;

5. providing reinforcement for the new behaviors;

6. creating an environment for sharing new learning across the work group by facilitating peer consultation; and

7. following up to ensure long-term maintenance of the new behaviors.

Overall, it is imperative for supervisors to make certain that workers have immediate opportunities to apply new learning and that there are measurable improvements in performance (Garrett & Barretta-Herman, 1995; Gist, Bavetta, & Stevens, 1990; Gregoire et al., 1998; Kreuger, Austin, & Hopkins, 2004; Lombardo & Eichinger, 2000; Love, 2007).

Development. Both workers and volunteers should be encouraged to be more responsible for their work, to be team builders, to be more innovative, and to help the agency continually improve its services and effectiveness (Hopkins, 2002b). The Gallup Organization's research on employee engagement with 3 million U.S. workers across employment fields shows that 71% of the workforce is not engaged, and it is engaged employees who significantly contribute to an organization's successful performance (Echols, 2005). Similarly, a recent Harris Interactive poll found that 3 out of 5 workers (59%) believe that their organization does not "tap into" their talents or potential, sparking Stephen Covey's (2007) development of the "8th habit of leadership—helping others to find their own voice" (p. 72).

It is the supervisor's responsibility to create an inclusive environment that values the contribution of all staff and volunteers and encourages them to take part in problem solving, and to create systems of reward, both financial and nonfinancial, that acknowledge competence and enhance retention (Krueger et al., 2004). Developing the knowledge and skills of staff and volunteers goes hand in hand with retaining them. Many organizations are now expanding their employees' and volunteers' opportunities for professional development and continuous learning for the purposes of improving quality of work life and managing transitions as staff move through agency careers (Pynes, 2004). Supervisors with a strong learning orientation can start by collaborating with their own unit or team in systematically teaching and sharing knowledge, successes, and failures; setting goals; consulting with each other; and promoting learning opportunities. For example, using regular staff or team meetings as "collaboration centers" to encourage creative thinking or brainstorming, sharing, and peer consultation instead of for information sharing purposes only, or instituting "customer-focused cross functional and cross departmental teams" to assess service delivery situations, develop solutions, and engage in collaborative problem solving (Austin & Hopkins, 2004; Garvin, 2000; Gregoire, 1994; Wisniewski & McMahon, 2005).

Supervisors also need to initiate an employee development plan with each supervisee that specifies knowledge needed or desired, competencies, skills, and career goals (see Table 13.5). Using an empowering approach, the worker identifies improvements or enhancements he or she wishes to make in his or her performance, and in collaboration with the supervisor, develops a specific written action plan with goals and objectives and a timeline for follow-up and review. The plan should focus on employee growth and career development within the organization, and it should include measurable objectives (Pynes, 2004). Specifying career goals and strategies within the current job not only serves to improve performance and guide future actions, but it also can enhance an employee's reputation/image and help with securing a mentor (Callanan & Greenhaus, 1994). Volunteers (and, subsequently, the organization) can also benefit from a development plan, using the same empowering approach that supervisors initiate with paid staff.

Development plans are only meaningful when they demonstrate the organization's "credible" commitment to the employee's development. Development plans achieve credible commitment when supervisors (and managers) expend the effort to tailor the plan to individual employee needs and desires and provide the resources and development opportunities to help achieve the employee's goals. In short, the plan has to be customized, achievable, have an impact on career goals, and the supervisor has to be committed to the plan (Corporate Leadership Council, 2005).

Besides participating in and being committed to employee development plans, supervisors facilitate career development through effective delegation. Delegation gives employees the opportunity to

1. demonstrate ability;

2. experience success;

3. be visible within the organization;

4. develop competence and confidence; and

5. experience variety and new challenges. (Bulin, 1995)

The effective use of delegation keeps workers from "getting in a rut" and allows them to try out new and different tasks while still consulting with the supervisor, at the same time sharing total responsibility for the outcome.

There are a variety of other activities and programs that are designed to develop or maintain the skills and attitudes necessary for staff and volunteers to perform effectively:

- Types of programs: orientations, staff meetings, conferences, brown-bag lunch discussions, sharing information from conferences, journal club
- Use of development alternatives: job rotation, shadowing with more experienced employee, group supervision, contracted consultation, peer teaching

Table 13.5   Components of an Employee Development Plan

1. Employee identifies career goals
2. Employee chooses one or more changes or enhancements to make in his or her performance at regular intervals

3. Supervisor and employee collaboratively develop plan that specifies
  a. knowledge needed or desired,
  b. competencies and skills,
  c. learning goals and objectives,
  d. action steps,
  e. evaluation of outcomes.

SOURCE: Adapted from Nielson (1993).

- Joint programs between agencies and local colleges to upgrade skills and work toward advancement in several career paths
- Design and implementation of programs for keeping staff and volunteers abreast of agency policies and service technologies
- Individual career counseling for developing career plans
- Managerial, executive, and leadership development programs
- Managerial accountability for employee development and providing feedback and coaching activities
- Promotion of internship opportunities in other departments or programs within the organizations to help employees advance
- Competency-based career progression: employees develop the abilities to perform in more demanding roles, either in multiple areas or in a single function
- Redeployment of employees who are retrained for open jobs

Supervisor Support for Worker Performance and Development

Supervisors who believe that "support" is a necessary component of their work behavior are more apt to engage in various developmental interactions with workers and volunteers than supervisors who believe their behavior should be purely task centered (Hopkins, 2002a). Social exchange theory has often been applied in organizational and management research to explain supportive behaviors by managers toward workers and volunteers. Social exchange theory proposes that "gestures of good will" are exchanged between subordinates and their superiors when particular actions warrant reciprocity (Blau, 1964; Levinson, 1964). For example, coaching and providing workers and volunteers with opportunities for professional development are viewed as important types of social exchange. When supervisors provide opportunities for workers/volunteers to grow and develop their skills,

workers/volunteers perceive that the organization has invested in them and is supportive of their growth. Therefore, they reciprocate with citizenship behaviors—extra-role activities not formally required by the job—that benefit both the organization and consumers (Hopkins, 2002b; Wayne, Shore, & Liden, 1997).

Supervisor support is one of the most important factors in enhancing exchange relationships with workers/volunteers. In fact, the relationship between an employee or volunteer and the immediate supervisor is perceived as the most important relationship the worker has in the organization (Cohen-Callow & Hopkins, 2005; Galinsky, 1988; Kaiser, 2004; Lambert & Hopkins, 1995; Ray & Miller, 1994; Repetti, 1987; Settoon, Bennett, & Liden, 1996). Because supervisors are in positions of leadership, workers/volunteers often come to them for advice, guidance, and help with their work problems as well as personal problems. Supervisors need to be responsive to workers/volunteers and be able to provide both emotional support and work supports that mitigate stress, enhance performance, and facilitate work-life integration. Supervisors are conduits of information, and they play an important gatekeeping role in workers/volunteers' knowledge and use of resources in the organization. Many workers learn about training, developmental, and helping resources in the organization through their supervisor, and supervisors are usually the people who help workers access these resources (Allen, 2000; Cohen-Callow & Hopkins, 2005; Hopkins, 1997; Lambert & Hopkins, 1995; Moen, Harris-Abbott, Lee, & Roehling, 2000).

Supervisors tend to develop different exchange relationships with workers/volunteers depending on the level of mutual trust, respect, loyalty, and support cultivated and experienced (Wayne & Green, 1993). As employee demographics change and more employees/volunteers bring different backgrounds, experiences, and lifestyles into the workplace, organizations are forced to develop a more inclusive and responsive culture in order to both attract and retain diverse, qualified workers and volunteers

(Hopkins, 2005). For supervisors, a major challenge lies in understanding how personal characteristics, especially gender and race, influence supervisors' supportive and developmental interactions with workers.

Greenhaus and Parasuraman's (1993; Greenhaus, Parasuraman, & Wormley, 1990) research on the role of gender and race in supervisors' assessment of job performance suggests that supervisors feel personally distant from employees who differ from them in gender and race. In general, the research supports that workers' gender and race combines with their supervisor's gender and race to shape workers' perceptions and experiences of supervisor support. One cannot assume that women workers' experiences differ from men's, or that minority workers' experiences differ from Caucasians, without also taking into account how those experiences, perceptions, and reactions may be altered depending on the gender or race of the supervisor (Gerstein, 1990; Greenhaus & Parasuraman, 1993; Hopkins, 2002a).

People, in general, tend to seek supportive and developmental relationships at work with members of their own race and gender (Thomas, 1996). Historically, in the United States, Caucasian males have held the majority of management and supervisory positions in the workplace. Therefore, it is not surprising that many women workers have not experienced a supportive or professionally developmental relationship with their supervisors. For example, women, more than men, perceive that their supervisors provide less support, are less trustworthy than other sources of support, communicate less frequently, and engage in lower quality discussions (Callan, 1993; Hopkins, 2002a, 2005). African American women report feeling significantly more isolated and alienated from their supervisors than other workers (Hopkins, 2002a). Thus, it is imperative for supervisors, especially Caucasian male supervisors, to learn to supportively interact with and develop employees (and volunteers) whose gender and race differs from their own.

Finally, it is important to note that the amount of support, training, and development that supervisors receive from upper management is likely to influence what happens at the supervisor-worker level. It is ultimately upper management's responsibility to create a supportive "learning and performing" environment that includes clear expectations, performance feedback, and positive attitudes toward training and development. However, no matter what is occurring in the upper ranks of the organization, supervisors have a responsibility to proactively develop a learning and performing work environment and create a supportive climate that encourages sensitivity, understanding, and development, regardless of demographic or cultural differences.

References

Allen, T. (2000). Family-supportive work environments: The role of organizational perceptions. *Journal of Vocational Behavior, 58*(3), 414–435.

Austin, M., & Hopkins, K. (Eds.). (2004). *Supervision as collaboration in the human services: Building a learning culture.* Thousand Oaks, CA: Sage.

Bettencourt, L. A., Gwinner, K. P., & Meuter, M. L. (2001). A comparison of attitude, personality, and knowledge predictors of service-oriented organizational citizenship behaviors. *Journal of Applied Psychology, 86,* 29–41.

Blau, P. (1964). *Exchange and power in social life.* New York: Wiley.

Bulin, J. (1995). *Supervision: Skills for managing work and leading people.* Boston: Houghton Mifflin.

Callan, V. (1993). Subordinate-manager communication in different sex dyads: Consequences for job satisfaction. *Journal of Occupational and Organizational Psychology, 66,* 13–27.

Callanan, G., & Greenhaus, J. (1994). *Career management.* New York: Dryden Press.

Clarke, N. (2002). Job/work environment factors influencing training transfer within a human service agency: Some indicative support for Baldwin and Ford's transfer climate construct. *International Journal of Training & Development, 6*(3), 146–162.

Cohen-Callow, A. (1998). Making magic by maximizing the potential of older volunteers: The transferable skills approach utilized by RSVP in New York City. *The Journal of Volunteer Administration, 4,* 14–20.

Cohen-Callow, A. (2007). *Factors associated with sustaining older adult volunteer activities: The relationship between psychological climate and volunteers' organizational withdrawal behaviors.* Unpublished doctoral dissertation, University of Maryland, Baltimore.

Cohen-Callow, A., & Hopkins, K. (2005). *Unlocking social worker stress: The relationship between supervisor emotional support and stress on the job.* Paper presented at the Society for Research and Social Work Conference, Miami.

Corporate Leadership Council. (2005). *Managing for high performance and retention.* Washington, DC: Corporate Executive Board.

Covey, S. (2007). *The 8th habit: From effectiveness to greatness.* West Valley City, UT: FranklinCovey.

Culbert, S. (1996). *Mind-set management.* New York: Oxford University Press.

Curry, D. (1997). *Factors affecting the perceived transfer of learning of child protection social workers.* Unpublished doctoral dissertation, Kent State University, Akron.

Davis, M. H., Hall, J. A., & Meyer, M. (2003). The first year: Influences on the satisfaction, involvement, and persistence of new community volunteers. *Personality and Social Psychology Bulletin, 29,* 248–260.

Dickinson, J. (2005). *Differential prediction of volunteer outcomes: Refining our knowledge of social service participation.* Unpublished dissertation, Clemson University.

Echols, M. (2005). Engaging employees to impact performance. *Chief Learning Officer, 4*(2), 44–49.

Foxon, M. (1987). Transfer of training—A practical application. *Journal of Education and Training, 11*(3), 17–20.

Galinsky, E. (1988). *The impact of supervisors' attitudes and company culture on work/family adjustment.* Paper presented at the Annual Convention of the American Psychological Association, Washington, DC.

Garrett, K., & Barretta-Herman, A. (1995). Moving from supervision to professional development. *The Clinical Supervisor, 13*(2), 97–110.

Garvin, D. (1998). Building a learning organization. In Harvard Business Review (Ed.), *Knowledge management* (pp. 47–80). Boston: Harvard Business School Press.

Garvin, D. (2000). *Learning in action: A guide to putting the learning organization to work.* Boston: Harvard Business School Press

Gerstein, L. (1990). The bystander-equity model of supervisory helping behavior: Past and future research on the prevention of employee problems. In P. M. Roman (Ed.), *Alcohol problem intervention in the work place: Employee assistance programs and strategic alternatives* (pp. 203–225).Westport, CT: Quorum Books.

Gist, M., Bavetta, A., & Stevens, C. (1990). Transfer training method: Its influence on skill generalization, skill repetition, and performance level. *Personnel Psychology, 43*(3), 501–523.

Goldstein, I., & Ford, J. (2002). *Training in organizations: Needs assessment, development and evaluation.* Belmont, CA: Wadsworth.

Greenhaus, J., & Parasuraman, S. (1993). Job performance attributions and career advancement prospects: An examination of gender and race effects. *Organizational Behavior and Human Decision Processes, 55,* 273–297.

Greenhaus, J., Parasuraman, S., & Wormley, W. (1990). Effects of race on organizational experiences, job performance evaluations, and career outcomes. *Academy of Management Journal, 33,* 64–86.

Gregoire, T. (1994). Assessing the benefits and increasing the utility of addiction training for public child welfare workers. *Child Welfare, 73,* 69–81.

Gregoire, T., Propp, J., & Poertner, J. (1998). The supervisor's role in the transfer of training. *Administration in Social Work, 22,* 1–17.

Grote, D. (1995). *Discipline without punishment.* New York: AMACOM.

Hager, M., & Brudney, J. (2004). *Volunteer management: Practices and retention of volunteers.* Washington, DC: The Urban Institute.

Hopkins, K. (1997). Influences on formal and informal supervisor intervention with workers experiencing personal and family problems. *Employee Assistance Quarterly, 13*(1), 33–51.

Hopkins, K. (2002a). Interactions of gender and race in workers' help seeking for personal and family problems: Perceptions of supervisor support and intervention. *The Journal of Applied Behavioral Science, 38*(2), 156–176.

Hopkins, K. (2002b). Organizational citizenship in social service agencies. *Administration in Social Work, 26*(2), 1–15.

Hopkins, K. (2005). Supervisor support and work-life integration. In E. Kossek & S. Lambert (Eds.), *Work and life integration in organizations: New directions for theory and practice* (pp. 445–467). Mahwah, NJ: Lawrence Erlbaum Associates.

Hopkins, K., & Austin, M. (2004a). The changing nature of human services and supervision. In M. Austin & K. Hopkins (Eds.), *Supervision as collaboration in the human services: Building a learning culture* (pp. 3–10). Thousand Oaks, CA: Sage.

Hopkins, K., & Austin, M. (2004b). Coaching employees with performance problems. In M. Austin & K. Hopkins (Eds.), *Supervision as collaboration in the human services: Building a learning culture* (pp. 215–226). Thousand Oaks, CA: Sage.

Hopkins, K., Cohen-Callow, A., Salliey, A., Barnes, G., Golden, G. & Morton, C. (2007). *Maryland child welfare workforce recruitment, selection and retention study.* Final Report, University of Maryland, Baltimore.

Hopkins, K., Mudrick, N., & Rudolph, C. (1999). University-agency partnerships in child welfare: Impact on organizations, workers, and work activities. *Child Welfare, 78*(6), 749–773.

Kaiser, T. (2004). Supervisory relationships. In M. Austin & K. Hopkins (Eds.), *Supervision as collaboration in the human services: Building a learning culture* (pp. 21–34). Thousand Oaks, CA: Sage.

Kreuger, M., Austin, M., & Hopkins, K. (2004). Creating a supportive culture for developing staff. In M. Austin & K. Hopkins (Eds.), *Supervision as collaboration in the human services: Building a learning culture* (pp. 176–186). Thousand Oaks, CA: Sage.

Lambert, S., & Hopkins, K. (1995). Occupational conditions and workers' sense of community: Variations by gender and race. *American Journal of Community Psychology, 23*(2), 151–179.

Levinson, H. (1964). *Emotional health in the world of work.* New York: Harper & Row.

Lombardo, M., & Eichinger, R. (2000). *For your improvement: A development and coaching guide.* Minneapolis, MN: Lominger.

Love, P. (2007). *Examining the effects of a goal setting intervention on transfer of training by Department of Social Services.* Unpublished doctoral dissertation, University of Maryland, Baltimore.

Moen, P., Harris-Abbott, D., Lee, S., & Roehling, P. (2000). Promoting workforce effectiveness and life quality: Early evidence from the Cornell Couples and Careers Study. In E. Applebaum (Ed.), *Balancing acts: Easing the burden and improving the options for working families* (pp. 61–84). Washington, DC: Economic Policy Institute.

Nielsen, D. (1993). *Partnering with employees.* San Francisco: Jossey-Bass.

Noe, R. A., & Schmitt, N. (1986). The influence of trainee attitudes on training effectiveness. *Academy of Management Review, 39,* 497–525.

Olson, H. (2000). *The 8 keys to becoming wildly successful and happy.* Owings Mills, MD: Maximum Potential.

Pynes, J. (2004). *Human resources management for public and nonprofit organizations.* San Francisco: Jossey-Bass.

Ray, E., & Miller, K. (1994). Social support, home/work stress, and burnout: Who can help? *Journal of Applied Behavioral Science, 30,* 357–373.

Repetti, R. (1987). Individual and common components of the social environment at work and psychological well-being. *Journal of Personality and Social Psychology, 52,* 710–720.

Settoon, R., Bennett, N., & Liden, R. (1996). Social exchange in organizations: Perceived organizational support, leader-member exchange, and employee reciprocity. *Journal of Applied Psychology, 81,* 219–227.

Thomas, R., Jr. (1996). *Redefining diversity.* New York: Amacom.

Tracey, E. M., & Pecora, P. J. (1988). Evaluating adult services training: Application of participant action plan approach. *Arete, 13*(2), 1–10.

United States Postal Service Foundation. (1998). *Managing volunteers.* A Report from United Parcel Service.

Wayne, S., & Green, S. (1993). The effects of leader-member exchange on employee citizenship and impression management behavior. *Human Relations, 46,* 1431–1440.

Wayne, S., Shore, L., & Liden, R. (1997, February). Perceived organizational support and leader-member exchange: A social exchange perspective. *Academy of Management Journal,* 82–111.

Wisniewski, B., & McMahon, K. (2005). Formalizing informal learning. *Chief Learning Officer, 4*(4), 29–33.

CHAPTER 14

Managing for Diversity and Empowerment in Human Services Agencies

Alfreda P. Iglehart

This chapter addresses managing for diversity and empowerment from two perspectives: the internal dynamics of the agency and the agency-community interface. Turner and Shera (2005) describe empowerment strategies that are intraorganizational as well as extraorganizational in nature, a duality that frames human services agencies. While this type of duality may exist with any organization, human services agencies have a unique dependency on environments that affect their internal functions and performance outcomes (see Chapter 20 for a discussion of environmental impacts).

This chapter will define diversity and empowerment management, emphasize its necessity, provide a theoretical foundation for understanding agency-based diversity and empowerment management, identify those barriers that impede the development of this type of management, and recommend a framework for promoting agency-based diversity and empowerment practice.

Understanding Diversity and Empowerment Management

Diversity and empowerment are concepts that are different and have different underlying assumptions. Diversity, as a broad term, generally refers to categories of people described by their race/ethnicity, physical disability, age, social class, religious identification, or sexual orientation. Unprecedented population shifts, combined with the visibility of and advocacy from many of these groups, appear to be contributing to a greater awareness of diversity among human services professionals (Dhooper & Moore, 2001; Fong, 2004). Much of this awareness has focused on the need for practitioners who are skilled in diversity practice with clients and the methods of educating these needed workers (Bankhead & Erlich, 2005; Lowery, 2002; Swank, Asada, & Lott, 2001; Williams, 2005). Effective agency intervention with diverse individuals and communities has been termed multicultural practice, diversity practice, ethnic-sensitive practice, and multicultural competency, among other designations.

Garcia (1995) captures the elements of this practice in a definition of multicultural diversity competence that includes the ability to respect, understand, communicate, and collaborate with individuals of diverse cultures. Management for diversity and empowerment within the agency and at the agency-community interface level suggests that the agency's practice with diverse communities also includes these elements of respect, understanding, communication, and collaboration. Emphasis on diversity practice at the management and administrative levels, however, has not been as prominent as the emphasis on diversity practice at the worker-client level. Furthermore, diversity training itself typically ignores the need for major changes in agency climate and structures (Brown, 1997).

The meaning of the term *diversity* varies according to the descriptors or nouns used with it. For example, *diversity practice,* as previously mentioned, tends to capture practice with a diverse clientele. *Cultural diversity* refers to the valuation of cultural differences, and *managing for diversity* signifies a competence (Choudhury, 1996). Managing for diversity encompasses those skills and techniques that are required for the effective and successful handling, directing, supervising, and administering of a diverse workforce.

Managing for diversity does not necessarily entail managing for empowerment, as the two are not synonymous. Empowerment is another widely used term in the human services professions, with numerous meanings as reflected in the numerous definitions of this term (Bartle, Couchonnal, Canda, & Staker, 2002; Boehm & Staples, 2002; Chadiha, Adams, Biegel, Auslander, & Gutierrez, 2004; Everett, Homstead, & Drisko, 2007; Hardina, 2005; Turner & Shera, 2005; Yip, 2004). Many of these definitions stress the process by which workers help clients, client groups, and communities increase their voice, input, self-direction, self-efficacy, capacity, strengths, resources, power, and control over their situations in order to erase or, at least, minimize their powerlessness.

Table 14.1 provides an overview of the different levels of empowerment that have been identified in the literature. Even though the levels move beyond the individual, individual empowerment is more prominent in the social work literature (Bartle et al., 2002; Boehm & Staples, 2002). It may be difficult, or near impossible, for disempowered workers to facilitate and support client empowerment (Hardina, 2005; Turner & Shera, 2005). Thus, worker empowerment may be a necessary ingredient for promoting client empowerment. Empowered workers can be more effective service providers, more powerful advocates, and more committed professionals. In this regard, the levels of empowerment may be interrelated and support each other.

In order to achieve empowerment practice at the agency level, management techniques are needed that minimize marginality, maximize integration, promote an equitable system of rewards, and foster skill development. In addition, the same or similar techniques are also needed to develop an effective agency-community relationship (Iglehart & Becerra, 1995). Examples of empowerment practice can be found at the public agency and the private, nonprofit agency levels. The Los Angeles County Department of Children and Family Services, for example, has stimulated the implementation of empowerment practice in its model of family preservation service delivery, which provides contracts for community agencies to collaborate for the formation of family preservation networks that serve diverse communities. These networks, composed of a lead agency and several satellite agencies, are required to provide culturally sensitive services, utilize culturally sensitive staff, create community advisory boards, and hold regular staff meetings to discuss issues affecting the service delivery process. While the participating agencies are committed to serving

Table 14.1   Levels of Empowerment

Level or Type	Description
Individual or personal empowerment, also referred to as psychological empowerment	This is the most frequently described type of empowerment. It encompasses self-determination, self-direction, self-efficacy, mastery, and individual competence. Service providers use their skills in a process that is aimed at decreasing the client's sense of powerlessness by promoting problem-solving and self-help behaviors (Everett et al., 2007; Lee, 2001). Yip (2004, p. 480) puts it more succinctly: "At the individual level, empowerment seeks to help clients make changes." From the psychological perspective, this empowerment is the sense or feeling of control (Everett et al., 2007).
Worker or staff empowerment	Empowered workers have a voice in agency decision making (Hardina, 2005). A Worker Empowerment Scale reviewed by Turner and Shera (2005, p. 81) included items on self-efficacy in work performance, degree to which workers felt valued by their organization, perception of control over resources, and perceptions of authority. A literature review by these authors highlighted gaps in the conceptualization of this type of empowerment.
Interpersonal empowerment	Through interpersonal empowerment, clients are able to use supportive networks to reduce their powerlessness (Yip, 2004, p. 480). Group connection and collective action are ways that clients can empower themselves because primary groups are instrumental forces in combating oppression (Lee, 2001).
Organizational empowerment	This empowerment can be found in the efforts, methods, and strategies used in organizations to reduce disempowering conditions (Turner & Shera, 2005). Empowered organizations support staff access to power (Fullam et al., 1998) and move "decision making down to the lowest level where a competent decision can be made" (Kreitner & Kinicki, 1998, as quoted in Fullam et al., 1998, p. 254).
Professional empowerment	This empowerment is not covered broadly in the literature (Yip, 2004). It highlights those professional traits that are necessary for workers to feel value toward their work and to practice their profession to the fullest extent (Fullam et al., 1998).
Community empowerment	At the community level, empowerment is the process by which community residents gain power and control over the conditions that affect their community existence (Fawcett, Paine-Andrews, Francisco, & Schultz, 1995).
Social or political empowerment	Social or political empowerment involves empowered individuals or groups engaging in actions that affect political processes and outcomes (Lee, 2001; Everett et al., 2007). Collective action seems to be a potential outcome of community empowerment.

diverse communities, the lucrative contract with this county agency also served as an incentive for the development of this empowerment practice. To a certain extent, agencies have had to alter their management techniques and the manner in which they relate to the communities they serve. Without the incentives, it is not clear that these empowering community-related activities would have taken place, because purchase of service contracts often provides the resources needed for the creation of new programs and services (Gibelman, 2003).

At the private, nonprofit level, the Women in Community (WIC) program emerged from a partnership between the Coro Southern California Leadership Center and the Women's Foundation of California. The program recruited women from underserved immigrant communities to build on their leadership strengths so they could mobilize, advocate, and promote positive community change. In this illustration, the catalyst for the program was its creator, who envisioned empowerment as the imparting of skills and information to indigenous leaders in the community. The collaboration between program staff and community residents was predicated on the view that the community had strengths and assets that could be mined for community change. Both examples indicate that diversity and empowerment management can coexist when the necessary conditions are met.

Why Manage for Diversity and Empowerment?

Diversity management and empowerment management are both processes and outcomes. As a *process,* diversity management involves those skills, strategies, and techniques that are used to ensure that all workers are managed in a fair and equitable manner. Access to information, resources, and rewards is not governed by capriciousness or opaque discretion. Administrative decisions are fairly transparent, and the lines of communication remain open. As an *outcome,*

effective diversity management can yield stable workers who are committed to the agency. For example, Schmid (2002), in reviewing the literature on organizational properties and organizational effectiveness, found a positive correlation between workers' perceptions of equitable reward allocation and trust in management, reduced turnover, quality of services, and organizational effectiveness. Because workers need to feel organizational acceptance, belonging, and commitment (Fullam, Lando, Johansen, Reyes, & Szaloczy, 1998), administrative actions that foster these feelings should be emphasized.

Organizational cultural/diversity competence is denoted by the racial/ethnic composition of its staff, agency mission statements that emphasize diversity, staff training in diversity, and an agency climate that is accepting of diverse staff and clients (Uttal, 2006). Through effective management strategies, administrators can reduce the stress and tension that often accompany the introduction of new, diverse members into the organization. Human resource consultants in the private sector are extolling the benefits of attracting and retaining qualified employees because this human capital represents a significant organizational investment (Gardenswartz & Rowe, 1998; Herman, 1998). With sound management practices, all employees can feel valued and respected and experience a promotional system that is fair and open. The organization suffers when workers feel excluded, disregarded, or shut out; time is spent on conflicts and misunderstandings; and communication breakdown occurs because of cultural conflicts (Charlton & Huey, 1992; Gardenswartz & Rowe, 1998). Furthermore, Mor Barak and Cherin (1998, p. 61) note that there is a growing body of evidence to support the connection between employees' perception of being accepted by the organization, their job satisfaction, and their organizational commitment. Organizations, therefore, should work to create a civic culture that emphasizes the relational values of equality and respect for differences (Chen & Eastman, 1997). Agency management can facilitate the development of such a culture.

As a *process*, empowerment management involves those skills, strategies, and techniques that are used to foster the value of the workers and their voices in agency matters. As an *outcome*, effective empowerment management can produce workers who are creative and innovative advocates for agency development. Empowered workers have the potential to provide effective services, overcome service delivery challenges, be flexible in responding to client needs, and maximize agency resources. Empowered workers are vital advocates for service and policy improvements (Hardina, 2005).

Synthesizing Diversity and Empowerment Management

A synthesis of diversity management and empowerment management will integrate the skills and strategies of both to produce stable, committed workers who provide valued input in determining agency goals and direction. Furthermore, with this synthesis, diverse staff members feel fairly treated and rewarded so that they are motivated to be risk-takers and advocates for program innovation. The value of effectively managing for diversity and empowerment cannot be overstated. According to Pine, Walsh, and Maluccio (1998, p. 21), racial and ethnic demographic shifts in both staff and client pools are amplifying the need to value diversity and to use this diversity as a means of improving service delivery and the workplace climate. These shifts are reflective of the major changes occurring in the United States. For example, in a press release, the United States Bureau of the Census (2007) noted that the ethnic minority population in the United States has surpassed 100 million. This minority population includes Hispanics (44.3 million), African Americans (40.2 million), Asians (14.9 million), American Indian and Alaska Natives (4.5 million), and native Hawaiian and other Pacific Islanders (1 million). Non-Hispanic whites make up 199 million of the population. Agency workers will be drawn from a labor pool

that is becoming more diverse in race/ethnicity, and the demand for services will come increasingly from clients and communities that are also becoming more diverse.

According to Gardenswartz and Rowe (1998), who are diversity trainers/consultants to businesses, bringing diverse workers together is a means of expanding organizational creativity. They further maintain that, in an environment marked by continuous change, the organization's resiliency, adaptability, viability, and flexibility are increased through workforce diversity. The organization's overall effectiveness and survivability are expected to increase when management practices support the integration of diverse workers into the organization. These outcomes, however, can only be achieved when this workforce feels empowered enough to express and implement creative ideas. Effective management for diversity and empowerment also leads to stronger agency-community interactions and interface. The community experiences the agency through its workers. Human services interventions aimed at developing community partnerships will not work if staff members are not empowered as professionals (Pine et al., 1998, p. 20). Adams and Nelson (1997, p. 74) also note that partnerships and collaborations mean empowering workers to, in turn, empower families and communities. The same kinds of techniques that support worker empowerment may be used to support community empowerment through the agency's community practice.

Theoretical Framework

Systems theory is used here to illuminate the agency's internal dynamics and the agency-community interface. Hardina, Middleton, Montana, and Simpson (2007) offer a discussion of the relevance of systems theory to organizational analysis. Bertalanffy (1974, p. 1100), one of the architects of this framework, asserted that a system is defined as a complex of components in mutual interaction. In an open system, energy is imported from the environment (inputs), transformed to create a technology, and then exported back into the environment (output). Significant features of an open system are interrelatedness of subsystems; boundary maintenance; system equilibrium; system functions (socialization, social control, communication, feedback); system adaptation and maintenance for survival; and the relationship between the system and its environment (Katz & Kahn, 1978; Netting, Kettner, & McMurtry, 2008). Schmid (Chapter 20 in this volume) provides a detailed discussion of organization adaptation theories and the strategies used by organizations in the adaptation process.

As an open system, the agency imports inputs from its environment that are needed for the agency to survive and conduct its daily business. These inputs vary from the tangible (staff, funding) to the intangible (values, beliefs, ideologies). The environment plays a pivotal role in the life of an agency, for it not only provides critical inputs but it also confers a legitimacy the agency needs for its existence. The particular manner in which an agency is structured and organized may also be imported from its environment. Consequently, trends in management practices and the identification of "appropriate" management techniques are also imported from and influenced by the environment.

While an agency is a system unto itself, it is also a system interacting with other systems as well as a subsystem of larger systems. As a bounded, distinct system, the agency interfaces with community systems as it engages in community practice. In addition, the agency and the community are both subsystems of a larger societal system. Many agencies have penetrated a community's boundaries to become part of that community's environment (Ringer & Lawless, 1989, p. 10). Hence, the systems framework permits the examination of agency management practices that address internal agency operations and those that address the agency in relation to other systems, such as communities.

Barriers to Diversity and Empowerment Management

While agencies are confronted with staff diversity issues and the need to respond to diverse communities, responses to these challenges are as varied as the agencies themselves. Some agencies appear to adapt to change with creativity, flexibility, and added growth. Others seem mired in a type of inertia that inhibits change and innovation. Factors that inhibit diversity and management for empowerment are worthy of discussion and seem to grow out of three contexts: societal, professional, and organizational. Understanding these barriers is essential to understanding an empowerment model of administration.

Barriers From Society

Because organizations are subsystems of the larger social system, they import societal values, beliefs, ideologies, and politics that are manifested in the attitudes and behaviors of the staff they recruit and the structures they create. Tensions, stress, and inequality between groups in the larger society (the agency's general environment) may be mirrored in the agency (see Chapter 20). In addition, the dependence of professions on the larger society for legitimacy compels professions and their organizations to accept and embrace problem definitions and problem interventions that amplify prevailing dominant social perspectives.

Current political issues and debates also penetrate the walls of the agency. Each decade, or even each year, may produce its own identifiable outgroups whose legitimacy and credibility are challenged. For example, public debates around undocumented immigrants and same-sex marriage may influence public attitudes about whether immigrants and the population of lesbian/gay/bisexual/transgendered individuals deserve services funded with public tax dollars. The resulting "War on Terrorism" and the Iraqi war in the aftermath of 9/11 may have inadvertently transformed Americans of Middle Eastern descent into another outgroup in the minds of many Americans. The political climate, therefore, may constrain and challenge an agency's ability to work with individuals and groups that do not share widespread public support. These examples capture the power of the agency's task environment in influencing agency legitimacy and controlling agency resources (see Chapter 20).

In the prevailing social context, the ideology of individual merit and the inability to resolve social conflict based on diversity may dictate that diversity issues can never be resolved by organizations (Donnellen & Kolb, 1994). With an ideology of individual merit that stresses performance as the sole basis for success, administrators may not believe that modifications in management strategies are necessary for a changing and more diverse workforce. Belief in individual merit mutes any consideration of social bias as a contributing factor to the ultimate fate of workers in the agency. In addition, managers may be reluctant to even consider the possibility that any type of social favoritism influenced their own ascendance to power. Furthermore, some managers may believe that conflict is inevitable because issues of race and ethnicity extend far beyond the agency's walls. Social service agencies influenced by these belief systems may merely perpetuate many of the tensions and conflict that plague society in general.

As society generates policy and other legislative responses to the changing social and political climate, these policies find expression in agency procedures and practices. Societal ambiguity surrounding the intent, goals, implementation, and enforcement of these policies often finds expression in social agencies. For example, how agencies interpret policies such as affirmative action and nondiscrimination clauses in contracts is often indicative of societal-level ambivalence about the structural and institutional causes and consequences of discrimination. The variations in agencies' responses to these policies capture much of this ambivalence.

Barriers in the Profession

Many agencies also appear uncertain about methods and approaches for implementing an empowerment perspective, while others appear to conduct business as usual despite a strong verbal adherence to an empowerment model. While this ambivalence may have been influenced by a conservative sociopolitical environment, the dominance of casework, direct practice, or micro social work over indirect practice or macro social work may have further constrained the evolution of empowerment practice and diversity competence in service delivery.

Confusion about which methods and approaches are most suitable for diversity and empowerment management may be attributed to the particular dimensions of empowerment upon which the profession has focused. Social work, as a profession, has advocated for individual or psychological empowerment rather than empowerment at the organizational and community levels. As noted in Table 14.1, and according to Zimmerman (1995, p. 581), organizational empowerment includes processes and structures that enhance members' skills and provide them with the mutual support necessary to effect community-level change. Community empowerment entails individuals, organizations, and linkages among organizations working together to improve the community (Zimmerman, 1995). Thus, a primary focus on psychological empowerment appears to minimize the need for empowerment at other system levels.

As noted in Table 14.1, psychological empowerment focuses on the beliefs, values, and attitudes of the clients—a familiar domain of the profession. Historically, the helping professions have stressed the social diagnosis of the individual and, in general, developed an ideology that supported a psychological orientation to social problems while ignoring institutional solutions. Institutional theory helps to explain how this conservative ideology may have been adopted. This framework proposes that the structure of certain classes of organizations, such as human services, is determined not by technology but by rules emanating from the institutional environment (Hasenfeld, 1992, p. 34; also see Chapter 3). In order to gain the legitimacy and acceptance that are conferred by the larger society, human services agencies and the professions that staff them may have had to endorse a psychological approach to social problem solving (see, e.g., Axinn & Levin, 1982; Gil, 1990; Jansson, 1997; Leiby, 1978; Martin, 1990; Schilling, Schinke, & Weatherly, 1988). This psychological approach may have been endorsed by prevailing public opinion, stakeholders, constituencies, and other groups with the power to shape the development of the profession.

The external or concrete dimension of empowerment, which includes providing tangible knowledge, information, competencies, skills, and especially the resources that enable one to take action (Parsons, 1998, p. 30), may receive less attention and support in social service agencies. This external dimension captures a more macro approach to practice. This type of empowerment practice seems most consistent with the needs and demands of diverse groups and communities that require information, skills, education, and resources in order to improve their quality of life. Psychological or personal empowerment alone may be insufficient to bring about the kinds of changes desired by disempowered groups.

Because of the primacy of micro practice, discussions about multicultural competence and empowerment practice often fail to address models of administrative practice that support multicultural competence. Practitioners who seek to develop skills in promoting intrapersonal empowerment among their clients have available to them a range of literature that describes models of empowerment practice and methods of implementing them. On the other hand, those practitioners who seek to facilitate organizational and community empowerment have a more limited array of literature and research to guide them. This imbalance may suggest to some professionals that one type of empowerment has priority over

another. Clearly, limitations observed in the field in the implementation of empowerment management techniques may be attributable to the lack of a sound knowledge and research base to guide the development of these managerial practices.

Barriers in the Agency

Agency-related barriers to effective management for diversity and empowerment include agency history, age, mission, degree of bureaucratization, public versus private nonprofit status, resource level, leadership, the workers themselves, and culture. Table 14.2 summarizes the manner in which these factors pose a challenge to diversity and empowerment management.

This overview of theoretical perspectives and barriers to diversity and empowerment practice can now be used to propose a process for managing and empowering a diverse workforce and for practice with diverse communities.

A Framework for Agency-Based Diversity and Empowerment Practice

The exploratory framework suggested here is a means of integrating empowerment and diversity practice in the agency and with the community. The values inherent in empowerment and diversity practice are operationalized through a process that facilitates both worker and community empowerment. With this conceptualization, empowerment practice and diversity practice have unifying elements that link all levels of macro practice. Implicit in this framework is the assumption that diversity and empowerment practice in the agency is a necessary precondition for diversity practice and empowerment practice with communities.

This framework uses the agency administrator as the change agent because she or he has the power of authority and control over resources. Clearly, agency change does not have to be top

Table 14.2   Factors in Diversity and Empowerment Management

Factor	Potential Effects
Agency's history	History may reveal a pattern of alienation from particular groups and communities that has perpetuated a negative agency reputation. History and tradition have dictated which individuals have been hired for specific positions in the agency (Bond & Pyle, 1998). In addition, the agency's tradition may entail particular organizational structures and processes that may inhibit worker empowerment.
Agency's age	Over time, organizations appear likely to experience inertia (Barnett & Carroll, 1995), with routines, structure, and technology so well-established that they defy change.
Agency's mission	Mission statements refer to the agency's purpose, why it exists, and what it seeks to accomplish (Gilbelman, 2003; Kirst-Ashman, 2008). Mission statements that disregard race, creed, and color as a basis for equitable treatment of staff and consumers and statements that espouse "one approach fits all" negate the need to explore alternative management models.
Agency's degree of bureaucratization	Bureaucratic routines have been associated with inertia and inflexibility (Feldman & Pentland, 2003). Bureaucratic characteristics that support routines (e.g., complexity, centralization, formalization, and specialization) may block organizational change, depending on the nature of the change under consideration (Barnett & Carroll, 1995; Brager & Holloway, 1978; Hasenfeld, 1983).
Public versus private nonprofit status	Public agencies are generally not lauded for their change ability. Change has long been held as the domain of agencies that could afford to be less responsive to political pressures and more experimental (Brager & Holloway, 1978, p. 43). Indeed, nonprofit agencies are generally viewed as more flexible, more innovative, and more responsive to client needs (Hardina et al., 2007).
Agency resource level	Agencies with slack (resources that exceed the minimum necessary to deliver outputs of programs and services) seem to be in a better position for innovation (Geiger & Cashen, 2002). Resource-rich agencies may have the luxury of mounting experimental or pilot efforts to test alternative management styles. With resource-poor agencies, the continuous quest for funds may place the need for more effective empowerment and diversity management low on the priority list.
Agency leadership	Leadership is vital to agency change (Armenakis et al., 1993; Donnellon & Kolb, 1994; Hardina et al., 2007; Hasenfeld, 1983; Kirst-Ashman, 2008; Mary, 2005). Here, the leaders are defined as those individuals who occupy top-level positions in organizations and will be referred to as administrators. Leaders who do not see value in diversity and empowerment management impede organizational development in this area. The presence of racial/ethnic minority leadership may, for some agencies, pose a unique challenge. For some agencies, the selection of a racial/ethnic minority administrator may be the

(Continued)

Table 14.2 (Continued)

Factor	Potential Effects
	extent of an agency's empowerment practice. In addition, some racial/ethnic minority administrators may be hesitant to launch dialogue on the subject for fear of being branded as biased in favor of their own group.
Agency staff	As Stanley, Meyer, and Topolnysky (2005) note, workers are often resistant to change. In addition, Donnellon and Kolb (1994) repeat the frequently cited statement that people with power act to retain that power. Indeed, staff members who perceive themselves as having higher status may act more assertively and may feel that they are entitled to the position and privileges that they enjoy (DiTomaso, Post, & Parks-Yancy, 2007). Change may be perceived as a threat to their power and, hence, workers may resist that change. In addition, Nicolini, Meznar, Stewart, and Manz (1995) note that workers have a general reluctance to move from old learning to new learning. Because of the sensitive nature of discussions of race/ethnicity and cultural diversity, workers may be even more likely to feel threatened and defensive.
Agency culture	Seren and Baykal (2007, p. 191) define organizational culture as the assumptions, values, norms, and customs of organizational members and further note that these interpersonal relationships affect members' work and agency operating outcomes. Agencies with cultures that do not support sensitivity toward and respect for diversity may be the most difficult to change because their members may not recognize their diversity issues or the need to address them.

down, and members in lower positions can form change systems and coalitions to engage in collective action (Donnellon & Kolb, 1994; Netting et al., 2008; Resnick, 1978). For this discussion, however, the focus is on the strategies and techniques that can be utilized by administrators.

The elements of the framework presented here will be applied first to the internal agency and then to the agency-community interface. Peterson and Zimmerman (2004) suggest a model of organizational empowerment that includes intraorganizational components as well as extraorganizational components. An intra- and extraorganizational focus shows the application of the systems perspective because the dynamics within the agency and the agency-community dynamics are highlighted. In the discussion of the internal agency, a case example will be presented to illustrate the application of the elements, and the same agency will be used throughout the discussion of the framework.

Table 14.3 outlines the key factors in the framework that will be discussed. While the focus of the agency change is increasing agency diversity, the steps and strategies utilized incorporate a worker empowerment framework. In this manner, management for diversity and management for empowerment converge. Through the empowerment of workers, diversity goals may be more readily embraced. After the element of agency leadership, the remaining elements reflect the steps in the problem-solving process that have been frequently mentioned in the literature (Brody, 1982; Kettner, Moroney, & Martin, 2007; Netting et al., 2008).

Leader Orientation

Because the administrator is expected to be a visionary for the agency and strive to move the agency closer to that vision, the administrator's specific orientation toward diversity and

Table 14.3   Elements of a Diversity and Empowerment Management Framework

Element	Description
Agency leadership	Leaders must possess the skills and traits that foster agency diversity and worker empowerment. The leader has a vision of the agency and seeks to bring that vision to fruition.
Information gathering	Any change process must include an assessment of current practices and issues. This information forms the knowledge base that is used to guide the direction of the change. Workers and other managers participate in this fact-gathering phase.
Formulation of a diversity intervention plan	The data and information gathered are used as the building blocks of a course of action. The plan must realistically address issues of resources, staff attitudes, and impact on the community. Workers and other managers participate in the formulation of the plan.
Implementation of the plan	The plan is put into action and monitored.
Evaluation	The effectiveness of the plan is assessed. Questions addressed include Were goals met? What were the problems?
Formalization of the plan	Policies are developed to make the plan a permanent feature of the agency. This institutionalization of the plan ensures its longevity.

empowerment is paramount. According to Fullam et al. (1998), leadership effectiveness is the extent to which the leader is able to lead the staff in achieving organizational goals. An agency's unique history and traditions establish the context for its diversity dynamics (Bond & Pyle, 1998, p. 604). Agency history has a similar impact on its empowerment dynamics. The visionary leader's orientation is informed by this history and the agency's mission so that the vision of the agency's future is realistic and feasible. If change that alters the fundamental structure, systems, orientation, and strategies of the organization is required, there must be recognition that this type of transformation is slow and tedious (for further discussion of leadership, see Chapter 7).

As was previously indicated, there must be a top-level commitment to diversity and empowerment that propels the administrator to take action. Orientation alone, however, is insufficient to begin the change process. The administrator's leadership ability and personal characteristics also shape his or her power. The empowering leader shares authority and relies on a team approach to problem solving (Shera & Page, 1995). A change agent's spheres of influence and dominance are also enhanced by such attributes of credibility, trustworthiness, sincerity, and expertise (Armenakis, Harris, & Mossholder, 1993). Indeed, Glisson's (1989) research on the effect of leadership on human services workers indicates that a leader's maturity, power, and intelligence can influence workers' level of organizational commitment. Leaders who are change agents should also inspire their workers and practice what they preach by demonstrating their own commitment to the vision and values they seek to promote (Kouzes & Posner, 2002, 2004). Leadership for diversity and empowerment seems to require the characteristics of a *transformational* leader. This type of leader is politically savvy, inspirational, a builder of an organizational community, a promoter of worker participation in forging agency vision, and is a sharer of organizational power (Hardina et al., 2007; Mary, 2005). The transformational leader is a key element of the organizational change process because his or her qualities and attributes are used as interventions in the agency change process. This type of leader envisions the agency as it can be and then works with staff to shape, plan, and implement that vision.

Because any attempt to change a system can be perceived as a threat to that system's equilibrium, agency resistance should be anticipated. Forces that propel the resistance and forces that counter the resistance should be identified and assessed. Administrators must be aware of the obstacles to be confronted and the strategies that can be effective in overcoming that resistance. The administrator's own risk-taking propensity has to also be assessed because resistance can often pose challenges that may test and/or weaken his or her commitment to diversity and empowerment. Administrators' efforts to reduce resistance should include utilizing a response style that neutralizes conflict rather than exacerbates it, continuously emphasizing a commitment to worker growth and development, and creating a nonpunitive agency climate that encourages the expression of ideas. These efforts should emanate from the administrator's own values and goals and should, therefore, carry with them a sincere and honest tone. In some extreme situations, resistance may be strong enough to defeat any change endeavors. For these situations, the change effort may need to focus on creating a climate that at least supports open discussion of change. This may be the first needed step in an incremental process that can conceivably take years to complete.

The Agency. Administrators have particular perspectives of the diversity and empowerment management issues in their agencies. For those with a vision of identifying management techniques that support and encourage diversity and worker participation, the orientation is to create, as much as possible, a stress-free climate in which cultural conflicts are acknowledged, appropriately addressed, and are in some process of resolution. This is also a climate in which workers learn to be at ease with each other and learn that their views and visions are valued. Cultural diversity and worker

empowerment are perceived as assets to the agency that enrich the agency for workers and service consumers. Because there may always be some type of tension around cultural diversity issues, administrators who value diversity and worker empowerment are concerned with creating a workplace or a system that can effectively address and resolve this tension in a constructive manner.

A first step in creating this type of agency environment may be the critical review of agency personnel policies and procedures; the employee grievance and appeal process; employee evaluation process; and agency recruiting, hiring, and promotion patterns. In this examination, the administrator is seeking to determine whether the agency is doing all it can to attract, retain, and promote workers from diverse groups. Such a task can be undertaken with the assistance of workers and other managers in the agency. The involvement of workers in this review communicates that workers' experiences and opinions are important and useful. Workers can share stories of situations they have observed or experienced. They may have crucial input that will clarify and inform. By beginning the process with an emphasis on openness and togetherness (e.g., "We are all in this together"), workers may have their first exposure to an empowerment model.

Several factors from Table 14.1 are operative with leader orientation. The agency may have a history and mission that target particular service delivery areas and/or populations. This history may include the hiring of certain personnel as a means of reaffirming the mission statement. The agency's age could suggest that its formal and informal organizational practices are so firmly entrenched that change can only take place incrementally and over a long period of time. The agency's culture may be closed to the hiring of individuals perceived to be "outsiders" so that resistance to increasing agency diversity may be almost impenetrable.

In this initial stage, the examination of policies and procedures for the purpose of assessing the agency's hiring and promoting practices may, in itself, increase tension in the agency. Workers may perceive these efforts as an indirect criticism

CASE STUDY

The newly appointed director of a family service agency in a community that was undergoing a demographic shift from primarily African American residents to both Hispanic and African American members was surprised to note that all the staff members were African American despite the increasing request for services from Hispanic residents. In reviewing agency recruitment and hiring practices, she further observed that policies specifically targeted the hiring of individuals who were knowledgeable about the African American community. The director's orientation supported service delivery to the entire community, and this orientation guided her in the review of agency policy.

aimed at them. To minimize staff fears and apprehensions, administrators may have to provide a clear explanation to staff of the nature and intent of the review. The extent (detailed or general) and form (verbal or written) of this explanation should be determined by the degree of formality administrators wish to achieve. Clear messages from the administrators are often needed to offset the speculation, gossip, and innuendo that are likely to arise in the agency.

The Agency-Community Interface. The administrator's orientation to diverse communities helps determine the agency's relationship with these communities. Again, the agency's history and mission with diverse groups can often be used to explain current relationships. To promote diversity and empowerment in the agency's relationship with communities, the administrator sees the worker as a crucial component. Thus, the orientation is to empower workers with the skills, knowledge, and resources necessary for empowerment practice at the community level. The administrator values and respects the diversity of the community and approaches this diversity as an asset.

A review of written materials on agency services and programs is undertaken to determine the extent to which they incorporate this value and respect for diversity. Workers and other managers can assist in this review. The goal here is to carefully examine program policies and procedures for an articulation of goals and objectives that support diversity. In particular, the

review can focus on identifying those goals and objectives that support worker, organizational, and community empowerment and diversity practice. Key areas to identify in the review include the improved/enhanced functioning of individual clients, the agency itself, and the community. While it may seem unusual for services and programs to target agency improvement, numerous programs do have the agency as the service beneficiary. Programs and services that involve activities such as staff training, program development, program evaluation, agency site visits from sponsors, community outreach, community feedback, and community participation provide valuable information about the agency's organizational and community practices.

Information

The policy and program review is preparatory to the gathering of information from primary sources. While the administrator has his or her opinion of what the agency looks like, how it operates, and what defines its culture, these opinions may be biased and only partially correct. In addition, from the position of administrator, the agency is seen from a top-down vantage point, and others in positions of lesser authority may certainly have a much different set of observations.

The Agency. The administrator has to identify those questions and issues to be addressed by workers. These issues and questions should emerge from the policy and program review and from her or his vision of the agency's future. These questions may address worker attitudes about the hiring of particular groups of people, service delivery to particular communities, ideologies about diversity, worker issues about diversity, agency directions in this area, and definitions of key elements of the agency's culture.

There are numerous methods for gathering information about the diversity needs of the agency from those within the agency. Surveys, self-administered questionnaires, and focus groups are examples. The administrator should also decide whether this information gathering is conducted by individuals within the agency or by outside consultants. Donnellon and Kolb (1994) assert that an organizational diagnosis conducted by insiders is in danger of being too narrow while attempting to avoid conclusions that could possibly stress the system. It may be in the agency's best interest to engage the services of an external consultant. If resources do not permit the hiring of an external consultant, another alternative is the use of a volunteer consultant.

This fact-finding mission does not have to be complex, protracted, or expensive. The administrator's goal is to obtain candid, open, honest feedback from staff members about the diversity issues she or he has identified, while at the same time allowing workers the opportunity to add, modify, and otherwise comment on diversity in the agency. Each method of information gathering has advantages and disadvantages. One-on-one interviews with staff members can provide invaluable information and the safety of confidentiality but may encourage socially desirable, political correct responses. Even so, this method communicates to the workers the administrator's interest in and commitment to this area. The confidential questionnaire has the advantage of protecting the identity of the respondent and may lead to more candid observations. An outside consultant may be able to stimulate candid discussions from workers that cannot be elicited by those in the agency.

Administrator observations should not be overlooked in this fact-finding phase. By walking around the agency, engaging in casual conversation with staff and clients, and observing what goes on in various parts of the agency, the administrator garners additional insight that may serve to further clarify and demystify some of the results obtained through other methods.

CASE STUDY

The director previously mentioned informally surveyed her staff for their opinions about adding Hispanic staff members and serving more Hispanic clients. While all workers said they were open to such changes, they were also quick to identify the reasons for not undertaking these changes at the present time (i.e., agency had limited resources, other agencies could do a better job of serving Hispanic families, there were so many more pressing priorities). From these informal conversations, the director became aware of those staff attitudes that impeded staff and service expansion to reach the Hispanic segment of the community.

The director appointed a task force of workers to also review agency staffing and hiring patterns. This task force was charged with obtaining worker feedback about agency personnel needs, client needs, community needs, and recommendations for meeting those needs. Through this task force, workers had a more formal avenue for communicating their positions. While attempting to increase staff diversity, the director was also empowering the workers to be involved in the change process.

The director also wanted to obtain information from the community. She used student interns from a local social work program to conduct community focus groups. Questions centered on community knowledge of and attitudes toward the agency. She also used the focus groups to discuss community needs, suggest best methods of disseminating information to the community, and identify indigenous leaders.

The Agency-Community Interface. Here, the administrator seeks to determine staff attitudes about the community and the community's attitudes about the agency. The administrator has to formulate those questions to be posed to staff members by the task force and those to be posed to community members in the focus groups.

Staff questions can include How do staff members define multicultural community practice? Is there really a need for this kind of practice? What types of skills are needed for this practice? What can the agency do to better support this practice? What kinds of staff members are needed for this practice? How should staff be evaluated in this area? Staff questions can be included in the agency fact-finding discussed above.

In the agency-community interface, several areas stand out as requiring information and feedback from the community. One area addresses the agency's image and reputation in the community. Another area is the community's definitions of its needs and priorities. Community questions can include What are community perceptions of the agency? What kind of reputation does the agency have in the community? When the agency's name is mentioned, what comes to mind? What are the community's pressing needs and priorities? What can the agency do to respond to these needs and priorities? Who are the leaders in the community? Where do residents typically go for assistance? What are the community's agency service utilization patterns? What are the barriers or obstacles to using the agency's services? Data-gathering methods include community surveys and questionnaires, surveys of present and former clients from the community, interviews with community individuals knowledgeable about the community (key informants), and use of focus groups. The review of secondary data about the community (e.g., community surveys conducted by other agencies) can also provide useful data about the community.

Any fact-finding mission should not be limited by the resources the agency has available. Clearly, the resource-rich agency may be in a better position to utilize paid consultants and more sophisticated methods; however, other agencies can benefit from the use of volunteer consultants and students who serve as social work interns. The administrator has to be creative in maximizing all the possibilities for data-gathering resources.

Formulation of an Intervention Plan

In the formulation of any intervention plan, workers and managers work to forge objectives that are clear, precise, and tied to the agency's bottom line. For some human services agencies, the bottom line may be values and agency mission. For others, it may be contract and funding mandates. All diversity objectives should have a clear relevance to what the agency and its members deem to be important. The process of debating and discussing objectives should serve as another means of fostering worker empowerment in the agency.

The resulting objectives should reflect consensus and compromise for the workers and for the director. In this situation, the director is not imposing a vision or plan on the staff and the staff is not merely rubber-stamping the director's ideas. All-staff meetings, smaller staff meetings, agency retreats, community panels, and speakers can be used to help move the agency to consensus. The consensus-building process may be lengthy, but it is needed for a plan that has the support of all the stakeholders. This process also is needed to promote worker empowerment. The agreed-upon objectives then become embodied in the interventions that are formulated.

The administrator must consider how the plan will affect the agency's relationship with its environment. Plans that are consonant with the values, ideologies, and technologies in the prevailing environment may have the endorsement of agency constituencies. Plans that are out of step with the stakeholders in the task environment, particularly those that control agency resources, may have to be reformulated or new sources of inputs may have to be tapped.

With the policy review and the information from staff and the community, the administrator is ready to embark on the formulation of strategies for promoting diversity and empowerment. While the content of the plan is crucial, the process of the plan's formulation is also of equal significance.

In the Agency. Worker participation in the formulation of a plan and in the decision making around its implementation is imperative for the plan's success. The participation of workers in the strategic planning activities can lead to insights about the issues facing the agency (Armenakis et al., 1993). This participation and involvement can further help the administrator understand the agency's culture (Zamanou & Glaser, 1994). According to Pine et al. (1998, p. 20), participatory management is a commitment to carrying out a set of strategies that involve workers in organizational decisions. This participation fosters collaboration between members of the agency that encourages all parties to cooperate in the plan's implementation. Participation leads to worker commitment and ownership of the proposed interventions.

For the administrator seeking to increase diversity in the agency, strategic plans could potentially emphasize the recruitment and hiring of workers from diverse groups through the placement of job advertisements in ethnic or community-based newspapers and on ethnic radio stations and the restructuring of the application and interview process to make it more user-friendly. In the absence of professionally qualified applicants who are members of diverse groups, the plan may consist of reviewing the role of the paraprofessional in the agency. While slots for paraprofessionals may be more likely to be filled by racial/ethnic minority group members or persons from other diverse groups, the administrator should be careful to avoid the creation of a two-tier staff system with the racial/ethnic group members occupying the lower tier.

For agencies with a diverse work force, strategic plans may target governance procedures and staff conflict issues. Agencies with diverse staff often utilize hidden approaches to intergroup conflict because of management discomfort in addressing this tension. These hidden approaches can include ignoring the problem (remaining silent in the face of conflict), using the confidential manager-employee conference, and writing letters of reprimand for employee files. The administrator may desire to move some issues (those that appear to be recurring or patterned) to a more open agenda through, for example, staff meeting discussions, the creation of a cross-cultural peer complaint board, the use of a diversity task force as part of a pre-formal complaint review, the appointment of an ombudsman, or the establishment of a multi-step complaint resolution process. With this approach, structures and processes are designed to specifically mediate and resolve multicultural conflict issues.

If the intervention is a rewriting of the personnel manual and the agency's goals and objectives to include statements about diversity, a task force, ad hoc committee, or other work group with staff representation may be convened to tackle the issue. In addition, a process for communicating group deliberations and outcomes should be developed so that all members of the agency have an opportunity to review and comment on the proposals. Again, the intent here is to maintain an open and fair process that values feedback, collaboration, and cooperation.

If the intervention identifies training as the agency need, the success of the training depends on a work environment that nurtures and supports new skills. Top-down directed mandatory training may be met with resistance (Gregoire, Propp, & Poertner, 1998). Workers should participate in identifying their training needs and the training should be tailored to meet those needs. In addition, training may be needed for all levels of staff, including management, if the new learning is to be diffused throughout the agency.

Empowerment practice can also be used to help resolve conflict in the agency. Because of the sensitivity surrounding diversity issues, the administrator is striving to put forth an open agenda that encourages the discussion of sensitive topics and the participation of all workers in this discussion. The veil of silence may be perpetuating suspicion and cynicism that can be combated by these frank, direct discussions. The administrator becomes a role model for conducting and participating in these discussions and using his or her oral persuasive communication ability to influence others. Oral persuasive communication involves the transmitting of explicit, direct messages through meetings and other personal presentations (Armenakis et al., 1993).

CASE STUDY

In the historically African American agency situated in a community with a growing Hispanic population, the director used the agency's goal of increasing its funding base as an opportunity to initiate discussions of increasing agency staff and client diversity. Staff members enthusiastically encouraged the director to pursue a sizable contract with a county agency to provide welfare-to-work supportive services for its community welfare recipients. The application required a detailed description of the community, its welfare recipients, and the agency's capacity to respond to the needs of these recipients.

The director formed a task force to assist with the completion of the application and used a portion of several staff meetings to engage workers in discussions of the application and its implications for the agency. The need to expand the staff to include bilingual, bicultural members was integrally linked with the agency's bottom line of survival and growth. The agency outlined the strategies it would use to recruit, screen, hire, and retain the additional staff it needed. These strategies included using Spanish-language media (newspapers and radio stations) to advertise job openings and meeting with Hispanic community groups to recruit applicants and to publicize the program. Other strategies focused on training existing staff to enable them to work more effectively with Hispanic individuals and families. The agency was successful in signing a multi-year contract with the county.

The Agency-Community Interface. The principle of participation is also operative as the administrator begins to outline tentative interventions at the agency-community level. Empowerment agencies must have key leaders who support the empowerment of both staff and program beneficiaries (Hardina, 2005). Community task forces, key informants, and previously identified community leaders can offer the administrator feedback and input about interventions under consideration. Through these interventions, the administrator seeks to support the community's diversity through the provision of services and programs that advance community empowerment.

If the intervention is staff training, community input may help to focus and guide the training agenda to better meet the community's needs. If the intervention is community training, the community can also help outline training priorities, appropriate training times, possible training sites in the community, and methods of recruiting training participants. If particular services and programs are under consideration, community feedback can help structure these programs and services. If the community's needs and priorities are beyond the mandates of the agency, community observations may help channel agency attention

to developing and providing a referral list, engaging in advocacy activities on behalf of the agency, and/or forging partnerships and collaborations with other community-based agencies.

Implementation

The formulated diversity plan is put into action and should have a schedule and set of benchmarks to monitor its progress. All roles should be carefully described so that all active parties in the implementation phase are aware of the expectations and demands facing them. The plan's clarity is essential for its success. Ambiguity can result when workers are allowed to use their discretion in interpreting the meaning and intent of the plan. The use of discretion may jeopardize consistency and uniformity in implementation in critical areas of the plan. Those areas that are flexible and open for workers to use their discretion should be discussed and identified. If there are particular areas that must be uniformly and consistently implemented across all workers, then they should also be discussed and identified. While no plan can cover all contingencies, some general rules may be developed to serve as guidelines for making decisions.

Because agencies are dynamic entities that do change, the plan should be periodically reviewed and, when necessary, modified and updated.

A reward structure should also accompany the implementation of the plan so that staff members know the value the agency attaches to the plan. In addition to money, promotions, status changes, recognition, and appreciation can be included in agency reward systems (Sager, 1995). Sanctions should also be imposed when staff members fail in implementing their part of the plan. Rewards and sanctions communicate to workers that specific behaviors are now being rewarded while others will no longer be overlooked. Whatever the reward structure, it should be equitably applied and include procedures for grievance.

In the Agency. Despite all the steps preceding it, the plan may still be met with staff resistance. Empowerment practice can be used to respond to this staff resistance. The administrator must search out the sources of this resistance and attempt to counter it with forces that support the change. This is not a task that can be accomplished by one person. It may be necessary to hold special meetings (open forum) to address employee concerns, to meet with some staff members as a group, to approach individual employees directly, and/or to enlist the active assistance of employee leaders to overcome the resistance. Incentives may have to be offered to encourage staff support. There may be staff members who are unwilling to accept a changing organization regardless of the incentives offered. These staff members may decide to retire, seek other employment, or remain with the agency. If they remain with the agency, they may be assigned projects that do not interfere with agency goal achievement.

Monitoring the plan and providing feedback to the staff helps to keep the plan and its goals in the forefront of employee attention. This agency goal is presented and treated as a priority. The administrator's public and open support of the plan and the accompanying reward structure further stress the centrality of the plan to the agency's mission. Thus, monitoring becomes a norm for making sure the plan remains on track and meets identified benchmarks.

With the implementation of new techniques, resources may have to be redistributed to support the change effort. Those workers with the skills and expertise required to implement it will rise in status and importance, while those who cannot develop appropriate skills may suffer a loss of power. In the implementation of the plan, new factions and power alliances may be created that alter the agency's usual way of doing business. This alteration may represent a temporary disruption of the agency's equilibrium, and it is expected that, over time, the new plan will establish a new agency homeostasis.

CASE STUDY

Although everyone at the African American agency was excited about being awarded the welfare-to-work contract, that excitement was not as widespread during staff training sessions and during the new worker recruitment period. While some staff members embraced the new learning as a way of moving the agency forward, other workers saw the training as an unnecessary imposition and inconvenience. To help overcome this resistance, the director solicited worker input about the training topics to be covered, schedule of the training sessions, length of the sessions, and names of potential trainers. Each session was evaluated and worker feedback was shared with trainers in preparation for the subsequent sessions. The director also attended the first series of training sessions as a participant to convey her need for this new knowledge. Although some resistance remained, the director was able to garner a significant level of worker support so that the disgruntled faction represented only a small part of the staff.

The Agency-Community Interface. Here, too, a schedule, benchmarks, and reward structure are necessary to the plan's success. Monitoring entails feedback from both the staff and the community. Staff resistance to the agency's community practice plan has to be overcome with some of the same strategies that were noted above.

The importance of the plan can be communicated to the community through administrator presentations at community meetings, worker presentations, media coverage, key informants, community leaders, and other community residents. The collaborative planning process should enable the agency to receive support for its community-focused intervention.

Evaluation

Following the implementation phase, the effectiveness of the plan has to be evaluated. The clearly articulated objectives serve to guide the focus of the evaluation. The objectives define the criteria for success so that expected outcomes can be measured.

In the Agency. Evaluation typically highlights agency changes that were caused by or related to the intervention. Evaluation questions may include Does the agency have a more diverse workforce at Time 2 in comparison to Time 1? Has agency conflict and tension been reduced? How many times did the Diversity Task Force meet to resolve conflict and what were the conflicts? Has more staff integration occurred? Do the perceptions of the culturally diverse staff (continue to) differ from those of the majority staff? Has the number of grievances been reduced? Has the agency been able to retain a higher percentage of its staff? Has worker morale and satisfaction improved?

Evaluation methods may include surveys, questionnaires, and content analysis of records/documents and may be administered at specific points in the implementation process. Surveys of current staff, exiting staff, and former staff may also reveal aspects of the plan's effectiveness. Document analysis can pinpoint changes in the applicant pool and the workforce.

The evaluation methods used are dependent on the agency resources and, again, volunteer consultants and student interns may be used by agencies with limited resources. The administrator can also use his or her observations of the agency to inform him or her about changes, but these observations should be augmented with data from more objective sources.

The Agency-Community Interface. Evaluation of the agency's community empowerment practice plan calls for measures taken of both the staff and the community. Staff members have their views about the effectiveness of the intervention, but these views may not be the same as those held by community residents. Observations from both sources provide a more comprehensive overview of the plan's effects. Also, feedback from workers and from the community can support the empowerment of both groups.

The evaluation methodology employed is dependent on the intervention, the intervention objectives, the evaluation questions, and available agency resources.

CASE STUDY

In the African American agency used as an example, evaluation was based on worker feedback about the training, the size and diversity of the new applicant pool, and the actual hiring of bicultural, bilingual staff.

Formalization of the Plan

Good ideas often leave the agency with the good administrator who had them. These good ideas may have been captured in particular agency activities and patterns that were established during the tenure of that administrator. With the exodus of this person, those patterns may become eroded or replaced by the activities of the next administrator. The administrator's authority of position and control of resources are powerful enough for staff members to abide by his or her wishes, suggestions, and gentle prodding. Such compliance may lull the administrator into thinking that this negates the need for policy. In the absence of sound policy, discretion continues to dominate.

In the Agency. After the implementation has been evaluated, decisions have to be made. Should the plan be modified and then implemented again? Should all or part of the plan be incorporated into the permanent agency structures? If the plan proves to be effective, steps should be taken to institutionalize it through formalized policy mandates. With policy, discretion is circumscribed and all agency personnel are mandated to follow the policy guidelines. A revised personnel manual that includes statements about the value of diversity practice skills and the evaluation of staff diversity practice skills communicates very loudly that the agency is serious about this type of practice. Policies that authorize the use of ethnic media for advertising job vacancies also let the staff and the community know that the recruitment of members from diverse groups is

an agency priority. Policies that dictate the manner in which grievances and conflicts will be handled also minimize the role of discretion in resolving these conflicts. Task forces, staff work groups, and mediation groups can become institutionalized as part of the agency structure through the establishment of policy. In this manner, all the good ideas do not have to leave the agency when the innovative administrator leaves. Also, this example of staff empowerment also becomes institutionalized.

The Agency-Community Interface. While community practice that supports empowerment practice can vary according to the changing needs and demands of the community, mechanisms for community input in the agency planning and decision-making process can be institutionalized through policy. Board diversity can be mandated by policy, and this diversity can boost organizational responsiveness by granting the community a voice in the agency. The community's voice can also be heard through the creation of special community advisory boards or task forces that are formalized in agency policy. The resources that community residents bring to the board, advisory group, or task force are perceived as just as valuable as the resources brought by affluent board members. In this view, community representation becomes associated with the agency's bottom line.

Structures and patterns that are vital to the agency diversity mission should not be left to chance or the good intentions of administrators. Those activities and patterns that are valued by the agency find expression in agency policy that identifies the rewards/sanctions associated with

CASE STUDY

For the African American agency under discussion, workers and other managers helped to modify the personnel policies to include the recruitment of workers knowledgeable in African American and/or Hispanic culture. Staff input was also instrumental in modifying staff performance reviews to include review of the provision of culturally relevant and culturally sensitive service. Client exit interviews were instituted as one of several factors used to assess client experiences with the agency.

those defined organizational behaviors. Agencies that profess a commitment to management practices that support diversity and empowerment but have not formalized this commitment are giving their workers and the community mixed messages. Policies are an agency's attempt to formally perpetuate a value, ideology, and/or a structure. Policies then become crucial in holding agencies accountable for behaviors and outcomes. In time, as such policies are effectively implemented they tend to become embedded in agency culture, which also serves to perpetuate agency priorities concerning diversity and empowerment. In the end, cultural acceptance emerges as a powerful means for ensuring the continuation of policies and for protecting the agency against policy drift.

Conclusion

The country is changing and social service agencies must change with it. Adapting to and accepting diversity can only serve to strengthen agency goal achievement. This adaptation and acceptance can occur more easily in agencies that embrace the inevitability of this change. Diversity for diversity's sake is insufficient grounds for motivating workers to value diversity. Empowered workers who are committed to the agency may be more likely to realize that diversity plays a key role in agency goal and mission achievement. Agency performance and survival may be predicated on empowered, diverse workers who are skilled in service delivery to clients and communities. But first, agencies must take care of business in-house before they can effectively intervene with the communities they serve. For agencies to empower disenfranchised clients and communities, they must first empower workers and value the diversity they bring to the agency. Diversity carries with it a number of meanings, reactions, and perspectives. In addition, the systems and institutional frameworks show that social services operate in an environment that shapes the ideologies within agencies.

Effective management for diversity and empowerment may be difficult to accomplish.

Numerous barriers in society, in the profession, and in the agency exist to mute candid diversity discourse and, consequently, hinder attempts at organizational change. If this change is tied to the agency's bottom line, whatever it may be, then efforts to embrace techniques for the management of diversity and empowerment can be tested.

A framework was offered that bridged the agency and the community because empowered workers can then work to empower the community. In order to support the empowerment of the community, an agency must first support the empowerment of its workers. In the framework, leader orientation, information gathering, plan formulation, plan implementation, evaluation, and formalization offered a process through which administrators can begin to apply the tenets of empowerment in their agency and in the agency-community interface. This framework advocated an orientation that valued diversity and supported empowerment through an inclusive, participatory management style that sought feedback from all levels in the agency and, when appropriate, from the community as well.

Diversity is a reality; yet, empowerment still seems to be an ideal. Agencies continue to face the challenge of developing organizational structures and management techniques that reflect the values the professions hold for individuals. These values do not just apply to individual clients; they apply to service providers and communities as well.

References

Adams, P., & Nelson, K. (1997). Reclaiming community: An integrative approach to human services. *Administration in Social Work, 21,* 67–81.

Armenakis, A., Harris, S., & Mossholder, K. (1993). Creating readiness for organizational change. *Human Relations, 46,* 681–702.

Axinn, J., & Levin, H. (1982). *Social welfare: A history of the American response to need.* New York: Harper and Row.

Bankhead, T., & Erlich, J. (2005). Diverse populations and community practice. In M. Weil (Ed.), *The handbook of community practice* (pp. 59–83). Thousands Oaks, CA: Sage.

Barnett, W., & Carroll, G. (1995). Modeling internal organizational change. *Annual Review of Sociology, 21,* 217–236.

Bartle, E. E., Couchonnal, G., Canda, E. R., & Staker, M. D. (2002). Empowerment as a dynamically developing concept for practice: Lessons learned from organizational ethnography. *Social Work, 47,* 32–34.

Bertalanffy, L. (1974). General systems theory and psychiatry. In S. Arieti (Ed.), *American handbook of psychiatry* (2nd ed., Vol. I). New York: Basic Books.

Boehm, A., & Staples, L. H. (2002). The functions of the social worker in empowering: The voices of consumers and professionals. *Social Work, 47,* 449–460.

Bond, M. A., & Pyle, J. L. (1998). The ecology of diversity in organizational settings: Lessons from a case study. *Human Relations, 51,* 589–623.

Brager, G., & Holloway, S. (1978). *Changing human service organizations.* New York: The Free Press.

Brody, R. (1982). *Problem solving.* New York: Human Sciences Press.

Brown, C. D. (1997). An essay: Diversity and unspoken conflicts. In C. D. Brown, C. C. Snedeker, & B. Sykes (Eds.), *Conflict and diversity* (pp. 217–226). Cresskill, NJ: Hampton Press.

Chadiha, L. A., Adams, P., Biegel, D. E., Auslander, W., & Gutierrez, L. (2004). Empowering African American women informal caregivers: A literature synthesis and practice strategies. *Social Work, 49,* 97–108.

Charlton, A., & Huey, J. (1992). Breaking cultural barriers. *Quality Progress, 25,* 47–49.

Chen, C., & Eastman, W. (1997). Toward a civic culture for multicultural organizations. *Journal of Applied Behavioral Science, 33,* 454–471.

Choudhury, E. H. (1996). The nature and significance of workforce diversity: Orientations of state and urban administrators. *International Journal of Public Administration, 19,* 399–423.

Dhooper, S. S., & Moore, S. E. (2001). *Social work practice with culturally diverse people.* Thousand Oaks, CA: Sage.

DiTomaso, N., Post, C., & Parks-Yancy, R. (2007). Workforce diversity and inequality: Power, status and numbers. *Annual Review of Sociology, 33,* 473–501.

Donnellon, A., & Kolb, D. (1994). Constructive for whom? The fate of diversity disputes in organizations. *Journal of Social Issues, 50,* 139–155.

Everett, J. E., Homstead, K., & Drisko, J. (2007). Frontline worker perceptions of the empowerment process in community-based agencies. *Social Work, 52,* 161–170.

Fawcett, S. B., Paine-Andrews, A., Francisco, V. T., & Schultz, J. A. (1995). Using empowerment theory in collaborative partnerships for community health and development. *Community Journal of Community Psychology, 23,* 677–697.

Feldman, M., & Pentland, B. (2003). Reconceptualizing organizational routines as a source of flexibility and change. *Administrative Science Quarterly, 48,* 94–118.

Fong, R. (2004). Overview of immigrant and refugee children and families. In R. Fong (Ed.), *Culturally competent practice with immigrant and refugee children and families* (pp. 1–18). New York: Guilford Press.

Fullam, C., Lando, A. R., Johansen, M. L., Reyes, A., & Szaloczy, D. M. (1998). The triad of empowerment: Leadership, environment, and professional traits. *Nursing Economics, 16,* 254–258.

Garcia, M. (1995). An anthropological approach to multicultural diversity training. *Journal of Applied Behavioral Science, 31,* 490–504.

Gardenswartz, L., & Rowe, A. (1998). Why diversity matters. *HR Focus, 75,* S1–S3.

Geiger, S. W., & Cashen, L. H. (2002). A multidimensional examination of slack and its impact on innovation. *Journal of Managerial Issues, 14,* 68–84.

Gibelman, M. (2003). *Navigating human service organizations.* Chicago: Lyceum Books.

Gil, D. (1990). Implications of conservative tendencies for practice and education in social welfare. *Journal of Sociology and Social Welfare, 17,* 5–27.

Glisson, C. (1989). The effect of leadership on workers in human service organizations. *Administration in Social Work, 13,* 99–116.

Gregoire, T., Propp, J., & Poertner, J. (1998). The supervisor's role in the transfer of training. *Administration in Social Work, 22,* 1–18.

Hardina, D. (2005). Ten characteristics of empowerment-oriented social service organizations. *Administration in Social Work, 29,* 23–42.

Hardina, D., Middleton, J., Montana, S., & Simpson, R. (2007). *An empowering approach to managing social service organizations.* New York: Springer.

Hasenfeld, Y. (1983). *Human services organizations.* Englewood Cliffs, NJ: Prentice Hall.

Hasenfeld, Y. (1992). *Human services as complex organizations.* Newbury Park, CA: Sage.

Herman, R. (1998). You've got to change to retain. *HR Focus, 75,* S1.

Iglehart, A., & Becerra, R. (1995). *Social services and the ethnic community.* Boston: Allyn & Bacon.

Jansson, B. (1997). *The reluctant welfare state* (3rd ed.). Pacific Grove, CA: Brooks/Cole.

Katz, D., & Kahn, R. (1978). *The social psychology of organizations* (2nd ed.). New York: John Wiley and Sons.

Kettner, P. M., Moroney, R. S., & Martin, L. L. (2007). *Designing and managing programs* (3rd ed.). Thousand Oaks, CA: Sage.

Kirst-Ashman, K. K. (2008). *Human behavior, communities, organizations, and groups in the macro social environment* (2nd ed.). Belmont, CA: Thomson-Brooks/Cole.

Kouzes, J. M., & Posner, B. Z. (2002). *The leadership challenge* (3rd ed.). San Francisco: Jossey-Bass.

Kouzes, J. M., & Posner, B. M. (2004, July/August). A prescription for leading in cynical times. *Ivey Business Journal Online,* 1–7.

Lee, J. (2001). *The empowerment approach to social work practice.* New York: Columbia University Press.

Leiby, J. (1978). *A history of social welfare and social work in the United States.* New York: Columbia University Press.

Lowery, C. T. (2002). Diversity, ethnic competence, and social justice. In M. A. Mattaini, C. T. Lowery, & C. H. Meyers (Eds.), *Foundations of social work practice* (3rd ed., pp. 73–94). Washington, DC: NASW Press.

Martin, G., Jr. (1990). *Social policy in the welfare state.* Englewood Cliffs, NJ: Prentice Hall.

Mary, N. L. (2005). Transformational leadership in human service organizations. *Administration in Social Work, 29,* 105–118.

Mor Barak, M., & Cherin, D. (1998). A tool to expand organizational understanding of workforce diversity: Exploring a measure of inclusion-exclusion. *Administration in Social Work, 22,* 47–64.

Netting, F. E., Kettner, P. M., & McMurtry, S. (2008). *Social work macro practice* (4th ed.). Boston: Allyn & Bacon.

Nicolini, D., Meznar, M., Stewart, G., & Manz, C. (1995). The social construction of organizational learning: Conceptual and practical issues in the field. *Human Relations, 48,* 727–746.

Parsons, R. (1988). Empowerment for alternatives for low income minority girls: A group work approach. *Social Work with Groups, 11,* 27–45.

Peterson, N. A., & Zimmerman, M. A. (2004). Beyond the individual: Toward a nomological network of organizational empowerment. *American Journal of Community Psychology, 34,* 129–145.

Pine, B., Walsh, R., & Maluccio, A. (1998). Participatory management in a public child welfare agency: A key to effective change. *Administration in Social Work, 22,* 19–32.

Resnick, H. (1978). Tasks in changing the organization from within (COFW). *Administration in Social Work, 2,* 29–44.

Ringer, B., & Lawless, E. (1989). *Race-ethnicity and society.* New York: Routledge.

Sager, J. (1995). Change levers for improving organizational performance and staff morale. In J. Rothman, J. Erlich, & J. Tropman (Eds.), *Strategies of community intervention* (5th ed., pp. 401–416). Itasca, IL: F. E. Peacock.

Schilling, R., Schinke, S., & Weatherly, R. (1988). Service trends in a conservative era: Social workers rediscover their past. *Social Work, 33,* 5–9.

Schmid, H. (2002). Relationships between organizational properties and organizational effectiveness in three types of nonprofit human service organizations. *Public Personnel Management, 31,* 377–395.

Seren, S., & Baykal, U. (2007). Relationships between change and organizational culture in hospitals. *Journal of Nursing Scholarship, 39,* 191–197.

Shera, W., & Page, J. (1995). Creating more effective human service organizations through strategies of empowerment. *Administration in Social Work, 19,* 1–14.

Stanley, D. J., Meyer, J. P., & Topolnysky, L. (2005). Employee cynicism and resistance to organizational change. *Journal of Business and Psychology, 19,* 429–459.

Swank, E., Asada, H, & Lott, J. (2001). Student acceptance of a multicultural education: Exploring the role of a social work curriculum, demographics, and symbolic racism. *Journal of Ethnic & Cultural Diversity in Social Work, 10,* 85–103.

Turner, L. M., & Shera, W. (2005). Empowerment of human service workers: Beyond intra-organizational strategies. *Administration in Social Work, 29,* 79–94.

United States Bureau of the Census. (2007, May 17). *Minority population tops 100 million* [Press release]. Washington, DC: Author. Retrieved May 18, 2007, http://www.census.gov/Press-Release.

Uttal, L. (2006). Organizational cultural competency: Shifting programs for Latino immigrants from a client-centered to a community-based orientation. *American Journal of Community Psychology, 38,* 251–262.

Williams, C. C. (2005). Training for cultural competence: Individual and group processes. *Journal of Ethnic & Cultural Diversity in Social Work, 14,* 111–143.

Yip, K. (2004). The empowerment model: A critical reflection of empowerment in Chinese culture. *Social Work, 49,* 479–487.

Zamanou, S., & Glaser, S. (1994). Moving toward participation and involvement: Managing and measuring organizational culture. *Group & Organizational Management, 19,* 475–502.

Zimmerman, M. (1995). Psychological empowerment: Issues and illustrations. *American Journal of Community Psychology, 23,* 581–599.

PART 4

Developing and Managing Programs and Resources

The chapters in Part 4 are largely devoted to developing and managing the governance, strategic, programmatic, and fiscal infrastructures necessary to support the agency's core service mission, anticipate future needs and opportunities, and acquire and account for agency resources. The coordination of these processes is essential for providing clear direction for the agency and a coherent framework for its day-to-day operations. While these management processes sometimes seem far removed from the service delivery process, they are organically related to it. Indeed, to the extent these processes are not orchestrated, the agency's viability can be at risk.

Recent experience in the human services suggests that the environment of human services agencies (policies, funding arrangements, technologies, etc.) is changing at an accelerating rate. Agency planning is the process by which organizations anticipate these changes, proactively address the inherent risks and opportunities, and seek to position themselves advantageously. In Chapter 15, Austin and Solomon provide a broad perspective on factors that drive agencies to plan in today's world; guidelines for how to conduct planning at several agency levels; and the challenges of articulating strategic, program/operational, and fiscal planning processes.

Chapter 16, a new entry in this edition, complements the previous Chapter 15 by providing a closer look at program planning. This responsibility falls primarily to middle managers and provides the means through which agency resources, technologies, and staffs deliver services to clients. Larry Martin places program planning in the context of strategic planning and then takes us through the steps on defining a program, needs assessment, design, costing, marketing, and implementation and monitoring, all necessary steps for insuring that programs reach their intended audiences.

Public and private agencies alike rely largely on third parties for resources—government contracts, federated agencies, foundations, donors—to fund their operations. While, as we saw in Chapters 1 and 4, there are large expenditures for human services, the competition for these resources has become quite demanding. In Chapter 17, a new addition to the book, Armand Lauffer assesses the reasons for this competitive environment, discuses ways in which agencies can learn about the preferences of potential publics and respond to them, and describes an array of fundraising strategies and mechanisms. In addition to complementing the other chapters in this section, Professor Lauffer's chapter can be read in tandem with Chapters 20 and 21, which address related material on organization-environment relations.

In Chapter 18, Sheldon Gelman discusses the functions of the boards of directors of nonprofit agencies. As the nonprofit sector agencies have grown in size and complexity, so too have the responsibilities of boards. The skills and capabilities they bring to board membership are increasingly important to effective governance, fundraising, and strategic planning. But board members are volunteers, and as Professor Gellman discusses, it falls to the agency managers to develop and support their capabilities if boards are to serve the agency well.

Human services agencies are increasingly accountable for how they spend their funds. In Chapter 19, Mark Ezell discusses the fiscal and regulatory contexts in which human services agencies operate. Contextual factors such as managed care and purchase of service contracting are reviewed, as are federal laws and regulations, the Internal Revenue Service requirements for nonprofits, and the handling of unrelated business income. Professor Ezell gives a detailed description of the tasks associated with each stage in the budgetary cycle and discusses common financial management issues faced by human services organizations. This chapter expands on several fiscally related subjects addressed in Chapters 16 and 18.

CHAPTER 15

Managing the Planning Process

Michael J. Austin

Jeffrey R. Solomon

For most human services agencies, planning is viewed as a luxury, especially when the demand for services exceeds the supply. In our recent post-World War II history, the limited amount of planning was usually long-range planning that paralleled the growth of the economy and social programs from 1945 to 1980. However, with government cutbacks in social programs, the expansion of military expenditures, and the global competitiveness that fostered the trend of downsizing and mergers in the 1980s, long-range planning was replaced by strategic planning in both the for-profit and nonprofit sectors. Long-range planning was characterized as "extrapolational," whereby planners extrapolated from current realities and trends 10 to 15 years into the future, assuming continued growth. This was logical in the post-World War II environment of steady economic growth and the steady expansion of government-supported social programs.

A new era of strategic planning in the human services emerged out of the curtailment of the growth of social programs during the Reagan Era of 1980 to 1992. This form of planning was characterized as transformational, in essence a planning process designed to transform organizations in the short term (three to five years), not long range. The goal was to be far more strategic with respect to external competition, environmental forces (threats and opportunities), and internal forces (strengths and weaknesses).

Organizational planning has shifted dramatically from being a luxury in an era of long-range planning to being a necessity in an era of strategic planning. Some of the profound changes in the economy of human services need to be noted here, even though they are beyond the scope of this chapter. The arrival of managed care in the health care sector has led to significant changes in the financing, organization, patient care, and

321

management of health and mental health services. Strategic planning has become essential as health care institutions are restructured, merged, closed, centralized, decentralized, and funded on a capitated basis. Similarly, the arrival of welfare reform has led to the restructuring of state and local social service agencies as well as community-based nonprofit contract provider agencies. The shift from benefit eligibility to job-ready employability has had a profound impact on redefining clients as future employees and social service personnel as employment and workplace-support specialists.

With this brief historical overview, it is possible to see how strategic planning provides an important tool for understanding how public and nonprofit human services agencies can address their respective futures. The planning process can assist human services organizations with managing the uncertain and changing environment in the following ways:

- Planning involves adjusting the internal structures and processes to account for changes in the external environment, especially acquiring the tools and capabilities to assess the external environment in terms of legislation, economic forecasts, changes in housing and transportation, changes in demand for support services such as child care and health care, and changes in the role of faith-based organizations in the delivery of human services.
- Planning involves increased interest in the organizational learning and strategic management that are necessary to position agencies to be responsive to the changing needs of client populations.
- Planning involves a profound shift in management philosophy, from reactive crisis management to proactive strategic management, in which middle and senior managers are equally attentive to efficient internal operations and effective external community relations.
- Planning involves renewed interest in understanding and assessing the community

context of human services organizations; directors of public social service agencies spend far more time educating elected officials and opinion leaders, and nonprofit agency directors devote more time to educating and shaping their boards of directors to be more concerned with external developments and involved in networking, fundraising, lobbying, marketing, and so on.

- Planning involves shifting from plans being an end-goal document to plans becoming the first step in a larger process of change: Strategic issues/directions/initiatives are translated into specific action plans that rely on strategic management and ultimately lead to the measurement of outcomes in terms of both quality and quantity.
- Planning involves new roles for program managers and agency directors in at least four areas of agency planning: (a) strategic planning, (b) strategic management related to implementing the plan, (c) operations and program planning related to restructuring current programs/systems and developing new service programs and systems, and (d) evaluation planning related to the design and implementation of new information systems and policy analysis capabilities.

With these significant changes in mind, this chapter focuses on strategic planning, implementation of the plan in the midst of ongoing operations/program planning, and the relationship between planning and implementation. Case examples from the public and nonprofit sectors are used to illustrate key planning activities, and the chapter concludes with a discussion of the challenges facing agency-based planning. Strategic planning is only as good as the process used to implement the plan and monitor the change process. Therefore, the dual perspective of planning and implementation is a central theme throughout this chapter, and each perspective is defined along with the interrelationship between planning and operations.

Defining Strategic Planning

As Berman (1998) has noted, strategic planning is a set of procedures that help organizations and communities to align their priorities with changing conditions and new opportunities. He approaches strategic planning from both a community and organizational perspective and notes that it is used to

- design a future that better meets their needs and to develop paths and guideposts;
- build consensus among often disparate individuals and organizations and shape different points of view (board, staff, clients, community, etc.);
- motivate organizations to respond to a changing environment;
- address the need for consolidation, reorganization, or restoration of balance among different organizational services.

From a slightly different perspective, Bryson (2004) views strategic planning as a disciplined effort to produce fundamental decisions that can shape the nature and direction of organizational activities. He notes that strategic planning can

- help revitalize, redirect, and improve organizational performance;
- provide an opportunity to make connections and changes across programs, as well as integrate policies and programs;
- build bridges with individuals and groups who are affected by or can affect the future of the organization;
- help make important decisions related to four fundamental questions: (a) Where are we going (mission)? (b) How do we get there (strategic programs)? (c) What is our blueprint for action (budgets and program plans)? and (d) How do we know if we are on track (monitoring and assessment)?
- be used effectively in highly politicized environments, provided extra attention is given to both client/member and stakeholder analysis.

Bryson (2004) notes that the most important feature of strategic planning is promoting the development of strategic thinking. This characteristic clearly distinguishes the old approaches of long-range planning from the new methods of strategic planning. Thinking strategically is somewhat like thinking critically, in terms of (a) developing a keen awareness of organizational cultures, histories, and external environments; (b) pursuing an intense examination of assumptions underlying different aspects of organizational life; and (c) engaging in imaginative speculation in which alternatives and viable options are generated. Strategic thinking also involves assessing how others view strategic planning, the topic of the next section.

The Key Elements of Strategic Planning

Based on a review of the limited literature on strategic planning and management in the human services, it is possible to identify three general themes. One segment of the literature focuses on the definition of strategic planning, the specific planning steps, and the benefits of strategic planning (Austin, 2002; Eadie, 1983; Julian & Lyons, 1992; Kaufman & Jacobs, 1987; Koontz, 1981; Sorkin, Ferris, & Hudak, 1984; Steiner, Gross, Ruffolo, & Murray, 1994; Ziegenfuss, 1989). Another segment includes discussions of the relationship among organizational characteristics, strategic planning, and performance (Siciliano, 1997; Vogel & Patterson, 1986; Webster & Wylie, 1988a, 1988b). A third segment focuses on some of the administrative and supervisory issues that need to be taken into account when implementing a strategic plan (Bryson, 2004; Eldridge, 1983; Gowdy & Freeman, 1993). With regard to the definition and relevance of strategic planning, Steiner et al. (1994) have identified certain internal and external factors. Among the most important external factors are (a) decreased funding; (b) changing social, political, and economic priorities in the external environment; (c) increased competition; (d) societal demographic, social, political, and economic changes; and (e) changing regulatory requirements. The most important internal conditions include (a) change in leadership or high turnover; (b) conditions of stagnancy, crisis, or loss of focus; and (c) rapid increases or decreases in demand for services. All of these factors also contribute to public pressures on public and nonprofit social services agencies to become more accountable (Siciliano, 1997; Steiner et al., 1994; Webster & Wylie, 1988b). Consequently, human services agencies have been placing greater emphasis on strategic planning over the past two decades

With respect to linking strategic planning to organizational characteristics, Webster and Wylie (1988a) found that agencies receiving funds from the United Way were more likely to engage in strategic planning if (a) their client population was changing rapidly, (b) they experienced pressures from regulatory agencies to plan, and (c) they had attended a workshop on strategic planning. Almost 90% of the agencies felt that they had benefited from the strategic planning process by changing their mission, adding/eliminating services, and/or restructuring the organization, with almost 50% of the agencies characterizing the benefits as major. Webster and Wylie (1988a) also found that large agencies using outside consultants to develop a comprehensive strategic planning process reported major changes as a result of the process. In addition, they found that, in some cases, eliciting widespread stakeholder participation detracted from securing major changes and was associated with lower agency satisfaction with the process (see Chapter 21 for further discussion of stakeholder involvement).

Similarly, in a survey of 240 YMCAs, Siciliano (1997) found that (a) the active involvement of board members can enhance the effectiveness of the strategic planning process, especially through their involvement on strategic planning committees; (b) financially secure organizations were more likely to engage in effective strategic planning; and (c) effective strategic planning leads to better financial and operational performance. With respect to implementing strategic plans,

Eldridge (1983) identifies the following factors that can keep the agency from fully benefiting from the plan: (a) inadequate staff involvement, (b) inability to anticipate and manage conflicts, (c) insufficient teamwork and coordination, (d) lack of staff empowerment, and (e) poor use of procedures to implement a plan (timelines, delegated responsibilities, and decision-making authority). As Gowdy and Freeman (1993) note with respect to program supervision, it is one thing to create a new program (or strategic plan) and quite another thing to change or reshape a program (or agency) to be responsive to changing conditions.

Steps in Strategic Planning

The specific activities involved in developing an effective strategic plan vary considerably depending on the focus, size, location, and external and internal environment of an agency. However, certain broadly defined activities, usually carried out simultaneously, are common to the development of an agency's strategic plan, namely (a) reassessing the agency's mission and developing a future vision of the agency, (b) assessing the external environment and competition, (c) assessing the internal operations and client services, and (d) developing a plan that includes strategies, tasks, outcomes, timelines, and implementation steps (Allison & Kaye, 2005; Bryson, 2004; Eadie, 1983; Julian & Lyons, 1992; Steiner et al., 1994). These broadly defined activities can be itemized in terms of key questions to be addressed, as noted in Figure 15.1.

Clarifying Mission, Goals, and Objectives. One of the initial steps in the strategic planning process is to reassess the organization's mission statement. If this process has not been done since the agency was established, it means a return to its charter or articles of incorporation to find the stated purpose of the organization. The mission statement often includes the agency's major goals. However, in periods of rapid external and internal change, some goals may have become

---

Strategic Planning Guide

I. Mission Statement Development/Review

    A. Does it reflect the organization's strengths and areas for continuous improvement?

    B. Does it adequately describe the clients, major programs/services, staff, and board?

    C. Does it reflect the unique assets of the organization?

    D. Does it reflect the organization's history and philosophy in terms of core values?

II. Assessing the External Environment

    A. What are some of the local and national factors affecting the organization: (1) social and political factors (shifting values, rising expectations, emerging groups, changing demographics, etc.), (2) economic factors (financial markets, local economy, tax policies, housing market, etc.), and (3) technological factors (information systems, Internet, cellular communications, etc.)?

    B. Given these external factors, what are the organization's major opportunities and threats?

III. Identifying Best Practices and the Nature of Our Competition

    A. What are some of the best practices (programs, processes, procedures) being carried out in similar organizations locally, regionally, nationally, and internationally?

    B. How do we compare with the competition in terms of (1) client services/fees, (2) staff salaries, (3) facilities, (4) reputation, and (5) administrative capacities (program development, marketing, and service effectiveness/efficiency)?

IV. Client/Stakeholder Analysis

    A. Who are the clients/stakeholders, and how have they changed over the past five years (age, ethnicity, gender, urban/suburban, occupations, incomes)?

    B. Why do they seek/use the organization's services (satisfaction/expectations)?

    C. What does the staff/board want to change (programs, service mix, staff/volunteer roles, etc.)?

    D. What are our efforts to reach prospective clients/stakeholders?

V. Assessing Internal Operations

    A. How well do we manage our operations: (1) finances (budgetary trends over past 5 years), (2) facilities (space utilization and building maintenance), (3) staff (personnel systems and professional development), (4) volunteers (recruitment, training, deployment, evaluation, recognition), (5) service programs (design, update, market, implement, evaluate), (6) communications (printed, information, and referral coordination), and (7) board leadership (board development and leadership succession) and client relations (including outreach)?

    B. How well do we plan and evaluate service programs?

    C. What are the major strengths and limitations of our organization's internal operations?

VI. Developing the Components of the Plan

    A. What are the cross-cutting themes that emerge as new directions/initiatives from items I to V?

    B. What strategies, tasks, and outcomes can be identified to address each initiative?

Figure 15.1   A Strategic Planning Guide

---

obsolete or require clarification in relationship to changing client needs, new regulatory requirements, funding priorities, and/or societal values. To be effective, agency goals need to be achievable, manageable, operational, and small in number. The process of clarifying goals should involve all relevant stakeholders (staff, clients, advocacy groups, funding organizations, and regulatory agencies) in order to develop a sense of ownership. A clearly articulated, generally accepted, and comprehensive set of goals in a mission statement is important for generating energy, cohesion, and motivation to deal with internal and external challenges.

As noted in Figure 15.2, the mission statement for a large Jewish fundraising organization in New York City includes four components: (a) a brief history of the organization, reflecting its roots and traditions; (b) a listing of its core values, which are used to guide daily operations; (c) a listing of the primary goals that structure the current operations; and (d) a listing of the methods used to achieve those goals. Not all mission statements are this elaborate, and some agencies pride themselves on the use of very brief mission statements. For example, a brief mission statement drawn from Figure 15.2 might be "To ensure the continuity of the Jewish people, to enhance the quality of Jewish life, and to build a strong and unified Jewish community in New York, Israel, and throughout the world." However, such brief statements do not always help others understand the full dimensions of an organization's mission.

Whereas a mission statement focuses primarily on the present and immediate future of the agency, a vision statement is designed to help the organization envision a time in the distant future (e.g., 15 years from now) by encouraging all parties in the planning process to dream. The primary assumptions needed to develop a vision statement are that the agency will have all the resources it needs (money, staff, facilities, etc.) to create and operate an ideal set of services for a target audience with a particular reputation and core set of values readily apparent to the community. For many, the development of a vision statement is extremely challenging and time-consuming, given the extensive pressures to deal with the present. However, the exercise can be very informative as it stretches the best minds of the stakeholders in the organization to envision a future condition that could provide a roadmap into the future.

Scanning the Environment. One of the factors that can distinguish strategic planning from long-range planning is the active scanning of the external environment (also see Chapter 20 in this volume). Identifying threats and opportunities due to social, political, and economic changes provides important information for continuously testing the relevance and feasibility of the agency's goals. Scanning can also identify problems and prospects that an agency may face in the future. These issues include the general condition of the economy, immigration trends, corporate policies, technological changes, and changes in societal values. These issues could affect the size of caseloads, contribute to changing client needs, and/or influence the flow of future funding. Consequently, agencies need to develop the capacity to foresee the impact of a broad range of factors on their agencies and client populations.

Environmental scanning is most effective when it is carried out on a continuous basis, especially during periods of rapid change. It requires access to sources of information in order to track information related to social, economic, and political changes at the local, state, and federal levels. Although newspapers and magazines can be important sources of information, other sources include informal channels of information used by the agency's board of directors, local leaders, advocates, and public officials. For example, community leaders may provide useful insights about the changing nature of client problems, whereas legislators may provide useful information about impending changes that may affect the revenue base of an agency. Assessments of the complex external environment are usually difficult and expensive for human services agencies to purchase, and therefore, senior agency staff members need to acquire the expertise to engage in effective environmental scanning (Farmby, 2004). Scanning the environment could be one of the most important components of the strategic planning process.

Another aspect of scanning the environment includes assessing competition and best practices. Although most human services agencies do not conceive of themselves as operating in a competitive environment, it is clear that such

---

Mission Statement of the United Jewish Appeal

Our History

UJA-Federation, the primary philanthropic arm of the Greater New York Jewish community, continues long and distinguished traditions of serving the Jewish community in New York, Israel, and throughout the world. Since its founding in 1917, the Federation of Jewish Philanthropies of New York helped—through united fundraising and other means—a diverse and growing network of agencies to minister the human service needs of the Jewish community and to advance and improve Jewish education.

In 1938, as a direct reaction to Kristallnacht and the Nazi threat to Jewish survival, the United Jewish Appeal was founded to finance the rescue, relief, and rehabilitation of Jews in Nazi Germany and throughout the world. In 1948, with the establishment of the State of Israel, UJA became the principal means for American Jews to assist in the absorption of Jewish immigrants and the building of the Jewish State.

In 1973, as the Yom Kippur War threatened the existence of the State of Israel, UJA and Federation united their fundraising efforts but retained their separate administrative and other operations. In 1986, to further the interests of the Jewish community, the merger of the two organizations was completed.

Our Values and Commitments

UJA-Federation exists in the largest and most diverse Jewish community in the world. We strive to advance the shared values and commitments of the overwhelming majority of that community:

- Philanthropy as an act of righteousness (tzedakah); the historic Jewish ideal of social justice for all; and the responsibility of Jews everywhere, each for the other
- The profound importance and vital role of Israel in Jewish history and Jewish life today
- The responsibility to help, rescue, and liberate Jews everywhere they may be in danger
- The unity of the Jewish people, while maintaining respect for the diversity of Jewish experience and ideas
- The importance of Jewish education and the synagogue to convey Jewish identity and values

Our Mission

It is the Mission of UJA-Federation:

- To ensure the continuity of the Jewish people, to enhance the quality of Jewish life, and to build a strong and unified Jewish community-in New York, Israel, and throughout the world
- To help, through a network of affiliated agencies, individuals and families in need—the old and young, the unemployed, the homeless, the sick and poor—and to resettle those who are persecuted or oppressed.
- To help meet human needs in the State of Israel and to strengthen the relationship between the people of Israel and the Diaspora

In order to fulfill our Mission, we must

- Strengthen the UJA-Federation role as the primary arm of the Jewish community of Greater New York for fundraising, communal planning, and allocation of resources
- Strengthen our partnership with the network of human and community service agencies, synagogues, Jewish education, and rescue agencies serving New York, Israel, and other countries; seek the active participation of all sectors of the Jewish community and bring all Jews more closely together
- Work in concert with government, other voluntary agencies, and other ethnic and religious communities in New York
- Educate the members of the Jewish community about the importance of supporting—with their talent, energy, and material resources—the UJA-Federation Mission

---

Figure 15.2   Mission Statement of the United Jewish Appeal-Federation of Jewish Philanthropies of New York, Inc. Approved November 30, 1989

environments exist and may be increasing with the arrival of managed care and welfare reform. Most public agencies are instrumental in creating boundaries around competition through the use of contracting with providers who can deliver services most efficiently, effectively, and cheaply. In contrast, nonprofit agencies are experiencing considerable competition as they seek multiple sources of funding, including funds from foundations, and find themselves under increased pressure to collaborate with other agencies, co-locate service, merge with or acquire other agencies, or go out of business.

One of the most productive approaches to assessing the competition is to identify promising practices. This approach involves scanning the environment in order to learn about the effective practices, policies, and/or procedures used by other agencies locally, regionally, nationally, and internationally. By comparing, agencies are then able to reassess their own services and explore the possibility of adapting and/or including some of the promising practices learned from the scanning process.

Assessing Operations. Within the context of the external threats and opportunities, an agency also needs to develop a comprehensive understanding of its own strengths and limitations, especially as they impact the relationship between operations and the resources needed (services, finance, personnel, facilities, communications, policies/procedures, and governance).

It is important to fully involve all levels of agency staff and board members in order to identify the agency's strengths and limitations. For example, top management needs to provide staff with the opportunity to assess organizational strengths and limitations through the use of open dialogue, criticism, and self-reflection. One of the goals of this process is to learn how staff members perceive their roles in relationship to others in the organization. Participation in program and strategic planning helps staff members transcend the narrow perspectives of their own jobs and become less defensive about evaluation activities as they understand how the larger

systemic issues influence their individual practice (Gowdy & Freeman, 1993). Similarly, dialogue and feedback from clients, advocacy groups, funders, and the general community are necessary to acquire other points of view (Austin & Vu, 2007). Frequently, a facilitator or organizational development consultant can help to identify organizational strengths and limitations as well as assist with the environmental assessment and the construction of the strategic plan.

Most strategic plans include a set of strategies or directions that the organization has chosen to pursue. An example of one of these strategies is noted in Figure 15.3 related to a national Jewish women's organization (Hadassah), namely, strengthening organizational structures and processes, which was one of five strategies. The others were related to expanding membership and fundraising, increasing targeting of programs at the local level, improving governance, and strengthening the volunteer-staff relationship (Austin, 2002).

Central to assessing internal operations is the process of analyzing the client or stakeholder population. As noted in Figure 15.1, many questions can be addressed in constructing a picture of the population currently being served as well as previous populations. It is also important to note how the client or stakeholder population has changed over time. When looking back over the past five years, has the population become older or younger, have the needs/interests of clients or members changed, and is the organization responsive to any of these changes? This form of client/stakeholder analysis relies heavily on recent satisfaction surveys, focus group meetings, interviews, and/or reviews of client/member records. Although most human services organizations possess an immense amount of client data, it is rarely reviewed from the perspective of contributing to a strategic plan. As a result, client analysis is an essential component of assessing internal operations.

Constructing the Strategic Plan. The previous steps on assessing the environment and internal operations involve collecting relevant information for

---

Strategy 3: Organizational Structure and Processes

Throughout the strategic planning committee reports, there was a consistent theme that the current organizational structure did not facilitate effective communication, flexibility in programming, quick response to changing environments and issues, and a personal sense of job enrichment. The following action plans need to be designed and implemented to address Strategy 3:

- Developing an interdepartmental structure for conducting annual or every-other-year evaluations of Hadassah programs, including all Israel and American projects, to assess levels of success and the potential for new ventures. Included in the structure needs to be a mechanism for evaluating new pilot proposals and the review of existing pilot projects.
- Conducting an in-depth assessment of Hadassah's current organizational structure in New York (the need for specific departments under a particular division, the need for eight divisions, role of the division coordinator, etc.) linked to an assessment of the structure of regions, the potential for satellite offices, and the role of regional consultants.
- Developing specific processes to foster greater interdepartmental communication to share annual work plans reflecting goals and measurable objectives as well as share departmental assessment of needs in the regions. In addition, it is important to address the multiple issues of improving meeting management within and between departments (e.g., use of agendas, coordinated meeting schedules, clarity about volunteer and/or staff participation, use of visuals, etc.).
- Conducting a communications audit to assess Hadassah's public relations capacity to share successes and important human-interest stories, assess the merits of a Hadassah House newsletter, and investigate the capacity to test-market issues and program ideas on a national basis. Special attention should be given to how Hadassah House communicates with chapters and regions.
- Conducting an office management audit to assess the adequacy of office equipment (desk-top publishing, teleconferencing, word processing, electronic mail, etc.) and the efficiency of current methods of managing the mail, distributing materials, and recycling.

Many of these issues should be handled by a senior management group that is responsible for the overall management of Hadassah House operations.

Figure 15.3   Hadassah Strategic Plan (1993)

NOTE: Hadassah is an American Jewish women's organization with 300,000 members, which provides educational programs and generates financial support for health, education, and community services in Israel.

---

use in developing the written plan. The final step in the strategic planning process includes the design of specific strategies to achieve the agency goals. It is based on an analysis of the internal strengths and weaknesses and external threats and opportunities. For example, the three major themes and the nine directions in the strategic plan of a public human services agency are noted in Figure 15.4. Each one of the nine directions would require considerable staff energy and a timeline of several years to implement. Simply communicating the considerable ramifications of the plan with all levels of staff, let alone the community, can be a significant challenge for senior management.

The formulation of strategies involves specifying what will be done, how it will be done, by whom, and when. Strategies involve concrete programs, policies, procedures, and action plans. These all flow from the agency's updated mission statement and reflect detailed and specific guidelines for future action. Once the overall strategic plan is ready, the next step is to design an implementation plan that links the strategic plan to the regular operations of the agency (Ziegenfuss, 1989). This includes the process of developing specific and measurable objectives, outcomes, and performance indicators for each program. These indices should serve as useful benchmarks for annually evaluating the implementation of the strategic plan. A key element of the implementation plan is the identification of the specific human and physical resource requirements

---

Theme I: Implement a Proactive, Outcomes-Oriented, High-Impact Philosophy of Service

Strategic Direction 1: We will promote a proactive, outcomes-oriented approach to meeting consumer needs through continuous training and support for Human Services Agency (HSA) and other service provider staff to provide assistance to consumers in advocating for their own needs.

Strategic Direction 2: Policymakers, program managers, and individual service providers at all levels (private, public, volunteer) will make decisions on the most effective utilization of resources by considering a common set of values:

    a. We will achieve the most long-term, widespread impact at the lowest cost, as determined by the best available consumer-defined outcome measures.
    b. We will focus on prevention and the earliest possible intervention, promote self-sufficiency, and strengthen families and individuals within their familial and support environments.
    c. We will treat all consumers with respect.
    d. We will assure, at a minimum, that all consumers receive assistance in identifying their needs and information and referral on available options for food, clothing, shelter, and health care.

Theme II: Extend the Boundaries of the Human Services System

Strategic Direction 3: We will create a seamless system of public/private service by fostering cooperation and partnerships among government, nonprofit, and private sector organizations and individuals through the development of shared vision and values, common interests and objectives, and coordinated implementation strategies.

Strategic Direction 4: We will build support for addressing human service needs through separate and joint public education efforts.

Strategic Direction 5: We will promote waivers and legislation that remove disincentives to prevention and early intervention services, attainment of consumer self-sufficiency, and provision of assistance that strengthens consumers' family and support environments.

Theme III: Deliver Services That Respond to the Self-Identified Needs of Consumers

Strategic Direction 6: We will develop an integrated single intake system, with multiple physical entry points, that provides consumer access to all available resources, both public and private, as well as a system of needs assessment, information, and referral that supports a coordinated delivery of services and offers consumers choices in both definition of needs and selection and design of solutions.

Strategic Direction 7: We will create accessibility to services for all consumers.

Strategic Direction 8: We will use data collected while serving consumers to plan, operate, and evaluate human services programs and activity.

Strategic Direction 9: We will make changes needed to expand service delivery of child care, affordable housing, and job training to consumers identified as the "working poor."

Figure 15.4   Strategic Planning Directions-San Mateo County (California) Human Services Agency (1993)

---

for each objective. This element provides the basis for developing the budget needed to implement the strategic plan.

The budget and its justification need to specify the proposed expenditures for each program, department, and activity based on the resource requirements and assigned responsibilities. The next component of an implementation plan is allocating the responsibility for implementation

and monitoring. Despite the growing popularity of strategic planning for human services organizations, the following factors continue to restrict the ability of the agencies to fully benefit from such planning (Eldridge, 1983):

- Inadequate staff involvement, including insufficient authority to make decisions, lack of access to analytical tools, lack of available information, and insufficient attention by top management to involve staff who have the relevant information

- Inability to anticipate and manage conflicts, especially within the strategic planning teams, when members may have different disciplines/backgrounds and senior administrators are unable to manage these conflicts
- Insufficient teamwork and coordination, especially when the planning teams are too large and unwieldy to function effectively (small teams of staff with different responsibilities can ensure more productive participation)
- Lack of empowerment, especially when the planning team is overwhelmed by the external demands on the agency and perceives little room for devising creative solutions
- Poor use of the planning procedures, especially when the deadlines for different tasks, responsibilities, and decisions are not clearly defined, that can lead to haphazard, random, and biased decision making

In a case study of a youth agency, Vogel and Patterson (1986) found that a team-based organizational structure can contribute to more effective strategic planning when work tasks and worker skills are combined to achieve goals. In contrast to the top-down bureaucratic approach, the team-based approach can greatly facilitate the development of strategic plans that call for changing the internal environment of the agency in response to external demands.

As noted earlier in the chapter, developing a strategic plan is one thing, but implementing it can be quite challenging. The implementation process usually occurs while staff members are carrying out ongoing agency activities and programs. Implementing the plan can be seen as an added burden (sometimes likened to changing a tire on your car while proceeding down the road at 60 mph). In the next section, we explore the issues of strategic management associated with planning and implementing ongoing operations and programs (Stone, Bigelow, & Crittenden, 1999).

The Messiness of Strategic Planning

Up to this point, the framework of strategic planning may appear logical and linear. However, real life strategic planning always requires adjustments along the way. For example, financial and human resources are often required. If a public sector human services agency engages in strategic planning, staff members will usually draw upon outside expertise in the form of a consultant. If a nonprofit human services agency decides on the development of a strategic plan, it is also conceivable that additional financial resources will be needed to support the effort, for example, to pay consultation fees or to support staff and board retreats. In either case, the next issue usually involves securing the necessary human resources as well as determining the degree to which staff and board members are to be involved in the planning process. Given that most agency staff members are already overloaded and board members are often consumed with their board responsibilities, other agency stakeholders may need to be recruited. For example, a congregation that wants to develop a plan may require the extensive use of knowledgeable and experienced members along with the selective use of staff. For small nonprofits, strategic planning may require abbreviated versions of the planning steps in the form of one-day board and staff retreats, board member involvement in completing other steps, and extensive involvement of the agency director.

Irrespective of the financial and human resources required for the strategic planning process, various crises will most likely occur and therefore need to be anticipated. Sometimes the planning process is delayed by unanticipated dilemmas facing the agency. Other times, the process is moving ahead nicely until the personalities of some of the planning committee members get entangled. For lay leaders, this may be reflected in their lack of diplomatic communications skills, and for others, it may be the distractions of their business or professional obligations that take precedence over their volunteer roles. The leadership capacities of lay leaders as well as staff are critical to the successful strategic planning process. For example, while some lay leaders may bring strategic planning experiences from their businesses or law firms, it is important to keep in mind that their involvement in the nonprofit sector is usually a learning experience for them. While it may appear surprising, some of them do not know how to effectively demonstrate meeting management skills (e.g., "My way or the highway").

And finally, while most agency directors may understand the strategic planning process, they may not have had the opportunity or experience needed to facilitate the process. Therefore, the agency director plays a critical role in assisting staff and/or a consultant in carrying out the planning process. One of the biggest decisions that an agency director, along with his/her board representative, makes is the selection of a strategic planning consultant. Some consultants view the process primarily as a set of data collection activities where multiple stakeholders are interviewed or surveyed and a report is produced. Others focus more on empowering lay leaders to own the process by helping them engage in extensive committee work and report writing where the consultant plays a more facilitating and synthesizing role. In essence, since most human services organizations operate in a unique environment and have developed their own organizational culture, the strategic planning process is different for each nonprofit or public sector human services organization.

Key Elements of Operations/Program Planning

While strategic planning provides a framework for setting agency directions with a focused mission statement, program and operations planning are the key components of day-to-day agency life. They tend to be tactical and emerge from four compelling sources: (a) the strategic plan itself, (b) ongoing program evaluation, (c) contingency planning, and (d) annual budget planning (also see Chapter 16).

Strategic Plan Implementation

Operational planning involves the transformation of the major strategic planning initiatives into specific goals and objectives that include action steps for staff and others to carry out. It is generally assumed that the implementation teams include many more people than the number who developed the strategic plan. Similarly, it is necessary to identify a range of resources needed to implement the initiatives in the strategic plan. In many settings, strategic plan implementation is driven by a conscious effort to involve busy staff and others in either changing the way they do business or adding new expectations to existing workloads. As Stacey (1992) notes, the controlled behavior (of staff and others) needs to have some overall coherence or pattern (i.e., internally connected and constrained rather than haphazard, unconnected thinking and acting without any pattern). In essence, staff members need to see how implementing the strategic plan relates to their current responsibilities and how they need to be re-prioritized to make room for new initiatives or processes.

Strategic plan implementation is built on the assumption that organizations need to change. Therefore, the operational plans for each initiative in the strategic plan need to be spelled out. Agencies often link the implementation of a strategic plan to its ongoing annual operations plan, which generally includes the following components (Allison & Kaye, 2005):

- Specified process and outcome objectives
- Identified staff responsible for implementing the plan
- A user-friendly monitoring template to note progress made
- Continuous reference to implementing the strategic plan
- Continuous assessment to make sure that the operational plan is realistic
- Continuous opportunities to provide suggestions for future annual plans

The most common error in strategic planning is to believe that the task is completed when the plan is approved. Agency staff members can use a variety of techniques to assure that the plan is continuously cited throughout the implementation process. For example, a simple, self-monitoring approach can be used when the key elements of the strategic plan are "boiled down" into specific action steps with projected outcomes, due dates, and people responsible for completing the work, as noted in Table 15.1. This chart could be updated monthly and shared with the agency's governing board on a quarterly basis, with a discussion focused on the status of each recommendation and the barriers preventing full implementation. The combination of board member oversight with staff accountability helps to maintain the focus and momentum needed to implement the strategic plan.

Program Planning and Evaluation

Well-administered, disciplined agencies engage in serious program planning and evaluation as part of their ongoing functioning. As Kettner, Moroney, and Martin (2003) note, the major elements of program planning are design and implementation. The design component includes the following: (1) defining the problem, (2) assessing needs, (3) setting goals and objectives, and (4) selecting intervention strategies. The implementation component of program planning consists of (1) operationalizing goals and objectives in the form of action steps and activities, (2) specifying elements of the program design in the form of services or interventions, (3) utilizing information systems to provide a database for monitoring and evaluation, (4) budgeting and planning for the allocation of human resources, and (5) evaluating the relationship between the design and implementation process to identify outcomes and problems inadequately addressed by the original design. It is critical to formally create a feedback loop from evaluation to program planning to assure that the lessons learned in these evaluative activities are translated to program and agency policies and procedures. For example, in the geriatric mental health program of a South Florida agency, accessibility was an important part of

Table 15.1   The Operational Steps Needed to Implement the Strategic Plan

Recommendation	Action Steps	Outcomes	Due Dates	People Responsible
Recommendation 1				
1.1	1.	1.	1.	1.
1.2	2.	2.	2.	2.
1.3	3.	3.	3.	3.
Recommendation 2				
2.1				
2.2				
Recommendation 3				
3.1				
3.2				

assessing client services. In looking at the populations served by the agency as compared to the target population in the catchment area, it was discovered that both men and Hispanics were significantly underrepresented in the client population. Through formal program planning sessions involving senior management, program evaluators, and clinical and supervisory staff to identify potential reasons for an underrepresentation of men, it was concluded that the center's hours of operation (8:30 a.m. to 5:30 p.m. Monday through Friday) might be a barrier to the employed older, disproportionately male population. Data from a review of intake inquiries suggested that, indeed, this might be a factor, and the hours of operation were changed to include evening hours, which helped to increase male service utilization (Austin, 1983).

Even though the program was multilingual (including Spanish), a focused outreach effort was developed based on concepts of "personalismo," a concept that suggested that the personal relationship between referral sources and Spanish-speaking clinical staff was more important than traditional institutional liaison arrangements. Again, the operational changes that included the outreach of Spanish-speaking clinical staff to traditional referral sources resulted in significantly greater service accessibility for the Latino population. The measurement of service outcomes, program accountability, and information management are addressed elsewhere in this volume (see Chapters 8 and 9). They are critical elements for effective operations planning (Szapocznik, Lasaga, Perry, & Solomon, 1979).

Contingency Planning

Day-to-day agency life is filled with the drama of unexpected events. Despite the finest strategic and operational plans, effective organizations are not always able to respond quickly and opportunistically to sudden changes in the environment. For example, a mid-year reduction in public support, a fire in an agency facility, a serious untoward incident involving an agency

client, an agency labor dispute, or an inability to find qualified credentialed staff to fill vacant positions are unexpected changes that illustrate why contingency planning can become a critical component of an agency's capacity to manage change. As a form of operations planning, contingency planning involves the converting of crises into organizational opportunities. This requires special attention to using a disciplined approach to systematically (a) refer to the agency mission on a regular basis, (b) seek out available information, (c) promote the active participation of appropriate staff and lay leaders, and (d) engage in extensive monitoring and follow-up. Contingency plans are much easier to implement if a strategic plan provides overall guidance for the future allocation of scarce agency resources.

Perhaps the most common contingency is a change in the flow of agency revenues that threatens the survival of the agency and its programs. In the case of a large city fundraising agency that allocates funds annually to a group of beneficiary agencies, experience with agency financial failures led to the development of a management tool that reduced the need for crisis management and focused the agency's board of directors and senior management on rational contingency planning tied to the agency's mission and plan. The tool was an early warning system that uses a combination of financial analyses (balance sheet ratios), agency-by-agency trend data, assessment analyses, and comparisons to identify those agencies that were within one to two years of financial crisis. In many cases, this led to contingency financial planning that altered the direction of the agency. In some cases, the agency mission could best be served by launching discussions on the value of a merger with another agency.

Most human services managers believe strongly in their agency mission and the value of its services, and they tend to view budgetary threats with unfettered optimism. However, budgets are projections that cannot always take into account changes in the external funding environment. As a result, managers tend to delay serious cuts as long as possible and to limit those cuts to overhead expenses rather than direct service delivery or across-the-board cuts in service expenditures, waiting for each contingency to become a crisis before acting. Ironically, fiscal crisis is often an unusual opportunity to reshape the agency in line with strategic planning recommendations. A fiscal crisis provides management with the ability to move far more decisively and quickly than in times of stability. The availability of time is a critical factor in contingency planning. If there is not enough time to meet the monthly payroll due to the financial crisis, it may be too late for contingency planning and drastic measures may be needed.

Budgetary Planning

Annual budgets represent the major link between implementing a strategic plan and the ongoing priorities reflected in the annual operations plans that accompany most budgets. Many organizations do program and operations planning on the basis of the agency's fiscal year. The budgetary allocation of funds often requires clear and measurable objectives in order to quantify the resources needed to achieve the goals and objectives related to revenues and expenses. This form of budgeting helps to assure that the budget preparation process is driven more by agency program and mission considerations than simply by the availability of financial resources (program driven rather than finance driven). Effective managers use budget planning as a valuable adjunct to implementing a strategic plan (also see Chapter 19).

For example, a national planning and service agency recently conducted a strategic plan that built the budgetary process into the planning process. The technique involved the use of a parallel budgetary planning process conducted at the same time as the strategic plan was being developed. The strategic planning included six major task forces. As each task force developed its recommendations, management was asked to prepare budget projections related to each of the recommendations, and agency department heads

were asked to identify the implications of each recommendation for staff implementation. By linking the planning and budgeting processes together, this agency improved its capacity to understand the implementation implications of the proposed components of the plan. At the same time, it involved the financial staff in thinking carefully about the financial and human resource implications of each recommendation in the strategic plan. In gaining board approval of the plan, staff used a budget template to demonstrate the budgetary changes needed to implement each recommendation. This technique helped to raise the level of confidence among all involved with respect to the realistic possibilities of implementing the strategic plan.

Revisiting the Relationship Between Strategic Planning and Operational Planning

The culture of strategic and operational planning requires agency leadership to be prepared to openly and objectively look at its current practices with the expectation and belief that things can be improved. Quality strategic planning is an interactive process that invites all stakeholders to participate actively in constructive criticism. The best planning processes have as many stakeholders as possible feeling that they are contributing to the activities. Whether it is in the process of holding formal hearings or engaging in focus groups, town meetings, and other methods of reaching all stakeholders, communication is a key element to planning.

An effective planning process is not simply an analytic exercise. It is one that blends art with science: the science of an analytic mindset to complete a comprehensive organizational assessment and the artistry to foster the broadest level of participation, touching the hearts and minds of all stakeholders with core organizational values and hopes for the future. Strategic planning involves change and managerial leadership. To paraphrase an observation by Lao Tse centuries ago, "leaders are individuals whom the people hardly know exist, but good leaders, when their work is done, their aims fulfilled, become truly invisible when the people say 'We did this ourselves.'" The quest for continuous improvement can motivate staff and board members alike, especially when they build together an environment where creativity leads to shared satisfaction and the status quo is not an acceptable condition.

Conclusion

In this chapter, we have explored the dynamics of strategic planning and operations planning and implementation. We have emphasized the linkage between planning and implementation and the importance of involving staff and board members throughout the process. Strategic planning is characterized as proactive and linear in that it seeks to analyze data from a variety of sources to develop a course of action. Not everyone identifies with the importance of planning. In the for-profit arena, an increasing number of entrepreneurs tend to minimize planning in order to be able to respond to opportunities that could not have been foreseen (Mintzberg, 1994). Some human services administrators identify with this entrepreneurial model, either because of the presumed flexibility involved or because the planning process is seen as too labor intensive and costly when involving staff, board members, and/or a consultant/facilitator. These reactions to planning call for more research on the process and outcomes of strategic planning. Although there is research on the benefits of strategic planning, there is little research to document the consequences of not planning, except for case studies of failed businesses or agencies. We need more information about when and why strategic planning works in human services organizations.

The operational and program planning required to implement a strategic plan clearly requires staff to understand the full context and details of the strategic plan in order to develop a sense of ownership. This ownership is critical if the unanticipated changes and crises that emerge daily in human services agencies are not allowed to derail the implementation process. This is easily said but not easily done. Both planning and implementation are creative processes. The analytic aspects of a strategic plan need to be matched by the interactional skills of managers and staff, if the future vision of the agency is to have any meaning within the daily realities of organizational life. There is an artistry to both planning and implementation. This observation has become even more relevant as agencies seek to implement strategic plans by paying attention to the processes of change management.

Change management is an organizational process that recognizes the importance of involving staff at all levels in "modifying the way we do business" (sometimes likened to the process of moving a graveyard). The forces for change and the forces of resistance need to be managed. Although change management is a topic for another chapter (McLennan, 1989; O'Toole, 1995; Senge, 1990), it is important to note that some human services organizations are recognizing the need for internal organization development specialists to assist with the teambuilding, communications enhancement, and intra-organizational restructuring that are often called for in the implementation and monitoring of strategic plans (Dubrow, Wocher, & Austin, 2001).

The value of strategic planning as a managerial tool has increased dramatically in the context of reinventing government and redefining the role of human services. As we move from an industrial society to a service and information society, the computer-based informational tools that allow us to look at our practices more systematically have become both widespread and inexpensive. These tools can be used quite successfully to inform the strategic planning process. Finally, with the end of the Cold War, the globalization of the economy, and fluctuation in economic growth, service consumers have increased their expectations for high-quality services. The human services administrator has a responsibility to anticipate and respond to this expectation through the use of strategic and operational planning as an essential component of human services management.

References

Allison, M., & Kaye, J. (2005). *Strategic planning for non-profit organizations: A practical guide and workbook* (2nd ed.). New York: John Wiley.

Austin, D. (1983). Program design issues in the improved administration of human services programs. *Administration in Social Work, 7*(1), 1–11.

Austin, M. J. (2002). Mapping the future: Strategic planning in the American Jewish community. *Journal of Jewish Communal Services, 79*(1), 29–36.

Austin, M. J., & Vu, C. (2007). Assessing organizations from multiple perspectives: Clients, staff, management, and funders. In W. Rowe & L. Rapp-Paglicci (Eds.), *Comprehensive handbook of social work and social welfare* (Vol. 3, pp. 533–555). New York: J. Wiley.

Berman, E. M. (1998). *Productivity in public and non-profit organizations.* Thousand Oaks, CA: Sage.

Bryson, J. M. (2004). *Strategic planning for public and nonprofit organizations: A guide to strengthening and sustaining organizational effectiveness* (3rd ed.). San Francisco: Jossey-Bass.

DuBrow, A., Wocher, D., & Austin, M. J. (2001). Introducing organizational development (OD) practices into a county human services agency. *Administration in Social Work, 25*(4), 46–59.

Eadie, D. (1983). Putting a powerful tool to practical use: The application of strategic planning in the public sector. *Public Administration Review, 43*(5), 447–452.

Eldridge, W. (1983). Aids to administrative planning in social agencies. *Child Welfare, 62*(2), 119–127.

Farmby, K. (2004). Environmental scanning for nonprofit human service organizations. In M. J. Austin & K. Hopkins (Eds.), *Supervision as collaboration in the human services: Building a learning culture* (pp. 252–260). Thousand Oaks, CA: Sage.

Gowdy, E., & Freeman, E. (1993). Program supervision: Facilitating staff participation in program analysis, planning, and change. *Administration in Social Work, 17*(3), 59–79.

Julian, D., & Lyons, T. (1992). A strategic planning model for human services: Problem solving at the local level. *Evaluation and Program Planning, 15,* 247–254.

Kaufman, J., & Jacobs, H. (1987). A public planning perspective on strategic planning. *Journal of American Planning Association, 53*(1), 23–33.

Kettner, P. M., Moroney, R. M., & Martin, L. L. (2003). *Designing and managing programs: An effectiveness-based approach* (2nd ed.). Thousand Oaks, CA: Sage.

Koontz, H. (1981). Making strategic planning work. In L. Reinharth, H. Shapiro, & E. Kellman (Eds.), *The practice of planning: Strategic, administrative, and operational* (pp. 29–41). New York: Van Nostrand Reinhold.

McLennan, R. (1989). *Managing organizational change.* Englewood Cliffs, NJ: Prentice Hall.

Mintzberg, H. (1994). *The rise and fall of strategic planning: Reconceiving roles for planning, plans, planners.* New York: Free Press.

O'Toole, J. (1995). *Leading change: Overcoming the ideology of comfort and the tyranny of custom.* San Francisco: Jossey-Bass.

Senge, P. (1990). *The fifth discipline: The art and practice of the learning organization.* New York: Doubleday.

Siciliano, J. (1997). The relationship between formal planning and performance in nonprofit organizations. *Nonprofit Management and Leadership, 7*(4), 387–403.

Sorkin, D., Ferris, N., & Hudak, J. (1984). *Strategies for cities and counties: A strategic planning guide.* Washington, DC: Public Technology.

Stacey, R. D. (1992). *Managing the unknowable: Strategic boundaries between order and chaos in organizations.* San Francisco: Jossey-Bass.

Steiner, J., Gross, G., Ruffolo, M., & Murray, J. (1994). Strategic planning in nonprofits: Profit from it. *Administration in Social Work, 18*(2), 87–106.

Stone, M., Bigelow, B., & Crittenden, W. (1999). Research on strategic management in nonprofit organizations: Synthesis, analysis, and future directions. *Administration & Society, 31*(3), 378–423.

Szapocznik, J., Lasaga, J., Perry, P. R., & Solomon, J. R. (1979). Outreach in the delivery of mental health services to Hispanic elders. *Hispanic Journal of Behavioral Sciences, 1*(1), 21–40.

Vogel, L., & Patterson, I. (1986). Strategy and structure: A case study of the implications of strategic planning for organizational structure and management practice. *Administration in Social Work, 10*(2), 53–66.

Webster, S., & Wylie, M. (1988a). Strategic planning in competitive environments. *Administration in Social Work, 12*(3), 25–43.

Webster, S., & Wylie, M. (1988b). Strategic planning in human service agencies. *Journal of Sociology and Social Welfare, 15*(3), 47–64.

Ziegenfuss, J. (1989). *Designing organizational futures.* Springfield, IL: Charles C Thomas.

CHAPTER 16

Program Planning and Management

Lawrence L. Martin

Introduction

This chapter deals with the topic of program planning and management in human services agencies. The chapter begins with a discussion of what constitutes a program and how program planning differs from strategic planning. The remainder of the chapter is divided into two major sections: (1) program planning issues and (2) program management and implementation issues. It is important at the outset to stress the overview nature of this chapter. Attempting to deal with the topic of program planning and management in a single chapter is a challenge. Whole textbooks have been written on this subject. Because of the limitations on length, the discussion here is abbreviated and should be considered only as an introduction to the topic.

What Is a Program?

A *program* is the basic organizational building block of a human services agency. Some small human services agencies may operate only one program. However, most human services agencies have multiple programs (Weinbach, 2003). The number and types of programs operated by a human services agency is referred to as its *program structure* (Martin, 2001).

Various definitions of *program* have been proposed over the years (e.g., Kettner, Moroney, & Martin, 2008; Martin, 2001; Rapp & Poertner, 1992; Weinbach, 2003). By synthesizing these various attempts, a consensus definition can be derived (see Definition of a Program, below). As this definition makes explicit, a program is a major ongoing activity or service. Not every activity or service engaged in by a human services

> ## DEFINITION OF A PROGRAM
>
> A major ongoing agency activity or service with its own sets of policies, goals, objectives, and budgets that produces a defined product or service.

agency warrants being designated as a program. A program is one of the important few ongoing activities or services provided by a human services agency.

To further distinguish it from other activities and services, a program generally has its own set of policies, goals, objectives, and budgets (Kettner, Moroney, & Martin, 2008). In particular, the acid test for a program is whether it has its own budget (Smith & Lynch, 2004). Finally, a program produces something, a defined product or service. For example, a home-delivered meals program produces "meals," a counseling program produces "hours of counseling," and an adoption program produces "adoptions." Conversely, accounting, public relations, and secretarial functions do not produce defined products or services.

With the emphasis placed on accountability and performance measurement today, a program must be able to demonstrate that it produces a product or service that achieves some result, impact, or accomplishment (Austin, 2002; Government Performance and Results Act of 1993 [GPRA]; Governmental Accounting Standards Board [GASB], 1993; Lohmann & Lohmann, 2002; McDavid & Hawthorn, 2006).

Program Planning Versus Strategic Planning

Program planning differs from strategic planning in at least two important ways (see Table 16.1). In terms of *focus*, strategic planning is concerned with the overall agency and providing overall direction through the agency's mission, vision, values, goals, and allocation of resources (Bryson, 2004; Cohen & Emicke, 1998). In program planning, the focus is on the individual program. This distinction is not to suggest that program planning is unaffected by strategic planning. Strategic planning creates the overall agency environment and framework in which program planning takes place.

Table 16.1   Differences Between Program Planning and Strategic Planning

Dimension	Strategic Planning	Program Planning
Focus	Agency	Program
Involvement	Board of directors and top management	Top and middle managers and supervisors

In terms of *involvement*, strategic planning is generally initiated and led by the upper echelons of a human services agency and involves top management and the agency's board of directors, with participation of middle management and direct service staff. Program planning takes place primarily at the mid-management level (Weinbach, 2003). While these distinctions are somewhat oversimplified, they do provide a demarcation between strategic planning and program planning (for a further discussion of strategic planning, see Chapter 15).

Program Planning Issues

This section deals with the conceptualization and design of a human services program. The discussion is organized into five topic areas: (1) initially conceptualizing the program, (2) determining the need for the program, (3) marketing considerations, (4) the elements of program design, and (5) budgeting issues. Before proceeding to the discussion of these five topic areas, however, some mention needs to be made of bottom-up program planning versus top-down program planning.

Bottom-Up Versus Top-Down Program Planning

Historically, program planning has tended to follow the bottom-up approach. The bottom-up approach begins with a human services agency deciding to provide or expand a program and then seeking grant funding from government, the United Way, a foundation, or some other source. In the bottom-up approach, the human services agency makes most, if not all, of the program planning decisions, including designating the target group to be served, identifying the service area, and specifying the service delivery strategy.

The top-down approach begins with a funding source deciding that a particular program should be provided or expanded. The funding source may also specify the target group to be served, the service delivery strategy to be employed, the geographical area to be served, and other considerations. The funding source then invites human services agencies to submit bids or proposals to provide the program, usually under a contractual or quasi-contractual arrangement.

Today, the top-down approach is just as prevalent as, and may perhaps be even more prevalent than, the bottom-up approach. In the sections below, the traditional bottom-up approach to program planning is utilized. It should be understood, however, that these program planning issues may be either dealt with by the human services agency itself or predetermined by

a funder. Regardless of the approach taken (bottom-up or top-down), certain key program planning issues need to be addressed concerning how the human services program is conceptualized and designed.

Initial Conceptualization of the Program

When initially conceptualizing a human services program, several questions need to be asked and answered. What is the target population? What is the program's purpose? And how will the program work? This process can be thought of as moving from a vague idea to a more concrete, but still incomplete, description of a human services program.

What Is the Target Group? There are a number of individuals and groups worthy and deserving of having a human services program developed to assist them with some problem or need. The question is which individuals or which group should be served? The individuals or group to be served are frequently referred to as the target group or target population. The term *target group* will be used here. A target group is defined by one or more shared characteristics (see Figure 16.1).

As Figure 16.1 demonstrates, determining the target group is a process of "drilling down" within a general classification of people (children, women, elderly) to identify a specific subgroup that a proposed program is designed to help (Rapp & Poertner, 1992). This drill-down procedure serves several purposes. First, individuals or a group can have a myriad of problems, issues, and needs. Consequently, it is useful to think in more concrete terms about the specific problem, issue, or need to be addressed by the proposed human services program. Second, problems, issues, and needs can be "place sensitive," meaning they can vary significantly depending upon geography (e.g., Northeast versus Southwest, urban versus rural, ethnic minority community versus white middle-class

Children

— at risk of abuse or neglect

• in need of out-of-home placements

o residing in the city of Orlando, Florida

Women

— in abusive relationships

• in need of shelter, care, and counseling

o residing in the New York City Borough of Queens

Elderly

— living alone

• in need of in-home support services

o residing on reservations in Northern Arizona

Figure 16.1 Target Groups

community). Third, there is generally insufficient funding to address all problems, issues, and needs. Consequently, choices have to be made. The decision to expend resources on one target group creates an "opportunity loss" because those same funds are no longer available to serve other target groups. Fourth, the more clearly defined the target group, the greater the probability of designing an effective human services program (Kettner et al., 2008). There are no clear decision rules here to guide practice. However, the values and ethics that underlie social work and other human services professions can and do provide guidance (Rapp & Poertner, 1992).

What Is the Program's Purpose? What specifically is the program trying to accomplish? The elderly target group identified in Figure 16.1 can be utilized as an example. The target group is elderly Native Americans living alone on reservations. The issue here may be one of assisting the target group to continue living independently, or reasonably independently, by providing in-home support services. Thus, the program purpose is to *keep people living independently through the provision of in-home support services.* But what, specifically, is meant by in-home support services?

How Will the Program Work? This question concerns what activities, tasks, or actions comprise in-home services. The best way to answer this question is to already know something about the target group, ask somebody for guidance who is an expert on the target group, or conduct a survey or focus group with target group members. Elderly Native Americans living alone on reservations in Northern Arizona will probably need assistance (among other activities, tasks, and actions) with gathering and chopping firewood and hauling water. The importance of "place sensitive" policies is highlighted here. Gathering and chopping firewood and hauling water may not be considered legitimate component parts of in-home services in many parts of the country, but they can be on some reservations.

To summarize, the purpose of initially conceptualizing a human services program is to begin clarifying the target group to be served; the purpose of the program (what the program is trying to accomplish); and the major activities, tasks, and actions that comprise the program (how the program will work). As these planning issues, as well as the ones that follow, are considered, planners may well find themselves returning to previous stages as they learn more or encounter barriers.

Determining the Need for the Program

Determining the need for the program involves attempting to identify the number of target group individuals who can reasonably be expected to (a) benefit from the program and (b) participate in the program. The argument can be made that this task should be dealt with first. Why bother, one can argue, spending time conceptualizing a program if there is no need for it? The answer is that it is a "chicken and egg" thing. How do you know whether there is a need for a program until the program has been conceptualized, and how do you conceptualize a program if you don't know something about the need for it? Need can affect how a program is conceptualized and how a program is conceptualized can affect the determination of need.

Need. A full discussion of the concept of need is beyond the scope of this chapter. For the sake of brevity, there are four generally recognized types of need: normative, perceived, expressed, and relative (Kettner et al., 2008; Reviere, 1996). Normative need is related to some standard, such as the poverty level. Relative need is the gap between the level of a particular human services problem in one area compared to another area (e.g., the number of unemployed in one community compared to another community). Perceived need is what people think they need. Expressed need is the extent to which individuals have actually attempted to access a human services program. Regardless of the type of need (normative, perceived, expressed, or relative), the challenge is attempting to determine how many or what proportion of a target group are in need of the program and will actually participate in the program.

Needs Assessments. Several approaches exist to conducting needs assessments. *Secondary data analysis of* existing studies can be done. *Surveys* (telephone or face-to-face) can be conducted. *Focus groups* can be held. *Resource inventories* can be compiled by contacting other human services agencies in the same geographical area to determine whether they already provide the same or a similar program and the numbers of clients they already serve. Or a combination of one or more of these approaches can be used. All of these approaches, however, have inherent limitations. Secondary data analysis requires research skills and statistical expertise. Surveys can be expensive and time consuming. Getting a representative cross section of target group individuals to participate in a focus group can be difficult. Compiling a resource inventory can be difficult, particularly if other human services agencies are not willing to provide information about their programs and the numbers of clients served. The important point here is that even in the best of situations,

determining the need for a human services program is difficult, and the measure of need is seldom any more than an estimation. It should be noted that in top-down planning, a needs assessment has probably already been done by the funding source, but the human services agency may still want to conduct some confirmatory assessment to insure that the need profile is valid.

At this point, a comment about unmet need is in order. Needs assessments provide an overall estimate of the need for a human services program. In order for a human services agency to make an informed decision about starting or expanding a program, it is necessary to estimate what proportion of the need is currently being met. This information is essential in order to estimate *unmet need.*

$$\text{Unmet} = \text{Need} - \text{Proportion of Need Currently Being Met}$$

Unfortunately, data and information on the proportion of need currently being met are difficult to obtain. Many human services agencies are reluctant to share this information for fear it will somehow be used against them, perhaps to help a competitor. Determining the proportion of need currently being met has always been the Achilles heel of needs assessments.

To summarize, needs assessments are concerned with attempting to estimate the number or proportion of the target group that potentially "need" a human services program and would potentially participate in it.

Marketing Considerations

While the needs assessment approach to program planning is the dominant paradigm in the human services, it does suffer from some inherent limitations. The needs assessment paradigm does not take into consideration such issues as, Who is the competition? Who are the customers? And what should be the marketing mix? These are all questions that fall outside the framework of the needs assessment paradigm, but fortunately they are addressed from a marketing perspective (Herron, 1997).

Who Is the Competition? Thinking about competition and competitors has never been part of the mindset of human services agencies. Historically, human services agencies have always maintained that they do not compete with each other (e.g., Martin & Parker, 1994). Whether or not a "golden age" existed at some time in the past when human services agencies and programs truly did not compete with each other, this situation clearly does not exist today. Resources for human services programs have steadily declined over the last two decades, while the number of nonprofit human services agencies has increased. These two trends have combined to create an environment in which more and more human services agencies and programs are competing for fewer and fewer available dollars (Fischer, 2005).

As part of the planning process, a human services agency should know who its competitors are and how strong they are. Based on an assessment of the competition and its relative strength, a human services agency considering starting a new program or expanding an existing one should ask itself such questions as, Can we compete? How can we compete? What is our "competitive advantage" (e.g., higher quality services, lower cost, accessibility for persons with disabilities, better outcomes)? And perhaps most important, should we compete? The three initial questions address the agency's organizational abilities and capacity. The last question goes to issues of community norms, networks, and politics. Deciding to compete to provide a particular program in a particular community may disrupt historic service delivery patterns and agency relationships and can have detrimental consequences for client customers, human services agencies, and the community itself. Sometimes, the most appropriate response for a human services agency is to consider issues other than its own organizational needs and decide not to compete.

Who Are the Customers? Marketing is said to involve determining what customers want and then providing it (e.g., Johnson & Venkatesan, 2001; Herron, 1997). There is an old adage about the difference between marketing and advertising. *Advertising* is about selling customers a product or service that already exists. *Marketing* is about designing a product or service around what consumers want, and then it sells itself.

The human services have two classes of customers: clients and funders. This realization only became clear as a result of the total quality management (TQM) movement (Gunther & Hawkins, 1996; Martin, 1993). Client customers consume products and services, but usually they do not pay for them. Funders pay for products and services, but generally they do not consume them. In designing a program, a human services agency needs to consider the preferences of both types of customers.

What Is the Marketing Mix? In this discussion, the terms *product* and service are used interchangeably. The marketing mix involves considerations of *p*roduct (or service), *p*romotion, *p*lacement, and *p*rice, also know as the 4Ps:

- *Product:* Marketing and program planning share a common perspective with respect to product: They are both concerned with designing a human services program that is as attractive as possible to customers.
- *Placement:* Placement deals with service delivery issues such as hours of program availability (e.g., 24/7), location (i.e., geographical service area), cultural competencies (e.g., Hispanic, African American), and other considerations.
- *Promotion:* Promotion deals with how the product is to be presented to client and funding source customers. What characteristics of the human services program should be emphasized in order to differentiate it from the same or similar programs offered by other human services agencies (e.g., the program is provided by licensed social

Figure 16.2   The Expanded System Model

SOURCE: Martin (2001), Martin and Kettner (1996), Martin (1993).

workers, the program is accredited by a professional association, client customers say it is the best program in the community)?

- *Price:* Considerations of price are important, for there is little to be gained from conceptualizing and designing a human services program that no one can afford. There is usually a tradeoff between quality and price (Martin, 1993). The higher the quality, the higher the price (e.g., more staff with higher professional qualifications means higher program costs). Part of program conceptualization and design of a human services program is attempting to find the right balance of program quality and cost so that the price will be acceptable to client customers as well as funding source customers.

To summarize, a marketing perspective augments the needs assessment approach by introducing additional considerations (competition, customers, and marketing mix) that are important in conceptualizing and planning a human services program. (Also see Chapter 17 for additional discussion of social marketing.)

Program Design Issues

Program design concerns the detailed specification of the elements that comprise a human services program (Kettner et al., 2008). The elements of program design generally follow what can be referred to as the "expanded systems model" (see Figure 16.2).

The expanded systems model augments the traditional systems model by adding quality and outcomes. The rationale for this action is that the quality management movement, the performance measurement movement, and the outcome movement all occurred after the development of the basic systems model and need to be included today in order to constitute a comprehensive systems approach (see Chapter 8 for additional discussion of quality and outcome measures).

- *Input* is what goes into a human services program (e.g., staff, facilities, equipment, clients, presenting problems).
- *Activities,* also known as *process,* deal with service delivery strategies, treatment modalities, and all those activities and actions that are considered essential to the operation of a human services program.
- *Output* is what a human services program produces. Outputs are also referred to as *units of service.* The purpose of an output is to provide a measure of service volume (how much service is provided). There are three basic types of outputs: time (e.g., one hour, one day, one month), episode (e.g., one visit, one appointment), and material (e.g. one meal, one prescription).
- *Quality* refers to one or more dimensions by which the quality of a human services program is evaluated. Quality dimensions include empathy, humaneness, responsiveness, security, durability, assurance, and accessibility (Martin, 1993).
- *Outcome* refers to the results, accomplishments, or impacts of human services programs (GPRA, 1993; GASB, 1993) and are usually expressed as measures of "quality

of life changes in clients" (Martin & Kettner, 1996). Clients' outcomes are sometimes said to be measured by the ABCs (positive changes in client *a*ctions, *b*ehaviors, or *c*onditions).

Logic Models. In recent years, the use of logic models has become popular as a way of thinking about program design and how the links (input, activities, output, quality, and outcome) of human services programs are related (Rossi, Lipsey, & Freeman, 2004; Valley of the Sun United Way, 2006; W. K. Kellogg Foundation, 2004). There is no single logic model (W. K. Kellogg Foundation, 2004). The term logic model is really an umbrella term that includes various approaches, depending upon the starting point and ending point of the logic chain. Figure 16.3 illustrates some of the more frequently encountered logic models.

In the *social problem approach*, the logic chain begins with the social problem the program addresses (Martin & Kettner, 1996). All links in the logic model are directly tied to the social problem and must demonstrate how they address the social problem. In the *community need approach*, the logic model begins with an identified community need (e.g., children at risk), and all subsequent links must demonstrate how the design of the human services program

addresses the identified community need (Valley of the Sun United Way, 2006). While there is some overlap between the social problem approach and the community need approach, their purposes are sufficiently different to warrant being treated as different logic model variations. In the *agency strategic plan approach*, the logic model chain begins with an agency's strategic plan, and all subsequent links must demonstrate how the design of the human services program flows from and supports the agency's strategic plan.

The output and outcome approaches are determined by the end point at which their logic models terminate. The *output approach* is favored by international funding organizations like the World Bank (Brook & Smith, 2001). In developing countries, it is difficult to develop and measure program outcomes, so international funding organizations prefer to end their logic models at outputs. In the *outcome approach*, the logic chain ends with the results, accomplishments, or impacts (outcomes) of human services programs. The outcome approach is favored by the federal government because of the GPRA. An example of a logic model utilizing both the social problem approach and the outcome approach is illustrated in Figure 16.4.

As Figure 16.4 illustrates, the logic model approach helps ensure that all aspects of a human

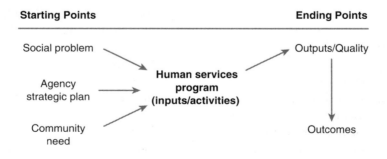

Figure 16.3   Different Types of Logic Models

services program are in alignment, beginning with the motivation for the program and continuing through to the outcome measure for the program.

Costing the Program

A critical aspect of the program planning process is determining how much the program will cost. (Also see Chapter 19 for additional discussion of this issue.) As a general rule, human services agencies have difficulty in this area.

The total cost, or full cost, of a human services program is the sum of its direct and indirect costs (Kettner et al., 2008; Martin, 2001). A *direct cost* benefits one and only one program, for example, the salary of a program director who works 100% of her time on one program and no other programs. An indirect cost is one that benefits two or more programs. Indirect costs are sometimes called overhead costs or operation and maintenance costs. For example, the executive director of a human services agency is an indirect cost because he or she works for all the agency's programs.

To determine the direct costs of a human services program, a line-item budget is frequently developed. However, a line-item budget generally

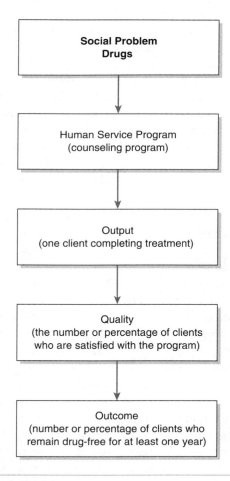

Figure 16.4   Example of Logic Model

contains only direct costs. Human services agencies usually allocate a portion of the agency's indirect costs to each program according to the agency's "cost allocation plan." A full discussion of direct and indirect costs and cost allocation plans is outside the scope of this chapter. The important point here is that indirect costs must be included in determining the cost of a human services program. If this is not done, the program will be underpricing its services. (For an additional discussion of cost and budgetary issues, see Chapter 19.)

Program Management and Implementation Issues

Human services programs are not self-implementing. While considerable attention is usually paid to program planning issues, less attention is paid to management and implementation issues. This section deals with two of the most important management and implementation issues: (a) selecting the service delivery approach and (b) monitoring implementation and taking corrective action when necessary.

Selecting a Service Delivery Strategy

Selecting a service delivery strategy is an issue that confronts government human services agencies more than nonprofits (i.e., whether the program is to be delivered by the human services agency itself or is to be co-produced or outsourced to another organization). However, even some nonprofit human services agencies today are beginning to consider alternative methods of delivering services.

At one time, there was essentially only one service delivery strategy: direct service delivery. A decision to provide a new service was de facto also a decision to provide the service directly. Today, there are a number of alternative service delivery strategies: contracting, vouchers, co-production, public-private partnerships, and others (Salamon, 2002).

Contracting, also called *privatization* and *community-based care,* is the preferred government service delivery approach today (Martin, 2005; Mayers, 2004). There are a number of advantages to contracting:

- lower service delivery cost,
- promotion of government/nonprofit cooperation,
- access to community based nonprofit service delivery expertise not available in government,
- equal or better service quality, and
- ability to experiment with different service delivery approaches.

As a general rule, contracting usually results in lower service delivery costs and equal or better service quality (Martin & Miller, 2006).

Government human services agencies that contract for services with nonprofit community-based organizations are increasingly utilizing performance-based contracting (PBC). In PBC, funding is tied to the achievement of output, quality, and outcome performance measures, which means that community-based nonprofits acting as contractors need to be highly accurate in estimating their program costs as well as their program performance (Martin, 2005).

Monitoring

An important aspect of program management and implementation is the conduct of monitoring. Monitoring can be defined as determining whether the human services program is being implemented as intended (Rossi et al., 2004). Monitoring comes from the Latin word *monere* meaning *to warn.* Monitoring can be seen as an early warning system designed to alert a human services agency when one of its programs is not being implemented as intended. Monitoring provides feedback on the current status of a human services program and is concerned with providing data and information on issues such as the following: What proportion of the need for the program is currently being met?

Table 16.2   Monitoring, Performance Measurement, and Program Evaluation

	1st Quarter	2nd Quarter	3rd Quarter	4th Quarter
Total number of persons served	175	200	225	250
Minority	50	75	75	75
Persons with disabilities	25	25	25	50
Women	50	50	75	75
Other	50	50	50	50
Outputs (hours of service)	4,200	4,500	4,700	5,000
Outcomes achieved	100	125	135	145

Are only eligible target group members being served? Are women, minorities, persons with disabilities, and other special interest groups being served in appropriate numbers?

Armed with these types of data, program managers can take corrective action should program implementation deviate from its intended direction.

Some people refer to monitoring as formative evaluation because its purpose is to provide data and information that can be used to make program improvements during implementation (Rossi et al., 2004). Thus, there is some overlap between monitoring and program evaluation (McDavid & Hawthorn, 2006). Monitoring is also concerned with the performance of a human services program. In this respect, there is also overlap between performance measurement and program monitoring (see Table 16.2; also see Chapter 8).

As Table 16.2 points out, the data collected and reported on a quarterly (Q) basis can be used for performance measurement, monitoring, or formative program evaluation. The same data can also be reviewed at the end of the program (summative evaluation) and used to make programmatic changes during the following year.

program planning and management generally take place at the mid-management level, these functions are no less important to a human services agency than is strategic planning. Program planning involves taking what is frequently only a vague notion of wanting to help someone or some group and translating that desire into a concrete plan of action that includes a defined target group, a designated service area, a prescribed service delivery methodology, and defined program elements (inputs, activities, outputs, quality, and outcomes).

Program planning also involves thinking about a human services program's customers, its competition, and how the program will be marketed. Costing and budgetary issues are also part of program planning and are essential to determining what price client customers and funding source customers will be willing to pay for the program.

Finally, program management and implementation involves the selection of the service delivery strategy (direct or alternative) and the monitoring of program implementation. Program management also involves taking corrective action when implementation does not proceed according to plan.

Summary and Conclusion

Program planning and management are important functions of any human services agency. While

References

Austin, D. (2002). *Human services management.* New York: Columbia University Press.

Brook, P. J., & Smith, S. M. (Eds.). (2001). *Contracting for public services: Output-based aid and its applications.* Washington, DC: The International Bank for Reconstruction and Development. Retrieved from http://rru.worldbank.org/Features/OBABook.aspx

Bryson, J. (2004). *Strategic planning for public and nonprofit organizations* (3rd ed.). San Francisco: Jossey-Bass.

Cohen, S., & Eimicke, W. (1998). Tools for innovators. San Francisco: Jossey-Bass.

Fischer, E. (2005). Facing the challenges of outcome measurement: The role of transformational leadership. *Administration in Social Work, 29*(4), 35–49.

Government Performance and Results Act of 1993, Pub. L. No. 103-62, 107 Stat. 285 (1993).

Governmental Accounting Standards Board. (1993). *Proposed statement of the Governmental Accounting Standards Board on concepts related to service efforts and accomplishments reporting.* Norwalk, CT: Author.

Gunther, J., & Hawkins, F. (Eds.). (1996). *Total quality management in human service organizations.* New York: Springer.

Herron, D. (1997). *Marketing nonprofit programs and services.* San Francisco: Jossey-Bass.

Johnson, E., & Venkatesan, M. (2001). Marketing. In T. Connors (Ed.), *The nonprofit handbook.* New York: John Wiley & Sons.

Kettner, P., Moroney, R., & Martin, L. (2008). *Designing and managing program: An effectiveness-based approach.* Thousand Oaks, CA: Sage.

Lohmann, R., & Lohmann, N. (2002). *Social administration.* New York: Columbia University Press.

Martin, L. L. (1993). *Total quality management in human service organizations.* Newbury Park, CA: Sage.

Martin, L. L. (2001). *Financial management for human service administrators.* Boston: Allyn & Bacon.

Martin, L. L. (2005). Performance based contracting: Does it work? *Administration in Social Work, 29*(1), 63–77.

Martin, L. L., & Kettner, P. (1996). *Measuring the performance of human service programs.* Thousand Oaks, CA: Sage.

Martin, L. L., & Miller, J. (2006). *Contracting for public sector services.* Herndon, VA: National Institute of Governmental Purchasing.

Martin, L. L., & Parker, M. (1994). Has the time come for social service vouchers? In H. Karger & J. Midgley (Eds.), *Controversial issues in social policy* (pp. 119–130). Boston: Allyn & Bacon.

Mayers, R. (2004). *Financial management for nonprofit human service organizations.* Springfield, IL: Charles C Thomas.

McDavid, J., & Hawthorn, L. (2006). *Program evaluation and performance measurement: An introduction to practice.* Thousand Oaks, CA: Sage.

Rapp, C., & Poertner, J. (1992). *Social administration: A client centered approach.* New York: Longman.

Reviere, R. (1996). *Needs assessment: A creative and practical guide for social scientists.* London: Taylor & Francis.

Rossi, P., Lipsey, M., & Freeman, H. (2004). *Evaluation: A systematic approach* (7th ed.). Thousand Oaks, CA: Sage.

Salamon, L. (2002). *The tools of government: A guide to the new governance.* New York: Oxford University Press.

Smith, R., & Lynch, T. (2004). *Public budgeting in America* (5th ed.). Englewood Cliffs, NJ: Prentice Hall.

Valley of the Sun United Way. (2006). *Logic model handbook—2007.* Phoenix, AZ: Author.

Weinbach, R. (2003). *The social worker as manager.* Boston: Allyn & Bacon.

W. K. Kellogg Foundation. (2004). *Logic model development guide.* Battle Creek, MI: Author.

CHAPTER 17

Confronting Fundraising Challenges

Armand Lauffer

Today's fundraising challenges are greater than ever and take up more and more nonprofit managerial time.[1] While management of high-performance human services organizations is complex and multifaceted, the acquisition of resources is fundamental to this practice.

The chapter is divided into four sections, beginning with an analysis of the challenges posed by increasingly competitive funding environments, rapid demographic changes, and the transforming impact of technology. New methods for assessing and responding to environmental preferences are followed by a description of funding mechanisms ranging from institutional grants to planned giving. The chapter concludes with an assessment of several strategic fundraising options, including exploiting prior fundraising successes and/or exploring new and potentially risky alternatives, reengineering organizational and fundraising operations,

and increasing productive cross-organizational collaboration.

These are followed by recommendations for a print and electronic library useful in fundraising and resource development and a Web address for suggested course- and agency-based learning exercises.

Environmental Challenges

Rapid transformations in funding and operating environments provide both immediate and long-term challenges to nonprofit and other human services managers and fundraisers. These stem from the following:

1. increasing competition for funding and other resources,

2. changing demographics, and

3. the transforming impact of technology.

Increased Competition for Funding

From year to year, there appear to be more nonprofits and other competitors chasing fewer government and philanthropic dollars. Success in fundraising requires understanding of both the competition and the sources of supply.

More Competitors

In the 15 years from 1990 to 2005, the number of charitable organizations in the United States doubled to more than 800,000. This growth is driven, at least in part, by government efforts to downsize through privatization. Privatization is achieved by contracting with others to conduct publicly mandated services. Such outsourcing has encouraged for-profit entities to compete with nonprofits for the new dollars available. To remain competitive, some nonprofits have merged with others or formed large conglomerates that offer a wider array of services with reduced overhead and greater efficiencies. Others have created more limited local or specialized services that serve niche markets.

More (and Bigger) Philanthropy

Government officials, legislators, and others had expressed the expectation that philanthropy, including that supporting faith-based initiatives, could overcome any cutback-related shortfalls in public spending. That did not happen, but philanthropy did grow. In 2006, charitable giving in the U.S. passed the $295 billion mark, almost $12 billion more than the previous year (Giving USA Foundation, 2007). Of this amount, 76.5% was donated by individuals and families representing 65% of all Americans, accounting for just under 3% of donor income. Because richer Americans, especially the super-rich, make bigger contributions, their mega-gifts are likely to generate headlines. It is no longer uncommon to learn of one-time donations of $20 to $100 million, gifts that are larger than the entire corpus of the vast majority of philanthropic foundations.

Foundations and corporations account for 11%–12% of philanthropic giving. Their giving patterns, too, are increasingly overshadowed by the super-endowed among them. In 2006, the Gates Foundation's giving represented 20% of all American foundation charitable allocations.[2] Mega-corporate gifts may not be far behind. When Google went public a few years ago, its founders promised shareholders they would use 1% of the company's equity and profits for philanthropy—about $900 million. Between 12% and 13% of charitable giving is funneled through federated and other voluntary sector fundraising and allocating bodies.

More Advisors

Philanthropy has become big business and, to cope with its complexity, donors have sought advice and assistance on how to give and to what. Some have formed self-help "giving circles," in which participants share information and often collaborate in making joint charitable investments. Investment firms have created charitable giving funds that enable investors to save on taxes while redirecting profits to nonprofit programs (Panel on the Nonprofit Sector, 2005). Many community foundations and federated giving programs provide "charity investment" counsel, sometimes in coordination with financial investment counselors, and conduct related training sessions for local investment firms.

More Regulations and Accountability

Growth in the nonprofit sector is often accompanied by public concern over (1) results achieved for the dollars and volunteer time expended, and (2) NPO management and accounting practices. By the mid-1990s, the American news media were carrying almost daily reports on such abuses as excessive CEO salaries, fundraising expenses that exceeded the costs of service, board member conflicts of interests, and improper tax accounting. In 2006, the *Independent Sector* issued a report that recommended the use of improved legal and regulatory mechanisms to promote accountability (Bernanke, 2006). The IRS followed suit with a revised annual tax report form for charities and posted an online mini-course on how to obtain and maintain 501(c)(3) tax exempt status (Internal Revenue Service, n.d.). These were supported by the emergence of new tools for measuring, record-ing, and communicating program outcomes.[3]

Changing Demographics

Demographic changes have a way of sneaking up on a community and can often overwhelm the capacity of public and civic institutions to deal with them.[4] Examples include the impact of large migrations which can lead to significant changes in fertility rates, family size, educational levels, or age characteristics and even language use.[5] Such changes can have serious implications for a non-profit's programs, consumers, staffing, communi-cation networks, and income needs and options.

Baby Boomer Retirees

For purpose of illustration, we'll select one demographic category, baby boomers—adults who were born between 1946 and 1968—in order to examine how their retirement could impact federal spending. Born during the post-WW II fertility boom, they entered a more crowded and competitive workforce where they sought the occupational successes that may have been denied their parents. Initially, baby boomers were known as the "generation of the Sixties," often character-ized by idealism and commitments to social justice.[6] They currently make up the core of America's managers and professionals, and they represent a large proportion of American taxpay-ers and contributors to charitable organizations.

In 2008, the first members of the baby-boom generation reached the minimum age for receiv-ing Social Security benefits. In 2030, when they will all have reached retirement age, those who qualify for Social Security and Medicare will have grown from the current 12% of all Americans to

19%. Spending on these two programs will increase from roughly 7% of the U.S. gross domestic product to 11%. In 2008, the contribu-tions of five American taxpayers covered the ben-efits for one retiree. However, given the changing proportion of workers to retirees, by 2030 only three taxpayers will be available to cover each retiree's health and social security benefits.

There will be pressures from retirees to retain benefits and from taxpayers to reduce costs. Currently, the proposed policy options for deal-ing with these pressures include (1) raising fed-eral taxes; (2) reducing federal expenditures, including cutting Medicare and Social Security benefits; or (3) requiring employees to increase their pre-retirement savings to cover post-retirement costs (see also Chapters 12 and 19). Tentative steps have already been taken to pursue options (2) and (3).

Impact on Nonprofits and Fundraising

The retirement of baby boomers not only affects public policy and spending; it is likely to affect their geographic distribution as well as their service needs. As is true of other, relatively affluent Americans, some boomers may move to the Sun Belt or elsewhere. This may require new housing units, expansion of health services, and expansion of both cultural and recreational resources in the areas to which they move. But it may also depress the housing values and general economies in the areas they leave.

Some fundraisers are looking to baby boomers to help address these challenges. They believe that boomers' reputed success orientation, when com-bined with rekindled commitments to social jus-tice, may lead to generous donations of both time and money to charitable enterprises.

Technology and Organizational Transformation

Perhaps no environmental force has had greater impact on organizational behaviors and nonprofit fundraising than the emergence and proliferation of information and organizational technology.[7]

Communication and Information Technologies

Organizational technology draws on the intersections of information and communication technologies. Using both computers and pre-cybernetic tools (radio, TV, and telephone), communications technology facilitates rapid, broad, and multidirectional interaction. Electronic messaging (e-mail) and both tele- and videoconferencing not only reduce distance, they also change the way in which messages are framed and understood. Computer-based information technology (IT) makes it possible to generate, store, retrieve, use, and transfer information. Computer-assisted management tools such as TQM (Total Quality Management) can be used to evaluate programs and report their results (Kettner, Moroney, & Martin, 2008; see also Chapter 9).

The Internet is becoming a principal resource for fundraisers, with its expanding capacity for information storage and dissemination and its millions of Web sites and opportunities for interactive communication. Some Web sites were designed specifically for donors or fundraisers.[8] For example, in the nonprofit sector, donors can access *Charity Navigator* (www.charitynavigator .org/) to evaluate potential grant recipients. Nonprofits can access *GuideStar* (www.guidestar .org) to share information on their missions, goals, programs, needs, and accomplishments. In 2007, 1500 nonprofits used *MySpace* (http:// myspace.com/) to share news and promotional materials with the general public. One site, *People Helping People* (www.peoplehelpingpeople.org/), engages more than 18,000 individuals in activities that promote the common good. Blogs,[9] occupationally oriented Listservs,[10] project-oriented Intranets,[11] and teleconferencing are among the variety of other instruments used by fundraisers to share information and experiences.

Organizational Technology and Organizational Change

Organizational technology creates an organizational environment in which information is widely available, easily transmittable, and rapidly updated. When donors can access independent information on social needs and NPO performance, and when nonprofits have ready access to information on funder preferences and the interests of potential collaborators, organizational attention is shifted from current operations to future possibilities.

Organizational decision making about programs and funding tends to shift from individuals in positions of authority (top managers, board chairpersons) to staff and volunteers who are likely to be influenced by their interactions with counterparts in other organizations as much as, or more than, colleagues within their own organizations (Corner, Kinicki, & Keats, 1994).

In the more nimble nonprofits, this may lead to the emergence of network forms in which a wide range of employees and volunteers initiate and manage resource procurement and other exchanges within and across organizations (Malhotra, 1999).

The Challenge of Environmental Preferences

The ability to secure necessary resources from the environment depends on what an organization can deliver in return. The application of marketing concepts to nonprofits reached maturity in the mid-1980s and since then has been increasingly applied to assessing environmental preferences[12] and in fundraising (Andreasen, 2005; Andreasen & Kotler, 2002; Lauffer, 1984).

What Marketing Is and Is Not

Marketing is not a specific action tool. It's a process of thinking about how to optimize the benefits of environmental interaction by adjusting organizational responses to environmental preferences. Although it overlaps with both the sales and the traditional program planning approaches used in many nonprofits, marketing can be differentiated from each.[13]

Marketing Is Not Selling. Nonprofits that use a sales approach to fundraising depend primarily on promotional means to convince potential donors to make or increase their contributions. They may stress the importance of the organization and its products, their location, or their relative price and other advantages. In contrast, market-oriented nonprofits are more likely to use a *donor-oriented* approach, in which the interests and capacities of donors and other key publics often precede the formation of a funding request and may impact product design or modification.

Marketing Is Not Traditional Program Planning. Although it does not supplant the traditional program planning approaches used in many nonprofits, it does provide another dimension. The traditional approach to program planning, often associated with social work and other helping professions, begins with an assessment either of needs or of a problem to be addressed. It then progresses through a process of goal selection, strategy development, resource procurement, and program implementation and evaluation (see Kettner, Moroney, & Martin, 2007). Where marketing differs is that it begins with an assessment of demand, rather than an assumption of need.[14]

Marketing Is Responding to and Managing Demand. Demand is generally understood to be an expression of an interest in something backed by a capacity to act on that interest.[15] Successful fundraisers are aware that they may need to adjust one or the other. It does not make much sense to approach a small family foundation to fully fund a home handyman program, if the funder clearly does not have the financial capacity to do so. However, if a fundraiser could tap another source of supply—say, volunteers recruited from local churches who are able to supply much of the work through volunteer time and expertise—the foundation might be prepared to cover the project's full management cost.

Demand is rarely static. It can be actual or potential, excessive, faltering or insufficient. *Actual demand* is reflected in what consumers, funders, auspice providers and staff *do* in relation to participating in or supporting a program. *Potential demand* reflects an assessment of what they *would* do, if they were interested or had the capacity to do it. When demand is *excessive,* a nonprofit may have to develop procedures to limit or deflect it. When it is *faltering or insufficient,* a nonprofit will need to increase potential interest or capacity on the part of targeted publics.

When there is capacity but no interest, the marketing challenge is to stimulate it. That might require relocating to a more attractive place, finding new leadership, or expanding the range of program offerings. When the interest exists but donors do not have the capacity to act on it in terms of time, money, or other resources, then the marketing challenge is to reduce the cost in time and dollars or to increase program benefits to outweigh the costs.

The 5 Ps of Nonprofit Marketing

Many business texts refer to the "4 Ps" of marketing, a shorthand way of reminding users about who might be interested in a nonprofit and its programs: products, price, place, and promotions. A fifth P, for *publics,* helps distinguish nonprofit marketing. Publics are the actual and potential stakeholders in a nonprofit organization, its mission, or its programs, those publics for whom what the nonprofit does could make a difference.

Publics

In the for-profit world, the term *markets* is generally used to refer to all potential *consumer* publics. But nonprofits are dependent not only on consumers to pay for services, but also on *suppliers* of other inputs, without which they could not sustain themselves. These include both donor and nondonor publics, in effect all the actual and potential stakeholders in an organization and its programs.[16] Nondonor publics include legitimators, collaborators, and both staff and volunteers. *Legitimators* might include certifying bodies like a professional accreditation body, a state licensing agency, or a board that includes community leaders who are presumed to vouch that the organization follows recognized standards.

Collaborators may include other organizations whose activities make it possible for the nonprofit to do its business. *Internal publics,* such as staff and volunteers, are included because their commitment to the nonprofit's mission and programs provides the commitment and expertise that are major factors in product development and delivery. Their creativity, energy, and competence may contribute to the organization or to the program's attractiveness to funders.

Donor publics (funders) include all those who provide funding or non-cash equivalents for current or future use.[17] Included are individual or family gift givers; philanthropic (private or community) foundations; corporations and other business organizations; voluntary sector funding bodies (such as United Way and sectarian or special interest federations); federal, regional, state, or local government agencies; other service providers; and service consumers. Consumers—such as service clients, students, concertgoers, and others—are often thought of as funders because their fees and other payments are an increasingly central component in nonprofit financing.

Products and Product Lines

An NPO's *products* can be defined as tangible services and other activities conducted by staff and volunteers and offered to a consumer public. Smaller nonprofits may offer only a single service to a very distinct population, in a specific location. More complex organizations may offer a number of product lines, each composed of

different services.[18] Frequently, these are grouped into departments by age (e.g., preschoolers, seniors) or function (e.g., child placement, health care, community building, or theater and dance).

Finding the right fit between funders and specific programs is a major marketing challenge even if the sums sought are modest. For example, assistance from a foundation might be sought to underwrite a product line (e.g., the community center's dance program), whereas a member-initiated end-of-the-year concert may be used to cover the costs of costumes for next year's youth dance program. Although many funders appear to be interested only in specific projects that have clear beginnings and endings,[19] others provide infrastructure support for the total (nonprofit) organization or a network of organizations.

Price

Price refers to the costs funders may be willing to pay to support a program (product or product line) or the organization providing it. The price may be paid by service recipients, subsidized by third party payers (via grants, contracts, or other mechanisms), or through gifts. Payments may be in cash or in kind.[20] In addition to paying the costs associated with project or infrastructure support, donors may also find themselves paying opportunity costs. These refer not to what is paid out but to what might have been gained from making similar commitments elsewhere.

Place

The term *place* most often refers to the geographic location of a service agency or the area from which clients and other resources are drawn. For example, mental health centers are mandated to provide services to residents of designated catchment areas, but some may seek clients from other locales in order to maintain programs that could otherwise not be justified on the basis of local demand. For some donors, interest in particular locales may change over time. The baby boomers, discussed earlier, are a case in point. Some boomers may choose to invest in the communities where they raised their families and spent most of their work years. Those who move to the Sun Belt may prefer to invest in their new communities, where their philanthropy may be one of the means of getting connected to those already engaged in charity work.

Corporate donors tend to give primarily in communities where the company is headquartered or does business. Community foundations have clear geographic limits, beyond which they may not provide funding to beneficiaries. However, the foundation may be permitted to provide expert assistance (e.g., consultation) to other funders as a courtesy or for a fee. Some organizations permit a degree of donor choice regarding geographic boundaries. For example, some sectarian or health care federations permit contributors to target a percentage of their allocations to overseas relief instead of local services. Many local United Way agencies permit donors to the annual campaign to designate the locales to which they want all or parts of their gifts to go.

Promotion

Promotion refers to the persuasive communication that takes place between producers and distributors and their various publics. It could include advertising new services, consciousness raising about community needs, or generating support for the agency itself. When promotion is all one way—between a nonprofit and its potential funders—it is in danger of becoming a sales pitch aimed at inducing more or bigger gifts. Aggressive and over-frequent fundraising promotions, whether aimed at institutional funders or individual donors, tend to alienate potential contributors.[21]

Among the most effective promotional efforts are those that are multidimensional or convey the special nature of the connections between members of a donor group;[22] between donors and the recipient charity; or between donors and the program, population, or cause supported. For example, some radio and TV stations not only thank donors on the air, but engage them in discussions about their interests and preferences.

A number use blogs to encourage member (donor) interaction.

Given the increasing detachment that donors and others feel in an increasingly faceless society, when direct interpersonal contact is not possible, some fundraisers attempt to use interactive digital media not only to reach populations that would not be accessible by other means, but also to enrich them via the communication. For example, although social network Web sites like *Facebook* (http://www.facebook.com/) are designed to promote communication among friends and others interested in similar issues, especially younger users, they also have fundraising potential. Nonprofits have successfully used *Facebook* to raise critical consciousness and to promote cause giving by including information from trusted sources (friends and other "people like me"). They've already proven themselves in connection with environmental and relief efforts.

Funder Interests and Capacities

Market-oriented nonprofit managers and fundraisers are likely to tailor communication to the interests and capacities of different publics. They do so through a process referred to as *market segmentation*.

Market Segmentation

Market segmentation generally refers to a process of partitioning the consumer and supplier publics according some criteria that may be useful in determining levels of potential demand for specific products. Among those already discussed are price, place, and demographics. Also important are program interests, often defined in terms of service categories (e.g., health, formal and informal education, housing, employment). Two additional characteristics speak to how funders and donor publics understand themselves and what motivates them: funder roles and funder interests.

Funder Roles. Both individual and institutional funders may perceive themselves as performing the roles of benefactors, buyers, investors, partners, or allocating agencies. For example, many individual donors may perceive themselves as benefactors of an organization, its cause, or the populations-in-need it serves. Foundations and corporations might understand their grantmaking as vehicles through which they perform their benefactor and/or their investor roles. Government agencies are more likely to view themselves as buyers, contracting for specific services in the public interest, than as benefactors.

Collaborators in program development or implementation are often understood to be partners who both contribute to a joint venture and may also share in its benefits. Allocators of funds, such as federations and other fundraising organizations, may view themselves as supporting the mandate of the organization or donors on whose behalf they are acting, not necessarily as acting in the interest of the recipient. Misunderstandings can occur when there is role ambiguity and when role expectations are changed or challenged by donors, fundraisers, or recipients.

Funder Role-Related Interests. Funders' interests are generally connected to the roles they play. Although most funders' contributions are motivated by the possibility of achieving highly valued outcomes at a reasonable cost, the nature of those outcomes may be role-related.

- *Benefactors* may be interested in achieving something of value for the community or populations served by a nonprofit through improving their circumstances or sustaining an organization and its programs.
- *Investors* may be seeking to promote something new or different and/or help a recipient organization become increasingly self-sustaining.
- *Buyers* expect to purchase services that can be provided at a lower cost or more effectively than they might be able to provide directly.
- Organizations that make *allocations* may understand their function to be the

transferring of funds from a central body to those organizations or divisions responsible for performing designated tasks.
- *Partners* are concerned with meeting their own service goals, which may only be achievable through a partnering process.

These interests reflect what donors and donor institutions state about themselves or their funding programs and are often reflected in annual reports, mission statements, and promotional materials. Potential recipients who ignore those interests are not likely to receive a positive hearing. However, in practice, a funder's actions may also reflect unstated expectations, those that reflect personal or institutional interests and that only become understood through personal contacts with funders or others who understand what those funders may not say about themselves.

Almost all funders are motivated by the expectation that their contributions may yield material, relationship, or growth-oriented benefits. *Material benefits* include tax writeoffs, long-term financial security through charitable remainder trusts, and even those mundane premiums that are used to stimulate higher giving levels.[23] *Relationship benefits* include those that generate recognition or esteem for the donor and extend the nature of the donor's personal or institutional relationships to esteemed publics.[24] *Growth-oriented benefits* are likely when funders learn from their experiences with specific projects, organizations, service programs, or populations served, and that learning is understood to lead to improvements in their own practices.

This is as true for institutional as for individual funders. Many business firms invest in their communities as a way of expanding the bottom line, by improving their corporate images, reducing their tax exposures, or serving the needs of their employees and reducing turnover.[25] Foundations may be motivated to respond to changing needs or to board member preferences[26] or to opportunities for expanding the interests of other potential contributors to a common project.[27]

The Funding Mechanism Challenge

Fundraising has become a complex industry in which a wide range of mechanisms are used to both raise and distribute funds.[28] These are described under the following categories: (1) organizational funding mechanisms, (2) those used to generate income from individuals, and (3) alternative sources of supply such as reserve funds and investments.

Organizational Funding Mechanisms

The primary tools used by institutional funders are allocations, grants, and contracts. In general, grants provide recipients with the greatest amount of discretion, whereas contracts provide the least.

Allocations

Allocations are distributions from a central source to a program unit, usually on an annual basis, barring unforeseen circumstances. The source can be external or internal.[29] The application procedure for an allocation may be as simple as a report on the previous year's programs and overall expenditure, a budget table that compares this year with next year's projected expenditures, and a request for continued funding for the coming fiscal year.

Until recently, many nonprofit programs could assume annual or multi-year allocations, with minor adjustments for rising costs or changes in client demand. Today, this is less likely in some arenas. Since the early 1990s, a number of United Way organizations have substituted competitive grants for allocations. These are open to all qualifying nonprofits rather than to a more limited group of federation "member" organizations.

Grants

Grants may be limited to only one or a small number of years. Renewals are subject to funding availability and recipient performance. They permit recipients to pursue activities of their own design within a set of guidelines provided by a funder (often a foundation, business firm, or government agency). They may be awarded to individuals, organizations, or networks. Grants made to individuals are almost always for specific purposes, such as travel or tuition grants. Grants to organizations tend to be awarded for the conduct of the tasks associated with a project, or to supplement the organization's overall budget for such activities as staffing and in-service training, one-time equipment purchases, or special events. Long-term grant support, if available, is often tied to a requirement for cross-organizational collaboration that has broad community impact or that may include multiple-source funding.[30] Grant applicants are generally required to complete written proposals that include a narrative response to a number of questions, plus a budget, timeframe, and evaluation plan.[31]

Contracts

A *contract* is legal agreement between a contractor and a vendor in which the former specifies what is to be done, by whom, to whom or to what, within what timeframe, following what standards. The vendor agrees to do the work in return for a specified remuneration. Purchase-of-service contracts (POSCs) are used by governments to buy the services of either voluntary (nonprofit) or proprietary (private, for-profit) organizations.[32] They may also be used by nonprofits to subcontract with individuals and other organizations to perform specific tasks. Examples of contracting with individuals include hiring a consultant to manage a fundraising campaign or contracting nutritionists, on an hourly basis, to perform assessments on selected health clinic clients.

Government contracts generally begin with the issuance of an RFP (Request for Proposal) or RFQ (Request for Quote), which is published in the Commerce Business Daily (for federal programs) or state and local newspapers. Notices may also be distributed to a list of potential bidders.

If the program and its requirements are new, the funding agency may conduct one or more regionally based bidder's conferences at which the program and its requirements are explained.

Like grants, contracts tend to be time limited, often designed to initiate or conclude a specific project with a beginning and an end. Most contracts require competitive bidding, but there are exceptions. A *sole source* may be awarded when time is limited or there is clearly only one applicant available who is considered to have the capacity to perform the designed tasks. In contrast with grantmaker proposal forms, contracting agencies may use "bidding" forms in which the contracting agency spells out exactly what it wants done, how, by whom, and by when. The application form may be limited to requests for information on the bidder's costs, facilities, and staff qualifications.[33]

Individual Fundraising Mechanisms

Support for nonprofits comes from individuals through fees for service, campaigns, and other approaches to generating charitable gifts, sales, and a wide range of grassroots funding activities.

Fees for Service

Some nonprofit direct services are paid all or in part through fees and tuition payments. Sliding scales may be used to accommodate user ability to pay. Fees paid on behalf of users by other organizations are called *third party payments*. In the health field, this mechanism is used extensively by both private insurers and public programs like Medicare and Medicaid. In education, third party payments also include employer, government, or philanthropic tuition grants and subsidies.

Given the increase in funding requests, it is not unusual for grants or contract-making institutions to insist that their award recipients increase fee income, especially from publics that are presumed to be able to afford the increases. Nor is it unusual for nonprofits to seek additional payments from consumers when costs rise or available allocations, grants, or contracts are no longer sufficient to subsidize service. Sometimes fees are supplemented through sales to consumers and other supporters, such as hats and T-shirts sold to campers, various booster products sold to students, or gift shop sales in hospitals.

Campaigns

Campaigns are generally time-limited events that use direct appeals to generate support for a single organization or cause. A capital (bricks and mortar) campaign for a mosque or synagogue may be a one-time event, conducted by a single organization for the purpose of building or improving a facility. Ongoing campaigns tend to be annual or semi-annual, often identified with specific dates that resonate with donors (the start of summer, end of the month, Memorial Day or a religious holiday, the start or end of the school year, etc.). Some campaigns are mass in appeal. Many are more narrowly targeted to those identified with a cause (e.g., addressing environmental issues). Others are member focused (e.g., college alumni, fellow parishioners, block club members and other neighborhood residents affiliated with an ethnic minority or faith-based movement).

More than three of every four dollars in charitable gifts are contributed by individuals directly, or indirectly through fundraising organizations such as sectarian federations,[34] the United Way, and other federations such as those affiliated with the Combined Federal Campaign.[35] Campaigns almost always require the creation of organizational structure in which people are assigned to the roles of solicitors, coordinators, event managers, publicists, and so on. Some mass appeal campaigns contract with business firms to conduct the campaigns using paid staff. In contrast, member-oriented campaigns may use paid staff or contract out for campaign management, but involve member volunteers as solicitors.

Campaign planners often segment their donor publics. They may do so on the basis of occupational identity, residence location, gender or sexual identity, generational characteristics, ethnic or religious identity, specific interests, and previous or anticipated gift size. Solicitors are often selected on the basis of their fit with potential donors. For example, members of the same occupational group may solicit their peers. Big givers will be recruited to solicit others who have the potential for making substantial contributions. Alumni solicitors will contact graduates from the same school or graduating class. Donor cards are used to record gifts and pledges as well as other relevant information (donor interests, questions about the organization, best times to contact them, etc.).

Campaigns may also record information on prospects not reached by the campaign but who may have found out about the charity through other means. These include friends and colleagues, employers, membership organizations, and public sources such as newspaper articles and TV news reports, Web site entries, entertainment sites, blogs, and so on.[36]

Planned Giving

Cash gifts may be given in the present or deferred, as when a pledge has a long-term pay-off schedule or a bequest is payable only when the donor's estate is settled, a format referred to as *planned giving*. Planned gifts can be used to transfer assets to a charity now or after the donor's death. In return, the donor (or a designee) retains income for life. The planned giving process can be complex and may need expert advice from trained professionals. It generally includes consideration of income, gift, and estate taxes (see Hopkins, 2006). The following are some of the instruments used in planned giving:

- Wills and bequests, which spell out the percentage remaining in an estate on the donor's death that is to be transferred to a charity (may be done directly or by means of a charitable trust);
- Pooled income funds, in which a donor's funds are comingled with those of other donors and transferred to the charity on a regular basis, finally to be fully transferred on the donor's death;

- Charitable remainder trusts, into which the donor deposits appreciating property or cash, which is managed by the charity but from which the donor may draw an agreed upon annual income, annually through an annuity or similar means; and
- Life insurance trusts, in which a donor names a charity as the recipient of all or part of the insurance payment on the donor's death.

Private Sector and Hybrid Innovations

Some federated fundraisers, having reached what they believe is a plateau or decline in campaign giving, have created alternative vehicles for potentially large donors. These include trusts and deferred giving programs, emulating the successes of many community foundations. As noted earlier, the crossover potential of philanthropic and income investments was recognized in the private sector as well. The practice of linking investment advice to philanthropy appears to have emerged during the economic boom of the 1990s. At the time, many brokerage firms, bank trust departments, and personal financial advisors began to encourage their clients to build charitable gifts as part of their investment portfolios. In addition to tax benefits associated with charitable giving, such hybrids also provide assistance to the newly affluent who, having done well financially, now want to do good socially.

Venture philanthropy, a recent innovation, combines the principles of venture capital investment developed in the high tech field with traditional grant making and gift giving (Romirowsky, 2007). Some venture philanthropists have attempted to support the growth of social innovation through the use of *social incubators,* laboratories for experimenting with something new while reducing the costly risks of missteps through untested early application.

Grassroots Fundraising and Sales

Grassroots fundraising is used for two purposes: (1) raising money and consciousness, and

(2) building the organization and community. They are called "grassroots" because they often involve consumers of a nonprofit's services and other community members as volunteers in the fundraising efforts or as purchasers of goods and services, some of which yields income to a non-profit enterprise, for example,

- sales, such as community-wide garage sales and thrift shops, bake sales;
- bazaars and auctions of commercial goods and services;
- social/cultural activities like potlucks and prepared dinners, dances, bingo and casino nights, trips, picnics, bike-a-thons, holiday celebrations, concerts and theater parties; or
- third-party contributions, such as super-market donations of a percentage of all sales on a given day to a designated charity. (Flanagan, 1982, 2002)

Recently, some differences between for-profits and nonprofits may have become blurred, as some NPOs create their own (and decidedly not grass-roots) for-profit enterprises, designed specifically to generate income for the nonprofits (Dees, 1999), and some for-profit enterprises designate all profits to be used for charitable purposes.[37]

With some limitations, nonprofit organiza-tions are permitted to sponsor commercial activ-ities without paying taxes on income. However, the activity must meet the "test of relatedness." This means that it must contribute importantly to the performance of the organization's tax-exempt purpose.[38] By engaging staff and volunteers in the effort, such activities can increase community involvement, educate the participants and broader public about a need or problem, and build leadership for other activities. Some grass-roots efforts generate big dollars, whereas others generate modest gifts from donors.

Alternative Sources of Supply

Fundraising also includes (1) in-kind (non-cash) gifts that may be transferable to cash or a cash value, and (2) the income generated from reserve funds and related investment income.

In-Kind Contributions

Some grassroots efforts build on non-cash contributions by individuals, business firms, partners, and others. These are called *in-kind* because they can be used in lieu of cash or trans-formed into cash equivalents. These can include either outright transfers or loans, and they can be useful as is or as converted to cash and other kinds of exchanges. Examples of ownership transfers include the following:

- real estate, such as a home, vacation retreat, campsite, city lots;[39]
- securities like stocks and bonds that may have accrued in value;
- equipment, such as used cars and comput-ers, gardening or sports equipment;
- arts, antiques, and items reflecting ethnic or religious heritage;
- treasures for trash items (generally for sale), including used clothing, equipment, books, tools;
- disposable items, like office supplies or food for a soup kitchen.

Similar items might be available on loan or at a subsidized cost. These might include equip-ment, such as a van or school bus used to trans-port children or the infirm to nonprofit agency service sites; and office or program space, such as church basement for use in preschool programs when it is not otherwise in use.

In-kinds can include volunteer time, in the form of time-limited assignments of skilled pro-fessionals and other personnel from for-profit and volunteer associations to NPOs.[40] Skilled tasks might include fundraising, bookkeeping, training and other management activities, med-ical treatment, counseling, museum guiding, or teaching. Less skilled volunteers can be trained to provide such services as friendly visiting, food preparation and distribution, and assistance in sitting in a shelter.

Although in-kinds are often used to supplement or improve NPO services, they can also be at the core of a program. Examples include the food in some food redistribution programs and the work of volunteer docents in many museums. Sometimes one non-cash contribution can be turned into another. For example, a van that transports children to day care might be on loan to an adult day care program during the hours children do not need transportation. In return, the adult care participants might prepare snacks and meals for the children. Often, existing volunteer programs can be worked into a more complex nonprofit intervention. For example, a Habitat for Humanity house building activity might include some local residents in construction efforts that are integral to a broader network of collaborations that make up a neighborhood renewal project.

The importance of non-cash contributions and the readiness of many individuals and organizations to contribute to them have led to creation of a number of Web sites that appeal to both national and international publics and serve as matchmakers between charities and potential donors.[41] Non-cash contributions lead to a broader involvement of citizens and organizations in the nonprofit sector and open new opportunities for nonprofit organizations to expand the range and quality of their services.

Reserve Funds

Reserve funds are dollars set aside for use in the future. They include assets that are not committed to covering program costs during the current fiscal year (see Lohmann, 1980). Made up of what is left over after all expenses are covered, they include vouchered items or other encumbrances and pay-backs.

Reserve funds may be banked for use in addressing emerging and unanticipated needs. If a nonprofit can't meet its payroll obligations until a donor has transferred grant funds, the reserves may be dipped into, temporarily. Reserves are not income, per se, but they can be turned into income when and if the NPO has no other options but to deplete them, in whole or in part. For example, should an economic downturn reduce the fee income anticipated from student tuition payments, reserves may be used to create a time-limited scholarship or loan program. Sometimes they are set aside for designated purposes—such as relief payments in the event of a weather-generated catastrophe.

In order to avoid the risk of not being able to replenish reserves because of use or inflation, nonprofits often invest reserves in such liquid assets as interest-bearing money market funds and certificates of deposit, and in riskier securities.[42] Others invest in upgrading their fundraising capacities. Examples might include covering the up-front costs for launching a fundraising campaign or covering the up-front cost of a fundraising event, such as renting space for a community fair.

The Strategic Challenge

To succeed in an increasingly competitive fundraising environment, nonprofit managers are faced with a choice of funding strategies that (1) build on their current and past success or explore new and potentially more rewarding approaches, (2) emphasize competition or collaboration, and (3) focus on organizational or network interests.

Building on the Past or Seeking New Opportunities

Most nonprofits use only a relatively limited number of fundraising mechanisms and have access to a small number of funding publics. Some choose a "building on strength" strategy, aimed at increasing fundraising effectiveness and efficiency in familiar areas. Others seek new opportunities for expanding their resource pools through alternative funding sources and by trying out new funding mechanisms.[43]

Building on Strength

When a nonprofit organization has had a successful fundraising history, there is much to recommend staying with what works, but doing it better. A fundraising campaign can be improved by (a) sharpening up its message, (b) more appropriately assigning solicitors, and (c) addressing donor expectations. It can reduce the costs of a campaign by substituting the Internet for more expensive means of communication, replacing paid staff with trained volunteers, or finding a lower-cost contractor to conduct the campaign.

Routine relationships with a long-term institutional funder can be reinvigorated by providing more detailed and accessible reports or offering to help the funder transfer a successful innovation to other nonprofits.[44] The scope of a planned giving effort might be significantly expanded by collaborating with investment firms on combined investment and philanthropic portfolios.

By building on both relationships and experience, nonprofits are able to maintain continuity with their own past and cohesion with donors and other publics. They succeed by not only doing what they already know how to do, but by doing it more effectively, cheaper, faster, and with more depth. The organization can also reduce its need for funds through the cost savings achieved using more efficient means of service delivery, better screening of clients, or by contracting out for some services and partnering on others. These examples represent attempts to control costs through downsizing and reengineering instead of seeking funds from alternative sources or using untried mechanisms.

Seeking New Opportunities

Some nonprofits are apt to explore previously unused fundraising mechanisms or untapped resource, especially when (a) accustomed fundraising efforts are no longer productive; (b) the availability of current funding sources is threatened; or (c) when decision makers are aware that other possibilities might be more productive.

Although changing an organization's approach to fundraising can be highly remunerative, it is rarely accomplished in a single step, or immediately successful. Organizational change can be described as a kind of journey, with stops and occasional changes in direction and with no certainty that the journey won't be aborted (Van de Ven, Polley, Garud, & Venkataraman, 1999).

Because the change journey often requires entering uncharted waters, it entails a good many unknowns and some risks. A radical change in funding sources may require significant alteration in the NPO's programs and purpose without assurance that its consumer public will go along. The use of new fundraising mechanisms may bring the organization into contact with new publics to which it is now accountable, in addition to rivals for the same resources.[45]

To deal with unpredictability, and to minimize risk, experienced fundraisers often use one or more of the following approaches in adapting new fundraising approaches:

- *partialization* of the innovation by (a) trying it out in a small section of the organization or (b) applying only a part of the innovation throughout the entire NPO;
- *sharing the risk* by collaborating with other organizations in a new fundraising effort;
- *using teams* to manage the innovation, thereby increasing the number and expertise of players available to address unanticipated occurrences;
- *adopting* and *adapting* innovations that have proven themselves elsewhere.[46]

Competing and Collaborating

The decision to seek new opportunities is often influenced by the continued availability of resources from prior sources or the presumed availability from new sources. Competition for scarce resources, *rivalry,* occurs when there are too many petitioners in a crowded field and too few resources to go around. Collaboration between nonprofits occurs when each of the partners understands that working together serves its own organizational interest or some greater good.

Rivals

Rivals can make themselves more competitive by addressing issues of price, place, and product. That means reducing costs to consumer or funder publics, changing a program's locale to increase accessibility, or differentiating the program from competing offerings. Programs can be made more appealing by more effective targeting of consumer and donor interests and by demonstrating shared values, beliefs, and norms. However, nonprofits may find it more effective to turn rivalry into some form of collaboration, including co-optation, absorption, coalition formation, and partnering.

For example, potential competitors might be co-opted by inviting them to share in the sponsorship of a community fundraising fair. A rival agency and its service programs might be absorbed by a more stable nonprofit. Potential collaborators might be induced to join a coalitional effort at fundraising or a community-wide advocacy effort. More permanent legal arrangements might be used to create partnerships in which each of the member organizations retains some independence. But such independence is limited by the obligations of and benefits for each partner. For example, although federation members may agree to limit their fundraising efforts and refrain from any solicitations during the federated campaign season, they share in the funds generated collectively.[47]

Getting to Yes

Each of these arrangements requires a bargaining process that leads to an agreement on the obligations of each of the parties. Some negotiations are *distributive* in their aims; that is, they distribute benefits and costs between the rivals in some manner that is acceptable, at least for a time.

Other negotiations aim for *integrative* outcomes, in which all the participants aim for a shared gain that outweighs the costs incurred and might generate a new value unachievable without collaboration (Fisher, Ury, & Patton, 1993).

Because funders, donors, and other key publics in the nonprofit world often base their program rationales on communal rather than private interests, they tend to aim their negotiations at value creation for all the parties involved. That often requires a shared trust between the potential collaborators. Fundseekers who concentrate primarily on their own organizational interests may lose out on the trust needed achieve common objectives. They may miss opportunities to think creatively with their negotiating partners about how to move from the satisfaction of individual NPO interests to optimizing those of all parties involved.

Focusing on Network or Organizational Interests

The propensity for collaboration is propelled by instability in the funding environment and the need for nonprofit organizations to adapt to changing environmental interests. Those needs are often best addressed at the periphery of organizations where intelligence is gathered and shared and where new cross-organizational marketing opportunities may be discovered though joint explorations.

Unicentric or Multicentric Structures

In nonprofits that retain a traditional top-down or highly centralized authority structure, it is common practice for central administrators to do all or most of the fundraising or to delegate it to one or more staff specialists, external consultants, or contractors. In the past, this may have been both efficient and effective. But in today's funding environment, overly centralized decision making may result in a great many missed opportunities. More diverse structures that include an increasing number of lateral relationships are required.[48] These draw decision making from the organizational center to its periphery and lead to creation of new roles and specialized expertise for dealing with resource procurement, program development, and coordination.[49]

When semi-autonomous units in different organizations collaborate on specific projects or processes, organizational alliances tend to be temporary, reflecting emerging interests and resource availability. They are project rather than organization specific.

This network orientation is not without problems (Castells, 2000). It may disconnect an organization from its own history as new relationships substitute for traditional arrangements. Because lateral coordination requires consensus building, it can be very time consuming. Although cross-organizational teams may help a nonprofit better attune itself to environmental complexity, they are difficult to manage. When several teams are in operation at the same time, some with only a few overlapping participants, their efforts may result in noncomplimentary outcomes. Those outcomes may not be in the best interests of the publics that some of the participating organizations purport to serve.[50]

Stability and Continuity

In fundraising, as in other managerial functions, most nonprofits appear to opt for some continuity, building on past experiences or integrating new approaches into ongoing operations. March (2002) argues that to survive and thrive in a destabilizing environment, organizations need to develop adaptive strategies that balance continuity and change and the exploitation of strengths with the exploration of new possibilities. In so doing, he suggests, they should avoid two common traps: repeatable failures and unrepeatable successes.

Rigid organizations that rely only on the exploitation of past strengths—and are good at doing so in the short run—are likely to dig themselves into a hole. They fail over the long haul

because of their inability or unwillingness to explore new arrangements that include novel sources of funding, funding mechanisms, or networking possibilities. Organizations that do succeed in locating new resources, often through networking and other collaborative relationships, may also risk failure. By not adequately exploiting their own strengths, they may reduce the possibility of integrating new fundraising successes into ongoing operations and community relationships.

Over time, success in getting funding but inability build it into stable support for an enduring program may contribute to the kind of continuity few nonprofits may want—the continuous starting and stopping of programs doomed to failure because of inadequate attention to connecting the organization's past to its possible future.

Conclusion

Confronting fundraising challenges turns out to much more complex than finding the right funder for a specific program or developing greater skill in the application of various fundraising mechanisms. It requires increasing the capacity of organizations to assess and respond to environmental preferences. It forces nonprofits to find the right balance between building on familiarity and prior successes and exploring new and emerging opportunities. And it goads them into responding to a competitive environment by seeking collaborative opportunities.

The chapter began and ended with an examination of destabilizing environments that impact both fundraising and other organizational processes. Those processes are affected by the proliferation of communication networks between organizations and their publics, which, in turn, promote cross-organizational and often transitory collaborations.

In this context, the fundraising challenge may be shifting from the question of "How to?" to "What if?"

Notes

1. Because fundraising is generally associated with charitable giving in the U.S., this chapter deals primarily with nonprofit organizations. However, some of the fundraising mechanisms covered—such as grants or contracts—are also used to transfer funds to for-profit organizations. Moreover, both for-profit and public institutions may, under certain circumstances, conduct charitable activities through nonprofit subsidiaries or affiliated citizen groups.

2. Following a gift of over $30 billion by Warren Buffet in 2006, the Gates Foundation is now five times as large as the Ford Foundation, formerly number one in size.

3. For more details on accountability requirements, see Chapters 18 and 19.

4. Examples include migrations from Middle Eastern countries to Western Europe and from Latin America and parts of Asia to the United States. Each of these has impacted local cultural and occupational patterns and generated programmatic responses from the public, private, and nonprofit sectors.

5. The U.S. Census Bureau found that 43% of California residents spoke a language other than English at home. In Los Angeles, the percentage was 10% higher (*N.Y. Times This Week*, Sept. 16, 2007).

6. "Socially idealistic" and "competitive" are *psychographic* rather than demographic characteristics. Psychographic descriptors refer to lifestyle patterns, an intersection of demographic with psychological and social behaviors.

7. Technology is a broad concept generally referring to the application of science and engineering to shape and manage the environment.

8. A wide range of such Web sites can be accessed via the University of Michigan School of Social Work *GRANTS, ETC.* site (http://www.ssw.umich.edu/resources/index2.html?collection=grants).

9. For access to more than 40 blogs and blog sites relevant to nonprofit management and fundraising, see http://www.lucasmcdonnell.com/essential-knowledge-management-sites-and-blogs/. For example, it includes the SupportingAdvancement.com Online Community (http://www.supportingadvancement.net/community/), which has a number of subunits dealing with such topics as telemarketing, annual funding drives, and e-solicitation.

10. Many Listservs can be accessed through professional associations or located through Google.

11. Intranets are designed for use by specific publics, such as staff or board members. They are used to provide ready access to databases or evaluation reports and to share "best practices" between members of a professional group or community coalition. See Smith, N. (1999). *Intranet planning guide*. Available at http://www.intranetjournal.com/planning/030899intraguide.html.

12. A term used to describe the interests of various organizations, groups, and individuals with which an organization currently or potentially interacts, with regard to specific program or fundraising concerns.

13. See Chapter 16 for a discussion of marketing as a component of program planning.

14. See also Chapter 16.

15. For example, there is not likely to be much demand for an environmentally friendly hybrid car in a community where there's little concern for the environment (or confidence that the product available would contribute much to reducing carbon emissions), if there are few or no model choices available, or if the purchase price is unreachable by the intended buyers.

16. The point of including nondonor publics in a chapter on fundraising is that donor interest in a product or organization is likely to be influenced by the involvement of such other parties as the nondonor publics listed.

17. "Deferred" giving might include pledges or cash gifts made now, but redeemable at some later date.

18. For example, a think tank may include research, community, and publishing divisions, each with several product lines. The community division may include consulting services, courses and workshops, and policy conferences. The publishing division may produce books and policy papers as well as training guides that can be used with the think tank's trainees or sold to consumer organizations and individuals.

19. For example, a funder may be interested in contributing to the development of a training DVD for use at a conference and for its distribution after the conference's close.

20. Examples include facilities, equipment, supplies, salable items, or volunteer time that can substitute for, or be turned into, cash.

21. Individual donors often express dissatisfaction about being bombarded with mass mailings, often complaining that they are only contacted when their

money is needed and rarely get responses to their questions or recommendations.

22. For some donors, group affiliation contributes powerfully to their personal identity and serves as a motivator of philanthropic behavior.

23. For example, a packet of wildflower seeds is included in a fundraising letter from an environmental group—in this case, the premium is provided in advance. Public radio semi-annual fundraisers often provide a range of inducements, from a coffee mug or T-shirt to an invitation to a special event. At grassroots fundraising events, like community rummage sales or in thrift shops, the inexpensive purchase may be more motivating than the gift to charity.

24. For example, being identified with donors whose community prestige is great, and with whom a potential donor may wish to be associated.

25. An example of an employee-serving program is the Monsanto Corporation's renowned child care programs, which were designed to make it possible for employees to bring young children to the workplace (reducing employee turnover). An example of an employee-initiated program is Credit Suisse in New York and Levi-Strauss in San Francisco, both of which give preference in grantmaking to employee-initiated projects (Perry, 2000).

26. The Carnegie Foundation moved from an initial interest in promoting literacy through the construction of community libraries and library collections, to promoting community-based innovations in education, and now engages in global education for peace endeavors.

27. The Cleveland Foundation's response to the federal government's Renaissance Zone initiative led to a community-wide redevelopment effort that generated more than $5 billion for investment in schools, jobs, and physical infrastructure development. In Oakland, California, the community foundation established a partnership with Lucas Films to create a successful family-centered approach to teaching and learning in a failing school district (Lauffer, 1997).

28. Historically, various funder publics have been associated with one or more funding mechanisms. For example, government agencies have used grants and contracts to transfer funds to local communities. United Way and other federations of member agencies use fundraising campaigns to generate the income transferred to nonprofits through the use of allocations and grants.

29. A county social service department that allocates funds to a domestic violence shelter is an example of an external source. An internal source might be the board of a community center that allocates parts of its annual budget to semi-independent subunits like the day camp, senior citizen's drop-in lounge, or a concert and lecture series. Each of these might be responsible for raising additional funds through fees for service, sales, and special events.

30. A number of grantmakers have begun to promote longer-term grant support, which, when combined with capacity-building consultation, mentoring, and technical assistance, is intended to help nonprofits to become more entrepreneurial and experimental and/or more self-sustaining (C. S. Mott Foundation, 2007).

31. For examples of proposal forms used in common by many foundations, see the common application forms on the National Network of Grantmakers Web site: http://www.nng.org/assets/Common_Grant_Application.doc

32. POSCs and third-party payments have become the preferred means of government funding because of the belief that both mechanisms lead to (a) cost cutting and improved efficiency, (b) better quality of service, and (c) improved fiscal accountability. When a government agency wants to initiate a program, expand services to new populations, or either replace or expand the number of current providers, it will seek new bidders. First, an RFP (Request for Proposal) or RFQ (Request for Quote) is published and distributed to a list of potential bidders. If the program and its requirements are new—like the job training and child care programs that accompanied welfare reform—the agency may conduct one or more regionally based bidders' conferences, at which the program and its requirements are explained. Interested parties may receive consultation or training on how to prepare acceptable proposals.

33. Some aspects of a grant or contract award may be negotiable. The recipient organization may be permitted some leeway in terms of the total dollar amount requested or the time-frame for completion. Funders often permit some renegotiation of the initial agreement over the life of a project.

34. The history of federated fundraising is covered in Chapters 2 and 4.

35. Initiated in 1987, the *Combined Federal Campaign* provides federal employees with workplace federated giving opportunities in 500 locales. Many

state, county, and local governments have chosen the federal government's CFC as a vehicle for increasing gift-making choices for their employees.

36. Also including specialized publications such as corporate, church, club, or professional association newsletters and such national publications as the *Chronicle of Philanthropy* (http://www.philanthropy .com/).

37. For example, actor Paul Newman's company that designates all profits from its spaghetti sauce and other products to support residential programs for children in need.

38. See Chapter 19 for further discussion of taxation of proceeds from commercial activity.

39. A donor's home might be part of a deferred gift, as when ownership is transferred in the present, but the house remains available to the donor until death.

40. Skilled services are also made available through local business firms or voluntary associations like the local Chamber of Commerce or a fraternal association. Some groups of retired professionals, like former accountants and money managers found in many communities, provide volunteer services to local nonprofits.

41. Examples include (a) Gifts In Kind International, http://www.giftsinkind.org/; (b) Volunteer Match, http://www.volunteermatch.org/; and (c) Canadian Charity Village's Volunteer Postings, http://www.charityvillage.com/applicant/volunteer.asp

42. A caution: The Internal Revenue Service requires extensive reporting of income-producing activities (see Part VII of Form 990). These include program-relevant revenues such as dues and fees, investment revenue, sales of assets, and many fundraising activities and events. Reported income must be categorized as excludable or nonexcludable for tax purposes. For-"profit" income is not tax exempt unless it is directly related to the organization's charitable purposes.

43. Some may just try to weather the storm by hunkering down and hoping it might pass over, only to discover belatedly they are the ones who were passed over (see Meyer & Zucker, 1989).

44. For example, a community school's director offers to share her experience with other schools applying to the grantmaking foundation.

45. Pettigrew (2003) points out that change is rarely only a multilinear, step-by-step process; it may also have a multivariate impact on many components of an organization.

46. An advantage of adapting innovations developed in peer institutions is that many of the bugs may have been worked on elsewhere, and consultation may be available for the transfer process.

47. See Chapter 21 for a further discussion of interorganizational collaborative arrangements.

48. In the literature, such organizations are generally referred to as (a) *network organizations* formed by cross-cutting linkages between several separate organizations (see Powell, 1990) or (b) *postbureaucratic organizations* because of their relative absence of rules and hierarchy and heavy reliance on networks (see Heckscher & Donellon, 1994).

49. The Gilbert Center (http://www.gilbert .org/Journals/) has recently launched three journals of interest: (a) *Online and Integrated Fundraising* (JOIF), (b) *Information Technology in Social Change* (JITSC), and (c) *Networks and Civil Society* (JNCS).

50. More extensive discussions of this issue are found in Chapters 21 and 22. Readers may also be interested in a description of organizational reframing in the context of environmental instability and emerging preferences, in Bolman and Deal (1997).

References

Andreasen, A. R. (2005). *Social marketing in the 21st century.* Thousand Oaks, CA: Sage.

Andreasen, A. R., & Kotler, P. (2002). *Strategic marketing for nonprofit organizations* (6th ed.). Englewood Cliffs, NJ: Prentice Hall.

Bernanke, B. S. (2006, October 4). *The coming demographic transition: Will we treat future generations fairly?* Presentation to The Washington Economic Club, Washington, D.C.

Bolman, L. G., & Deal, T. E. (1997). *Reframing organizations: Artistry, choice and leadership* (2nd ed.). San Francisco: Jossey-Bass.

Castells, M. (2000). *The information age: Economy society and culture, volume I, the rise of the network society.* Oxford: Blackwell.

Corner, P., Kinicki, A., & Keats, B. (1994). Integrating organizational and individual information processing perspectives on choice. *Organizational Science, 5,* 294–308.

C. S. Mott Foundation. (2007). *The long-term capacity-building initiative.* Flint, MI: Author.

Dees, J. G. (1999). Enterprising nonprofits. In *Harvard business review on nonprofits* (pp. 135–166). Cambridge, MA: Harvard Business School Press.

Fisher, R., Ury, W. L., & Patton, B. (1993). *Getting to yes* (2nd ed). Boston: Houghton-Mifflin.

Flanagan, J. (1982). *The grass roots fundraising book.* New York: Contemporary Books.

Flanagan, J. (2002). *Successful fundraisers: A complete handbook for volunteers and professionals* (2nd ed.). New York: McGraw-Hill.

Giving USA Foundation. (2007). *The annual report on philanthropy.* Retrieved from http://www.aafrc.org/gusa/

Heckscher, C., & Donellon, A. (Eds.). (1994). *The post-bureaucratic organization: New perspectives on organizational change.* Thousand Oaks, CA: Sage.

Hopkins, B. R. (2006). *Charitable giving law made easy.* New York: John Wiley & Sons.

Internal Revenue Service. (n.d.). *Stay exempt: Tax basics for exempt organizations.* Retrieved from http://www.stayexempt.org

Kettner, P. M., Moroney, R. M., & Martin, L. L. (2007). *Designing and managing programs: An effectiveness-based approach* (2nd ed.). Thousand Oaks, CA: Sage.

Kettner, P. M., Moroney, R. M., & Martin, L. L. (2008). *Designing and managing programs: An effectiveness-based approach* (3rd ed.). Thousand Oaks, CA: Sage.

Lauffer, A. (1984). *Strategic marketing for not-for-profit organizations.* New York: The Free Press.

Lauffer, A. (1997). *Grants, etc.* Thousand Oaks, CA: Sage.

Lohmann, R. A. (1980). *Breaking even: Financial management in human service organizations.* Philadelphia: Temple University Press.

Malhotra, Y. (1999). *Role of information technology in managing organizational change and organizational interdependence.* Retrieved from http://www.brint.com/papers/change/

March, J. G. (2002). The future, disposable organizations, and the rigidities of imagination. In S. R. Clegg (Ed.), *Central currents in organizational studies II: Contemporary trends* (Vol. 9). London: Sage.

Meyer, M. W., & Zucker, L. (1989). *Permanently failing organizations.* Thousand Oaks, CA: Sage.

Panel on the Nonprofit Sector. (2005). *Strengthening transparency, governance, accountability of charitable organizations: A final report to congress and the nonprofit sector.* Washington, DC: The Independent Sector. Retrieved from http://www.nonprofitpanel.org/report/final/

Perry, S. (2000, December 7). Banking on volunteers. *The Chronicle of Philanthropy.* Available at http://philanthropy.com/free/articles/v19/i05/0001401.htm

Pettigrew, A. (2003). *Innovative forms of organizing.* London: Sage.

Powell, W. W. (1990). Neither market nor hierarchy: Network forms of organization. *Research in Organizational Behavior, 12*(3), 259–336.

Romirowsky, R. (2007, Winter/Spring). A venture worth taking? Sustaining 21st-century nonprofit organizations through social venture philanthropy. *Journal of Jewish Communal Service, 82*(1/2), 129–138.

Van de Ven, A. H., Polley, D. E., Garud, R., & Venkataraman, S. (1999). *The innovation journey.* Oxford: Oxford University Press.

Additional Resources

New and Recent Books

Achilles, C. M., & Ruskin, K. B. (1995). *Grant writing, fundraising and partnerships: Strategies that work.* Thousand Oaks, CA: Sage.

Ahern, T. (2007). *How to write fundraising materials that raise more money.* Medfield, MA: Emerson and Church.

Alexander, G. D., & Carlson, K. (2005). *Essential principles for fundraising success: An answer manual for everyday challenges.* New York: John Wiley & Sons.

Allen, J. (2000). *Event planning: The ultimate success guide to meetings, corporate events, fundraising galas, conferences, conventions, incentives and other special events.* New York: John Wiley & Sons.

Andreasen, A. R., & Kotler, P. (2002). *Strategic marketing for nonprofit organizations* (6th ed.). Englewood Cliffs, NJ: Prentice Hall.

Arrossi, E., et al. (1994). *Funding community initiatives: The role of NGOs in the third world.* London: United Nations Development Programme.

Bassoff, M. (2001). *Relationships: Revolutionary fundraising.* New York: Robert D Reed.

Bauer, D. G. (1999). *The "how to" grants manual: Successful grantseeking techniques for obtaining public and private grants.* Westport, CT: Greenwood.

Brav, I. (2005). *Effective fundraising for nonprofits.* Portland, OR: NOLO Press.

Burnett, K., & Thompson, J. (2002). *Relationship fundraising: A donor-based approach.* San Francisco: Jossey-Bass.

Callahan, K. L. (1997). *Effective church finances: A complete guide to budgeting, fund-raising, and setting and achieving financial goals.* San Francisco: Jossey-Bass.

Carlson, M., & Clarke, C. A. (2002). *Team-based fundraising, step by step.* New York: John Wiley & Sons.

Coley, S. M., & Scheinberg, C. A. (2007). *Proposal writing* (3rd ed.). Thousand Oaks, CA: Sage.

Dove, K. E. (2000). *Conducting a successful capital campaign* (2nd ed.). San Francisco: Jossey-Bass.

Edles, L. P. (2007). *Fundraising: Hands-on tactics for nonprofits* (2nd ed.). New York: McGraw Hill.

Fischer, M. (2000). *Ethical decision making in fundraising.* New York: John Wiley & Sons.

Fogal, R. E., Seiler, T. L., & Williams, C. (2002). *Fundraising in diverse cultural and giving environments.* New York: John Wiley & Sons.

Freedman, H. A., & Feldman, K. (1998). *The business of special events: Fundraising strategies for changing times.* Sarasota, FL: Pineapple Press.

Golden, S. L. (1997). *Secrets of successful grantsmanship: A guerilla guide to raising money.* San Francisco: Jossey-Bass.

Grace, K. S. (1997). *Beyond fundraising: New strategies for non-profit innovation and investment.* New York: John Wiley & Sons.

Greenfield, J. E. (2002). *Fundraising fundamentals: A guide to annual giving for professionals and volunteers.* New York: John Wiley & Sons.

Grobman, G. M., & Grant, G. B. (2006). *Fundraising online: Using the internet to raise serious money for your nonprofit organization.* Harrisburg, PA: White Hat Communications.

Hart, N. (2005). *Funding your cause with direct mail.* New York: Jameson Books.

Hart, T., Greenfield, J. M., & Haji, S. D. (2007). *People to people fundraising.* New York: John Wiley & Sons.

Hodgkinson, V. A., Weitzman, M. S., & Kirsch, A. D. (1993). *From belief to commitment: The activities and finances of religious congregations in the United States.* Washington, DC: The Independent Sector.

Hopkins, B. T. (2007). *The law of fundraising* (3rd ed.). New York: John Wiley & Sons.

Joseph, J. A. (1998). *Black philanthropy: The potential and limits of private generosity in a civil society.* Washington, DC: Association of Black Foundation Executives.

Joyaux, S. P. (1997). *Strategic fund development: Building profitable relationships that last.* Gaithersburg, MD: Aspen.

Keegan, P. B. (1994). *Fundraising for non-profits: How to build a community partnership.* New York: HarperCollins.

Kihlstedt, A., & Schwartz, C. P. (1997). *Capital campaigns: Strategies that work.* Aspen, CO: Aspen.

Klein, K. (2006). *Fundraising for social change* (5th ed.). New York: Chardon Press, John Wiley & Sons.

Kosmin, B., & Ritterband, P. (Eds.). (1991). *Contemporary Jewish philanthropy in America.* Savage, MD: Rowman & Littlefield.

Lauffer, A. (1997). *GRANTS, ETC: Grantgetting, contracting and fundraising for nonprofits.* Thousand Oaks, CA: Sage.

Miner, L. E., Miner, J. T., & Griffith, J. (1998). *Proposal planning and writing* (2nd ed.). Phoenix, AZ: Oryx Press.

Mintzer, S., & Friedman, R. (2003). *Everything fundraising: Create a strategy, plan events, increase visibility, and raise money.* Avon, MA: Adams Media Corp.

Nichols, J. E. (1999). *Transforming fundraising: Fundraising to grow with change.* San Francisco: Jossey-Bass.

Novom, M. L. (2007). *The fundraising feasibility study.* New York: John Wiley & Sons.

Ostrander, S. A. (1997). *Money for change: Social movement philanthropy.* Philadelphia: Temple University Press.

Petty, J. G. (2001). *Cultivating diversity in fundraising.* New York: John Wiley & Sons.

Shaw, S. C., & Taylor, M. A. (1995). *Reinventing fundraising: Realizing the potential of women's philanthropy.* San Francisco: Jossey-Bass.

Sherman, L., & Rooney, P. (Eds.). (2005). *Exploring black philanthropy.* New York: John Wiley & Sons.

Sprinkle, J. (2005). Beyond fundraising: New strategies for nonprofit fundraising and investment (2nd ed.). New York: John Wiley & Sons.

Warwick, M., Allen, N., & Hart, T. (Eds.). (2002). *Fundraising on the internet.* San Francisco: Jossey-Bass.

White, D. E. (1995). *The art of planned giving: Understanding donors and the culture of giving.* New York: John Wiley & Sons.

Williams, K. A. (1997). *Donor focused strategies for annual giving.* Gaithersburg, MD: Aspen.

Short List of Directories and Source Books (updated annually)

Public Funding

- *The Catalog of Domestic Federal Assistance.* Washington, DC: U.S. Government Printing Office

- Domouchel, R. *Government Assistance Almanac.* Detroit, MI: Omni Graphics
- Each state's list of grant and contract programs and procedures. These are often available from a state's Attorney General's office or its state "League for the Human Services."

Private and Voluntary Funding

- *Guide to U.S. Foundations, Their Trustees, Officers and Donors*
- *Foundation Directory*
- *Corporate Foundation Profiles*
- *Corporate-500 Directory of Corporate Philanthropy*
- *Matching Gift Details*
- *National Directory of Corporate Giving*
- See also Foundation Center Web site: http://www.foundationcenter.org

- *Fundraising Know How.com**
- *Fundraising Management Newsletter*
- *Grant Advisor*
- *Grants Magazine*
- *Grantsmanship Center Magazine*
- *Grassroots Fundraising Journal*
- *Health Grants and Contracts Weekly*
- *Minority Funding Report*
- *New Directions in Philanthropy and Fundraising*
- *Nonprofit and Public Sector Marketing*
- *Nonprofit and Voluntary Sector Quarterly*
- *Nonprofit Management and Leadership*
- *NonProfit Times**
- *Nonprofit World**
- *Philanthropy Journal**
- *Professional Fundraising**
- *Public Economics*
- *Religious Funding Monitor*

Journals and Periodicals

Items with asterisks are also found, all or in part, on the Internet.

- *Business and Society Review*
- *Chicago Philanthropy Quarterly*
- *The Chronicle of Philanthropy**
- *ERC Newsbriefs** (Ecumenical Resources Committee and Development Council)
- *Education Funding News*
- *Federal Grants and Contracts Weekly*
- *Foundation News and Commentary**

Internet Resources

The easiest way to locate fundraising resources on the Internet is to use one of the many powerful search engines. The two that appear, at this writing, to be used most frequently are http://www.google.com/ and http://www.yahoo.com/.

GRANTS, ETC. is another option (for location, see note 8 on p. 367). This site was created by students in a fundraising course over several years and is updated periodically. It is divided into sections dealing with funding sources and fundraising learning resources.

CHAPTER 18

Nonprofit Boards

Developing and Managing a Vital Resource

Sheldon R. Gelman

With the assistance of Tiferet Unterman

I n the not-for-profit world, which continues to grow as governments retreat from directly providing services, volunteers play critical roles in organizational development, maintenance, and operation. Key among the roles assumed by volunteers is service on the board of directors. This chapter will examine the roles and functions performed by boards as well as their relations with executive and agency staff.

Obligations and Responsibilities

Laws relating to the creation of not-for-profit organizations require formal incorporation and the identification of individuals to serve on the board of directors. Boards of directors or trustees of private or voluntary organizations are charged with the general direction and control of those organizations (Mitton, 1974). The board is the policymaking body of the organization, with a legal duty to ensure that the organization's actions are consistent with its goals and objectives.

Board members of a not-for-profit organization, in their volunteer role, have a legal and moral obligation to keep themselves fully informed about the agency's operations. Boards typically fulfill the following six functions:

1. Maintaining the general direction and control of the agency (policy development)

2. Directing short- and long-term planning (program development)

AUTHOR'S NOTE: This chapter is dedicated to the memory of Margaret Gibelman, a valued colleague and collaborator.

3. Hiring competent administrative staff (personnel)

4. Facilitating access to necessary resources (finance)

5. Interpreting the organization to the community at large (public relations)

6. Evaluating operations (accountability) (Gelman, 1995)

A more detailed set of responsibilities for boards has been identified by BoardSource in its various publications:[1]

- Determine the organization's mission
- Select the chief executive
- Provide financial oversight
- Ensure adequate resources
- Ensure legal and ethical integrity while maintaining accountability
- Ensure effective planning, implementation, and monitoring of the organization's goals
- Recruit, orient, and evaluate board members
- Promote the organization's mission and accomplishments in public forums
- Monitor the effectiveness of the organization's programs and services
- Assess the performance of the chief executive (Ingram, 2003)

Under established principles of not-for-profit and corporation law, a board member must meet certain standards of conduct in carrying out his or her responsibilities to the organization. These standards are usually described as follows:

- the duty of care,
- the duty of loyalty, and
- the duty of obedience (Leifer & Glomb, 1992; Vanden Berk, 2002).

The board, as a group, manages the nonprofit corporation, delegating responsibilities to staff but remaining ultimately accountable for the agency's image and its performance (Hanson & Marmaduke, 1972). The board is legally responsible and morally accountable to the agency's various constituencies for its actions or inactions.

Board members share collective responsibility for the fiscal and programmatic aspects of the organization's performance (Gelman, 1995). The board is responsible to funding sources, to the community, to governmental and private regulatory bodies, and to consumers of the agency's services. It is the board that sets directions through short- and long-term strategic planning, in concert with professional staff. The board hires the chief executive officer and supervises and evaluates his or her performance. Legal responsibility and fiduciary duty, which is based on a special relationship of trust, rest with the board, not the professional staff (Gelman, 1987, 1995; Gelman, Gibelman, Pollack, & Schnall, 1996; Gibelman & Gelman, 1999, 2002).

Countless books and scholarly articles have been devoted to the subject of developing a "good board" (Bradshaw, Maori, & Wolpin, 1992; Carver & Charney, 2004; Drucker, 1990; Forbes, 1998; Herman & Associates, 1994; Nanua & Dobbs, 1999; Scott, 2000). The role of the board is often described as a sacred trust, an exemplar of the democratic ideals, volunteerism at its best, and communitarianism in action (Brooks, 2002; Etizoni, 1994; Janoski, 1998; Kramer, 1998; Salamon, 1990). The high and almost sacrosanct status afforded to not-for-profit boards is most evident in human services organizations, the mission of which is to promote the well-being of citizens, often those most vulnerable to the ravages of poverty, homelessness, mental illness, and disease (Gibelman, 2004; Wagner, 2000).

The formal authority of the board is set forth in sections of the articles of incorporation, which are filed with the state government and in the organization's bylaws. These documents

- describe the organization's structure, size, and responsibilities of the governing body;
- establish the mechanisms for selection, rotation, and duration of membership and for elections of officers;
- set the minimum number of formal meetings of the full board;

- set the quorum for these meetings. (Gibelman, 2000)

Board members must, in their fiduciary role, act in the best interest of the organization. There is no exception to this obligation. Deviation from it can have significant consequences and can be costly in terms of dollars, reputation, and community good will. The board of directors, composed of volunteers, is the bedrock of every not-for-profit organization. Thus, "a board which fails in its function of both determining policy and evaluating achievement in support of those policies is negligent in performing its mandated functions" (Gelman, 1983, p. 88).

Governance

The board of directors is responsible for identifying a mission and vision for the organization, setting its policies, defining its services, guiding its development, and ensuring its accountability to the constituencies it serves. The organizational structure and size of the board should be adequate to carry out appropriate responsibilities; select and evaluate the chief executive officer it hires to manage the day-to-day operations; and engage in ongoing strategic planning, financial oversight, resource development, and relationships with the community (Chait, Ryan, & Taylor, 2004; Ostrower, 2007; Wertheimer, 2008). Good governance requires open and transparent oversight and communication as well as vision and respect. This is the ideal form of board functioning and governance for a not-for-profit organization. Unfortunately, it is an ideal that is not uniformly achieved.

Throughout the 1990s and well into this decade, articles about wrongdoing in not-for-profit organizations have appeared in the press. Some of the most glaring examples of organizational wrongdoing were perpetrated by staff of prominent not-for-profit organizations such as the United Way of America, American Parkinson's Disease Association, and Goodwill Industries of Santa Clara, California:

- *The United Way of America (UWA)*. Perhaps the biggest nonprofit story of the 1990s is that of the United Way of America, a national organization with a $29 million annual budget, and its long-time president, William Aramony. The United Way, a network of 2,100 local organizations, raised more than $3 billion a year for charity. In 1992, in response to concerns expressed by local UWA affiliates, the United Way board of governors set up an independent investigation of the allegations against Mr. Aramony. The resulting report concluded that Mr. Aramony's "haphazard" management style resulted in a breach of the trust placed in him by the board of governors and the public. Specifically, Aramony was accused of using charitable donations to finance a lavish lifestyle, including support of an expensive condominium, use of a limousine, and trips on the Concorde, a supersonic jet. Other allegations included his involvement in satellite corporations spun off from the main UWA operations. His salary of $463,000, including fringe benefits, also fueled the fires of public outrage.

- *American Parkinson's Disease Association*. With charismatic leadership, Frank L. Williams oversaw the expansion of the American Parkinson's Disease Association to 90 chapters nationwide. But over a period of seven years, Mr. Williams had quietly embezzled contribution checks worth more than $1 million. He told federal investigators that he stole because his $109,000 a year salary was half that earned by the chief executive officers of comparable charities. According to the organization's president, "at first it had a terrible impact. . . . some people blamed us for it and some still do."

- *Goodwill Industries of Santa Clara*. Goodwill Industries of Santa Clara, California, is one of the 187 autonomous local Goodwill affiliates in the United States and Canada. At least seven individuals who were related to the alleged mastermind Linda Fay Marcil systematically stole more that $15 million by selling donated clothing and pocketing the proceeds. The systematic looting of proceeds took place over a period of almost 25 years.

Money was skimmed from cash registers and donated clothing was sold by the barrelful to private dealers. One Goodwill official, Carol Marr, committed suicide. More that $400,000 in cash was found in the home and office of Linda Marcil, and more than $1 million in accounts held by Carol Marr (Gibelman & Gelman, 2001).

The above examples represent only a fraction of the problems that have come to light in recent years. Wrongdoing in the form of fraud, embezzlement, and exploitation have occurred locally, nationally, and internationally and have occurred in religious and secular voluntary agencies (Gibelman & Gelman, 2001, 2002, 2003, 2004).

The incidents of wrongdoing appear to be motivated by self-interest (greed), psychiatric aberrations, and perceived entitlement on the part of trusted staff members (Gibelman & Gelman, 2001, 2002, 2004). Most of the reported wrongdoing occurred over an extended period of time. "Situational opportunity," characterized by a lack of board oversight, allowed for the wrongdoing to go undetected. In other words, there was negligence, a failure of the ideal governance structure to operate as it was intended.

Gelman (1988) identified six areas in which charges of negligence can involve board members:

- Failure to manage and supervise the activities of the corporation
- Neglect or waste of corporation assets
- Conflicts of interest or self-benefit
- Improper delegation of authority
- Harm done to third parties through tort (wrongful action)
- Breach of contract
- Offenses against taxing authorities

Any or all of these breaches of responsibility can have detrimental and long-lasting impact on the organization.

Although these incidents of "scandal" have rocked the not-for-profit world, both domestically and internationally, are they isolated examples or part of a more widespread phenomenon?

Are not-for-profit organizations under greater scrutiny today than in the past? Are there inherent structural vulnerabilities that are just now surfacing? Or has the growth of the not-for-profit sector and the re-engineering of the not-for-profit world (Salamon, 2003b) missed the mark?

Growth of Not-for-Profits

The growth and development of the not-for-profit sector in the last quarter of the 20th century relates, in part, to a quest to find alternatives to government service provision, a quest largely borne out of disillusionment with government's handling of the welfare state (Eisenberg, 2000; Hall & Reed, 1998; Harris, 2000; Kramer, 1998; McDonald, 1997; Salamon, 1990; Wagner, 2000). This shift in service auspices requires increased numbers of volunteers at a time when not-for-profit organizations are having difficulty recruiting and retaining volunteers (Pollak & Blackwood, 2006). This is complicated further by the emergence of increasing numbers of small "faith based" organizations entering the arena of human services provision. These organizations rely heavily on volunteers and lack the infrastructure of larger, well-established organizations (Banerjee, 2006). Can the not-for-profit sector meet the expectations and demands for accountability?

As indicated previously, there has been a systematic shift away from the direct provision of services by the government to those in need. This shift has led to the dramatic growth in the number and auspices of not-for-profit organizations. The use of voluntary agencies, both secular and faith based, allows government to fulfill its historic responsibility to its citizens in what is believed by many to be a more cost-effective and efficient manner. While some of the shift has been accomplished by grant programs, the major stream of funding has come via purchase of service contracts. The acceptance of government grants and/or purchase of service contracts, in turn, has dramatically changed the nature and operation of not-for-profits. New operational structures and procedures had to be developed in response to new funding streams and requirements. In other words, the infusion of government funds, which requires compliance with federal regulations, alters the way not-for-profits conduct business. It also expanded the oversight responsibilities and obligations of those individuals serving as board members (Gibelman, 1995).

Fortunately or unfortunately, the governance of not-for-profit organizations, like their for-profit cousins, has come under increased scrutiny (Salamon, 2003a) and promoted new legislation and administrative rules intended to curb the excesses discussed above. In July of 1996, President Clinton signed legislation requiring charitable organizations (501 corporations) with gross receipts of more than $25,000 per year to make available their annual 990 IRS filing to anyone requesting it (Hopkins & Tesdahl, 1997). The 990 lists the amount of compensation paid to its highest paid employees. Oversight was further expanded with the passage of the Sarbanes-Oxley Act of 2002 (Public Company Accounting Reform and Investor Protection Act of 2002, Pub.L. No. 107-204). This act requires that organizations must report on the extent of their financial oversight and auditing practices, the level of compensation authorized by the board for the chief executive officer, and potential conflicts of interest that may exist involving board members in their service to the organization (Jackson, 2007).

The Internal Revenue Service has recently released a draft of a new version of its Form 990, which not-for-profits are required to file. Organizations will be asked about management and governance policies and practices, including executive compensation, fundraising expenses, protection for whistleblowers, and record retention policies (Schwinn, 2007; Williams, 2007). Beginning in 2008, smaller not-for-profits, those with annual gross receipts of less than $25,000, will be required to submit a form 990-N if they want to retain their tax-exempt status (Lipman, 2007).

Orientation, Training, and Development in an Era of Increased Scrutiny

How do volunteer boards prepare themselves for this heightened scrutiny and increasing demands for accountability?

New board members need a formal period of orientation, and continuing members need ongoing training to perform their required roles effectively. Board members need to understand their roles and responsibilities, as well as the time commitments that are required. All members should be provided with copies of the organization's charter and bylaws and with written descriptions of role expectations and obligations. Members of the board should become familiar with the agency and its facilities, programs, services, and personnel. An orientation manual or board handbook should be developed, disseminated, and periodically revised. Board members need to be familiar with legal standards that guide their actions, including the business judgment standard (directors are required to act in good faith and exercise their unbiased judgment in conducting the affairs of the organization), the reasonable care standard (the care required of an ordinarily prudent person in conducting his or her personal affairs), and the trustee or fiduciary rule (a director must exercise the highest level of care, that is, care greater than expected of an ordinarily prudent person; Gelman, 1995).

Unfortunately, many nonprofits provide insufficient training for board members to prepare them for their roles. Recent history demonstrates that assumptions should not be made about the innate ability of board members to understand and carry out their role (Gibelman & Gelman, 1999).

Orientation and training of board members needs to be specific to the circumstances and to the particular environment of the agency. The focus of training should be on knowledge building and developing skills and using these to reduce legal vulnerability through prevention-oriented (risk management) practices.

BoardSource (2005), in its publication *Board Member*, details 12 tips for successful board member orientation:

- Plan the orientation for the most convenient time and location for all board members. Set the date well in advance.
- Keep it simple. Provide an overview of important information and what board members should be looking for in the future.
- Pace the presentation to fit the time allotted. Create a timed agenda and stick to the schedule.
- Allow time for board members to get to know each other better.
- For half-day or day-long orientations, plan breaks for snacks, beverages, and a meal.
- Pay attention to the room's seating arrangements. Seat participants around a U-shaped table or in an informal circle with comfortable chairs or couches.
- Ask seasoned or emeritus board members attending to share stories from the organization's past.
- Include an official "swearing in" ceremony, at which time new board members pledge their service to the organization and formally acknowledge their responsibilities as board members.
- Fill board members in on some of the more informal board procedures.
- Pair a new board member with a seasoned board member to serve as a mentor.
- Maintain a sense of humor.
- Learn from experience.

Board member orientation cannot be simply a show-and-tell presentation, but must engage members in interaction and dialogue that conveys a sense of both belonging and responsibility. The failure to institute board development programs on a continuing basis often reflects an unwillingness of the board to invest scarce agency resources in itself. Instead, priority is given to using available dollars for organizational programs and services. While this may look good to contributors and keeps administrative and governance costs down, it is "penny wise, pound foolish." Systematic and ongoing board training is essential to knowledgeable and effective governance (Gibelman & Gelman, 1999). Good governance requires open and transparent communication, vision, and respect.

Board Composition and Selection

In setting up a board, it is crucial to select individuals whose personal commitment, energy, and areas of knowledge are appropriate to the agency's mission and to the specific tasks that need to be performed. Above all, board members must have the time, interest, and willingness to be of service to the agency. Power, position, and status are not substitutes for interest and commitment. Individuals who are overcommitted, or who spend much time away from the community, slow down the board in carrying out its mandated responsibilities. Unavailable or irresponsible board members force committed members to assume more responsibility than they desire, which in turn limits effectiveness and increases risk. The lack of regular and consistent attendance at board meetings is one indicator of a board member's failure to meet the required standard of care.

Individuals who serve on boards need to reflect the diversity of the community and the constituencies that are served. Members of the board should have legitimacy or standing in the community and be recognized as credible and responsible individuals, which may require verification through formal background checks. Individuals who serve on boards should be able to work cooperatively and tactfully with one another. Interpersonal skills are critical because board members interact not only with their peers on the board but also with the agency's director and staff, with community leaders and public officials, and with members of the community at large who may also be clients of the agency (Bubis

& Dauber, 1987). A board member who is an expert on everything and cannot take in information or input from others compromises the board's effectiveness and makes it more difficult to enlist others to board service.

Although the agency's charter may require that the board include bankers, politicians, clergy, and representatives of various professions and designated constituencies, every prospective member should be screened for interest and relevant expertise. Care should be taken to recruit board members with diverse knowledge and expertise, which includes financial expertise. It may be advisable to appoint prestigious community leaders as honorary members of the board, thus preventing their potential lack of time, interest, or commitment from hindering the board in the conduct of its business. Many organizations have expanded board membership to include former consumers of service and/or members of their families.

All board members should fully understand the nature of the organization and their individual and collective responsibilities. Given the possibility of personal liability, all board members need to participate in a planned and comprehensive orientation program and be covered by directors' and officers' insurance (Gelman, 1995; Gibelman & Gelman, 1999, 2002, 2005).

Who Serves and Why?

Individuals agree to serve as members of a not-for-profit board for a variety of reasons. Generally, board members are successful community members who donate their time to community service activities. Some have a passion or vested personal interest in a particular cause or issue (e.g., a disabled relative). According to Klein (1968), others are motivated because "charitable and related activities are, in our culture, a source of social prestige, and occasionally auxiliary means of access to the power structure" (p. 194). Although some individuals may be motivated by a quest for prestige or political power or by some other self-interest, Stein (1962) observed that others serve for purely altruistic reasons. Many individuals

serve on boards of charitable or not-for-profit agencies as an expression of religious or moral obligation; others do so because of professional commitment. Historically, many boards were composed of community leaders and/or stay-at-home women who had time to devote to worthy causes. Today, with more women in the workforce and concerns about time commitments, disclosure requirements, and potential liability, finding individuals willing and able to serve has created problems for many organizations in their effort to recruit board members. It is incumbent on organizations to make board membership a meaningful and worthwhile experience. If service is viewed as a chore or burden, board members will be difficult to find and retain. Similarly, the potential liability associated with board service may limit the willingness of individuals to serve.

Consumer presence is mandatory on the advisory boards of most public agencies, and consumer representation is increasingly found on the boards of private not-for-profit organizations in the health, mental health, and disability fields. The growth of the self-help and self-advocacy movement has contributed to this involvement and has resulted in greater awareness, understanding, and responsiveness by board members to clients' needs and concerns. Regardless of the motivation for serving, acceptance of a board position brings with it an obligation that must be met with care and diligence.

Board Size

The optimal size of the board of directors of a nonprofit organization is difficult to specify. Often the size and composition are dictated by the agency's charter or bylaws. In other instances, it is reflective of the size and budget of the organization. Although Weber (1975) suggested that boards be composed of 30–36 members, this may be too large to permit the development of effective group process. Excessively large boards tend to lack strong feelings of commitment and obligation, resulting in poor or sporadic participation by members. A board that is too small, however, will not have sufficient members to accomplish its work. There must be enough board members regularly present to ensure a division of labor so that no member or small group has to carry disproportionate responsibility. A sufficient number of board members also prevents one or two dominant individuals or a clique from dominating the processes that the board must engage in. Size and composition should, therefore, be related specifically to the agency's goals and objectives. A board of 15 to 18 members usually is sufficient to monitor the six areas of board responsibility previously identified.

A board must have sufficient collective expertise to monitor and evaluate the various elements of the agency's operation. The size of the board should be reasonable given the size of its budget and its geographic coverage. Ideally, each member's individual role and unique contribution to the overall effectiveness of the agency should be clear, and the board should strive to develop itself into a cohesive work group.

Length of Service

Terms of board service should be limited to three years. Reappointment to a second three-year term should be an option for those members who have fulfilled their obligations and functioned effectively. Those who have been unable to meet the expectations set for board members, or who can no longer commit themselves to board service, should not be recommended for reelection or reappointment. Individuals who fail to meet their obligations should be asked to resign or should not be reappointed (Swanson, 1984).

Board members should serve on a rotating basis, with one-third of the board's positions replaced each year. Such a format promotes continuity, allows ongoing monitoring of the enterprise, and provides for a regular infusion of new talent and the grooming of new leaders. The systematic addition of new members with identified expertise and commitment and the ongoing training of board members help the agency to become self-evaluating. According to many authors

(Austin, Cox, Gottlieb, Hawkins, Kruzich, & Rauch, 1982; Blythe & Goodman, 1987; Gelman, 1983; Gibelman & Gelman, 1999; Newman & Van Wijk, 1980; Wildavsky, 1972), the development of a capacity for self-evaluation is the only way that an agency can be responsible for and accountable to its goals, mission, and constituencies.

Board-Staff Relationships

The Executive

The executive director or chief executive officer (CEO) is an employee of the organization and serves at the pleasure of the board. He or she is a professional who is knowledgeable about people, management techniques, service provision, evaluation, fundraising, and conflict resolution and excels as a politician and communicator (Carlton-LaNey, 1987; Gummer, 1984). The executive is a skilled technician who motivates, educates, and trains both lay leaders and staff to act on behalf of the goals of the organization (Glenn, 1985). The executive director is delegated the responsibility for managing the organization and implements strategies designed to achieve organizational objectives (Gibelman, 2000). The executive director draws on the energy, expertise, and resources of the board members by involving them and keeping them informed (Blythe & Goodman, 1987; Gelman, 1983). The executive is accountable to the board in terms of the organization's performance related to identified goals and objectives. Above all else, the executive must be ethical and of good character.

Board-Executive Relations

The literature (Blau & Scott, 1962; Robins & Blackburn, 1974; Senor, 1965; Wiehe, 1978) is filled with contradictory statements about board-executive relationships and with cautions about duplications and overlapping roles and functions. While a number of authors recognize the interdependence of the relationship, they view it as a partnership with shared and overlapping functions (Bradshaw, 2002; Bubis, 1999; Bubis & Dauber, 1987; Conrad & Glen, 1976; Gibelman, 2000; O'Connell, 1976). Although *management* and *leadership* are often used interchangeably, Gibelman (2004) observes that the role of management may have to be separated from the role of leadership. While leadership can be assumed by both the board and the executive, management of organizational operations is an executive responsibility.

Some authors (Tripodi, 1976; Volunteer Bureau of Pasadena, 1972) have suggested that an agency executive must provide leadership for the board in policymaking. This works well when there is mutual respect and the executive identifies new issues or directions as the organization evolves. However, such a shared arrangement may conflict with both the agency's charter and the requirements of law if the board defers to the executive in policy formulation. According to Harris (1977), many formulations that deal with board-executive relations treat the subject as if two separable spheres of activity exist, one occupied by the board and the other by the professional executive. Senor (1965) warned that although the executive may be an ex officio member of the board, granting the executive the right to vote on policy matters creates a potential conflict of interest. It also grants the executive disproportionate power because the executive controls the information the board needs to do its job. An executive who keeps the board in the dark is an executive who does not serve the interests of the organization.

Bubis (1999), in his interesting volume titled *The Director Had a Heart Attack and the President Resigned,* identifies several problematic issues that arise in board-staff relations: blurring of roles, internal power struggles, increased dehumanizing and brutalizing of staff, and stereotyping of volunteer leaders. These issues must be addressed and resolved if an organization is to meet its goal in an effective and efficient manner. The executive and the board must work together, but the executive needs to understand that the organization and the board that employs him or her have their own history and culture

(Gibelman, 2004). The board is responsible for evaluating the executive and the agency's operations at regular intervals. The executive director is delegated authority for the agency's day-to-day operations and for handling most personnel matters, while the board must limit the tendency of individual members to become overinvolved in the day-to-day workings of the organization. The executive must also understand and respect the fact that the board is empowered by law, and the agency's charter invests the board with the power and authority to make policy. In other words, the ultimate responsibility for agency functioning and for the performance of the executive and staff resides with the board. Kramer (1985) concluded that most relationships between executives and boards involve elements of power and dependency and may take on a conflictive bent. This creative tension and interdependency can work to the advantage of the organization as long as respect exists and the give-and-take is roughly equal. When a strong executive continually butts heads with a strong board chair, the organization suffers.

The key, therefore, is the degree to which the board retains its mandated role. Although the board can draw on the executive's expertise and knowledge, it cannot allow its legal responsibility to be diluted or co-opted by overdependence. A collegial working relationship, a partnership, is essential between the board and the executive, but the executive, no matter how seasoned, remains an employee of the organization. The following capacities describe the ideal skill set needed by both board members and staff that leads to best practices (Bubis, 1999):

- The capacity to understand systems, their problems, possibilities, and limits
- The capacity to communicate well through the written and spoken word
- The capacity to facilitate interaction between people and, through them, units within and between organizations
- The capacity to have consideration and respect for others (not just volunteer leaders)

- The capacity to envision change without defensiveness
- The capacity to promote others' capacities and productivity
- The capacity to analyze and produce homeostasis when needed and enable others to prepare for change when needed
- The capacity to share information, power, and responsibility
- The capacity to master fiscal matters

Best practices are the best form of risk management (Gibelman & Gelman, 1999).

Board-Staff Relations

According to Trecker (1981), appropriate, effective, and efficient board-staff relations are based on a clear and common understanding of their respective functions and responsibilities within the organization. The board is responsible for developing and establishing policies that guide the organization, and staff members are responsible for implementing the policies adopted by the board of directors and transmitted through the executive. In implementing and achieving board policy, staff member may choose among several alternatives, but the board is ultimately responsible and therefore must hold staff, including the executive, accountable. Although the evaluation of staff should rest with the designated administrator or supervisory staff, the staff's performance reflects on the agency's goal or mission and on the performance of the board.

This analysis may appear unbalanced in the board's favor. However, ongoing interaction between board and staff is essential to the development of a responsive and accountable agency. It is crucial for staff members to have regular opportunities to report to the board about their experience in implementing board policies, about obstacles they encounter, and about unmet needs they identify. In this way, the board can adjust or modify its policies based on staff experiences. Staff members should know and feel comfortable with members of the board who are assigned to review various programs.

A three-way partnership should thus exist among board, administrator, and staff (Swanson, 1984). Such a partnership is facilitated by clear job descriptions that specify obligations and responsibilities. Personnel standards that help to clarify the rights, responsibilities, and expectations of employees are critical. Similarly, an understanding of the necessity and desirability of creating a self-evaluating agency and a commitment to this objective by all parties are essential to the achievement of agency goals.

Risk Management

Concerns about agency accountability are paramount. Charitable immunity has largely disappeared as a shield against harm caused by agency oversight or actions (Gelman, 1988, 1992; Gibelman & Gelman, 1999, 2001; Monagle, 1985; Tremper, 1989; Zelman, 1977). In response, many agencies have developed risk management strategies as a means of limiting their liability exposure (Jennings & Shipper, 1989; Litan & Winston, 1988; Olson, 1988). Risk management involves the ongoing study and assessment of activities and practices that potentially could lead to legal vulnerability (Bryant & Korsak, 1988; Salman, 1986). Risk management is a preventive activity that falls within the fiduciary purview of boards.

Boards of directors should understand and routinely engage in risk management activities on behalf of the organization. Unfortunately, the leadership of an organization, both voluntary and paid staff, may lack understanding about risk and managing risk, or board and paid staff may assume that risk management is the responsibility of the other. Risk management involves costs to the organization, typically in the form of time, effort, and insurance premiums. The costs are ongoing and apparent, while potential losses are more amorphous, less tangible, and more devastating.

Protected status is no longer afforded to the nonprofit (Kurzman, 1995; Tremper, 1994). Although some states have enacted various laws limiting the liability of charity organizations, immunity has disappeared in every state except Arkansas (Tremper, 1994). While limited liability may cap the number of dollars for which an organization is liable, or limit certain types of claims, volunteers and staff are not immune from suit. Not-for-profit organizations are liable for the harm they cause to the same degree as for-profit enterprises. As one New Jersey court ruled,

> Due care is to be expected of all, and when an organization's negligent conduct injures another there should, in all justice and equity, be a basis for recovery without regard to whether the defendant is a private charity. (Rupp v. Brookdale Baptist Church, 1990, at 190)

Risk management involves the policies, procedures, and processes that an organization engages in that are designed to reduce the chances of liability exposure. Risk management strategies are actualized through the board of directors and its delegates to reduce legal vulnerability (Bryant & Korsak, 1988; Gelman, 1987, 1992; Gibelman & Gelman, 1999, 2001, 2002, 2005; Monagle, 1985). In a proactive manner, risk management implies that the organization manages its business in accord with both sound financial practices and applicable laws, regulations, and professional requirements. The business of the organization is conducted to reduce risk, through evaluation of potential risks it may assume and implementation of strategic plans to ensure legal, ethical, and professional accountability. Managing risk is a preventive and ongoing activity designed to improve the quality of services and prevent negative outcomes (Tremper, 1994).

The need to minimize risk is both good practice and an organizational requirement, given the rise in the actual and potential number of complaints against not-for-profit organizations and their personnel. The need for practical tools that can help develop and guide good practice based on legal, ethical, and sound business principles is clear. Areas in which not-for-profit organizations are increasingly vulnerable include negligence, breach of duty through acts of omission or commission, conflict of interest, confidentiality, privileged communication, informed consent, quality of service, contracts, and "unorthodox" treatment (Antler, 1985; Besharov, 1985; Gelman, 1983, 1995; Joseph, 1989). The range of complaints against not-for-profit agencies and/or their staff include sexual improprieties, incompetence and/or incorrect treatment, breach of confidentiality/privacy, misrepresentation through marketing, breach of duty/failure to warn, abandonment of clients, defamation/libel/slander, and exerting undue influence (Gelman, 1988; Gibelman & Gelman, 1999, 2002; Roswell, 1988).

Risk management is more than preventing bad things from happening. It implies an overarching consideration on the part of the organization with achieving its mission as effectively as possible (Kurzman, 1995). Risk management is also not confined to business practices, per se, but extends to and incorporates the quality of services provided and how effective those services are in meeting needs or accomplishing stated goals and objectives.

Conclusion

While volunteers are the life blood of not-for-profit organizations, those who choose to express their voluntarism through service on the board of directors must understand their role and responsibilities. Unfortunately, many organizations do not devote sufficient time or resources to the orientation and training of board members. Board members must understand their fiduciary responsibilities and that they are individually and collectively responsible to multiple constituencies for the performance of the organization. Board membership requires more than altruism and interest; it requires an investment of quality time for both learning and oversight. Board members, in partnership with the executive and staff, need to work together in creating, developing, and monitoring an effective and accountable organization characterized by openness, responsiveness, transparency, and respect.

Failure to achieve this level of mutuality poses risks for the organization that have long-term consequences for the individuals involved and the population they serve.

Notes

1. BoardSource (http://www.boardsource.org), formerly the National Center for Nonprofit Boards, publishes the bimonthly *Board Member* and other resources designed to assist not-for-profit organizations.

References

Antler, S. (1985). *Child welfare at the crossroads: Professional liability.* Boston: NASW, Massachusetts Chapter.

Austin, M. J., Cox, G., Gottlieb, N., Hawkins, J. D., Kruzich, J. M., & Rauch, R. (1982). *Evaluating your agency's programs.* Beverly Hills, CA: Sage.

Banerjee, N. (2006, July 19). Report faults safeguards in religion program. *The New York Times,* p. A16.

Besharov, D. J. (1985). *The vulnerable social worker.* Silver Spring, MD: National Association of Social Workers.

Blau, P. M., & Scott, W. R. (1962). *Formal organizations.* San Francisco: Chandler.

Blythe, B. J., & Goodman, D. R. (1987). Agency board members as research staff. *Social Work, 32,* 544–545.

BoardSource. (2005). *The source 12: Twelve principles of governance that power exceptional boards.* Washington, DC: Author.

Bradshaw, P. (2002). Reframing board-staff relations: Exploring the governance function using a storytelling metaphor. *Nonprofit Management & Leadership, 12*(4), 471–484.

Bradshaw, P., Maori, V., & Wolpin, J. (1992). Do non-profit boards make a difference? An exploration of the relationships among board structure, process and effectiveness. *Nonprofit and Voluntary Sector Quarterly, 21*(3), 227–249.

Brooks, A. C. (2002). Does civil society stop the downward spiral of bad government or speed it up? *Nonprofit and Voluntary Sector Quarterly, 31*(1), 140–144.

Bryant, Y., & Korsak, A. (1988). Who is the risk manager and what does he do? *Hospitals, 52,* 42–43.

Bubis, G. B. (1999). *The director had a heart attack and the president resigned: Board-staff relations for the 21st century.* Israel: Jerusalem Center for Public Affairs.

Bubis, G. B., & Dauber, J. (1987). The delicate balance: Board-staff relations. *Journal of Jewish Communal Service, 63*(3), 187–196.

Carlton-LaNey, I. (1987). County social services director's perceptions of their policy boards. *Administration in Social Work, 11*(1), 25–36.

Carver, M., & Charney, B. (2004). *The board members' playbook: Using policy governance to solve problems, make decisions and build a stronger board.* San Francisco: Jossey-Bass.

Chait, R. P., Ryan, W. P., & Taylor, B. (2004). *Governance as leadership: Reframing the work of nonprofit boards.* San Francisco: Jossey-Bass.

Conrad, W., & Glen, W. (1976). *The effective voluntary board of directors.* Boulder, CO: National Center for Voluntary Action.

Drucker, P. F. (1990). Lessons for successful nonprofit governance. *Nonprofit Management & Leadership, 1*(1), 7–14.

Eisenberg, P. (2000). The nonprofit sector in a changing world. *Nonprofit and Voluntary Sector Quarterly, 29*(3), 325–330.

Etizoni, A. (1994). *Rights and the common good: The communication perspective.* Belmont, CA: Wadsworth.

Forbes, D. P. (1998). Measuring the unmeasurable: Empirical studies of nonprofit organization effectiveness from 1977 to 1997. *Nonprofit and Voluntary Sector Quarterly, 27*(2), 183–202.

Gelman, S. R. (1983). The board of directors and agency accountability. *Social Casework, 64*(2), 83–91.

Gelman, S. R. (1987). Board of directors. In A. Minahan (Ed.-in-chief), *Encyclopedia of social work* (18th ed., Vol. 2, pp. 206–218). Silver Spring, MD: NASW Press.

Gelman, S. R. (1988). Roles, responsibilities, and liabilities of agency boards. In M. P. Janicki, M. W. Krauss, & M. Seltzer (Eds.), *Community residences for persons with developmental disabilities: Here to stay* (pp. 57–68). Baltimore, MD: Paul H. Brooks.

Gelman, S. R. (1992). Risk management through client access to case records. *Social Work, 37*(1), 73–79.

Gelman, S. R. (1995). Boards of directors. In R. Edwards (Ed.-in-chief), *Encyclopedia of social work* (19th ed., pp. 305–312). Washington, DC: NASW Press.

Gelman, S. R., Gibelman, M., Pollack, D., & Schnall, D. J. (1996). Boards of directors on the line: Roles, realities and prospects. *Journal of Jewish Communal Service, 72*(3), 185–194.

Gibelman, M. (1995) Doing a difficult task "right": Firing employees. *Administration in Social Work, 19*(1), 75–87.

Gibelman, M. (2000). Structural and fiscal characteristics of social service agencies. In R. Patti (Ed.), *The handbook of social welfare management* (pp. 113–133). Thousand Oaks, CA: Sage.

Gibelman, M. (2004). On boards and board membership. *Administration in Social Work, 28*(2), 49–62.

Gibelman, M., & Gelman, S. R. (1999). Safeguarding the nonprofit agency: The role of the board of directors in risk management. *Journal of Residential Treatment for Children and Youth, 16*(4), 19–37.

Gibelman, M., & Gelman, S. R. (2001). Very public scandals: Nongovernmental organizations in trouble. *Voluntas: International Journal of Voluntary and Nonprofit Organizations, 12*(1), 49–66.

Gibelman, M., & Gelman, S. R. (2002). Should we have faith in faith-based social services? Rhetoric versus realistic expectation. *Non-Profit Management & Leadership, 13*(1), 49–65.

Gibelman, M., & Gelman, S. R. (2003). The promise of faith-based social services? Perception versus reality. *Social Thought: Journal of Religion in the Social Services, 22*(1), 5–23.

Gibelman, M., & Gelman, S. R. (2004). A loss of credibility: Patterns of wrongdoing among nongovernmental organizations. *Voluntas: International Journal of Voluntary and Nonprofit Organizations, 15*(4), 355–381.

Gibelman, M., & Gelman, S. R. (2005). Ethical considerations in the changing environment of human service organizations. In M. L. Pava & P. Primeaux (Eds.), *Crisis and opportunity in the professions: Research in ethical issues in organizations* (Vol. 6, pp. 1–19). Oxford: Elsevier.

Glenn, W. E. (1985). Board and staff relations. In E. Anthes, J. Cronin, & M. Jackson (Eds.), *The nonprofit board book: Strategies for organizational success* (pp. 87–102). West Memphis and Hampton, AK: Independent Community Consultants.

Gummer, B. (1984). The social administrator as politician. In F. D. Perlmutter (Ed.), *Human services at risk* (pp. 23–36). Lexington, MA: Lexington Books.

Hall, M. H., & Reed, P. B. (1998). Shifting the burden: How much can government download to the non-profit sector? *Canadian Public Administration, 41*, 1–20.

Hanson, P. L., & Marmaduke, C. T. (1972). *The board member-decision maker for the nonprofit corporation.* Sacramento, CA: HAN/MAR.

Harris, J. E. (1977). The internal organization of hospitals. *Bell Journal of Economics, 8*(2), 467–482.

Harris, M. (2000). The changing challenges of management and leadership in the UK voluntary sector: An interview with Stuart Etherington. *Nonprofit Management & Leadership, 10,* 319–324.

Herman, R. D., & Associates. (Ed.). (1994). *Jossey-Bass handbook of nonprofit leadership and management.* San Francisco: Jossey-Bass.

Hopkins, B. R., & Tesdahl, D. B. (1997). *Intermediate sanctions: Curbing nonprofit abuse.* New York: John Wiley & Sons.

Ingram, R. T. (2003). *Ten basic responsibilities of nonprofit boards* (Rev. Ed.). Washington, DC: BoardSource.

Jackson, P. M. (2007). *Sarbanes-Oxley for nonprofit boards.* Hoboken, NJ: John Wiley & Sons.

Janoski, T. (1998). *Citizenship and civil society: A framework of rights and obligations in liberal, traditional, and social democratic regimes.* Cambridge, UK: Cambridge University Press.

Jennings, M. M., & Shipper, F. (1989). *Avoiding and surviving lawsuits.* San Francisco: Jossey-Bass.

Joseph, M. V. (1989, October 14). *At risk: Legal vulnerability and what to do about it.* Presentation at the 1989 NASW Annual Conference, San Francisco, CA.

Klein, P. (1968). *From philanthropy to social welfare.* San Francisco: Jossey-Bass.

Kramer, R. M. (1985). Toward a contingency model of board-executive relations. *Administration in Social Work, 9*(3), 15–33.

Kramer, R. M. (1998). *Nonprofit organizations in the 21st century: Will sector matter?* Nonprofit Sector Research Fund, Working Paper Series. Washington, DC: Aspen Institute.

Kurzman, P. A. (1995). Professional liability and malpractice. In R. L. Edwards (Ed.-in-chief), *Encyclopedia of social work* (19th ed., pp. 1921–1927). Washington, DC: NASW Press.

Leifer, J. C., & Glomb, M. B. (1992). *The legal obligations of nonprofit boards: A guide book for board members.* Washington, DC: National Center for Nonprofit Boards.

Lipman, H. (2007, July 31). Small nonprofits must now deal with something new: Taxes. *The Record,* p. B1.

Litan, R. E., & Winston, C. (Eds.). (1988). *Liability: Perspectives and policy.* Washington, DC: Brookings Institution.

McDonald, C. (1997). Deinstitutionalised or reinstitutionalised? Developments in the nonprofit human services sector. *Australian Journal of Social Issues, 32,* 341–363.

Mitton, D. G. (1974). Utilizing the board of trustees: A unique structural design. *Child Welfare, 53*(6), 345–351.

Monagle, J. F. (1985). *Risk management: A guide for health care professionals.* Rockville, MD: Aspen.

Nanua, B., & Dobbs, S. M. (1999). *Leaders who make a difference: Essential strategies for meeting the nonprofit challenge.* San Francisco: Jossey-Bass.

Newman, H., & Van Wijk, A. (1980). *Self-evaluation for human service organizations.* New York: Greater New York Fund/United Way.

O'Connell, B. (1976). *Effective leadership in voluntary organizations.* New York: Association Press.

Olson, W. (Ed.). (1988). *New directions in liability law.* New York: Academy of Political Science.

Ostrower, F. (2007). *Nonprofit governance in the United States: Findings on performance and accountability from the first national representative study.* Washington, DC: The Urban Institute.

Pollak, T. H., & Blackwood, A. (2006). *The nonprofit sector in brief: Facts and figures from the nonprofit almanac.* Washington, DC: The Urban Institute.

Robins, A. J., & Blackburn, C. (1974, Summer). Governing boards in mental health: Roles and training needs. *Administration in Mental Health,* 37–45.

Roswell, V. A. (1988). Professional liability: Issues for behavior therapists in the 1980s and 1990s. *The Behavior Therapist, 11*(8), 163–171.

Rupp v. Brookdale Baptist Church, 577 A.2d 188 (N.J. Super A.D. 1990).

Salamon, L. M. (1990). *America's nonprofit sector: A primer* (Rev. ed.). New York: Foundation Center.

Salamon, L. (2003a, May 29). Charities shouldn't be urged to act like Enron. *Chronicle of Philanthropy,* p. 3.

Salamon, L. (2003b). *The state of nonprofit America.* Washington, DC: Brookings Institution.

Salman, S. L. (1986). Risk management process and functions. In G. T. Troyer & S. L. Salman (Eds.), *Handbook of health care management* (pp. 149–182). Rockville, MD: Aspen.

Schwinn, E. (2007, June 14). A big makeover coming for charity tax form. *The Chronicle of Philanthropy,* pp. 35–37.

Scott, K. T. (2000). *Creating caring and capable boards.* San Francisco: Jossey-Bass.

Senor, J. M. (1965). Another look at the executive board relationship. In M. N. Zald (Ed.), *Social welfare institutions: A sociological reader* (pp. 418–427). New York: John Wiley and Sons.

Stein, H. D. (1962). Board, executive and staff. In H. Millman (Ed.), *The social welfare forum* (pp. 215–230). New York: Columbia University Press.

Swanson, A. (1984). *Building a better board: A guide to effective leadership.* Washington, DC: Taft Corporation.

Trecker, H. B. (1981). *Boards of human service agencies: Challenges and responsibilities in the 1980s.* New York: Federation of Protestant Welfare Agencies.

Tremper, C. (1989). *Reconsidering legal liability and insurance for nonprofit organizations.* Lincoln, NB: Law College Education Services.

Tremper, C. (1994). Risk management. In R. D. Herman & Associates (Ed.), *The Jossey-Bass handbook of nonprofit leadership and management* (pp. 485–508). San Francisco: Jossey-Bass.

Tripodi, T. (1976). Social workers as community practitioners, social welfare administrators and social policy developers. In T. Tripodi, P. Fellin, I. Epstein, & R. Lind (Eds.), *Social workers at work* (2nd ed., pp. 162–169). Itasca, IL: F. E. Peacock.

Vanden Berk, K. M. (2002, Summer). What you need to know about the legal responsibilities of nonprofit officers and directors. *Alliance for Children & Families Magazine,* pp. 29–31.

Volunteer Bureau of Pasadena. (1972). *So. . . . you serve on a board.* Pasadena, CA: Author.

Wagner, D. (2000, February 24). The "virtue" of charity: Debunking an American myth. *The Chronicle of Philanthropy,* pp. 42–43.

Weber, J. (1975). *Managing the board of directors.* New York: Greater New York Fund.

Wertheimer, M. R. (2008). *The board chair handbook* (2nd ed.) Washington, DC: BoardSource.

Wiehe, V. R. (1978). Role expectations among agency personnel. *Social Work, 22,* 270–274.

Wildavsky, A. (1972). The self-evaluating organization. *Public Administration Review, 32,* 509–520.

Williams, G. (2007, June 28). A new form takes shape. *The Chronicle of Philanthropy,* p. 33.

Zelman, W. N. (1977). Liability for social agency boards. *Social Work, 22,* 270–274.

CHAPTER 19

Managing Financial Resources

Mark Ezell

Financial Management and Agency Performance

There is little doubt that planning for and using financial resources challenges human services managers unlike many of their other responsibilities. A significant portion of the challenge is the demand for accountability to numerous internal and external groups. All agency stakeholders, from clients to staff and boards to funders, have significant interests in the effective management of fiscal resources during all stages of the budget cycle. Clients are concerned about financial management because they believe that service quality and intended outcomes are more likely to be achieved with effective budget planning, implementation, control, and assessment. Employees are interested because of their salaries and benefits, but also because ongoing work conditions,

client outcomes, and their sense of efficacy depend on the prudent use of dollars. It goes without saying that funders are interested in the effective utilization of funds for such reasons as the accomplishment of client service objectives, ongoing community support, and accountability to their constituents.

We do not need research to tell us that program and agency survival are at risk when managing finances; too many programs and agencies have closed not just because of the inability to acquire funding, but also because of ineffective use and accounting of financial resources. Some mismanaged agencies have to close their doors, but far more stumble along with inadequate planning, control, and evaluation of finances. Short of closure, there is a long list of negative consequences for the community, staff, and clients when financial matters are mishandled.

AUTHOR'S NOTE: Information included in this chapter is general guidance and should not be construed as professional counsel. Please consult your tax/legal advisor for specific guidance.

This raises the important question, What is the empirical, causal connection between managers' financial management competence and subsequent client outcomes, service quality, client satisfaction, and employee morale?

Simply put, there is almost no research in the human services field on this question. We take as given the causal relationship that seems apparent in practice and, further, design graduate school curricula around the premise. Research in the for-profit sector shows that executives strongly influence organizational performance (Ritchie & Eastwood, 2006). By studying chief executives of nonprofit university and college foundations, Ritchie and Eastwood found that executives' years of experience in five areas (i.e., accounting, finance, production, operations, marketing) is related to financial performance. Their measures of financial performance appear to be better approximations of the ability to *acquire* resources rather than *manage* resources. This research is a beginning, and one should be cautious about overgeneralizing the findings. Three major challenges prevent making grand statements about the relationship between the financial management competence of managers and client outcomes: (1) it is highly likely that university and college foundations are, in many ways, distinct from human services nonprofits; (2) because the research was cross-sectional, we cannot be sure about the direction of the empirical relationship; and (3) the dependent variables measured fundraising, not effective financial management or a more client-centered measure of organizational performance. It is quite possible, however, that very little research on the relationships between managers' financial management skills and agency service performance has been conducted because it seems so obvious that underfunding, inefficiency, inadequate financial controls, and misallocation of funds are major reasons for the poor performance of programs and services. Also, we are all too aware that poor financial management undermines the credibility of agencies with funders and, as such, jeopardizes ongoing funding.

It is also noteworthy to examine two recent articles that reviewed the literature in search of organizational and managerial variables associated with client outcomes in human services. Neither the article by Poertner (2006) nor the one by Yoo, Brooks, and Patti (2007) identified any empirical research that demonstrates that better client outcomes are achieved in agencies with competence in financial management. In the 11 studies Poertner identified with empirical associations between management behavior and client outcomes, none of the independent variables included the financial management competence of managers. Yoo et al. extensively reviewed the child welfare literature, and they observed that very little research had examined the influence of organizational constructs, such as management and leadership, on client outcomes. The experience of workers was identified as an important variable, but there was no specific mention of managers or their financial management skills and knowledge.

Despite the absence of supportive research, there is little doubt that boards of directors will require that chief executive officers (CEOs) and other executive managers have knowledge and skills in financial management or, at least, the ability to supervise a chief financial officer (CFO) and/or others with specific financial management duties.[1] The performance record of agencies that have ignored this wisdom is not very good and, sometimes, is disastrous. It may not be necessary for CEOs and other executive-level managers to have technical financial management skills (e.g., accounting), but they need to know how to interpret various financial statements and monitoring reports (to be discussed later). They also need to insure that budget planning and program planning go hand in hand. One of the many contributions of Vinter and Kish (1984) is their emphasis on the link between these two, "how to think about the *budgeting* [italics added] process as a tool for accomplishing *program* [italics added] objectives" (p. 3), and how budget reports provide essential information about program performance.

In addition, an agency's strategic plan should influence annual budgets as agency priorities change and agency leaders navigate opportunities for the agency in constantly dynamic environments. It is a good idea for the strategic plan to include a multi-year revenue and expenditure budget painted in broad brush strokes (see Chapter 15 on strategic planning). Also, it should almost go without saying, but as program plans are created and revised—the targeted client group, the intensity and duration of services, staff qualifications, and caseload size, for example—expense and revenue budgets need to be revised (see Chapter 16 on program planning).

Financial Management: A Key Skill

Notwithstanding the importance of financial management, students frequently contemplate their budgeting class with great trepidation (if one is even available). Human services managers, who are often promoted from the ranks of direct service workers, frequently share these feelings. Whether the trepidation stems from math phobia or the sometimes technical nature of this work remains to be seen, but as Lohmann (1980) rightly points out, they "must eventually come to terms with these topics. For the truth is that management knowledge cannot be considered complete without *some knowledge* [italics added] of the working of financial resources in organizations and of the decisions which regulate their movement" (pp. 123–124). Almost 30 years after Lohmann's statement, it seems clear that it should be changed from "some knowledge" to *extensive* knowledge.

Even though budgeting duties are very important and frequently time consuming, one of the major challenges facing human services managers is to avoid "budget obsession," or what has become the frequent complaint of nonmanagement staff, "only focusing on the bottom line." All too often, budgets are treated as immutable law and become of singular importance in agencies.

Budgets and budget compliance should be seen as means to facilitate all aspects of service effectiveness (Patti, 1985) and employee satisfaction. The relevance and value of budgeting and other financial management functions should be evaluated in terms of how well they contribute to positive client outcomes, service quality and program integrity, client satisfaction, and positive staff morale. "The more the organization knows about where and how it uses resources, the better service job it can do" (Vinter & Kish, 1984, p. 2).

This chapter begins with a discussion of the fiscal and regulatory context within which human services agencies operate. Contextual factors such as managed care and purchase of service contracting are reviewed, as are federal laws and regulations, the Internal Revenue Service, and unrelated business income. The next section explains numerous fiscally related administrative tasks in each of the major stages of the budgeting cycle. The final section includes an in-depth discussion of common financial management issues faced by human services organizations.

The Context for Agency Financial Management

Human services agencies are accountable to external constituencies for how they use and record their financial resources. The most prominent external constituencies are the various funders, both public and private. To a large degree, the funders dictate budget formats, report types and frequencies, and accounting and auditing procedures. Nonprofit human services organizations also need to comply with the policies and procedures of their boards of directors and the Internal Revenue Service (IRS). Even without all these specific dictates, social service agencies must have well-developed financial management systems in order to compete in the current fiscal and policy environment.

Besides complying with the requirements of specific funders, human services agencies and their managers operate in an environment strongly shaped by contemporary funding mechanisms such as managed care and different contracting approaches (e.g., fee-for-service, case rate). It is becoming very rare for human services nonprofits to have a single source of funding, such as United Way. It is very common for both large and small nonprofits to rely on multiple funding streams, including government and foundation grants, government contracts, managed care agreements, individual donations, and proceeds from endowments.

Bidding for private insurance and public contracts is increasingly competitive, and when reimbursement rates are part of the bid, human services administrators need to know how much it costs to deliver services to particular types of clients and how many clients are needed for a specific program to break even (Meyer & Sherraden, 1985). Agencies that bid successfully will need to develop and operate financial and client information systems that can invoice the payer(s) for the specific set of services provided to each client at the agreed-upon rates. State contracts with private providers (both for- and nonprofit) frequently reimburse agencies on an hourly basis, depending on the nature of the service delivered (e.g., transportation, therapy) and on the type of staff delivering the services (e.g., professional, paraprofessional). This requires detailed record keeping, billing, and monitoring systems.

Federal Legislative Action

An important federal law passed in 2002 with implications for human services nonprofits increased the complexity of the financial management environment. The Sarbanes-Oxley Act (P.L. 107-204)—abbreviated as SOX—was developed as a result of "wrongdoing and fiscal mismanagement in public companies" (Jackson & Fogarty, 2005, p. 1).[2] In a joint publication by the Independent Sector and BoardSource (BoardSource & Independent Sector, 2006), it was reported, "several state legislatures have already passed or are considering legislation containing elements of the Sarbanes-Oxley Act to be applied to nonprofit organizations" (p. 2). Jackson and Fogarty (2005) advise the following:

> While it is true that the majority of the SOX provisions currently only apply to publicly traded corporations and not to nonprofit organizations, nonprofits could benefit operationally from adopting some of the SOX provisions as "best practices." In addition, voluntarily adhering to the SOX standards would create greater credibility and the ability to recruit high quality board members, and attract the favorable attention of major donors, foundations, and other funding sources. (p. 22)

Space limitations prohibit an in-depth analysis of SOX. Helpful resources are increasingly available for human services managers. For example, United Way of America (n.d.) published a useful pamphlet with a section-by-section summary of the law and recommendations for nonprofits. Web sites for the following organizations have materials and publications on SOX: The Independent Sector, BoardSource, GuideStar, and the National Council on Nonprofit Associations.

SOX includes two provisions to which nonprofits *must* adhere: (1) whistleblower protection, and (2) required policies on document preservation/destruction. Nonprofits must develop and implement policies that protect staff and volunteers who make reports of problems with accounting, internal controls, and audits. The policy must include a process to investigate reports and release findings. Document management and preservation policies are intended to prevent someone who wants to obstruct an investigation from hiding, altering, or destroying agency documents. Violations of the document preservation policy can result in a person being punished by fines and imprisonment.

As mentioned above, there are many other provisions that are not required but are recommended by leaders in the nonprofit sector: several provisions relating to the auditors, their work, and their ongoing relationship with the non-profit agency; requirements regarding the audit committee of the board; directives regarding accounting procedures, financial statements, and internal controls; and constraints on the CEO and CFO.

Before nonprofit managers think there is little else to be concerned about, they should note that the U.S. Senate Finance Committee recently held hearings and is studying nonprofit accountability. The 2004 and 2005 hearings included statements by the IRS Commissioner including plans for greater oversight and enforcement (Panel on the Nonprofit Sector, 2005). Commissioner Everson said the IRS would begin programs to examine the compensation levels of individuals employed by nonprofits and the independence of boards' oversight of salaries and duties, to examine the failure of some nonprofits to file Form 990, to increase the number of enforcement staff for exempt organizations, and to revise Form 990 to make it easier to complete and to produce information needed by IRS agents (Jackson & Fogarty, 2005, pp. 34–39). As a result of the Committee's work, a White Paper was published that includes draft recommendations for discussion (U.S. Senate Finance Committee, 2004). The White Paper includes too many proposals to discuss here, but a significant result of the hearings was the convening of the Panel on the Nonprofit Sector by the Independent Sector. The Panel released its report in June, 2005 and a Supplemental Report in April, 2006 (both are available at www.NonprofitPanel.org). The Panel developed eight guiding principles for accountability and governance of charities (see pp. 20–22 of the 2005 Report) and approximately 140 recommendations on two dozen topics.

In August, 2006, the President signed the Pension Protection Act (P.L. 109-280), which included some of the changes recommended by the Panel. "The bill contains an important package of reasonable safeguards intended to strengthen the work of the charitable sector by deterring potential abuse of tax-exempt organizations and creating additional protections to ensure that donated funds are used for charitable purposes" (Independent Sector, 2007, p. 1). The charitable giving provisions only impact contributions made in 2006 and 2007. Nonprofits formerly exempt from filing Form 990 because their annual gross receipts are $25,000 or less are now required to file the new electronic Form 990-N. Also, organizations are now required to make public their unrelated business income tax returns.

Internal Revenue Service

Just like individuals, nonprofits have to file income tax returns with the IRS. Specifically, they must file Form 990. As discussed above, the IRS is changing reporting requirements as well as enforcement activities. There is little doubt that more change will be coming. Recent changes include the December, 2007 release of a revised Form 990 (to be used for 2008); the requirement that Form 990-T, Exempt Organization Business Income Tax Return, be made public; increased guidance on allowable political activities; and the development of online courses to help organizations maintain their exempt status (see http://stayexempt.org/; GuideStar, 2007).

As a result of the policy and fiscal environment, many nonprofits engage in revenue-generating activities that are unrelated to their exempt purposes (Ezell & Wiggs, 1989). Administrators should seek expert advice on the definition of "unrelated business income" and whether it applies in their specific situation because the regulations are very complex. Business activities that are not directly related to the exempt purposes of the organization and are regularly carried on may generate a profit on which the nonprofit must pay unrelated business income tax. A very common misconception is that net profits from unrelated activities can be used to subsidize underfunded, exempt activities, and no income tax will be owed. The IRS does not consider the expenditure of the profits, just whether the activities that generated the profits are related or unrelated to nonprofits' exempt purposes. Instead of operating unrelated businesses within nonprofit corporations, many organizations have opted to create for-profit subsidiaries to generate revenues for the nonprofit (Goldstein, 1998). The advantage of this arrangement is that the nonprofit receives tax-free income from the for-profit subsidiary, and the subsidiary writes off its charitable donation. Tax laws and accounting practices are very different for these types of corporations. Obviously, unrelated business activities—whether housed in the nonprofit or a subsidiary—can consume a great deal of administrators' attention, as well as other resources, and might draw attention and focus away from the central human services mission of the organization. In either case, administrators should proceed with great caution and should seek advice from tax attorneys and CPAs.

Government Audits

Another contextual influence is that public and private agencies receiving federal funding must comply with Circular A-133, Audits of States, Local Governments, and Non-Profit Organizations (Office of Management and Budget, 2003).[3] Circular A-133 is intended to unify auditing standards used by the federal government when auditing nonfederal organizations that expend federal funds. In most cases, nonfederal agencies do not have to conduct audits as specified in the Circular if they receive less than $300,000 of federal awards per year. If agencies are subject to the provisions of Circular A-133, they must prepare certain financial statements. The audits seek to determine the following: (1) Are the financial statements prepared in accordance with generally accepted accounting practices? (2) Do internal controls ensure compliance with relevant laws and regulations? (3) Has the agency complied with laws, regulations, and the provisions of contracts or grant agreements? (4) Has

the agency corrected problems identified in prior audits (Kalin, Hardiman, Corfman, & Hunter, 1990)? Because audits may be conducted on the entire operation of the agency and not just the organizational units that expend federal funds, agencies are strongly encouraged to design fiscal systems that are consistent with expectations outlined in Circular A-133.

Performance Measurement

The growing and maturing movement toward performance measurement is an additional context affecting financial management in human services organizations (also see Chapter 8 for additional discussion of performance measurement). Joyce (1997) discusses whether and how performance measures can be used in the budgeting process. He reminds us that zero-based budgeting as well as program budgeting, both of which have been around for quite awhile, require a great deal of work. Performance budgeting, discussed in more detail below, attempts to use program results for budgeting purposes, but experience with this approach to date has received mixed reviews. At the federal level, agencies are required to report on performance measures as part of their annual budget requests. This requirement was included in the Government Performance and Results Act of 1993 (P. L. 103-62; Martin & Kettner, 1996). It remains to be seen how much these requirements will change agency budgeting practices.

Auspice and Financial Management

Inherent in the discussion to this point is that agency auspice is a significant contextual factor. The financial management differences between public and private agencies are profound, as are those between private for-profits and private nonprofits. Also, while not all private agencies are small, almost all public human services agencies are large. Auspice in combination with agency size creates one of the major differences between managing public versus private agencies. Public managers generally have less input into the design of financial management systems. Those responsible for recording, reporting, and monitoring financial transactions are likely to be in a separate organizational unit than those delivering services, giving the human services manager less influence over the form and frequency of financial reports. The author's experience is that monthly financial statements in public agencies, for example, are not always made available but are generally less user-friendly than the similar reports in nonprofits, largely because the reports are prepared by and primarily for the use of budget specialists.

Internally, nonprofit social agencies are accountable to boards of directors, with whom ultimate legal fiduciary responsibility rests. Many boards create finance committees to work closely with agency staff and to save the remainder of the board from having to review numerous, detailed financial reports. The division of labor between the board and the staff is a delicate, evolutionary dynamic. As a staff person, the author has felt that board members tried to micro-manage; as a board member, he has felt that staff were too involved in policymaking. Nevertheless, the organization as a whole benefits, and the manager is best protected when board members are actively involved in all stages of the budget cycle. One issue that especially needs board involvement is the challenge of what to do with cash reserves and endowments. Wolf (1990) advises that when reserve funds grow large, "the board [should] designate a portion of the reserves as 'funds functioning as endowment'" (p. 149). Endowments, whether created from reserves or specific contributions, involve investing the principal and only spending the earnings for specified purposes. Clearly, managers need to work with and depend on their boards to establish investment policies regarding whether to invest endowment funds and cash reserves in savings accounts, mutual funds, and other investment vehicles.

Fiscal Responsibilities of the Human Services Administrator

Being accountable to internal and external constituents is only one aspect of financial management. Managers' time will also be devoted to planning, monitoring, and evaluating the use of financial resources in such a way as to achieve the goals and service objectives of the agency. This section will explain the three major stages of the budget cycle and the associated managerial tasks of each. Since another chapter is devoted to fundraising (see Chapter 17), this chapter will treat that task as a fait accompli. (Wouldn't it be nice if it were that easy!)

The stages of the budget process are not as sequential as this chapter and many books seem to depict. At any given time, administrators are simultaneously concerned with at least three different fiscal years: prior, current, and next. The exception to this, of course, is when an agency or program is brand new, as in the case of a grant proposal being written for a new service. Next year's budget, the continuation budget, must be developed long before the current fiscal year is complete. A fiscal year has to be completed and all expenses and revenues recorded before an audit or a cost analysis can be done. This does not happen until a new budget year is well under way. Figure 19.1 illustrates this scenario. Further complicating matters is the reality that many agencies and programs have multiple funding sources, and the different funders may operate on different fiscal years. Standard fiscal years are October 1st to the end of the following September (e.g., federal government), July 1st to June 30th (state governments), and January 1st to December 31st (many United Ways). The timetables for the stages and tasks, therefore, are dictated by the funding sources. One highly recommended technique to cope with the melange of due dates is to develop a budget calendar that includes the elements presented in Figure 19.2.

Before discussing each budget stage and its associated managerial tasks specifically, two

FY –1 (prior)			FY 0 (current)			FY +1 (next)		
Assess FY –2	Implement FY –1	Plan FY 0	Assess FY –1	Implement FY 0	Plan FY +1	Assess FY 0	Implement FY +1	Plan FY +2
			Audit	Allocate funds	Project revenues			
			Analyze costs	Manage	Plan program & budget			
			Report	Control	Estimate costs			
				Adjust	Negotiate			
				Report				

Figure 19.1   Three Fiscal Years of Concern and Budget Stages

Elements of Budget Calendar

- What are the tasks and subtasks, in chronological order, necessary to develop, implement, and assess the budget? (Column #2)
- When should each of the above be started and finished? (Column #1)
- Who will take primary leadership for each of the tasks? (Column #3)
- Who else should participate in each task, and whose review or approval is necessary in order to move on? (Column #4)
- When are internal and external reports due? (Item #2 under Budget Activity)

Budget Calendar for Agency XYZ (Fiscal Year—January Through December)

1. Dates	2. Budget Activity	3. Lead Responsibility	4. Involve
Start: April 1 Finish: April 30	Prepare brief proposals for new programs/ services	Program Coordinators	Program Staff
Start: April 1 Finish: April 15	Prepare first quarterly report for fiscal year	Executive Director	Program Coordinators
Start: May 1 Finish: May 15	Review proposals for new services, prioritizing by feasibility, need, and fundability	Executive Director	Program Coordinators
Start: May 16 Finish: June 15	Conduct prospect research on two most promising new services.	Fund Developer	Program Coordinators
Start: June 1 Finish: June 30	Review all programs for underfunded aspects, need for program changes, and efficiencies that could be introduced	Program Coordinators	Program Staff and Clients
Start: June 1 Finish: June 15	Estimate revenues for next fiscal year	Executive Director	Executive Committee
Start: June 15 Finish: June 30	Decide on cost-of-living raises and amount available for merit increases; prepare budget instructions for program coordinators	Executive Director	Executive Committee

Figure 19.2   Elements of a Budget Calendar With a Sample Calendar

important notes are warranted. First, the following discussion focuses on *what* has to be done, not *how* to do it. The material tries to be "management style neutral." A specific manager's style might be unilateral and "top-down," participative, or eclectic. The choice of management style, or combinations of styles, is constrained by time, energy, staff and their skill level, and other programmatic obligations.

Second, while administrators do not necessarily do all budgeting tasks personally (e.g., bookkeeping), they must, at least, oversee the following:

- hire and supervise appropriate personnel;
- be able to talk the language and communicate with fiscal staff;
- be able to select and work with external auditors;
- associate fiscal issues with program matters and client concerns;
- translate fiscal reports to appropriate audiences; and
- insure quality control of the financial systems.

In addition to this list, another skill is to be able to ask the right questions at the right times. Small agencies may not be able to hire a CPA on staff, and clerical staff, untrained in bookkeeping, are made responsible for many fiscal activities. In these cases, supervision and consultation are very important, as are the functions of the external auditor. The author's observation is that more and more agencies are contracting for payroll services to save money and anguish. Financial management/bookkeeping software is becoming more sophisticated and user-friendly, which is good, but many agencies fail to pay attention to important security and backup issues. Notwithstanding the size of an agency and the skills of staff, more attention should be paid to internal fiscal controls. This is discussed at greater length in the next section.

Types of Budgets and Planning Processes

There are several well-known approaches to budgeting (i.e., budget planning processes) as there are several types of budgets, but they are not one and the same. "Type of budget" refers to the format of budget documents, the layout of the budget on paper. The format of a budget usually does not reveal the underlying planning process. Mayers (2004) provides an extensive discussion of budget planning and budget documents with more detail than can be provided here. The most common and simplest budgeting *process* is incremental or, unfortunately, decremental, where an agreed-upon percentage—frequently an inflationary factor or change in the cost of living—is added to or subtracted from the prior year's budget. Two other well-known budget processes, zero-based budgeting (ZBB) and planning programming budgeting system (PPBS), are both derived from a rational planning model and are time consuming and somewhat technical approaches if every step is followed. Over time, however, both have lost favor because the payoff is less than the investment of time and energy. ZBB, unlike incremental budgeting, does not take the prior year's budget as its starting point but rebuilds budgets and programs from the ground up. It is frequently the case that managers combine the best and most convenient features of different budgeting processes and utilize different budget formats for various audiences and purposes. There are several situations in which ZBB (or "quasi-ZBB") is recommended: (1) when major change (e.g., reorganization) occurs, (2) when a new CEO is hired to implement a new strategic plan, and (3) when competition for contracts is strong and bids are awarded on the basis of cost.

Line Item Budget. The most common *budget format* is a line item budget, also known as an object classification budget (Granof, 1998). This form of budget includes a vertical listing of the sources of revenue (e.g., grants, donations, fees) and the input items to be purchased to run the program (e.g., salaries, benefits, travel, rent).[4] Funders such as United Way (as well as others) require agencies to use a standardized list of line items, and the level of specificity varies. Due to the inconsistent expectations of different funders, including the line items on the IRS Form 990, many nonprofits find it overly time consuming to meet everyone's demands for budget formats. Several organizations have coalesced to develop and advocate for a Unified Chart of Accounts (UCOA) to make financial reporting more efficient (Editors, 2001). "A chart of accounts is a system for classifying transactions" (p. 1). The UCOA cross-references IRS Forms 990 and 990 EZ and the United Way of America Accounting Guide. The items on the UCOA are very specific, and with computers can be easily collapsed into more general categories, depending on the audience. (For more information on the Unified Chart of Accounts, see http://nccs.urban.org/projects/ucoa.cfm.)

The horizontal axis of a line item budget frequently includes columns that represent the prior and current year budgets as well as next year's proposed budget for all of the revenue and expense items. This allows a year-by-year comparison of changes and plans. In the case of an agency that operates multiple programs, an agency-wide line item budget, such as that described here, makes it impossible to determine which programs are being increased or decreased.

A very common alternative to this format shows the same line items down the first column, but the horizontal axis shows either programs or organizational units. For example, a children's agency might have programs such as recreation, tutoring, and counseling, and each of these has a column with the planned revenues and expenditures. A public child welfare agency could show organizational units such as child protective services, foster care, adoption, and family preservation.[5] One of the great contributions computers have made to financial management is that it is very easy to develop these different formats and change between them. For example, an agency's executive director, the board of directors, and the local United Way may all want the budget layout to be slightly different. Most financial software can do this with ease.

Functional Budget. An examination of IRS Form 990 reveals that expenditure items are broken down into three functional categories: program services, management and general, and fundraising. (See pp. 26–27 in the IRS 2006 Instructions for Form 990 and Form 990 EZ for specific definitions.) This is what a *functional budget* looks like. "The functional classification of expenses involves grouping expenses by major classes of program activities and supporting services" (Larkin & DiTommaso, 2007, p. 181). Vinter and Kish (1984) are strong proponents of functional budgeting as a way to allocate, control, and analyze costs within a program and across functions or sets of activities. Wolf (1990) refers to this as project budgeting. Vinter and Kish's book uses the case example of a youth diversion program that can be broken down into several interdependent functions: screening and intake, referral, counseling, consultation and referral, and administration. This approach is particularly valuable when different clients of the same program receive different "packages" of services. As in Vinter and Kish's case example above, clients are initially screened, and a certain subset of clients is determined to be ineligible and cases are closed. Another subset of clients receives screening and is then referred for services to another agency. Still another subset receives screening and then counseling. As is probably obvious, detailed functional budgeting such as the example above, coupled with an understanding of different client case flows, allows managers to conduct much more accurate cost analyses.

Performance Budget. The final form of budgeting to be mentioned here is *performance budgeting.* This is a budget that focuses on an organization's or program's outputs, such as workloads, efforts, or outcomes, emphasizing units of work produced and their cost per unit. Table 19.1 shows a performance budget for a hypothetical child welfare agency. It is rarely the case that an agency uses a performance budget like this without other information. Both internally and externally, stakeholders wish for more specific accountability and control than that offered by a performance budget. Performance information such as this is very frequently included in budget documents that accompany a line item, program, or functional budget.

Table 19.1   Performance Budget of Hypothetical Child Welfare Agency, FY2010

Program Activity	Budget
Investigate 30,000 reports of child abuse and neglect	$30,000,000
Provide 2,007,500 days of foster care	$180,675,000
Recruit 500 new foster homes	$500,000
Train 750 foster parents	$250,000
Prevent foster care placement of 500 children	$1,750,000
Place 300 children for adoption	$4,200,000

The Language of Budgeting

Many budgeting and accounting terms are confusing and are used differently in common parlance versus the language of budget experts. Three primary villains are "administrative costs," "indirect costs," and "overhead." For an organizational unit to show *indirect costs* in its budget, there must be a "parent" agency. For example, the social work department is one organizational unit in a hospital; a school of social work is one unit in a university. If a school of social work, for example, receives a federal research grant, some expenses are experienced directly by the school, while others borne by the university are considered indirect expenses. These are real costs to the university, the parent organization, for a subunit to operate a grant program. Because the school utilizes the personnel and bookkeeping units in the university, for example, when implementing a research grant, those costs are part of an agreed-upon rate that is collected by the university, the parent organization. Indirect costs rates are established between an agency and a funding agency (usually a federal or state agency or private foundation) after audits and negotiations.

Vinter and Kish (1984) equate "overhead" with indirect costs, which makes sense given the visualization of a parent agency.

"Indirect costs" and "administrative costs," often used interchangeably, are not the same thing. Programs and agencies have direct expenses that are immediately associated with service delivery (i.e., program services) and there are other expenses related to the management of the agency, fundraising, and membership development. Grouped together, these latter three are called "supporting services" by the Financial Accounting Standards Board and in common parlance are referred to as *administrative costs*. Donors are very interested to know what percentage of their donated dollars actually go to service delivery versus supporting services.[6] There are subtle distinctions between the costs that can be attributed to program services and administration, for which a CPA should be consulted.

The Budget Cycle

Planning and Development Stage

The first stage of the budget cycle is planning and development. The specific managerial tasks in this stage will differ depending on whether a budget is being prepared for a new or a continuing program, and depending on the specific *budgeting process* used. The first task in the budget development stage is to understand the agency's or program's revenue sources, amounts, and related policies. Questions such as the following should be asked and answered: How much funding is approved for what amount of time? How is the revenue received (e.g., reimbursed on a per client basis, periodic lump sums)? In what instances does the manager have budget discretion and when is prior approval needed? What are allowable and unallowable costs? What are the fiscal and programmatic reporting requirements?

Related to this task is the forecasting of revenues. The forecast for some revenue sources is straightforward, such as grants and some contracts, when the upcoming year's level of funding is known. Public agencies depend on somewhat unpredictable legislative processes to establish their revenue levels. In other instances, however, when revenue is based on factors such as the volume of services delivered, fundraising efforts, the number of clients, client fees, and reimbursement rates, the trends need to be studied and projection techniques utilized. Three pieces of advice are offered here. First, estimate revenues conservatively and expenses liberally so that the agency will be protected if you are wrong in both cases. Second, forecast revenues before estimating expenses. When expenses are estimated first, there is a strong tendency to project revenues at a level to match or exceed expenditures, as opposed to a more realistic and safer level. Finally, Wolf (1990) suggests that managers include a contingency/reserve line item in their budgets that should be as high as 5%, especially if revenue sources are unpredictable. Using a line item like this is another instance in which board policy is needed to guide decisions on when reserve funds can be spent.

Program planning is another major task during this stage. The program plan must include an estimate of the number of clients to be served and must be specific enough to estimate how much of different types of resources are needed (see Chapter 16 on program planning). In human services programs, the major resource is almost always staff, so that is a good place to start. What types of staff (e.g., BSWs, MSWs, MDs) are needed to deliver the intended service? How many of each are needed, and what will be their level of compensation? After those determinations, it is fairly straightforward to estimate the costs of fringe benefits and payroll taxes. To estimate the next set of costs, ask, "What types of facilities, space, and materials are necessary to deliver the intended services and how much of each will be needed to serve the estimated number of clients?" For example, if a counseling program will use treatment groups, they will need meeting space conducive to this type of intervention. This, of course, will only provide managers with estimates of the basics. A very strong reminder for this task is that the cost estimates

cannot be made without adequate program plans. Program staff and financial staff should not work in isolation from one another but should communicate frequently and circulate drafts of the budget and program plan. Here is where the very important link between programming and budgeting is often lost.

The final managerial task in this stage of the budget cycle is negotiation. Whether the budget is being submitted to external funders, legislative bodies, or a board of directors, these bodies are frequently looking to cut costs, increase efficiencies, and increase productivity. Managers must defend their budget requests and their programs and advocate for their clients and staff (Ezell, 1991). While there are many different ways to be persuasive in these situations, human services managers will be well served if they have program evaluation results that demonstrate service effectiveness, cost analysis findings to substantiate budget requests, and needs assessment statistics to show the necessity of their program.

Implementation

The next stage of the budget cycle begins once the budget and program have been approved by the appropriate powers that be and the program is initiated. The organizational level at which these activities are conducted and decisions made differs by organization. In organizations that become more decentralized, budget implementation is "pushed down" to lower and lower levels of the hierarchy. As public agencies have made budget cuts or slowed their growth, they have attempted to maintain direct services by cutting middle management staff. This, too, gives budget discretion to staff closer to the front lines.

An early task in this stage is the allocation of funds to specific program activities (i.e., functions) and cost centers. "Cost centers represent clusters of distinguishable activities that accrue costs, to which expenditures can be assigned" (Vinter & Kish, 1984, p. 114). Allocating resources in this manner firmly establishes which and how much of the different resources (e.g., staff time, space, client financial assistance) will be devoted to various program activities. A functional budget facilitates this task just as this task supports the control function.

Exercising programmatic and fiscal control demands managerial vigilance. It is easy to understand the importance of fiscal control by remembering that revenues were projected, programs planned, and costs estimated far in advance—sometimes more than a year—of the actual delivery of services. Much can change between the planning and the implementation stage. Also, largely unique to the human services enterprise is the fact that all clients are different and each of them brings a different set of strengths and challenges that will consume more and different resources than anticipated. "Control" consists of three activities: (1) monitoring revenues and expenditures, (2) comparing the data collected from monitoring to standards or benchmarks, and (3) taking corrective action, if necessary. The budget, broken down into monthly or quarterly increments, serves as the benchmark. Managers need to develop procedures for recording revenue and expenses and install a system that will produce timely monitoring reports that include variances from budget and year-end estimates. The reports need to be detailed so that warning flags, such as unexpected expenditures or reduced revenues, pop up easily and early; once a warning flag comes up, the manager needs to start asking questions. A warning flag does not mean that something untoward is happening. It may only reveal that the original budget needs adjusting due to unforeseen rate hikes (e.g., postage, insurance). It can indicate that services are being implemented differently than planned or that fundraising activities are being less productive than hoped. Warning flags might also announce that the client population is harder to reach and serve than anticipated. Flags should pop up when revenue collections are falling short and when expenditures are either over or under budget.

This stage includes interim financial reporting to both internal and external constituents. Nonprofits provide financial reports to the Internal Revenue Service (Form 990), funders, boards of directors, and members. Public agencies report to their respective legislative bodies and to other governmental agencies, such as the federal government when a state has a federal grant. This stage of the budget cycle, just like the previous, can involve more negotiations. Funders' permission to amend the expenditure budget may be sought when major changes are necessary. Most funders allow managers a certain amount of budget discretion without review, but commonly, if any line item needs to be reduced or increased by more than 10%, prior approval is required. If revenue collections are falling below budget, expenses will need to be cut unless reserve funds can be tapped. Undoubtedly, this will require internal negotiations among staff and various programs as well as legislative bodies and boards of directors. Complicating matters further, it may be necessary to report to the IRS, for example, in the middle of a funder's or program's fiscal year.

The implementation stage also includes the recording of transactions. The Financial Accounting Standards Board (FASB) sets standards for nonprofits. The Securities and Exchange Commission and the American Institute of Certified Public Accountants both recognize the FASB. There is also a Governmental Accounting Standards Board (Zietlow, Hankin, & Seidner, 2007). In general, the guidelines from FASB are referred to as Generally Accepted Accounting Principles (GAAP). "In order to have a CPA audit your organization and give your organization an unqualified opinion on your financial statements, you *must* present those statements according to GAAP" (Zietlow et al., 2007, p. 171). (Specific financial statements are discussed below.)

Budget Assessment

The third stage of the budget cycle begins once the fiscal year has been completed and all income and expenditures have been recorded. Managers need to file end-of-year program and financial reports with the appropriate authorities and demonstrate that objectives were met and funds used appropriately. Three specific financial statements should be prepared at this point: statement of financial position (also called a balance sheet), statement of activity (also called a statement of net revenue), and statement of cash flows. The statement of financial position is a point-in-time description of the agency's assets and liabilities. "The statement of activity indicates to what extent an organization's revenues exceeded its expenses in a given period" (Zietlow et al., 2007, p. 176). The statement of cash flows is very useful in that it is not a snapshot but shows the amount of cash from one quarter/year to the next.[7]

It is at this point that managers either choose to conduct an audit or are informed that their agency/program will be audited. There are many different definitions of auditing (McKinney, 1995), many types of audits, and numerous agencies that can serve as auditors, ranging from CPA firms to legislative and governmental auditing offices.

> *Financial and compliance audits* or *fiscal audits* assess whether financial operations are properly conducted. They evaluate whether an entity's financial statements are presented fairly and in compliance with applicable laws, policies, procedures, and regulations. (McKinney, 1995, p. 407)

It should go without saying that human services administrators are expected to give their full cooperation to auditors. The author's experience is that auditors hired by the agency can be extremely helpful, especially when they review and make suggestions regarding the adequacy of internal fiscal controls. Nonprofit managers and boards are frequently hesitant to pay for audits every year, but such practices represent false economies. It is far better to get critical feedback from accountants who are working for you rather than unexpectedly to be handed a list of audit exceptions by auditors for the IRS, the General Accounting Office, or other governmental bodies whose loyalties are elsewhere.

Cost Analysis

The final managerial task to be discussed here is cost analysis. Far too few human services agencies conduct appropriate analysis of their costs, and, therefore, they lack the ability to state with confidence what it costs to serve different kinds of clients. In the current world of managed care, privatization, and fee-for-service contracts, this puts these agencies not only at a huge disadvantage but also at great financial risk. Cost analysis is a technique that calculates the use of resources by different types of clients, outputs, or outcomes. This process links expenditures with program operations and outcomes.

Flowcharts tracing client careers (Vinter & Kish, 1984, p. 258) and functional budgets are necessary to disaggregate program components and determine the cumulative costs for different client careers. A word of caution here about using the results of a cost analysis to negotiate contracts. As previously mentioned, human services administrators are disadvantaged without this information, but they may also be in a situation where a little information is a dangerous thing. Managers should not lose sight of the fact that an analysis of this type calculates the *average* cost per client or service unit, and "average" is a mathematical concept and does not represent a "real" client or service unit. This means that administrators must not only conduct cost analyses but also be very familiar with the characteristics of and challenges involved in serving the intended client population. Again, knowing just the dollars is not enough.

Funders typically insist that agencies define and report outcomes, as well as the average cost per outcome. Equally concerned about outcomes are those agencies that have signed performance contracts that may be required to return funds if they fail to reach agreed-upon levels of success (Else, Groze, Hornby, Mirr, & Wheelock, 1992: also see Chapter 16 on performance-based contracts). Analyzing costs per positive outcome will require agencies to collect one or more outcome measures for clients served. McCready, Pierce,

Rahn, and Were (1996) discuss a useful example of a technique to associate costs with outcomes.

Common Financial Management Issues

Social service agencies tend to have several financial management challenges in common. For over 20 years, the author has worked with numerous public and private agencies as they wrestled with financial management challenges in a changing policy and fiscal environment. Based on that experience, it is possible to identify frequent challenges and exemplary financial practices designed to solve them. While some cautions have been previously mentioned, this section discusses several challenges in more detail.

Revenue Forecasting

The first issue involves revenue forecasting. As discussed earlier, if grants have been awarded, the amount of revenue is known. However, other funding mechanisms reimburse based on the volume of services delivered within agreed-upon ceilings defined in the contracts. The challenge becomes to predict the volume of cases (or service units, if not cases) and, sometimes, the intensity of services. Many managers develop their estimates unsystematically with "guesstimates" based on their experience. Sometimes they project the number of cases that just happens to balance their budget. On matters involving program revenue, human services managers should make these forecasts conservatively *and* analytically.

Many human services administrators have begun using simple mathematical projections and have found them useful. They do not depend on these as their sole source of estimates but weigh them along with their practice wisdom, knowledge of the field, clients, and conversations they have with the funding and referral sources. Figure 19.3 includes 12 months of hypothetical data on case closings and graphs them over time. This hypothetical example is relevant in situations when funders reimburse providers and/or agencies collect client fees. The specific question confronting the manager is, "How many cases will we close next fiscal year and, therefore, how much revenue will that generate?"

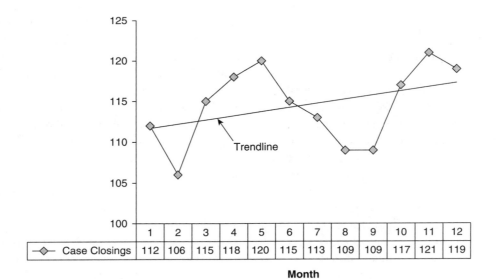

	1	2	3	4	5	6	7	8	9	10	11	12
Case Closings	112	106	115	118	120	115	113	109	109	117	121	119

Month

Figure 19.3   FY07: Case Closings per Month (Hypothetical Data)

The manager could use the FY07 case closings, averaging 114.5 per month, to project next year's number. This method predicts 1,374 case closings for the upcoming year, the same as FY07. This is often done, eyeballed, and then increased by some factor—often 5% or 10%. Using an average such as this ignores the overall trend of increased closings as the year progressed and the real possibility that the trend may continue next year and, if it does, that expenses will increase. This trend can be easily identified with spreadsheet software, as was done in Figure 19.3. It is very easy to graph the FY07 data and use the software to add a trend line to it. (Microsoft Excel was used here.) Somewhere way back in high school math, we learned that this line has an equation that describes it (in this case, $y = .5105x + 111.18$, where "x" is the month number and "y" the number of case closings). This equation can be used to estimate how many cases will be closed in months 13 through 24. Totaling these for the next fiscal year estimates that a total of 1,448 cases will be closed, an annual increase of 5.3% and an average of 120.6 closings per month. The software does almost all the work. Once these numbers are generated, managers should treat them as hypothetical and try to determine the real likelihood of the trend continuing.

Monitoring Reports

The second issue of concern is the preparation and formatting of periodic reports used to monitor revenues and expenses. These reports are essential in human services management. Even if the agency heavily invests in budget and program planning, there are so many unknowns that variances between the plan and actual experience are bound to occur. There are a number of common practices that make monitoring reports less useful than they could be and cause them to fail to provide early warnings of financial problems. Since budget planning is, at best, highly approximate, managers need a monitoring system that will provide them with warnings as early as possible that revenue and expenditures may be off track.

It should be obvious that if monitoring reports are prepared monthly, for example, then the original revenue and expense budgets should be broken down into monthly increments so that useful benchmarks are established (see Table 19.2). A monitoring system is no better than the quality of the benchmarks, and, unfortunately, monthly benchmarks developed as if one-twelfth of the revenues will come in every month and one-twelfth of the expenses will occur will not help a manager spot problems. This may be a reasonable assumption on some line items, like salaries and benefits, but travel, insurance, tax payments, and a number of other items are expended on different and variable schedules. Much depends on the type of program and when certain activities occur. Also, if the organization holds one major fundraising event per year, both the costs of putting it on and the revenue generated will occur irregularly. Because of this, managers frequently review and act on monthly statements based on faulty benchmarks.

A similar problem occurs when managers use monitoring information to project their end-of-year financial position. This is an ongoing managerial concern as they ask, "Given my program and budget experience up to now, will I be over or under budget at the end of the year?" Monitoring reports frequently include a column that shows—either item by item and/or program by program—how much has been spent (or received) year-to-date. Another column indicates the remainder to be spent or amounts to be collected based on the approved budget. There is nothing to help them project their year-end balances.

Many administrators have learned that adding a column that represents their best projection of how much will be spent or received in the remaining months makes the year-end projections much more accurate. This column is not created mathematically but is derived by asking several questions. For example, if managers review mid-year monitoring reports, they can ask these questions to create this "accrual column for each line item": (1) Will the last six months' spending pattern on this item continue? (2) Do program plans anticipate more or less spending

Table 19.2 Monthly Monitoring Report

Agency for the Prevention of Bad Things, Inc.
Expenditures (Cash Only) July, 2007

Account	Budget Total	Monthly Average	Spent Prior to This Month	Current Month	Total YTD	Budget Balance	Projected YTD	Over/(Under) Projected YTD
Salaries	66,300	5,525.00	33,121.69	5,609.00	38,730.69	27,569.31	38,675.00	55.69
Benefits	14,200	1,183.34	7,576.25	646.34	8,222.59	5,977.41	8,283.38	(60.79)
Payroll Taxes	5,167	430.58	2,631.59	472.48	3,104.07	2,062.93	3,014.06	90.01
Professional Fees	2,000	166.67	2,000.00	0	2,000.00	0	1,166.69	833.31
Office Supplies	3,300	275.00	1,178.23	63.21	1,241.44	2,058.56	1,925.00	(683.56)
Phones, Postage, Printing	6,340	528.33	4,212.50	640.82	4,853.32	1,486.68	3,698.31	1,155.01
Utilities	466	38.83	375.23	65.07	440.30	25.70	271.81	168.49
Equipment	1,133	94.41	615.92	47.20	663.12	469.88	660.87	2.25
Subscriptions	200	16.67	168.50	0	168.50	31.50	116.69	51.81
Travel	1,865	155.42	944.71	274.21	1,218.92	646.08	1,087.94	130.98
Conference Supplies	1,200	100.00	0	137.22	137.22	1,062.78	700.00	(562.78)
Meeting Space	5,800	483.33	1,302.58	329.04	1,631.62	4,168.38	3,383.31	(1,751.69)
Membership Dues	250	20.83	237.50	275.00	512.50	(262.50)	145.81	366.69
Miscellaneous	100	8.33	63.02	7.38	70.40	29.60	58.31	12.09
Total	108,321	9,026.74	54,427.72	8,566.97	62,994.69	45,326.31	63,187.18	(192.49)

NOTE: The layout of the report and data come from a real agency. It has been slightly adapted for educational purposes.

on this item in the next six months? (3) Are any rate, caseload, or staffing changes expected in the next six months? The figure derived from this thought process added to the amount already spent shows how much is expected to be spent by the end of the year. This is the figure that should be compared to the original budget to estimate over- or underspending.

A challenge associated with monitoring revenues and expenditures is managing cash flow. Unfortunately, even though human services administrators may have successfully negotiated a contract and a fair reimbursement rate, it can take one to three months after invoicing to receive payment. For the specifics of how to conduct cash flow projections, see Wolf (1990), but a small addition to the monthly monitoring reports can be immediately useful. Show the cash balance at the beginning of the month; the monthly net of revenue and expenses; the cash balance at the end of the month; and finally, the projected net of revenue versus expenses for the next month. Comparing the end-of-month cash balance with next month's projection will reveal whether there will be cash on hand at the end of the month or whether funds need to be moved from the reserve account. Besides projecting and monitoring cash flow, agencies must have sizable cash reserves or lines of credit due to lengthy delays in payments.

Improving the formatting of these reports can make them easier to use (Oster, 1995). Frequently, a lot of numbers are jammed onto a page that is poorly labeled. Consider different formats for different audiences. The administrator with program responsibility can be given detailed reports while the board of directors might receive a report with aggregated numbers or collapsed categories. For example, while it is possible to report expenditures line item by line item, they can be summarized into categories such as personnel (salaries, benefits, and employee taxes) and operating costs (e.g., rent, travel, supplies, equipment). Graphics such as line charts and bar graphs are also very useful when making comparisons. Managers should consider utilizing

Poertner and Rapp's (2007) very useful principles for designing management reports.

Last, many nonprofits use software or bookkeeping services that create the standard financial statements on a monthly basis for the purpose of monitoring revenues and expenses. It is the author's opinion that these financial statements are rarely designed well enough to provide early warnings of under- or overspending and low revenue collections in enough detail—by program and line item—to allow managers to take appropriate corrective actions.

Internal Controls

Another ongoing challenge for human services agencies, especially small ones, is the absence of an internal control system. Generally, internal control policies and procedures are intended to insure that resources are used for their intended purposes and to reduce the chance of fraud and embezzlement. One of the major practices in an internal control system is "separation of duties." This creates a check and balance system where there are different people who reconcile an account and who write the checks, for example, or different staff open the mail and record checks. Another safeguard is the bonding of employees with fiscal responsibilities. Bonding employees essentially involves purchase of an insurance policy that helps the agency recover its losses, but it can also involve in-depth screening of employees (Mayers, 2004).

According to McMillan (2006), one of the most common vulnerabilities of nonprofits is the receipt and handling of donation and payment checks. There is no known technique that absolutely can prevent theft, especially if two or more employees collude to do so. Assuming that it will never happen in your agency is not a workable approach, nor is the belief that you can tell whether someone is dishonest. There are a number of resources available to help design and evaluate systems of internal controls. The agency auditor is a great resource on this. Besides the practices identified above, there are a number of other measures that might prevent embezzlement: (1) thorough background checks of staff, (2) policies against nepotism, (3) personnel policies that require the reporting of suspected fraudulent or unethical activity, (4) protection of whistleblowers, (5) requiring two signatures on checks, (6) regular backup of computers, and (7) very strict policies on the use of agency credit cards (McMillan, 2006).

Staff Diversity and Cultural Competence

Is financial management different for agencies serving or composed of people from historically oppressed groups? Based on a review of IRS regulations, federal laws, and other funders' requirements for reporting and accountability, the answer seems to be "no." Human services managers, however, have many issues to consider related to the composition of their staff and/or the nature of their target populations. Most, if not all, have implications for programming, budgeting, and/or personnel policies. An agency's efforts and commitments in this area should be visible in its budget.

Many clients from historically oppressed groups are difficult to locate, must be served where they are (as opposed to the agency office building), and experience many other barriers to service access. Have funds been set aside for outreach, staff travel to get to clients, for dependent care, for translators or signers, to remodel facilities to increase access, and any other relevant expenses necessary for service delivery to oppressed persons? Staff may need special and/or extensive knowledge and skills to serve people from historically oppressed groups. Is there money in the budget for training and consultation? (See Chapter 14 for additional discussion of this issue.)

Funds are needed both to increase the diversity of staff, volunteers, and board members and to create and maintain healthy, inclusive work environments. Extensive advertising and networking may be necessary to increase the number of applicants from oppressed groups. Good personnel policies and benefit packages, not to mention salaries, are necessary to attract and keep a diverse workforce. It takes funding to underwrite bereavement policies, different religious holidays, benefits for domestic partners, and revised definitions of "family" and "dependents." It is increasingly important in a diverse society to endorse initiatives such as this, and little progress will be made without earmarking funds.

When agencies are required to absorb budget cuts, it is important for managers to think through the consequences of potential cuts on staff and clients from oppressed groups. Due to the subtle ways in which biases and stereotypes influence decision making, many people should closely scrutinize budget revision plans, asking many questions, not the least of which are (1) Will potential cuts affect certain staff more than others, and (2) Will particular client groups be disproportionately affected? In both cases, managers must avoid "discrimination on the basis of race, ethnicity, national origin, color, sex, sexual orientation, age, marital status, political belief, religion, or mental or physical disability" (National Association of Social Workers, 1996, pp. 22–23). Sadly, for example, women have been laid off because of the misconception that husbands are primary breadwinners.

Conclusion

This chapter is an introduction to the financial management responsibilities of human services administrators. A discussion of the fiscal, regulatory, and policy context that influences the practice of financial management served as the background to describe necessary financial management skills and knowledge. Second, the chapter reviewed the three major stages of the budget cycle and specific tasks that managers must accomplish during each stage. Finally, several common financial management challenges were discussed in greater depth.

Managing the finances for a human services program is a major responsibility that involves many large and small decisions, the use of influence and power, and the need for creative thinking. The effectiveness of financial management should be judged on the basis of how well it contributes to service effectiveness, to staff morale, and to the continuing viability of the agency in the community. Balancing the budget and staying "in the black" cannot be ignored, by any means. The budget, which is merely a plan on how to use resources, should be handled as a very powerful tool to help accomplish service objectives and human services goals.

Notes

1. This is less often the case when hiring executive managers in public agencies, due to wide separation of budget and program planning, implementation, and evaluation.

2. Although most commonly referred to as the Sarbanes-Oxley Act, its official name is the Public Company Accounting Reform and Investor Protection Act.

3. In March, 2007, OMB published a Compliance Supplement to assist auditors. It can be found on the OMB Web site.

4. Experience has taught the author that most people only think of expenses when the term "budget" is mentioned. Revenue budgets may or may not be a separate document, but a big warning flag should go up if an agency has no revenue budget.

5. Organizational units and programs are frequently, but not always, one and the same.

6. The specific definitions of *supporting services* can be found in Statement of Financial Accounting Standards #117, ¶ 17, pp. 11–12 (Financial Accounting Standards Board, 1993).

7. More detail on financial statements can be found in Larkin and DiTommaso (2007), Martin (2001), and Zietlow and colleagues (2007).

Internet Resources

Note: These addresses are accurate as the manuscript is prepared, but Internet addresses change frequently. The author is not endorsing any of these organizations or certifying the accuracy of their materials.

BoardSource: http://www.boardsource.org

Financial Accounting Standards Board: http://www.fasb.org

GuideStar (Philanthropic Research, Inc.): http://www.guidestar.org

Independent Sector: http://www.independent sector.org

Internal Revenue Service: http://www.irs.gov
  ○ IRS Online Training: Stay Exempt: http:// stayexempt.org/

Management Assistance Program for Nonprofits: http://www.mapfornonprofits.org

National Council of Nonprofit Associations: http://www.ncna.org

Office of Management and Budget (federal): http://www.whitehouse.gov/omb/

The Nonprofit Quarterly: http://www.non profitquarterly.org/

United Way of America: http://www.united way.org

Urban Institute: http://www.urban.org
  ○ National Center for Charitable Statistics: http://nccsdataweb.urban.org/faq/ index.php?category=31
  ○ Center on Nonprofits and Philanthropy: http://www.urban.org/center/ cnp/index.cfm

References

BoardSource & Independent Sector. (2006). *The Sarbanes-Oxley Act and implications for nonprofit organizations.* Retrieved June, 2007, from http:// www.boardsource.org/Knowledge.asp?ID=7.300

Editors. (2001). Initiative for a unified chart of accounts: An attempt to define our own terms. *The Nonprofit Quarterly, 8*(1). Boston, MA: Third Sector New England.

Else, J. F., Groze, V., Hornby, H., Mirr, R. K., & Wheelock, J. (1992). Performance-based contracting: The case of residential foster care. *Child Welfare, LXXI*(6), 513–526.

Ezell, M. (1991). Administrators as advocates. *Administration in Social Work, 15*(4), 1–18.

Ezell, M., & Wiggs, M. (1989). Surviving the threats from small business advocates. *The Child and Youth Care Administrator, 2*(1), 47–53.

Financial Accounting Standards Board. (1993). *Statement of financial accounting standards # 117: Financial statements of not-for-profit organizations.* Norwalk, CT: Author.

Goldstein, H. (1998). Making charities' for-profit arms more accountable. *The Chronicle of Philanthropy.* Retrieved April 9, 1998, from http://philanthropy .com/premium/articles/v10/i12/12004501.htm

Granof, M. H. (1998). *Government and not-for-profit accounting: Concepts and practices.* New York: John Wiley & Sons.

GuideStar. (2007). *IRS updates, June 2007: Public disclosure of IRS Form 990-T and political activities of exempt organizations.* Retrieved June, 2007, from http://www.guidestar.org/DisplayArticle.do?arti cleid=1136

Independent Sector. (2007). *Analysis of charitable reforms & incentives in the "Pension Protection Act of 2006" (Pub. Law 109-280).* Washington, DC: Author. Retrieved May 7, 2007, from http://www.independent sector.org/programs/gr/Pension_Bill_Summary.pdf

Jackson, P. M., & Fogarty, T. E. (2005). *Sarbanes-Oxley for nonprofits: A guide to gaining competitive advantage.* Hoboken, NJ: John Wiley & Sons.

Joyce, P. G. (1997). Using performance measures for budgeting: A new beat, or is it the same old tune? In K. E. Newcomer (Ed.), *Using performance measurement to improve public and nonprofit programs* (pp. 45–61). San Francisco: Jossey-Bass.

Kalin, D. H., Hardiman, P. F., Corfman, S., & Hunter, C. (1990). Auditing nonprofit entities under Circular A-133. *The CPA Journal, LX*(2), 32–43.

Larkin, R. F., & DiTommaso, M. (2007). *Not-for-profit GAAP 2007: Interpretation and application of generally accepted accounting principles for not-for-profit organizations.* Hoboken, NJ: John Wiley & Sons.

Lohmann, R. (1980). Financial management and social administration. In F. D. Perlmutter & S. Slavin (Eds.), *Leadership in social administration* (pp. 123–141). Philadelphia: Temple University Press.

Martin, L. L. (2001). *Financial management for human service administrators.* Needham Heights, MA: Allyn & Bacon.

Martin, L. L., & Kettner, P. M. (1996). *Measuring the performance of human service programs.* Thousand Oaks, CA: Sage.

Mayers, R. S. (2004). *Financial management for nonprofit human service agencies* (2nd ed.). Springfield, IL: Thomas.

McCready, D. J., Pierce, S., Rahn, S. L., & Were, K. (1996). Third generation information systems: Integrating costs and outcomes. Tools for professional development and program evaluation. *Administration in Social Work, 20*(1), 1–15.

McKinney, J. B. (1995). *Effective financial management in public and nonprofit agencies* (2nd ed.). Westport, CT: Quorum Books.

McMillan, E. J. (2006). *Preventing fraud in nonprofit organizations.* Hoboken, NJ: John Wiley & Sons.

Meyer, D. R., & Sherraden, M. W. (1985). Toward improved financial planning: Further applications of break-even analysis in not-for-profit organizations. *Administration in Social Work, 9*(3), 57–68.

National Association of Social Workers. (1996). *Code of ethics.* Washington, DC: Author.

Office of Management and Budget. (2003). *Circular No. A-133—Audits of states, local governments, and non-profit organizations.* Washington DC: Author.

Oster, S. M. (1995). *Strategic management for nonprofit organizations: Theory and cases.* New York: Oxford University Press.

Panel on the Nonprofit Sector. (2005). *Strengthening transparency governance accountability of charitable organizations.* Washington, DC: Independent Sector. Retrieved March, 2007, from http://www .NonprofitPanel.org

Patti, R. J. (1985). In search of purpose for social welfare administration. *Administration in Social Work, 9*(3), 1–14.

Poertner, J. (2006). Social administration and outcomes for consumers: What do we know? *Administration in Social Work, 30*(2), 11–24.

Poertner, J., & Rapp, C. A. (2007). *Textbook of social administration: The consumer-centered approach* (2nd ed.). New York: Haworth Press.

Ritchie, W. J., & Eastwood, K. (2006). Executive functional experience and its relationship to the financial performance of nonprofit organizations. *Nonprofit Management and Leadership, 17*(1), 67–82.

United Way of America. (n.d.). *A United Way guide to Sarbanes-Oxley*. Alexandria, VA: Author.

U.S. Senate Finance Committee. (2004, June). *Staff discussion paper released in conjunction with June 2004 hearings on charity oversight and reform: Keeping bad things from happening to good charities*. Washington, DC: Author.

Vinter, R. D., & Kish, R. K. (1984). *Budgeting for not-for-profit organizations*. New York: The Free Press.

Wolf, T. (1990). *Managing a nonprofit organization*. New York: Fireside.

Yoo, J., Brooks, D., & Patti, R. J. (2007). Organizational constructs as predictors of service effectiveness in child welfare interventions. *Child Welfare, 8*(1), 53–78.

Zietlow, J., Hankin, J. A., & Seidner, A. (2007). *Financial management for nonprofit organizations: Policies and procedures*. Hoboken, NJ: John Wiley & Sons.

PART 5

Leadership in the Agency Environment

Managers, especially those at upper levels, give a good deal of time and personal resources to influencing relationships between their agencies and external groups and constituencies. This aspect of managerial leadership, which has historically received little attention, is now among the most important functions performed by administrators in an environment characterized by turbulence, scarcity, and competition.

In Chapter 20, Professor Hillel Schmid provides a broad-ranging discussion of theoretical perspectives on how human services agencies acquire the legitimacy and resources from their environments needed for growth and survival. The author analyzes this fundamental issue through the prisms of adaptation, ecological, and institutional theories. The chapter also deals with strategies managers use to adapt to changing environments, as well as administrative and structural implications these strategies may have for the agency.

In Chapter 21, Catherine Alter focuses on a key aspect of how agencies relate to their environments: building collaborative relations. The forces that press agencies to engage in collaborative networks; the array of collaborative arrangements available; and the various purposes, advantages, and limitations of each are addressed. Professor Alter also addresses the stages in the development of collaborative and management skills used to negotiate this process.

As we have seen in the preceding chapter and in previous discussions of strategic planning and fundraising, human services agencies that fail to devote resources to understanding and shaping their environments are likely to fare badly. In Chapter 22, a new entry in this revised edition, Jennifer Mosely addresses a little-examined aspect of management practice: advocacy and lobbying. After discussing the incentives for agencies to become involved in advocacy and the constraints associated with this activity, the chapter explores what organizational and environmental factors managers should consider when developing an advocacy agenda. Professor Mosely concludes by reviewing useful strategies and tactics.

CHAPTER 20

Agency-Environment Relations

Understanding External and Natural Environments

Hillel Schmid

This chapter presents the main theoretical approaches that describe and analyze the relations between organizations and their environments. The first part provides a definition of organizational environment and a typology of environments, followed by a presentation of the main theoretical approaches: organization adaptation theories, ecological theory, and institutional theory. The discussion highlights the unique contribution of each theory toward understanding organization-environment relations, as well as the connections between the theories. In addition, the chapter deals with strategies of adaptation to changing environments and presents the implications for management of human services organizations. The concluding section analyzes the relationships that emerge between characteristics of the environment and strategies, organizational structure, administrative processes, and organizational performance.

Organizational Environments: Definition

Environment has been defined as all external conditions that actually or potentially affect an organization (Hawley, 1968), or as conditions and constraints outside the organization that might affect its functioning. The environment includes individuals, groups, and organizations, as well as state and institutional systems. It encompasses social, economic, cultural, political, religious, technological, military, legal, demographic, geographic, ecological, and physical elements representing ethics, beliefs, and norms existing in the society.

One major approach to describing organization-environment relations emphasizes the difference between the real environment and the cognized or perceived environment. The *real environment* refers to the set of economic, social, political, demographic, and other characteristics that can be evaluated and measured objectively, for example, official indices of inflation, cost of living, unemployment rates, number of people below the poverty line, migration rates, and political changes that are published by government institutions such as the Census Bureau, Bureau of Labor Statistics, Department of Health and Human Services, and other institutions. Interpretations of those indices reflect the *perceived or cognized environment,* which is the product of the individual's perceptions of environmental conditions and is based on individual attributes (Duncan, 1972; Weick, 1979). According to this approach, organizations respond to what they perceive, and unnoticed events do not affect them (Sharma, 2000; Yasai-Ardekani, 1986). Organizations may, however, perceive the same environments differently. "The same environment one organization perceives as unpredictable, complex, and evanescent, another organization might see as static and easily understood" (Starbuck, 1976, p. 1080).

Organizations not only perceive and interpret their environments, they also create and influence them. It is assumed that "if one defines situations as real, their outcomes are real" (Thomas, 1928). Weick (1979) uses the term *enactment* to emphasize the more active role played by individuals and organizational participants in defining the environments they confront. According to Weick (1979), "the concept of an enacted environment is not synonymous with the concept of a perceived environment." Rather, the label *enactment* "is meant to emphasize that managers construct, rearrange, single out, and demolish many objective features of their surroundings" (p. 164). The process of enacting is one in which "the subject partly interacts with and constitutes the object" (p. 165). The organization does more than observe and interpret: It modifies and directly influences the state of their environments through their own actions (Scott, 2003), and "through information and the creation of meaning" (Kreps, 1986, p. 116).

Within the environment, the organization defines its domain. The domain identifies the points at which the organization is dependent on resources from the environment (Thompson, 1967, p. 27) and consists of the claims it makes with respect to products or services provided, the technology employed, population served, and services rendered (Levine & White, 1961). In defining its domain, the organization has to create a unique identity that differentiates it from other organizations. The organization must determine its added value, in addition to developing its distinctive competence and organizational capacity in terms of human, material, and technological relative advantages and competitiveness. To the extent that the organization succeeds in defining its unique identity and distinctiveness, it will be able to change power-dependence relations with its natural environment and ensure a steady flow of resources needed for its survival and operations.

The organization also determines its boundaries through negotiations and bargaining with other organizations and with a variety of stakeholders in its natural environment. In this process, the organization should be attentive to changes in its environment and to the legitimized goals of other organizations and populations. In the case of human, community, and voluntary organizations, the boundaries cannot be so rigid and high that they obstruct mutual influence and accessibility to clients. Clients must be able to voice their opinions and must engage in policy making, as well as in formulating service programs (Boris & Krehely, 2003; Hasenfeld & Schmid, 1989; Shemer & Schmid, 2006).

Given this situation, it has been argued that "the establishment of a domain cannot be an arbitrary, unilateral action. Only if the organization's claims to domain are recognized by those who can provide the necessary support, by the task environment, can a domain be operational" (Thompson, 1967, p. 28). This is the *domain consensus,* which Thompson defines as "a set of expectations both for members of an organization and for others with whom they interact about what the organization will and will not do" (p. 26). In other words, both formal and informal legitimation of the organization's domain are necessary for its existence. Specifically, legitimation means acquiring formal and social support and approval from actors in the surrounding environment, which ensures the organization's resources.

Legitimacy is a resource for new ventures, and is at least as important as other resources such as capital, technology, personnel, customer goodwill, and networks (Zimmerman & Zeitz, 2002). Suchman (1995) defines legitimacy as "a generalized conception or assumption that the actions of an entity are desirable, proper, or appropriate within some socially constructed systems of norms, values, beliefs, and definitions" (p. 574). Three types of legitimacy are most important and relevant to the organization's existence: regulatory, normative, and cognitive (Suchman, 1995). Regulatory legitimacy is derived from regulations, rules, standards, and expectations created by institutions such as the government and from credentialing of associations, professional bodies, and other powerful organizations. Normative legitimacy is derived from the norms and values of society or from a level of the societal environment that is relevant to the new agency. Cognitive legitimacy can be derived from addressing "widely held beliefs and taken-for-granted assumptions that provide a framework for everyday routines, as well as the more specialized, explicit, and codified knowledge and belief systems promulgated by various professional and scientific bodies" (Scott, 1994, p. 81). Zimmerman and Zeitz (2002) argue that legitimacy is crucial in the early years of an agency or a program or for the existence of new ventures even before they begin to generate any product or service. Studies show that it is important for organizations to establish formal work procedures, mainly in the early stages of their life cycle. Established procedures are a source of stabilization, and they have an impact on gaining trust from providers of legitimation and resources (Sine, Mitsuhashi, & Kirsch, 2006). Such structural characteristics are found in large and veteran organizations, and they have an impact on achieving high levels of organizational performance (Aldrich & Reuf, 2006; Ethiraj & Levinthal, 2004).

On the informal level, legitimation is provided by clients, who consume the products and/or services offered by the organization. The greater the extent of legitimacy, the stronger the position of the organization in its natural environment and the greater its ability to make elements in the environment more dependent on its capabilities and capacities.

Typology of Environments: General and Natural Environments

Classic organizational literature distinguishes between general environments and task environments, as well as between milieus and niches. We propose the term "natural environment" as a substitute for the term "task environment," which reflects the environment in which the organization exists and operates (Anderson & Bateman, 2000; Aragón-Correa, 1998). The natural environment is actually a *niche*, consisting of external actors with whom the local organization transacts directly and whom the organization can influence. Whereas *niche* refers to the natural environment, the term *milieu* refers to the general environment (i.e., the external conditions of the organization, which do not necessarily have a direct impact on it). The attempt to differentiate between these types of environments seems to be obsolete and irrelevant, due to the rapid changes that have shrunk the world into a global village. In fact, political, social, economic, technological, and demographic changes often have an impact on local organizations. For example, security issues raised in one part of the world directly affect organizations in different localities and countries. The distinctions between niche and milieu are increasingly blurred in today's reality. Thus, for example, the different elements and constraints in the general and immediate environment have an impact on the organization itself.

National and international economics have an immediate impact on the economic stability of organizations. Decisions related to monetary or fiscal changes have implications for the decisions and behavior of organizations, whereas economic prosperity and recession affect decision making and allocation of resources in those organizations. Under conditions of full employment, excess demand or insufficient demand affects the organization's strategic activity, as well as its ability to raise funds and hire staff.

Social tensions as well as political and economic inequalities between groups in society affect the way organizations organize themselves to provide services. Cultural values, attitudes, and prevailing beliefs have an effect and are reflected in the structure and processes within the organization. The political interests of groups affect the ideology, policies, and espoused goals of the organization as well as allocation of resources for various service programs with different priorities. Moreover, new legislation or revisions to existing legislation affect the existence and survival of organizations (Edelman & Suchman, 1997). Advanced information technology systems affect the management of organizations, including their division of labor, relations with clients, and provision of services, as well as issues of efficiency and effectiveness.

Clearly, the demographic composition of the environment also affects the nature of services provided, as well as the organization's very survival. For example, aging of the population in a given geographic region can lead to closure of kindergartens, schools, and other agencies that serve children and adolescents. Demographic changes such as increased ethnic diversity call for the establishment of organizations, institutions, and programs that provide universal responses on the one hand and particularistic responses on the other, in an attempt to address the differential needs of those population groups.

This is also the case with regard to the development of advanced patterns of management, which address the cultural differences among the diverse population groups (Mor Barak, 2005). Furthermore, religiosity affects the organization's goals and operation; that is, the stronger the religious elements in the environment, the more religious groups there are, and the more the organization needs to gear its service programs to the unique characteristics of those clients. Moreover, in recent years, faith-based organizations

have entered the arena of human and social services, which had been dominated almost exclusively by public and secular social service agencies in the past (Chaves, 2004; Cnaan, 2002). In those environments, organizations are often required to recruit staff with specific personal characteristics who are aware of the needs of the clients and are able to communicate with them effectively and provide appropriate responses.

In particular, organizations maintain working relations with elements in their natural environment and engage in continuous negotiations with those elements to ensure their position in the environment as well as to attain scarce resources. The elements in the organization's natural environment include clients; providers of resources, raw materials, workers, capital, funds, and equipment; competitors for markets and resources; formal and state organizations, as well as institutions that are responsible for legislation and establishment of regulations and bylaws pertaining directly to the organization's goals and activity; and providers of complementary and supplementary services (Aldrich & Reuf, 2006).

Characteristics of the Environment

Environments can be characterized according to various criteria and dimensions. Possible classifications are based on the degree of uncertainty, the extent to which resources are concentrated, the rate and intensity of changes in the environment, as well as the stability and availability of resources. According to this perspective, several types of criteria for classifying environments can be distinguished (Dess & Beard, 1984; Emery & Trist, 1965; Hasenfeld, 1983; Scott, 2003):

- *Placidity and stability versus turbulence and instability:* Determines the dynamics of the environment in terms of changing goals, values, and extent to which the organization has knowledge of environmental characteristics. Placid environments are characterized by political, economic, and social stability with a low level of change. Turbulent environments are characterized by high levels of political, social, economic, and technological change, which make it difficult for the organization to project and plan for the long range.

- *Homogeneity versus heterogeneity:* Homogeneity is defined as the extent to which there is similarity between groups of organizations in terms of the services they provide, their service technologies, and the needs of their target populations. Heterogeneity highlights the differences between organizations.
- *Richness versus paucity:* Determined on the basis of the existence and accessibility of resources required by the organization; also defined as the extent to which the environment can support and sustain a rate of organizational growth (Dess & Beard, 1984).
- *Stability versus instability:* Determined according to the level and rate of changes in the environment.
- *Simple versus complex:* Defined as proliferation and diversity of factors and issues in the environment (Tan & Litschert, 1994). The greater the number of factors in the external environment and the greater the differences among those factors, the more complex the environment.
- *Organized versus unorganized:* Determined according to the presence of mobilized individuals, groups, coalitions, and organizations representing the interests of clients, consumers, and residents.
- *Certainty versus uncertainty:* Determined by the extent of information available to the organization in its relations with the environment. This criterion reflects the gap between potential information existing in the environment and information controlled by the organization. The larger the gap, the greater the uncertainty in organization-environment relations. Under those conditions, it is difficult for the organization to develop an appropriate strategy for adapting to the external environment.

To adapt to its environment, the organization must learn and recognize the inherent opportunities and threats, as well as the risks and opportunities, in the environment. The more turbulent, dynamic, uncertain, and unpredictable the environment is, the more difficult it will be for the organization to learn about its characteristic behavior and develop mechanisms of adaptation. At the same time, turbulent, rapidly changing environments stimulate learning and enhance the organization's ability to provide innovative and creative solutions to acute needs and dilemmas that arise. In contrast, stable, placid, and certain environments enable the organization to sustain its routine and maintain its mechanisms of adaptation. In those contexts, administrative responses are usually routine, and employees' development and creativity are limited, to some extent (Schmid, 1992). Notwithstanding these distinctions, it should be mentioned that almost all human services organizations operate in dynamic, uncertain, and constantly changing environments. The changes and uncertainty have been generated by ideological and political struggles regarding the role of welfare in general and social services in particular. In that process, legitimation for social services has declined, and human services organizations have faced continuous budget cuts. These conditions of uncertainty and instability impede the functioning of human services organizations and make it difficult for them to achieve their espoused goals.

Understanding Relations Between the Organization and Its Environment: Theoretical Approaches

This section will discuss the main theoretical approaches to understanding the relations between the organization and its environment: (a) organization adaptation theories; (b) ecological theory; (c) institutional theory.

Organization Adaptation Theories

These theories are based on the concept of *adaptation,* which is defined as the process of evolutionary change by which the organization provides a better and better solution to the problem, and the end result is the state of being adapted (Lewontin, 1978). A state of adaptation, in a biological sense, describes a state of survival for an organism. Analogously, a state of adaptation for an organization is one in which it can survive in the conditions of its environment (Chakravarthy, 1982). It involves sensing and understanding both internal and external environments, as well as taking action to achieve a fit between the two (Weick, 1995).

In this process, the organization may be forced to alter part of its identity or distinctive characteristics because adaptation to the complexities of the environment also demands changes in goals, objectives, service technologies, and operating procedures. Therefore, in the adaptation process, the organization should develop what Motamedi (1977) called "copability," that is, *coping* and *ability,* which means the internal ability of an organization to maintain its identity and overcome the problem of change. The essence of copability is the ability of a system to maintain its integrity and distinct characteristics, or "to hold one's own" (Motamedi, 1977). In order to ensure organizational effectiveness, it is necessary to combine adaptability and copability, which preserves the organization's identity as well as its ability to adapt to changes in the environment.

Adaptation can also be described as a learning process. Organizations learn their environment, and the better they do this, the more effectively they can adapt and ensure their survival (Hedberg, 1981). As in every learning process, the stimulus-response paradigm is applied. Accordingly, organizations react to stimuli from their external environment and respond after filtering, coding, and processing the information that flows into them. By receiving and decoding stimuli, the organization learns the strengths and weaknesses of other organizations in the environment, which are actual or potential competitors or partners. The organization not only responds to stimuli, but also scans its environment in order to identify needs for which it has developed solutions. By scanning and gathering information, the organization discovers new environmental spaces for expansion of its domain. The process of learning is reciprocal, and the organization internalizes it by developing new and creative mechanisms of adaptation to changing and emerging needs. In that context, the organization also develops structures and administrative processes that require permanent creativity, in an attempt to respond to the challenges and opportunities generated by the environment (Senge, 1990; Senge, Kliener, Roberts, Ross, Roth, & Smith, 1999).

The main theoretical approaches attesting to this active process of adaptation between the organization and its environment are contingency theory, political economy theory, and resource dependence theory.

Contingency theory provides an important paradigm for analyzing organizational structure. According to this theory, there is no single organizational structure that is effective for all organizations (Donaldson, 1996). Rather, organizational structures have to be matched with the contextual demands of contingency factors, such as size, environment, and technology (Ethiraj & Levinthal, 2004). According to this theory, organizations that fit the contextual features of their environment are more likely to have higher performance levels as well as better chances of survival than those that do not (Lawrence & Lorsch, 1967; Thompson, 1967).

Burns and Stalker (1961) were among the first scholars to develop this approach. In a study of the electronics industry in Britain, they distinguished between mechanistic and organic structures. A mechanistic structure is one characterized by a clear hierarchy and division of tasks, formal systems of communication and coordination, and formal reporting procedures. This organizational structure develops primarily in organizations operating in stable, certain environments characterized by gradual change and easy access to information. In contrast, organic structures are characterized by a low level of formality, lack of a clear hierarchy, and informal flow of communication, which is not channeled through the lines of hierarchy and command. This kind of structure fits organizations operating in rapidly changing environments with high uncertainty and instability. Recently, however, Sine et al. (2006) revealed that new ventures in the emergent Internet sector and in other emergent economic sectors, which operate in turbulent environments, have higher founding team formalization, specialization, and administrative intensity that enable them to outperform organizations with more organic structures. These findings are in total contradiction to Burns and Stalker's (1961) approach, which argues that a simple organic structure is the most appropriate one to achieve the organization's goals and reach a high level of performance under conditions of turbulence.

During the same period, another British researcher examined the relationships between organizational structure and contingency factors in manufacturing organizations (Woodward, 1965). Those studies, however, revealed no relationship between the structure and size of these organizations and argued that operations technology is the key correlate of organizational structure. Specifically, Woodward found that organizations with simple, manual production technology tend to be informal and organic, whereas those with complex technology based on mass production (e.g., automobile assembly plants) tend to be formal and mechanistic. Woodward's conclusions also indicate that organizations with a growing volume of complex work tend to integrate organic elements such as task groups, which deviate from the organizations' strictly mechanistic overall structure. Integration of these of these organic elements also contributes to higher performance.

In a similar vein, Lawrence and Lorsch (1967) proposed a theory based on their study of three types of industries in the United States: containers, processed foods, and plastics. According to Lawrence and Lorsch, the level and rate of changes in the external environment affect the extent of differentiation and integration in the organization itself. In environments characterized by rapid change and heterogeneous needs and demands, organizations are required to develop a high level of differentiation, which includes, for example, specialized organizational units that focus on development of knowledge, ideas, and research. These units scan and map the environment in an attempt to reduce uncertainty in the organization. Under these circumstances, the organization also requires a higher level of integration in order to tighten the connection between organizational units and enhance effectiveness. The balance between differentiation and integration is the only way to ensure that the organization will be able to adapt itself to contingency factors originating in the external environment.

In line with this approach, Thompson (1967) argued that organizations structure themselves in response to the differential needs of the environment. Similarly, Perrow (1986) argued that knowledge technology is a contingency of organizational structure. According to this perspective, the clearer and more specific the interpretations of the knowledge, and the fewer exceptions to the rules, the greater the tendency of the organization to adopt a hierarchical, centralized structure.

Critics of this approach have questioned the relevance of contingency theory to analysis of interrelations between characteristics of the external environment and organizational structures and strategies (Mintzberg, 1979; Pennings, 1992). Moreover, it has been argued that the contingency approach focuses on a few environmental variables and often ignores essential intervening variables, particularly those relating to strategic choice (Child, 1972; Pfeffer & Salancik, 1978). According to this argument, there is a mutual relationship between organizations and their environment. Specifically, not only does the environment influence organizations and their structure, but organizations influence their environment and try to change it. This is especially true of large organizations, which have a strong influence on the development of their environments and on creating new areas of activity. Critics of the contingency approach also emphasize the strong bias toward cross-sectional analysis rather than longitudinal studies of organizations, as well as the proclivity to draw sample-wide conclusions about relationships among variables, even when the sample includes diverse types of organizations (Miller, 1979). This approach also assumes that organizational adaptation is characterized by symmetry ("if this, then that"), particularly with respect to adapting structures and administrative processes to changing conditions. However, in recent years, researchers have criticized this approach (Moon et al., 2004). In their view, organizations are characterized by asymmetric adaptability, and they do not develop adaptive structures in response to every single change in the environment. For example, the change required in the transition from a functional organizational structure to a divisional structure is relatively uncomplicated and does not arouse strong resistance. However, the transition from a divisional to a functional structure involves changes that can be implemented only when the existing environmental conditions and constraints allow for it. In addition, it is argued that contingency theorists have characterized the external environment in objective terms, totally disregarding subjective perceptions of the environment that might influence organizational activities. However, notwithstanding the critique of the contingency approach, the essential implication of this approach is that a fundamental responsibility of the executive is to respond to the changing environment by continuously adapting to the contingencies that the organization confronts.

Political Economy Theory. The second approach to understanding how organizations adapt to their environments, political economy theory (Wamseley & Zald, 1976; Zald, 1970), recognizes that in order to survive and produce services, the organization must garner two fundamental types of resources: legitimacy and power (i.e., political) and production resources (i.e., economic). The underlying premise of this approach is the organization's dependence on resources controlled by agents and interest groups in the external environment. The greater the organization's dependence on these resources, the stronger the influence of external interest groups on processes within the organization.

A further derivative of this approach is resource dependence theory, which provides a general conceptual framework that applies ideas from social exchange theory (Blau, 1964; Emerson, 1962). This theory claims that "power is a property of the social relations; it is not an attribute of the actor" (Emerson, 1962, p. 32) and that the power of actor A over actor B is the inverse of B's dependence on A. This framework explains interorganizational dependencies created by the need of all organizations to acquire scarce resources. Based on that premise, resource dependence theory (Aldrich & Pfeffer, 1976; Aldrich & Reuf, 2006; Pfeffer & Salancik, 2003) proposes that organizations often become dependent on their environments for resources that are critical for their survival. Dependence generates uncertainty. According to Pfeffer and Salancik (1978), "the underlying premise of the external perspective on organizations is that organizational activities and outcomes are accounted for by the context in which the organization is embedded" (p. 39). The extent of an organization's dependence on the external environment is affected by the importance of a particular resource to the organization and by the extent to which those who control that resource have a monopoly on it and discretion over its allocation (Frooman, 1999; Pfeffer & Salancik, 2003). Thus, "organizations will (and should) respond more to the demands of those organizations or groups in the environment that control critical resources" (Pfeffer, 1982, p. 193). Moreover, exchange of resources with the environment enables the organization to acquire the various resources it needs to survive. In this process, organizational directors must manage their environment at least as much as, or perhaps more than, they manage their organizations, in order to ensure an adequate resource supply (Aldrich & Pfeffer, 1976; Aldrich & Reuf, 2006). The organization must change its power-dependence relations with the environment and direct activities toward (a) reducing dependence on the external environment as much as possible by controlling necessary resources, and (b) increasing dependence of agents in the environment on the distinctive services and/or products of the organization. By adopting this approach, the organization can attain more discretion and achieve a relative advantage in acquiring necessary resources (Mizruchi & Galaskiewicz, 1993). In this process, the organization develops strategies based on cooperation to reduce its dependence on the environment, as well as strategies of competition and disruption (see "Strategies of Adaptation to Changing Environments" below and Chapter 21).

Notwithstanding the contribution of resource dependence theory to understanding power-dependence relations between organizations and their environments, it does not sufficiently stress environmental constraints on strategic choice (Child, 1972; Galaskiewicz, 1985). For example, organizations and directors do not accept the environment as a constraint that unilaterally influences their domain, goals, and internal behavior. Furthermore, although this approach recognizes the impact of environmental constraints such as formal restrictions on organizational behavior (Edelman & Suchman, 1997), it tends to ignore other forms of institutional restriction such as the material environment (Reitan, 1998, p. 296).

Despite the ambiguities in this theory, researchers in the field have continued to refer to it for nearly 30 years. Until 2002, over 2,321 citations of Pfeffer and Salancik's (1978) book were recorded in the professional literature. However, Casciaro and Piskorski (2005) argue that resource dependence theory does not sufficiently address concepts such as power imbalance and mutual dependence, which reflect the asymmetry in relations between organizations on the one hand and the environment that controls resources on the other. Notably, an imbalance in power relations influences the behavior of organizations. In addition, Pfeffer and Salancik (2003) note that "there is a limited amount of empirical work explicitly extending and testing this theory and its central tenets" (p. xvi). Regarding the relevance of this theory to human services organizations, the main drawback is that it ignores other important factors that may affect organization-environment interaction, such as

ideologies, values, norms, ethics, and the commitments that they evoke.

Notwithstanding the limitation of these theoretical perspectives, adaptation theory in general has important implications for management of human services agencies by focusing on the development of unique services and the added value of special programs that distinguish the organization from its competitors. Executives should make efforts to develop the organization's distinctive competence and create the structural, physical, technological, and human infrastructure that will enable the organization to survive in a competitive environment and change power-dependence relations. Organizations that effectively exploit their distinctiveness can substantially reduce their dependence on agencies in the environment and create dependence on their products and services.

Ecological Theories

Ecological theories derive from the Darwinian and genetic schools, which argue that genetic variations can be traced to processes of mutation and natural selection, expressed as "survival of the fittest." This approach has been adopted in studies of organization-environment relations and is known as the *population ecology theory* (Aldrich & Reuf, 2006; Baum, 1996; Baum & Amburgey, 2005; Baum & Singh, 1994a; Hannan & Freeman, 1977, 1984). Unlike the adaptation theories, which focused on individual organizations, the basic unit of analysis here is a population of organizations, that is, all organizations that share the following characteristics: (a) common dependence on resources controlled by the environment, (b) similar organizational structure, (c) organizational features that remain relatively stable over time (Hannan & Freeman, 1977), and (d) a similar extent of homogeneity in terms of vulnerability to external constraints (Hannan & Carroll, 1992) that expose the organization to dramatic changes that endanger its survival.

The key concept of this theory is the existence of a niche. Based on Hutchinson's (1957) biological definition, Hannan and Freeman (1977) state that a *niche* is an "an area in constraint space (the space whose dimensions are levels of resources, etc.) in which the (species) population out competes all other local (species) populations" (p. 947). The *ecological niche,* therefore, is resource space that determines the carrying capacity that limits the number of organizations able to operate in the niche (Baum, 1996; Baum & Singh, 1994b). Two dimensions may characterize niches: breadth and depth. *Breadth* indicates the extent to which organizations attract resources from many actors in a niche, while *depth* indicates the extent to which focal organizations are dependent on the other organizations. The niche can also change its size and shape. For example, the Israeli Long-Term Care Insurance Law (1988) created a new ecological niche for provision of government-financed home care services to frail elderly persons. During the years immediately following implementation of the law, most of the mandated home care services (70%) were provided by voluntary nonprofit organizations (VNPOs). Today, however, almost 20 years after the law took effect, the majority of home care service providers (70%) are private for-profit organizations, whereas the share of VNPOs has been reduced to only 30%.

In organizations, as in other forms of life, the life cycle is characterized by stages of variation, selection, and retention. The variation stage relates to different types of organizational life, to different organizational patterns, and to the changes that occur in organizations. In the selection stage, some types of organizational life and some organizations are selected to live, whereas others cease to exist. Selection itself results from the behavior of the markets where the organizations operate, as well as from pressure generated by competition with other organizations for scarce resources. Selection is also affected by internal organizational processes such as mismanagement, which can weaken the organization and threaten its survival. Organizations that survive within the ecological niche are those that possess the unique characteristics required by the environment. The

environment selects the most appropriate organizations, whereas the individual organizations have relatively little influence (Aldrich, 1979). Finally, the retention stage refers to preservation of the organizations that have been chosen for survival. This stage also involves a process of institutionalization, in which organizations stabilize their activity and structure based on formal and institutional dynamics (Aldrich & Reuf, 2006).

Critics of this approach have argued that it views organizations as passively accepting environmental constraints. In their view, the environment can threaten the survival of an organization only to a partial and limited extent. It can cause part of the organization to stop functioning, but it does not necessarily lead to the demise of the entire organization (Henderson & Stern, 2004). Thus, for example, directors of social services can eliminate certain programs that are unsuccessful even before the environment causes them to discontinue. They can also transfer resources from programs that are not in demand to those that are needed.

In addition, critics of the ecological approach argue that biological development models are inappropriate for social organizations (Young, 1988), mainly on the grounds that they lack a clear concept of the environment. According to Perrow (1986), for example, the ecological model tends to be mystic, and disregards power relations, conflicts, disturbances, and power struggles among interest groups in the organization. The theory recognizes the considerable power of the environment and its deterministic processes, but fails to acknowledge the ability of organizations to alter their environments.

Moreover, social and human services organizations do not disappear easily. Instead, they change their strategies or target populations. In fact, this is the most common way that organizations can ensure their survival without being completely dissolved. For example, in the process of deinstitutionalization, mental health institutions have sent clients out into the community and received new clients, and the same is true of other human services agencies. This reflects a new cycle of dissolution, life, and renewal in organizations. Thus, as long as there is a social interest or human need that requires a response, social service organizations tend to survive.

At the same time, it is clear that the risk of dissolution or death in these organizations can be traced to two causes: ecological and institutional. These contexts change rapidly, while organizations find it difficult to adapt at the same pace. The process of adaptation entails modifications in the organization's ideology, strategies, structure, internal processes, and in its management of human resources. All of this requires a major organizational effort as well as investment of time and resources that are not always at the organization's disposal. Failure to adapt rapidly and reorganize systems creates a gap that threatens the organization's survival. The adaptation process is complex, and organizations that have difficulty identifying what and how to change are likely to face dissolution because they are unable to keep up with the pace of rapidly changing environments.

In addition, attempts to apply this model to selection of organizations and organization-environment relations have not provided clear explanations of the natural selection process. Nor do they explain why some organizations survive while others dissolve. Moreover, this approach assumes that organizations have no influence on shaping the environment and behave according to the power of the "invisible hand" (i.e., their behavior is reactive and passive). In reality, however, organizations actively scan, learn, and influence their environment (Child, 1972). Similarly, decisions made by organizational directors are not arbitrary, but derive from planned activities aimed at attaining the goals of the organization and at mobilizing support from the task environment (Pennings, 1981).

Institutional Theory

Institutional theory asserts that organizations are driven to incorporate the practices and procedures defined by prevailing rationalized and institutionalized concepts of organizational operations. For example, to ensure a steady flow of resources, human services organizations often adopt the espoused ideologies and goals of the government, which are not always attainable. These ideologies and goals can be expressed as "closing social gaps and reducing inequality between haves and have nots," "the need to redistribute power and transfer it to peripheral units," "integration of populations," and "changing attitudes toward minorities." Organizations that succeed in achieving those goals increase their legitimacy and, consequently, their prospects for survival, irrespective of the immediate efficacy of the required practices and procedures.

Institutional theorists (Dacin, Goodstein, & Scott, 2002; DiMaggio & Powell, 1983; Meyer & Rowan, 1977, 1983; Powell & DiMaggio, 1991; Scott, 1994, 2004; Tolbert & Zucker, 1996; Zucker, 1987, 1988, 1991) suggest that changes in the formal structure of organizations are often introduced to make organizations more aligned with the changing institutional environment of "rationalized myths" (Meyer & Rowan, 1977, p. 346).

Organizations that conform to the requirements and expectations of the institutional environment gain the legitimacy and resources needed to survive and grow, even if they do not intend to realize rationalized myths (Meyer & Rowan, 1983). This is also true of firms in the business sector that earn environmental legitimacy when their performance conforms to stakeholders' expectations. Bansal and Clelland (2004) found that firms can attenuate the effect of low legitimacy by expressing commitment to the natural environment. This process results in institutional isomorphism (either coercive, mimetic, or normative), which means developing identical processes, increasing similarity, and copying organizational forms (D'Aunno, Sutton, & Price, 1991). This, in turn, generates increased bureaucratization, formalism, and standardization in the organizations themselves (Meyer, Scott, Strang, & Creighton, 1988).

In the case of human services organizations, legitimacy and social support are derived less from the distinctive products (services) they offer than from adopting a system of social values accepted in the society and community. These organizations garner support for their espoused goals by accepting prevailing institutional ideologies (Perrow, 1986; Zald, 1970). In light of this situation, executives should realize that although conformist behavior may ensure the survival of the organization, it might also restrict the organization's ability to respond to diverse and changing needs of clients. In addition, they should be aware of the potential for loss of organizational identity, an erosion of agency ideology and values, and a decline in the organization's capacity for creativity and innovation (Deakin, 1996; Schmid, 2003; Schmid & Hasenfeld, 2008).

Critics of this approach argue that it is deterministic and that institutional agencies such as the government largely determine the destiny of organizations. This is especially true of human services organizations, which are highly dependent on resources controlled by the external environment. In this connection, Tolbert and Zucker (1996) proposed that the organizations themselves are not passive in their conformance to institutional rules. Rather, they are actively involved in shaping the process of institutionalization. In their encounters with governmental agencies, executives not only have to accept their regulations and restrictions, but they should also try to change the attitudes of government officials regarding the essential role of social services in societies where the gaps between the haves and have nots are constantly widening. In addition, executives cannot afford to refrain from involvement in processes of legislation that affect the activities of the organization as well as its prospects for development and survival. It is also argued that the institutional approach ignores internal organizational elements that have the ability to make choices and decisions. These elements influence the destiny of the organization and constantly aspire to achieve the organization's goals. Moreover, it is argued that this theory ignores changes and conflicts in the institutional environment (Reitan, 1998) and that it tends to be mystical, introverted, and distrustful.

Comparison of the Resource Dependence, Ecological, and Institutional Theories

We will begin by comparing the resource dependence and population ecology theories and highlighting the differences between them (Scott, 2003; see Table 20.1). Afterwards, we will deal with the relationship between those two theories and institutional theory.

First, differences were found in the levels and units of analysis. Population ecology theory focuses primarily on populations of organizations rather than on specific organizations (Baum & Oliver, 1992).

Second, the theories differ in terms of their time perspectives. Population ecology theory is based on a long-range perspective, whereas resource dependence theory is short range. Specifically, the population ecology theory focuses on the organizational life cycle, which requires comprehensive longitudinal analysis. In contrast, examination of the adaptation of individual organizations is often incremental and continues for short, specified periods.

Third, there are several differences between the two approaches with regard to conceptualization of the environment, even though they also share some perspectives in common. Both theories emphasize the critical importance of environmental characteristics in terms of abundance and scarcity of resources, and both emphasize the dimensions of certainty and uncertainty. However, ecological theories argue that when exogenous environments change over time, it is not as a result of actions taken by organizations, whereas resource dependence theory argues that environmental change is partly a function of the actions taken by the organization to manage problems of interdependence (Pfeffer, 1982).

Fourth, population ecology theory deals with processes of organizational birth and death, which are not addressed at all by resource dependence theory.

Fifth, there are differences regarding the extent of rationalism underlying each of the approaches. The orientation of the population

Table 20.1 Resource Dependence and Population Ecology Theories: A Comparative Analysis

Focus of Interest	Population Ecology	Resource Dependence
Level and unit of analysis	Populations of organizations	Individual organizations
Time perspective	Long range	Short range, incremental
Conceptualizing the environment	Focus on exogenous environments	Focus on exogenous environments as well as changes within the organization
Organizational life cycle	Focus on organizational birth and death	Ignores organizational birth and death
Rationale of approach	Less normative, emphasis on randomness	More normative, emphasis on deliberate action
The organization	Not concerned with events in the organization itself	Concerned with the organization, its decisions and actions
Power and influence of environments	Environments are powerful and determine the organization's survival	Organizations determine their own survival through effective adaptation
Organization's strategic behavior	Reactive	Proactive

ecology approach is less normative than that of the resource dependence theory and places more emphasis on randomness as opposed to deliberate action.

Sixth, population ecology theory is less concerned with events and processes within the organization than it is with long-term trends and changes in the population of organizations.

Seventh, according to population ecology theory, the organizational environment plays an extremely powerful role and determines whether or not the organization will survive. In contrast, resource dependence theory argues that the organization determines its own destiny in the ongoing struggle with its environment and with other organizations in that environment. The ability of organizations to survive can be attributed to continuous improvements and appropriate strategic choices, which enable effective adaptation and ensure the organization's survival.

Eighth, according to the population ecology approach, the organization is characterized by passive behavior (i.e., it reacts to events in the external environment that force it to adopt a structure that fits the environmental constraints). However, according to resource dependence theory, organizations play an active role in their relationship with the external environment and constantly attempt to change their dependency relations with the agents that control resources and power. In this context, the organization seeks new domains of activity while enhancing its independence and making other agents dependent on it.

Ecological theories have major implications for management of social service agencies. Notwithstanding the considerable power of the environment, executives in human services organizations need to be aware of trends and changes in their environments. Prior awareness and comprehensive understanding of existing and potential events can help executives create responses aimed at preventing shocks that may jeopardize the organization's survival. Thus, for example, creating organizational slack with appropriate financial reserves and human resources (staff vacancies) may mitigate the impact of external factors such as budget cutbacks. In this way, the organization has room to maneuver and can continue to exist under conditions of rapid change.

The relationships between those theories and institutional theory are also noteworthy. It has been argued, for example, that the relationship between ecological and institutional theories is complementary and that they should be synthesized into a single explanatory framework (Baum, 1996; Hannan & Carrol, 1992; Hannan & Freeman, 1989; Zucker, 1989). Others conceive of institutional theory as contextual to ecological theory and argue that the relationship between them is not only complementary but also hierarchical (Tucker, Baum, & Singh, 1992).

The attempt to integrate these theories indicates that the institutional elements in the organization's ecological niche have a considerable impact on its continued existence. Thus, for example, it is argued that the government can enact legislation and amendments that influence organizational behavior and determine whether or not organizations survive (Barnett & Carroll, 1993; Baum, 1996; Baum & Oliver, 1992; Schmid & Hasenfeld, 1993; Singh, Tucker, & Meinhard, 1991).

Integration of resource dependence and institutional theories reveals another perspective, particularly with respect to human services organizations (Scott, 1994; Sherer & Lee, 2002; Sutton, Dobbin, Meyer, & Scott, 1994). These organizations lack their own resources and are dependent on the external environment to provide for their needs. Thus, they tend to accept the norms, values, and social and national myths as a condition for attaining legitimation. By adopting behavior that conforms with the standards of government agencies, these organizations ensure a steady flow of resources.

Strategies of Adaptation to Changing Environments

In this section, we address the various strategies employed by human services agencies to manage the environments in which they operate.

Competition Versus Cooperation. To reduce dependence on external resources controlled by agents in the environment, the organization adopts several strategies, some of which are competitive and some of which are cooperative (Alexander, 2003; Gidron & Hasenfeld, 1994; Oster, 1995; Schmid, 1995; Yankey, 1991; York & Zychlinski, 1996).

Competition is a pattern of rivalry between two or more organizations that compete for scarce resources, for their share of the environment, for influence, and for support from clients. When resources are scarce, competition is often inevitable to ensure the survival of organizations (Najam, 2000). Thus, for example, competition between the nonprofit and for-profit organizations has intensified following the entry of for-profit organizations into the arena of social services, which were previously dominated by nonprofits.

Bargaining is a type of negotiation that leads to agreements for the exchange of products or resources between two or more organizations. In some cases, organizations negotiate for domains of activity and strive to defend the territory in which they operate. In this process, organizations are subject to oversight and control by other agencies. Thus, they cannot operate arbitrarily or unilaterally to further their own interests without considering the other parties and reaching an agreement or compromise.

Co-optation is a strategy of bringing in opponents and absorbing them into the organization system, as well as into its leadership and governance. In this way, the organization tries to diminish existing and potential threats and pressures. It can be argued that governments co-opt advocacy and civil society organizations by supporting and financing their programs, thus preventing them from engaging in political activities and from raising their voices against government policies (Child & Grønbjerg, 2008).

Coalition is a pattern of cooperation between two or more organizations seeking to achieve a common goal. Coalitions are commonly formed among nonprofit human services organizations, which struggle to attain the resources they need to finance their activities. Recognition of the relative advantage of each partner in the coalition enables them to attain a higher level of partnership and organizational synergy in terms of acquiring resources as well as in terms of achieving their espoused goals (Frooman, 1999). Nonetheless, cooperation through coalitions has some drawbacks. When coalitions are formed, organizations expose their strategies and modes of operation, and relatively autonomous decision-making processes are inhibited, which include setting priorities and allocating resources for different programs. Mergers and joint ventures are forms of cooperation. A merger refers to a situation in which two or more independent organizations become a single collective actor (Pfeffer, 1972), and a joint venture refers to collaboration of two or more organizations that creates a new organization to pursue a common purpose (Pfeffer & Novak, 1976).

Another related strategy is *exerting authority and power.* For example, in certain situations, organizations with power and control over resources dictate the conditions and behavior they desire from the other party. This strategy is authoritative in the sense that the party dictating the conditions uses its power to determine the other party's activities, without necessarily providing encouragement or rewards. The ability to utilize this strategy is measured by the extent to which the party dictating the conditions is able to exercise control and impose the conditions on the other party, if necessary. Government agencies that control resources and have the power to make decisions about various programs often use this strategy vis-à-vis welfare agencies contracted by the government to provide services (Schmid, 2003). A government that finances the services imposes other policies and standards on the provider-contractors, in addition to imposing service programs and technologies. In certain cases, the financing agent even intervenes in internal organizational processes, to impose professional criteria to be met by employees, the number of job positions, and modes of supervision and control within the organization itself. Use of coercive power can also be accompanied by sanctions against organizations that fail to conform to the policies, programs, and standards set by the funding sources.

Another strategy is *disruption,* in which one party breaks rules and violates codes of fairness, thus preventing the other party from attaining its goals. For example, when two organizations depend on one source of funding, they can use aggressive tactics against one another, including campaigns that portray the competitor's activities in a negative light and that highlight the potential harm that can be caused to clients as a result of those activities. Such campaigns also include personal accusations against the directors of the competing organization, casting doubt on their integrity, their ethical and professional standards, and their commitment to clients. In this way, one party threatens the other and prevents it in various ways from attaining the legitimacy and resources it needs for its activities. Strategies of disruption are chosen by organizations under certain conditions:

1. The organization strives at all costs to enter the arena of service provision, and the other organizations prevent it from doing so.

2. The organization is powerless vis-à-vis the elements operating in the environment, which ignore its demands and needs.

3. The organization has little to lose in the struggle with its competitors, and uses any means at its disposal to prevail.

4. An ideological dispute and conflict of interest exists between the organization and competitive agencies that struggle for scarce resources. Organizations that adopt

this strategy must be aware of the potential for counterattacks from other agencies that may threaten the organizations' existence or withhold resources.

Generalism Versus Specialism. The strategy of *generalism* encompasses a wide array of activities aimed at incorporating a diverse range of relations with environmental elements for the optimal utilization of existing and potential resources. Organizations adopting this strategy offer a variety of products, services, and programs aimed at different market segments. Miller and Shamsie (1999) found that the greater the uncertainty in the environment, the greater the firm's tendency to produce a variety of products or services, which in turn leads to greater innovation. In uncertain environments, the most innovative firms were the ones with the best industry performance because they achieved differentiation and a reduction of uncertainty.

Specialism, in contrast, entails concentrating activities within a relatively narrow range of the environmental domain, as well as developing a distinctive competence that confers a relative advantage regarding products and/or services exported by the organization to its environment. Especially in placid, certain, and stable environments, organizations that adopt the strategy of specialism have a relative advantage in comparison to those that disperse their resources and efforts among a variety of products and services in an attempt to attain a high level of performance.

Complementary to the issue of generalism versus specialism are the "first movers" (R) versus the "slow movers" (K) strategies. According to Brittain and Freeman's (1980) definition, "pure R strategists are organizations that move quickly to exploit resources as they first become available . . . they trade on speed of expansion" (p. 311). Operationally, the R strategy is associated with being the first to market, so as to optimize one's chances for extensive resource exploitation. Organizations that adopt that strategy will be first to consider the suitability of their structures, technologies, and human resources when they decide to enter a certain market in

which they see a potential for growth. In that way, they can be more innovative and attain a competitive advantage over others because they have learned the market faster than their competitors. Studies also reveal that organizations adopting this strategy do not conform to their institutional environment and do not operate according to the policies and regulations of the government. Their proactivity and initiative has been found to contribute to improved performance (Aragón-Correa & Sharma, 2003). Community service organizations, for example, provide a wide array of programs for all age groups. They are in constant competition with other social service organizations and organize quickly when a governmental or other funding agency allocates resources to promote social and educational projects. In that way, they attain stronger control in their task environments, and they become the leaders in the field by establishing new programs to deal with emerging problems before their competitors have organized themselves to do so.

K-strategists, in contrast, seek to gain a competitive advantage through efficiency of operations. In essence, they trade off expansion opportunities for more certain control of resources in established domains. Organizations that adopt this strategy learn their environment more gradually and cautiously. They prefer to lay the organizational, human, and professional groundwork before entering a given market that has the potential to expand. They join the niche and develop specific services at a later stage in their life cycle, when they see that the conditions are ripe for them to enter a new or growing market. These organizations also learn from the successes and failures of others that entered the market earlier. This information is essential for organizations that adopt the K strategy, because it enhances their perception of the need to operate efficiently, systematically, and gradually rather than "jumping" quickly at every opportunity to mobilize resources.

The activities of organizations are often determined by a combination of the two pairs of strategies: specialism and generalism, and R and K processes (Romanelli, 1987). In effect, there are four possible paths of adaptation. Whereas R-specialists exploit available resources rapidly within a relatively narrow domain, R-generalists exploit resources rapidly within a broad range of domains. Similarly, K-specialists emphasize efficiency of operations within a narrow domain, while K-generalists emphasize efficiency in a broad range of domains. Research has revealed that focusing organizational efforts in one direction (i.e., specialism) provides the advantage of gaining a lead and concentrating expertise in a confined market segment. Moreover, this strategic approach allows for more efficient utilization of limited resources and enhances the organization's ability to respond quickly to the changing needs of clients. Thus, it creates environmental dependence on the organization in its area of specialization as well as a competitive advantage that arises from the development of valuable organizational capabilities, such as continuous innovation, organizational learning, and stakeholder integration (Romanelli, 1987; Sharma & Vredenburg, 1998). Generalism requires complex management of diverse organizational units, whereas concentration on a single product or service is considered risky, in the sense of "putting all of their eggs into one basket." Generalism enables the organization to spread risks among several programs or products, whereas specialization makes the organization more vulnerable to technological, economic, demographic, and other changes. In addition, there is a danger of total extinction as substitute or improved products or services are introduced by other organizations operating in the domain. For example, human services organizations that offer a wide array of services do not endanger their survival in changing environments. In contrast, organizations that specialize in a specific type of services (e.g., home care for elderly people) are endangered when new agencies begin to offer the same services in addition to other supplementary and complementary services. The resources available to the specialist organizations diminish drastically as a result of the competition, and their continued activity is in danger.

Organizations also adopt proactive or reactive strategies (Miles & Snow, 1978; Miller & Friesen, 1983), depending on the changing environments and on the leadership's perception of the environments as conducive and enabling or as inhibiting growth and development. A "proactive strategy" is defined as one that frequently seeks to initiate and offer new service programs and that consistently looks for new, financially attractive markets. Proactive organizations envision future trends and develop mechanisms to prevent the negative influences of the environment (Sharma & Vredenburg, 1998). Conversely, organizations using reactive strategies are those that offer programs and/or products when the external environment produces stimuli and presents new needs to which the organizations can react through their existing programs. Studies have shown that proactive organizations dictate policies and processes in the markets in which they are active. They also control a larger share of the market and tend to perform at a higher level (Aragón-Correa, 1998).

Relationships Between Environment Characteristics, Strategy, Administrative Processes, and Structure of the Organization

The nature of organization-environment relations affects a number of processes occurring within the organization. Organizations in environments that change slowly have little difficulty collecting information. Organizational strategies are long range, while tactics are derived from those strategies and adapted to the moderate changes. However, organizations operating in unstable environments characterized by extensive change encounter difficulty in scanning and gathering information. The process of formulating strategic policies is complex, tactics change frequently, and operational programs are short term.

Organizations operating in relatively stable, certain environments usually adopt strategies of cooperation and specialism, as well as strategies that emphasize becoming established and attaining effectiveness before entering new market sectors and environments. In relatively placid, stable environments, the strategy of specialism is the most suitable for optimal utilization of the resources and opportunities provided by the environment and for the attainment of high levels of performance. By contrast, organizations operating in unstable, dynamic, uncertain, and turbulent environments tend to adopt the generalist strategy, which has the best potential for enabling high levels of performance.

The environment also affects organizational structure. For example, turbulent and uncertain environments affect organizational structure in a different way than do placid, homogeneous, and stable environments (Lawrence & Lorsch, 1967; Yasai-Ardekani, 1989). Organizations operating in turbulent environments, where there is a high demand for their product and a high level of change, tend to develop decentralized structures based on organic mechanisms (e.g., participation, mutual agreement, open communication, lack of hierarchy). They also operate as loosely coupling systems that can respond independently to changing needs and require minimal coordination and collaboration with the different units of the organization (Weick, 1976).

This structure enables the organization to develop mechanisms for sensing, scanning, and absorbing stimuli from the environment without being hampered by formal, bureaucratic systems. The ability of these organizations to survive and the extent to which the units are adapted is determined by the dynamics that prevail in the environment. If the stability of one organizational unit is undermined, the overall agency is not affected. In this organizational setting, costs of coordination and communication are relatively low. Another suitable structure for these environments is the matrix organization, which is based on pooling of efforts among different task forces that operate independently to attain their goals. This structure tends to be an organic, flat, and informal one that allows for flexible adaptation to rapidly changing environmental conditions.

In placid, stable, certain environments characterized by a slow rate of change, the organizational structure tends to be relatively centralized, mechanistic, formal, and functional. Work procedures are standardized, and the mechanisms of coordination and control are relatively simple. In these conditions, organizations can plan for the long range and invest resources in strategic planning. The probability of realizing their goals and programs under these conditions is greater than in uncertain and unstable environments, which concentrate on tactical and relatively short-range planning. In general, it can be argued that the more congruence there is between the organizations' strategies and structures, and where processes are adjusted to environmental exigencies, the higher the organizations' level of performance.

Summary

The chapter presents the main theories and concepts pertaining to organization-environment relations and discusses the contribution of these theories to understanding how organizations adapt to rapid changes in their environment. Ecological theory argues that deterministic processes affect the organization's survival. Advocates of this approach contend that the dynamics characterizing the external environment are more rapid and powerful than the ability of organizations to adapt to changes. In this context, adaptation is construed as adopting an appropriate strategy, adapting structure and procedures, training staff to cope with internal changes caused by the transition from one structural pattern to another, changing service technologies, and establishing new relations with elements that provide legitimacy and resources. The gap between the rapid changes in the external environment and the ability of organizations to adapt their activity at various levels can generate a profound crisis and even threaten their survival.

Adaptation theory, in contrast, argues that the organization learns its environments and reacts to events and also initiates activities and changes aimed at influencing the environment. According to this approach, social service organizations do not accept environmental constraints as given and unchangeable. Rather, organizations and their management have a choice of making their own decisions, setting and even changing priorities, and allocating resources for various activities and influencing elements in the environment, particularly their clientele. The process of learning environments is continuous and dynamic. It is a daily experience that involves scanning and mapping the environment, as well as identifying needs, threats, and opportunities inherent in the environment. Organizations that fail to learn their environments may find themselves in an inferior position vis-à-vis other organizations that can take over their functions, particularly in the era of increasing competition between human services and social welfare organizations.

Finally, institutional environments have a strong influence on the administrative behavior of organizations, their structure, and their performance. The institutional environment, which has been referred to as an "iron cage" (DiMaggio & Powell, 1983), has the power to be a regulator that imposes rules, processes, and procedures on organizations in their direct relationships with governmental agencies, which also finance a large share of their activities. Under those conditions, organizations develop behavior that conforms to the values and standards and programs dictated by the government as well as to other institutional forces. Thus, they do not develop innovative and new programs beyond what the government expects them to. Instead, they develop formal and rigid organizational structures with institutionalized and standard administrative and bureaucratic processes (D'Aunno et al., 1991; Meyer et al., 1988).

Learning the environment and interpreting events is largely subjective and depends on the way the environment is construed by directors and members of the organization. The chapter places special emphasis on the distinction between the objective and subjective, or perceived, environment. This distinction suggests that different possible strategies derive from the organization's perception of the environment. Environments can be characterized in terms of

economic, social, technological, and other indicators (e.g., rates of growth in the economy, unemployment rates, cost of living indices, the level of social tension between different population sectors, inequality in distribution of income, rates of change, and technological innovations). Nonetheless, it is the subjective interpretations of these measures that play a decisive role in adopting strategies of operation in organizations as they attempt to adapt to the external environment. The adaptation process itself is not limited to immediate elements in the natural environment, but also refers to major developments that have turned the world into a village. In the "global village," political changes generate economic changes, and decisions to introduce technological changes affect the functioning and structure of organizations. Similarly, economic and political crises in one part of the world affect other regions because the economies of different countries are interconnected. However, organizations do not always have a chance to follow international events without being directly involved or affected by them. Therefore, organizations must develop sensors and mechanisms for observation, in an attempt to obtain information that may be critical in determining their fate and their ability to cope effectively with crises and changes.

References

Aldrich, H. E. (1979). *Organizations and environments.* Englewood Cliffs, NJ: Prentice Hall.

Aldrich, H. E., & Pfeffer, J. (1976). Environments of organizations. *Annual Review of Sociology, 11,* 79–105.

Aldrich, H. E., & Reuf, M. (2006). *Organizations evolving.* Thousand Oaks, CA: Sage.

Alexander, J. (2003). Adaptive strategies of nonprofit human service organizations in an era of devolution and new public management. *Nonprofit Management & Leadership, 10,* 287–303.

Anderson, L. M., & Bateman, T. S. (2000). Individual environment initiative: Championing natural environmental issues in U.S. business organizations. *Academy of Management Journal, 43,* 548–570.

Aragón-Correa, J. A. (1998). Strategic productivity and firm approach to the natural environment. *Academy of Management Journal, 41,* 556–567.

Aragón-Correa, J. A., & Sharma, S. (2003). A contingent resource-based view of proactive corporate environmental strategy. *Academy of Management Review, 28,* 71–88.

Bansal, P., & Clelland, I. (2004). Talking trash: Legitimacy, impression management and unsystematic risk in the context of the natural environment. *Academy of Management Journal, 47,* 93–103.

Barnett, W. P., & Carroll, G. R. (1993). How institutional constraints affected the organization of early American telephony. *Journal of Law, Economics, and Organization, 9,* 98–126.

Baum, J. A. C. (1996). Organizational ecology. In S. R. Clegg, C. Hardy, & W. R. Nord (Eds.), *Handbook of organization studies* (pp. 77–114). Thousand Oaks, CA: Sage.

Baum, J. A. C., & Amburgey, T. L. (2005). Organizational ecology. In J. A. C. Baum (Ed.), *Comparison to organizations* (pp. 304–326). Somerset, UK: Blackwell.

Baum, J. A. C., & Oliver, C. (1992). Institutional embeddedness and the dynamics of organizational populations. *American Sociological Review, 57,* 540–559.

Baum, J. A. C., & Singh, J. V. (1994a). *Evolutionary dynamics of organizations.* New York: Oxford University Press.

Baum, J. A. C., & Singh, J. V. (1994b). Organizational niches and the dynamics of organizational mortality. *American Journal of Sociology, 100,* 346–380.

Blau, P. M. (1964). *Exchange and power in social life.* New York: Wiley.

Boris, E., & Krehely, J. (2003). Civic participation and advocacy. In L. M. Salamon (Ed.), *The state of nonprofit America* (pp. 299–330). Washington, DC: Brookings Institution Press.

Brittain, J. W., & Freeman, J. H. (1980). Organizational proliferation and density dependent selection. In J. R. Kimberly & R. H. Miles (Eds.), *The organizational life cycle* (pp. 291–338). San Francisco: Jossey-Bass.

Burns, T., & Stalker, G. M. (1961). *The management of innovation.* Chicago: Quadrangle.

Casciaro, T., & Piskorski, M. J. (2005). Power imbalance, mutual dependence and constraint absorption: A closer look at resource dependence theory. *Administrative Science Quarterly, 50,* 167–199.

Chakravarthy, B. S. (1982). Adaptation: A promising metaphor for strategic management. *Academy of Management Review, 7*(1), 35–44.

Chaves, M. (2004). *Congregations in America.* Cambridge, MA: Harvard University Press.

Child, C. D., & Grønbjerg, K. A. (2008). Nonprofit advocacy organizations: Their characteristics and activities. *Social Science Quarterly, 88,* 259–281.

Child, J. (1972). Organizational structure, environment and performance: The role of strategic choice. *Sociology, 6,* 1–22.

Cnaan, R. A. (2002). *The invisible caring hand: American congregations and the provision of welfare.* New York: New York University Press.

Dacin, M. T., Goodstein, J., & Scott, W. R. (2002). Institutional theory and institutional change: Introduction to the special research forum. *Academy of Management Journal, 45,* 45–57.

D'Aunno, T., Sutton, R., & Price, R. (1991). Isomorphism and external support in conflicting institutional environments: A study of drug abuse treatment units. *Academy of Management Journal, 34,* 636–661.

Deakin, N. (1996). What does contracting do to users? In D. Billis & M. Harris (Eds.), *Voluntary agencies: Challenges of organization and management* (pp. 113–129). London: Macmillan.

Dess, G., & Beard, D. (1984). Dimensions of organizational task environments. *Administrative Science Quarterly, 29,* 52–73.

DiMaggio, P. D., & Powell, W. (1983). The iron cage revisited: Institutional isomorphism and collective rationality in organizational fields. *American Sociological Review, 48,* 147–160.

Donaldson, L. (1996). The normal science of structural contingency theory. In S. R. Clegg, C. Hardy, & W. R. Nord (Eds.), *Handbook of organization studies* (pp. 57–76). Thousand Oaks, CA: Sage.

Duncan, R. B. (1972). Characteristics of organizational environment and perceived environmental uncertainty. *Administrative Science Quarterly, 17,* 313–327.

Edelman, L. B., & Suchman, M. C. (1997). The legal environments of organizations. *Annual Review of Sociology, 23,* 479–515.

Emerson, P. M. (1962). Power dependence relations. *American Sociological Review, 26,* 31–41.

Emery, F. E., & Trist, E. L. (1965). The causal texture of organizational environments. *Human Relations, 18,* 21–32.

Ethiraj, S. K., & Levinthal, D. (2004). Bounded rationality and the search for organizational architecture: An evolutionary perspective on the design of organizations and their evolvability. *Administrative Science Quarterly, 49*, 404–437.

Frooman, J. (1999). Stakeholder influence strategies. *Academy of Management Review, 24*, 191–205.

Galaskiewicz, Y. (1985). Interorganizational relations. *Annual Review of Sociology, 82*, 929–964.

Gidron, B., & Hasenfeld, Y. (1994). Human service organizations and self-help groups: Can they collaborate? *Nonprofit Management and Leadership, 5*(2), 159–172.

Hannan, M. T., & Carroll, G. R. (1992). *Dynamics of organizational populations: Density, competition, and legitimation.* New York: Oxford University Press.

Hannan, M. T., & Freeman, J. (1977). The population ecology of organizations. *American Journal of Sociology, 82*, 929–964.

Hannan, M. T., & Freeman, J. (1984). Structural inertia and organizational change. *American Sociological Review, 49*, 149–164.

Hannan, M. T., & Freeman, J. (1989). *Organizational ecology.* Cambridge, MA: Harvard University Press.

Hasenfeld, Y. (1983). *Human service organizations.* Englewood Cliffs, NJ: Prentice Hall.

Hasenfeld, Y., & Schmid, H. (1989). The community center as a human service organization. *Nonprofit and Voluntary Sector Quarterly, 18*(1), 47–61.

Hawley, A. (1968). Human ecology. In D. L. Sills (Ed.), *International encyclopedia of social sciences* (pp. 328–337). New York: Macmillan.

Hedberg, B. (1981). How organizations learn and unlearn. In P. C. Nystrom & W. H. Starbuck (Eds.), *Handbook of organizational design* (pp. 3–27). London: Oxford University Press.

Henderson, H. D., & Stern, I. (2004). Selection-based learning: The coevolution of internal and external selection in high-velocity environments. *Administrative Science Quarterly, 49*, 39–75.

Hutchinson, G. E. (1957). Concluding remarks: *Cold Spring Harbor Symposium on Quantitative Biology, 22*, 415–427.

Kreps, G. L. (1986). *Organizational communication: Theory and practice.* New York: Longman.

Lawrence, P. R., & Lorsch, J. W. (1967). *Organization and environment: Managing differentiation and integration.* Boston: Harvard University, Graduate School of Business Administration.

Levine, S., & White, P. E. (1961). Exchange as a conceptual framework for the study of interorganizational relationships. *Administrative Science Quarterly, 5*, 583–601.

Lewontin, R. C. (1978). Adaptation. *Scientific American, 239*, 212–230.

Meyer, J. W., & Rowan, B. (1977). Institutionalized organizations: Formal structure as myth and ceremony. *American Journal of Sociology, 83*, 340–363.

Meyer, J. W., & Rowan, B. (1983). The structure of educational organization. In J. W. Meyer & W. R. Scott (Eds.), *Organizational environments: Ritual and rationality* (pp. 71–98). Beverly Hills, CA: Sage.

Meyer, J. W, Scott, W. R., Strang, D., & Creighton, A. (1988). Bureaucratization without centralization: Changes in the organizational system of U.S. public education, 1940–1980. In L. Zucker (Ed.), *Institutional patterns and organizations* (pp. 139–168). Cambridge, MA: Ballinger.

Miles, R., & Snow, C. (1978). *Organizational strategy, structure and process.* New York: McGraw-Hill.

Miller, D. (1979). Strategy, structure, and environment: Context influences on bivariate associations. *Journal of Management Studies, 16*, 294–316.

Miller, D., & Friesen, P. (1983). Strategy making and environment: The third link. *Strategic Management Journal, 4*, 221–235.

Miller, D., & Shamsie, J. (1999). Strategic responses to three kinds of uncertainty: Product-line simplicity at the Hollywood film studios. *Journal of Management, 25*, 97–116.

Mintzberg, H. (1979). *The structuring of organizations.* Englewood Cliffs, NJ: Prentice Hall.

Mizruchi, M. S., & Galaskiewicz, J. (1993). Networks of interorganizational relations. *Sociological Methods and Research, 22*, 46–70.

Moon, H., Hollenbeck, J. R., Humphrey, S. E., Ilgen, D. R., West, B., Ellis, A. P., et al. (2004). Asymmetric adaptability: Dynamic team structures as one-way streets. *Academy of Management Journal, 47*, 681–695.

Mor Barak, M. (2005). *Managing diversity: Toward a globally inclusive workplace.* Thousand Oaks, CA: Sage.

Motamedi, K. K. (1977). Adaptability and copability: A study of social systems, their environment, and survival. *Group and Organization Studies, 2*(4), 480–490.

Najam, A. (2000). The four C's of third sector-government relations: Cooperation, confrontation, complementarity, and co-option. *Nonprofit Management & Leadership, 10*, 375–397.

Oster, S. M. (1995). *Strategic management for nonprofit organizations.* New York: Oxford University Press.

Pennings, J. (1981). Strategically interdependent organizations. In P. C. Nystrom & W. H. Starbuck

(Eds.), *Handbook of organizational design* (Vol. 2, pp. 28–64). London: Oxford University Press.

Pennings, J. (1992). Structural contingency theory: A reappraisal. *Research in organization behavior, 14,* 267–309.

Perrow, C. (1986). *Complex organizations: A critical essay* (3rd ed.). New York: Random House.

Pfeffer, J. (1972). Merger as a response to organizational interdependence. *Administrative Science Quarterly, 17,* 218–228.

Pfeffer, J. (1982). *Organizations and organization theory.* Marshfield, MA: Pitman.

Pfeffer, J., & Novak, P. (1976). Joint ventures and interorganizational dependence. *Administrative Science Quarterly, 17,* 218–228.

Pfeffer, J., & Salancik, G. R. (1978). *The external control of organizations.* New York: Harper & Row.

Pfeffer, J. & Salancik, G. R. (2003). *The external control of organizations: A resource dependence perspective* (2nd ed.). Stanford, CA: Stanford University Press.

Powell, W. W., & DiMaggio, P. J. (Eds.). (1991). *The new institutionalism in organizational analysis.* Chicago: University of Chicago Press.

Reitan, T. C. (1998). Theories of interorganizational relations in the human services. *Social Service Review, 72*(3), 285–309.

Romanelli, E. (1987). *Contexts and strategies of organization creation: Patterns in performance.* Paper presented at the Annual Meeting of the Academy of Management.

Schmid, H. (1992). Strategic and structural change in human service organizations: The role of the environment. *Administration in Social Work, 16*(3-4), 167–186.

Schmid, H. (1995). Merging nonprofit organizations: Analysis of a case study. *Nonprofit Management and Leadership, 5*(4), 377–391.

Schmid, H. (2003). Rethinking the policy of contracting out social services to nongovernmental organizations. *Public Management Review, 5,* 167–189.

Schmid, H., & Hasenfeld, Y. (1993). Organizational dilemmas in the provision of home care services. *Social Service Review, 67*(1), 40–54.

Schmid, H., & Hasenfeld, Y. (2008). Contracting out social services. In T. Mizrahi & L. E. Davis (Eds.), *Encyclopedia of social work* (pp. 454–457). New York: Oxford University Press.

Scott, W. R. (1994). Institutional analysis: Variance and process theory approaches. In W. R. Scott & J. W. Meyer (Eds.), *Institutional environments and organizations: Structural complexity and individualism* (pp. 81–99). Thousand Oaks, CA: Sage.

Scott, W. R. (2003). *Organizations, rational, natural, and open systems.* Englewood Cliffs, NJ: Prentice Hall.

Scott, W. R. (2004). Institutional theory. In G. Ritzer (Ed.), *Encyclopedia of social theory* (pp. 408–414). Thousand Oaks, CA: Sage.

Senge, P. M. (1990). *The fifth discipline: The art and practice of the learning organizations.* New York: Doubleday/Currency.

Senge, P. M., Kliener, A., Roberts, C., Ross, R., Roth, G., & Smith, B. (1999). *The dance of change: The challenges of sustaining momentum in learning organizations.* New York: Doubleday/Currency.

Sharma, S. (2000). Managerial interpretations and organizational context as predictors of corporate choice of environmental strategy. *Academy of Management Journal, 43,* 681–697.

Sharma, S., & Vredenburg, H. (1998). Proactive corporate environmental strategy and the development of competitively valuable organizational capabilities. *Strategic Management Journal, 19,* 729–753.

Shemer, O., & Schmid, H. (2006). Toward a redefinition of community partnership: A three-dimensional approach. *Hevra Urevaha [Society and Welfare], 26,* 307–354.

Sherer, P. D., & Lee, K. (2002). Institutional change in large law firms: A resource dependence and institutional perspective. *Academy of Management Journal, 45,* 102–119.

Sine, W. D., Mitsuhashi, H., & Kirsch, D. A. (2006). Revisiting Burns and Stalker: Formal structure and new venture performance in emerging economic sectors. *Academy of Management Journal, 49,* 121–132.

Singh, J. V., Tucker, D. J., & Meinhard, A. G. (1991). Institutional change and ecological dynamics. In W. W. Powell & P. J. DiMaggio (Eds.), *The new institutionalism in organizational analysis* (pp. 390–422). Chicago: University of Chicago Press.

Starbuck, W. H. (1976). Organizations and their environments. In M. Dunnette (Ed.), *Handbook of organizational and industrial psychology* (pp. 1069–1123). Chicago: Rand McNally.

Suchman, M. C. (1995). Managing legitimacy: Strategic and institutional approaches. *Academy of Management Review, 20,* 571–610.

Sutton, J., Dobbin, F., Meyer, J., & Scott, W. R. (1994). The legislation of the workplace. *American Journal of Sociology, 99,* 944–971.

Tan, J. J., & Litschert, R. J. (1994). Environment-strategy relationships and its performance implications: An empirical study of the Chinese electronics industry. *Strategic Management Journal, 15*, 1–20.

Thomas, W. I. (1928). *The child in America.* New York: Alfred Knopf.

Thompson, J. D. (1967). *Organization in action.* New York: McGraw-Hill.

Tolbert, P. M., & Zucker, L. G. (1996). The institutionalization of institutional theory. In S. R. Clegg, C. Hardy, and W. R. Nord (Eds.). *Handbook of organization studies* (pp. 175–190). Thousand Oaks, CA: Sage.

Tucker, D. J., Baum, J. A. C., & Singh, J. V. (1992). The institutional ecology of human service organizations. In Y. Hasenfeld (Ed.), *Human services as complex organizations* (pp. 47–72). Newbury Park, CA: Sage.

Wamseley, G. L., & Zald, M. N. (1976). *The political economy of public organizations.* Lexington, MA: Heath.

Weick, K. E. (1976). Educational organizations as loosely coupled systems. *Administrative Science Quarterly, 21*(1), 1–19.

Weick, K. E. (1979). *The social psychology of organizations.* New York: Addison-Wesley.

Weick, K. E. (1995). *Sense making in organizations.* Thousand Oaks, CA: Sage.

Woodward, J. (1965). *Industrial organization: Theory and practice.* London: Oxford University Press.

Yankey, J. A. (1991). *Mergers, acquisitions and consolidations in the nonprofit sector: Trends, processes, and lessons.* Paper presented at the Research Conference on Nonprofit Organizations in a Market Economy, Cleveland, Ohio.

Yasai-Ardekani, M. (1986). Structural adaptations to environments. *Academy of Management Review, 11*(1), 9–21.

Yasai-Ardekani, M. (1989). Effects of environmental scarcity and munificence on the relationships of context to organizational structure. *Academy of Management Journal, 32*, 131–156.

York, A., & Zychlinski, E. (1996). Competing nonprofit organizations also collaborate. *Nonprofit Management and Leadership, 7*(1), 15–27.

Young, R. C. (1988). Is population ecology a useful paradigm for the study of organizations? *American Journal of Sociology, 94*(1), 1–24.

Zald, M. N. (1970). Political economy: A framework of comparative analysis. In M. N. Zald (Ed.), *Power in organizations* (pp. 221–261). Nashville, TN: The Vanderbilt University Press.

Zimmerman, M. A., & Zeitz, G. J. (2002). Beyond survival: Achieving new venture growth by building legitimacy. *Academy of Management Review, 27*, 414–431.

Zucker, L. G. (1987). Institutional theories of organizations. *Annual Review of Sociology, 13*, 443–464.

Zucker, L. G. (1988). Where do institutional patterns come from? Organizations as actors in social systems. In L. Zucker (Ed.), *Institutional patterns and organizations* (pp. 23–52). Cambridge, MA: Ballinger.

Zucker, L. G. (1989). Combining institutional theory and population ecology: No legitimacy, no history. *American Sociological Review, 54*, 542–545.

Zucker, L. G. (1991). The role of institutions in cultural persistence. In W. W. Powell & P. J. DiMaggio (Eds.), *The new institutionalism in organizational analysis* (pp. 83–107). Chicago: University of Chicago Press.

CHAPTER 21

Building Community Partnerships and Networks

Catherine Foster Alter

Introduction

Few human services organizations survive today completely on their own. Regardless of their size or mission, organizations must build collaborations and networks with other organizations to manage the external task environment, adapt to fast-changing conditions, and acquire resources essential for the organization's survival. Today, most successful organizations are linked to a web of lateral and/or vertical interorganizational relationships (IORs), and successful managers know they must spend a significant part of their time developing and maintaining these interorganizational alliances (Alter & Hage, 1993; Bailey & Koney, 2000; Considine, 1988; Schmid, 2004). In today's world, IORs are not an option; they are a necessity. If the capacity to collaborate is not among an organization's competencies, managers need to develop these networking skills. However, before reading this overview of current IOR topics, please take note of a few caveats.

First, IORs have never been a panacea for every ill that organizations face; for example, they cannot overcome managerial stagnation and/or organizational error (Argyris, 1982; Silver, 2006). What they can do, under the right circumstances, is extend the existing resources and competencies of organizations to accomplish objectives beyond their current reach.

Second, collaboration requires managers to have more than a superficial understanding of strategic planning and IOR structures and processes. For example, successful managers do not enter into IORs without allocating sufficient time and effort for IOR building, and they must be able to articulate a collaborative vision and market that vision to internal and external constituencies (Patti, Packard, Daly, Tucker-Tatlow, & Prosek, 2002). They must be willing to spend as much time on external work as they do with internal management. Menefee and Thompson (1994, p. 19; see also Chapter 5) concluded that social work managers need to split their time equally between intraorganizational and interorganizational tasks—a strong endorsement for the content of this chapter. As a part of systems and subsystems of community service delivery, human services organizations are impacted by complex sets of stakeholders and multiple funding streams. To survive in this increasingly complex environment, managers must understand these forces and how to use them.

Third, development and maintenance of IORs require a considerable financial investment. Although unwilling to include the actual costs of collaboration in most contracts and grants, funders nevertheless often mandate that community organizations achieve "services integration" with other community organizations that serve the same client population. This directive is meant to reduce service duplication, plug service gaps, and create a "seamless" service system, that is, to overcome the rigidity of federal and state fragmentation by means of local collaboration. Although services integration is certainly possible and very commendable, smart managers know its costs are high. Despite the challenges and costs associated with building IORs, ample anecdotal and empirical evidence shows that managers influence and shape their organizations' environments as much as they are influenced and shaped by them (Hardina, 2007; Simonin, 2002).

A word about terms. This chapter describes a set of general principles and practices that apply to all IORs, defined here as a relationship between an autonomous organization and one or more other organizations that join to achieve a goal none could achieve on its own. In other words, the focus of this chapter is collaboration across the boundaries of organizations (Hassett & Austin, 1997; Lendrum, 2004; Mathiesen, 1971). Many nouns are commonly used to describe IORs—"alliances," "collaboratives," "partnerships," "strategic alliances," "consortia," "collectives," "networks," "service systems," and so on—and much space has been devoted to trying to differentiate them in terms of structure. Similarly, many verbs are employed to describe the act of creating and maintaining IORs. Terms

such as "boundary spanning," "cooperating," "collaborating," "coordinating," "integrating," and "networking" are often used interchangeably. To date, the literature has not reached consensus on standard definitions for these terms, although a number of taxonomies have been designed with this goal in mind (Alter & Hage, 1993; Astley & Fombrun, 1983; Bailey & Koney, 2000; Contractor & Lorange, 2002). For the purposes of this chapter, the term "partnership" is used to refer to joint ventures with limited numbers of members, while "network" refers to ventures with larger memberships.

Theoretical Context

Differentiating Collaborative IORs

Rather than trying to differentiate IORs in terms of their structure (e.g., size, configuration, centrality, complexity, connectivity), a more useful scheme is to focus on purpose as the distinguishing feature. After all, a favorite truism in organizational studies is "form follows function," and IORs differ significantly in the functions for which they are created and maintained.

Obligational IORs. Partnerships and networks that come together to exchange resources have been called "obligational" collaborative forms (Alter & Hage, 1993). They are loosely linked, informal, and may depend on personal and friendship relationships. They provide a means of obtaining critical resources, such as information and knowledge that is unobtainable through other channels (Bell & Dennis, 1991; Benson, 1975; Das & Teng, 2002). Obligational partnerships and networks are built on the principle of reciprocity—you give me something of value and I will return the favor. They can be ad hoc, formed to meet a time-limited need, or they can be maintained for many years as a useful form of mutual exchange (Mathiesen, 1971). One example is community welfare councils that survive for decades because they link members in order to share information. Obligational IORs can be "flat," with little centralization of control among member organizations because of their reciprocal and low-risk nature.

Promotional IORs. Promotional IORs are partnerships and networks that form to accomplish a goal or objective that no single organization could accomplish on its own, are by necessity more tightly linked, are somewhat formal (if significant investments are required), and enable managers to pool their resources through various means (e.g., interagency teams with formal division of roles; Alter & Hage, 1993; Kitzi, 2002; Vervest, 2005). Because they function to accomplish a common objective, they require a good measure of task coordination to ensure that "the left hand knows what the right hand is doing." They can be ad hoc, as when a specific political or legislative objective is tackled by a consortium of organizations, or they can be more permanent, as with a trade or professional association that represents the interests of its member organizations in policy arenas for many decades. Promotional IORS require some degree of centralization because of the high level of coordination needed and because of the significant investments required of the IOR members.

Systemic IORs. Partnerships and networks that form in order to enable organizations to jointly provide a service or product are a "systemic" form of collaboration (Hassett & Austin, 1997; Schmid, 2004). They must be tightly linked and formal to enable organizations to integrate their resources and human assets horizontally across organizational boundaries. In an integrated service delivery system, managers work together to create and maintain common plans and protocols; their staffs are often combined and/or colocated so they can work together face to face. Because systemic IORs must combine staffs and other resources, clients may not know which agency is serving them nor be able to differentiate workers in terms of their employers. This form of collaboration is said to be "seamless" and

requires a high degree of centralization in order to control the complexity of managing multiple organizations' work processes.

Consolidated IORs. Partnerships that progress to such a high degree of centralization that integration has to occur vertically as well as horizontally may create what is commonly termed a "merger." In this case, organizational boundaries become identical and centralization is complete. The nonprofit sector often witnesses organizations voluntarily consolidating their assets when their missions become identical, resources are scarce, vertical integration is needed, and/or the benefits outweigh the costs (Kassirer, 2001). Technically, this form is not an IOR but is included here to illustrate that IOR structures lie on a continuum from little or no central control to total control.

Differences among these IOR forms may be difficult to discern in communities because in reality, IOR work processes are often not very visible and they often overlap. However, in an ideal sense, they constitute a framework that describes a continuum of collaborative forms, each with different purposes, work processes, degrees of centralization, and outcomes (Alter & Hage, 1993). This continuum of IOR forms is summarized in Table 21.1.

This simplified taxonomy postulates a continuum of forms that vary widely in their functions and work processes. Thus, managers who are contemplating linking with another organization need to be clear about the nature of the proposed collaboration. Are they seeking to (1) communicate and exchange resources with others, (2) coordinate resources through joint activities, (3) integrate resources and actions, or (4) consolidate all resources and assets into a unified whole? The question of purpose is important because each subsequent form requires a larger investment of time and money and thus represents an increasingly larger risk to the participating organizations. Put another way, "Don't buy a Cadillac if a Chevy will do."

This framework is not a developmental theory—it does not assert that an obligational IOR

Table 21.1   Continuum of IOR Forms

| | *Embryonic* ⟶ *Developing* ⟶ *Consolidateded* | | | |
	Obligational	*Promotional*	*Systemic*	*Merger*
Purpose	Increase availability of tangible/ intangible resources	Mesh activities to achieve common objective	Bring together work processes to produce joint product/service	Combine assets of two or more organizations into a single entity
Work processes	• Linking • Exchanging	• Coordinating • Pooling	• Integrating • Combining	• Solidifying • Unifying
Necessary degree of central control	Little to none	Medium	High	Complete
Examples	• Buying groups • Welfare councils	• CSWE • United Way	• Juvenile justice systems • Community-based hospices	• Unified school districts

has to be created before a promotional IOR can be attempted. For example, a partnership or network of organizations could be mandated to jointly establish a juvenile justice and child welfare "service system" without any prior experience with collaboration, in which case it can be thought of as a "production system" with inputs, throughputs, and outputs. Such an organizational network would have had no chance to learn the tasks of exchange and pooling of resources. However, even though this theory is not developmental, it does assert that the collaborative tasks necessary for an obligational IOR are also necessary for each succeeding form in order for it to be successful. In other words, personnel in juvenile justice systems must be practiced at sharing information and resources, coordinating their work, *and* working together as teams in order for the system to function effectively.

The Changing Environment

Nothing about IORs is new; they have been in use since formal organizations were invented during the Greek and Egyptian civilizations.

What is new is their scope, number, and changing forms. The use of partnerships and networks in commerce and human services delivery increased dramatically during the last several decades (Alter & Hage, 1993; Austin, 2004; Kegler & Harris, 2003). We see them all around us: the U.S. government joins the big three automakers in a $1 billion research and development effort to design more fuel-efficient cars; the Colorado Symphony, more than $5 million in debt in 1989, transforms itself into a cooperative with linkages to community organizations and private industry and becomes remarkably successful in building support, increases ticket sales, and becomes a vital member of the City of Denver; and, in child welfare systems, public and private agencies jointly establish common referral networks and case management programs in order to improve the quality of their services. Across government, commerce, industry, and human services, autonomous organizations increasingly form partnerships and networks to accomplish supraordinate goals.

The force driving partnership and network formation is multifaceted change, which increases in speed and intensity by the year (Morrison,

1996). Like the Santa Ana winds, this change is constant, intense, and unpredictable and affects every aspect of organizations and their environments. Today, managers can be heard to say, "In the old days . . . last year, that is. . . ."

The rapid pace of change, in turn, is fueled by the continuous growth in knowledge. One of the most important factors shaping the structure and processes of service delivery has been the growth of knowledge and the resulting new technologies (Alexander & Randolph, 1985). These factors are important determinants of the ways in which professionals and organizations work together. As our knowledge base grows, society's perceptions of human and organizational behavior become increasingly more complex (Hage & Powers, 1992); this complexity has had two impacts on human services professions and their organizations. The first is society's increasing willingness and capacity to identify and respond to new social problems; the second is society's unwillingness to adequately fund solutions for these problems.

As understanding of human problems deepens, society views them more complexly and holistically (Lefton & Rosengren, 1966). We identify many more human conditions as representing a community "problem" than we did in the past. For instance, take recent efforts by large cities such as Philadelphia and Denver to reduce and eventually eradicate homelessness by using multisystemic interventions such as transitional and affordable housing, mental health and substance abuse treatment, training and employment, transportation services, and case coordination. Homelessness is not a new problem—hobos and transients have been with us since the Industrial Revolution. What is new is our response. We now understand that categorical programs created to treat one problem with one intervention are less effective than those that take a comprehensive approach to individual and family problems, which are most often multifaceted (Austin, 2004; Dryfoos, 1991). Thus, federal, state, and local communities strive to develop multidisciplinary approaches to a wide range of human problems. Not surprisingly, professions,

disciplines, organizations, and communities are exhorted to engage in interdisciplinary research and practice (Israel, Schulz, Parker, & Becker, 1998), and organizations are mandated to form IORs in order to provide more comprehensive and accessible services (Agranoff, 1991).

Post-industrial society is characterized by an exponential growth in knowledge and technology (Hage & Powers, 1992) made possible by our increasing ability to think in more complex ways (e.g., multivariate cognitive processes, dialectical thinking, cause/effect analysis). Multisystemic thinking is another byproduct of the knowledge explosion, and it is an important prerequisite to building successful partnerships and networks. Even when organizations are driven toward collaboration by government mandate or the needs discussed below, managers will probably be resistant and/or unsuccessful if they lack an appreciation of environmental complexity or lack the ability to think in multisystemic ways (Carlson & Donohoe, 2003).

IORs as a Response to Change

If an organization has all the resources necessary to fulfill its mission (i.e., human assets such as knowledge and skills, state-of-the-art technologies, positive community image and sanction, a supportive policy environment that strives to meet human needs in a comprehensive and effective manner), then administrators should not consider networking to be essential. If, however, resources are inadequate for strengthening a service, breaking into a new service market, or meeting unmet community needs, then collaboration can play a key role (Bell & Dennis, 1991; Kitzi, 2002). Managers most often form partnerships and networks for the purpose of obtaining needed resources, sharing risk, co-opting or competing with competitors, improving adaptability, achieving economies of scale, or building community capacity (Chaskin, 2001).

The Need for Resources. The most frequently cited reason for interorganizational collaboration is the need for resources to accomplish organizational objectives. In many instances, collaboratives are an efficient way to gain resources, especially those that are highly specialized, tacit, or dependent on political and policy experience. Once embedded within an organization, these competencies can be leveraged into expanded activities of the alliance (Benson, 1975). For example, a community-based economic development organization in a Midwestern state decided to establish a self-employment program for women on TANF. However, TANF eligibility rules, namely those concerned with assets, prevented poor women from accumulating the resources needed for a micro-enterprise start-up. Consequently, the organization allied itself with the trade association of the banking industry and, through education and the influence of several of its board members, enticed the association into working for legislative reform. A TANF waiver was adopted by the legislature and the program was launched. Now, after nearly 20 years, the state has over 1,200 small businesses owned by formerly low-income women, and the state has a high level of commercial lending to start-up micro-enterprises (Institute for Social and Economic Development, 1998).

The Need to Expand. In the business sector during the past decade, companies have been forced by market forces to downsize and focus on a more narrow range of activities, but, simultaneously, they have entered new markets (Bergquist, Betwee, & Meuel, 1995; Vervest, 2005). This presumes that a single company will have "in shop" all necessary resources and makes it less likely that the firm can risk what it does have in order to exploit new opportunities. A solution is found by combining separate resources to produce new activities that are better than the sum of the previous parts (Yuen & Owens, 1996). Although research is scanty in the nonprofit sector, anecdotal data suggests that the same circumstances are currently present in many health and welfare organizations. For example, a hospice organization on the East Coast decided to establish a specialized program for terminally ill AIDS patients but was reluctant because the needed specialized knowledge and skill were lacking. Members of the hospice board located a university teaching hospital that had a specialization in immune deficiency disease and was willing to provide technical consultation and supervision in return for an opportunity to develop medical internships. Some time after the AIDS hospice began, the organization leveraged its newly gained knowledge by initiating an extensive 10-state training program for AIDS caregivers.

The Need to Compete. Of course, turning a potential competitor into an ally via collaborative activities is not always desirable or possible. Sometimes competition cannot be avoided. This circumstance was illustrated by Organization A (a community-based mental health center) when it needed to neutralize or block Organization B (a national for-profit behavioral managed care company) in order to win a state-funded contract. Organization A's least costly means of overcoming Organization B might have been co-option—making Organization B an ally. But even if co-option had been possible, it would have been a marriage between David and Goliath. Further, the chances of winning the large managed care contract head-to-head against Organization B seemed slim. After a thorough community needs assessment, Organization A partnered with Organization C, a local Latino service organization, and submitted an integrated proposal that won the bid. The components of diversity and community embeddedness offered by the local partnership outweighed the advantages offered by the national corporation (Rodriguez, Pereira, & Brodnax, 2004). By competing with Organization B, Organization A triumphed and survived (Gargiulo, 1993). In an age of managed care, successful competition is often the difference between an organization that closes its doors and one that creates new stability and growth.

The Need to Move Quickly. Grant funding and managed care systems often require organizations to move with speed. Unfortunately, adaptability and speed require excess organizational capacity not available in many health and welfare organizations today. One way to overcome this need for speed is to form interorganizational collaboratives that have agreed-upon divisions of labor. In a partnership between three family service organizations, for example, each provided one specialist—a social welfare planner/policy analyst, a researcher/statistician, and a grant writer/editor. These three, working as a team and in concert with their three managers, developed an annual work plan that benefited each organization equally. The cost-benefit ratio of this pooling of resources was highly successful from the first year.

The Need to Achieve Economies of Scale and Contain Costs. The expectation is that collaboration with at least some level of central control can result in significant savings (Hassett & Austin, 1997), an expectation that was not realized in the nationally funded Services Integration Targets of Opportunity (SITO) projects of the 1970s (Agranoff, 1991; Agranoff & Pattakos, 1979; Lendrum, 2004). On the other hand, little or no data exists on small, successful, community-based service integration projects to determine whether economies of scale across participating programs have been achieved. Common sense dictates that case coordination, as an added value, certainly must add cost. But what about real service integration? When several community-based organizations who serve the same client population can eliminate the duplication of program components such as intake, assessment, and case planning, common sense also dictates that overall service costs can be lowered.

Potentially, interorganizational collaboration has a number of important strategic advantages; for example, acquiring scarce or specialized human assets that enable organizations to improve their speed and adaptability and thus compete more successfully over time. However, IORs also have costs that need to be clearly understood. The balancing of costs and benefits is not always an easy matter.

IOR Practice: Collaborating and Networking

The Calculus of IOR Collaboration: Balancing Risk and Gain

Before entering into collaborations or networks, managers should clearly understand not only the potential utility of IORs but also the potential costs and benefits. They need to carry out a calculus of the factors that are likely to affect the success or failure of the proposed venture. A summary of the costs and benefits of collaboration are shown in Table 21.2. This table is not meant to be an exhaustive list, but it is a brief summary of the many costs and benefits identified in the literature.

Each item in Table 21.2 has a quid pro quo, but this does not mean there is a potentially equal loss or gain in each area. The table does suggest that smart managers should estimate the overall costs and benefits of collaboration and conclude that the benefits outweigh the costs before they move ahead with collaborative efforts. For example, a perceived loss of autonomy may be offset by a newfound ability to specialize, and with greater specialization there is less likelihood of direct competition.

A wide range of motivators and risks are associated with collaborative relationships, and different theorists and researchers have focused on different aspects of this calculus. For example, Benson (1975) placed a much greater emphasis on the potential loss of resources; McCann and Gray (1986) focused on the power of collaboratives; Litwak and Hylton (1962) emphasized the opportunities. Tjosvold (1986) concentrated on the opportunities to gain information and expertise rapidly, thus creating the capability for program expansion. Others tend to emphasize the economics of services integration (Hasset & Austin, 1997). For managers, the operative words are "depending on the circumstances" because each opportunity for IOR collaboration presents a different set of costs and benefits.

Table 21.2 Calculus of Interorganizational Collaboration

Costs	Benefits
Loss of resources—time, money, and information (Benson, 1975; Litwak & Hylton, 1962).	Gain of resources—time, money, and information (Litwak & Hylton, 1962); utilization of unused organizational capacity.
Being linked with failure; sharing the costs of failing such as loss of reputation, status, legitimacy, and financial position (Alter & Hage, 1993).	Sharing the risks of program development; moving more quickly, developing higher quality, gaining greater market share (Bergquist, Betwee, & Meuel, 1995).
Loss of technological superiority; loss of human assets with technological edge or with specialized intervention skills (Provan, 1984).	Opportunities to learn and adopt new technologies, develop competencies, jointly develop new services (Jaskyte & Lee, 2006).
Loss of autonomy; loss of ability to unilaterally control outcomes (Gray & Hay, 1986), goal displacement (Beder, 1984).	Gain of influence over domain; ability to penetrate new markets; competitive positioning with new service in current markets (Bailey & Koney, 2000).
Loss of stability; increase in feelings of uncertainty and dislocation; loss of known time-tested technology (Beder, 1984).	Ability to manage uncertainty: ability to solve complex problems (Hage, 1988); ability to specialize or diversify (Alter, 1988); ability to fend off competitors (Sosin, 1985).
Conflict over domain, goals, methods (Alter, 1990).	Gain of synergy; increase in mutual support and harmonious working relationships (Bergquist, Betwee, & Meuel, 1995).
Delays in finding solutions due to problems with communication and coordination; frustration over delay in seeing outcomes (Linden, 2002).	Improvement in response rate; rapid response to changing market demands; fewer delays in use of new technologies (Linden, 2002).

SOURCE: Adapted from Alter and Hage (1993, pp. 36–37).

Prerequisites of Collaboration

The potential for organizational survival discussed above may be obvious to all organizational members, but without certain prerequisites the chances of success can be limited. The three most important prerequisites are (1) the necessary resources (Litwak & Hylton, 1962), (2) a willingness to be a risk taker (Hudson, 1987), and (3) overall intra- and interorganizational capacity (Link, 2000).

Considerable time and money are necessary to establish and then maintain interorganizational relationships, and the investment increases from obligational, to promotional, to systemic partnerships. Managers must invest enormous amounts of time in seemingly nonproductive social and community activities before ideas and opportunities present themselves. Initial meetings are often nonproductive, while numerous starts and stops commonly occur as organizations search for allies who can create truly synergistic and creative relationships. Thus, stakeholders must be realistic about the true costs before initiating collaborative efforts (Silver, 2006).

Administrators must also have an innate sense of adventure, be horizon scanners, possess a positive attitude toward change, be visionaries (Hardina, 2007), and, at the same time, understand that reengineering organizations takes time and attention to the needs and fears of staff (Patti et al., 2002). They need to view innovation as an evolutionary process that adds value to previous initiatives (Ashkenas, Ulrich, Jick, & Kerr, 1995). In order to initiate collaboration, managers must not only initiate, motivate, and lead within their own organizations, they must also accomplish the same future-oriented processes with colleagues in other autonomous organizations (Carlson & Donohoe, 2003; Patti et al., 2002). Partnerships always require some risk taking. As in marriage, where spouses unconditionally trust each other's intentions and competencies, so in interorganizational relationships: Managers must be able to make similar commitments that have no guarantee of success.

Initial Phase: Seeking Partners

Developing partnerships and networks is essentially a political process because power in partnerships and networks must be shared. Especially in the initial phases of collaboration, power struggles can erupt between those who are best served by the status quo and those who want to introduce an innovation. Regardless of whether power or persuasion is used, overcoming resistance to change is a political process that requires strategic thinking as well as skill in negotiation and conflict resolution. This process is also complex because organizations contain mixed motives; that is, organizational members often share some common interests, but also hold some conflicting ones. The resulting relationships are, therefore, simultaneously interdependent and conflicting. Making sense of these cross-cutting motives can be an analytical challenge, but understanding them is essential in building interorganizational partnerships.

Gray (1985, 1990) described an approach that is particularly useful in the initial phase for building interorganizational partnerships because it focuses on managers' interpersonal skills. Her approach conceptualizes three basic tasks that must be accomplished in order for partnerships to develop successfully: (1) establish communication, (2) develop a shared vision, and (3) establish permanence through trust. Like all political processes, these tasks are not performed in a linear fashion, although that is the way they are described below. In reality, they are integrated parts of a circular process characterized by a considerable amount of reformulation and mutual adjustment. Accomplishment of these tasks is essential for all types of collaboration, whether voluntary or mandated, because all working relationships are hampered without open communication and trust. While resistance may be greater when collaboration is mandated, collaboration can certainly occur in any situation. It should be noted that many so-called voluntary associations, when initiated to obtain badly needed resources, may be infused with as much conflict as any mandated relationship. The lesson is that all types of networking require open channels of communication and opportunities for conflict resolution.

Task 1: Establish Common Ground Through Negotiation and Conflict Resolution. The first step in seeking new partners is initiation of communication with organizations that you believe may be a "good fit" in terms of your unmet goals, history and experience, commonality of vision and values, and complementary resources. To identify likely partners, study the distribution of power and resources horizontally and vertically throughout your community or region. Seek to discover the organizations that have something to gain or lose by implementing your idea(s) and then approach those who seem to be a fit.

This identification of potential stakeholders and their enlistment in negotiation is a crucial step; if important stakeholders are inadvertently left out of the process, sanction for the collaboration may never be obtainable. On the other hand, if organizations are wrongly identified as potential stakeholders and brought into negotiation, the process can become sidetracked and/or sabotaged.

Likewise, if too many organizations are included, the process can become unwieldy. In the initial phase, the tendency to include every possible partner should be avoided because the process may become so unwieldy that individual interests and fears cannot be identified and adequately explored. This sorting out of nonessential actors is vital for successful collaboration and requires skill and patience. Effective sorting is best achieved through a large number of interactions between potential stakeholders in informal conversations and among groups in semiformal and formal meetings.

Once potential partners are identified and sorted, the next step is to entice them into a conversational process that focuses on a concrete proposal. The object of these conversations is to explore potential partners' motives for joining (or not joining) and determine whether common goals exist. Realize that potential partners' goals may vary along a continuum that ranges from highly objective, such as financial considerations, to very subjective, such as socially constructed values concerning the "right way to do things." This process must reconcile potential partners' seemingly divergent motives by identifying where trade-offs can be found. By this process, you may discover that dissimilar interests are so in conflict that they require partners to compromise on uncompromisable interests. To find this mutual agreement, you must envision potential partners collectively as a field of mixed motives (Alter, 1990) and place yourself in the middle of these often dissimilar interests. A clear resolution to this negotiation process should establish the common ground on which to build the partnership or network.

Task 2: Develop a Common Cognitive Structure. Once common ground is established, moving toward a "common cognitive structure" is possible (Gray, 1985). Sometimes termed a "shared vision," this process is often mistakenly overlooked or given short shrift. Without this step, participants will lack a common definition of the problem to be addressed, making agreement on an action plan difficult to achieve.

Almost always, people have very different cognitive conceptions about the same phenomenon even though they use similar terms. For successful partnering in the initial stage, all participants must have similar images and definitions of those images. Sometimes a fully fleshed out cognitive picture of the goal is all that is needed, but most often a shared and clear understanding of the problem is also necessary. Sometimes stakeholders are operating with extremely broad concepts of their goal—such as "comprehensive," "integrated," and "multidisciplinary"—and are unaware that going from such an abstraction to an operational model can be difficult and time consuming. Considerable intellectual effort is often needed to translate abstract mental images into concrete plans that are feasible and cost effective. Managers may be unaware they do not have a model that can be implemented, and thus their expectations of the partnership and the collaborative process may be unrealistic. When operations finally commence, partners may quickly become frustrated and withdraw prematurely from the partnership. For both of these reasons, time spent on cognitive mapping and logic modeling is time very well spent (Alter & Egan, 1997).

In communities where partnerships and networks have been tried and failed in the past, trying to forge a common cognitive structure is difficult because the conversations are dominated by retrospective and negative recitals of past failure, and then the process becomes one of avoiding failure—a tautology that gets you nowhere. If this is the situation, be sure the first step in the planning process is a goal that is far reaching and positive: "Achieve a place at the table in our managed care environment"; "Provide the best care and support of homeless families in our community." This is a normative process (Gilbert & Specht, 1977) and in these situations is preferable to focusing on the problem that has brought the group of organizations together.

Conflict is often a part of negotiating and a necessary part of achieving a common cognitive structure. Be sensitive to the potential for conflict as well as the opportunity to use conflict to push the negotiation forward. Differences and incompatible ideas usually must be resolved, and you can sometimes use anger and frustration to expose contradictions that potential partners would rather hide. Conflict is often necessary to stimulate creative processes when change is proposed; it becomes destructive only if it escalates beyond a level at which it can be controlled (Alter, 1990).

Thus, through negotiative communication, potential partners accomplish the process of defining a common cognitive structure. This model or plan for change should be clearly articulated with enough detail to describe the effort you wish to undertake. Considerable time and energy are usually spent in developing a common vision because it is here, during this phase, that the basic ideas about efficacy are thrashed out. Negotiations may at times seem frustrating and futile! These feelings can be tempered if you remain focused on the goal and keep the development process moving. As the plan is revised through many discussions characterized by a conscious dialectic of conflict and resolution, you will be able to work potential partners toward a common vision of how the partnership should function. Although skeptical in the initial phase of this process, partners may gradually become more cooperative and enthusiastic.

Achieving a shared cognitive structure also requires that a mutual understanding be reached by all participants regarding their contributions to the joint project and their expectations regarding payoffs for their cooperation. In simple terms, policy makers, administrators, supervisors, and line staff must be clear about what they are agreeing to do and, in turn, what benefits they expect to receive from their efforts.

Task 3: Achieve Trust. Many partnerships and networks fail or do not achieve their potential because the initial phase was never completely addressed or completed. One outcome of reaching consensus on a common cognitive structure is a deeper understanding of each other that leads to mutual respect and the concomitant ability to make a substantial commitment to the partnership. This process is called achieving trust.

In a study of collaboration, Bergquist et al. (1995) compiled 55 case studies of partnerships and found they often succeeded or failed not because of tangible elements such as resources or expertise, but because of the quality of interpersonal relationships. They concluded that successful partners must share something more than the basic bargain they forged.

> Sometimes this is an appreciation for the complementary skills or perspective a partner brings to solving problems . . . or common values or goals . . . or basic human qualities such as integrity, loyalty, kindness, humor, and tolerance . . . or desire to learn from each other. Typically, it is a rich combination of some or all of the above. (p. 65)

One result of fully knowing and understanding partners is that we are clear about their strengths and weaknesses and can begin to rely on them; to rely on others is to trust them.

Bergquist et al.'s (1995) analysis of trusting relationships is helpful because it is multidimensional; they propose at least three components to a fully trusting relationship. The first component is *intentions.* If you feel that potential partners are interested in your organization's welfare as well as their own, then you will tend to believe that the relationship is based not only on self-interest but also on mutual interest. The partners believe they are committed to an effort in which all will benefit. The second component is *competence.* You may believe that a potential partner is very committed to your organization's future, but if you are not convinced that your partner has the knowledge and skill to benefit your organization, then you will be reluctant to put your organization's future in that partner's hands.

The third component is trust in *perspective.* You may have trust in potential partners' intentions and competence, but if you believe that their world view is different from yours and that your agreement on a common cognitive structure cannot be embedded within the culture of their organization, then the probability is that, in time, the partnership will flounder in discord and conflict. When we feel uncertain about a potential partner, one of these dimensions may be missing, or perhaps there is a dissonance between organizations' perspectives. Perspective is a particularly important form of trust, especially when partnerships are composed of individuals from diverse cultures and ethnicities.

In building successful partnerships and networks, the object is to grow trusting relationships into group solidarity and esprit de corps such that single organizations are willing to surrender autonomy and invest resources (Zaheer et al., 2002). Hechter (1987) believes that group solidarity is a function of two independent elements: (1) the extensiveness of the normative obligations individuals are willing to assume by virtue of their participation in a given group, and (2) the extent to which they actually comply with these normative obligations. Hechter's theory holds that the greater the average proportion of each partner's private resources contributed to the collective goal, the greater the solidarity of the group. In other words, partners will give up resources to gain access to collective ones, as well as act in ways consistent with collective standards of conduct out of fear of losing their investment. Thus, when the cost of obligation is high, solidarity will be high, and vice versa. The emphasis of this model is on the costs and benefits of joining partnerships and networks; the potential loss of autonomy is one of the costs that partners must bear in order to achieve the group goal.

Of course, interorganizational partnerships and networks are not groups of individuals, but tasks institutions developed to achieve supra-organizational goals. However, the idea of built-in incentives to trust makes intuitive sense. We all have felt, at times, we have so much invested in a project that we cannot afford to abandon it. Once time (and time *is* money) is spent on developing a collaboration, a correlation is in place between the partners' willingness to trust and stick with the process and the amount of the investment (Hechter, 1987). Though not a perfect correlation, leadership can use this inevitable dynamic in subtle ways to keep things together when the going gets tough.

While the foregoing generalizations regarding trust and commitment seem to apply more to small partnerships, researchers have found they apply equally to large, interorganizational networks (Bergquist et al., 1995; Tjosvold, 1986). Like individuals, organizations have personalities, values, specific ways of looking at opportunities, and other attributes that make up what is known as organizational culture. Similarly, then, they can clash just as fiercely as do people involved together in a small business. Therefore, establishing open communication systems that can manage conflict is essential for successful partnering between organizations. Likewise, achieving consensus on a shared vision and building trust are also basic ingredients of successful partnerships. Partnerships often fail, in part, because insufficient time is devoted to these basic tasks, which, if accomplished, lay the foundation for effective and rewarding relationships.

Implementation Phase: Establishing Operational Plans

"Turning vision into value" requires building effective relationships within an IOR. But, in addition, managers need to design structures and processes that will be effective for maintaining these relationships once they are formed. Horizontally linked autonomous organizations that form an IOR have distinctly different governance needs than does a single organization. Since partnerships and networks, by definition, are non-hierarchical, IORs present a different set of challenges concerning structure than do single organizations. Consequently, for IORs, the answers need to be based on the nature of the work and not on abstract notions about the desirability of integration for its own sake (Silver, 2006).

Task 1: Establish Effective Governance and Work Processes. To maintain a partnership and its shared vision of the future, clear and permanent governance structures and operational processes are necessary. Maintenance of any IOR requires a governance structure that, at a minimum, supports the ongoing operation so that the shared vision will be developed and maintained (Considine, 1988). At the other extreme, complex and highly integrated IORs require a governance structure that provides a high level of central control. Again, decisions about IOR structure must be arrived at through a dialogue that includes all parties and that is inclusive and frank. Each partner must be clear about who controls what, when, and how.

In single organizations, accountability is often achieved through monitoring and control (Considine, 1988), although in current literature, the emphasis is often on achieving accountability by building commitment to organizational goals. By contrast, management of IORs is most often a matter of achieving control through various methods of collaboration: linking, coordinating, and integrating (Kitzi, 2002).

Above, it was asserted that post-industrial society has seen a steady movement toward more complex institutional arrangements and complex collaborative mechanisms. The growth of knowledge in social and biological sciences has meant the recognition of more complex medical and social problems, producing a proliferation of new interventions, agencies, and interorganizational arrangements. Over 40 years ago, Lawrence and Lorsch (1967) hypothesized that as the environment changes rapidly, new and different demands are made of organizations—demands for higher quality and broader ranges of services at lower costs. To meet these demands and compete successfully in the changing environment, organizations must become more complex and differentiated while the tasks that staff perform become increasingly specialized. Various units and departments take on roles, responsibilities, and styles of operation that differentiate them from other units and departments to which they were previously similar.

Many writers point out that this trend is not only inevitable but can be a healthy development for organizations (Contractor & Lorange, 2002; Kitzi, 2002). Increasing specialization and task complexity (Brown & Konrad, 1996) lead to interdependencies because workers can no longer perform all the necessary tasks and must rely on others to accomplish some of the work of the organization. Thus, the greater the specialization and division of labor of the whole, the greater the need for interdependent parts. Put simply, in complex organizational structures we need and have to depend on each other.

This trend toward increasing differentiation and specialization applies especially to partnerships and interorganizational networks. The central idea, that structural differentiation demands increasing levels of collaboration and that differentiation and collaboration must increase in tandem in order for organizations to avoid poor performance, is probably truer of interorganizational collaborations than it is of single organizations (Alter & Hage, 1993). Given this thesis, processes and methods that achieve increasing levels of interdependence across the boundaries of organizations must be identified. Put more simply, the more complex the efforts of IORs, the greater the level of collaboration required.

Earlier, three types of partnerships/networks were identified—obligational, promotional, and systemic—each requiring progressively more complex forms of interorganizational structures and processes. Further, this taxonomy asserted that partnerships/networks, given a specific purpose, will not be successful unless all levels of the participant organizations are working together in a complementary manner. Putting these two ideas together produces Table 21.3, which lists methods for achieving increasing levels of collaboration in service delivery (1) horizontally across the three different types of partnerships/networks and (2) vertically across policymaking/administrative, program management/supervision, and direct practice levels of the member autonomous organizations. It should be noted that as the intensity of collaboration increases, the costs of collaboration also increase.

As an example of how the intensity of collaboration can increase, Table 21.3 contrasts referral agreements, coalitions, and interagency executive

Table 21.3   Methods for Increasing Levels of Collaboration in Interorganizational Service Delivery Systems

Obligational Partnerships/ Networks: Methods of Exchanging and Linking	Promotional Partnerships/ Networks: Methods of Pooling and Meshing	Systemic Partnerships/ Networks: Methods of Integrating
Policymaking/Administration		
• Referral agreements concerning which agencies (units) will accept which clients under what conditions. • Resource acquisition MOUs that provide resources needed for IOR referral systems, i.e., MIS systems, computer networks, specialized staff.	• Coalitions that make and clarify policies, do collaborative needs assessment and planning, and solve policy problems when they arise. • Resource acquisition MOUs that provide resources necessary for filling service gaps and implementing policies and plans.	• IOR Executive Committees that develop seamless services through the pooling of resources and colocation of staff. • Joint resource acquisition MOUs that provide new resources that benefit the whole system and that support integrated services.
Program Management/Supervision		
Protocols that operationalize the mechanics of a referral system, such as what information is required by all participating organizations, forms and procedures to follow, timing, etc.	Program plans that implement coordinated service delivery; define the roles of participating agencies in terms of intake, assessment, and treatment services; and ensure that all program components of the system operate smoothly.	Management tools that support the integrated operation of services: procedures for integrating the hiring, supervision, and evaluation of pooled staff; integrated budgets and operating plans; methods for integrated program evaluation.
Direct Practice		
• In-service training for staff of all participating organizations that provides comprehensive information about services available to clients of the system; conferences and retreats. • Social and professional functions that promote mutual awareness and understanding between staff who make and receive referrals in participating organizations.	• Case conferences/IOR staffings that share information about client assessment, planning, and intervention and offer mutual case adjustment/ planning opportunities. • Case coordinators who insure that all necessary client information is shared, detect intervention problems, and negotiate adjustments in participating agencies' case plans if necessary.	• IOR teams that jointly do client assessment and develop and implement an integrated case plan. • Case integrators who ensure that all necessary information is shared among participating team members, monitor team members' compliance with the case plan, mediate changes in the case plan, and jointly evaluate outcomes.

committees as methods of bringing increasing collaboration to the policymaking and administrative functions of partnerships and networks. Likewise, Table 21.3 contrasts in-service training of participants' staff, interagency case conferences, and permanent interagency teams as means of achieving increasing collaborative intensity among the direct practice staffs of member organizations. This illustration is cast in the language of service systems—collaboratives that operate via referral agreements, coordinated service delivery, and truly integrated seamless systems. Nevertheless, the table also lays out a framework of collaborative methods that can be applied to many other types of interorganizational collaboration, such as legislative action and community resource development projects.

When partnerships and networks are being implemented, the primary task is to create stable yet flexible governance structures that will support frequent and open communication among partners and preserve the shared vision that brought them together in the first place. The other major task is to create work processes that fit the necessary degree of specialization and produce the required level of collaboration. Certainly, installing overly integrative methods that are a waste of resources and everyone's time and energy is possible; however, even more likely are insufficient levels of collaboration during start-up and implementation. These principles are similar to management practices within all types of complex organizations. The major difference is the absence of traditional, central management control in networks that must be replaced by various methods of collaboration selected from the vast range of such methods shown in Table 21.3.

Task 2: Move the IOR to Becoming a Learning Community. All methods of IOR collaboration depend not only on consistent and flexible work structures and processes, but also on the capacity of multiple layers of staff in member organizations to communicate horizontally with each other in a timely and effective manner. We all understand the importance of communication

within single organizations; however, we often underestimate the challenge of communication across organizational boundaries in IORs.

One key to understanding the difficulties inherent in IOR communication is to distinguish between explicit and tacit knowledge. Explicit knowledge consists of facts and their contexts that are easily communicated because they can be readily articulated through oral or written language. Tacit knowledge, however, includes facts and understandings that are carried in individuals' minds, where they are difficult to access and not easy to articulate. Individuals in organizations are often not even conscious of the extent to which they possess and rely on tacit knowledge, and they are unaware that it is valuable to others. Further, tacit knowledge is also embedded in organizational culture and thus is not readily accessible to those who are not part of that culture (Maierhofer, Kabanoff, & Griffin, 2002; Polanyi, 1966/1983; Schein, 1992). This is why the dissemination and infusion of tacit knowledge across organizational boundaries is so problematic. For example, being able to facilitate a multiorganizational planning meeting of personnel from multiple health care organizations requires a good measure of tacit knowledge. You can take a course or read a book on team building, but study will not give you the on-the-ground skill for leading planning groups composed of individuals from different professions and organizations who lack a common language and vision. In most cases, you would have to learn this kind of facilitation by doing it, rather than through education and training.

An understanding of tacit knowledge is important in IOR practice because tacit knowledge is a vital element in any innovation process (Morel-Guimaraes, Khalil, & Hosni, 2005). The hard work of building a common vision and plan for an IOR is the drawing out of tacit knowledge from participants and transforming that knowledge into explicit knowledge (Terra & Angeloni, 2005). IORs' ability to mutually develop a new joint program or service depends substantially on your ability to leverage participants' tacit knowledge into effective communication, mutual understanding, and trust. By its very nature, innovation is a journey into the unknown and thus depends greatly on the collectivity of tacit knowledge possessed by the innovators. In their book on innovation, Nonaka and Takeuchi (1995) suggested that Japanese firms are substantially more innovative than their Western counterparts because of their culturally acquired skill in "collectivizing individuals' tacit knowledge to the firm." In our social welfare organizations, with highly specialized intervention programs, infusing tacit knowledge throughout the organization and across its borders is equally time consuming and important.

A second key to understanding the dimensions of IOR communication is contained in the lesson of Table 21.1. Just as the need for flexible structures and processes with central coordination and control increases across obligational, promotional, and systemic partnerships and networks, so, too, does the need for intensity in communication. For example, in an obligational IOR, where an Adoption Exchange is exchanging information about adoptable children or a group of food banks is exchanging commodities, most communication is explicit and can be handled by systemized channels such as computer mediated interorganizational information systems (IOS). By contrast, a community-based case management program for frail elderly cannot be effective without some face-to-face communication regarding workers' deep understanding of clients' circumstances, strengths, and liabilities. At the far extreme are systemic partnerships and networks that require the most intense level of communication such that IOR personnel interact with intimacy as if they are on the same staff. Thus, the level of communication intensity that is needed, like the level of central control, is driven by the purpose of the IOR.

In IORs where the transformation of tacit into explicit knowledge is crucial for success, learning communities may emerge. This process of knowledge acquisition among partnerships and networks is the focus of much research and discussion in the technology literature (Duguid,

2005; Orlikowski, 2000; Pohlmann, Gebhardt, & Etzkowitz, 2005). Sometimes termed "learning communities" (Roth & Lee, 2006) and extended into the computer-mediated world as "virtual communities of practice" (VCoP; Etzioni & Etzioni, 1999), the focus of this work is on how independent organizations can intertwine their personnel to create synergies and innovation through the process of learning together. The aim of these new organizational forms is to leverage and transfer explicit and tacit knowledge between organizations in order to (1) cultivate and sustain new technological capabilities, (2) create continuously improving (CI) practice (Bessant & Francis, 2005), and (3) extend and sustain the technological capabilities of both firms (Lynskey, 1999). The factors necessary for successful implementation of learning communities are the same as those needed for IORs but with additional emphasis on internal information systems and shared computer standards (Lu, Huang, & Heng, 2006).

Etzioni and Etzioni (1999) offer us a concise definition of organizational communities—those that materialize in face-to-face (f2f) encounters and those that develop through computer-mediated exchanges (VCoPs). They claim that three conditions must be present for a VCoP to evolve and be sustained. First, members must have a high level of "encompassing" rather than specific knowledge about each other so they can form "broad and inclusive images" of all others and be able to trust the content of their communication. Called "bonding," such communication must allow members to believe that not only is the collective trustworthy, but that a mechanism exists to enforce accountability and punish irresponsible or antisocial behavior. VCoPs emerge because a web of affect-laden relationships exists that encompasses the entire group—"relationships that crisscross and reinforce one another, rather than simply a chain of one-on-one relationships" (p. 241).

Last, for interorganizational learning communities to develop with this level of bonding, IOR members must have access to one another. Almost all IORs today will have f2f and e-mail capability. Other, more sophisticated IORs will have computer-mediated systems that support regular video conferencing, computer-mediated (CM) video/audio communication from office workstations, and online synchronous chat capabilities. A question occupying many minds at present is whether VCoPs that have the characteristics of learning communities can develop if access is limited to just CM methods of communication. Some believe that it is a mistake to assume that f2f is vastly more effective than CM methods at satisfying the communication needs of learning communities. Although research is inconclusive, most feel f2f is better for some tasks (i.e., building encompassing knowledge and bonding) and CM methods are better for other tasks (i.e., storing, retrieving, and analyzing information). At this point in time, the consensus is that IORs that combine both f2f and CM systems will be more successful in building learning communities than those that rely on only one communication method.

Lessons Learned

Societies are weak in their interorganizational capability, as compared with their capability at the level of the single organization, though here also, the higher level of interdependence present in the contemporary environment is rendering traditional bureaucratic models dysfunctional. Debureaucratization of single organizations is necessary but not sufficient. Needed also are advances in institution-building at the level of interorganizational domains. (Trist, 1983, p. 269)

The art of interorganizational practice has progressed significantly in the 25 years since Eric Trist (1983) wrote that "societies are weak in their interorganizational capability" (p. 269), in spite of the fact that little empirical study has been done on the efficacy of interorganizational partnerships and networks (Olk, 2002).

The SITO evaluation is one of a limited number of rigorous studies that we have (Agranoff, 1991; Agranoff & Pattakos, 1979). The major

findings from these projects were that (1) few projects were implemented quickly enough to satisfy all stakeholders; (2) expectations that service integration would result in cost savings were not met; and (3) resistance from staff contributed to significant program slippage (Hassett & Austin, 1997).

Based on these findings, the following advice is certainly intuitive, if not validated by multiple scientific studies. First, managers and program planners need to have a long-term vision of the possibilities of their interorganizational efforts. Several years of cultivation and relationship building may be necessary for common vision and trust to develop. IOR building is an incremental process. Small successful efforts that build sequentially toward the goal are absolutely necessary in order to keep the potential partners engaged and willing to continue their investment.

Second, all partners need to have realistic expectations about the short- and long-term outcomes. We would never expect to create a complex social service organization and have it up and running with favorable benchmarks in place within a year. Why, then, would we expect the same or more of partnerships and networks that must be created without the advantage of intraorganizational control? Although dependent on the depth and scope of the collaboration, effective operational systems will take more time and a greater investment across organizational boundaries than within them.

Third, if clearly defined and behaviorally specific objectives for human services organizations are important today, then the same is true of collaborative partnerships. Logic models, if carefully constructed during the planning process by all who will have responsibility for delivering the product, put all stakeholders on the same page and may prevent serious misunderstandings and program slippage as the partnership develops.

Further, potential partners should prepare at the outset for exit. They should construct ways and means of dissolving the partnership if it does not work. Much as a prenuptial agreement can eliminate unnecessary arguments at the time of marital separation or divorce, so, too, can preconstructed methods eliminate misunderstandings and hard feeling when an organizational partnership is forced to dissolve.

The knowledge and documented experience of interorganizational collaboration is limited, partly because federal agencies have only been interested in funding evaluations of large scale, top-down, integrated service delivery systems. The fact is that these projects are only the visible tip of the iceberg. In every community and in every service sector, multiple networks of informal, reciprocal, friendship relationships exist among line workers and staff. Clearly, without these relationships, client services would be far less effective and efficient than they actually are. In building formal interorganizational systems, managers would do well to identify, learn from, and build on the relationships that already exist.

References

Agranoff, R. (1991, November/December). Human services integration: Past and present challenges in public administration [Monograph]. *Public Administration Review* (No. 6).

Agranoff, R., & Pattakos, A. N. (1979). *Dimensions of services integration.* Rockville, MD: Project SHARE Monographs.

Alexander, J., & Randolph, W. A. (1985). The fit between technology and structure as a predictor of performance in nursing subunits. *Academy of Management Journal, 28*(4), 844–859.

Alter, C. (1988). Function, form and change of juvenile justice systems. *Children and Youth Services Review, 10*(2), 71–99.

Alter, C. (1990). Conflict and cooperation in interorganizational service delivery systems. *Academy of Management Journal, 33*(3), 478–502.

Alter, C., & Egan, M. (1997). Logic modeling: A tool for teaching critical thinking in social work practice. *Journal of Social Work Education, 33*(1), 85–102.

Alter, C., & Hage, J. (1993). *Organizations working together.* Newbury Park, CA: Sage.

Argyris, C. (1982). *Reasoning, learning, and action: Individual and organizational.* San Francisco: Jossey-Bass.

Ashkenas, R., Ulrich, D., Jick, T., & Kerr, S. (1995). *The boundaryless organization: Breaking the chains of organizational structure.* San Francisco: Jossey-Bass.

Astley, W. G., & Fombrun, C. J. (1983). Collective strategy: Social ecology of organizational environments. *Academy of Management Review, 8,* 576–587.

Austin, M. J. (2004). *Changing welfare services: Case studies of local welfare reform programs.* New York: Haworth Press.

Bailey, D., & Koney, K. M. (2000). *Strategic alliances among health and human services organizations.* Thousand Oaks, CA: Sage.

Beder, H. (1984). *Realizing the potential of interorganizational cooperation.* San Francisco: Jossey-Bass.

Bell, G. H., & Dennis, S. (1991). Special needs development, networking and managing for change. *European Journal of Special Needs Education, 6*(2), 133–146.

Benson, J. (1975). The interorganizational network as a political economy. *Administrative Science Quarterly, 20*(2), 229–249.

Bergquist, W., Betwee, J., & Meuel, D. (1995). *Building strategic relationships: How to extend your organization's reach through partnerships, alliances, and joint ventures.* San Francisco: Jossey-Bass.

Bessant, J., & Francis, D. (2005). Transferring soft technologies: Exploring adaptive theory. *International Journal of Technology Management and Sustainable Development, 4*(2), 93–112.

Brown, D. W., & Konrad, A. M. (1996). Task complexity and information exchange: The impact of nurses' networking activities on organizational influence. *Sociological Focus, 29*(2), 107–124.

Carlson, M., & Donohoe, M. (2003). *The executive director's survival guide: Thriving as a nonprofit leader.* San Francisco: Jossey-Bass.

Chaskin, R. J. (2001). *Building community capacity.* New York: Aldine de Gruyter.

Considine, M. (1988). Bureaucracy and the structure of collaboration. *Australian Journal of Public Administration, 47*(3), 277–280.

Contractor, F. J., & Lorange, P. (Eds.). (2002). *Cooperative strategies and alliances.* Amsterdam, Boston: Elsevier Science.

Das, T. K., & Teng, B. S. (2002). Social exchange theory of strategic alliances. In F. J. Contractor & P. Lorange (Eds.), *Cooperative strategies and alliances* (pp. 439–460). Amsterdam, Boston: Elsevier Science.

Dryfoos, J. D. (1991). *Adolescents at risk: Prevalence and prevention.* New York: Oxford University Press.

Duguid, P. (2005). "The art of knowing": Social and tacit dimensions of knowledge and the limits of the community of practice. *Information Society, 21*(2), 109–118.

Etzioni, A., & Etzioni, O. (1999). Face-to-face and computer-mediated communities: A comparative analysis. *The Information Society, 15,* 241–248.

Gargiulo, M. (1993). Two-step leverage: Managing constraint in organizational politics. *Administrative Science Quarterly, 38,* 1–19.

Gilbert, N., & Specht, H. (1977). *Planning for social welfare.* Englewood Cliffs, NJ: Prentice Hall.

Gray, B. (1985). Conditions facilitating interorganizational collaboration. *Human Relations, 39*(10), 911–936.

Gray, B. (1990). Building interorganizational alliances: Planned change in a global environment. In R. Woodman & W. Padmore (Eds.), *Research in organizational development* (pp. 23–28). Greenwich, CT: JAI Press.

Gray, B., & Hay, T. (1986). Political limits to interorganizational consensus and change. *The Journal of Applied Behavioral Science, 22*(2), 95–112.

Hage, J. (Ed.). (1988). *Futures of organizations: Innovating to adapt strategy and human resources to rapid technological change.* Lexington, MA: Lexington Books.

Hage, J., & Powers, C. (1992). *Post-industrial lives.* Newbury Park, CA: Sage.

Hardina, D. (2007). *An empowering approach to managing social service organizations.* New York: Springer.

Hassett, S., & Austin, M. J. (1997). Service integration: Something old and something new. *Administration in Social Work, 21*(3/4), 9–29.

Hechter, M. (1987). *Principles of group solidarity.* Berkeley: University of California Press.

Hudson, B. (1987). Collaboration in social welfare: A framework for analysis. *Policy and Politics, 15*(3), 175–182.

Institute for Social and Economic Development. (1998). *Annual report.* Iowa City, IA: Author.

Israel, B., Schulz, A., Parker, E., & Becker, A. (1998). Review of community-based research: Assessing partnership approaches to improving public health. *Annual Review of Public Health, 19,* 173–202.

Jaskyte, K., & Lee, M. (2006). Interorganizational relationships: A source of innovation in non profit organizations? *Administration in Social Work, 30*(3), 43–54.

Kassirer, J. P. (2001). Mergers and acquisitions—Who benefits? Who loses? In C. Harrington (Ed.), *Health policy: Crisis and reform in the U.S. health care system* (pp. 132–136). Sudbury, MA: Jones and Bartlett.

Kegler, M., & Harris, V. (2003). A multiple case study of neighborhood partnerships for positive youth development. *American Journal of Health Behavior, 27*(2), 156–170.

Kitzi, J. (2002). Cooperative strategy: Building networks, partnerships & alliances. In J. G. Dees, J. Emerson, & P. Economy (Eds.), *Strategic tools for social entrepreneurs: Enhancing performance of your enterprising nonprofit* (pp. 45–70). New York: Wiley.

Lawrence, P. F., & Lorsch, J. W. (1967). Differentiation and integration in complex organizations. *Administrative Science Quarterly, 12,* 1–47.

Lefton, M., & Rosengren, W. (1966). Organizations and clients: Lateral and longitudinal dimensions. *American Sociological Review, 31*(6), 802–810.

Lendrum, T. (2004). *The strategic partnering pocketbook: Building strategic partnerships and alliances.* Sydney, New York: McGraw-Hill.

Linden, R. M. (2002). *Working across boundaries: Making collaboration work in government and nonprofit organizations.* San Francisco: Jossey-Bass.

Link, A. (2000). Private-sector and public-sector strategies to encourage technology alliances. In J. de la Mothe & A. Link (Eds.), *Networks, alliances and partnerships in the innovative process* (pp. 7–28). Boston: Kluwer Academic.

Litwak, E., & Hylton, L. F. (1962). Towards the theory and practice of coordination between formal organizations. In W. Rosengren & M. Lefton (Eds.), *Organizations and clients* (pp. 137–186). Columbus, OH: Charles E. Merrill.

Lu, X. H., Huang, L. H., & Heng, M. (2006). Critical success factors of inter-organizational information systems—A case study of Cisco and Xiao Tong in China. *Information & Management, 43,* 395–408.

Lynskey, M. (1999). The transfer of resources and competencies for developing technological capabilities—The case of Fujisu-ICL. *Technology Analysis and Strategic Management, 11*(3), 317–336.

Maierhofer, N., Kabanoff, B., & Griffin, M. (2002). The influence of values in organizations: Linking values and outcomes at multiple levels of analysis. In

C. Cooper & I. Robertson (Eds.), *International review of industrial and organizational psychology* (Vol. 17, pp. 217–163). New York, Chichester: Wiley. Retrieved May 14, 2008, from http://eprints.qut.edu.au/archive/00009936/

Mathiesen, T. (1971). *Across the boundaries of organizations.* Berkeley, CA: Flendessary Press.

McCann, J. E., & Gray, B. (1986). Power and collaboration in human service domains. *The International Journal of Sociology and Social Policy, 6*(3), 58–67.

Menefee, D. T., & Thompson, J. J. (1994). Identifying and comparing competence for social work management: A practice driven approach. *Administration in Social Work, 18*(3), 1–25.

Morel-Guimaraes, L., Khalil, T., & Hosni, Y. (Eds.). (2005). *Management of technology: Key success factors for innovation and sustainable development.* Selected papers from the Twelfth International Conference on Management of Technology. Amsterdam, Boston: Elsevier Science.

Morrison, T. (1996). Partnership and collaboration: Rhetoric and reality. *Child Abuse & Neglect, 20*(2), 127–140.

Nonaka, I., & Takeuchi, H. (1995). *The knowledge creating company.* New York: Oxford University Press.

Olk, P. (2002). Evaluating strategic alliance performance. In F. J. Contractor & P. Lorange (Eds.), *Cooperative strategies and alliances* (pp. 119–144). Amsterdam, Boston: Elsevier Science.

Orlikowski, W. (2000). Using technology and constituting structures: A practice lens for studying technology in organizations. *Organization Science, 11*(4), 404–428.

Patti, R., Packard, T., Daly, D., Tucker-Tatlow, J. & Prosek, K. (2002). *Seeking a better performance through interagency collaboration: Prospects and challenges.* A report submitted to the Southern Area Consortium of Human Services (SACHS), California.

Pohlmann, M., Gebhardt, C., & Etzkowitz, H. (2005). The development of innovation systems and the art of innovation management—Strategy, control and the culture of innovation. *Technology Analysis & Strategic Management, 17*(1), 1–7.

Polanyi, M. (1983). *The tacit dimension.* Gloucester, MA: Peter Smith. (Original work published 1966)

Provan, K. G. (1984). Technological and interorganizational activity as predictors of client referrals. *Academy of Management Journal, 27*(4), 811–829.

Rodriguez, A., Pereira, J. A., & Brodnax, S. (2004). Latino nonprofits: The role of intermediaries in organizational capacity building. In D. Maurrasse & C. Jones (Eds.), *A future for everyone: Innovative social responsibility and community partnerships* (pp. 79–100). New York: Routledge.

Roth, W. M., & Lee, Y. J. (2006). Contradictions in theorizing and implementing communities in education. *Educational Research Review, 1*(1), 27–40.

Schein, E. H. (1992). *Organizational culture and leadership.* San Francisco: Jossey-Bass.

Schmid, H. (2004). The role of nonprofit human service organizations in providing social services: A prefatory essay. In H. Schmid (Ed.), *Organizational and structural dilemmas in nonprofit service organizations* (pp. 1–22). New York: Haworth Press.

Silver, I. (2006). *Unequal partnerships: Beyond the rhetoric of philanthropic collaboration.* New York: Routledge.

Simonin, B. (2002). Nature of collaborative know-how. In F. J. Contractor & P. Lorange (Eds.), *Cooperative strategies and alliances* (pp. 237–266). Amsterdam, Boston: Elsevier Science.

Sosin, M. (1985). Social problems covered by private agencies: An application of niche theory. *Social Services Review, 59,* 75–93.

Terra, J. C., & Angeloni, T. (2005). Understanding the difference between information management and knowledge management. In L. Morel-Guimaraes, T. Khalil, & Y. Hosni (Eds.), *Management of technology: Key success factors for innovation and sustainable development* (pp. 3–14). Amsterdam, Boston: Elsevier Science.

Tjosvold, D. (1986). The dynamics of interdependence in organizations. *Human Relations, 39*(4), 517–540.

Trist, E. (1983). Referent organizations and the development of inter-organizational domains. *Human Relations, 36*(1), 269–284.

Vervest, P. (2005). *Smart business networks.* New York: Springer.

Yuen, F., & Owens, J. (1996). Power in partnership. *International Journal of Nursing Practice, 2,* 138–141.

Zaheer, A., Lofstrom, S., & George V. (2002). Interpersonal and interorganizational trust in alliances. In F. J. Contractor & P. Lorange (Eds.), *Cooperative strategies and alliances* (pp. 347–380). Amsterdam, Boston: Elsevier Science.

CHAPTER 22

Policy Advocacy and Lobbying in Human Services Organizations

Jennifer E. Mosley

I think absolutely that [the] policy impact [of my organization] is even more important than service provision. There has to be some kind of communication to policymakers.

> —Executive director of mid-sized youth development
> organization in a low-income neighborhood

Participating in advocacy is an issue of time. But the way I see it is that we can't afford not to be advocates.

> —Director of mid-sized residential drug and alcohol treatment center

I spend more time on advocacy than on fundraising. It's a better payoff. A bigger responsibility.

> —Executive director of small organization providing
> employment assistance for the elderly

The above quotes reflect the importance of an often overlooked, but critical, skill for managers of human service organizations: the ability to conduct meaningful policy advocacy in order to boost awareness of and resources available to an organization, its clients, and its community. The quotes also reflect some of the tradeoffs involved in advocacy: participating takes time, is sometimes perceived as detracting from service provision goals, and can involve financial costs.

This chapter begins by outlining both the important reasons for managers to develop advocacy skills and the barriers that keep some from participating in political activities. Unfortunately, what is known about advocacy by human services organizations is spread out across several disparate literatures, including work on social movements, interest groups, nonprofit organizations, and community organizing. This chapter seeks to critically interpret this wide-ranging literature in terms of its relevance for administration and leadership in human service organizations. Misunderstanding of the legal context, as well as lack of resources or knowledge, keeps many human service managers from pursuing advocacy goals. After discussing these incentives and constraints, this chapter explores the organizational and environmental factors managers should consider when developing an advocacy agenda and concludes by reviewing useful strategies and tactics.

Advocacy in the Human Services

As a tool to advance social justice, advocacy has historically been an important part of the practice of social workers and other human service professionals. Human service administrators have played a particularly important role in conducting advocacy, and in the early settlement house movement, administration and advocacy were seen to be organically related. Indeed, many of the idealized models for social change and advocacy in social welfare history were administrators. Jane Addams and her contemporaries, such as Lillian Wald and Julia Lathrop, were tireless advocates during the Progressive Era, participating actively in lobbying activity, even during a time when women were denied the right to vote. Their legacy has resulted in advocacy and political activity always being included side by side with service provision on the agendas of social work professional associations (Schneider & Lester, 2001).

Today, the importance of teaching advocacy skills is recognized by the Council on Social Work Education, and active, not passive, involvement in advocacy and social change is also in the National Association of Social Workers' (NASW) Code of Ethics as part of social work's ethical responsibility to broader society. Section 6.04 states that "Social workers should be aware of the impact of the political arena on practice and should advocate for changes in policy and legislation to improve social conditions in order to meet basic human needs and promote social justice" (NASW, 1999). Policy advocacy is an integral part of good social work practice and a responsibility of social work leaders, including administrators (Alexander, 1982).

Policy advocacy is different from case advocacy, which is advocacy on behalf of individuals or families. Defined as "any attempt to influence the decisions of any institutional elite on behalf of a collective interest" (Jenkins, 1987, p. 297), policy advocacy has the potential to impact much larger groups of people through the process of incremental social change. Policy advocacy tactics are the specific actions taken, and targets are those people or communities whom the advocacy is intended to influence (Lofland, 1996). As is clear from the definition given above, policy advocacy is a broad term that encompasses many different tactics, including everything from sitting on government committees and testifying before Congress to sponsoring protests or boycotts. Similarly, advocacy campaigns can target many different groups. For example, federal legislators may be targeted in a lobbying campaign to bring about a badly needed policy change. Alternatively, state- or county-level administrative agencies may be targeted when advocating for an administrative rule change or to protect a vital funding stream that is at risk. In other situations, community members may be targeted in a public education campaign. Human service organizations can and do participate in all of these activities.

One special kind of advocacy, lobbying, is defined as advocating for or against specific legislation and is limited, but not prohibited, by the IRS for 501(c)(3) nonprofit organizations. All the other activities mentioned above may be freely undertaken. The legal environment surrounding policy advocacy will be discussed more below, but it should be mentioned that while advocacy activities are conceived of and carried out by individuals, manager-advocates are generally representing and speaking for their organization, not themselves. This has some important legal implications, which make the rules governing advocacy different for managers of nonprofits versus managers of public organizations. According to the U.S. Office of Special Council, managers of public organizations face special rules and restrictions when participating in political advocacy, pursuant to the 1939 Hatch Act, which governs the activities of federal employees. Often, similar legislation exists at the state level. For the most part, public employees may not lobby while on the job, may not use agency resources to lobby, and may not speak for their agencies. They may, however, provide impartial, factual information about pending legislation. Additionally, most public employees may participate in advocacy and political campaigns on their own time, but they must be careful to speak as private citizens rather than as public employees. The Supreme Court has recently upheld the view that when public employees speak as part of their official duties, their First Amendment rights are limited (*Garcetti v. Ceballos*, 126 S.Ct. 1951 [2006]).

For this reason, this chapter will focus on nonprofit human services organizations, which have more leeway when it comes to policy advocacy, employ large numbers of human services professionals as administrators, and serve significant numbers of the needy and underrepresented. Indeed, nonprofits are often considered to have a special responsibility to participate in policy advocacy as part of their mission to serve the public good. It has been argued that by speaking for underrepresented classes of people, nonprofit advocacy facilitates the democratic process and leads to increased political participation and a stronger civil society (Berry, 2003; Reid, 1999). Although some of their advocacy

tactics and constraints are shared by other kinds of organizations, such as social movement organizations, think tanks, and grassroots interest groups, human services nonprofits face particular incentives and challenges as they try to balance their commitment to service provision with their desire to help create social change.

Importance of the Advocacy Role in Human Services Management: Why Should Managers Choose to Advocate?

Given the importance of policy advocacy in the pursuit of social justice, and the special role social workers and other administrators of human services nonprofits have in conducting it, we must ask, What is the actual prevalence of advocacy among human services organizations? The question is harder to answer than it seems. Different investigations have produced very different estimates over time, partly depending on how the researchers defined advocacy and what group of organizations they studied. In one of the earlier investigations, Sosin (1986) found that only 11% of the social service organizations he studied were involved in political activities. Pawlak and Flynn (1990) found a drastically different number just a few years later, however, with over 90% of the executive directors of human services organizations that they studied reporting involvement in some kind of advocacy activity. A few years after that, Salamon (1995) reported that only about 18% of human services nonprofits responding to a national survey reported involvement in advocacy. In 2003, however, Berry reported that about 28% of the human services nonprofits in his national sample said they met "frequently" with government officials. That same year, Mosley, Katz, Hasenfeld, and Anheier (2003) found that over half the human service nonprofits in Los Angeles County reported advocacy activity when it was defined broadly. This varied, however, from 83% of the largest organizations (expenditures over $5 million) to 39% of the smallest (expenditures under $100,000).

Most recently, Child and Grønbjerg (2008) found that 27% of nonprofits in Indiana participated in advocacy, again defined broadly.

Regardless of the exact number of organizations participating in advocacy, reports of low rates are troubling because there are so many reasons for managers to involve their organizations in advocacy. Managers trying to decide whether to involve their organizations in advocacy, or who are seeking to convince relevant organizational stakeholders of the importance of advocacy, need to consider a variety of different arguments. Perhaps the most important reason, however, is that advocacy is an important service for clients. The clients of human services nonprofits are often needy and underrepresented and frequently lack substantial political power (Mondros & Wilson, 1994). Policy advocacy by human service organizations can help address this important social justice issue (Dodd & Gutierrez, 1990).

In addition to this, increased services for vulnerable communities, improved service delivery systems, and increased resources for human service organizations are all possible payoffs. Advocacy by human service nonprofits can improve public policy by providing vital feedback to policymakers regarding how policy is working "on the ground." Managers of human service organizations have a front row seat to see which policies are working and how others could be improved (Alexander, 1982). For example, over the last 20 years, advocates working with homeless children in a variety of settings witnessed their special needs, some of which were being overlooked by current policy. By lobbying everyone from school districts to the federal government, they have contributed to improvements in multiple reauthorizations of the McKinney-Vento Act, which resulted in new policies protecting preschool-age children and those living in domestic violence shelters. The policies establish homeless children's categorical eligibility for free lunches and preserve the right of students to remain in their school of origin when they experience homelessness (Jozefowicz-Simbeni & Israel, 2006).

Participation in policy advocacy can also contribute to the health of the organization itself. Human service nonprofits are often directly impacted by policy mandates in terms of regulations, eligibility for services, and funding. Clearly, it is in their best interest, both in terms of organizational growth and effective service delivery, to advocate policies that create new funding and service opportunities. As Pfeffer and Salancik (1978) write, "the political context is a place for formally institutionalizing the survival of the organization, guaranteeing it access to the resources it needs" (p. 190). An example of this is the Violence Against Women Act, which was brought about largely because of nonprofit advocacy (Kurz, 1998). Beyond the important goal of helping to reduce domestic violence, another direct result of that Act was drastically increased funding for domestic violence work. Overall, advocacy can help organizations influence their task environment in order to promote the legitimacy of their preferred service technology and help achieve domain consensus.

Research has also demonstrated how advocacy can help reconceptualize a field of practice, opening up new funding possibilities and creating badly needed new services. One example is efforts by youth services advocates to promote programs that emphasize positive youth development, rather than services that primarily see youth as delinquents needing intervention. Scott, Deschenes, Hopkins, Newman, and McLaughlin (2006) have documented how youth services advocates in the San Francisco Bay area have made significant progress in changing the terms of the youth services debate by building coalitions that opposed punitive legislation. Advocacy helped organizations practicing positive youth development gain increased legitimacy, ultimately transforming the organizational field.

For all of the reasons given above, advocacy is increasingly becoming a critical area of involvement for managers. Menefee (2000) argues that advocacy is one of the 11 key activities of human service managers and that its importance is growing in an increasingly turbulent environment. Frumkin and Andre-Clark (2000) agree with this assessment, arguing that as for-profit organizations increasingly enter the human services, nonprofit organizations can best compete with them by highlighting the mission-driven dimension of their programming. One key way to do this is to express organizational values through advocacy. Finally, Eisenberg (2000a) argues that if human service managers really want to make a difference in their chosen areas, they must pay more attention to their role as advocates and not let day-to-day programmatic or bureaucratic concerns derail their efforts.

Reports from human service leaders who have been actively involved in advocacy support these findings. Pawlak and Flynn (1990) found that when asked about the consequences of their political participation, almost all of the executive directors they studied reported little to no lasting negative consequences from advocacy participation and cited many more positive consequences. The consequences they mentioned included creating new funding opportunities, staving off cutbacks, winning desired new legislation or regulations, increasing access to key decision makers, and witnessing improvements in how policymakers understood important community issues.

Overcoming Barriers to Involvement

Given these excellent reasons to be involved, what is holding managers of human service organizations back? There are three primary areas of constraint: legal restrictions and misunderstandings, leadership initiative and training, and organizational capacity.

Legal Restrictions and Misunderstandings

The first, fear of violating the law, is a very real concern as the legal environment surrounding nonprofit advocacy is complex and the penalties for breaking the lobbying laws are severe—an organization's 501(c)(3) status can be revoked for engaging in excessive lobbying. The complexity has led to the mistaken belief by many social welfare administrators that their organizations are more restricted legally than they actually are. There is also evidence that some managers limit their organizations' advocacy activity even when they are not participating in lobbying because they are fearful and confused about the IRS rules and thus stay out of the political arena altogether (Salkin & Rutigliano, 1998).

Berry (2003) quizzed nonprofit leaders about their knowledge of lobbying regulations and found striking differences regarding their knowledge of what the tax code allows regarding their political participation. He found that very few nonprofits that had not taken the H election (see the text box titled "Lobbying and the Legal Environment" for more information on the H election) knew the basics about their political rights. For example, only 54% knew that it was acceptable for them to support or oppose legislation, and only 32% knew it was legal to lobby if their organization accepted government funds (it is, just not with the government funding itself). Organizations that had taken the H election were much more knowledgeable about what was allowed, answering correctly between 70–98% of the time.

LOBBYING AND THE LEGAL ENVIRONMENT

One reason managers of human service organizations may stay away from advocacy is the fear that they are doing something illegal. For most organizations, this is not the case. In a legal sense, there are essentially three forms of advocacy. The first is electioneering or "express advocacy," which includes supporting or opposing specific candidates or political parties. This type of partisan activity

(Continued)

(Continued)

is prohibited for 501(c)(3)s. The second is lobbying, which is explicitly regulated by the IRS for 501(c)(3)s. The third category comprises everything else and is basically unregulated.

Also known as legislative advocacy, lobbying is the common term used for efforts to influence legislation. There are two forms of lobbying and each is regulated differently. Direct lobbying occurs when organizations directly contact decision makers in support of or against specific legislation. Grassroots lobbying occurs when organizations encourage their membership or the general public to contact decision makers in support of or against specific legislation. Other related public policy activities, such as contacting legislators about specific regulations or conducting public education, are not lobbying and so are not limited. The important distinction between grassroots lobbying and public education is that grassroots lobbying contains a "call to action" and public education does not.

The rules for what is allowed and what is not are complicated by the IRS's two different regulation policies. Prior to 1976, all 501(c)(3)s were faced with the same regulation—expenditures on lobbying were limited to being an "insubstantial" part of a nonprofit's activities. What was substantial and what was not was not defined, and staff and volunteer time and effort were included. In 1976, however, Congress passed the Tax Reform Act, which allowed nonprofits to make the "501(h)" election, which, if an organization chooses it, provides clear guidelines about limits on lobbying expenditures. Hard to measure elements, such as staff and volunteer time, are not factored in as expenditures. In general, an H elector may spend 20% of its first $500,000 on lobbying, 15% of the next $500,000, and so on, up to a total limit of $1,000,000. However, only 25% of that can be spent on grassroots lobbying (Raffa, 2000). Organizations that do not elect to be governed by the H election (only about 2.5% make the election) simply continue to be governed by the "insubstantial" test. Taking the H election is easy—organizations simply fill out the one-page Form 5768 and send it to the IRS.

Human service managers should also be aware of the numerous challenges to nonprofit advocacy rights that have been appearing before Congress with ever-greater frequency (Bass, Guinane, & Turner, 2003). The best known of these attacks on the right of nonprofits to advocate was Rep. Ernest Istook's failed 1995 attempt to amend a major appropriations bill with language that would have prohibited nonprofits who accept any government funding to lobby at all. This would have had clear implications for the heavily government-financed human services sector. Currently, nonprofits that accept government funding may lobby, but they may not use government-provided funds to do so. Other, more recent threats include several bills that have included amendment language restricting the rights of government grantees to participate in nonpartisan voter registration and advocacy, though as of yet none have passed. These bills include the authorization of major funding streams for affordable housing programs, Head Start, and legal services. Human service administrators should be aware of this trend and monitor its development because further restrictions would have serious implications regarding the ability of human service professionals, agencies, and managers to speak for their clients or inform policy debates.

Leadership Initiative and Training

The second reason advocacy often does not occur in human service organizations is a lack of initiative on the part of managers themselves. Schneider and Lester (2001) list several reasons social workers hold back from advocacy, many of which are applicable to human service managers. These include a preoccupation with a service role, lack of professional norms and standards around advocacy, lack of training, concern with professionalism, and disagreement with any commonly proposed solutions to social problems.

Some of these barriers might be resolved if advocacy skills were given greater weight in graduate programs. Many schools of social work do not offer courses on advocacy specifically, the literature on advocacy is slim compared to the literature on many other managerial skills, and appropriate field placements and internships seem to be particularly lacking. Mor Barak, Travis, and Bess (2004) found that most social work managers did not see their fieldwork experience as providing them with sufficient training in administration skills, including advocacy. Furthermore, Wolk, Pray, Weismiller, and Dempsey (1996) found that only 33% of social work programs they surveyed had policy advocacy placements available, even for second-year MSW students. Of course, this is a vicious cycle because the lack of placements in advocacy settings is partly due to the paucity of MSWs who are able and willing to supervise students in this kind of practice.

Lack of political involvement may also have to do with the overwhelming time constraints many managers face. Advocacy can be very time consuming and does not always have an immediate payoff. Pawlak and Flynn (1990) found that the top complaints cited by executive directors who were involved with advocacy were that it led them to work too many hours and intruded on their personal lives. Additionally, leaders must ensure that other agency functions are attended to while the administrator is engaged in advocacy work. Overworked human service managers may simply feel they do not have time to participate in another activity in addition to supporting existing service programs and fundraising.

This is reflective of the fact that executive leadership is generally not rewarded for attempts to achieve broad community objectives. Rather, they are encouraged to focus on more narrow organizational goals (Eisenberg, 2000b). This means that it often requires the personal commitment of a leader to maintain an active advocacy program. However, managers who have strong leadership skills can fight pressures to focus on short-term, intra-agency goals.

Educating key organizational stakeholders, particularly the board of directors, about the payoffs for advocacy is crucial (Gibelman & Kraft, 1996; Pawlak & Flynn, 1990). Marwell (2004) found that leaders who have a strong interest in political activity can boost acceptance of this activity in an organization, even when institutional pressures to avoid it are strong.

In short, leadership is critical in order for human service organizations to be active in advocating on behalf of people they serve. Because the responsibility to initiate an advocacy program often falls to the executive director, administrators must have the drive to pursue it, educate themselves on how to communicate with policymakers, and motivate both their staff and board in the belief that involvement in advocacy will benefit the organization and its clients.

Organizational Capacity

The final set of reasons many managers choose not to involve their organizations in advocacy is related to organizational capacity. Kirsten Grønbjerg and her colleagues (Grønbjerg, Cheney, Leadingham, & Liu, 2007) found that about 80% of the nonprofits they surveyed identified challenges regarding capacity for networking and advocacy. Over half the organizations surveyed specifically mentioned four areas as particular challenges: enhancing the public understanding of key policy issues, strengthening relationships with key policymakers, responding effectively to community expectations, and interacting with other organizations to learn better practices. When asked what types of assistance were most needed to help them meet these challenges, over half mentioned specific forms of financial assistance, namely, increased multi-year funding, funding for general overhead, and increased availability of small grants for networking and advocacy. Clearly, financial constraints are a major concern when managers consider their capacity to build an effective advocacy program.

It is true that it can be very difficult to get advocacy funded. A major study cosponsored by the Independent Sector and the Foundation Center found that only 11% of the grant money given by the largest U.S. foundations goes to social justice concerns (Lawrence, Jalandoni, & Smith, 2005). Barriers mentioned by those foundations include an adverse political climate, little collaboration in the field, and a sense that resources were not sufficient to meet increasingly severe needs. Other scholars have argued that foundations are essentially conservative and hesitant to fund advocacy that, if successful, would result in disruptions to the status quo (McAdam, 1982; Roelofs, 2003). Many foundations essentially limit the amount of advocacy and lobbying their grantees can participate in by using restrictive language in their grant agreements, even though it is legal for the recipient organizations to spend money on advocacy (Reid, 1999). This is partly because foundations face their own set of IRS regulations over how much of the grant money they give out can be spent on lobbying. Others have argued that foundations sometimes hold back on funding advocacy because it is hard to measure outcomes and return on investment, although Scott and Carson (2003) have shown that when lobbying efforts are successful, the payoff can be huge. They give an example of a $1 million advocacy campaign conducted by nonprofits participating in the AmeriCorps program that resulted in an extra $100 million in AmeriCorps funding.

The difficulty in raising funds specifically for advocacy means that larger organizations with more "slack" in their budget often have greater capacity for advocacy. Many studies have shown that larger organizations are more likely to participate in advocacy, or to have more developed advocacy programs (Child & Grønbjerg, 2008; Mosley et al., 2003; Nicholson-Crotty, 2007). Organizational size also conveys status and stability, both factors that can increase access to important decision makers (Berry, 2003).

Having more resources to go around can also lessen the impression that advocacy is "taking away" from programs for clients. It is vitally important for managers to remember the common perception that every dollar spent on advocacy means money not spent on the agency's core services. This tradeoff can create tension within the organization, with some staff or board members questioning the utility of advocacy (Berry, 2003). However, there is some indication that, if supported, staff members may be eager to participate in greater levels of advocacy. Herbert and Mould (1992) found that child welfare workers had high levels of interest in pursuing more advocacy, but lack of support by their agency and lack of education on how to conduct advocacy kept them from participating. They also found that organizational leaders generally did not solicit workers' feedback about what in the system needed to change.

Other organizational characteristics beyond size can also increase capacity for advocacy. Research on interest groups has shown that the ability to mobilize large numbers of people makes up for some lack of financial resources (Berry, 2003). In a study of nonprofits engaged in advocacy for children, researchers from the Urban Institute (DeVita, Montilla, Reid, & Fatiregun, 2004) found that although capacity needs differed between organizations depending on their political goals, there were particular strategies that could be used to strengthen advocacy programs overall. The first was having leadership that was skilled at maintaining networks, promoting collaborations, and doing outreach, both within and outside the organization. The second was having a policy advisory committee, and the third was utilizing feedback from constituents to improve communications. It is these kinds of strategies and tactics that skilled human services managers consider when building or expanding advocacy programs.

Advocacy Toolbox: Strategies and Tactics for the Human Service Manager

Even for managers who are committed to involving their organization in advocacy and have developed the organizational support to do so, thinking about strategy and how best to conduct a specific advocacy campaign can be daunting. Planning is vital. Managers must think about which issues they will choose to become involved in by considering what is most important to various stakeholders (clients, board members), what outcomes may have the greatest payoff to the organization, and what campaigns are truly winnable (Gibelman & Kraft, 1996). Short-term as well as long-term goals need to be spelled out regardless of how large or small the issue is.

There is a wide range of advocacy tactics available to human services organizations. Tactics that have traditionally been known as "outsider," or extra-institutional (Gamson, 1975), include conducting or participating in demonstrations and boycotts or performing other types of social action. Community organizing is sometimes thought of as an outsider tactic. "Insider" tactics involve dealing directly with traditional electoral, judicial, and lobbying systems. Human service organizations also often use tactics that don't fall neatly into one of these categories, such as writing letters to the editor, participating in coalitions, or providing public education.

Turner and Killian (1987) argue that managers should think strategically about how effective a given tactic will be, given its costs, while also trying to choose tactics that meet the symbolic character of the cause and build sympathy and commitment. They also outline how organizations choose different tactics and targets depending on their advocacy goal. When the goal is to impact policy directly, elite targets such as administrators, legislators, and funders are generally chosen, and insider tactics, like lobbying or administrative advocacy, are used. When the goal is societal transformation, or "changing the hearts and minds of people," targeting the general public is generally chosen. This can be done through a variety of tactics. Conducting public education, issuing policy reports, and working with the media can help inform people and persuade them to take action or change their position. Social action, like protests and boycotts, can show the commitment of supporters and draw attention to the cause.

Coalitions

A popular tactic engaged in by many human service nonprofits is to join advocacy-related coalitions (also see Chapter 21 for further discussion of coalitions). Coalitions are groups of affiliated organizations advocating on issues in which they have a shared interest, whether a similar client population, a similar service technology, or a shared geographical location. Coalition work has both advantages and disadvantages. The major advantages include having increased leverage through the appearance of unity, the ability to pursue multiple policy goals at once, increased access to information, exposure to new advocacy skills, and the ability to network around other issues, such as service coordination or fundraising (DeVita et al., 2004; Dluhy, 1990).

Coalitions also have serious disadvantages, however, including a loss of autonomy for each member, time delays, difficulties in finding ways to work together, and disagreement about goals (Hojnacki, 1997; Mulroy, 2003). Balancing the need for broad-based support in a coalition and maintaining a consistent message is an inherent problem in coalition work. Often members are involved for slightly different reasons or have different beliefs about the nature of the problem and disagree about preferred solutions. Finding a message that can unite the voices of all participants without excluding or offending anyone is difficult and calls for creativity and flexibility.

To ensure the effectiveness of a coalition, a number of factors must be considered, some of which may be difficult to address. Goodwin (2001) warns that for coalitions to be maximally effective, they should be formed before the identified problem has reached a point of urgency. Most important, coalitions should be strategic about selecting goals, establishing time frames, and determining which targets and tactics are appropriate (Dluhy, 1990). Other characteristics of effective advocacy coalitions include having enduring, flexible memberships; a lack of organizational ego issues; a clear vision; and good communication with one another (Goodwin, 2001).

Media Communications

Working with the media can be intimidating, but it can be extremely effective when it is successful. It is also an essential skill because it is relevant to many different tactics. For example, in order for a boycott to be successful, people must know about it. Alternatively, if an organization is lobbying to protect funding for homeless shelters, it may be helpful to place a story in the paper highlighting how overcrowded shelters are having to turn needy families away.

Common advice regarding how to use media communications effectively includes the following. First, many stories compete every day for limited space, and a story is more likely to get picked up if it is about something new and interesting. A press release about an important issue that is not framed in a compelling and innovative way may not be able to compete with the latest news from Hollywood. Also, the frequency of the message is important. Research has shown that people may not remember or feel compelled to act on an issue until they have heard about it at least four times (Story, 2001). Third, never underestimate the power of a real-life example. An issue that has a human face will stay with people and be the story that gets repeated to others. Finally, when working with the media, it is important to select a format that best fits the news you are promoting (Richan, 1996). An event may be more likely to get picked up by radio or a local newsletter or special interest weekly. An issue of local concern may have luck at a larger newspaper, such as a regional daily. Having an issue that you can put a human face to—a human interest story—is often the only way to get television news coverage.

Framing the Issue

The concept of "framing" political issues has recently become a topic of much discussion, partly due to several popular analyses of political campaign strategies (e.g., Lakoff, 2004). The notion has a much longer history in the academic literature, however, beginning with the work of Erving Goffman (1974) and Tversky and Kahneman (1981). More recently, Benford and Snow (2000) defined frames as "action-oriented sets of beliefs and meanings that inspire and legitimate the actions" of an organization (p. 614). Frames are important because they provide direction about how to think about a problem. They guide attributions about the cause of the problem, as well as which solutions will be seen as preferable. Opinions have been shown to be quite malleable and sensitive to the way problems are framed (Iyengar, 1990). How an organization frames a message also helps determine which groups of people will be most likely to hear it. Surveying members or otherwise soliciting how they understand important issues is one way that organizations can help frame their messages in ways that resonate with the people they are trying to reach (DeVita et al., 2004).

Frames are strategic, dynamic, and ongoing rather than static. Political and cultural changes, as well as other changes in the policy environment, impact frame construction, leading organizations to reconsider and reframe their beliefs and their messages. For example, advocates concerned about teen pregnancy might frame the problem as being about morals, negative outside influences, or the availability of accurate information about sex. The same advocate might use these different messages to motivate different audiences, or they may be chosen by different advocates who have different preferred policy solutions. Different frames also require presenting different kinds of information, for example, statistics about the extent of a problem versus stories that put a human face on a problem.

Master frames are frames that are used by many different groups on many different issues because they are so flexible, inclusive, and culturally resonant (Benford & Snow, 2000). These include frames about "justice," "human rights," "choice," and "democracy." Using a frame of this type can be useful because it is difficult for opponents to argue "against" justice or "against" human rights. Not infrequently, both sides of an issue will claim to be representing one or more of these values. For example, in the welfare reform debate of 1996, advocates for welfare rights claimed that time limits for income assistance were un*just* because they would negatively impact innocent children, while opponents argued that letting families receive welfare without time limits was un*just* to taxpayers who worked and did not receive welfare.

New Technologies

Another strategy that more and more human service organizations are contemplating is how best to use the Internet to mobilize community members, communicate with allies, provide information, or conduct outreach. Indeed, the rise of the Internet has made many forms of advocacy easier for nonprofits and has possibly even opened up new opportunities. Hick and McNutt (2002) argue that the Internet can be particularly useful for contacting policymakers, organizing allies, and "getting the word out." Delany (2006) warns that when using the Internet, however, it is important to consider your audience and to make sure that your message, design, and tools resonate with the people you are trying to reach. People who are looking at an organization's Web site are often already interested in the issue at hand, so a Web site is a good place to provide additional in-depth information. It may also be useful to frame your information differently to suit the culture, perspective, and history of those you are trying to reach. Things to consider are age, political persuasion, and educational level. It should also be remembered that measuring the impact of Internet-related communication strategies is often quite difficult and that the impact of Internet-related advocacy strategies may be reduced for organizations that are trying to reach low-income populations or constituencies that speak languages other than English (DeVita et al., 2004).

Who Should Participate?

Finally, managers may find it helpful to structure participation in their organization's advocacy activity in different ways, depending on the size of the organization. Although in many organizations responsibility for advocacy falls to the executive director, advocacy can be something that all staff members are encouraged to participate in, or it can be the stated job responsibility of one or more staff members. Staff can be very effective advocates because they are often the ones who see how policies are playing out on the front lines and know personal stories that can serve as powerful advocacy tools (Hayes & Mickelson, 2000). They may also feel empowered by advocating for their clients, resulting in increased feelings of empathy and lower rates of "burn-out" (Gutierrez, 1992). Ezell (1994) found that agency-level characteristics and preferences strongly influenced the advocacy activity of social workers. He also found that while administrators were more involved in policy advocacy than direct service workers, the latter were more involved with case advocacy.

Members of the board of directors should also not be overlooked when it comes to advocacy activity, nor should other volunteers from the community or past and present agency clients. Board members are often chosen to be involved in the organization partly because of their strong influence and networks in the community. Mobilizing this social capital on behalf of the organization can be an extremely effective tool in terms of gaining access to decision makers. Involving clients has the added benefit of adding legitimacy to the organization's message and is thought to be an empowering intervention for clients (Gibelman & Kraft, 1996; Mondros & Wilson, 1994). Involving community members in advocacy efforts to change policy can sometimes be a step in helping the community to resolve the factors that led to the problems in the first place (Donnelly & Majka, 1998; Ferre, 1987). This involvement can also lay the groundwork for future mobilization efforts and increase community capacity (Chaskin, Brown, Venkatesh, & Vidal, 2001).

Striving for Effectiveness

Choosing the most effective advocacy strategy will depend on the capacity of the organization and the goal of the advocacy. However, a few studies have pointed to some general rules of thumb. Susan Rees (1999) studied the structure and activities of 12 national nonprofits that policymakers themselves identified as "highly effective." Some of the activities or traits she found most important were taking a bipartisan approach; spending the majority of time and resources on one top priority; and disseminating information to lawmakers in a way that makes their job easier, such as providing statistics about the extent of a problem in a community. Rees also found it was helpful to expose policymakers to people experiencing the problem firsthand, so as to make the issue come alive—an activity that should come easily to most human services organizations. A final recommendation she mentioned, also emphasized by others (Gibelman & Kraft, 1996), is to maintain a constant presence with policymakers, rather than just showing up when there is an urgent issue to address. This is important advice to remember for cash-strapped human service organizations that may try to save money by only participating in advocacy when they are experiencing an immediate problem. Maintaining ongoing relationships can make a vital difference when there is a crisis.

Obviously, ongoing advocacy can be draining on organizational resources, especially for small organizations. Two ways to overcome this were already mentioned above. The first is increasing the capacity and reach of the organization by mobilizing volunteers, board members, and community members to participate in advocacy-related work. The second is to form or join ongoing advocacy coalitions for this purpose. Advocacy coalitions hold much promise for boosting effectiveness while sharing advocacy-related costs, but coalitions often work on an ad hoc basis when specific bills or issues of concern are in play. Groups of organizations working together over time in order to achieve larger long-term goals could significantly increase the capacity

of each organization to achieve agenda success. Another way is to join an umbrella organization—a voluntary association created either by leaders in the field or by an association of organizations (Gibelman & Kraft, 1996). Umbrella organizations typically have an independent existence outside the founding players and choose issues to be involved in on a long-term basis. In California, for example, the California Welfare Directors Association has played an important role in influencing welfare policy at the state level. The Mental Health Association in New York State has played a similar role influencing mental health policy in that state. Advocacy participation through these types of interest groups typically reduces costs and increases anonymity for organizations concerned about retribution.

Dear and Patti (1981) have given classic advice, suggesting several important tactics for legislative advocacy, especially when advocates plan to be highly involved with a single bill. They write that these tactics are aimed specifically at advocates who face constraints in terms of power and resources, although both would clearly smooth the process, especially with the increasing influence of lobbyists and the growth of "pay-to-play" politics (McChesney, 2000). Their recommendations include making sure the bill gets introduced early, having more than one legislator sponsor the bill, making sure those legislators have sufficient influence in the chamber to move the bill along, considering the reality of partisan politics and making sure that the bill has bipartisan or majority party support, seeking additional support from executive-level policymakers, arranging expert witnesses to give testimony at committee hearings, and being ready to compromise through the amendatory process.

Berry (2003) suggests that administrative advocacy may be a particularly effective type of advocacy for human service nonprofits to be involved in because access comes easier at the local level, and nonprofits may wield more power in that sphere. Recognizing that many human service organizations have very limited resources and struggle to gain a seat at the table, he recommends that nonprofits think of what they have to offer policymakers and capitalize on that. Local government needs human service organizations to administer needed programs and often turns to local service providers for information about the extent or severity of a problem. Developing a relationship with the local government officials overseeing services in the organization's area of expertise (homelessness, child welfare, domestic violence, etc.) can be a way to influence the rules and regulations that impact the agency's functioning as well as ensure that adequate funding is available and that emerging issues are addressed.

Other scholars (Schneider & Lester, 2001; Sherraden, Slosar, & Sherraden, 2002) have made similar arguments, pointing out that devolution has increased the power wielded by state-level decision makers, and that advocacy at the state level is considerably more accessible and less intimidating than federal-level advocacy. Geographically, it also makes coalition building easier because organizations can join with others who serve the same population, or who receive funding from the same local agency. Others have argued, however, that devolution has not led to increased access and that many nonprofits are finding it difficult to communicate with state-level officials (DeVita, 1999). Additionally, in areas with considerable federal oversight, the power of state-level officials to change regulations may be limited.

Whether at the local, state, or federal level, influencing the regulation-writing process can be a highly effective way of influencing social welfare policy. This often-overlooked point is in line with research on policy implementation, which has argued that implementation details, often worked out in the regulatory process by administrators, not legislators, is key to how policy is experienced at the ground level (Brodkin, 1990). To do this effectively, Hoefer and Ferguson (2007) argue that advocates must enter the regulation-writing process early, avoid conflict, and have access to key players. Hoefer (2001) has also proposed several other tactics for shaping regulation, based on the activities of influential interest groups in Washington, D.C., such as bringing current regulations to executive branch attention or suggesting changes to proposed regulations to the issuing agency.

Conclusion

Regardless of the tactics used or level of resources available, advocacy is an important skill for managers in the human services. Whether motivated by social justice concerns, professional values, or organizational self-interest, managers who involve their organizations in advocacy will raise the profile of their organization as well as that of their clients. Managers of human service organizations play a vital mediating role between policy and practice. Increased participation in policy advocacy has the potential to improve both, resulting in improved organizational health and more stable funding streams, while helping to reduce the racial, economic, and social inequalities that are still so pervasive in our society.

ONLINE ADVOCACY RESOURCES

As well as a tool for conducting advocacy and mobilizing constituents, the Internet is a rich resource for information about how to carry out effective and legal advocacy and lobbying campaigns. Below is a nonexhaustive list of some of the most comprehensive sites.

Nonprofit Advocacy Information and Legal Information About Lobbying

- Center for Lobbying in the Public Interest: http://www.clpi.org
- OMB Watch: http://www.ombwatch.org
- Alliance for Justice: http://www.afj.org

(Continued)

(Continued)

Leadership and Coalition Building

- Institute for Sustainable Communities Advocacy and Leadership Center: http://www.iscvt.org/what_we_do/advocacy_and_leadership_center/

Communication Strategies and Working With the Media

- The Spin Project: http://www.spinproject.org

Internet and Online Advocacy

- e.politics: http://www.epolitics.com
- Net Action: http://www.netaction.org

Foundations and Policy Advocacy

- National Committee for Responsive Philanthropy: http://www.ncrp.org
- Donors Forum of Illinois: http://www.donorsforum.org/policy/pubpol.html

Social Justice-Focused Policymaking

- The Praxis Project: http://www.thepraxisproject.org

References

Alexander, C. A. (1982). Professional social workers and political responsibility. In M. Mahaffey & J. W. Hanks (Eds.), *Practical politics: Social work and political responsibility* (pp. 15–31). Silver Spring, MD: National Association of Social Workers.

Bass, G., Guinane, K., & Turner, R. (2003). *An attack on nonprofit speech: Death by a thousand cuts.* Washington, DC: OMB Watch.

Benford, R. D., & Snow, D. A. (2000). Framing processes and social movements: An overview and assessment. *Annual Review of Sociology, 26,* 611–639.

Berry, J. M. (2003). *A voice for nonprofits.* Washington, DC: Brookings Institution Press.

Brodkin, E. Z. (1990). Implementation as policy politics. In D. J. C. Palumbo & J. Donald (Ed.), *Implementation and the policy process: Opening up the black box* (pp. 107–118). Westport, CT: Greenwood Press.

Chaskin, R. J., Brown, P., Venkatesh, S., & Vidal, A. (2001). *Building community capacity.* New York: Aldine De Gruyter.

Child, C. D., & Grønbjerg, K. A. (2008). Nonprofit advocacy organizations: Their characteristics and activities. *Social Science Quarterly, 88*(1), 259–281.

Dear, R. B., & Patti, R. J. (1981). Legislative advocacy: Seven effective tactics. *Social Work, 26*(4), 289–296.

Delany, C. (2006). *Online politics 101.* Retrieved July 31, 2007, from http://www.epolitics.com/onlinepolitics101.pdf

DeVita, C. J. (1999). Nonprofits and devolution: What do we know? In E. T. Boris & C. E. Steuerle (Eds.), *Nonprofits and government: Collaboration and conflict* (pp. 213–233). Washington, DC: Urban Institute Press.

DeVita, C. J., Montilla, M., Reid, E. J., & Fatiregun, O. (2004). *Organizational factors influencing advocacy for children.* Washington, DC: The Urban Institute.

Dluhy, M. J. (1990). *Building coalitions in the human services.* Newbury Park, CA: Sage.

Dodd, P., & Gutierrez, L. M. (1990). Preparing students for the future: A power perspective on community practice. *Administration in Social Work, 14*(2), 63–78.

Donnelly, P. G., & Majka, T. J. (1998). Residents' efforts at neighborhood stabilization: Facing the challenges of inner-city neighborhoods. *Sociological Forum, 13*(2), 189–213.

Eisenberg, P. (2000a). The nonprofit sector in a changing world. *Nonprofit and Voluntary Sector Quarterly, 29*(2), 325–330.

Eisenberg, P. (2000b). Separate, we lose. *The Nonprofit Quarterly, 7*(2), 26–30.

Ezell, M. (1994). Advocacy practice of social workers. *Families in Society: The Journal of Contemporary Human Services, 75*(1), 36–46.

Ferre, M. I. (1987). Prevention and control of violence through community revitalization, individual dignity, and personal self-confidence. *Annals of the American Academy of Political and Social Science, 494,* 27–36.

Frumkin, P., & Andre-Clark, A. (2000). When missions, markets, and politics collide: Values and strategy in the nonprofit human services. *Nonprofit and Voluntary Sector Quarterly, 29,* 141–163.

Gamson, W. A. (1975). *The strategy of social protest.* Homewood, IL: The Dorsey Press.

Gibelman, M., & Kraft, S. (1996). Advocacy as a core agency program: Planning considerations for voluntary human service agencies. *Administration in Social Work, 20*(4), 43–59.

Goffman, E. (1974). *Frame analysis: An essay on the organization of experience.* Cambridge, MA: Harvard University Press.

Goodwin, R. K. (2001). Developing partnerships for greater success. In W. P. Pidgeon (Ed.), *The legislative labyrinth: A map for not-for-profits* (pp. 92–110). New York: John Wiley & Sons.

Grønbjerg, K. A., Cheney, L., Leadingham, S., & Liu, H. (2007). *Indiana capacity assessment: Indiana charities, 2007.* Bloomington: Indiana University School of Public and Environmental Affairs.

Gutierrez, L. M. (1992). Empowering ethnic minorities in the twenty-first century: The role of human service organizations. In Y. Hasenfeld (Ed.), *Human services as complex organizations* (pp. 320–338). Newbury Park, CA: Sage.

Hayes, K. S., & Mickelson, J. S. (2000). *Affecting change: Social workers in the political arena.* Boston: Allyn & Bacon.

Herbert, M. D., & Mould, J. W. (1992). The advocacy role in public child welfare. *Child Welfare, 71*(2), 114–130.

Hick, S. F., & McNutt, J. G. (Eds.). (2002). *Advocacy, activism and the internet: Community organization and social policy.* Chicago: Lyceum Books.

Hoefer, R. (2001). Highly effective human service interest groups: Seven key practices. *Journal of Community Practice, 9*(2), 1–13.

Hoefer, R., & Ferguson, K. (2007). Controlling the levers of power: How advocacy organizations affect the regulation writing process. *Journal of Sociology & Social Welfare, 34*(1), 83–108.

Hojnacki, M. (1997). Interest groups' decisions to join alliances or work alone. *American Journal of Political Science, 41*(1), 61–87.

Iyengar, S. (1990). Framing responsibility for political issues: The case of poverty. *Political Behavior, 12*(1), 19–40.

Jenkins, J. C. (1987). Nonprofit organizations and policy advocacy. In W. W. Powell (Ed.), *The nonprofit sector: A research handbook* (pp. 296–315). New Haven, CT: Yale University Press.

Jozefowicz-Simbeni, D. M. H., & Israel, N. (2006). Services to homeless students and families: The McKinney-Vento Act and its implications for school social work practice. *Children and Schools, 28*(1), 37–44.

Kurz, D. (1998). Women, welfare, and domestic violence. *Social Justice, 25*(1), 105–118.

Lakoff, G. (2004). *Don't think of an elephant! Know your values and frame the debate: The essential guide for progressives.* White River Junction, VT: Chelsea Green.

Lawrence, S., Jalandoni, N. T., & Smith, B. K. (2005). *Social justice grantmaking: A report on foundation trends.* New York: The Foundation Center.

Lofland, J. (1996). *Social movement organizations: Guide to research on insurgent realities.* New York: Aldine De Gruyter.

Marwell, N. P. (2004). Privatizing the welfare state: Nonprofit community-based organizations as political actors. *American Sociological Review, 69,* 265–291.

McAdam, D. (1982). *Political process and the development of black insurgency, 1930–1970.* Chicago: The University of Chicago Press.

McChesney, F. S. (2000). The practical economics of "pay to play" politics. In E. J. Reid (Ed.), *Structuring the inquiry into advocacy* (pp. 35–49). Washington, DC: Urban Institute Press.

Menefee, D. (2000). What managers do and why they do it. In R. Patti (Ed.), *The handbook of social welfare management* (pp. 247–266). Thousand Oaks, CA: Sage.

Mondros, J., & Wilson, S. (1994). *Organizing for power and empowerment.* New York: Columbia University Press.

Mor Barak, M. E., Travis, D., & Bess, G. (2004). Exploring managers' and administrators' retrospective perceptions of their MSW fieldwork experience: A national study. *Administration in Social Work, 28*(1), 21–44.

Mosley, J. E., Katz, H., Hasenfeld, Y., & Anheier, H. K. (2003). *The challenge of meeting social needs in Los Angeles: Nonprofit human service organizations in a diverse community.* Los Angeles: UCLA School of Public Policy and Social Research.

Mulroy, E. A. (2003). Community as a factor in implementing interorganizational partnerships: Issues, constraints, and adaptations. *Nonprofit Management and Leadership, 14,* 47–66.

NASW. (1999). *Code of ethics of the National Association of Social Workers.* Washington, DC: NASW Press.

Nicholson-Crotty, J. (2007). Politics, policy and the motivations for advocacy in nonprofit reproductive health and family planning providers. *Nonprofit and Voluntary Sector Quarterly, 36*(1), 5–21.

Pawlak, E. J., & Flynn, J. P. (1990). Executive directors' political activities. *Social Work, 35*(4), 307–312.

Pfeffer, J., & Salancik, G. R. (1978). *The external control of organizations: A resource dependence perspective.* New York: Harper & Row.

Raffa, T. (2000). Advocacy and lobbying without fear: What is allowed within a 501(c)(3) charitable organization. *The Nonprofit Quarterly, 7*(2), 44–47.

Rees, S. (1999). Strategic choices for nonprofit advocates. *Nonprofit and Voluntary Sector Quarterly, 28*(1), 65–73.

Reid, E. J. (1999). Nonprofit advocacy and political participation. In E. T. Boris & C. E. Steuerle (Eds.), *Nonprofits and government: Collaboration and conflict* (pp. 291–325). Washington, DC: Urban Institute Press.

Richan, W. C. (1996). *Lobbying for social change* (2nd ed.). New York: The Haworth Press.

Roelofs, J. (2003). *Foundations and public policy: The mask of pluralism.* Albany: State University of New York Press.

Salamon, L. M. (1995). *Partners in public service: Government-nonprofit relations in the modern welfare state.* Baltimore, MD: Johns Hopkins University Press.

Salkin, P. E., & Rutigliano, C. (1998). *Communications between New York nonprofits and government: Restrictions on lobbying.* Albany, NY: Government Law Center of Albany Law School.

Schneider, R. L., & Lester, L. (2001). *Social work advocacy: A new framework for action.* Belmont, CA: Brooks/Cole.

Scott, J., & Carson, N. (2003). Who's afraid of real returns? *Alliance, 8*(3), 35–37.

Scott, W. R., Deschenes, S., Hopkins, K., Newman, A., & McLaughlin, M. (2006). Advocacy organizations and the field of youth services: Ongoing efforts to restructure a field. *Nonprofit and Voluntary Sector Quarterly, 35*(4), 691714.

Sherraden, M. S., Slosar, B., & Sherraden, M. (2002). Innovation in social policy: Collaborative policy advocacy. *Social Work, 47*(3), 209–221.

Sosin, M. (1986). *Private benefits: Material assistance in the private sector.* Orlando, FL: Academic Press.

Story, R. (2001). Adding light to the heat: Using the mass media to support your issues. In W. P. Pidgeon (Ed.), *The legislative labyrinth: A map for not-for-profits.* New York: John Wiley & Sons.

Turner, R. H., & Killian, L. M. (1987). *Collective behavior* (3rd ed.). Englewood Cliffs, NJ: Prentice Hall.

Tversky, A., & Kahneman, D. (1981). The framing of decisions and the psychology of choice. *Science, 211*(4481), 453–458.

Wolk, J. L., Pray, J. E., Weismiller, T., & Dempsey, D. (1996). Political practica: Educating social work students for policymaking. *Journal of Social Work Education, 32*(1), 91–100.

PART 6

Looking to the Future: Practice Trends and Management Education

P art 6 looks at likely future directions of human services management from two perspectives: managers themselves and academics who prepare students for administrative careers. While each group necessarily focuses on somewhat different issues, it is interesting to see the points at which they converge. This is encouraging because there is a pressing need for these two communities to collaborate far more extensively than they have typically done in past years. Managers play a role in this collaboration by participating in the teaching of management both as adjunct professors and intern instructors and, importantly, by articulating the kinds of skills future managers will need to be effective. Academics, for their part, should build more bridges to the practice community so they can better track changes occurring in a rapidly evolving field of practice, to strengthen the relevance of their curricula and inform their research.

In Chapter 23, Gary Bess, a former administrator and long-time consultant to social agencies, reports on the results of intensive interviews with seasoned human services managers regarding future practice trends. These views are especially interesting because they provide an unadorned view of the constraints and pressures facing agency managers and changes that are occurring in the industry that have important implications for administration. They also resonate many of the themes presented in previous chapters regarding, for example, the pressures for performance and accountability, the demands of leadership, the challenges of motivating workers, fundraising, information technology, and others.

The final chapter, by Rick Hoefer, critically examines the state of management education in schools of social work. Although social work education has been educating managers for several decades, Professor Hoefer argues that these programs may not offer sufficient breadth and depth and instructional capability to adequately prepare students for leadership positions in this field (though they seem to do a better job with preparation for middle management). A number of the instructional and structural challenges facing schools are addressed, as are several strategies schools might pursue to improve the quality of management education.

CHAPTER 23

Practitioners' Views on the Future of Human Service Management

Gary Bess

A good way to consider the future of human services management is to talk with human services managers who have been successful in their careers and ask them to think about what the future will require of them and others in light of changing expectations, values, technology, and resource requirements. This chapter's discussion was developed from a consensus of input from human services managers who were interviewed concerning challenges facing their institutions and their views about the next 10 to 15 years and what will be required of them and their institutions. What will be expected of leaders? Will competition for resources increase? How will accountability be measured? How will workforce competition change?

In one of the opening scenes in the 1974 classic *The Towering Inferno,* a simple flashing warning light triggered by a sensor foreshadows the poorly constructed 135-story skyscraper's demise. In a similar way, many of the insights and observations made by our panel of experts foretell a future in human services management that is dependent on an infrastructure that can withstand today's onslaught of predictable as well as unpredictable events. To withstand the latter, which will be discussed below, an organization requires the capacity to temporarily deal with the unexpected, sufficient resources to respond, and the resiliency to absorb an unanticipated impact.

The panel of 20 managers interviewed for this chapter was composed of master's and PhD-level social workers currently employed as CEOs or senior managers or working as consultants to a wide array of health and human services organizations. They each had more than 20 years of mid- and executive-level human services management responsibility and were well regarded among peers for their professionalism and success on behalf of their organizations. Many were also

Certified Social Work Managers, a peer-reviewed designation given by the National Network for Social Work Managers based on 12 competencies that range from human resources management to advocacy and ethics to program design, evaluation, and budgeting (Wimpheimer, 2004). Each interview was conducted by this author, and respondents were asked to reflect on the continuing importance of the management competency levels espoused by the Network, as well as their views on leadership, consumer involvement, technology, and organizational accountability. The open-ended interview format, while obtaining input on currently acknowledged competencies, also allowed for a wide range of exploration of possible new competencies and standards for social work management.

Complexity in Management and Leadership

Managers underscored the complexity of leading an organization today, a trend that all said will become even more challenging in the future. Interviewees across sectors and service disciplines emphasized growing regulatory and accountability standards that require well-recorded documentation of their services, their developmental and programmatic activities related to new initiatives, and their financial management. This complexity is compounded by multiple streams of funding among large organizations and differing definitions of clients, service units, and permissible expenditures, and all agreed that teams of high-functioning middle and senior managers will be required to comply with requirements established by regulatory, oversight, and funding organizations. Senior managers and CEOs, most of whom were 25 or more years post-graduate school, were quick to add that younger workers were more adept at using technology to track and comply with requirements and that these skills will continue to be necessary in the future.

Along with the left brain function of compiling, managing, and reporting information, right brain functions such as creatively managing people and teams will also be a continuing requirement for managers. People management skills were cited as a key leadership attribute and something that comes naturally to some, but not to all. While returning e-mails after hours or via their Blackberry allowed them to communicate with their staffs, most expressed a conviction that this was not a replacement for "face time," when they could discuss matters of importance to the organization, talk personally about their expectations, and provide encouragement.

While transparently fair employment practices and adherence to laws comprise one important facet of a manager's role as a supervisor in today's litigious environment, motivating employees to see the big picture and understand how their actions contribute to the organization's fulfillment of its mission is an everyday and sometimes daunting challenge. (See Chapter 7 for further discussion of leadership functions.) The respondents observed that while employees of human services organizations are motivated by more than remuneration, a shift in workforce composition has occurred as organizations have grown and become more specialized and technologically dependent. Senior managers and CEOs report that because of the complexity of the work to be done, they have chosen skill over commitment in hiring new employees, though they value both, believing that the latter can be inculcated through the work environment and the supervising manager's influence. Leadership through the modeling of qualities that make for a humanistic organization was cited by many as an ongoing challenge and responsibility, often mitigated by competing priorities that left insufficient time for quality interactions.

A related challenge in complex multiservice organizations is addressing competing priorities and deadlines. CEOs and senior managers expressed their desire to support their staffs in determining what is most important among their several looming deadlines and responsibilities. All respondents reported that they and their subordinates have never been busier in their careers, using such phrases as multitasking or shifting gears to describe their constant movement from one issue to the next. They emphasized the importance of having realistic expectations of employees, understanding that even competent workers may not easily transition from issue to issue and that sensitivity on the part of managers is necessary. Many saw their role as the fulcrum for the management of employee workloads and feared that asking too much of subordinates too quickly would adversely affect employee morale. CEOs and senior managers reported that they monitored workloads and due dates along with their employees to make sure that deadlines would be met and that staff and other resources were sufficient for each assignment.

All emphasized the importance of sense making, priority setting, and negotiating (and buffering) for their staffs in the face of unrealistic or conflicting report deadlines from internal as well as external sources. Political as well as intellectual skills in priority setting were identified as necessary qualities for managers.

Several CEOs and senior managers also discussed their relationships with external funders and regulatory bodies, such as project officers for private foundations and public agencies responsible for monitoring grants and contracts, and with accreditation and credentialing bodies. A universal theme was redundancy and inconsistency of information reporting within and across these institutions. This is not a new issue per se; conflicting methods for counting service units, defining encounters, determining eligibility, and tracking the frequency and intensity of user services have been regularly cited over the years as inefficient and often irreconcilable.

One difference, however, is that some CEOs and senior managers discussed their collaborative involvement with similar service providers and within their professional associations to advocate for changing these policies and practices, including meeting with regulatory body representatives and working with elected officials to introduce legislation that would encourage consistency among public agencies. Though they acknowledged their dependency on these institutions and did not want to jeopardize their

relationships, CEOs and senior managers expressed guarded optimism that in some areas, especially within similar systems (e.g., the federal Departments of Health and Human Services, Education), increased comparability of reporting requirements could be achieved.

Consumer Involvement

CEOs and senior managers foresaw a continuing emphasis on ethical practice principles and client-centered services. They also expressed their struggle with the application of these values in their agencies and what they perceived as sometimes unrealistic expectations by grantors and oversight organizations with regard to consumer (client) involvement. One example cited was the establishment of consumer majorities on boards of directors of large complex organizations. This is a requirement, for example, of the federal Bureau of Primary Heath Care as a condition of a nonprofit community health center's designation as a Federally Qualified Health Center (FQHC). The requirement is that low-income patients— bona fide consumers of services—possibly without experience in governance, finance and budgeting, healthcare services delivery, human resources, and other management expertise, must comprise the majority of the board.

The panelists reported that meaningful consumer involvement represented a training and education challenge for them as managers and for nonconsumer volunteer board members. These expectations will likely remain and, consequently, human services managers will be challenged to provide the training and support that those without governance experience will need to fulfill their responsibilities as board members. They also discussed resistance that they sometimes observe from other members of the board who hail from higher socioeconomic circumstances than the consumers, and they admitted to struggling with their own biases in narrowly defining consumer roles and competencies. CEOs and senior managers reported that among their priorities is working with their present board's leadership to accept new members with backgrounds and life experiences different from their own and to educate consumers, many of whom have little formal education or even bank accounts, to function at a level that supports the mission and goals of the organization.

While the FQHC experience may seem extreme, there are comparable movements to include mental health, substance abuse, and youth consumers on boards and committees and to hire them as staff. Respondents acknowledged that they saw benefits in the growing emphasis on consumer involvement, including assurances that quality services were being delivered and the agency remained responsive to client needs, and they emphasized their responsibility to make sure that consumers and former clients were prepared for these roles in the organization.

Governance

In addition to discussing the emerging role of consumers in organizations and on boards, CEOs and senior managers also discussed the dynamics between management staff and volunteer boards. Several organizations have adopted a corporate model of governance, whereby the executive director is the chief executive officer (CEO), the finance director is the chief financial officer (CFO), the development director is the chief development officer (CDO), the program director is the chief program officer (CPO), and so on. Their counterparts on the board include conventional positions of chair, vice chairs, treasurer, and secretary (see Chapter 18 for further discussion of boards of nonprofit human services agencies).

Some organizations have also moved to allowing executive management to serve as voting board members, and in some instances, the CEO also holds the dual title of corporation president. Some observers suggested that the change in nomenclature is an acknowledgment that professionalism in human services management is regarded with the same esteem as applied to titans of industry or commerce who share the same titles, and that they elevate the holder's

position when representing his or her institution to corporate bodies and elected officials. Some also say that it clarifies roles and responsibilities, emphasizing high-level management expectations for senior staff.

While this trend continues, some managers also discussed their concern that as their organizations have grown, the commitment of their volunteer board members to the organization's mission and bottom line was less than their own, which created an imbalance in their respective dedication to the agency. Votes by the board on high-stake decisions affecting the nonprofit corporation were, at times, considered by scant quorums of members who had not reviewed collateral materials sent in advance for the meeting. A few members said that they were not averse to compensating members if it would increase their level of involvement.

Managers also discussed strategies to engage their boards, such as mandatory annual retreats, performance reviews, and attendance policies, and they saw these tactics as necessary to increase board member involvement. Some reflected on the changes that management has experienced in the past 10 to 15 years, such as increasing emphasis on quality assurance, risk management, outcome measurements, and a work environment of potentially litigious situations involving employees, clients, or vendors, and questioned whether their boards understood these new challenges. Yet, believing that a strong and involved board and a strong and involved management staff was still the best governance model for viable human services organizations, CEOs and senior managers said that their board's understanding of issues could no longer be taken for granted and that education of board members vis-à-vis a board development plan was necessary and increasingly important, in order for their organizations to go forward.

Technology

Not surprisingly, staying current with rapidly developing technologies that enhance health and human services management and accountability was universally identified as important. While having general competency in managing e-mail, word processing, and using simple databases were seen as indispensable skills for most human services employees, including CEOs and senior managers, the frontier of new technologies (e.g., electronic client records, wireless data transfer from the field, or video conferencing for meetings and consults) were reportedly just beginning to take hold (see Chapter 9 for further discussion of information technologies). Managers discussed the relative advantage of these information technology wonders in terms of return on investment and their impact on efficiency (e.g., cost savings and improved access to services), quality of care, and staff morale. Many of them were just beginning to select practice management systems or to substantially improve their current systems.

Panelists discussed the benefits of improving efficiencies in data management for service reporting to funders and stakeholders and the indispensable utility of database software for program planning. Combining descriptive information on clients with their service utilization histories or being able to map client residences using Geographic Information System (GIS) software are among the current and new possibilities that are associated with practice management databases. This information, they said, informs their staffs of client utilization patterns and allows them to monitor trends from baseline reports. It also generates data for new grant funders by providing accurate and up-to-date information on current users of services. For detailed comparative analysis, this information can easily be cross-tabulated by selected patient or service utilization variables, such as age, gender, race/ethnicity, frequency of visit, or diagnosis.

Deciding when to take the leap and to purchase these technologies was an often-cited challenge. The dilemma of not knowing for sure that the technology will do the job and that something even better or less costly is not around the corner was an ever-present concern among managers. Cost also figured substantially into their decision making because most systems required, in addition to capital expenses associated with hardware and software acquisition, maintenance and subscription outlays as well. New line items in budgets, such as IT (Information Technology), were emerging as general fund expenses, which, managers lamented, were difficult to assign to grants and contracts, though some were attempting to establish indirect (overhead) rates that would account for these costs. Most organizations had one or more IT specialists on their staff, having found it less expensive than contracting for this expertise (see Chapter 9 for pros and cons of this decision).

Large-scale conversion to new technologies had its own set of concerns. While the apocryphal notion that younger employees are more adept at and receptive to new technologies was often expressed, systems changes, which required staff retraining in procedures, equipment usage, and terminology, were viewed as among the most complex and challenging of undertakings for an organization. Those who had been through the process emphasized the importance of planning and preparing staff for the transition. Discussing the benefits of the technology and involving staff in the process of determining systems and design, where customization is possible, was reported to increase buy-in, as well as improve utilization. Having personable trainers available on site to immediately respond to questions and to explain procedures was also viewed as key to reducing frustration and accelerating adaptation.

Work Flexibility

Workplace expectations among a younger workforce were reported to be changing, and several managers discussed their struggles in competing for and accommodating qualified employees by offering flexible work arrangements. Some organizations had moved to four-day work weeks, and others offered earlier starting times to support commuting employees who otherwise would be caught in rush hour traffic or others with children or aging parents to pick up or drop off. Some said that the time clock was a thing of the past and that accountability was being measured by output and outcome, not by the number of hours on task. This, they said, was also true for clerical and reception employees, who could be anywhere and working from offsite computers on the Internet to type and file or answer and transfer calls.

Some also reported on a trend toward hiring older workers as second careerists. Valuing their maturity and work ethic, and understanding preferences for less than full-time employment, managers said that they were rethinking job requirements to accommodate part-time and possibly alternative schedule workers. Some second careerists, managers reported, could step into management positions such as human resources, finance, and operations, while others, by virtue of their life experiences, could be deployed as case managers or intake staff or trainers. Some older workers were also returning to school, pursuing certificates or degrees in healthcare and social work management and mental heath and substance abuse counseling.

Believing that the most qualified people should be hired, CEOs and managers said that in today's and tomorrow's high-tech era, work flexibility is an important inducement for new employees. While certain positions remain agency-based, such as reception for walk-in traffic and clinical care and management, certain administrative functions can often be handled offsite or in fewer hours. This opens up a wide range of employment possibilities and structures.

Social Marketing and Outreach

Increasing competition for clients, as well as the difficulty of reaching treatment-resistant populations, were seen as challenges that were expected to continue and expand. In some fields, like healthcare, substance abuse, mental health, and education, there is competition for users of services who participate in publicly funded or private managed care programs, who receive Medicaid or SSI benefits, who have private insurance, or who can be qualified for other payer sources that cover all or part of their treatment.

Historically, human services organizations have passively advertised their availability by providing information about their services but not actively promoting them or offering incentives for clients to enroll. Today, however, terms such as *social marketing* and *service branding* are part of the lexicon used by resource developers and managers to describe their proactive service marketing strategies (see Chapter 16 for a discussion of marketing in the human services).

This development is a dramatic change from times past. Today, managers and finance officers calculate break-even points based on client composition and their payer sources and establish targets for the number of beds or counseling sessions that need to be filled in order to maintain a balanced budget. They also make assumptions about the levels of reimbursement by first and third parties and the amount of funds that will be disallowed due to weak documentation because numerous grants and contracts require organizations to document the units of service provided based on client eligibility and to demonstrate improvements in health, well-being, functionality, employment, or other desirable transformations resulting from their services. While resisting on ethical grounds the temptation to *cream*—select clients considered especially amenable to the organization's services—there is clearly competition for new clients. Some human services organizations rely on marketing professionals to advise on strategies, to produce promotional materials, and to augment their outreach staff's efforts through targeted materials and promotions. One agency executive of a residential substance abuse treatment program reported that he had authorized the development of several printed brochures and a new Web site based on market analysis and the identification of the following six potentially distinct referral sources:

- *Families and friends,* who often become aware of the addiction before their loved one does;
- *Employers,* who do not want to lose valuable employees and colleagues;

- *Clergy,* who are approached for pastoral counseling;
- *Therapists,* who are called to intervene in family and/or personal crises and realize that addiction is a precipitating component;
- *Physicians,* whose patients seek medical excuses for absences due to headaches or stress or who fear that excess alcohol consumption will cause adverse reactions to prescription drugs; and
- *Treatment Center Professionals* seeking outpatient resources for clients completing inpatient/primary care services.

Though common in the business and sales worlds, this form of promotion is just beginning to take root in the human services field and is likely to continue. Some organizations, such as those in the healthcare field with managed care contracts, also reported offering incentives for clients to change providers and to enroll and remain with their agencies. These incentives included compensation for completing enrollment forms and fast food meal vouchers.

Grants and Contracts Compliance

Maintaining accountability to donors and funders, with a concomitant emphasis on credibility, which is sometimes referred to as *trust,* has led some organizations to create the position of *compliance officer* to oversee grants and contracts. Generally responsible for assuring that a grant or contract is being administered according to the original proposal's plan or funder expectations and that mechanisms are in place to document and report service levels and short- and long-term outcomes, the compliance officer is the linchpin for coordinating reports from program management, financial management, and IT staff.

In recent years, agencies and grantors have become increasingly driven by measurable outcomes. Both parties have developed sophistication in understanding and measuring program

impacts (for further discussion of outcome measurement, see Chapter 8). CEOs and senior managers point to the importance of developing practical assessment and measurement designs. Relying at times on evaluation consultants to help in planning and assessment oversight, human services organizations are sometimes challenged by grantors to justify their interventions with evidence that their methods work. With different standards for evidence-based practice, however, and the unevenness in research across service areas, it is not always possible to identify an effective practice. Even so, the organization's capacity to operationalize and document outcomes in client functioning and well-being will continue to be expected and can make the difference in its ability to successfully compete for grants and contracts. Once funding is received, the organization needs to put into place the necessary infrastructure to obtain and compile documentation showing that the outcomes were achieved.

Timely compilation of service information is often tied to financial reimbursements and is dependent upon integrated practice management and/or other database systems. With growing frequency, reports can be generated in formats or on forms acceptable to contract agencies, thus eliminating the need to re-record information before it is submitted. In some instances, financial information must accompany program reports and is expected to be commensurate with reported service levels. The compliance officer is responsible for preparing reports to funders that are accurate and complete, minimizing disallowed costs and/or returned payment requests due to errors in calculation, and reconciling discontinuities between reporting periods or discontinuities between expenditure reports and program reports.

Progress and final reports are also often electronically submitted, which requires technical knowledge in that information is often encrypted before being transmitted. Several federal and state offices require electronic submission and have also moved toward system-wide data reporting. For example, the federal Health and

Both sides of the equation

Human Services Administration's reliance on the Government Performance Results Act (GPRA) of 1993 for compiling comparable information across grantees requires the use of standard forms and progressive online submissions of data. Some organizations have dedicated IT staff to manage these data and have hired or contracted with evaluators to oversee these requirements. With greater use of the Internet and the ability to electronically manipulate and transfer program and financial information without ever having a hard copy in hand, CEOs and senior managers reported that organizations will increasingly require the internal capacity and resources (e.g., hardware, integrated software, and personnel) to conform to heightened paperless transmission expectations.

Implications

There is strong support among CEOs and senior managers for bringing social workers into management rather than managers into social work. Several stated that they believe that client-centered humanistic organizations are the best form of human services delivery. They also expressed a conviction that social work education for managers, albeit not as rounded or as in-depth as they would prefer, was still the best of all alternatives for preparing the next generation of managers to take the helm of large, complex organizations. Additional preparation was considered desirable in the domains of budgeting, governance issues, human resources management and supervision, and resource development.

As may be apparent from the preceding discussion, there is considerable interplay and overlap in managerial skill sets and responsibilities. While the thread of humanistic values and client-centered services will continue to permeate their work, CEOs and senior managers acknowledged that the complexity of their roles means that while they rely on e-mail and cell phones to keep things moving along, they must also consciously carve out time to provide visible leadership to their organizations. Although technology is a

tool for improvements in management and services and must be embraced due to external expectations of technological competence, the need for face-to-face interactions is likely to continue, requiring managers to retain focus on their leadership responsibilities.

CEOs and senior managers also understand that their and their organization's success is tied to the role that their boards of directors play in representing the interests of the community and of consumers of services. These expectations, along with the ethical imperative to involve beneficiaries of services in the organization's governance and services structure, will require a commitment to this value and the time and training resources to prepare and fully integrate consumers. A comparable effort should also be directed to board members, recognizing that they may be resistant to a shift in board composition to include persons who hail from different socioeconomic strata and life experiences.

Volunteer boards also must be evaluated to ensure that they fulfill their fiduciary responsibilities to provide oversight for nonprofit human services corporations. As organizations have adopted corporate structures with management staff seated on the board as voting members, the role of board members needs to be reconsidered. Though agency boards will continue to assume legal responsibility for their organizations' action, selection and oversight of the CEO and senior managers is a critical function because board members defer to human services managers for the day-to-day running of the institution and for information on the agency's viability. There is also an increasing expectation that board members should be at least conversant in key standards of performance (e.g., understanding balance sheets and revenue and expenditure reports, quality assurance and outcome measurements, and legal and regulatory compliance requirements).

The use of alternative and part-time work arrangements is also likely to continue. Defining productivity based on output, rather than a measurement of time on task, is a different way of looking at job expectations and opens up possibilities for recruiting competent workers whose lives and/or lifestyles preclude full-time or conventional work hours. Finding fairness in employment flexibility in human services organizations, like other work settings, is challenging.

Social marketing and branding are now part of discussions in the human services field. While success with these kinds of focused efforts is seen as necessary for the organization, ethical considerations are imbedded in these strategic approaches to client recruitment and resource development. Although qualifying clients for programs to which they are entitled helps clients and represents resources that fuel the human services organization, CEOs and senior managers are held to a higher level of accountability than simply "truth in advertising." As social work managers they must ask, What is in the best interests of the vulnerable populations and who is the best provider of care? Taking service outreach and resource development to new levels is clearly necessary, and doing so will take skills and creative energies that social work managers may be uniquely positioned to apply.

Last, grant and contract accountability that relies on database management, the use of specialized software, integration of reports from finance and service functions, and dedicated IT and compliance staff will likely only expand. Much like an orchestra conductor, social work managers will continue to be required to direct the harmonious assimilation of informational components into comprehensive and accurate reporting. They also need to be schooled in program evaluation and assessment and remain current on evidence-based practices that are relevant to their service areas.

Judging from the panel's comments and the enthusiasm with which they were expressed, the next few years, like the last few, will be characterized by stunning advances in technology, new organizational structures and management roles, and a constant and accelerated flow of information within and across organizations. Amid these changes, however, there will also remain the need for grounded, humanistic, and client-centered manager-leaders.

Reference

Wimpheimer, S. (2004). Leadership and management competencies defined by practicing social work managers: An overview of standards developed by the National Network of Social Work Managers. *Administration in Social Work, 31*(4), 45–56.

CHAPTER 24

Preparing Managers for the Human Services

Identifying and Overcoming Current Barriers in Social Work Management Education

Richard Hoefer

S ocial work management education faces tremendous obstacles in preparing students for social work administration jobs. While we have learned what current managers and selected academics believe should be taught to administration students, several barriers prevent us from feeling comfortable as we view the present situation. First, evidence is lacking that social work faculty are adequately prepared to teach basic skills, much less the advanced skills students and alumni need to be hired in top-level positions. Second, social work schools have not developed an atmosphere that is truly supportive of management studies and students. Finally, social work administration education has not made a convincing case for the superiority of its degree programs compared to other management programs, such as the Master in Business or Master in Public Administration.

In this chapter, we examine the current context of social work administration and administration education and the purposes of social work professional training (particularly in administration). We ask what should be in the social work administration curriculum, whether schools of social work have the capability to teach it, how social work students perceive their management education, what current practitioners believe about social work administration education graduates, and, finally, what can be done to improve social work management education.

The Context of Social Work Administration and Administration Education

The larger context of social work administrative practice must be considered before any discussion of human services administration education can meaningfully take place. The literature is replete

483

with studies addressing how social work managers must be aware of, and deal with, changes in their agencies' worlds. Managed care (Jones, 2006; McBeath & Meezan, 2006), an uncertain political and economic climate (Golensky & Mulder, 2006; Hopkins & Hyde, 2002; Schmid, 2004), policy reform (Regehr, Chau, Leslie, & Howe, 2002; Reisch & Sommerfeld, 2003), requirements for outcome budgeting (Martin, 2000), and the introduction of performance measurement systems (Zimmermann & Stevens, 2006) are just a few topics affecting social work administrators today.

Although many trends are important, seven are described here as having significant impact on social work administrators and social work management education. The first three, while predominantly concerned with administrative practice, should be considered in designing and implementing social work education for administrators.

- *Administrators operate in an environment of scarce resources, increased competition for resources (if only because the number of human services nonprofits is increasing), and other boundary-spanning concerns.* Challenges are greater now for human services agencies than ever before (Adams & Perlmutter, 1995; Hopkins & Hyde, 2002). The range of skills needed to cope with this difficult environment is also greater than in the past (Golensky & Mulder, 2006). Administrators not only need to be competent at internally oriented activities such as budgeting, grant writing, supervision, and other internally oriented capabilities; they also need skill in externally oriented capacities such as advocacy, community collaboration, and strategic planning (Alexander, 2000; Golensky & Mulder, 2006; Hoefer, 2003; Hopkins & Hyde, 2002; Menefee, 2000; Menefee & Thompson, 1994). Increasingly, cross-sector partnerships involving the government, business, and nonprofit sectors are the way to achieve progress on social issues (Selsky & Parker, 2005). Social work managers thus must respect and understand how to collaborate with counterparts in other sectors. Social work management educators must incorporate knowledge of other sectors into their courses.

- *Evidence-based practice and research/program evaluation are becoming more important to funders and other stakeholders.* As the need to compete for resources intensifies, human services agencies must become more effective. One way to accomplish this is to use service technologies that have research to support their claims of helping solve client problems. The movement towards evidence-based practice, while compelling theoretically, may require culture change within agencies (Johnson & Austin, 2006). As difficult as this is to accomplish, some grant-providing agencies, such as the federal Substance Abuse and Mental Health Services Administration (SAMHSA), provide strong incentives and greater funding opportunities for agencies willing to use program models that have been tested empirically and have evidence of effectiveness. Interventions that have received research validation are listed on the National Registry of Evidence-Based Programs and Practices (available online at www.nrepp .samhsa.gov/). Additional reviews of evidence-based social work practice are located on the Web site for the Campbell Collaboration (www.camp bellcollaboration.org) and elsewhere. Similarly, research and program evaluation within agencies is usually required as a condition of receiving a grant, and agencies struggle with how to cope with such demands, having neither the staff time nor the knowledge base to analyze data they collect (Stoecker, 2007; also see Chapter 23 for managers' perspectives on this issue). Performance measurement, within the context of program evaluation and accountability, is a salient example of the need for additional research skills for nonprofit managers (Zimmermann & Stevens, 2006). Salipante and Aram (2003) argue that nonprofit managers must move beyond being users of knowledge to becoming generators of knowledge. Education for social work administration should stress the ability to collect, manage, and analyze data to make management decisions.

- *A crisis in social work leadership of human services agencies has emerged.* Social work education is currently producing fewer administrative practice students than in the past (Ezell, Chernesky,

& Healy, 2004). In addition, it seems clear that the social work profession has lost ground in leading agencies in core fields such as aging, mental health, disabilities, housing, and homelessness (Perlmutter, 2006; Wuenschel, 2006). At the same time, the number of business schools, schools of public administration, and programs in nonprofit management producing graduates who compete with social workers for administrative jobs has increased rapidly (Mirabella, 2007; Packard, 2004). Research shows that experienced leaders in nonprofit institutions (whether social workers or not) are leaving the field (Birdsell & Muzzio, 2003; Faffer & Friedland, 2007; Teegarden, 2004). Not only are current leaders retiring, but many direct service social workers, their supervisors, and even middle-level managers exhibit little desire to take over top positions within their agencies (Faffer & Friedland, 2007). Social work education, more so than ever, must find ways to entice and enroll more students, particularly women and people of color, who aspire to positions of leadership.

The Educational Context

In addition to these three trends affecting the practice world of social work administration, management education in social work has its own context and concerns. Four factors are addressed here: the emphasis within social work education on direct practice, the assumption that administration students need the same foundation for practice that direct practice students need, accreditation standards for social work education, and the expansion in the number of social work education programs.

- *The main goal of social work education has always been to train professionals in direct practice.* Most schools of social work educate the vast majority of their students in direct practice skills. Only a tiny minority specialize in administration (about 3% of MSW students; Patti, 2000). When only about 1,000 students across the country matriculate in the social work administration

specialization, Deans, Provosts, and University Presidents are unlikely to allocate larger shares of financial resources to schools of social work for that purpose. It must seem more strategic to promote new programs in other academic units that have broader appeal (Wuenschel, 2006). This process leads to a downward spiral. Fewer administration students in a program leads to fewer resources (faculty time, class sections, fieldwork opportunities). Fewer opportunities in administration education leads to students choosing a different concentration or degree option, and the cycle continues.

- *An assumption exists, expressed in the accreditation requirements for schools of social work, that all social workers should have the same educational foundation.* The accrediting body for social work education, the Council on Social Work Education (CSWE), is thus involved in the plight of administration education. Because all social work education programs must be accredited by CSWE, programs follow the Educational Policy and Accreditation Standards (EPAS), which state that specializations (such as administration) must build upon a professional foundation. This reduces a potential two-year administration education by nearly half, as administration students complete credits in direct practice theories and techniques (Perlmutter, 2006). This dilutes students' management education considerably, compared to what is received by students in the Master of Business Administration (MBA), Master of Public Administration (MPA), and Master of Nonprofit Organizations (MNO). Less coursework and internship experience in administration may mean that MSW students are not as well-qualified as graduates of other programs for administrative jobs.

- *Controversy and frequent changes in CSWE standards for accreditation.* Social work education is embroiled in controversy, both from without and within. The National Association of Scholars (2007), a self-avowed conservative organization, has attacked the accreditation standards of CSWE for indoctrinating, rather than educating, students. Controversy exists inside social work education, as well. Stoesz (2002) believes that CSWE has been captured by various interest groups who have been able to insert their desired topics into the required foundation curriculum components. At least eight elements must be included in the foundation year: values and ethics, diversity, populations at risk and social and economic justice, human behavior and the social environment, social welfare policy and services, social work practice, research, and field education. Given that there may only be 30 credit hours of course work to cover all eight topics, the level of knowledge on any one topic attained by students is surely diluted. In addition to the problem of attenuated education, CSWE standards for accreditation change frequently, meaning that schools generally do not respond to the same standards from one reaffirmation self-study to the next. (Recent examples of this are the requirement to use different measures of educational outcomes than just a few years ago, and the new standards being drafted as this book goes to press. A school could thus have begun a reaffirmation round under one set of standards, been judged according to a second set, and be looking at needing to incorporate a third set into its next reaffirmation process.) Such constant change makes it difficult for schools to learn from past efforts. It also lessens their ability to gather longitudinal data about students and graduates because data collection efforts become outdated when new goals are adopted to match ever-changing CSWE standards.

- *CSWE has accredited large numbers of programs in recent years at both the bachelor and master's levels, which may compromise the quality of faculty and students.* While there is no doubt that some programs have accomplished faculty and strong students, it is likely that an overall dilution of talent is occurring. One result of increasing the number of accredited programs is to lower admission standards as new programs compete with established ones for students (Stoesz, 2002). Another result is to weaken the strength of social

work education as a whole as new programs must hire from an academic pool that is growing slowly, if at all. These new educators may be, as a group, less experienced and less rigorously educated in their specializations than faculty members hired before the expansion of accredited programs. Doctoral programs are not producing new graduates at the rate that retirements are occurring among an aging social work professoriate, so it is difficult to see how new programs are being staffed with faculty as academically well-prepared as the current cohort. The use of adjuncts has increased tremendously to keep pace with enrollments and manage class sizes. Students are not as academically qualified as those in other professional schools, either. Stoesz (2002) notes that social work student Graduate Record Exam scores are the lowest of all major disciplinary categories in the three areas of the test—verbal, quantitative, and analytical. Anecdotal reports suggest that students' education for administrative practice may be hampered by low-level skills in writing, use of numbers, and critical thinking and analysis. This, and the use of instructors who may have limited exposure to social work education themselves, can lead to less qualified students who are generally less qualified graduates. A tacit admission of the problem was made by the Social Work Congress, a group of over 400 leaders from the National Association of Social Workers, the Association of Baccalaureate Program Directors, the Council on Social Work Education, and the National Association of Deans and Directors of Schools of Social Work, which adopted the following statement as an imperative to be accomplished within 10 years: "Increase the value proposition of social work by raising standards and increasing academic rigor of social work education programs" (Social Work Congress, 2005).

Anyone trying to improve future prospects for social work administration education must begin by understanding the current situation. With this contextual information as a backdrop, we next examine the purposes of social work administration education.

The Purposes of Social Work Administration Education

A process is said to fail when it does not accomplish its goals. What are (or should be) the goals of social work education when it comes to human services administration at the master's level? Agreement does not exist on the answer to this question (Au, 1994). The CSWE (2007) describes the purposes of social work education as to "prepare competent and effective professionals, to develop social work knowledge, and to provide leadership in the development of service delivery systems."

The CSWE formulation is noticeably short on details, befitting an organization moving toward greater diversity in programmatic and educational approaches, with more emphasis on measuring educational program outcomes than on directing what the specific outcomes should be. Still, more specificity about what social work administration students are supposed to learn is important.

A more precise view regarding the purpose of a social work professional education is provided by Armitage and Clark (1975), who argue that

1. the ultimate purpose of a profession is practice,

2. the purpose of professional education is to effectively teach practice behaviors,

3. practice behaviors can be specified as the operational objectives of social work education. (cited in Gingerich, Kaye, & Bailey, 1999, p. 120)

Following this formulation, graduates of administration-focused social work education should be able to perform the practice behaviors of social work administrators, a topic covered in detail below. This is similar in spirit to Patti's statement:

If graduate education has not instilled ways of thinking about organizational issues and

managerial strategies for addressing them, if it has not socialized graduates to the expectations of managers, if it has not imparted technical skills and language, then potential employers are not likely to perceive graduates as credible candidates for managerial jobs (Patti, 2000, p. 18).

I propose two goals for social work administration education programs. First, students should obtain required knowledge, learn managerial skills, and develop the attitudes and ethical perspectives necessary to become successful administration practitioners. Student knowledge should come from both classroom and field experiences. Second, the MSW administration degree should be viewed as the preferred. degree for managers to have at all levels of human services agency management. Thus, alumni should be positioned in the job market to obtain employment as managers at all levels to a greater extent than graduates of other types of academic programs.

As we move through the rest of this chapter, we will see just how well social work education's realities match these two rather innocuous-seeming goals. We address the following questions:

1. Do we know what should be in a social work administration curriculum?

2. If so, do schools of social work have the capability to adequately teach this material, and, if they do, can schools of social work teach the material at least as well as in competitive fields of study?

3. Do students have an environment conducive to learning the material?

4. What do people currently in agency leadership positions think about the social work master's degree with a specialization in administration, particularly compared to other management degrees?

5. What can be done to improve the situation?

What Should Be in a Social Work Administration Curriculum?

In order to answer this question, we first look at several studies indicating what social work administrators do in their jobs currently and what they believe are important skills, values, experiences, and knowledge sets for social work managers to possess. Then we examine the quality of textbooks in social work administration.

Studies of What Social Work Managers Do and Should Know

The mid-1990s saw considerable research to answer basic questions in the field of social work administration. Two vital questions addressed are "What *do* human services managers *do?*" and "What *should* human services managers *know how to do?*"

Menefee and Thompson (1994) rightly state that "Understanding what contemporary social work managers do, how frequently they do it, and how important it is . . . may provide the social work management educator with ideas for improving or updating course designs and teaching methods" (p. 2). This section looks at three major recent comprehensive lists of job skills that have been put forward by academics and practitioners in social work. Hoefer (1993, 2003), Menefee and Thompson (1994), and the National Network of Social Work Managers, as articulated by Wimpfheimer (2004), have compiled extensive lists of what human services administrators should know how to do. Educators must understand what are considered the important skills for their graduates in order to provide a firm educational foundation to their students. (Also see Chapter 5 for discussion of management roles and tasks.) Previous scholars, such as Patti (1985) and Slavin (1977), have also contributed significantly to our knowledge base, but we will examine only these three more recent studies.

Hoefer (1993, with a follow-up article in 2003) addresses the questions of what should be taught and where it should be taught. Hoefer (1993) uses a sample of human services administrators

from Chicago and later (Hoefer, 2003) adds social work educators, government program managers, and public administration educators to the pool of raters. His results show that 37 skills, attitudes, and knowledge areas found in the literature could be rated individually in terms of importance. They could also be condensed into four categories (people skills, attitudes and experiences, substantive knowledge, and management skills) to determine what social work administrators should know how to do. The level of agreement among the different groups asked to rate the skills was high, with Spearman's Rho correlations between the four groups of raters significant at the .001 level for entry, middle, and top levels of management. Hoefer develops three primary conclusions based on the ratings of the 37 identified skills and the four grouped skill sets:

- "Strong agreement exists regarding which skills are most important at the three different levels of administration across disciplines and types of administrators." (p. 41)
- The desired knowledge, skills sets, and attitudes of human services administrators do not change very much as they move from lower levels of administration to higher levels. But it is important to become more accomplished in each of the areas as one reaches a higher level of administration.
- "For all respondents, at all levels, 'people skills' are the most important and 'management' skills are the least important." (p. 38)

This empirical work, while useful, is hampered in its utility by having no theoretical or conceptual basis. Nevertheless, because the list of skills was drawn from the literature, it has high face validity, and the four sets of respondents ranking them provide additional support for their importance as vital elements of social work management practice.

Menefee and Thompson (1994) conducted their research to provide a "comprehensive perspective on what social work managers report they do today" (p. 6). Menefee (1998) conducted a follow-up study that confirmed these results. In the initial study, Menefee and Thompson surveyed members of the National Network for Social Work Managers plus 80 social work managers throughout Tennessee regarding how often they performed 35 administrative competencies and how important they ranked 163 skills organized and listed by competency.

After analyzing their results, Menefee and Thompson (1994) argue that what managers do can be categorized into 12 management dimensions, each of which is composed of a number of key skills. Going beyond a simple listing of what skills and dimensions are most often performed, they also asked about the importance of each skill. Combining how frequently tasks were done with the perceived importance of the tasks, Menefee and Thompson develop an overall ranking regarding each management dimension. In order from most to least important, they are communicating (1st), supervising (2nd), boundary spanning (tied for 3rd), futuring (tied for 3rd), facilitating (tied for 5th), teaming (tied for 5th), aligning (7th), evaluating (8th), policy practice (9th), managing resources (10th), leveraging resources (11th), and advocating (12th). Austin and Kruzich (2004) place these 12 dimensions into 3 larger sets of managerial roles: leadership roles, interactional roles, and analytic roles.

Based on their data, Menefee and Thompson (1994) paint a picture of a social work management skill set that changed drastically in just a decade: "The role of the social work manager has transitioned from one primarily concerned with the internal functioning of the agency to one that concerns itself primarily with the strategic positioning of the agency in relation to its external environment" (p. 20). Menefee's (1998) follow-up results add additional support to the importance of these identified skills.

A third conceptualization of what social work managers should know was developed by the National Network for Social Work Managers (NNSWM, 2004) and discussed in Wimpfheimer (2004). Developed through a lengthy process of consultations with practitioners and academics, 14 competency areas are considered vital for

social work managers. In order to receive the "Certified Social Work Manager" credential from the NNSWM, applicants must demonstrate their abilities in these areas. The standards of the NNSWM are not minimum standards but are the competencies that are for experienced and academically trained managers (NNSWM, 2004). A total of 51 skills flesh out the 14 areas. The 14 competency areas are as follows:

Advocacy

Communication and interpersonal relationships

Ethics

Evaluation

Financial development

Financial management

Governance

Human resource management and development

Information technology

Leadership

Planning

Program development and organizational management

Public/community relations and marketing

Public policy

These standards have no explicit theoretical foundation but also have solid face validity, given the process used to develop and refine the list (NNSWM, 2004).

Table 24.1 presents these three answers to what social work managers do or should do side by side, in order to show that they have considerable overlap. Thus, despite the seeming differences between the authors on what should be known by human services administrators, the amount of agreement far exceeds the amount of disagreement. The independent processes used to arrive at

Table 24.1   Comparing Desired Management Skills

	Hoefer (1993, 2003)[a] Rankings in parentheses	Menefee and Thompson (1994)[b] Rankings in parentheses	National Network for Social Work Managers (2004)[c]
People Skills	• Leadership (1) • Oral communication (2) • Written communication (4) • Conflict resolution (7) • Group dynamics (9) • Meeting management (13) • Negotiation (16)	• Communicating (1) • Supervising (2) • Boundary spanning (3.5-tied) • Teaming (5.5-tied)	• Communication • Governance • Leadership
Attitudes and Experiences	• Professionalism (5) • Identify with agency (6) • Commitment to clients (8) • Tolerance for ambiguity (18) • Entrepreneurial attitude (24) • Previous work in an agency (27) • Previous work in that agency (34) • Political connections (37)	Facilitating (5.5-tied)	Ethics
Substantive Knowledge	• Administrative law (28) • Agency policy area (10) • Organization theory (19) • Knowledge of community (20) • Policy process (21) • Service technology (22) • Social policy (25)	• Policy practice (9) • Advocating (12)	• Advocacy • Public policy
Management Skills	• Decision making (3) • Strategic planning (11) • Personnel management (12) • Program planning (15) • Coordination (14) • Budgeting (17) • Evaluation (23) • Marketing (26) • MIS (29) • Statistics (30) • Computer spread sheet (31) • Accounting (32) • Fundraising (33) • Computer database (35) • Word processing (36)	• Futuring (3.5-tied) • Aligning (7) • Evaluating (8) • Managing resources (10) • Leveraging resources (11)	• Evaluation • Financial development • Financial management • Information technology • Human resource management and development • Management program development and organizational planning • Public relations

a. The rankings here are from nonprofit administrators.
b. The rankings here are the combined rankings of the frequency of use of each management dimension and its importance.
c. These skills are not ranked.

these lists provides further confidence regarding what to teach to social work administration students. Thus, as Hoefer (2003) states, "There is strong agreement . . . on which skills are considered important" across all levels of management and all four categories of respondents (p. 36).

To summarize this section, the answer to the question "Do we know what should be in a social work administration curriculum?" is a strong "Yes." While the research available to us is not in complete agreement, a great deal of core material is agreed upon within and between the practice community and selected academics. Knowing what should be taught to managers, it is interesting to determine whether management texts reflect this knowledge. Unfortunately, available textbooks do not necessarily present these agreed-upon skills fully.

Quality of Textbooks

The state of the art within most disciplines can be gleaned from the major textbooks of the field. When this principle is applied to our topic, we come to a sobering conclusion: Social work administration texts are woefully inadequate. Au (1994) notes many problems among the 13 administration texts reviewed:

- Lack of a strong theoretical base for the texts
- Lack of agreement among text authors on whether and how human services organizations are different than other types of organizations
- Lack of clearly defined purpose for human services management, making empirical research about outcomes difficult
- Too many unsubstantiated claims about managerial tasks in the texts
- Lack of discussion or acknowledgment regarding differences in managerial or administrative tasks according to level of administration

Austin and Kruzich (2004) provide an updated analysis of social work administration texts. They also find significant problems: Most texts display considerable gaps in knowledge, as well as a lack of attention to skill development (compared to knowledge acquisition); case-based and problem-centered learning techniques are frequently omitted; the amount of attention paid to social environment theory as an input into administrative practice is small; and empirical research on the nature of managerial practice is not used to develop the texts to a strong enough extent.

Management Curricula and Instructional Capability in Schools of Social Work

Having answered the question as to what *should* be taught, it is important to know what *is* being taught in social work administration classes. This helps us know what are the current capabilities for instruction.

An early effort to capture what social work education programs taught is McNutt's (1995) survey of macro practice curricula. He notes that administration is a part of every surveyed school's macro concentration, with 20% of the 44 responses having an administration-only concentration. He concludes that,

> While there is a core of agreement over which areas must be covered, several technical areas (financial management and personnel management) are either ignored or treated in a superficial manner. The data suggest that the stress is on interpersonal/interactional skills (such as communication and participatory management). (p. 71)

More recent research compares coursework across MSW, MBA, MPA, and MNO programs (Wish & Mirabella, 1998). Comparing the coursework across disciplines shows the strengths and weaknesses of each.

Social work schools emphasize acquisition and management of financial resources as well as other internal management issues. Courses on advocacy, public policy and community organizing are more likely to be found in social work schools than in other programs, whereas courses in philanthropy, the third sector and boundary spanning are not. (p. 105)

Business schools offering a nonprofit management program offer many courses on fundraising and financial management, boundary spanning, and internal management issues. They are not likely to offer courses on human resource management, philanthropy, or advocacy (Wish & Mirabella, 1998). Master of Public Administration programs are more likely to offer all the types of courses deemed desirable for nonprofit administration, emphasizing fundraising and internal management skills, and are more likely to offer courses on philanthropy and human resources than are social work or business degrees (Wish & Mirabella, 1998).

Mirabella and Wish (2000) state, "We find an overwhelming preponderance of 'inside function' courses among all degree programs—66 percent within the MBA, 61 percent within the MPA, 50 percent within the MSW and 49 percent within the MNO" (p. 226). These findings suggest that the MSW degree is more, not less, concerned with agencies' external contexts than other degree programs, which makes them better aligned with the need for knowledge and skills regarding environmental issues and boundary spanning, as discussed by Menefee and Thompson (1994).

Mirabella (2007) has recently updated her earlier work. She notes a large increase in the number of universities offering education in nonprofit management. Depending on how nonprofit management programs are defined, the number of universities offering such education has increased by as much as 50%. Between 1996 and 2006, she finds an increase in the number of nonprofit management education programs located within schools of business and public administration, but a small decrease among schools of social work (Mirabella, 2007, p. 15S).

Knowing what *should* be taught and what *is* being taught allows us to ask whether social work administration professors have both the academic and experiential knowledge necessary to teach these topics. While experience in management may not be mandatory, surely instructors with real-world experience would bring an additional dimension to classroom teaching. CSWE standards require instructors of required practice courses to have at least two years post-BSW social work practice experience (CSWE, 2007). This might seem to protect the profession from underqualified teachers, but there is room for doubt. The current requirement, for example, is weaker than the previous standard of two years of post-MSW practice experience. In addition, post-BSW experience in direct practice presumably counts toward the practice requirements for teaching administrative practice courses.

Additional concerns have been raised about the ability of social work faculty to provide adequate knowledge of administration topics to students. There are reasons for this concern. First, as social work programs have become more firmly tied to academic norms of research and publication as criteria for faculty selection and promotion, a doctorate degree is now widely required for tenure-track positions. Once hired, academics seeking tenure must focus on conducting research and publishing in peer-reviewed journals. Such research may not be directly helpful to practitioners. The hiring and tenuring process tends to work against having social work administration faculty with significant levels of administrative experience. Administrators with high levels of experience are typically paid more than assistant (nontenured) social work professors. Experienced managers face a strong financial disincentive to begin a new career in academia when it is added to the several years of frequently demanding doctoral education and its attendant expenses.

Another element discouraging top-level administrators from taking on full-time jobs in social work education is the relative lack of opportunities for well-paid consultancies working with nonprofit organizations. Colleagues in business schools, by contrast, are able to tap into a market (for-profit organizations) that frequently pays well for a professor's time. Because of financial constraints, nonprofits are more apt to request pro-bono consultations.

A different way to have instructors with a strong management background in the classroom is to hire adjunct faculty from among working or retired managers. While this option is logical, adjunct faculty without a strong academic background may rely too much on their own experiences (the proverbial "war stories") rather than subject matter specified in the curriculum plan for the administration concentration. Adjuncts may also neglect or give superficial attention to theory and research because of the preparation time that is required and, in some cases, because they lack formal education in the subject matter. Gaps in the curriculum can certainly arise from a number of sources, but incorporating adjuncts into the world of the classroom is not always easy or well done. This is particularly true if many adjuncts are used to provide instruction because they are not always involved in designing the curriculum or in the socialization activities of other faculty members (including meetings to discuss issues and concerns regarding coursework and students). In addition, adjuncts are typically paid poorly, so the proposition may not seem financially attractive to seasoned managers who frequently have to contend with long and unpredictable hours at their regular jobs.

While we know that administrative content is being taught, we have unanswered questions about the capabilities of the instructors themselves that require additional research. The main concerns is that we simply do not have enough information about the level of practice experience of tenured and tenure-track faculty and the ability of adjuncts to present theory and practice to students. Adjuncts, particularly, may lack the time, collegial support, and incentives to invest fully in the academic enterprise.

Let us now turn to the recipients of the curriculum to see what insights students and alumni of administration education programs can provide. If they are, by and large, happy with their experiences, we can rest a bit more easily.

Students' Perceptions of Their Management Education

Little research exists on how students feel about their administration education. Statistics indicate that fewer social work students specialize in administrative practice, and a lower percentage of NASW members identify themselves as administrators or supervisors than in the past (Ezell et al., 2004). No definitive answer to the question "Why?" has been discovered.

Martin, Pines, and Healy (1999) present data from social work administration graduates who perceived their education as adequate to good, with most of them satisfied with their careers. About three-fourths of these alumni were employed in middle and upper-level management positions after 15 years in the workforce.

As a contrast, in a limited, but instructive, study, Ezell et al. (2004) asked whether the climate for administration students within schools of social work might be part of the reason the numbers in administration concentrations are down. Reports show that administration students are not pleased with what they experience. Specifically, they concluded,

> Nonadministration students were perceived to be critical of students who selected administration concentrations and administration as a career path, that majorities [in several schools] of students experienced anti-management comments and attitudes in a variety of forms, and that administration students thought that their foundation courses provided inadequate background for their advanced studies. (pp. 57–58)

If the climate for administration students presents a "negative psychological climate" (Ezell et al., 2004, p. 72), then perhaps the other element of social work education, field education, provides an antidote to this inhospitable environment. According to the CSWE *Educational Policy and Accreditation Standards* (EPAS), field education in social work is equal in value to classroom instruction. In fact, social work professional education relies on fieldwork as its signature pedagogy, that is, "the form of instruction and learning in which a profession socializes its students to perform the role of practitioner" (CSWE, 2007).

Field education is not without problems, however. Current issues include having to handle more students as pressures for enrollment growth in schools of social work abound, dealing with more students with psychological and social problems, and a widening gap between social work education and social work practice (Lager & Robbins, 2004).

Mor Barak, Travis, and Bess (2004) surveyed all members of the NNSWM to determine their retrospective views of their MSW fieldwork. The response rate was 63% (200 out of 317), which indicates that the results are fairly representative of all members of the organization. Of most importance for this chapter, results show that nearly half of the respondents (48%) had a combined macro and micro focus during their social work education, nearly one-fifth (19%) had solely a macro educational experience, and one-third (33%) had solely a micro focus. Thus, approximately two-thirds of the respondents had exposure to a macro-focused curriculum, and about one-third had little or no exposure. About 10% of the total respondents obtained another master's degree after their MSW, mainly in business, management, or public administration (Mor Borak et al., 2004).

When asked to rate the quality and intensity of their fieldwork, NNSWM administrators said they were in the "poor" to "good" range. The good news is that students with at least some macro focus (macro-only or macro-micro combined) rated the quality of their management-related field experiences higher than did former students with a micro focus. Additionally, macro-focused students rated the intensity of their fieldwork in management as between "minimal" and

"moderate." This is compared to micro-focused students, who rated fieldwork as being between "no experience" and "minimal experience" for management tasks (Mor Barak et al., 2004). As the authors point out, however, the bad news is that the field practicum was not seen as excellent or even very good, the other possible responses. The most common fieldwork experiences reported were "planning and program development, program evaluation and advocacy" (p. 40). These three areas, while important, do not constitute sufficient breadth for respondents to feel content with their field experience. One of the conclusions of this report is that there is a need to "provide students with more and better field practicum experiences that focus on contemporary management skills" (p. 38). These results are similar to Zunz's (1995) finding that a majority of child welfare managers in her study lacked a substantive internship experience to develop their management skills.

To summarize, the picture painted thus far in the chapter is not entirely positive for social work administrative practice education. It is true that we have a good idea what should be taught. We also know that instructors (of uncertain ability and training) are providing courses in many of the relevant areas. Students going into administration concentrations are decreasing in number, perhaps because their nonadministration colleagues make their lives uncomfortable and cause them to doubt their choice to work in administrative positions. Fieldwork for administration students does not elicit positive memories, a result that might be linked to the rather limited set of tasks that interns are allowed to complete. The next section describes how others perceive the MSW degree compared to other management degrees.

Practitioners' Assessments of Management Education in Social Work

One of the two goals proposed for social work management education noted earlier was that capable social work administration graduates should have an advantage in the management job market in human services, compared to graduates of other types of management programs and particularly compared to those who do not receive any management education. Do social work graduates have such an advantage? Is their degree well-respected?

Some research, both qualitative and quantitative, has been conducted to answer these questions. Anecdotal information is discouraging. Perlmutter (2006) reports her conversations with 14 CEOs/Executive Directors in an array of social service organizations. Among other problems noted, four are salient: a seeming lack of pride in the social work profession, a lack of commitment to data-driven decision making, an absence of the high analytic skills needed to use data, and a need for more effective written and verbal communication skills. The directors interviewed noted that these skills, not found frequently enough in social work graduates, were more often found among MBA, MPA, and urban planning alumni (Perlmutter, 2006). Patti (2003) also found such sentiments on the part of human services managers. One author, Dr. Frederick Lane, from the field of public administration, sums up the view of many with a terse comment: "Few social work schools seem serious about management education" (Hall, O'Neill, Vinokur-Kaplan, Young & Lane, 2001, p. 75).

Survey research substantiates that the MSW degree is not highly regarded in the field for the highest levels of leadership. Haas and Robinson (1998) found that organizations with larger budgets preferred MBA degrees for their chief executives, and agencies heavily reliant on government funding preferred MPA degrees. Nonetheless, "the strongest and most consistent association is between the respondents' own degrees and their degree preferences; the degrees and degree preferences tend to match" (Haas & Robinson, 1998, p. 358). If MSW graduates are doing the hiring, in other words, MSW applicants have a better chance of being hired in the future. This illuminates the current problem of fewer MSWs currently in positions of leadership and shows how

the current situation may spiral downward. People with MBAs, MPAs, and MNOs, the degrees with increasing popularity, are more likely to hire their colleagues in the future, leaving MSW graduates with fewer options.

Additionally, a study by Hoefer (2003) found that nonprofit administrators believe that a social work administration master's degree is useful, but only at the lower levels of administration. In the three levels of administration, an MSW is ranked second (out of four options) most useful (after "no degree") for entry-level administration, most useful at the middle level of administration, and third most useful (behind an MBA or an MPA, but ahead of "no degree") at the top level. This finding, sadly, echoes the other results reported over the last 30 years (Keys & Cupaiuolo, 1987; Patti & Rauch, 1978).

Administrators in the Texas State government Mental Health and Mental Retardation agency rank a MSW (administration track) degree more highly, saying it is the best option at both the entry and middle levels. Similar to the nonprofit administrators, however, they believe that the MSW ranks behind MPA and MBA degrees for top-level administrators. It is still better than "no degree" (Hoefer, 2003).

It appears, then, that students graduating with an MSW administration degree can expect to receive a positive reception from governmental and nonprofit agencies when applying for entry- and middle-level administration jobs. The difficulty appears to emerge when the MSW competes with the MBA and MPA graduates for top-level jobs in human services and government agency positions. Still, many social workers are hired into administrative positions with little or no management education (Mor Barak et al., 2004; Patti, 2000; Preston, 2004). Thus, we can say that social work education is viewed as valuable preparation for lower and middle management, but is less well regarded as preparation for upper level management when compared to business and public administration.

We definitely have a glass one-fourth full or three-quarters empty situation, in terms of social work education leadership for social work administration. In the first edition of this book, Patti (2000) reached a similar conclusion: "It does not seem that social work education is serving the management needs of social welfare very well" (p. 19). The next section provides suggestions for filling the glass more fully so that progress can be made in the next decade.

Improving Social Work Management Education

Social work academics and management professionals realize that a problem exists regarding human services administration and social work education. "Professional social work associations and schools of social work should take the lead in advocating for the Master of Social Work as the most credible degree not only for entry-level management but top administration levels of social service agencies" (Wuenschel, 2006, p. 17). Unfortunately for social work education, no evidence suggests that such a position is defensible, and some evidence suggests the opposite. Hopkins and Hyde (2002), based on interviews with 115 top-level social work managers working in a broad cross-section of agencies, flatly state, "The overall picture that emerges regarding the ability of managers to address the challenges of human service work is distressing" (p. 13).

Still, it is not enough to say that we have not succeeded in meeting the goals for management education set out above. We must search for ways to improve the situation. Proposed suggestions range from those requiring minimal change to those that require more substantial change.

Make Incremental Improvements

Some authors suggest ways to improve social work education on the margin, without making structural changes. Many of these ideas relate to improving what is taught. Examples include turning to existing practitioners for advice on how to make the program more relevant and responsive to practitioner needs (Packard, 2004; Wimpfheimer, 2004), using environmental scanning and strategic planning to keep the curriculum for administration education fresh (Packard, 2004), and basing the curriculum on evidence-based administration techniques (Poertner, 2006).

Because of the documented tension between administration and direct practice students (Ezell et al., 2004), suggestions have been made to change the internal dynamics within schools of social work to make them friendlier to administration students. This can be accomplished by surfacing the topic among all students and faculty, providing opportunities for students to work across the micro-macro divide, and improving the balance of micro and macro to include more administrative topics in foundation coursework (Ezell et al., 2004).

Other aspects of administrative practice education are highlighted in additional suggestions. We are encouraged to improve texts and other instructional techniques (Au, 1994; Austin & Kruzich, 2004) and to attract more and better students into macro concentrations, including raising student entrance requirements (Stoesz, 2002). If students are more capable in quantitative abilities, for example, budgeting will not seem such a daunting course. Once more highly qualified students are enrolled, administration fieldwork opportunities can become more challenging and interesting (Mor Barak et al., 2004). Another idea is to market the administration concentration better, if only by emphasizing how many direct practice MSW graduates work in administrative positions without adequate academic preparation (Raymond, Teare, & Atherton, 1996).

An issue scarcely mentioned in the literature is the need to find ways to make management education more attractive to female students and to students of color. Males, particularly white males, continue to be overrepresented among high level social work administrators. Given that the vast majority of social work students and social workers are female, this imbalance is troubling (see Chapter 1 for additional discussion of this issue). Also, as social work becomes an ever more diverse field, we must make renewed efforts to ensure that the opportunity, interest, and ability to advance on the job exist for all.

Social work administration education can also begin to make changes in its models of teaching. The use of technology could possibly reach additional or different types of students. Online courses, with or without the use of technologies such as podcasting, interactive Web sites, virtual life simulations, and other learning opportunities, could be harnessed to reach out to students with managerial ambitions and skills.

Nonacademic, Post-degree Education and Training

Nonprofit management outreach programs have expanded quickly in recent years (Mirabella & Renz, 2001). Post-degree training can include, but should not be limited to, professional education or continuing education opportunities (Raymond et al., 1996). Indeed, Dolan's (2002) research (which asked agencies to indicate how their training needs were met) shows that many of the training needs of nonprofit administrators are fulfilled "in-house" (50%) and by other nonprofit organizations (34%). Only 30% is provided by academic institutions. For colleges and universities to expand their level of training, they should "give consideration to the less traditional means of meeting the needs of nonprofit management" (p. 287). In this study, academic graduate programs were considered the sixth best approach out of eight options by current nonprofit managers. Scoring more highly were, in descending order, half-day seminars, day-long seminars, luncheon sessions, certificate programs, and breakfast sessions. The only two options considered worse than traditional graduate education programs were intensive courses and traditional undergraduate courses.

Preston (2004) finds that post-degree training for new and mid-level child welfare managers ranges from adequate to good, but frequently ignores important topics that should be

included. Austin, Weisner, Schrandt, Glezos-Bell, and Murtaza (2006) found that an executive development program for human services managers can be an effective way to improve a person's knowledge base, but that these trainees require a supportive manager, the opportunity to network with other trainees to process the experience, and appropriate work tasks for the training to be most effective (Patti, 2003 provides a brief description of such programs).

Reinvigorate Joint Degree and Interdisciplinary Programs

Patti (2000) discusses the concept of joint degree programs, which is that students receive two degrees, one in social work and another in, for example, business or public administration. Students are required to take up to an extra year of coursework to receive such a joint degree. Social work schools apparently largely abandoned joint degree programs during the 1990s (Patti, 2000), but no research exists describing what the barriers and strengths of the approach were.

Another approach to interdisciplinary management education combines social work with other programs (business, public administration, nonprofit management). This approach goes beyond a joint program in that only one degree is received but students can fashion a program from two or more existing schools or departments. The concept of comparative advantage applies here. Social work programs lead all other types of programs in teaching advocacy and community organizing, for example, but lag behind in other areas, such as quantitative analysis, strategic planning, and marketing (Mirabella & Wish, 2000). Vinokur-Kaplan discusses how joining together with an MBA and an MPA program was instituted at the University of Michigan (Hall, O'Neill, Vinokur-Kaplan, Young & Lane, 2001). Stoesz (2002) argues that social work should blend with other practice-oriented disciplines to become a new field, human services, with different degree requirements altogether.

Some, like Nessof (2007), do not want to devalue social workers' uniqueness. He argues that without social work values and direct social service practice experience, there is no difference between social workers and other managers, except that social workers have a weaker background in necessary technical skills. A combined degree may work around this objection, but the insistence on a foundation year involving direct practice courses may make this approach difficult to maintain.

A Two-Year Advanced-Placement-Only Social Work Management Degree Program

Perlmutter (2006) and others (including Patti, 2000) have long advocated for increased specialized management training at the MSW level. Leaving behind the dualism of current foundation (micro/macro) education and second-year specialization, we could see a new emphasis on social work, administration, and leadership if social work education at the master's level relied on the BSW as the source of foundation material. The post-BSW program could then be a two-year program that focused students' education on management within a social work perspective.

The advantage of this approach over a combined program is the more complete control of the curriculum, including reinforcing the particular values of the social work profession. Because such programs would be costly to run and would appeal to only a limited number of students who first must have a BSW, few schools of social work could take such a drastic step. Those that did, however, could become the Harvard and Yale of the social work administration education world, attracting the best faculty and students from across the country. While this approach might require working closely with CSWE to ensure an accredited program, such a concentration of talent would likely spur advances in social work administration theory, teaching, and practice.

Conclusion: Providing Better Leadership for Social Work Administration?

The barriers facing social work education's efforts to provide leadership for the field of human services administration are many and formidable. This is not to say that all educators are inadequate or that all students are graduated without the ability to succeed. In fact, despite the concerns described here, we can observe social work instructors and students in our classrooms who are more than a match for their colleagues from other management degree programs. Still, on the whole, we cannot claim to have met the twin goals of learning the correct things to teach and producing graduates who are respected in the marketplace for having unique qualifications for human services management positions. Poertner's (2006) literature review of the connections between social administration skills and outcomes for consumers reminds us why it is vital for social work administration graduates to have proper training and education: "Supervisory behavior is both positively and negatively associated with outcomes for consumers" (p. 11).

Two specific initiatives have been taken that show promise of advancing the practice of social workers in management: the creation of the Association for Community Organization and Social Administration, a niche organization within social work education dedicated to advancing teaching and research in macro practice; and the establishment of the National Network for Social Work Managers, which has, among other things, provided a forum for collaboration between the academic and professional communities. Of the approximately 225 individual and 21 organizational members, about one-third are academics and two-thirds practitioners (Bruce Friedman, President, NNSWM, personal communication, Dec. 3, 2007).

Although these are important and welcome efforts, it appears that the realities of competition from other management degree programs and difficulties in recruiting motivated and talented students are causing social work academics to seek an accommodation with those other programs, with a further weakening of the prognosis for stand-alone social work programs. It is, however, as yet unnecessary to eliminate social work administration programs entirely, if only because we have not attempted all feasible options to improve the situation. More programs should try the alternatives suggested above to see which are more useful and which are less so. Researchers and educators comparing notes at conferences and via electronic roundtables may be able to provide enriched opportunities to the students and alumni of the future. The generation of social work educators who first developed management education in social work schools may leave the job unfinished, but by standing on their shoulders, the next wave of administration instructors may be able to see over the existing barriers to a more hospitable landscape.

Beyond the clear problems discussed here, there is another way that social work education, and the profession as a whole, can assist human services managers. As noted early in this chapter, the environment for social work administrators is increasingly difficult, particularly due to resource constraints and competition. Perhaps social work students and practitioners working in management positions simply are facing a nearly impossible task, for which no curriculum can adequately prepare practitioners. Thus, it is incumbent upon the leaders of today to make the practice world more amenable to realistic work expectations. Successful advocacy for increased resources and organizing for positive change, among other macro level actions, may, in the end, be every bit as important in preparing social work administrators to do well as would be altering a curriculum or developing more classes or continuing education offerings.

References

Adams, C., & Perlmutter, F. (1995). Leadership in hard times: Are nonprofits well served? *Nonprofit and Voluntary Sector Quarterly, 24*, 253–262.

Alexander, J. (2000). Adaptive strategies of nonprofit human service organizations in an era of devolution and new public management. *Nonprofit Management and Leadership, 10*(3), 287–303.

Armitage, A., & Clark, F. (1975). Design issues in the performance-based curriculum. *Journal of Education for Social Work, 11*(1), 22–29.

Au, C. (1994). The status of theory and knowledge development in social welfare administration. *Administration in Social Work, 18*(3), 27–57.

Austin, M., & Kruzich, J. (2004). Assessing recent textbooks and casebooks in human services administration: Implications and future directions. *Administration in Social Work, 28*(1), 115–137.

Austin, M., Weisner, S., Schrandt, E., Glezos-Bell, S., & Murtaza, N. (2006). Exploring the transfer of learning from an executive development program for human service managers. *Administration in Social Work, 30*(2), 71–90.

Birdsell, D., & Muzzio, D. (2003). *The next leaders: UWNYC leadership development and succession management needs.* New York: United Way of New York City.

Council on Social Work Education. (2007). *Educational policy and accreditation standards,* Draft of September 24, 2007. Retrieved October 28, 2007, from http://www.cswe.org/NR/rdon lyres/450CD3CE-3525-4CE1-9031-59EA4DC77 EDA/0/EPASDraftSeptember242007Rev1012207 .pdf

Dolan, D. (2002). Training needs of administrators in the nonprofit sector: What are they and how should we address them? *Nonprofit Management and Leadership, 12*(3), 277–292.

Ezell, M., Chernesky, R., & Healy, L. (2004). The learning climate for administration students. *Administration in Social Work, 28*(1), 57–76.

Faffer, J., & Friedland, S. (2007). Addressing the professional leadership crisis in the Jewish family service field. *Journal of Jewish Communal Service, 82*(1/2), 139–144.

Gingerich, W., Kaye, K., & Bailey, D. (1999). Assessing quality in social work education: Focus on diversity. *Assessment & Evaluation in Higher Education, 24*(2), 119–129.

Golensky, M., & Mulder, C. (2006). Coping in a constrained economy: Survival strategies of nonprofit human service organizations. *Administration in Social Work, 30*(3), 5–24.

Haas, P., & Robinson, M. (1998). The views of non-profit executives on educating nonprofit managers. *Nonprofit Management and Leadership, 8*(4), 349–362.

Hall, P., O'Neill, M., Vinokur-Kaplan, D., Young, D., & Lane, F. (2001). Panel discussion: Where you stand depends on where you sit: The implications of organizational location for university-based programs in nonprofit management. *Public Performance and Management Review, 25*(1), 74–87.

Hoefer, R. (1993). A matter of degree: Job skills for human service administration. *Administration in Social Work, 17*(3), 1–20.

Hoefer, R. (2003). Administrative skills and degrees: The "best place" debate rages on. *Administration in Social Work, 27*(1), 25–46.

Hopkins, K., & Hyde, C. (2002). The human service managerial dilemma: New expectations, chronic challenges and old solutions. *Administration in Social Work, 26*(3), 1–15.

Johnson, M., & Austin, M. (2006). Evidence-based practice in the social services: Implications for organizational change. *Administration in Social Work, 30*(3), 75–104.

Jones, J. (2006). Understanding environmental influence on human service organizations: A study of the influence of managed care on child caring institutions. *Administration in Social Work, 30*(4), 63–90.

Keys, P., & Cupaiuolo, A. (1987). Rebuilding the relationship between social work and public welfare administration. *Administration in Social Work, 11*(1), 47–58.

Lager, P., & Robbins, V. (2004). Field education: Exploring the future, expanding the vision. *Journal of Social Work Education, 40*(1), 3–11.

Martin, L. (2000). Budgeting for outcomes in state human agencies. *Administration in Social Work, 24*(3), 71–88.

Martin, M., Pines, B., & Healy, L. (1999). Mining our strengths: Curriculum approaches for social work management. *Journal of Teaching in Social Work, 18*(1/2), 73–97.

McBeath, B., & Meezan, W. (2006). Nonprofit adaptation to performance-based, managed care contracting in Michigan's foster care system. *Administration in Social Work, 30*(2), 39–70.

McNutt, J. (1995). The macro practice curriculum in graduate social work education: Results of a national study. *Administration in Social Work, 19*(3), 59–74.

Menefee, D. (1998). Identifying and comparing competencies for social work management II: A replication study. *Administration in Social Work, 22*(4), 53–63.

Menefee, D. (2000). What managers do and why they do it. In R. Patti (Ed.), *The handbook of social welfare management* (pp. 247–266). Thousand Oaks, CA: Sage.

Menefee, D., & Thompson, J. (1994). Identifying and comparing competencies for social work management: A practice-driven approach. *Administration in Social Work, 18*(3), 1–25.

Mirabella, R. (2007). University-based educational programs in nonprofit management and philanthropic studies: A 10-year review and projections of future trends. *Nonprofit and Voluntary Sector Quarterly, Supplement, 36*(4), 11S–27S.

Mirabella, R., & Renz, D. (2001). Nonprofit management outreach programs: An examination of institutional mission and setting. *Public Performance and Management Review, 25*(1), 14–29.

Mirabella, R., & Wish, N. (2000). The "best place" debate: A comparison of graduate education program for nonprofit managers. *Public Administration Review, 60*(3), 219–229.

Mor Barak, M., Travis, D., & Bess, G. (2004). Exploring managers' and administrators' retrospective perceptions of their MSW fieldwork experience: A national study. *Administration in Social Work, 28*(1), 21–44.

National Association of Scholars. (2007). The scandal of social work education. Retrieved October 27, 2007, from http://www.nas.org/nas-initiatives/CSWE-initiative/soswe_scandal/scandal_soc-work ed_11sep07.pdf

National Network for Social Work Managers. (2004). *Leadership and management practice standards.* Retrieved October 8, 2007, from www.social workmanager.org/Standards.htm

Nessof, I. (2007). The importance of revitalizing management education for social workers. *Social Work, 52*(3), 283–285.

Packard, T. (2004). Issues in designing and adapting an administration concentration. *Administration in Social Work, 28*(1), 5–20.

Patti, R. (1985). In search of purpose for social welfare administration. *Administration in Social Work, 9*(3), 1–14.

Patti, R. (2000). The landscape of social welfare management. In R. Patti (Ed.), *The handbook of social welfare management* (pp. 3–25). Thousand Oaks, CA: Sage.

Patti, R. (2003). Reflections on the state of management in social work. *Administration in Social Work, 27*(2), 1–11.

Patti, R., & Rauch, R. (1978). Social work administration graduates in the job market: An analysis of managers' hiring preferences. *Social Service Review, 52*, 567–583.

Perlmutter, F. (2006). Ensuring social work administration. *Administration in Social Work, 30*(2), 3–10.

Poertner, J. (2006). Social administration and outcomes for consumers: What do we know? *Administration in Social Work, 30*(2), 11–24.

Preston, M. (2004). Mandatory management training for newly hired child welfare supervisors: A divergence between management research and training practice? *Administration in Social Work, 28*(2), 81–97.

Raymond, G., Teare, R., & Atherton, C. (1996). Do management tasks differ by field of practice? *Administration in Social Work, 20*(1), 17–30.

Regehr, C., Chau, S., Leslie, B., & Howe, P. (2002). An exploration of supervisors' and managers' responses to child welfare reform. *Administration in Social Work, 26*(3), 17–36.

Reisch, M., & Sommerfeld, D. (2003). Welfare reform and the future of nonprofit organizations. *Nonprofit Management and Leadership, 14*(1), 19–46.

Salipante, P., & Aram, J. (2003). Managers as knowledge generators: The nature of practitioner-scholar research in the nonprofit sector. *Nonprofit Management and Leadership, 14*(2), 129–150.

Schmid, H. (2004). Organization-environment relationships: Theory for management practice in human service organizations. *Administration in Social Work, 28*(1), 97–113.

Selsky, J., & Parker, B. (2005). Cross-sector partnerships to address social issues: Challenges to theory and practice. *Journal of Management, 31*(6), 849–873.

Slavin, S. (1977). A framework for selecting content for teaching about social administration. *Administration in Social Work, 1*, 245–257.

Social Work Congress. (2005). Social work imperatives for the next decade. Retrieved November 29, 2007, from http://www.socialworkers.org/congress/imperatives0605.pdf

Stoecker, R. (2007). The research practices and needs of nonprofit organizations in an urban center. *Journal of Sociology and Social Welfare, XXXIV*(4), 97–119.

Stoesz, D. (2002). From social work to human services. *Journal of Sociology and Social Welfare, XXIX*(4), 19–37.

Teegarden, P. H. (2004). *Change ahead, nonprofit executive leadership and transitions survey 2004.* Annie E. Casey Foundation. Retrieved March 10, 2007, from http://www.aecf.org/upload/PublicationFiles/executive_transition_survey_report2004.pdf

Wimpfheimer, S. (2004). Leadership and management competencies defined by practicing social work managers: An overview of standards developed by the National Network for Social Work Managers. *Administration in Social Work, 28*(1), 45–56.

Wish, N., & Mirabella, R. (1998). Curricula variations in nonprofit management graduate programs. *Nonprofit Management and Leadership, 9*(1), 99–109.

Wuenschel, P. (2006). The diminishing role of social work administrators in social service agencies: Issues for consideration. *Administration in Social Work, 30*(4), 5–18.

Zimmermann, J., & Stevens, B. (2006). The use of performance measurement in South Carolina nonprofits. *Nonprofit Management and Leadership, 16*(3), 315–327.

Zunz, S. (1995). The view from behind the desk: Child welfare managers and their roles. *Administration in Social Work, 19*(2), 63–80.

Index

About the Editor

Rino J. Patti is professor emeritus at the University of Southern California School of Social Work, where he was the dean until 1997. He retired in 2001. His teaching and research interests are focused on the organization and management of human services organizations, with particular attention to the conditions and processes that contribute to high quality, effective consumer services. He has authored or edited 5 books and more than 50 articles and served as the editor of the *Administration in Social Work* journal. He is the recipient of a 2003 Career Achievement Award from the Association for Community Organization and Social Administration (ACOSA) and the Faculty Lifetime Achievement Award from the University of Southern California.

About the Contributors

Catherine Foster Alter, PhD, MSW was director of the Iowa University School of Social Work (1986–1992) and the Graduate School of Social Work at the University of Denver (1997–2006), where she is professor emerita. Her practice background in urban planning and social service administration led to a continuing interest in building theory and knowledge about interorganizational networks and collaborations as a strategy for social change. Her book with Jerald Hage, *Organizations Working Together* (1993), is used today by doctoral students in many disciplines and countries. Her recent research focuses in two areas: (1) alleviating poverty using strategies such as micro enterprise and self-employment programs that enable low-income women to move toward self-sufficiency, and (2) programs for at-risk children and youth. She retired from the University of Denver in 2007 and currently resides in Asheville, NC.

Michael J. Austin is the Milton and Florence Krenz Mack Professor of Nonprofit Management at the School of Social Welfare, University of California, Berkeley. He is the former dean of the University of Pennsylvania, School of Social Work and teaches graduate students in the area of nonprofit management, community planning, and the social environment dimensions of human behavior. He received his doctorate in organizational research related to nonprofit human services organizations from the University of Pittsburgh School of Social Work (1970). He has taught at Florida State University (1970–1976), the University of Washington (1976–1985), the University of Pennsylvania (1985–1992), and the University of California, Berkeley (1992–present). In addition to writing more than 80 articles and numerous reports, he edited *Changing Welfare Services* (2004) and co-edited, with Karen Hopkins, *Supervision as Collaboration in the Human Services: Building a Learning Culture* (Sage Publications, 2004). He serves on the editorial boards of seven journals and is the associate editor of *Administration in Social Work*.

Gary Bess, PhD, holds two master's degrees in social work and applied sociology and a PhD in social work from the University of Southern California. For several years he directed nonprofit health and human services organizations in southern California. Since 1991, his consulting firm, Gary Bess Associates (www.garybess .com), has provided management consultation, needs assessment, program evaluation, and strategic planning services to a range of large and small public and private organizations. He teaches part time in the School of Social Work at California State University, Chico.

Mark Ezell, PhD, is professor of Social Welfare at the University of Kansas in Lawrence, Kansas where he has worked since 1998. His teaching and research interests include management practice in social work, child welfare contracting and privatization, juvenile justice, advocacy, research, and program evaluation. He has published widely in professional journals and presented numerous papers at conferences throughout the world. He is the author of *Advocacy in the Human Services* (Wadsworth, 2000). In 1997, he was selected by the U.S. Children's Bureau as a Child Welfare Research Fellow and received funding for research related to child welfare contracting.

Sheldon R. Gelman is professor and Schachne Dean at the Wurzweiler School of Social Work of Yeshiva University in New York. He also serves as associate vice president for academic affairs. He earned his bachelor's degree in psychology and his master's degree in social group work at the University of Pittsburgh. He received his PhD in welfare planning from the Heller School of Brandeis University and his MSL (Master of Studies in Law) from Yale University Law School. Dr. Gelman is a member of the Academy of Certified Social Workers and a Fellow of the American Association on Intellectual and Developmental Disabilities.

Margaret Gibelman was Professor and Director of the Doctoral Program at Yeshiva University, Wurzweiler School of Social Work. She published widely in the area of nonprofit organizations, including *The Privatization of Human Services* with Harold Demone.

Leon Ginsberg is director of the social work program at Appalachian State University in North Carolina. He served as dean of two other schools of social work and as Commissioner of Human Services for West Virginia in the 1970s and 1980s. His writings include several articles on social work management as well as books and articles on social welfare policy and rural social work. He co-edited two editions of *New Management for Human Services* (NASW Press) with Paul R. Keys.

Charles Glisson, PhD, is University Distinguished Research Professor and director of the University of Tennessee Children's Mental Health Services Research Center (CMHSRC). He received his doctorate in social work from Washington University, St. Louis in 1976 and has directed interdisciplinary, NIH-funded research continuously since founding the CMHSRC in 1988. The research conducted by the CMHSRC is concerned with children and families at risk of behavioral and mental health problems and targeted services provided by mental health, child welfare, and juvenile justice systems. Dr. Glisson's work has focused on the organizational characteristics of these systems and on organizational strategies to improve the quality and outcomes of the services they provide.

Yeheskel Hasenfeld is the Distinguished Professor of Social Welfare at the Department of Social Welfare, University of California, Los Angeles School of Public Affairs. His research focuses on the dynamic relations between social welfare policies, the organizations that implement these policies, and the people who use their services. He has written extensively on human services organizations, the implementation of welfare reform, and the nonprofit sector. His most recent book with Joel F. Handler is *Blame Welfare, Ignore Poverty and Inequality*.

Richard (Rick) Hoefer is professor of Social Work, University of Texas at Arlington. He specializes in human services management and social policy, with a particular emphasis on program evaluation and advocacy. Dr. Hoefer is the founding and continuing editor of *The Journal of Policy Practice* (formerly *The Social Policy Journal*). With numerous book chapters, journal articles, and conference presentations to his credit, his research has been published in venues such as *Social Work, Administration in Social Work, Nonprofit Management and Leadership,* and the *Journal of Sociology and Social Welfare.*

Karen M. Hopkins is an associate professor and co-chair of the management and community organization concentration at the Graduate School of Social Work, University of Maryland, Baltimore. She teaches program management, human resources management, and research methods in management and community practice. She also provides management development training, consultation, and program evaluation to human services organizations. Her research focuses on supervision/management practices and outcomes, organizational learning and citizenship, work-life integration, and child welfare workforce retention. Dr. Hopkins received a PhD from the University of Chicago and MSW from the University of Pittsburgh.

Alfreda P. Iglehart is associate professor in the Department of Social Welfare at the University of California, Los Angeles, School of Public Affairs. She has conducted research on and published in the areas of macro social service delivery, ethnic-sensitive macro practice, and child welfare. Her current interests include macro practice in a diverse society and the intersection of race, ethnicity, and public child welfare. She is co-author with Professor Rosina Becerra of *Social Services and the Ethnic Community* and is completing a book, *Aging Out of Foster Care: The Transition to Adulthood.*

Armand Lauffer is co-chair of the Sage Editorial Board for the Human Services and founding co-editor of two Sage series in the human services and nonprofit management. Author of more than 20 books on social work, nonprofit management, and community planning, Lauffer is professor emeritus of The University of Michigan. He and his wife currently make their home in Jerusalem, Israel. A consultant to several international and Israeli foundations and nonprofit organizations, he recently completed design of a cross-national MBA program in nonprofit management. In 2000, he received ACOSA's Lifetime Achievement Award for his contributions to community organization and social administration.

Lawrence L. Martin is professor of public affairs, public administration, and social work at the University of Central Florida in Orlando. He previously taught at Florida Atlantic University in Boca Raton and at Columbia University in New York City. His research interests are in the areas of contracting, performance measurement, and human services management and administration, and he has published widely in all of these areas.

David Menefee has more than 30 years of experience designing and conducting evaluation research for human services organizations. He earned his PhD in 1990 from the University of Washington and is currently the director of data and evaluation for the

Divisions of Mental Health and Alcohol and Drug Abuse in the State of Colorado. Dr. Menefee has held full-time faculty positions at Columbia University, University of Maryland, and University of Tennessee. His published works focus on organizational effectiveness and management in the nonprofit sector. His areas of practice include managerial leadership and performance management in human services.

Michàlle Mor Barak, PhD, is the Stein-Wood Professor of Social Work and Business in a Global Society at the University of Southern California, with a joint appointment at the School of Social Work and the Marshall School of Business. She has published extensively in peer-reviewed journals in the areas of global workforce diversity and cross-cultural aspects of work/family integration. Her most recent book, *Managing Diversity: Toward a Globally Inclusive Workplace* (Sage), won the prestigious 2006 Choice Award for Outstanding Academic Titles and the 2007 Academy of Management Terry Book Award for the "Most Significant Contribution to Management Knowledge."

Jennifer E. Mosley earned her MSW and PhD from the University of California, Los Angeles and is currently an assistant professor at the University of Chicago's School of Social Service Administration. Her areas of special interest include nonprofit organizations, policy advocacy and lobbying, organizational theory, civic engagement, and collaborative networks in service provision and advocacy. Overall, her work focuses on the role of nonprofit organizations as political actors, specifically the role nonprofits and other voluntary associations play in advocating for improved human services and underrepresented populations. Her current research seeks to explain how environmental and organizational pressures work to encourage or constrain different types of policy advocacy involvement by human services nonprofits.

Thomas Packard is an associate professor in the School of Social Work at San Diego State University. His teaching specialties are administration and social policy. He is a faculty consultant with the school's Academy for Professional Excellence, where he works with county human services directors in southern California, consults with their leadership development program, and conducts program evaluations. Prior to entering teaching, he was the director of two not-for-profit human services organizations. He has for more than 20 years been an organization development consultant specializing in government and not-for-profit organizations. His current research interests include organizational performance and organizational change.

Peter J. Pecora has a joint appointment as the senior director of research services for Casey Family Programs, and professor in the School of Social Work, University of Washington, Seattle. Peter has worked with a number of state departments of social services in the United States and in other countries to refine foster care programs; develop evaluation strategies; and implement intensive home-based services, child welfare training, and risk assessment systems for child protective services. He was recently appointed to the Institute of Medicine Committee on the Prevention of Mental Health Disorders and Substance Abuse for the Board on Children, Youth, and Families, to explore issues related to preventing mental disorders among children and young adults.

John Poertner, DSW, is professor emeritus, School of Social Welfare, University of Illinois at Urbana-Champaign, where he was associate dean before retiring. For many years, he has published in professional journals in the areas of child welfare and human services management. His interest in management is the relationship between management actions and outcomes for consumers of social services. He is co-author with Charles Rapp of *Social Administration: The Consumer-Centered Approach,* the second edition of which is forthcoming.

Michael Reisch, a professor at the University of Michigan, has published more than 20 books and monographs and nearly 100 articles and book chapters on the history and philosophy of social welfare, community organization theory and practice, the nonprofit sector, and contemporary policy issues. His work has been translated into French, Spanish, Italian, Korean, Japanese, Chinese, and Bulgarian. He has held leadership positions in local, state, and national advocacy and professional organizations and consulted with governments, nonprofits, advocacy groups, and political campaigns in five states, and has lectured and consulted in Europe, Latin America, Canada, and Australia.

Hillel Schmid, PhD, is a senior faculty member at the School of Social Work and Social Welfare at the Hebrew University of Jerusalem. He is the incumbent of the Centraide-L. Jacque Ménard Chair in Social Work for the Study of Volunteer and Nonprofit Organizations. From 2003 to 2006, Professor Schmid served as dean of the social work school, and he is currently director of the Center for the Study of Philanthropy in Israel at the Hebrew University of Jerusalem. Professor Schmid has also served as a visiting professor at the University of Michigan and Columbia University. His main areas of research are organization-environment relations, strategies of adaptation to changing environments, the role of nonprofits in providing human and social services, executive leadership, organizational change, and the political roles of human services organizations. He has published books and chapters in books, as well as numerous articles in leading scholarly journals.

Dick Schoech is the Dulak Professor in Administrative and Community Practice at the University of Texas at Arlington (UTA), School of Social Work. He received an interdisciplinary administration PhD from the UTA schools of Business, Social Work and Urban Studies. He is founder (1981) of the Computer Use in Social Services Network (CUSSN), the founding editor (1985) of the *Journal of Technology in Human Services,* and the founding chair of HUSITA, an international organization to further technology that serves humanity. He has had technology grants in child protective services, aging, HIV/AIDS, mental health, substance abuse, and developmental disabilities.

Jeffrey R. Solomon is the President of the Andrea and Charles Bronfman Philanthropies, a group of foundations operating in Canada, Israel, and the United States. Among the foundations' innovative launches are Birthright Israel and Reboot, two initiatives aimed at connecting young, assimilated Jews to their tradition; The Gift of New York, a powerful response to September 11, helping to heal families of victims through the power of culture; and Project Involvement, an educational reform program serving some 265,000 Israeli elementary school students.

He previously served as the Senior Vice President and Chief Operating Officer of UJA-Federation of New York.

Other past roles include executive positions at Altro Health and Rehabilitation Services, Miami Jewish Home and Hospital for the Aged, and Jewish Family and Children's Services in Miami. Dr. Solomon also served with city, state, and federal governments. An author of more than 70 publications, he served as an adjunct associate professor at New York University and sits on numerous nonprofit and foundation boards, including the FJC; a community foundation in New York; and the Council of Foundations, where he chaired the Committee on Ethics and Practice and serves on its Executive Committee. He is a founding trustee of the World Faiths Development Dialogue and has received a number of honors from professional associations and universities.

He is currently completing a book, *The Art of Giving: Where the Soul Meets the Business Plan,* with Charles Bronfman, to be published in December 2009.

Diane Vinokur-Kaplan, PhD, LMSW, is an associate professor at the School of Social Work, The University of Michigan, and past director of that university's Nonprofit and Public Management Center. She received her BA (cum laude, sociology) from Oberlin College and her MSW, MA, and a doctorate in social work and sociology from the University of Michigan. She serves on the editorial boards of *Administration in Social Work* and *Nonprofit and Voluntary Sector Quarterly.* Her current research, The Under One Roof Project, investigates the benefits and challenges, for both organizations and communities, of co-locating nonprofit organizations(www.ssw.umich.edu/underoneroof).